CONCISE SIXTH EDITION

LIBERTY, EQUALITY, POWER

A HISTORY OF THE AMERICAN PEOPLE

Volume 2: Since 1863

JOHN M. MURRIN
PRINCETON UNIVERSITY, EMERITUS

PAUL E. JOHNSON
UNIVERSITY OF SOUTH CAROLINA, EMERITUS

JAMES M. McPHERSON
PRINCETON UNIVERSITY, EMERITUS

ALICE FAHS
UNIVERSITY OF CALIFORNIA, IRVINE

GARY GERSTLE
VANDERBILT UNIVERSITY

EMILY S. ROSENBERG
UNIVERSITY OF CALIFORNIA, IRVINE

NORMAN L. ROSENBERG
MACALESTER COLLEGE

WADSWORTH
CENGAGE Learning

Australia • Brazil • Japan • Korea • Mexico • Singapore • Spain • United Kingdom • United States

Liberty, Equality, Power: A History of the American People, Concise Sixth Edition, Volume 2: Since 1863
Murrin/Johnson/McPherson/Fahs/Gerstle/Rosenberg/Rosenberg

Editor-in-Chief: Lyn Uhl
Senior Publisher: Suzanne Jeans
Senior Sponsoring Editor: Ann West
Senior Development Editor:
    Margaret McAndrew Beasley
Assistant Editor: Megan Chrisman
Editorial Assistant: Kati Coleman
Media Editor: Kate MacLean
Brand Manager: Melissa Larmon
Marketing Development Manager: Kyle Zimmerman
Marketing Coordinator: Lorreen R. Towle
Senior Content Project Manager: Carol Newman
Senior Art Director: Cate Rickard Barr
Print Buyer: Sandee Milewski
Senior Rights Acquisition Specialist:
    Jennifer Meyer Dare
Cover Designer: Cabbage Design
Cover Image:
    Untitled, 1985 by Romare Bearden (1911 – 1988)/
    Christie's Images /CORBIS ©Romare Bearden
    Foundation/Licensed by VAGA, New York, NY
Production Service and Compositor:
    Integra Software Services, Inc.

For product information and technology assistance, contact us at
Cengage Learning Customer & Sales Support, 1-800-354-9706

For permission to use material from this text or product, submit all requests online at **www.cengage.com/permissions**. Further permissions questions can be emailed to **permissionrequest@cengage.com**.

Library of Congress Control Number: 2012935928

Student Edition:
ISBN-13: 978-1-133-94774-5
ISBN-10: 1-133-94774-3

Wadsworth
20 Channel Center Street
Boston, MA 02210
USA

Cengage Learning is a leading provider of customized learning solutions with office locations around the globe, including Singapore, the United Kingdom, Australia, Mexico, Brazil and Japan. Locate your local office at **international.cengage.com/region**

Cengage Learning products are represented in Canada by Nelson Education, Ltd.

For your course and learning solutions, visit **www.cengage.com**.

Purchase any of our product at your local college store or at our preferred online store **www.cengagebrain.com**.

Instructors: Please visit **login.cengage.com** and log in to access instructor-specific resources.

Printed in the United States of America
3 4 5 6 7 16 15 14 13

JOHN M. MURRIN

Princeton University, Emeritus

John M. Murrin studies American colonial and revolutionary history and the early republic. He has edited one multivolume series and five books, including two essay collections, *Colonial America: Essays in Politics and Social Development*, Sixth Edition (2010), and *Saints and Revolutionaries: Essays in Early American History* (1984). His own essays range from ethnic tensions, the early history of trial by jury, the emergence of the legal profession, and the political culture of the colonies and the new nation, to the rise of professional baseball and college football in the 19th century. He served as president of the Society for Historians of the Early American Republic in 1998–1999.

PAUL E. JOHNSON

University of South Carolina,
Distinguished Professor Emeritus

A specialist in early national social and cultural history, Paul E. Johnson is also the author of *The Early American Republic, 1789–1829* (2006); *Sam Patch, the Famous Jumper* (2003); and *A Shopkeeper's Millennium: Society and Revivals in Rochester, New York, 1815–1837*, 25th Anniversary Edition (2004). He is coauthor (with Sean Wilentz) of *The Kingdom of Matthias: Sex and Salvation in 19th-Century America* (1994), and editor of *African-American Christianity: Essays in History* (1994). He has been awarded the Merle Curti Prize of the Organization of American Historians (1980), the Richard P. McCormack Prize of the New Jersey Historical Association (1989), and fellowships from the National Endowment for the Humanities (1985–1986), the John Simon Guggenheim Foundation (1995), the Gilder Lehrman Institute (2001), and the National Endowment for the Humanities We the People Fellowship (2006–2007).

JAMES M. MCPHERSON

Princeton University, Emeritus

James M. McPherson is a distinguished Civil War historian and was president of the American Historical Association in 2003. He won the 1989 Pulitzer Prize for his book *Battle Cry of Freedom: The Civil War Era*. His other publications include *Marching Toward Freedom: Blacks in the Civil War*, Second Edition (1991); *Ordeal by Fire: The Civil War and Reconstruction*, Third Edition (2001); *Abraham Lincoln and the Second American Revolution* (1991); *For Cause and Comrades: Why Men Fought in the Civil War* (1997), which won the Lincoln Prize in 1998; *Crossroads of Freedom: Antietam* (2002); and *Tried by War: Abraham Lincoln as Commander in Chief* (2008), which won the Lincoln Prize for 2009.

ALICE FAHS

University of California, Irvine

Alice Fahs is a specialist in American cultural history of the 19th and 20th centuries. Her 2001 *The Imagined Civil War: Popular Literature of the North and South, 1861–1865* was a finalist in 2002 for the Lincoln Prize. Together with Joan Waugh, she published the edited collection *The Memory of the Civil War in American Culture* in 2004; she has also edited Louisa May Alcott's *Hospital Sketches* (2004), an account of Alcott's nursing experiences during the Civil War first published in 1863. Fahs has been published on the cultural history of the Civil War and gender in such journals as the *Journal of American History and Civil War History*. Her honors include an American Council of Learned Societies Fellowship and a Gilder Lehrman Fellowship, as well as fellowships from the American Antiquarian Society, the Newberry Library, and the Huntington Library. She is currently at work on a study of popular literary culture in the late 19th and early 20th centuries, focused on the emergence of mass-market newspapers during an age of imperialism.

GARY GERSTLE

Vanderbilt University

Gary Gerstle is the James G. Stahlman Professor of American History at Vanderbilt. A historian of the 20th-century United States, he is the author, coauthor, and coeditor of six books and the author of more than 30 articles. His books include *Working-Class Americanism: The Politics of Labor in a Textile City, 1914–1960* (1989); *American Crucible: Race and Nation in the Twentieth Century* (2001), winner of the Saloutos Prize for the best work in immigration and ethnic history; *The Rise and Fall of the New Deal Order, 1930–1980* (1989); and *Ruling America: Wealth and Power in a Democracy* (2005). He has served on the board of editors of both the *Journal of American*

History and *The American Historical Review*. His honors include a National Endowment for the Humanities Fellowship, a John Simon Guggenheim Memorial Fellowship, the Harmsworth Professorship of American History at the University of Oxford, and membership in the Society of American Historians.

EMILY S. ROSENBERG
University of California, Irvine

Emily S. Rosenberg specializes in U.S. foreign relations in the 20th century and is the author of *Spreading the American Dream: American Economic and Cultural Expansion, 1890–1945* (1982); *Financial Missionaries to the World: The Politics and Culture of Dollar Diplomacy* (1999), which won the Ferrell Book Award; and *A Date Which Will Live: Pearl Harbor in American Memory* (2004). Her other publications include (with Norman L. Rosenberg) *In Our Times: America Since 1945*, Seventh Edition (2003), and numerous articles dealing with foreign relations in the context of international finance, American culture, and gender ideology. She has served on the board of the Organization of American Historians, on the board of editors of the *Journal of American History*, and as president of the Society for Historians of American Foreign Relations.

NORMAN L. ROSENBERG
Macalester College

Norman L. Rosenberg specializes in legal history with a particular interest in legal culture and First Amendment issues. His books include *Protecting the "Best Men": An Interpretive History of the Law of Libel* (1990) and (with Emily S. Rosenberg) *In Our Times: America Since 1945*, Seventh Edition (2003). He has published articles in the *Rutgers Law Review*, *UCLA Law Review*, *Constitutional Commentary*, *Law & History Review*, and many other journals and law-related anthologies.

BRIEF CONTENTS

17 RECONSTRUCTION, 1863–1877 385

18 A TRANSFORMED NATION: THE WEST AND THE NEW SOUTH, 1865–1900 407

19 THE RISE OF CORPORATE AMERICA, 1865–1914 432

20 CITIES, PEOPLES, CULTURES, 1890–1920 456

21 PROGRESSIVISM 478

22 BECOMING A WORLD POWER, 1898–1917 504

23 WAR AND SOCIETY, 1914–1920 527

24 THE 1920s 551

25 THE GREAT DEPRESSION AND THE NEW DEAL, 1929–1939 576

26 AMERICA DURING THE SECOND WORLD WAR 604

27 THE AGE OF CONTAINMENT, 1946–1953 632

28 AFFLUENCE AND ITS DISCONTENTS, 1953–1963 657

29 AMERICA DURING ITS LONGEST WAR, 1963–1974 685

30 UNCERTAIN TIMES, 1974–1992 712

31 ECONOMIC, SOCIAL, AND CULTURAL CHANGE IN THE LATE 20TH CENTURY 741

32 A TIME OF HOPE AND FEAR, 1993–2012 766

CONTENTS

LIST OF MAPS   XVII
LIST OF FEATURES   XIX
TO THE STUDENT   XXI
USING THE DISCOVERY SECTIONS   XXIII
PREFACE   XXV

17 RECONSTRUCTION, 1863–1877   385

WARTIME RECONSTRUCTION   386
   Radical Republicans and Reconstruction   387

ANDREW JOHNSON AND RECONSTRUCTION   387
   Johnson's Policy   388
   Southern Defiance   388
   The Black Codes   389
   Land and Labor in the Postwar South   389
   The Freedmen's Bureau   389
   Land for the Landless   390
   Education   390

THE ADVENT OF CONGRESSIONAL RECONSTRUCTION   391
   Schism between President and Congress   392
   The Fourteenth Amendment   392
   The 1866 Elections   392
   The Reconstruction Acts of 1867   393

THE IMPEACHMENT OF ANDREW JOHNSON   393
   The Completion of Formal Reconstruction   394
   The Fifteenth Amendment   394
   The Election of 1868   395

THE GRANT ADMINISTRATION   395
   Civil Service Reform and Foreign Policy Issues   396
   Reconstruction in the South   396
   Blacks in Office   397
   "Carpetbaggers"   397
   "Scalawags"   397

   The Ku Klux Klan   398
   The Election of 1872   398
HISTORY THROUGH FILM *Birth of a Nation* (1915)   399
   The Panic of 1873   400

THE RETREAT FROM RECONSTRUCTION   400
   The Mississippi Election of 1875   401
LINK TO THE PAST Frederick Douglass on the Supreme Court and Civil Rights   402
   The Supreme Court and Reconstruction   402
   The Election of 1876   403
   Disputed Results   403
   The Compromise of 1877   403
   The End of Reconstruction   404
   Conclusion   404

CHAPTER REVIEW   405

DISCOVERY   406

18 A TRANSFORMED NATION: THE WEST AND THE NEW SOUTH, 1865–1900   407

AN INDUSTRIALIZING WEST   408
   The Homestead Act   408
   Railroads   409
   Chinese Laborers and the Railroads   409
   Railroads and Borderland Communities   411
   Mining   411
   Cattle Drives and the Open Range   412
HISTORY THROUGH FILM *Oklahoma!* (1955)   413
   Industrial Ranching, Industrial Cowboys   414
   Mexican Americans   414
   Itinerant Laborers   415
   Homesteading and Farming   416
   The Experience of Homesteading   416
   Gender and Western Settlement   417

CONQUEST AND RESISTANCE: AMERICAN INDIANS IN THE TRANS-MISSISSIPPI WEST 417
Conflict with the Sioux 418
Suppression of Other Plains Indians 419
The "Peace Policy" 420
The Dawes Severalty Act and Indian Boarding Schools 420
VISUAL LINK TO THE PAST Indian Children at the Hampton Institute 421
The Ghost Dance 422
Sitting Bull and Buffalo Bill: Popular Myths of the West 422

INDUSTRIALIZATION AND THE NEW SOUTH 423
Race and Industrialization 423
Southern Agriculture 424
Exodusters and Emigrationists 424
Race Relations in the New South 425
The Emergence of an African American Middle Class 425
The Rise of Jim Crow 426

THE POLITICS OF STALEMATE 427
Knife-Edge Electoral Balance 427
Civil Service Reform 428
The Tariff Issue 428
Conclusion 429

CHAPTER REVIEW 430

DISCOVERY 431

19 THE RISE OF CORPORATE AMERICA, 1865–1914 432

A DYNAMIC CORPORATE ECONOMY 433
Engines of Economic Growth 434
Technological Innovation 434
The Rise of Big Business 434
Corporate Consolidation 435
Mass Production and Distribution 437
Revolution in Management 437

CORPORATIONS AND AMERICAN CULTURE 439
Standardized Time 439
A National Consumer Culture 439

Ideas of Wealth and Society 440
Sharpened Class Distinctions 440
Obsession with Physical and Racial Fitness 441

CHANGES IN MIDDLE-CLASS WOMEN'S LIVES 442
Middle-Class Women and Work 442
The Women's Club Movement 442
VISUAL LINK TO THE PAST The New Woman 443
The "New Woman" 444
Higher Education and Professional Organizations 444

WORKERS' RESISTANCE TO CORPORATIONS 444
Industrial Conditions 445
The Great Railroad Strike of 1877 445
The Knights of Labor 445
Haymarket 446
The American Federation of Labor (AFL) 447
The Homestead Strike 447
Coxey's Army 447
The Pullman Strike 448

FARMERS' MOVEMENTS 448
Resistance to Railroads 449
The Greenback and Silver Movements 449
Grangers and the Farmers' Alliance 450

THE RISE AND FALL OF THE PEOPLE'S PARTY 450
The Silver Issue 451
The Election of 1896 451

"ROBBER BARONS" NO MORE 453
Conclusion 454

CHAPTER REVIEW 454

DISCOVERY 455

20 CITIES, PEOPLES, CULTURES, 1890–1920 456

THE RISE OF THE CITY 457

IMMIGRATION 460
European Immigration 461
Chinese and Japanese Immigration 462

Immigrant Labor   464
Living Conditions   465

BUILDING ETHNIC COMMUNITIES   465
A Network of Institutions   465
The Emergence of an Ethnic Middle Class   465
Political Machines and Organized Crime   466

AFRICAN AMERICAN LABOR AND COMMUNITY   467
MUSICAL LINK TO THE PAST Ragtime   468

WORKING-CLASS AND COMMERCIAL CULTURE   469
Popular Literature   470
HISTORY THROUGH FILM *Coney Island*
(1917)   471

THE NEW SEXUALITY AND THE RISE OF FEMINISM   472

REIMAGINING AMERICAN NATIONALITY   473
Conclusion   475

CHAPTER REVIEW   476

DISCOVERY   477

21   PROGRESSIVISM   478

PROGRESSIVISM AND THE PROTESTANT SPIRIT   479

MUCKRAKERS AND THE TURN TOWARD "REALISM"   480

SETTLEMENT HOUSES AND WOMEN'S ACTIVISM   481
Hull House   481
The Cultural Conservatism of Progressive
Reformers   482
A Nation of Clubwomen   483

SOCIALISM   483
The Several Faces of Socialism   485
Socialists and Progressives   485

MUNICIPAL REFORM   485
The City Commission Plan   486
The City Manager Plan   486
The Costs of Reform   486

REFORM IN THE STATES   486
Restoring Sovereignty to "the People"   487
Creating a Virtuous Electorate   487
The Australian Ballot   487
Personal Registration Laws   487
Disfranchisement   488
Disillusionment with the Electorate   488
Woman Suffrage   488
Robert La Follette and Wisconsin Progressivism   490
LINK TO THE PAST Humor and the Woman Suffrage
Movement   491
Scientific Management on the Factory Floor   492

A CAMPAIGN FOR CIVIL RIGHTS   493
The Failure of Accommodationism   493
From the Niagara Movement to the NAACP   493

THE ROOSEVELT PRESIDENCY   494
Regulating the Trusts   494
Toward a "Square Deal"   495
Expanding Government Power: The Economy   495
Expanding Government Power: The
Environment   495
Progressivism: A Movement for the People?   496
The Republicans: A Divided Party   496

**THE TAFT PRESIDENCY: PROGRESSIVE DISAPPOINTMENT
AND RESURGENCE   497**
Battling Congress   497
The Ballinger-Pinchot Controversy   497
Roosevelt's Return   498
The Bull Moose Campaign   498
The Rise of Woodrow Wilson   498
The Election of 1912   499

THE WILSON PRESIDENCY   500
Tariff Reform and a Progressive Income Tax   500
The Federal Reserve Act   500
From the New Freedom to the New
Nationalism   501
Conclusion   501

CHAPTER REVIEW   502

DISCOVERY   503

22 BECOMING A WORLD POWER, 1898–1917 504

THE UNITED STATES LOOKS ABROAD 505
Protestant Missionaries 505
Businessmen 506
Imperialists 506

THE SPANISH–AMERICAN WAR 508
"A Splendid Little War" 509

THE UNITED STATES BECOMES A WORLD POWER 512
The Debate over the Treaty of Paris 513
The American–Filipino War 513
Controlling Cuba and Puerto Rico 514
MUSICAL LINK TO THE PAST Music for Patriots 515
China and the "Open Door" 516
HISTORY THROUGH FILM Tarzan, The Ape Man
(1932) 517

THEODORE ROOSEVELT, GEOPOLITICIAN 518
The Roosevelt Corollary 519
The Panama Canal 520
Keeping the Peace in East Asia 521

WILLIAM HOWARD TAFT, DOLLAR DIPLOMAT 522

WOODROW WILSON, STRUGGLING IDEALIST 523
Conclusion 524

CHAPTER REVIEW 525

DISCOVERY 526

23 WAR AND SOCIETY, 1914–1920 527

EUROPE'S DESCENT INTO WAR 528

AMERICAN NEUTRALITY 530
Submarine Warfare 531
The Peace Movement 532
Wilson's Vision: "Peace without Victory" 532
German Escalation 532

AMERICAN INTERVENTION 533

MOBILIZING FOR "TOTAL" WAR 534
Organizing Industry 534
LINK TO THE PAST "A Storm of Our People toward the
North" 535
Securing Workers, Keeping Labor Peace 535
Raising An Army 536
Paying the Bills 536
Arousing Patriotic Ardor 537
Wartime Repression 537

THE FAILURE OF THE INTERNATIONAL PEACE 540
The Paris Peace Conference and the Treaty of
Versailles 541
The League of Nations 541
Wilson versus Lodge: The Fight over
Ratification 542
The Treaty's Final Defeat 544

THE POSTWAR PERIOD: A SOCIETY IN CONVULSION 545
Labor–Capital Conflict 545
Radicals and the Red Scare 545
Racial Conflict and the Rise of Black
Nationalism 547
Conclusion 548

CHAPTER REVIEW 549

DISCOVERY 550

24 THE 1920S 551

PROSPERITY 552
A Consumer Society 552
A People's Capitalism 553
The Rise of Advertising and Mass Marketing 553
Changing Attitudes toward Marriage and
Sexuality 554
An Age of Celebrity 554
MUSICAL LINK TO THE PAST Women Singers and the
Birth of Modern Country Music 555
Celebrating a Business Civilization 556
Industrial Workers 557
Women and Work 557
The Women's Movement Adrift 558

THE POLITICS OF BUSINESS   559

Harding and the Politics of Personal Gain   559
Coolidge and Laissez-Faire Politics   560
Hoover and the Politics of Associationalism   560
The Politics of Business Abroad   561

FARMERS, SMALL-TOWN PROTESTANTS, AND MORAL TRADITIONALISTS   562

Agricultural Depression and Cultural Dislocation   562
Prohibition   563
The Ku Klux Klan   564
Immigration Restriction   564
Fundamentalism versus Liberal Protestantism   565
The Scopes Trial   566

ETHNIC AND RACIAL COMMUNITIES   567

European American Ethnics   567
African Americans   568
The Harlem Renaissance   569
HISTORY THROUGH FILM *The Jazz Singer* (1927)   570
Mexican Americans   571

THE "LOST GENERATION" AND DISILLUSIONED INTELLECTUALS   572

Democracy on the Defensive   573
Conclusion   573

CHAPTER REVIEW   574

DISCOVERY   575

25 THE GREAT DEPRESSION AND THE NEW DEAL, 1929–1939   576

CAUSES OF THE GREAT DEPRESSION   577

Stock Market Speculation   577
Ineffective Federal Policies   578
A Maldistribution of Wealth   578

HOOVER: THE FALL OF A SELF-MADE MAN   579

Hoover's Program   579
The Bonus Army   580

A CULTURE IN CRISIS   580

THE DEMOCRATIC ROOSEVELT   581

An Early Life of Privilege   581
Roosevelt Liberalism   582

THE FIRST NEW DEAL, 1933–1935   582

Saving the Banks   584
Economic Relief   584
Agricultural Reform   584
Industrial Reform   585
Rebuilding the Nation's Infrastructure   585
The TVA Alternative   585
The New Deal and Western Development   586

POLITICAL MOBILIZATION, POLITICAL UNREST, 1934–1935   588

Populist Critics of the New Deal   588
Labor Protests   588
Anger at the Polls   589
Radical Third Parties   589

THE SECOND NEW DEAL, 1935–1937   590

Philosophical Underpinnings   590
Legislation   590
Victory in 1936: The New Democratic Coalition   592
Rhetoric versus Reality   592
Men, Women, and Reform   593
Labor in Politics and Culture   594

AMERICA'S MINORITIES AND THE NEW DEAL   596

Eastern and Southern European Ethnics   596
African Americans   596
MUSICAL LINK TO THE PAST An African American Rhapsody   597
Mexican Americans   597
American Indians   598

THE NEW DEAL ABROAD   599

STALEMATE, 1937–1940   600

The Court-Packing Fiasco   600
The Recession of 1937–1938   600
Conclusion   600

CHAPTER REVIEW   602

DISCOVERY   603

26 AMERICA DURING THE SECOND WORLD WAR 604

THE ROAD TO WAR: AGGRESSION AND RESPONSE 605
The Rise of Aggressor States 606
U.S. Neutrality 606
The Mounting Crisis 607
The Outbreak of War in Europe 607
The U.S. Response to War in Europe 607
An "Arsenal of Democracy" 609
Pearl Harbor 609

FIGHTING THE WAR IN EUROPE AND THE PACIFIC 610
Campaigns in North Africa and Italy 610
Operation OVERLORD 611
HISTORY THROUGH FILM Saving Private Ryan
(1998) 612
Seizing the Offensive in the Pacific 614
China Policy 614
U.S. Strategy in the Pacific 614
A New President, the Atomic Bomb, and Japan's
Surrender 617

THE WAR AT HOME: THE ECONOMY 619
Government's Role in the Economy 619
Business and Finance 619
The Workforce 620
The Labor Front 621
A New Role for Government? 621

THE WAR AT HOME: SOCIAL ISSUES 622
Selling the War 622
Gender Issues 622
Racial Issues 623
Internment of Japanese Americans 624
Challenging Racial Inequality 625
LINK TO THE PAST Civil Liberties in Wartime: Korematsu v.
United States 626

SHAPING THE PEACE 627
International Organizations 627
Spheres of Interest and Postwar Settlements 628
Conclusion 629

CHAPTER REVIEW 630

DISCOVERY 631

27 THE AGE OF CONTAINMENT, 1946–1953 632

CREATING A NATIONAL SECURITY STATE,
1945–1949 633
Onset of the Cold War 633
The Truman Doctrine and Containment Abroad 634
Truman's Loyalty Program and Containment at
Home 635
The National Security Act, the Marshall Plan,
and the Berlin Crisis 635
The Election of 1948 636

THE ERA OF THE KOREAN WAR, 1949–1952 637
NATO, China, and the Bomb 637
NSC-68 and the Korean War 639
Korea and Containment 641

PURSUING NATIONAL SECURITY AT HOME 642
Anticommunism and the U.S. Labor
Movement 642
Containing Communism at Home 643
VISUAL LINK TO THE PAST It's Okay–We're Just Hunting
Communists 644
Targeting Difference 645
The "Great Fear" 645
Joseph McCarthy 646
The National Security Constitution and the Structure of
Governance 647

POSTWAR SOCIAL-ECONOMIC POLICY-MAKING 647
The Employment Act of 1946 and Economic
Growth 648
Truman's Fair Deal 648
Civil Rights 649

SIGNS OF A CHANGING CULTURE 650
The Baseball "Color Line" 650
The New Suburbia 651
Postwar Hollywood 652

THE ELECTION OF 1952 653
Continuing Containment 653
A Soldier–Politician 654
Conclusion 654

CHAPTER REVIEW 655

DISCOVERY 656

28 AFFLUENCE AND ITS DISCONTENTS, 1953–1963   657

REORIENTING CONTAINMENT, 1953–1960   658
Eisenhower Takes Command   658
The New Look, Global Alliances, and Summitry   659
Covert Action and Economic Leverage   659

THE THIRD WORLD   660

AFFLUENCE—A "PEOPLE OF PLENTY"   661
LINK TO THE PAST A Warning about the Future: President Dwight Eisenhower's Farewell Address, 1961   662
Economic Growth   662
Labor–Management Accord   663
Political Pluralism   663
A Religious People   665

DISCONTENTS OF AFFLUENCE   665
Conformity in an Affluent Society   665
Restive Youth   666
The Critique of Mass Culture   667

DEBATING THE ROLE OF GOVERNMENT   667
The New Conservatism   667
The Case for a More Active Government   668

NEW FRONTIERS, 1960–1963   669
The Election of 1960   669
Foreign Policy   670
Cuba and Berlin   670
Southeast Asia and Flexible Response   671

DOMESTIC POLICY-MAKING   672

THE POLITICS OF GENDER   672
The New Suburbs and Gender Politics   672
Signs of Women's Changing Roles   673
A New Women's Movement   673

THE EXPANDING CIVIL RIGHTS MOVEMENTS, 1953–1963   674
The Brown Cases, 1954–1955   674
The Montgomery Bus Boycott   676
The Politics of Civil Rights: From The Local to The Global   677

The Politics of American Indian Policy   677
Spanish-Speaking Communities and Civil Rights   678
Urban-Suburban Issues   679
New Forms of Direct Action, 1960–1963   679

NOVEMBER 1963   681
Policy Choices   681
The Assassination of John F. Kennedy   681
LINK TO THE PAST JFK (1991)   682
Conclusion   683

CHAPTER REVIEW   683

DISCOVERY   684

29 AMERICA DURING ITS LONGEST WAR, 1963–1974   685

THE GREAT SOCIETY   686
Closing the New Frontier   686
The Election of 1964   688
Lyndon Johnson's Great Society   689
Evaluating the Great Society   689

ESCALATION IN VIETNAM   690
The Gulf of Tonkin Resolution   690
The War Continues to Widen   692
VISUAL LINK TO THE PAST Shocking Images   693
The Media and the War   693

THE WAR AT HOME   694
The Movement of Movements   694
A New Left   695
The Counterculture   695
Civil Rights and Black Power   696
The Antiwar Movement   697

1968   698
Turmoil in Vietnam   698
Turmoil at Home   699
The Election of 1968   701

CONTINUED POLARIZATION, 1969–1974   701
Lawbreaking, Violence, and a New President   701
Social Policy   702

Environmentalism 702
Controversies over Rights 703
The Economy 704

FOREIGN POLICY IN A TIME OF TURMOIL, 1969–1974 705

Détente 705
Vietnamization and the Nixon Doctrine 706
The United States Leaves Vietnam 707
Expanding the Nixon Doctrine 707

A CRISIS OF GOVERNANCE, 1972–1974 708

The Election of 1972 708
The Watergate Investigations 708
Nixon's Resignation 709
Conclusion 710

CHAPTER REVIEW 710

DISCOVERY 711

30 UNCERTAIN TIMES, 1974–1992 712

SEARCHING FOR DIRECTION, 1974–1980 713

A Faltering Economy 714
Welfare and Energy Initiatives 715
Negotiation and Confrontation in Foreign Policy 715
The New Right 717

THE REAGAN REVOLUTION, 1981–1992 718

The Election of 1980 718
Supply-Side Economics 719
Curtailing Unions, Regulations, and Welfare 720
Reagan to Bush 721
HISTORY THROUGH FILM *The First Movie-Star President* 722

RENEWING AND ENDING THE COLD WAR 723

The Defense Buildup 723
Deploying Military Power 724
The Iran-*Contra* Controversy 724
The Cold War Eases 725
Post–Cold War Policy and the Persian Gulf War 726
The Election of 1992 728

THE POLITICS OF SOCIAL MOVEMENTS 729

Women's Issues 729
LINK TO THE PAST Cultural Disagreements: Equality for Women? 731
Sexual Politics 731
Activism among African Americans 733
Activism among American Indians 733
Activism in Spanish-Speaking Communities 734
Activism among Asian Americans 736
Anti-Government Activism 736
Conclusion 738

CHAPTER REVIEW 739

DISCOVERY 740

31 ECONOMIC, SOCIAL, AND CULTURAL CHANGE IN THE LATE 20TH CENTURY 741

A CHANGING PEOPLE 742

An Aging, Shifting Population 742
The New Immigration 744
The Metropolitan Nation 747

ECONOMIC TRANSFORMATIONS 749

New Technologies 749
Changes in the Structure and Operations of Business 750
The Financial Sector 752
The Sports-Entertainment Industry 753

CULTURE AND MEDIA 755

The Video Revolution 755
Hollywood 756
The Changing Media Environment for Pop Music 758
The New Mass Culture Debate 758
The Religious Landscape 759
MUSICAL LINK TO THE PAST Hip-Hop Leaps In 760
Conclusion 763

CHAPTER REVIEW 764

DISCOVERY 765

32 A TIME OF HOPE AND FEAR, 1993–2012 766

THE POLITICS OF POLARIZATION, 1993–2008 768
    A New Democrat 768
    A Decade of Legal Investigations and Trials 769
    The Investigation and Trial of a President 770
HISTORY THROUGH FILM *The Big Lebowski*
(1998) 771
    The Long Election and Trials of 2000 772
    A Conservative Washington, 2001–2008 773
    Politics and Social-Cultural Issues 775

FOREIGN POLICIES OF HOPE AND TERROR:
1993–2008 776
    Clinton's Internationalist Agenda 776
    Globalization 777
    Protecting the Planet 777
    September 11, 2001, and the Bush Doctrine 778
    Unilateralism and the Iraq War 778
    National Security and Presidential Power 781
    Divisions over Foreign Policy Direction 783

AN ECONOMY OF BUBBLE AND BUST,
1993–2008 783
    Deregulation of the Financial Sector during the
    1990s 784
    Economics for a New Century, 2000–2006 784
    The Bubble Bursts, 2006–2008 785
    The Election of 2008 786

CHANGING TIMES, 2009– 787
    Political Polarization 787
VISUAL LINK TO THE PAST The Future of Print
Media? 789
    The Culture of Social Networking and Liberty,
    Equality, Power 790
    The Election of 2012 790
    Conclusion 792

CHAPTER REVIEW 793

DISCOVERY 794

APPENDIX A-1

INDEX I-1

LIST OF MAPS

Map 18.1 Railroad Expansion, 1870–1890 **410**

Map 18.2 Indian Reservations, 1875 and 1900 **418**

Map 19.1 Industrial America, 1900–1920 **438**

Map 19.2 Presidential Election of 1896 **452**

Map 21.1 Cities and Towns Electing Socialists as Mayors or as Other Major Municipal Officers, 1911–1920 **484**

Map 21.2 Woman Suffrage before 1920 **490**

Map 21.3 Presidential Election, 1912 **499**

Map 22.1 Spanish–American War in Cuba, 1898 **510**

Map 22.2 American South Pacific Empire, 1900 **512**

Map 22.3 U.S. Presence in Latin America, 1895–1934 **519**

Map 22.4 Panama Canal Zone, 1914 **521**

Map 23.1 Europe Goes to War **529**

Map 23.2 Europe and the Near East after the First World War **542**

Map 24.1 Urbanization, 1920 **563**

Map 24.2 Presidential Election, 1928 **568**

Map 25.1 Presidential Election, 1932 **581**

Map 25.2 Tennessee Valley Authority **586**

Map 25.3 Federal Water Projects in California Built or Funded by the New Deal **587**

Map 25.4 Presidential Election, 1936 **593**

Map 26.1 German Expansion at Its Height **608**

Map 26.2 Allied Advances and Collapse of German Power **613**

Map 26.3 Pacific Theater Offensive Strategy and Final Assault Against Japan **616**

Map 27.1 Presidential Election, 1948 **637**

Map 27.2 Divided Germany and the NATO Alliance **638**

Map 27.3 Korean War **640**

Map 27.4 Presidential Election, 1952 **654**

Map 28.1 Presidential Election, 1960 **670**

Map 28.2 Shifts in African American Population Patterns, 1940–1960 **675**

Map 29.1 Vietnam War **691**

Map 29.2 Presidential Election, 1968 **701**

Map 30.1 Presidential Election, 1976 **714**

Map 30.2 Presidential Election, 1980 **719**

Map 30.3 Collapse of the Soviet Bloc **727**

Map 30.4 Presidential Election, 1992 **729**

Map 31.1 Population Shifts toward the Sun Belt **744**

Map 31.2 New Americans: Percentage of Persons Who Are Foreign Born and Foreign-Born Population by Region of Birth, 2000 **746**

Map 32.1 Presidential Election, 2000 **772**

Map 32.2 Presidential Election, 2008 **786**

LIST OF FEATURES

HISTORY THROUGH FILM

Birth of a Nation (1915) **399**

Oklahoma! (1955) **413**

Coney Island (1917) **471**

Tarzan, The Ape Man (1932) **517**

The Jazz Singer (1927) **570**

Saving Private Ryan (1998) **612**

JFK (1991) **682**

The First Movie-Star President **722**

The Big Lebowski (1998) **771**

MUSICAL LINKS TO THE PAST

Ragtime **468**

Music for Patriots **515**

Women Singers and the Birth of Modern Country Music **555**

An African American Rhapsody **597**

Hip-Hop Leaps In **760**

LINKS TO THE PAST

Frederick Douglass on the Supreme Court and
   Civil Rights **402**

Humor and the Woman Suffrage Movement **491**

"A Storm of Our People toward the North" **535**

Civil Liberties in Wartime: Korematsu v.
   United States **626**

A Warning about the Future: President Dwight Eisenhower's
   Farewell Address, 1961 **662**

Cultural Disagreements: Equality for Women? **731**

VISUAL LINKS TO THE PAST

Indian Children at the Hampton Institute **421**

The New Woman **443**

It's Okay—We're Hunting Communists **644**

Shocking Images **693**

The Future of Print Media? **789**

WHY STUDY HISTORY?

Why take a course in American history? This is a question that many college and university student ask. In many respects, students today are like the generations of Americans who have gone before them: optimistic and forward looking, far more eager to imagine where we as a nation might be going than to reflect on where we have been. If anything, this tendency has become more pronounced in recent years, as the Internet revolution has accelerated the pace and excitement of change and made even the recent past seem at best quaint, at worst uninteresting and irrelevant.

But it is precisely in these moments of change that a sense of the past can be indispensable in guiding our actions in the present and future. We can find in other periods of American history moments, like our own, of dizzying technological change and economic growth, rapid alterations in the concentration of wealth and power, and basic changes in patterns of work, residence, and play. How did Americans at those times create, embrace, and resist these changes? In earlier periods of American history, the United States was home, as it is today, to a broad array of ethnic and racial groups. How did earlier generations of Americans respond to the cultural conflicts and misunderstandings that often arise from conditions of diversity? How did immigrants of the early 1900s perceive their new land? How and when did they integrate themselves into American society? To study how ordinary Americans of the past struggled with these issues is to gain perspective on the opportunities and problems that we face today.

History also provides an important guide to affairs of state. What role should America assume in world affairs? Should we participate in international bodies such as the United Nations, or insist on our ability to act autonomously and without the consent of other nations? What is the proper role of government in economic and social life? Should the government regulate the economy? To what extent should the government enforce morality regarding religion, sexual practices, drinking and drugs, movies, TV, and other forms of mass culture? And what are our responsibilities as citizens to each other and to the nation? Americans of past generations have debated these issues with verve and conviction. Exploring these debates, and how they were resolved, will enrich our understanding of the policy possibilities for today and tomorrow.

History, finally, is about stories—stories that we all tell about ourselves; our families; our communities; our ethnicity, race, region, and religion; and our nation. They are stories of triumph and tragedy, of engagement and flight, and of high ideals and high comedy. When telling these stories, "American history" is often the furthest thing from our minds. But, often, an implicit sense of the past informs what we say about grandparents who immigrated many years ago; the suburb in which we live; the church, synagogue, or mosque at which we worship; or the ethnic or racial group to which we belong. How well, we might ask, do we really understand these individuals, institutions, and groups? Do our stories about them capture their history and complexity? Or do our stories wittingly or unwittingly simplify or alter what these individuals and groups experienced? A study of American history helps us first to ask these questions and then to answer them. In the process, we can embark on a journey of intellectual and personal discovery and situate ourselves more firmly than we had thought possible in relation to those who came before us. We can gain a firmer self-knowledge and a greater appreciation for the richness of our nation and, indeed, of all humanity.

Astronomers investigate the universe through telescopes. Biologists study the natural world by collecting plants and animals in the field and then examining them with microscopes. Sociologists and psychologists study human behavior through observation and controlled laboratory experiments.

Historians study the past by examining historical "evidence" or "source" materials—government documents; the records of private institutions ranging from religious and charitable organizations to labor unions, corporations, and lobbying groups; letters, advertisements, paintings, music, literature, movies, and cartoons; buildings, clothing, farm implements, industrial machinery, and landscapes—anything and everything written or created by our ancestors that gives clues about their lives and the times in which they lived.

Historians refer to written material as "documents." Excerpts of dozens of documents appear throughout the textbook—within the chapters and in the "Discovery" sections. Each chapter also includes many visual representations of the American past in the form of photographs of buildings, paintings, murals, individuals, cartoons, sculptures, and other historical evidence. As you read each chapter, the more you examine this "evidence," the more you will understand the main ideas of this book and of the course you are taking. The better you become at reading evidence, the better historian you will become.

"Discovery" sections at the end of each chapter assist you in practicing these skills by taking a closer look at specific images, quotes, or maps that will help you to connect the various threads of American history and to excel in your course.

DISCOVERY

What kind of culture emerged out of the market revolution that was discussed in Chapter 9? What was the impact on American families of the popular culture discussed in Chapter 10?

In thinking about this question, begin by breaking it down into the components shown below. A discussion of the significance of each component should appear in your answer.

The Impact of the Market on Family Life

Look at the illustration of domestic life on page 230. What does it suggest about how middle-class Americans saw their lives and their daily activities? What did the family want to reveal about their life at home? How does the illustration reflect the artist's definitions of *domesticity* and *sentimentality*? What would a photograph of your family suggest to future generations about the way you lived?

The Impact of the "New Popular Culture" on Family Life

Examine the image of an evening at the theater in the early 19th century. Does this activity seem to attract more men or women? How do you account for this gender difference? Is this gender difference important?

AN EARLY PRINT OF "JIM CROW" RICE AT NEW YORK'S BOWERY THEATER

Liberty, Equality, Power is a textbook admired for its successful integration of political, cultural, and social history; its thematic unity; its narrative clarity and eloquence; its extraordinary coverage of pre-Columbian America; its attention to war and conquest; its extended treatment of the Civil War; its history of economic growth and change; and its robust map and illustration programs. We have preserved and enhanced all these strengths in this Concise Sixth Edition. The concise version is intended to make the textbook more accessible to a broad range of students and give instructors maximum flexibility in their teaching. A brief edition, for example, makes it easier for instructors both to reach out to students who might be discouraged by a longer narrative and to supplement the textbook with readings, Web-based exercises, movies, and related materials of their own choosing.

THE LIBERTY, EQUALITY, POWER APPROACH

In this book we tell many small stories, and one large one: how America transformed itself, in a relatively brief era of world history, from a land inhabited by hunter-gatherer and agricultural Native American societies into the most powerful industrial nation on earth. This story has been told many times before, and those who have told it in the past have usually emphasized the political experiment in liberty and equality that took root here in the 18th century. We, too, stress the extraordinary and transformative impact that the ideals of liberty and equality exerted on American politics, society, and economics during the American Revolution and after. We show how the creation of a free economic environment, one that nourished entrepreneurship and technological innovation, underpinned American industrial might. We emphasize, too, the successful struggles for freedom that, over the course of the last 230 years, have brought—first to all white men, then to men of color, and finally to women— rights and opportunities that they had not previously known. But we have also identified a third factor in this pantheon of American ideals: power. We examine power in many forms— the accumulation of economic fortunes that dominated the economy and politics; the dispossession of Native Americans from land that they regarded as theirs; the enslavement of millions of Africans and their African American descendants for a period of almost 250 years; the relegation of women and of racial, ethnic, and religious minorities to subordinate places in American society; and the extension of American control over foreign peoples, such as Latin Americans and Filipinos, who would have preferred to be free and self-governing. We do not mean to suggest that American power has always been turned to negative purposes. To the contrary: Subordinate groups have themselves marshaled power to combat oppression, as in the abolitionist and civil rights crusades, the campaign for woman's suffrage, and the labor movement. In the 20th century, the federal government used its power to moderate poverty and to manage the economy in the interests of general prosperity. While one form of power sustained slavery over many generations, another, greater power abolished the institution in four years. Later, the federal government mobilized the nation's military might to defeat Nazi Germany, World War II Japan, the Cold War Soviet Union, and other enemies of freedom. The invocation of power as a variable in American history forces us to widen the lens through which we look at the past and to complicate the stories we tell. Ours has been a history of freedom and domination, of progress toward democracy and of delays and reverses, of abundance and poverty, of wars to free peoples from tyranny and battles to put foreign markets under American control.

In complicating our master narrative in this way, we think we have rendered American history more exciting and intriguing. Progress has not been automatic, but has been instead the product of ongoing struggles.

In this book we have also tried to capture the diversity of the American past, both in terms of outcomes and in terms of the variety of groups who have participated in America's making. We have not presented Native Americans simply as the victims of European aggression, but as a people diverse in their own ranks, with a variety of systems of social organization and cultural expression. We give equal treatment to the industrial titans of American history—the likes of Andrew Carnegie and John D. Rockefeller—and to those, such as small farmers and skilled workers, who resisted the corporate reorganization of economic life. We dwell on the achievements of 1863, when African Americans were freed from slavery, and of 1868, when they were made full citizens of the United States. But we also note how a majority of African Americans had to wait another 100 years, until the civil rights movement of the 1960s, to gain full access to American freedoms. We tell similarly complex stories about women, Latinos, and groups of ethnic Americans.

Political issues, of course, are only part of America's story. Americans have always pursued individuality and happiness and, in the process, have created the world's most vibrant popular culture. They have embraced technological innovations, especially those promising to make their lives easier and more fun. In light of this history, we have devoted considerable space to a discussion of popular culture, from the founding of the first newspapers in the 18th century to the rise of movies, jazz, and comics in the 20th century, to the cable television and Internet revolutions of recent years. We have pondered, too, how American industry has periodically altered home and personal life by making new products—such as clothing, cars, refrigerators, and computers— available to consumers. In such ways we hope to give our readers a rich portrait of how Americans spent their time, money, and leisure at various points in our history.

New to this edition

In preparing for this revision, we solicited feedback from professors and scholars throughout the country, many of whom have used the comprehensive or concise editions of *Liberty, Equality, Power* in their classrooms. Many of their suggestions have been incorporated into the Concise Sixth Edition. Thus, for example, at the prompting of reviewers, we have expanded our primary source program to include new "Visual Links to the Past," described below. We have also undertaken for this edition a major reorganization and overhaul of Chapters 19 and 20. The new Chapter 19 now brings together and reworks material on late 19th-century economics, technology, and labor that in earlier editions had appeared in multiple chapters. The new Chapter 20, in turn, focuses on cities, peoples, and cultures during that same period of time. Much of the material in Chapter 20 is new and deepens our textbook's engagement with cultural and intellectual history. Chapters 29, 30, and 32 have also been significantly revised and reorganized to provide new perspectives on the most recent past.

Finally, we have scrutinized each page of the textbook, making sure our prose is clear, the historical issues are well presented, and the scholarship is up to date. This review, guided by the scholarly feedback we received, caused us to make numerous revisions and additions. A list of notable content changes follows.

Specific Revisions to Content and Coverage

Chapter 1 New Link to the Past feature, Miguel León-Portilla, *The Broken Spears*. Deleted "Brazil" section.

Chapter 2 Condensed "Dutch and Swedish Settlements" section by shifting focus to the Dutch. New Link to the Past feature, "A City upon a Hill."

Chapter 3 New Visual Link to the Past feature, *A Pictish Man Holding a Human Head*, by John White; new map of Pueblo Revolt, 1680. Streamlined "Demographic Differences" section.

Chapter 4 New Visual Link to the Past feature, Benjamin West's *Benjamin Franklin Drawing Electricity from the Sky* (circa 1817). Rearranged and streamlined "Political Culture in the Colonies" section.

Chapter 5 Deleted sections on "The Feudal Revival and Rural Discontent" and "Regulator Movements in the Carolinas."

Chapter 6 Streamlined material on loyalists.

Chapter 7 New Link to the Past feature, "Washington's Republican Court."

Chapter 8 Deleted references to "safety-first" agriculture; condensed "The Decline of Patriarchy" section and moved to Chapter 12.

Chapter 9 New Visual Link to the Past feature, "A Southern View of Slavery"; increased coverage of crops and regions other than cotton; revised treatment of Denmark Vesey takes into account work of Michael Johnson; condensed treatment of government role in settlement; discussion of invention of the cotton gin revised to give less exclusive credit to Eli Whitney; added Link to the Past feature, "A Slave Mother and the Slave Trade"; revised Map 9.2 Distribution of Slave Population, 1790, 1820, and 1860.

Chapter 10 New Musical Link to the Past feature, "Oh Susannah"; moved discussions of *Uncle Tom's Cabin* and American Colonization Society to Chapter 12; deleted section entitled "Southern Entertainments" in response to reviewer feedback.

Chapter 11 Reworked Conclusion; added Focus Questions.

Chapter 12 New Visual Link to the Past feature, "An Abolitionist View of Slave Society"; reworked Introduction and Conclusion; deleted section on "Appetites"; expanded and revised treatments of antislavery movement and women's rights with increased emphasis on influence of blacks and women; condensed treatment of economic development.

Chapters 13 and 14 Added material in sections on Manifest Destiny, the Gold Rush, the Oregon Trail, and Harriet Beecher Stowe; Chapter 13 includes a new Visual Link to the Past feature, "Manifest Destiny."

Chapter 15 Condensed material on foreign relations, eliminating the section on the Trent affair.

Chapter 16 New Link to the Past feature, "'We Cannot Escape History': Abraham Lincoln."

Chapter 17 Condensed material on the Treaty of Washington. New Link to the Past feature, "Frederick Douglass on the Supreme Court and Civil Rights."

Chapter 18 New material on mining; condensed material on ranching and cowboys; new Visual Link to the Past feature, "Indian Children at the Hampton Institute."

Chapter 19 (MAJOR REVISION) Completely revised and reorganized. Now titled "The Rise of Corporate America, 1865–1914," it incorporates material from Fifth Edition Chapters 19 and 20 so that the story of the growth of American corporations is told in one place. New Visual Link to the Past feature, "The New Woman."

Chapter 20 (MAJOR REVISION) New title, Introduction, and Conclusion; added two substantial sections, "The Rise of the City" and "Reimagining American Nationality"; substantially revised section, "Working-Class and Commercial Culture" (formerly, "The Joys of the City"); new Musical Link to the Past feature, "Ragtime"; new History through Film feature, *Coney Island* (1917); added Focus Questions and glossary terms.

Chapter 21 Added sections on the IWW and Frederick W. Taylor and scientific management; added Focus Questions;

reduced number of major headings. New Link to the Past feature, "Humor and the Woman Suffrage Movement."

Chapter 23 New Link to the Past feature, "A Storm of Our People toward the North."

Chapter 24 Moved History through Film feature on *The Jazz Singer* here from Chapter 20.

Chapter 25 Condensed material on the Federal Reserve Board and the tariff; added Focus Questions.

Chapter 26 Streamlined and revised prose to provide stronger narrative; condensed sections on European and Pacific theaters into one; increased attention to role of West in "Business and Finance" section; expanded coverage of Japanese internment and added mention of Italian and German internees; revised Focus Questions; added History through Film feature, *Saving Private Ryan* (1998); new Link to the Past feature, "Civil Liberties in Wartime: *Korematsu v. United States*."

Chapter 27 Revised Korean War section, giving greater emphasis to war's impact; substantially revised discussion of containment; updated material on McCarthy; added material on farm issues; revised Fair Deal section; added discussion of integration of armed forces; revised end of chapter in light of recent scholarship on significance of election of 1952; new Visual Link to the Past feature, "It's Okay—We're Hunting Communists"; revised Focus Questions.

Chapter 28 Combined coverage of civil rights movement into one section; revised coverage of conservatism in sections "Debating the Role of Government" and "The Case for a More Active Government"; refocused final section of chapter; reorganized and streamlined the section "The Third World"; added material on rural America and farm policy; new Link to the Past feature, "A Warning about the Future: President Dwight Eisenhower's Farewell Address, 1961."

Chapter 29 (MAJOR REVISION) Streamlined and reorganized to clarify and focus narrative; reframed section, "A Crisis of Governance, 1972–1974"; reworked civil rights material; added discussion of environmentalism; revised accounts of 1964 election and Gulf of Tonkin; revised Focus Questions; new Visual Link to the Past feature, "Shocking Images."

Chapter 30 (MAJOR REVISION) Completely reorganized chapter along thematic lines; new section, "The Reagan Revolution, 1981–1992," includes a more focused discussion of the central themes of the administration of Ronald Reagan; added Link to the Past feature, "Cultural Disagreements: Equality for Women?"

Chapter 31 Revised section on the financial sector.

Chapter 32 (MAJOR REVISION) Revised and updated entire chapter; reworked economic discussion; new Visual Link to the Past feature, "The Future of Print Media?"; new History through Film feature, *The Big Lebowski* (1998); revised Focus Questions.

FEATURES

The success of our **Musical Link to the Past** feature has inspired us to expand our primary source program in new directions for this edition: We have added an entirely new feature, **Visual Link to the Past.** Each of the new Visual Links focuses on a single piece of art, material culture, or photography that reveals something important about the historical era in which it was produced. In an extended caption we explore the historical significance of the object in question, and then pose a question for students to answer. Examples include "Benjamin West's *Benjamin Franklin Drawing Electricity from the Sky* (circa 1817)" (Chapter 4); "Indian Children at the Hampton Institute" (Chapter 18); "The New Woman," featuring a John Singer Sargent portrait (Chapter 19); and a political cartoon "It's Okay—We're Hunting Communists" (Chapter 27).

The Concise Sixth Edition also incorporates some of the **Link to the Past** features that have appeared in the comprehensive version for several editions. These features explore important written documents from the American past and include an assignable question for individual response or classroom discussion. Featured documents include an 1852 letter from an enslaved woman to her husband expressing distress at the recent sale of their son (Chapter 9), a poem which takes a lighthearted look at woman suffrage (Chapter 21), and an excerpt from President Eisenhower's Farewell Address, warning about escalating the Cold War arms race (Chapter 28).

We've retained the Musical Link to the Past features, which cover a great range of songs and artists: from revolutionary era odes to liberty to 20th-century country music laments about women's domestic burdens; from John Philip Sousa to Duke Ellington and Grandmaster Flash. The Concise Sixth Edition includes two new entries: Stephen Foster, "Oh Susannah" (Chapter 10); and Scott Joplin, "Maple Leaf Rag" (Chapter 20). Dr. Harvey Cohen, a specialist in American cultural history who teaches at King's College London, drafted the texts of these musical features, and we wish to recognize his important contributions to this textbook. To make the Musical Links come alive in classrooms, we have assembled a **Musical Links to the Past CD** containing many of the musical selections that we discuss. All instructors who adopt our textbook are encouraged to request a free copy of this CD to play in their classrooms. In combination, the three Links features—musical, visual, and textual—endow our Concise Sixth Edition with one of the most comprehensive, diverse, and intriguing programs of primary sources available in a U.S. history textbook.

The popular **History through Film** essays summarize a film, note interesting historical questions that it raises, and offer commentary on the accuracy or inaccuracy of historical figures and events as seen through the lens of a camera. The Concise Sixth Edition includes 15 History through Film features, including *A Midwife's Tale* (Chapter 8), *Amistad* (Chapter 11), a new feature on *Coney Island* (Chapter 20), and *Saving Private Ryan* (Chapter 26).

Visually engaging **Timelines** help students understand the relationships among the events and movements of a particular era. Many chapter sections open with **Focus Questions** to aid students in grasping overarching themes and to organize the knowledge that they are acquiring. These reappear at the end of each chapter in the **Chapter Review**, which is supplemented by **Critical Thinking Questions** that encourage students to range widely and imaginatively in their thinking about what they have just learned. **Identification** lists at the end of the chapter highlight the key terms for study and review.

Quick Reviews and **Glossary Terms** further contribute to the emphasis we have placed on pedagogy. Quick Reviews appear periodically in the margins to summarize major events, ideas, and movements discussed in the text. Glossary Terms—individuals, ideas, events, legislation, and movements that we have deemed particularly important to an understanding of the historical period in question— appear boldface in the text and then are briefly defined in the margins.

SUPPLEMENTS

FOR THE INSTRUCTOR

The Instructor's Companion Web Site provides instructors access to all of the features of the Student Companion Web Site, along with the eInstructor's Resource Manual. This manual has many features, including instructional objectives, chapter outlines and summaries, lecture suggestions, suggested debate and research topics, cooperative learning activities, and suggested readings and resources.

The PowerLecture with ExamView and JoinIn, [ISBN: 9781285059334] a dual-platform, all-in-one multimedia resource, includes the Instructor's Resource Manual; Test Bank, revised by D. Antonio Cantù of Bradley University (includes key term identification, multiple-choice, short answer, essay, and map questions); Microsoft® PowerPoint® slides of both lecture outlines and images and maps from the text that can be used as offered, or customized by importing personal lecture slides or other material; and JoinIn® Power-Point® slides with clicker content. Also included is ExamView, an easy-to-use assessment and tutorial system that allows instructors to create, deliver, and customize tests in minutes. Instructors can build tests with as many as 250 questions using up to 12 question types, and using ExamView's complete word-processing capabilities, they can enter an unlimited number of new questions or edit existing ones.

Cengage Learning's History **CourseMate** brings course concepts to life with interactive learning, study, and exam preparation tools that support the printed textbook. Watch student comprehension soar as your class works with the printed textbook and the textbook-specific Web site. History CourseMate includes an integrated eBook, interactive teaching and learning tools including quizzes, revised by Thomas Born of Blinn College, flashcards, videos, and more, and EngagementTracker, a first-of-its-kind tool that monitors student engagement in the course. Learn more at www.cengagebrain.com.

Aplia™ is an online interactive learning solution that improves comprehension and outcomes by increasing student effort and engagement. Founded by a professor to enhance his own courses, Aplia provides automatically graded assignments with detailed, immediate explanations on every question and innovative teaching materials. Our easy-to-use system has been used by more than one million students at over 1,800 institutions. Features include "flip-book" navigation that allows students to easily scan the contents; chapter assignments, developed specifically for your textbook and customizable for your course, that are automatically graded and provide detailed responses to students; a course management system so you can post announcements, upload course materials, host student discussions, e-mail students, and manage your gradebook; and personalized support from a knowledgeable and friendly team. Our support team also offers assistance in customizing our assignments to your course schedule. To learn more, visit www.aplia.com.

FOR THE STUDENT

The Student Companion Web Site allows students to access a wide assortment of resources to help them master the subject matter. The Web site includes a glossary, flashcards, tutorial quizzes, essay questions, critical thinking exercises, Web links, and suggested readings. Throughout the text, icons direct students to relevant exercises and self-testing material located on the student companion Web site.

The History Handbook, Second Edition [ISBN: 9780495906766], by Carol Berkin of Baruch College, City University of New York, and Betty Anderson of Boston University, teaches students both basic and history-specific study skills such as how to read primary sources, research historical topics, and correctly cite sources. Substantially less expensive than comparable skill-building texts, *The History Handbook* also offers tips for Internet research and evaluating online sources.

Doing History: Research and Writing in the Digital Age, Second Edition [ISBN: 9781133587880], by Michael J. Galgano, J. Chris Arndt, and Raymond M. Hyser of James Madison University, is a perfect guide whether you are starting down the path of a history major or simply looking for a straightforward, systematic guide to writing a successful paper. This text is an indispensable handbook to historical research. Its "soup-to-nuts" approach to researching and writing about history addresses every step of the process, from locating your sources and gathering information, to writing clearly and making proper use of various citation styles to avoid plagiarism. You'll also learn how to make the most of every tool available to you—especially the technology that helps you conduct the process efficiently and effectively. The Second Edition includes a special appendix linked to CourseReader (see below), where you can examine and interpret primary sources online.

The Modern Researcher, Sixth Edition [ISBN: 9780495318705], by Jacques Barzun and Henry F. Graff of Columbia University, a classic introduction to the techniques of research and the art of expression, is used widely in history courses but is also appropriate for writing and research method courses in other departments. Barzun and Graff thoroughly cover every aspect of research, from the selection of a topic through the gathering, analysis, writing, revision, and publication of findings, presenting the process not as a set of rules but through actual cases that put the subtleties of research in a useful context. Part One covers the principles and methods of research; Part Two covers writing, speaking, and getting one's work published.

Rand McNally Atlas of American History, Second Edition [ISBN: 9780618842018], is a comprehensive atlas that features more than 80 maps, with new content covering global perspectives, including events in the Middle East from 1945 to 2005, as well as population trends in the United States and around the world. Additional maps document voyages of discovery; the settling of the colonies; major U.S. military engagements, including the American Revolution and World Wars I and II; and sources of immigrations, ethnic populations, and patterns of economic change.

Our new **CourseReader** lets you create a customized electronic reader in minutes. With our easy-to-use interface and assessment tool, you can choose exactly what your students will be assigned—simply search or browse Cengage Learning's extensive document database to preview and select your customized collection of readings.

Once you've made your choice, students will always receive the pedagogical support they need to succeed with the materials you've chosen: Each source document includes a descriptive headnote that puts the reading into context, and every selection is further supported by both critical thinking and multiple-choice questions designed to reinforce key points.

Acknowledgments

We recognize the contributions of these reviewers, who have provided feedback on *Liberty*, *Equality*, *Power*, Concise Edition:

David Arnold, Columbia Basin College

Mary Ann Bodayla, Southwest Tennessee Community College

Betty Brandon, University of Southern Alabama

Janet Brantley, Texarkana College

April L. Brown, NorthWest Arkansas Community College

B. R. Burg, Arizona State University

Gary Damron, Seward County Community College

Randy Finley, Georgia Perimeter College

Michael P. Gabriel, Kutztown University

Steven C. Garvey, Muskegon Community College

Wendy Gordon, SUNY Plattsburgh

Sally Hadden, Florida State University

Kevin E. Hall, University of South Florida

Ian Harrison, University of Nevada, Las Vegas

Mary Ann Heiss, Kent State University

Terry Isaacs, South Plains College

Volker Janssen, California State University, Fullerton

Catherine Kaplan, Arizona State University

Timothy K. Kinsella, Ursuline College

Greg Kiser, NorthWest Arkansas Community College

C. Douglas Kroll, College of the Desert

David F. Krugler, University of Wisconsin, Platteville

Joseph Lapsley, Columbia College of Art

Marianne F. McKnight, Salt Lake Community College

Joel McMahon, Baker College

Salvatore R. Mercogliano, Central Carolina Community College

Caryn E. Neumann, Miami University of Ohio

Margaret E. Newell, Ohio State University

Thomas Ott, University of North Alabama

George S. Pabis, Georgia Perimeter College

Birte Pfleger, California State University, Los Angeles

Geoffrey Plank, University of Cincinnati

G. David Price, Santa Fe Community College (FL)

John Putman, San Diego State University

Akim D. Reinhardt, Towson University

Jason Ripper, Everett Community College

Jerry Rodnitzky, University of Texas, Arlington

John Paul Rossi, Penn State Erie

Steven T. Sheehan, University of Wisconsin, Fox Valley

Megan Taylor Shockley, Clemson University

Adam M. Sowards, University of Idaho

Evelyn Sterne, University of Rhode Island

Kristen L. Streater, Collin County Community College, Preston Ridge Campus

Sean Taylor, Minnesota State University, Moorhead

Jerry Tiarsmith, Georgia Perimeter College

Leslie V. Tischauser, Prairie State College

Paul S. Vickery, Oral Roberts University

Stephen Webre, Louisiana Tech University

Bryan Wuthrich, Santa Fe Community College (FL)

We also wish to thank Carol Newman, senior content project manager, and other members of the Wadsworth staff who capably guided the revision and production of this edition. Special thanks to Ann West, senior sponsoring editor, for her wisdom, support, and mastery of textbook publishing, and to Rob Heinrich, freelance editor, for the quality of his editing. Our greatest debt once again is to our longtime developmental editor, Margaret McAndrew Beasley. Margaret's editing skills, organizational expertise, good sense, and belief in this book and its authors keep us going.

John M. Murrin
Paul E. Johnson
James M. McPherson
Alice Fahs
Gary Gerstle
Emily S. Rosenberg
Norman L. Rosenberg

LIBERTY, EQUALITY, POWER

RECONSTRUCTION, 1863–1877

WARTIME RECONSTRUCTION
Radical Republicans and Reconstruction

ANDREW JOHNSON AND RECONSTRUCTION
Johnson's Policy
Southern Defiance
The Black Codes
Land and Labor in the Postwar South
The Freedmen's Bureau
Land for the Landless
Education

THE ADVENT OF CONGRESSIONAL
RECONSTRUCTION
Schism between President and Congress
The Fourteenth Amendment
The 1866 Elections
The Reconstruction Acts of 1867

THE IMPEACHMENT OF ANDREW JOHNSON
The Completion of Formal Reconstruction
The Fifteenth Amendment
The Election of 1868

THE GRANT ADMINISTRATION
Civil Service Reform and Foreign Policy Issues
Reconstruction in the South
Blacks in Office
"Carpetbaggers"
"Scalawags"
The Ku Klux Klan
The Election of 1872
The Panic of 1873

THE RETREAT FROM RECONSTRUCTION
The Mississippi Election of 1875
The Supreme Court and Reconstruction
The Election of 1876
Disputed Results
The Compromise of 1877
The End of Reconstruction

From the beginning of the Civil War, the North fought to "reconstruct" the Union. Lincoln at first attempted to restore the Union as it had existed before 1861, but once the abolition of slavery became a northern war aim, the Union could never be reconstructed on its old foundations. Instead, it must experience a "new birth of freedom," as Lincoln had said at the dedication of the military cemetery at Gettysburg.

But precisely what did "a new birth of freedom" mean? At the very least it meant the end of slavery. But what would liberty look like for the four million freed slaves? Would they become citizens equal to their former masters in the eyes of the law? And on what terms should the Confederate states return to the Union? What would be the powers of the states and of the national government in a reconstructed Union?

1863	1865	1867	1869	1871	1873	1875	1877

■ **1863**
Lincoln issues Proclamation of Amnesty and Reconstruction

■ **1865**
Andrew Johnson becomes president, announces his reconstruction plan

1865–1869
Andrew Johnson presidency

■ **1866**
Congress passes civil rights bill and expands Freedmen's Bureau over Johnson's veto and approves Fourteenth Amendment

■ **1867**
Congress passes Reconstruction acts over Johnson's vetoes

■ **1868**
Andrew Johnson impeached but not convicted

1869–1877
Ulysses S. Grant presidency

■ **1870**
Fifteenth Amendment ratified

1871 ■
Congress passes Ku Klux Klan Act

■ **1872**
Liberal Republicans defect from party
• Grant wins reelection

1873 ■
Economic depression begins with the Panic

■ **1874**
Democrats win House of Representatives

■ **1876**
Disputed presidential election causes constitutional crisis

1877 ■
Compromise of 1877 installs Rutherford B. Hayes as president

Wartime reconstruction

Lincoln initially feared that whites in the South would never extend equal rights to the freed slaves. In 1862, he encouraged freedpeople to emigrate to all-black countries like Haiti. Black leaders, abolitionists, and many Republicans objected to that policy. Black people were Americans. Why should they not have the rights of American citizens instead of being urged to leave the country?

Lincoln eventually embraced the logic and justice of that view. But in beginning the process of reconstruction, he first reached out to southern *whites*, whose allegiance to the Confederacy was lukewarm. On December 8, 1863, Lincoln issued his Proclamation of **Amnesty** and Reconstruction, which offered presidential pardon to southern whites who took an oath of allegiance to the United States and accepted the abolition of slavery. The plan allowed southern states to form new governments if the number of adult white males who took the oath equaled 10 percent of the number of voters in 1860.

Because the war was still raging, this policy could be carried out only where Union troops controlled substantial portions of a Confederate state: Louisiana, Arkansas, and Tennessee in early 1864. Lincoln hoped that the process might

amnesty *General pardon granted to a large group of people.*

snowball as Union military victories convinced more and more Confederates that their cause was hopeless. But those military victories were long delayed, and reconstruction in most parts of the South did not begin until 1865.

Radical Republicans and Reconstruction

Growing opposition within Lincoln's own party slowed the process as well. Many Republicans believed that white men who had fought *against* the Union should not be rewarded with restoration of their political rights while black men who had fought *for* the Union were denied those rights. If the freedpeople were landless, Radical Republicans said, provide them with land by confiscating the plantations of leading Confederates. Radical Republicans also distrusted oaths of allegiance sworn by ex-Confederates. Rather than simply restoring the old ruling class to power, they asked, why not give freed slaves the vote, to provide a genuinely loyal nucleus of supporters in the South?

These radical positions did not command a majority of Congress in 1864. Yet the experience of Louisiana, the first state to reorganize under Lincoln's more moderate policy, convinced even nonradical Republicans to block Lincoln's program. Enough white men in the occupied portion of the state took the oath of allegiance to satisfy Lincoln's conditions. They adopted a new state constitution and formed a government that abolished slavery and provided a school system for blacks. But the new government did not grant blacks the right to vote. It also authorized planters to enforce restrictive labor policies on black plantation workers. Louisiana's actions alienated a majority of congressional Republicans, who refused to admit representatives and senators from the "reconstructed" state.

At the same time, though, Congress failed to enact a reconstruction policy of its own. This was not for lack of trying. Both houses passed the Wade-Davis reconstruction bill (named for Senator Benjamin Wade of Ohio and Representative Henry Winter Davis of Maryland) in July 1864. That bill did not enfranchise blacks, but it did impose such stringent loyalty requirements on southern whites that few of them could take the required oath. Lincoln therefore vetoed it.

Lincoln's action infuriated many Republicans, and the bitter squabble threatened for a time to destroy Lincoln's chances of being reelected. Union military success in the fall of 1864, however, reunited the Republicans behind Lincoln. The collapse of Confederate military resistance the following spring set the stage for compromise on a policy for the postwar South. But Lincoln's assassination changed everything.

ANDREW JOHNSON AND RECONSTRUCTION

In 1864, Republicans had adopted the name Union Party to attract the votes of War Democrats and border-state Unionists who could not bring themselves to vote Republican. For the same reason, they also nominated Andrew Johnson of Tennessee as Lincoln's running mate.

Of "poor white" heritage, Johnson had clawed his way up in the rough-and-tumble politics of east Tennessee. This region of small farms and few slaves held little love for the planters who controlled the state. Johnson denounced the planters as "stuck-up aristocrats" who had no empathy with the southern yeomen for whom Johnson became a self-appointed spokesman. Johnson was the only senator from a seceding state who refused to support the Confederacy.

FOCUS QUESTION

What were the positions of Presidents Abraham Lincoln and Andrew Johnson and of moderate and radical Republicans in Congress on the issues of restoring the South to the Union and protecting the rights of freed slaves?

Booth's bullet therefore elevated to the presidency a man who still thought of himself as primarily a Democrat and a southerner. But the trouble this might cause in a party that was mostly Republican and northern was not immediately apparent. In fact, Johnson's enmity toward the "stuck-up aristocrats" whom he blamed for leading the South into secession prompted him to utter dire threats. "Traitors must be impoverished," he said. "They must not only be punished, but their social power must be destroyed."

Radical Republicans liked the sound of this. Johnson seemed to promise the type of reconstruction they favored—one that would deny political power to ex-Confederates and enfranchise blacks. They envisioned a coalition between these new black voters and the small minority of southern whites who had never supported the Confederacy. These men could be expected to vote Republican. Republican governments in southern states would pass laws to provide civil rights and economic opportunity for freed slaves.

Johnson's Policy

From a combination of pragmatic, partisan, and idealistic motives, therefore, Radical Republicans prepared to implement a progressive reconstruction policy. But Johnson unexpectedly refused to cooperate. Instead of calling Congress into session, he moved ahead on his own and issued two proclamations on May 29, 1865. The first provided a blanket amnesty for all but the highest-ranking Confederate officials and military officers and those ex-Confederates with taxable property worth $20,000 or more. The second named a provisional governor for North Carolina and directed him to call an election of delegates to frame a new state constitution. Only white men who had received amnesty and taken an oath of allegiance could vote. Similar proclamations soon followed for other former Confederate states. Johnson's policy was clear: He would exclude both blacks and upper-class whites from the reconstruction process.

Many Republicans supported Johnson's policy at first, but the radicals feared that restricting the vote to whites would open the door to the restoration of the old power structure in the South. They began to sense that Johnson (who had owned slaves) was as dedicated to white supremacy as any Confederate. "White men alone must govern the South," he told a Democratic senator. Although moderate Republicans believed that black men should participate to some degree in the reconstruction process, in 1865 they were not yet prepared to break with the president. They regarded his policy as an "experiment" that would be modified as time went on.

Southern Defiance

As it happened, none of the state conventions enfranchised a single black. Some of them even balked at ratifying the Thirteenth Amendment. Reports from the South told of neo-Confederate violence against blacks and their white sympathizers. Johnson seemed to encourage such activities by allowing the organization of white militia units.

Then there was the matter of presidential pardons. After talking fiercely about punishing traitors, and after excluding several classes of them from his amnesty proclamation, Johnson began to issue special pardons to many ex-Confederates, restoring property and political rights. Under the new state constitutions southern voters were electing hundreds of ex-Confederates to state offices. Even more alarming to northerners, who thought they had won the war, was the election to Congress of no fewer than nine ex-Confederate congressmen, seven ex-Confederate state officials, four generals, four colonels, and even the former Confederate vice president, Alexander H. Stephens.

Somehow the aristocrats and traitors Johnson had denounced in April had taken over the reconstruction process. They did so by flattering the presidential ego.

Thousands of prominent ex-Confederates or their tearful female relatives applied for pardons, confessing the error of their ways and appealing for presidential mercy. Johnson reveled in his power over these once-haughty aristocrats. More important, perhaps, was the praise and support Johnson received from leading northern Democrats. That party's leaders enticed Johnson with visions of reelection as a Democrat in 1868 if he could manage to reconstruct the South in a manner that would preserve a Democratic majority there.

The Black Codes

In fall 1865, these newly reconstructed state legislatures sought to define the rights of four million former slaves. The option of treating them exactly like white citizens was scarcely considered. Instead, the states excluded black people from juries and the ballot box, did not permit them to testify against whites in court, banned interracial marriage, and punished blacks more severely than whites for certain crimes. Some states defined any unemployed black person as a vagrant and hired him out to a planter, forbade blacks to lease land, and apprenticed black youths out to whites.

Northern Republicans saw these **"Black Codes"** as a brazen attempt to reinstate a quasi-slavery. "We tell the white men of Mississippi," declared the *Chicago Tribune,* "that the men of the North will convert the State of Mississippi into a frog pond before they will allow such laws to disgrace one foot of the soil in which the bones of our soldiers sleep and over which the flag of freedom waves." The Union army's occupation forces suspended the implementation of Black Codes that discriminated on racial grounds.

Land and Labor in the Postwar South

The Black Codes, though discriminatory, were designed to address a genuine problem. The end of the war had left black–white relations in the South in a state of limbo. The South's economy was in a shambles. Most tangible assets except the land itself had been destroyed. Law and order broke down in many areas. The war had ended early enough in the spring to allow the planting of at least some food crops. But who would plant and cultivate them? One-quarter of the South's white farmers had been killed in the war; the slaves were slaves no more. "I never did a day's work in my life," lamented a South Carolina planter, "and I don't know how to begin."

Despite all of this trouble, life went on. Slaveless planters and their wives and soldiers' widows and their children plowed and planted. Confederate veterans drifted home and went to work. Former slave owners asked their former slaves to work the land for wages or shares of the crop, and many did so. Others refused, because for them to leave the old place was an essential part of freedom.

Thus the roads were alive with freedpeople on the move in summer 1865. Many signed on to work at farms just a few miles from their old homes. Others moved into town. Some looked for relatives who had been sold away during slavery or from whom they had been separated during the war. Some wandered aimlessly. Whites organized vigilante groups to discipline blacks and force them to work.

The Freedmen's Bureau

Into this vacuum stepped the U.S. army and the **Freedmen's Bureau.** Tens of thousands of troops remained in the South until civil government could be restored. The

Black Codes *Laws passed by southern states that restricted the rights and liberties of former slaves.*

Freedmen's Bureau *Federal agency created in 1865 to supervise newly freed people. It oversaw relations between whites and blacks in the South, issued food rations, and supervised labor contracts.*

SHARECROPPERS WORKING IN THE FIELDS. *This photograph shows two families of sharecroppers picking cotton. Freed slaves resisted landowners' efforts to work them in gangs as they had in slavery, so the owners rented land to black families in return for a share of the crop. These croppers do not appear to be overjoyed with the new system.* Photographs and Prints Division, Schomburg Center for Research in Black Culture, The New York Public Library, Astor, Lenox and Tilden Foundations.

share wages *Payment of workers' wages with a share of the crop rather than with cash.*

sharecropping *Working land in return for a share of the crops produced instead of paying cash rent.*

40 acres and a mule *Largely unfulfilled hope of many former slaves that they would receive free land from the confiscated property of ex-Confederates.*

Freedmen's Bureau (its official title was Bureau of Refugees, Freedmen, and Abandoned Lands), created by Congress in March 1865, became the principal agency for overseeing relations between former slaves and owners. Staffed by army officers, the bureau established posts throughout the South to supervise free-labor wage contracts between landowners and freedpeople. The Freedmen's Bureau also issued food rations to 150,000 people daily during 1865, one-third of them to whites. Southern whites viewed the Freedmen's Bureau with hostility, but, without it, the postwar chaos in the South would have been much greater. Bureau agents encouraged black people to sign free-labor contracts and return to work.

In negotiating labor contracts, the bureau tried to establish minimum wages. Lack of money in the South, however, caused many contracts to call for **share wages**— that is, paying workers with shares of the crop. At first, landowners worked their laborers in large groups called gangs. But many black workers resented this system as reminiscent of slavery. Thus, a new system evolved, called **sharecropping,** whereby a black family worked a specific piece of land in return for a share of the crop produced on it.

Land for the Landless

Freedpeople, of course, would have preferred to farm their own land. "What's de use of being free if you don't own land enough to be buried in?" asked one black sharecropper (dialect in original source). Some black farmers did manage to save up enough money to buy small plots. Demobilized black soldiers purchased land with their bounty payments, sometimes pooling their money to buy an entire plantation on which several black families settled. Northern philanthropists helped some freedmen buy land. But most ex-slaves found the purchase of land impossible. Few of them had money, and even if they did, whites often refused to sell.

Several northern radicals proposed legislation to confiscate ex-Confederate land and redistribute it to freedpeople, but those proposals went nowhere. The most promising effort to put thousands of slaves on land of their own also failed. In January 1865, after his march through Georgia, General William T. Sherman had issued a military order setting aside thousands of acres of abandoned plantation land in the Georgia and South Carolina lowcountry for settlement by freed slaves. The army even turned over some of its surplus mules to black farmers. The expectation of **"40 acres and a mule"** excited freedpeople in 1865, but President Johnson's Amnesty Proclamation and his issuance of pardons restored most of this property to ex-Confederates. The same thing happened to white-owned land elsewhere in the South.

Education

Abolitionists were more successful in helping freedpeople get an education. During the war, freedmen's aid societies and missionary societies founded by abolitionists had sent teachers to Union-occupied areas of the South to set up

NEW YORK, SATURDAY, MAY 26, 1866.

THE BURNING OF A FREEDMEN'S SCHOOL. *Because freedpeople's education symbolized black progress, whites who resented and resisted this progress sometimes attacked and burned freedmen's schools, as in this dramatic illustration of a white mob burning a school during antiblack riots in Memphis in May 1866.*

Library of Congress, Prints and Photographs Division

schools for freed slaves. After the war, this effort was expanded with the aid of the Freedmen's Bureau. Two thousand northern teachers, three-quarters of them women, fanned out into every part of the South to train black teachers. After 1870, missionary societies concentrated on making higher education available to African Americans. They founded many of the black colleges in the South. The education crusade reduced the southern black illiteracy rate to 70 percent by 1880 and to 48 percent by 1900.

THE ADVENT OF CONGRESSIONAL RECONSTRUCTION

Political reconstruction shaped the civil and political rights of freedpeople. By the time Congress met in December 1865, the Republican majority was determined to take control of the process by which former Confederate states would be restored to full representation. Congress refused to admit the representatives and senators elected by the former Confederate states under Johnson's reconstruction policy and set up a special committee to formulate new terms. The committee held hearings at which southern Unionists, freedpeople, and U.S. army officers testified to abuse and terrorism in the South. Their testimony convinced Republicans of the need for stronger federal intervention to define and protect the civil rights of freedpeople. Many radicals wanted to grant the vote to black men, but because racism was still strong in the North, the special committee instead decided to draft a constitutional amendment that would encourage southern states to enfranchise blacks but would not require them to do so.

Schism between President and Congress

Meanwhile, Congress passed two laws to protect the economic and civil rights of freedpeople. The first extended the life of the Freedmen's Bureau and expanded its powers. The second defined freedpeople as citizens with equal legal rights and gave federal courts appellate jurisdiction to enforce those rights. Johnson vetoed both measures. He then gave a speech to Democratic supporters in which he denounced Republican leaders as traitors who did not want to restore the Union except on terms that would degrade white southerners. Democratic newspapers applauded the president for vetoing bills that would "compound our race with niggers, gypsies, and baboons."

The Fourteenth Amendment

With better than a two-thirds majority in both houses, congressional Republicans passed the Freedmen's Bureau and Civil Rights bills over the president's vetoes. Then, on April 30, the special committee submitted to Congress its proposed Fourteenth Amendment to the Constitution. After lengthy debate, the amendment received the required two-thirds majority in Congress on June 13 and went to the states for ratification. Section 1 defined all native-born or naturalized persons, including blacks, as American citizens and prohibited the states from abridging the "privileges and immunities" of citizens, from depriving "any person of life, liberty, or property without due process of law," and from denying to any person "the equal protection of the laws." Section 2 gave states the option of either enfranchising black males or losing a proportionate number of congressional seats and electoral votes. Section 3 disqualified a significant number of ex-Confederates from holding federal or state office. Section 4 guaranteed the national debt and repudiated the Confederate debt. Section 5 empowered Congress to enforce the Fourteenth Amendment by "appropriate legislation." The Fourteenth Amendment had far-reaching consequences. Section 1 has become the most important provision in the Constitution for defining and enforcing civil rights.

The 1866 Elections

During the campaign for the 1866 congressional elections, Republicans made clear that any ex-Confederate state that ratified the Fourteenth Amendment would be declared "reconstructed" and that its representatives and senators would be seated in Congress. Tennessee ratified, but Johnson counseled other southern legislatures to reject the amendment, which they did. Johnson then created a National Union Party made up of a few conservative Republicans who disagreed with their party, some border-state Unionists who supported the president, and Democrats. But many northern Democrats still carried the taint of having opposed the war effort, and most northern voters did not trust them. Further, race riots in Memphis and New Orleans bolstered Republican arguments that national power was necessary to protect "the fruits of victory" in the South. Perhaps the biggest liability was Johnson himself. In a whistle-stop tour through the North, he traded insults with hecklers and embarrassed his supporters.

Republicans swept the election. Having rejected the reconstruction terms embodied in the Fourteenth Amendment, southern Democrats now faced far more stringent terms. "They would not cooperate in rebuilding what they destroyed," wrote an exasperated moderate Republican, so "we must remove the rubbish and rebuild from the bottom."

The Reconstruction Acts of 1867

The new Congress enacted over Johnson's vetoes the Reconstruction acts of 1867. The acts divided the 10 southern states into five military districts, directed army officers to register voters for the election of delegates to new constitutional conventions, and enfranchised males aged 21 and older (including blacks) to vote in those elections. When a state had adopted a new constitution that granted equal civil and political rights regardless of race and had ratified the Fourteenth Amendment, it would be declared reconstructed, and its newly elected congressmen would be seated.

These measures embodied a true revolution. Southerners were shorn of political power, with their former slaves not only freed but also politically empowered. Blacks and their white allies organized **Union Leagues** to mobilize the new black voters into the Republican Party. Democrats branded southern white Republicans as **"scalawags"** and northern settlers as **"carpetbaggers."** By September 1867, the 10 states had 735,000 black voters and only 635,000 white voters registered. At least one-third of the registered white voters were Republicans.

President Johnson did everything he could to block Reconstruction. He replaced several Republican generals with Democrats. He had his attorney general issue a ruling that interpreted the Reconstruction acts narrowly, thereby forcing a special session of Congress to pass a supplementary act in July 1867. He encouraged southern whites to obstruct the registration of voters and the election of convention delegates. Johnson aimed to slow the process until 1868 in the hope that northern voters would repudiate Reconstruction in the presidential election of that year, when Johnson planned to run as the Democratic candidate.

Union Leagues *Organizations that informed African American voters of, and mobilized them to support, the Republican Party.*

scalawags *Term used by southern Democrats to describe southern whites who worked with the Republicans.*

carpetbaggers *Northerners who settled in the South during Reconstruction.*

THE IMPEACHMENT OF ANDREW JOHNSON

Johnson struck even more boldly against Reconstruction after the 1867 elections, which saw Republicans suffer setbacks in several northern states. In February 1868, he removed from office Secretary of War Edwin M. Stanton, who had administered the War Department in support of the congressional Reconstruction policy. This appeared to violate the Tenure of Office Act, passed the year before over Johnson's veto, which required Senate consent for such removals. By a vote of 126 to 47 along party lines, the House **impeached** Johnson on February 24. The official reason for impeachment was that he had violated the Tenure of Office Act. The real reason was Johnson's stubborn defiance of Congress on Reconstruction.

The impeachment trial before the Senate proved to be long and complicated, which worked in Johnson's favor by allowing passions to cool. The Constitution specifies the grounds on which a president can be impeached and removed: "Treason, Bribery, or other high Crimes and Misdemeanors." The issue was whether Johnson was guilty of any of these acts. His able defense counsel exposed technical ambiguities in the Tenure of Office Act that raised doubts about whether Johnson had actually violated it. Behind the scenes, Johnson strengthened his case by promising to appoint the respected General John M. Schofield as secretary of war and to stop obstructing the Reconstruction acts. In the end, seven Republican senators plus all Democrats voted for acquittal on May 16, and the final tally fell one vote short of the necessary two-thirds majority.

FOCUS QUESTION

Why was Andrew Johnson impeached? Why was he acquitted?

impeach *To charge government officeholders with misconduct in office.*

© CORBIS

TWO MEMBERS OF THE KU KLUX KLAN. *Founded in Pulaski, Tennessee, in 1866 as a social organization similar to a college fraternity, the Klan evolved into a terrorist group whose purpose was intimidation of southern Republicans. The Klan, in which former Confederate soldiers played a prominent part, was responsible for the beating and murder of hundreds of blacks and whites alike from 1868 to 1871.*

universal male suffrage
System that allowed all adult males to vote without regard to property, religious, or race qualifications or limitations.

Ku Klux Klan *White terrorist organization in the South originally founded as a fraternal society in 1866.*

The Completion of Formal Reconstruction

The impeachment trial's end cleared the poisonous air in Washington, and Johnson quietly served out his term. Constitutional conventions met in the South during winter and spring 1867–1868. The constitutions they wrote were among the most progressive in the nation. They enacted **universal male suffrage.** Some disfranchised certain classes of ex-Confederates for several years, but by 1872, all such disqualifications had been removed. The constitutions mandated statewide public schools for both races for the first time in the South. Most states permitted segregated schools, but schools of any kind for blacks represented a great step forward. Most of the constitutions increased the state's responsibility for social welfare.

Violence in some parts of the South marred the voting on ratification. The **Ku Klux Klan,** a night-riding white terrorist organization, made its first appearance during the elections. Nevertheless, voters in seven states ratified their constitutions and elected new legislatures that ratified the Fourteenth Amendment in spring 1868. That amendment became part of the U.S. Constitution the following summer, and the newly elected representatives and senators from those seven states, nearly all Republicans, took their seats in the House and Senate.

The Fifteenth Amendment

The remaining three southern states completed the Reconstruction process in 1869 and 1870. Congress required them to ratify the Fifteenth as well as the Fourteenth Amendment. The Fifteenth Amendment prohibited states from denying the right to vote on grounds of race, color, or previous condition of servitude. Its purpose was not only to prevent any future revocation of black suffrage, but also to extend equal suffrage to the border states and to the North.

But the Fifteenth Amendment still left women disfranchised, and debates over whether or not to support the amendment split the women's rights movement. In 1866, male and female abolitionists formed the American Equal Rights Association (AERA) to work for both black and woman suffrage. Most members supported the Fifteenth Amendment, believing that woman suffrage would have to wait until public opinion could be educated up to the standard of gender equality. Arguing instead that the amendment would establish "the most odious form of aristocracy the world has ever seen: an aristocracy of sex," radical suffragists Elizabeth Cady Stanton and Susan B. Anthony left the AERA and founded the National Woman Suffrage Association. The remaining AERA members reorganized themselves as the American Woman Suffrage Association. For the next two decades, these rival organizations, working for the same cause, remained at odds.

The Election of 1868

Just as the presidential election of 1864 was a referendum on Lincoln's war policies, so the election of 1868 was a referendum on the Reconstruction policy of the Republicans. Although the Republican nominee, General **Ulysses S. Grant,** had no political experience, he commanded greater authority and prestige than anyone else in the country. Grant agreed to run for the presidency in order to preserve in peace the victory for Union and liberty he had won in war.

The Democrats turned away from Andrew Johnson and nominated Horatio Seymour, the wartime governor of New York. They denounced the Reconstruction acts as "unconstitutional, revolutionary, and void." Their militant platform also demanded "the abolition of the Freedmen's Bureau, and all political instrumentalities designed to secure negro supremacy." The vice presidential candidate, Frank Blair of Missouri, declared that the Democrats sought to "allow the white people to reorganize their own governments."

The only way to achieve this bold counterrevolutionary goal was to suppress Republican voters in the South. Federal troops had only limited success in preventing the violence of the Ku Klux Klan. In Louisiana, Georgia, Arkansas, and Tennessee, the Klan or Klan-like groups committed dozens of murders and intimidated thousands of black voters. The violence helped the Democratic cause in the South, but probably hurt it in the North, where many voters perceived the Klan as an organization of neo-Confederate paramilitary guerrillas.

Seymour did well in the South, carrying five former slave states and coming close in others despite the solid Republican vote of the newly enfranchised blacks. But Grant swept the electoral vote 214 to 80. Seymour actually won a slight majority of the white voters nationally; without black enfranchisement, Grant would have had a minority of the popular vote.

QUICK REVIEW

GOALS OF RECONSTRUCTION

- To bring ex-Confederate states back into the Union

- To define and protect the rights of ex-slaves

- Johnson's plan: rapid restoration of states to Union but minimal rights and economic opportunities for freedpeople

- Radical Republicans' plan: equal civil and political rights for freedpeople plus land and education

THE GRANT ADMINISTRATION

Upon taking office, Grant's inexperience and poor judgment betrayed him into several unwise appointments of officials who were later convicted of corruption. His back-to-back administrations were plagued by scandals. His secretary of war was impeached for selling appointments to army posts and Indian reservations, and his attorney general and secretary of the interior resigned under suspicion of malfeasance in 1875.

Grant was too trusting of subordinates, and he appointed military colleagues and family members to offices for which they were scarcely qualified. But in an era notorious for corruption at all levels of government, many of the scandals were not Grant's fault. The Tammany Hall "Ring" of "Boss" William Marcy Tweed in New York City may have stolen more money from taxpayers than all federal agencies combined. In Washington, one of the most widely publicized scandals, the **Credit Mobilier** affair, concerned Congress rather than the Grant administration. Several congressmen had accepted stock in the Credit Mobilier, a construction company for the Union Pacific Railroad, which received loans and land grants from the government in return for ensuring lax congressional supervision.

What accounted for this explosion of corruption? During the war, expansion of government contracts and the bureaucracy had created new opportunities for the unscrupulous. Following the intense sacrifices of the war years came a relaxation of tensions and standards. Rapid postwar economic growth, led by an extraordinary

Ulysses S. Grant *General-in-chief of Union armies who led those armies to victory in the Civil War*

Credit Mobilier *Construction company for the Union Pacific Railroad that gave shares of stock to some congressmen in return for favors.*

rush of railroad construction, encouraged greed and get-rich-quick schemes of the kind satirized by Mark Twain and Charles Dudley Warner in their 1873 novel *The Gilded Age*, which gave its name to the era.

Civil Service Reform and Foreign Policy Issues

Some of the apparent increase in corruption during the Gilded Age was more a matter of perception, as reformers focused on the dark corners of corruption hitherto unilluminated because of the nation's preoccupation with war and reconstruction. In reality, during the Grant administration, several government agencies made real progress in eliminating abuses that had flourished in earlier administrations.

The chief target of civil service reform was the **"spoils system."** With the slogan "To the victor belongs the spoils," the victorious party in an election rewarded party workers with government appointments. The spoils system politicized the bureaucracy and staffed it with unqualified personnel who spent more time working for their party than for the government. Civil service reformers wanted to separate the bureaucracy from politics by requiring competitive examinations for the appointment of civil servants. This movement gathered steam during the 1870s and finally achieved success in 1883 with the passage of the Pendleton Act, which established the modern structure of the civil service. When Grant took office, he seemed to share the sentiments of civil service reformers, but many congressmen, senators, and other politicians resisted reform because patronage greased political machines that kept them in office. They managed to subvert reform, sometimes using Grant as an unwitting ally and turning many reformers against the president.

A foreign policy fiasco added to Grant's woes. The irregular procedures by which his private secretary had negotiated a treaty to annex Santo Domingo (now the Dominican Republic) alienated leading Republican senators, who defeated ratification of the treaty. Politically inexperienced, Grant acted like a general who needed only to give orders rather than as a president who must cultivate supporters. The fallout from the Santo Domingo affair widened the fissure in the Republican Party between "spoilsmen" and "reformers."

But the Grant administration had some solid foreign policy achievements to its credit. Hamilton Fish, the able secretary of state, negotiated the Treaty of Washington in 1871 to settle the vexing "Alabama Claims." These were damage claims against Britain for the destruction of American shipping by the C.S.S. *Alabama* and other Confederate commerce raiders built in British shipyards. The treaty established an international tribunal to arbitrate the U.S. claims, resulting in the award of $15.5 million in damages to U.S. shipowners and a British expression of regret.

Reconstruction in the South

During Grant's two administrations, the "Southern Question" was the most intractable issue. With the ratification of the Fifteenth Amendment, many people breathed a sigh of relief at this apparent resolution of "the last great point that remained to be settled of the issues of the war." But Reconstruction was not over; it had hardly begun. State governments elected by black and white voters were in place in the South, but Democratic violence protesting Reconstruction and the instability of the Republican coalition that sustained it portended trouble.

spoils system *System by which the victorious political party rewarded its supporters with government jobs.*

Blacks in Office

In the North, the Republican Party represented the most prosperous, educated, and influential elements of the population, but in the South, most of its adherents were poor, illiterate, and landless. About 80 percent of southern Republican voters were black. Although most black leaders were educated and many had been free before the war, the mass of black voters were illiterate ex-slaves. Neither the leaders nor their constituents, however, were as ignorant as stereotypes have portrayed them. Of 14 black representatives and two black senators elected in the South between 1868 and 1876, all but three had attended secondary school and four had attended college. Several of the blacks elected to state offices were among the best-educated men of their day. For example, Jonathan Gibbs, secretary of state in Florida from 1868 to 1872 and state superintendent of education from 1872 to 1874, was a graduate of Dartmouth College and Princeton Theological Seminary.

It is true that some lower-level black officeholders, as well as their constituents, could not read or write, but the fault for that situation lay not with them but with the slave regime that had denied them an education. Illiteracy did not preclude an understanding of political issues for them any more than it did for Irish American voters in the North, some of whom also were illiterate. Participation in the Union League and the experience of voting were forms of education. Black churches and fraternal organizations proliferated during Reconstruction and tutored African Americans in their rights and responsibilities.

Linked to the myth of black incompetence was the legend of the "Africanization" of southern governments during Reconstruction. The theme of "Negro rule" was a staple of Democratic propaganda, but blacks in fact held only 15 to 20 percent of public offices, even at the height of Reconstruction in the early 1870s. There were no black governors and only one black state Supreme Court justice. Nowhere except in South Carolina did blacks hold office in numbers anywhere near their proportion of the population.

"Carpetbaggers"

Next to "Negro rule," carpetbagger corruption and scalawag rascality have been the prevailing myths of Reconstruction. Carpetbaggers did hold a disproportionate number of high political offices in southern state governments during Reconstruction. A few did resemble the proverbial adventurer who came south with nothing but a carpetbag in which to stow the loot plundered from a helpless people. But most were Union army officers who stayed on after the war as Freedmen's Bureau agents, teachers in black schools, or business investors. They hoped to rebuild Southern society in the image of the free-labor North. Many were college graduates. Most brought not empty carpetbags but considerable capital, which they invested in what they hoped would become a new South. But they underestimated the hostility of southern whites, most of whom regarded them as agents of an alien culture.

"Scalawags"

Most of the native-born whites who joined the southern Republican Party came from the upcountry Unionist areas of western North Carolina and Virginia and eastern Tennessee. Others were former Whigs. Republicans, said a North Carolina scalawag, were the "party of progress, of education, of development."

But Democrats saw that the southern Republican Party they abhorred was a fragile coalition of blacks and whites, Yankees and southerners, hill-country yeomen and lowcountry entrepreneurs, illiterates and college graduates. The party was weakest along the seams where these disparate elements joined, especially the racial seam. Democrats attacked that weakness with every weapon at their command, including violence.

The Ku Klux Klan

The generic name for the secret groups that terrorized the southern countryside was the Ku Klux Klan, but some went by other names (the Knights of the White Camelia in Louisiana, for example). Part of the Klan's purpose was social control of the black population. Sharecroppers who tried to extract better terms from landowners, or black people who were considered too "uppity," were likely to receive a midnight whipping—or worse—from white-sheeted Klansmen. Scores of black schools, perceived as a particular threat to white supremacy, went up in flames.

The Klan's main purpose was political: to destroy the Republican Party by terrorizing its voters and, if necessary, murdering its leaders. No one knows how many politically motivated killings took place—certainly hundreds, probably thousands. Nearly all the victims were Republicans; most of them were black. In one notorious incident, the Colfax Massacre in Louisiana (April 18, 1873), a clash between black militia and armed whites left three whites and nearly 100 blacks dead. In some places, notably Tennessee and Arkansas, Republican militias suppressed and disarmed the Klan, but in most areas the militias were outgunned and outmaneuvered by ex-Confederate veteran Klansmen. Some Republican governors were reluctant to use black militia against white guerrillas for fear of sparking a racial bloodbath, as happened at Colfax.

In 1870 and 1871, Congress responded to southern violence with three laws intended to enforce the Fourteenth and Fifteenth Amendments. Interference with voting rights became a federal offense, and any attempt to deprive another person of civil or political rights became a felony. The third law, passed on April 20, 1871, and popularly called the Ku Klux Klan Act, gave the president power to suspend the writ of **habeas corpus** and send in federal troops to suppress armed resistance to federal law.

Armed with these laws, the Grant administration moved against the Klan. Although Grant used his powers with restraint, suspending the writ of habeas corpus only in nine South Carolina counties, there and elsewhere federal marshals backed by troops arrested thousands of suspected Klansmen. Federal grand juries indicted more than 3,000, and several hundred defendants pleaded guilty in return for suspended sentences. About 600 Klansmen were convicted. Most of them received fines or light jail sentences, but 65 went to a federal penitentiary for terms of up to five years.

The Election of 1872

These measures broke the back of the Klan in time for the 1872 presidential election. A group of dissident Republicans had emerged to challenge Grant's reelection. They believed that conciliation of southern whites rather than continued military intervention was the only way to achieve peace in the South. Calling themselves Liberal Republicans, these dissidents nominated Horace Greeley, the famous editor of the *New York Tribune*. Under the slogan "Anything to beat Grant," the

habeas corpus *Right of an individual to have the legality of his arrest and detention decided by a court.*

HISTORY THROUGH FILM

Birth of a Nation (1915)

Directed by D. W. Griffith; starring Lillian Gish (Elsie Stoneman), Henry B. Walthall (Ben Cameron), Ralph Lewis (Austin Stoneman), George Siegmann (Silas Lynch)

Few films have had such a pernicious impact on historical understanding and race relations as *Birth of a Nation*. This movie popularized a version of Reconstruction that portrayed predatory carpetbaggers and stupid, brutish blacks plundering a prostrate South and lusting after white women. It perpetuated vicious stereotypes of rapacious black males. It glorified the Ku Klux Klan of the Reconstruction era, inspiring the founding of the "second Klan" in 1915 that became a powerful force in the 1920s (see Chapter 24). The first half of the film offers a conventional Victorian romance of the Civil War. The children of the northerner Austin Stoneman (a malevolent Radical Republican who is a thinly disguised Thaddeus Stevens) become friends with the children of the Cameron family, from South Carolina. The Civil War tragically separates the families. The Stoneman and Cameron boys enlist in the Union and Confederate armies and—predictably—face each other on the battlefield. Two Camerons and one Stoneman are killed in the war, and Ben Cameron, badly wounded, is captured, to be nursed back to health by Elsie Stoneman.

After the war the younger Camerons and Stonemans renew their friendship. The Stonemans visit South Carolina, and Ben Cameron and Elsie Stoneman, and Phil Stoneman and Flora Cameron, fall in love. If the story had stopped there, *Birth of a Nation* would have been just another Hollywood romance. But Austin Stoneman brings south with him Silas Lynch, an ambitious, leering mulatto demagogue who stirs up the animal passions of the ignorant black majority to demand "Equal Rights, Equal Politics, Equal Marriage." A "renegade Negro," Gus, stalks the youngest Cameron daughter, who saves herself from rape by jumping from a cliff to her death. Silas Lynch tries to force Elsie to marry him. "I will build a Black Empire," he tells the virginal Elsie (Lillian Gish, the Hollywood beauty queen of silent films), "and you as my queen shall rule by my side."

Finally provoked beyond endurance, white South Carolinians led by Ben Cameron organize the Ku Klux Klan to save "the Aryan race." Riding to the rescue of embattled whites in stirring scenes that anticipated the heroic actions of the cavalry against Indians in later Hollywood westerns, the Klan executes Gus, saves Elsie, disperses black soldiers and mobs, and carries the next election for white rule by intimidating black voters. The film ends with a double marriage that unites the Camerons and Stonemans in a symbolic rebirth of a nation, one rightfully based on the supremacy of "the Aryan race."

The son of a Confederate lieutenant colonel, David Wark (D. W.) Griffith was the foremost director of the silent movie era. *Birth of a Nation* was the first real full-length feature film, technically and artistically superior to anything before it. Apart from its place in the history of cinema, though, why should anyone today watch a movie that perpetuates such wrongheaded history and noxious racial stereotypes? Precisely *because* it reflects and amplifies an interpretation of Reconstruction that prevailed from the 1890s to the 1950s, and thereby shaped historical understanding as well as contemporary behavior—as in its inspiration for the Klan of the 1920s.

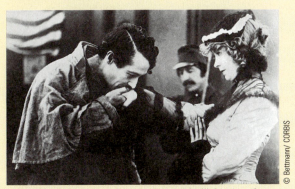

© Bettmann/ CORBIS

Colonel Ben Cameron (Henry B. Walthall) kissing the hand of Elsie Stoneman (Lillian Gish) in Birth of a Nation.

Democratic Party also endorsed Greeley's nomination. On a platform denouncing "bayonet rule" in the South, Greeley urged his fellow northerners to put the issues of the Civil War behind them.

Most voters in the North were still not prepared to trust Democrats or southern whites, however. Anti-Greeley cartoons by Thomas Nast showed Greeley shaking the hand of a Klansman dripping with the blood of a murdered black Republican. On Election Day Grant swamped Greeley. Republicans carried every northern state and 10 of the 16 southern and border states. But this apparent triumph of Republicanism and Reconstruction would soon unravel.

The Panic of 1873

The U.S. economy had grown at an unprecedented pace since recovering from a mild postwar recession. The first transcontinental railroad had been completed on May 10, 1869, at Promontory Summit, Utah Territory. But the building of a second transcontinental line, the Northern Pacific, precipitated a Wall Street panic in 1873 and plunged the economy into a five-year depression.

Jay Cooke's banking firm, fresh from its triumphant marketing of Union war bonds, took over the Northern Pacific in 1869. Cooke pyramided every conceivable kind of equity and loan financing to raise the money to begin laying rails west from Duluth, Minnesota. Other investment firms did the same as a fever of speculative financing gripped the country. In September 1873, the pyramid of paper collapsed. Cooke's firm was the first to go bankrupt. Like dominoes, hundreds of banks and businesses also collapsed. Unemployment rose to 14 percent, and hard times set in.

THE RETREAT FROM RECONSTRUCTION

FOCUS QUESTION

Why did a majority of the northern people and their political leaders turn against continued federal involvement in southern Reconstruction in the 1870s?

Democrats made large gains in the congressional elections of 1874, winning a majority in the House for the first time in 18 years. Public opinion also began to turn against Republican policies in the South. Intraparty battles among Republicans in southern states enabled Democrats to regain control of several state governments. Well-publicized corruption scandals also discredited Republican leaders. Although corruption was probably no worse in southern states than in many parts of the North, white Democrats scored propaganda points by claiming that corruption proved the incompetence of "Negro-carpetbag" regimes. Northerners grew increasingly weary of what seemed the endless turmoil of southern politics. Most of them had never had a very strong commitment to racial equality, and they were growing more and more willing to let white supremacy regain sway in the South.

By 1875 only four southern states remained under Republican control: South Carolina, Florida, Mississippi, and Louisiana. In those states, white Democrats had revived paramilitary organizations under various names: White Leagues (Louisiana); Rifle Clubs (Mississippi); and Red Shirts (South Carolina). Unlike the Klan, these groups operated openly. In Louisiana, they fought pitched battles with Republican militias in which scores were killed. When the Grant administration sent large numbers of federal troops to Louisiana, people in both the North and South cried out against military rule. The protests grew even louder when soldiers marched onto the floor of the Louisiana legislature in January 1875 and expelled several Democratic legislators after a contested election.

The Mississippi Election of 1875

The backlash against the Grant administration affected the Mississippi state election of 1875. Democrats there devised a strategy called the Mississippi Plan. The first step was to "persuade" the 10 to 15 percent of white voters still calling themselves Republicans to switch to the Democrats. Only a handful of carpetbaggers could resist the economic pressures, social ostracism, and threats.

The second step in the Mississippi Plan was to intimidate black voters, because even with all whites voting Democratic, the party could still be defeated by the 55 percent black majority. Economic coercion against black sharecroppers and workers kept some of them away from the polls, but violence was the most effective method. Democratic "rifle clubs" showed up at Republican rallies, provoked riots, and shot down dozens of blacks in the ensuing melees. Governor Adelbert Ames, a former Union general, called for federal troops to control the violence. Grant intended to comply, but Ohio Republicans warned him that if he sent troops to Mississippi, the Democrats would exploit the issue of bayonet rule to carry Ohio in that year's state elections. Grant yielded—in effect giving up for Ohio.

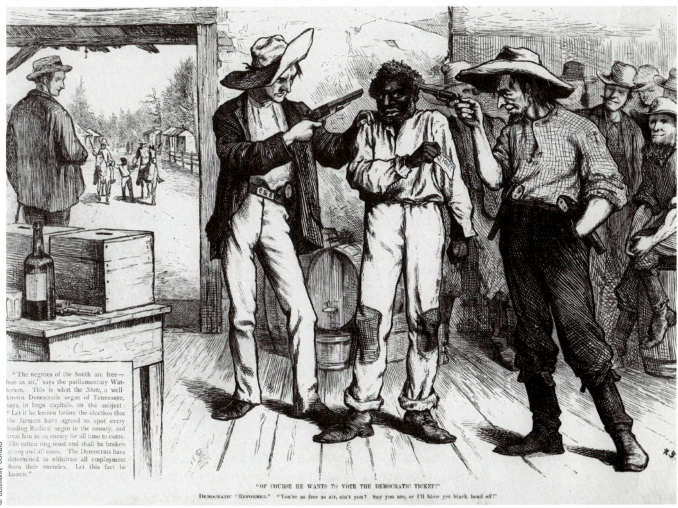

"The negroes of the South are free—free as air," says the parliamentary Watterson. This is what the *State*, a well-known Democratic organ of Tennessee, says, in huge capitals, on the subject: "Let it be known before the election that the farmers have agreed to spot every leading Radical negro in the county, and treat him as an enemy for all time to come. The rotten ring must and shall be broken at any and all costs. The Democrats have determined to withdraw all employment from their enemies. Let this fact be known."

"OF COURSE HE WANTS TO VOTE THE DEMOCRATIC TICKET!"

DEMOCRATIC "REFORMER." "You're as free as air, ain't you? Say you are, or I'll blow yer black head off!"

HOW THE MISSISSIPPI PLAN WORKED. *This cartoon shows how black counties could report large Democratic majorities in the Mississippi state election of 1875. The black voter holds a Democratic ticket while one of the men, described in the caption as a "Democratic reformer," holds a revolver to his head and says: "You're as free as air, ain't you? Say you are, or I'll blow your black head off!"*

LINK TO THE PAST

Frederick Douglass on the Supreme Court and Civil Rights

The Civil Rights Act of 1875 anticipated many of the provisions of the Civil Rights Act of 1964, which is the law of the land and has been upheld by the U.S. Supreme Court. But the law of 1875 was ahead of its time, or at least ahead of the Supreme Court of its time, which declared it unconstitutional on the grounds that the Fourteenth Amendment prohibited discrimination by states but not by individuals. The black civil rights leader Frederick Douglass denounced the Court's decision in language that anticipated the Supreme Court's reasoning in the last third of the 20th century.

> *This decision of the Supreme Court admits that the Fourteenth Amendment is a prohibition of the States. It admits that a State shall not abridge the privileges or immunities of citizens of the United States, but commits the seeming absurdity of allowing the people of a State to do what it prohibits the State itself from doing. . . . It is said that this decision will make no difference in the treatment of colored people; that the Civil Rights Bill was a dead letter, and could not be enforced. There is some truth in all this, but it is not the whole truth.*
>
> *That bill, like all advance legislation, was a banner on the outer wall of American liberty, a noble moral standard, uplifted for the education of the American people. . . .*
>
> *This law, though dead, did speak. It expressed the sentiment of justice and fair play. . . . If it is a bill for social equality, so is the Declaration of Independence, which declares that all men have equal rights; so is the Sermon on the Mount, so is the Golden Rule . . . so is the Constitution of the United States.*

FREDERICK DOUGLASS

From a speech in Washington, D.C., October 22, 1883

Q What is Douglass's response to the argument that the Civil Rights Act was a dead letter even before the Supreme Court declared it so?

The Mississippi Plan worked. In five of the state's counties with large black majorities, the Republicans polled 12, 7, 4, 2, and 0 votes, respectively. What had been a Republican majority of 30,000 in 1874 became a Democratic majority of 30,000 in 1875.

The Supreme Court and Reconstruction

Even if Grant had been willing to continue intervening in southern state elections, Congress and the courts would have constricted such efforts. The new Democratic majority in the House threatened to cut any appropriations intended for use in the South. In 1876, the Supreme Court handed down two decisions that declared parts of the 1870 and 1871 laws for enforcement of the Fourteenth and Fifteenth Amendments unconstitutional. In *U.S. v. Cruikshank* and *U.S. v. Reese,* the Court ruled that the Fourteenth and Fifteenth Amendments applied to actions by *states.* Therefore, the portions of these laws that empowered the federal government to prosecute *individuals* were unconstitutional. The Court did not say what could be done when states were controlled by white-supremacy Democrats who had no intention of enforcing equal rights.

Meanwhile, in the *Civil Rights Cases* (1883), the Court declared unconstitutional a civil rights law passed by Congress in 1875. That law banned racial discrimination in all forms of public transportation and public accommodations. If enforced, it would have effected a sweeping transformation of race relations—in the North as well as in the South. But even some of the congressmen who voted for the bill doubted its constitutionality, and the Justice Department had made little effort to enforce it. Several cases made their way to the Supreme Court, which in 1883 ruled the law unconstitutional—again on grounds that the Fourteenth Amendment applied only to states, not to individuals.

Chapter 17

— After "Free Slaves" ← ———— Disney land Versions
  - Slaves didn't know what to do
  - became sharecroppers
  + schools, but they're still segregated.

1930's.

— Lincoln thought it was impossible to make slaves equal.
  - makes colonies in other countries (Haiti, Africa)
— People who broke the law were just ordered
an oath, and they were back.
— Radical Republicans — Democrats.
— Black Codes — Slave Law's just no Slaves.
— KKK - Violence to keep down blacks.
  — kept Blacks in their place.
— Carpetbaggers - moved from North to South
to reconstruct. became rich.
— Scalawags - took government money to start a
project took money and used very little to project.
— Chicago Fire - "Cow knocked over lantern"
  - 250 people dead, 100,000 homeless, 24 hours
  to put fire out.
— Elizabeth Blackwell
  - medical school (entered as joke)
  - finished #1 and opened up clinic.
— Radical Republican layed a trap for Andrew
Johnoson's impeachment.
  - they didn't get the 2/3 required

THE RETREAT FROM RECONSTRUCTION

The Election of 1876

The mounting revelations of corruption at all levels of government ensured that reform would be the leading issue in the presidential election of 1876. Both major parties gave their presidential nominations to governors who had earned reform reputations in their states: Democrat Samuel J. Tilden of New York and Republican Rutherford B. Hayes of Ohio.

Democrats entered the campaign as favorites for the first time in two decades. It seemed likely that they could assemble an electoral majority from a "solid South" plus New York and two or three other northern states. To ensure a solid South, they looked to the lessons of the Mississippi Plan. In 1876, a new word came into use to describe Democratic techniques of intimidation: **bulldozing.** To bulldoze black voters meant to trample them down or keep them away from the polls. White vigilantes mobilized for an all-out bulldozing effort.

The most notorious incident, the Hamburg Massacre, occurred in the village of Hamburg, South Carolina, where a battle between a black militia unit and 200 Red Shirts resulted in the capture of several militiamen, five of whom were shot "while attempting to escape." This time Grant did send in federal troops. The federal government also put several thousand deputy marshals and election supervisors on duty in the South. Although they kept an uneasy peace at the polls, they could do little to prevent assaults, threats, and economic coercion in backcountry districts, which reduced the potential Republican tally in the former Confederate states by at least 250,000 votes.

Disputed Results

When the results were in, Tilden had carried four northern states, including New York with its 35 electoral votes, and all the former slave states except—apparently—Louisiana, South Carolina, and Florida, which produced disputed returns. Because Tilden needed only one of them to win the presidency, while Hayes needed all three, and because Tilden seemed to have carried Louisiana and Florida, it appeared initially that he had won the presidency. But fraud and irregularities reported from several bulldozed districts in the three states clouded the issue. For example, a Louisiana parish that had recorded 1,688 Republican votes in 1874 reported only 1 in 1876. The official returns ultimately sent to Washington gave all three states—and therefore the presidency—to Hayes, but the Democrats refused to recognize the results, and they controlled the House.

The country faced a serious constitutional crisis, and many people feared another civil war. The Constitution offered no clear guidance on how to deal with the matter. Congress created a special electoral commission consisting of five representatives, five senators, and five Supreme Court justices split evenly between the two parties, with one member, a Supreme Court justice, supposedly an independent—but in fact a Republican.

Tilden had won a national majority of 252,000 popular votes, and the raw returns gave him a majority in the three disputed states. But an estimated 250,000 southern Republicans had been bulldozed away from the polls. In a genuinely fair and free election, the Republicans might have carried Mississippi and North Carolina as well as the three disputed states.

The Compromise of 1877

In February 1877, three months after voters had gone to the polls, the electoral commission issued its ruling. By a partisan vote of 8 to 7—with the "independent" justice voting with the Republicans—it awarded all the disputed states to Hayes.

bulldozing *Using force to keep African Americans from voting.*

The Democrats cried foul and began a **filibuster** in the House to delay the final electoral count beyond the inauguration date of March 4. But, behind the scenes, a compromise began to take shape. Hayes promised his support as president for federal appropriations to rebuild war-destroyed levees on the lower Mississippi and federal aid for a southern transcontinental railroad. Hayes's lieutenants also hinted at the appointment of a southerner as postmaster general, who would have a considerable amount of patronage at his disposal. Most important, Hayes signaled his intention to end "bayonet rule." He believed that the goodwill and influence of southern moderates would offer better protection for black rights than federal troops could provide. In return for his commitment to withdraw the troops, Hayes asked for—and received—promises of fair treatment of freedpeople and respect for their constitutional rights.

The End of Reconstruction

Such promises were easier to make than to keep, as future years would reveal. In any case, the Democratic filibuster collapsed and Hayes was inaugurated on March 4. He soon fulfilled his part of the Compromise of 1877: Ex-Confederate Democrat David Key of Tennessee became postmaster general; in 1878, the South received more federal money for internal improvements than ever before; and federal troops left the capitals of Louisiana and South Carolina. The last two Republican state governments collapsed. Any remaining voices of protest could scarcely be heard above the sighs of relief that the crisis was over.

Conclusion

Before the Civil War, most Americans had viewed a powerful government as a threat to individual liberties. That is why the Bill of Rights imposed strict limits on the powers of the federal government. During the war and especially during Reconstruction, however, the national government had to exert an unprecedented amount of power to free the slaves and guarantee their equal rights as free citizens. That is why the Thirteenth, Fourteenth, and Fifteenth Amendments to the Constitution contained clauses stating that "Congress shall have power" to enforce these provisions for liberty and equal rights.

During the post–Civil War decade, Congress passed civil rights laws and enforcement legislation to accomplish this purpose. Federal marshals and troops patrolled the polls to protect black voters, arrested thousands of Klansmen, and even occupied state capitals to prevent Democratic paramilitary groups from overthrowing legitimately elected Republican state governments. But by 1875, many northerners had grown tired of or alarmed by this continued use of military power to intervene in the internal affairs of states. And the Supreme Court stripped the federal government of much of its authority to enforce certain provisions of the Fourteenth and Fifteenth Amendments.

The withdrawal of federal troops from the South in 1877 constituted both a symbolic and a substantive end of the era known as Reconstruction. Reconstruction had achieved the two great objectives inherited from the Civil War: to reincorporate the former Confederate states into the Union, and to accomplish a transition from slavery to freedom in the South. That transition was marred by the economic inequity of sharecropping and the social injustice of white supremacy. And a third goal of Reconstruction, enforcement of the equal civil and political rights promised in the Fourteenth and Fifteenth Amendments, was betrayed by the Compromise of 1877. In subsequent decades the freed slaves and their descendants suffered repression into segregated second-class citizenship.

filibuster *Congressional delaying tactic involving lengthy speeches that prevent legislation from being enacted.*

CHAPTER REVIEW

Review Questions

1. What were the positions of Presidents Abraham Lincoln and Andrew Johnson and of moderate and radical Republicans in Congress on the issues of restoring the South to the Union and protecting the rights of freed slaves?
2. Why was Andrew Johnson impeached? Why was he acquitted?
3. What were the achievements of Reconstruction? What were its failures?
4. Why did a majority of the northern people and their political leaders turn against continued federal involvement in southern Reconstruction in the 1870s?

Critical Thinking Questions

1. The two main goals of Reconstruction were to bring the former Confederate states back into the Union and to ensure the equal citizenship and rights of the former slaves. Why was the first goal more successfully achieved than the second?
2. Why have "carpetbaggers" and "scalawags" had such a bad historical image? Did they deserve it?

Identifications

Review your understanding of the following key terms, people, and events for this chapter.

amnesty, p. 386
Black Codes, p. 389
Freedmen's Bureau, p. 389
share wages, p. 390
sharecropping, p. 390
40 acres and a mule, p. 390
Union Leagues, p. 393
scalawags, p. 393
carpetbaggers, p. 393
impeach, p. 393
universal male suffrage, p. 394
Ku Klux Klan, p. 394
Ulysses S. Grant, p. 395
Credit Mobilier, p. 395
spoils system, p. 396
habeas corpus, p. 398
bulldozing, p. 403
filibuster, p. 404

DISCOVERY

Evaluate the success with which African Americans were integrated into American society during Reconstruction.

In thinking about this question, begin by breaking it down into the components shown below. A discussion of the significance of each component should appear in your answer.

Culture and Society

From your reading in this chapter and your examination of the illustrations shown here, what observations can you make about the role of violence and/or intimidation in suppressing Republican votes across the South in the 1870s? In the cartoon on the Mississippi Plan, how are the two gun-toting southern whites portrayed? Does this scene appear to represent a spontaneous, isolated incident or a systematic effort to influence votes? What is common between the two images?

TWO MEMBERS OF THE KU KLUX KLAN

HOW THE MISSISSIPPI PLAN WORKED

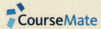
Visit the CourseMate website at www.cengagebrain.com for additional study tools and review materials for this chapter.

C H A P T E R

18

A TRANSFORMED NATION: THE WEST AND THE NEW SOUTH, 1865–1900

AN INDUSTRIALIZING WEST

The Homestead Act
Railroads
Chinese Laborers and the Railroads
Railroads and Borderland Communities
Mining
Cattle Drives and the Open Range
Industrial Ranching, Industrial Cowboys
Mexican Americans
Itinerant Laborers
Homesteading and Farming
The Experience of Homesteading
Gender and Western Settlement

CONQUEST AND RESISTANCE: AMERICAN INDIANS IN THE TRANS-MISSISSIPPI WEST

Conflict with the Sioux
Suppression of Other Plains Indians

The "Peace Policy"
The Dawes Severalty Act and Indian Boarding
    Schools
The Ghost Dance
Sitting Bull and Buffalo Bill: Popular Myths of the
    West

INDUSTRIALIZATION AND THE NEW SOUTH

Race and Industrialization
Southern Agriculture
Exodusters and Emigrationists
Race Relations in the New South
The Emergence of an African American Middle Class
The Rise of Jim Crow

THE POLITICS OF STALEMATE

Knife–Edge Electoral Balance
Civil Service Reform
The Tariff Issue

A wave of settlement transformed the West in the post–Civil War era. From 1865 to 1890, the white population in the trans-Mississippi West increased some 400 percent to 8,628,000—a figure that includes both native-born and white immigrants. The western lands also inspired African Americans, whose cherished hopes for liberty led hundreds of thousands to leave the South for points west from 1880 to 1910. At the same time, immigrants from China, Mexico, and other countries were drawn to the economic opportunities of the West as part of a global movement of peoples in this period.

All of these men and women were driven by the desire for a better life, but this motivation conflicted with the rights and desires of the diverse peoples who already inhabited the West, including, among others, a variety of Indian cultures and societies, borderland villages of Spanish-speaking peoples, settlements of Chinese miners and laborers, and Mexicans in California. Settlement set in motion conflict and resistance in numerous locations.

TIMELINE

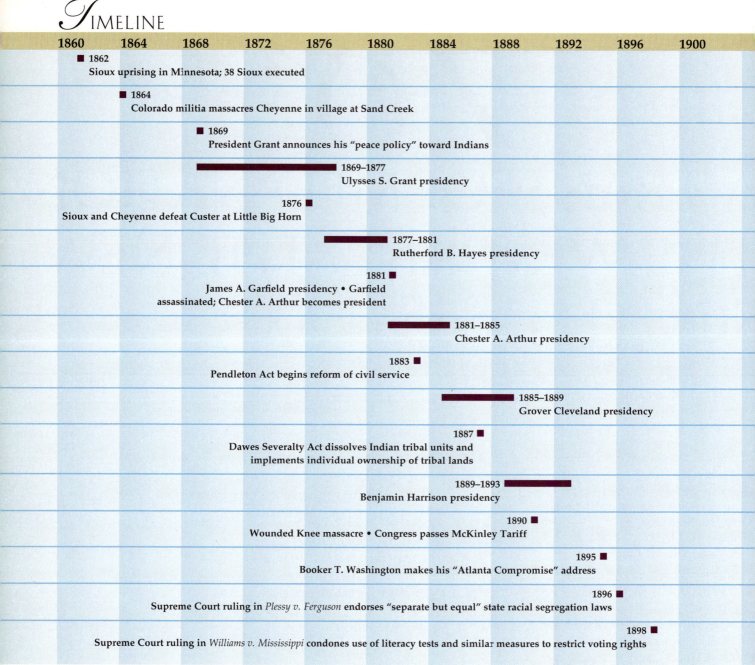

| 1860 | 1864 | 1868 | 1872 | 1876 | 1880 | 1884 | 1888 | 1892 | 1896 | 1900 |

■ 1862
Sioux uprising in Minnesota; 38 Sioux executed

■ 1864
Colorado militia massacres Cheyenne in village at Sand Creek

■ 1869
President Grant announces his "peace policy" toward Indians

1869–1877
Ulysses S. Grant presidency

1876 ■
Sioux and Cheyenne defeat Custer at Little Big Horn

1877–1881
Rutherford B. Hayes presidency

1881 ■
James A. Garfield presidency • Garfield
assassinated; Chester A. Arthur becomes president

1881–1885
Chester A. Arthur presidency

1883 ■
Pendleton Act begins reform of civil service

1885–1889
Grover Cleveland presidency

1887 ■
Dawes Severalty Act dissolves Indian tribal units and
implements individual ownership of tribal lands

1889–1893
Benjamin Harrison presidency

1890 ■
Wounded Knee massacre • Congress passes McKinley Tariff

1895 ■
Booker T. Washington makes his "Atlanta Compromise" address

1896 ■
Supreme Court ruling in *Plessy v. Ferguson* endorses "separate but equal" state racial segregation laws

1898 ■
Supreme Court ruling in *Williams v. Mississippi* condones use of literacy tests and similar measures to restrict voting rights

AN INDUSTRIALIZING WEST

FOCUS QUESTION

How did the industrialization of
the West change American lives?

Industrialization in the West had many linked components: the creation of farms, communities, and cities; the production of commodities such as cattle and timber that could be shipped east; the creation of western consumers and thus the demand for manufactured goods; the extraction of resources through mining and logging; and the shipment of commodities using a national transportation network.

The Homestead Act

Settlement of the West was part of the larger process of industrialization. Many migrants were able to become homesteaders because of legislation that took effect on January 1, 1863—the same day that the Emancipation Proclamation became law.

The Homestead Act embodied an American ideal that stretched back to the Jeffersonian era: the belief that individual landownership was the source of a virtuous citizenry and democratic republic.

The provisions of the Homestead Act were remarkably egalitarian for their day—up to a point. Both men and unmarried women were eligible to file for up to 160 acres of surveyed land in the public domain, as long as they were over the age of 21. (Married women were assumed to be dependents of their homesteading husbands.) Immigrants who affirmed their intention to become citizens were also eligible. As long as homesteaders lived on the land for five years, not only cultivating it but also "improving" it by building a house or barn, they could receive full title for a fee of only $10. White homesteaders ultimately claimed some 285 million acres of land.

Despite a surface egalitarianism, the Homestead Act privileged white farmers over African Americans and Hispanics, who rarely had the resources necessary to homestead. Even free land required tools and seed, plus costly transportation. The act also denied access to Chinese laborers, who could not become U.S. citizens and had few property rights. It made no provisions for the truly poor.

Furthermore, the Homestead Act was in fact a step in the process of conquest, driven by the twin pressures of industrialization and white settlement, through which Indians were irrevocably stripped of their lands. A final problem with the act was corruption in its implementation. Through chicanery, fraud, and government giveaways, more public land fell into the hands of railroads, corporations, and speculators than into the hands of individual farmers.

Railroads

Nothing was more important to the industrialization of the West than the railroad. In 1862, the year the government passed the Homestead Act, it also passed the Pacific Railroad Bill, which provided large loans and generous subsidies of land to two railroad companies, the Union Pacific (working west) and the Central Pacific (working east), in order to enable them to build a transcontinental line stretching from Omaha, Nebraska, to Sacramento, California. (Railroad lines already existed from Omaha to the east.) Two years later, the government also paid a monetary subsidy for each mile of track laid in the West. Ultimately, the government gave away 131 million acres of land to support transcontinental railroads.

These lavish subsidies set off a frenzy of railroad building. Having provided the subsidies, the government expected the railroads to obtain their own financing. Various railroads sold millions of dollars of stocks and bonds, often selling as much as the market would bear without much relationship to the actual value of the railroads. This "watered" stock was part of the runaway corruption that surrounded financing railroads.

Once they had arranged the financing for this complex venture, the Union Pacific and Central Pacific embarked on the daunting task that engaged some 20,000 workers at a time. From 1865 on, the two railroads raced against one another, as whoever laid the most track stood to gain in subsidies as well as later commerce. The Union Pacific employed primarily Irish laborers, while the Central Pacific employed a workforce that was by 1867 almost 90 percent Chinese.

Chinese Laborers and the Railroads

Thousands of Chinese laborers came to California during the Gold Rush, beginning in 1849. By 1870, approximately 63,000 Chinese lived in the United States, with over three-quarters settled in California. Almost entirely men, Chinese immigrants intended to be sojourners who planned to take their hard-earned savings home to

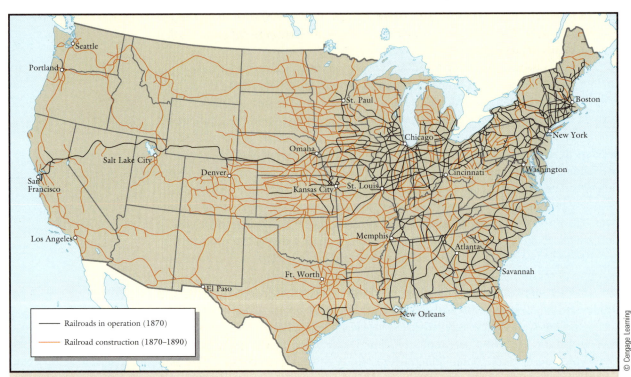

Map 18.1 **Railroad Expansion, 1870–1890.** *This map provides a vivid illustration of the spanning of the western half of the United States by steel rails in two short decades.*

the wives and families they had left behind. At first they worked as independent prospectors panning for gold, but as gold profits dwindled they moved into other areas of work.

In the 1860s, labor contractors in China recruited young men to come to America to build the transcontinental railroad. Some 12,000 Chinese laborers ultimately built the Central Pacific, often under exceptionally harsh conditions, and with substantially less pay than white workers. They also received less public recognition for their tireless labor. Chinese workers were present when the two railroads finally met on May 10, 1869, with the historic driving of a "golden spike" in Promontory Summit, Utah. But official photographs of the event leave them out—an absence that speaks volumes.

Even before they began working on the railroads, Chinese miners and laborers faced prejudice from whites. In 1850, the California State legislature responded to anti-foreigner agitation with a Foreign Miners' Tax on all foreigners; two years later the legislature specifically targeted Chinese immigrants. Violence against Chinese workers occurred throughout the West during the 1870s and 1880s, including a massacre in Rock Springs, Colorado, after the Union Pacific Railroad decided to hire Chinese workers.

At the local level, Chinese immigrants faced a host of discriminatory measures, from queue ordinances regulating the length of men's hair (forbidding the distinctive braid worn by Chinese men) to sidewalk ordinances preventing the carrying of baskets on shoulders. At the state level, California laws denied Chinese the right to own land, to testify in court, to intermarry with whites, and to immigrate. Under these conditions, Chinese workers created communities of their own. By 1850, a Chinatown had emerged in San Francisco, and Chinese sections emerged in numerous communities throughout the West.

In 1882, the federal government enacted its first discriminatory law targeting a specific immigrant group. The Chinese Exclusion Act suspended Chinese immigration for 10 years with the exception of a few job categories. Although wealthy Chinese businessmen and merchants were allowed entry, the law barred Chinese laborers, who were said to endanger "the good order of certain localities." Renewed in 1892, the Chinese Exclusion Act achieved its aim: The population of Chinese declined from 105,465 in 1880 to 89,863 in 1900, during a period in which immigration swelled for other groups.

Railroads and Borderland Communities

The arrival of the railroads, as well as the **Anglo** settlers who followed in their wake, dramatically changed the borderland communities of northern New Mexico and southern Colorado. In places like Rio Arriba County, New Mexico, Hispanic villagers who had done a thriving trade freighting—hauling goods by wagons—found themselves replaced by the railroads. As a result, communities that had combined trade with grazing and farming were now forced to go back only to farming and grazing, even though this combination had never produced enough for their needs. Even worse, in a pattern repeated throughout the West, Hispanic villagers found that Anglo settlement and fencing of once open lands reduced the range available for grazing.

As Anglo-owned livestock companies moved in, bringing in better breeds and buying up grazing land, they began to squeeze out the Hispanic farmers. By the 1890s villagers began to depend on credit for the first time; in the turbulent economy of that decade, many of them were unable to pay their debts. The end result was the loss of their sheep—and livelihood—to Anglo businessmen who had extended credit to them. Many ended up working for livestock companies, sometimes caring for herds they had once owned themselves. Eventually others ended up as miners, forced to become wage laborers. Still, some people resisted. In the 1880s, a secret organization, *las Gorras Blancas* (the White Caps), rode at night to cut fences, tear up railroad track, and burn bridges.

Mining

By the 1870s the majority of miners were also wage laborers who worked for corporations, not for themselves. Mining was big business, with groups of investors consolidating holdings in some of the richest mines. Other financiers invested in the industries related to mining, including railroads, lumber companies, and smelters.

Gold Rush prospectors had worked the surface of the earth with picks, shovels, and tin pans. But soon miners and mining companies developed new technologies to extract ore, whether on the surface of the earth or underground. **Hydraulic mining**, used as early as the 1850s, employed high-pressure jets of water to wash away banks of earth and even mountains in order to extract gold. By the 1880s, hydraulic mining produced 90 percent of California's gold, but it also ravaged the environment, tearing away at the soil and vegetation, clogging rivers, and causing floods.

Railroads played a central role in the development of industrial mining, not only providing access to mines but also enabling a new kind of mining late in the century. Copper mining became profitable because the railroads allowed the transportation of huge quantities of ore. Copper mines thrived in Butte, Montana—whose copper lode was known as the "richest hill on earth"—and in southern Arizona. Large-scale resource extraction was at the heart of western industrialization.

Working conditions in these heavily mechanized hard-rock mines grew steadily worse. Miners died from the extreme heat, poor ventilation, toxic gases, and equipment accidents. Accidents disabled 1 out of every 30 miners in the 1870s. By the end of the century, mining was the most dangerous industry in the country.

Anglos *English-speaking people.*

hydraulic mining *Use of high-pressure streams of water to wash gold or other minerals from soil.*

Unions gained a limited foothold during the 1870s and 1880s, but wage cuts in the early 1890s initiated a new burst of labor radicalism and resistance. After a violent confrontation between miners and the National Guard at Coeur d'Alene, Idaho, in 1892, mining unions met at Butte in 1893 to form the Western Federation of Miners (WFM), whose radical politics included a call to transform the American economic system. That year, a violent strike at Cripple Creek, Colorado, broke out over mine owners' attempts to move from an eight-hour to a ten-hour day. These strikes were a part of nationwide labor activism and resistance in the 1890s (see Chapter 19).

Cattle Drives and the Open Range

A postwar boom in the range cattle industry had its beginnings in southern Texas. The Spaniards had introduced **longhorn** cattle there in the 18th century, and by the 1850s millions roamed freely on the Texas plains. The market for them was limited, until the Civil War depleted the cattle supply in the older states, where prices rose to the unheard-of sum of $40 per head. The postwar expansion of population and railroads westward brought markets and **railheads** ever closer to western cattle that were free to anyone who rounded them up and branded them.

The longhorns represented a fortune on the hoof—if they could be driven northward the 800 miles to the railhead at Sedalia, Missouri. In spring 1866, cowboys hit the trail with 260,000 cattle in the first of the great drives. Disease, stampedes, bad weather, Indians, and irate farmers in Missouri (who were afraid that the Texas fever carried by longhorn herds would infect their stock) killed or ran off most of the cattle.

Only a few thousand head made it to Sedalia, but the prices they fetched convinced ranchers that the system would work, if they could find a better route. By 1867, the rails of the Kansas Pacific had reached Abilene, Kansas, 150 miles closer to Texas, making it possible to drive the herds through sparsely occupied Indian Territory. About 35,000 longhorns reached Abilene that summer, where they were loaded onto cattle cars for the trip to Kansas City or Chicago. The development of refrigerated rail cars in the 1870s enabled Chicago to ship dressed beef all over the country.

More than a million longhorns bellowed their way north on the Chisholm Trail to Abilene over the next four years, while the railhead crept westward to other Kansas towns, chiefly Dodge City, which became the most wide-open and famous of the cow towns. As buffalo and Indians disappeared from the grasslands north of Texas, ranches moved northward to take their place. Cattle drives grew shorter as railroads inched forward. Ranchers grazed their cattle for free on millions of acres of open, unfenced government land. But clashes with **"grangers"** (the ranchers' contemptuous term for farmers), on the one hand, and with a growing army of sheep ranchers on the other—not to mention rustlers—led to several "range wars." Most notable was the Johnson County War in Wyoming in 1892. Grangers and small ranchers there defeated the hired guns of the Stock Growers' Association, which represented larger ranchers.

By that time, open-range grazing was already in decline. The boom years of the early 1880s had overstocked the range and driven down prices. Then came record cold and blizzards on the southern range in winter 1884–1885, followed by even worse weather on the northern plains two years later. Hundreds of thousands of cattle froze or starved to death. These catastrophes spurred reforms that brought an end to open-range grazing.

longhorn *Breed of cattle introduced into the Southwest by the Spanish that became the main breed of livestock on the cattle frontier.*

railhead *End of a railroad line, or the farthest point on the track.*

grangers *Members of the Patrons of Husbandry (a farmers' organization) and a contemptuous name for farmers used by ranchers in the West.*

HISTORY THROUGH FILM

Oklahoma! (1955)

Directed by Fred Zinnemann; starring Gordon MacRae (Curly); Shirley Jones (Laurey); and Rod Steiger (Jud)

Only a history textbook would ask you to connect the great Rodgers & Hammerstein musical *Oklahoma!* to the range wars of the late 19th-century West. But think about it: When the cast sings "The Farmer and the Cowman" during a square dance, right before launching into a colorful fistfight, they express the different worldviews of farmers and cattle ranchers. "Whyn't those dirtscratchers stay in Missouri where they belong?" asks a cowman. Another protests that farmers "come out west and built a lot of fences! And built 'em right acrost our cattle ranges!" It's up to the song's refrain to tell us how to resolve this dispute:

The farmer and the cowman should be friends,
Oh, the farmer and the cowman should be friends.
One man likes to push a plow,
The other likes to chase a cow,
But that's no reason why they cain't be friends.

Oklahoma! is really about a mythic western space in the American imagination, where Americans come together in harmony at square dances and box suppers and where a cowboy like the masculine hero Curly is no wage laborer for life, but instead is about to become a prosperous farmer. *Oklahoma!* may be set in Indian Territory, but there are no Native Americans here. It is an entirely white, native-born world except for the peddler Ali Hakim—and he is clearly just passing through. There's certainly no indication of Oklahoma's arid climate and the devastating drought of the Great Depression, which would have been in recent memory when the musical was written in 1943. In fact, some of the people associated with the musical were uneasy about the title "Oklahoma" precisely because they were afraid it would remind audiences of the "Okies," poverty-stricken farmers forced to flee the "dust bowl" during the Depression. Instead, this is a world of green abundance where "the corn is as high as an elephant's eye." The only shadow in this sunlit world with its "bright golden haze on the meadow" is Jud, the hired hand.

Played with a heavy, menacing scowl by Rod Steiger, Jud is the dark side of the western dream, a man with a deep violent streak and an unhealthy liking for "girly pictures." These negative qualities are loaded onto his status as the "hired hand"—an uneasy reminder that class did exist in the West and that not everyone was on the brink of becoming prosperous. Jud is the only real problem in the mythic world of *Oklahoma!* and the musical blithely dispatches him by having him fall on his own knife in a fight with Curly.

A huge hit right in the midst of World War II, the show's determined exuberance and confidence struck deep chords. The show's choreographer, Agnes DeMille, remembered seeing soldiers and sailors weeping at the back of the theater, so deeply did *Oklahoma!* evoke what they considered the essence of America. "Oh what a beautiful mornin'," sings Curly at the beginning, and it reassured Americans that, having grown up on that mythic frontier, they were at the dawn of a new era.

Vibrant movie posters for the 1955 movie musical Oklahoma! *emphasized the fresh-faced, homespun appeal of romantic leads Gordon MacRae (Curly) and Shirley Jones (Laurey), who began her movie career with this role.*

BLACK COWBOYS. *Some studies of cowboys estimate that one-quarter of them were black. That estimate is probably too high for all cowboys, but it might be correct for Texas, where this photograph was taken.*

Erwin E. Smith Collection of the Library of Congress on deposit at the Amon Carter Museum, Fort Worth

Industrial Ranching, Industrial Cowboys

As open-range grazing declined, industrialized ranching expanded. By 1900, the California corporation Miller & Lux was one of the largest industrial enterprises in the country, having integrated raising cattle on vast landholdings together with meatpacking in San Francisco. Mobilizing large amounts of capital, they employed over a thousand laborers, building an operation that resembled other large corporations of the time.

Cowboys did not just ride the open range in cattle drives that had already become the stuff of legend; they also rode the extensive Miller & Lux landholdings. Before the 1870s, the most valuable of the firm's cowboys were *vaqueros*, Mexican cowboys who rounded up cattle, branded them, and drove them to San Francisco. Not surprisingly, the head *vaquero* at Miller & Lux was a Mexican American, Rafael Cuen, whose father had once owned (and lost) a piece of the Miller & Lux land. Cuen's was a position of skill and respect, yet his salary was not as high as that of his white coworkers, reflecting the prevalent discrimination against Mexicans. The arrival of railroads took a toll on the positions of *vaqueros* like Cuen: After the 1870s, cattle were shipped to market by rail.

Mexican Americans

Throughout the late 19th century Mexican Americans lost both property and political influence to incoming Anglo-American settlers. Even as early as 1849 in the northern California goldfields, resentment against "foreigners" provoked violence against Mexican American miners—and the Foreign Miners' Tax of 1850 effectively forced Mexican Americans out of the goldfields (even though they were not "foreigners"). As the 19th century progressed, hordes of Anglo-American "squatters" invaded the expansive holdings of the Mexican American elite, who sought relief in the courts. Although their claims were generally upheld, legal proceedings often stretched on for years. After exorbitant legal fees and other expenses were taken into account, a legal triumph was often a Pyrrhic victory. In the end, most Mexican American landholders in northern California had to sell the very lands they had fought to keep in order to pay their mounting debts.

The migration of Anglos into eastern Texas had played a role in fomenting the war for Texas independence and in bringing about the war with Mexico (see Chapter 13). By the latter half of the 19th century, eastern Texas was overwhelmingly Anglo; most *tejanos* (people of Mexican origin or descent) were concentrated in the Rio Grande valley of southern Texas. As in California, Anglos

QUICK REVIEW

WESTWARD EXPANSION

- Spurred the opening of western mines

- Marked by the expansion of cattle ranching and railroad construction

Kansas State Historical Society, Topeka, Kansas

DESTRUCTION OF THE BUFFALO. *By the 1880s, buffalo were almost extinct, leaving behind millions of bones, which were gathered in piles, as in this photograph of buffalo skulls, and shipped to plants that ground them into fertilizer.*

in Texas used force and intimidation, coupled with legal maneuvering, to disenfranchise the *tejanos*. The Texas Rangers often acted as an Anglo vigilante force that exacted retribution for the real or imagined crimes of Mexican Americans. Eventually, Mexican Americans in Texas were reduced to a virtual state of peonage, dependent on Anglo protectors for political and economic security.

Similar patterns prevailed in New Mexico, but the effects were mitigated somewhat because New Mexicans continued to outnumber Anglo-American settlers. Throughout the Southwest, Spanish-speaking peoples maintained their cultural traditions in the face of Anglo settlement, with the Roman Catholic Church an important center of community life. An influx of immigrants from Mexico toward the end of the century created a new basis for community as well.

Itinerant Laborers

The *vaquero* Rafael Cuen was highly skilled; he was one of the lucky employees who had long-term employment. But for many workers in the West, itinerancy was the norm. A virtual army of workers and wanderers traveled the western countryside.

Most low-level jobs in ranching were seasonal, meaning that workers were forced to move from place to place in search of work. As western industrialization uprooted their traditional lives, more and more people took to the road.

At Miller & Lux, itinerant laborers were Chinese, Portuguese, Italian, Mexican, and Mexican American, in addition to white, native-born Americans. One itinerant laborer on an irrigation crew, Joseph Warren Matthews, was a farmer who had heavy debts. To pay his debts he had taken on a series of grueling temporary jobs including wage labor at a lumber company in the Pacific Northwest, work in the Alaskan goldfields, pipe laying for a water company, ore smelting, and digging ditches. His situation underlines the precariousness of many lives in the industrializing West.

Homesteading and Farming

Homesteaders and farmers shared that precariousness: Not only were 49 percent of all homesteaders unable to "prove up" their claims, but many were ultimately forced off their homesteads by the unforgiving climate of the Great Plains. A great wave of settlement of the Great Plains occurred during the late 1870s to the mid-1880s, when rainfall was relatively abundant, but years of drought inevitably followed. The truth was that the average normal rainfall on the Great Plains was scarcely enough to support farming except in certain river valleys. Homesteaders and farmers in Minnesota, Iowa, and parts of Kansas and Nebraska were relatively lucky—those areas had rich soil and adequate rainfall. But other land was arid and unproductive, producing heartbreak for homesteaders and farmers. Between 1888 and 1892, half the population of Kansas and Nebraska were forced to give up and move back east to Illinois or Iowa.

The Experience of Homesteading

Homesteading families on the Great Plains built their houses from the ground up. In an environment without trees, they cut the dense prairie sod into blocks and stacked them up to form walls, providing a small window and a door in a "soddy" of around 18 by 24 feet. **Soddies** were a practical solution to a difficult problem on the plains, but they were also dark, dank, and claustrophobic.

As Kansas homesteader Mary Abell explained to her sister: "Imagine living in a place dug out of the side of a hill (one side to the weather with door and window—top covered with dirt and you have our place of abode). No one east would think of putting pigs in such a place." Abell's letters from 1871 to 1875 make clear the hard labor involved in homesteading. In addition to caring for five children, in the fall of 1873 she had been her husband's "sole help in getting up and stacking at least 25 tons of hay and oats." Less than a week later "one of those dreadful prairie fires" swept through the Abells' land, and they lost not only their hay and oats, but also chickens and farm equipment. In 1874, she faced both drought and grasshoppers, and wrote her family that "none of you have the least conception" of "actual want, destitution." In 1875, Abell died at the age of 29.

Not all homesteaders faced dire straits. Of the four million immigrants who came from Germany, the Czech region of the Austro-Hungarian Empire, and the Scandinavian countries from 1865 to 1890, many settled in the upper Midwest and northern plains and became successful farmers. The northern plains had the highest proportion of foreign-born residents in the nation. These European immigrants formed ethnic enclaves that maintained the distinctive culture and traditions of their homelands. Swedish immigrants in Minnesota, for instance, spoke Swedish

soddies *Homes constructed out of sod. Soddies were prevalent on the Great Plains.*

with one another and centered their lives around the Swedish Lutheran church; their children attended Swedish schools and learned to read the Swedish bible, sing Swedish songs, and recite Swedish history; both men and women wore traditional Swedish dress on holidays. By the end of the century, similarly homogenous communities of Germans, Czechs, Poles, Hungarians, and Norwegians dotted the northern landscape.

Gender and Western Settlement

The Homestead Act was unusual in allowing unmarried women to stake claims. Between 5 percent and 15 percent of homestead entries in different locales went to women in the late 19th century. Many of these women probably "proved up" only to sell their land immediately, rather than farm it themselves; but still, the existence of women homesteaders suggests just one way gender roles were different in the West.

The most pronounced difference was in mining camps and towns, which were overwhelmingly masculine. During the Gold Rush, California was up to 93 percent male, and many ranches, including Miller & Lux holdings, were exclusively male as well. Mining towns were violent, hardly a place for respectable family life.

Prostitutes from all over the world were drawn to mining towns, but nowhere except San Francisco were women systematically forced into sexual slavery. There, the situation of Chinese laborers encouraged an exploitative world trade in women. Although by the last decades of the century Chinese merchants were allowed to bring wives and daughters to America, laborers had no such rights. Furthermore, respectable single women were expected to stay home. The number of Chinese women in America never rose above 5,000 during the 19th century.

The absence of Chinese women encouraged a brutal international trade in prostitution. Chinese women kidnapped or purchased from poor parents were sold into indentured servitude or slavery and shipped to America to become prostitutes. In San Francisco, an estimated 85 to 97 percent of Chinese women were prostitutes in 1860; around 72 percent in 1870; and 21 to 50 percent in 1880. They faced a harsh existence. However, a number of women managed to escape prostitution. Some married men who had saved up enough money to purchase the contracts that bound them. Protestant missionaries also worked to rescue prostitutes.

CONQUEST AND RESISTANCE: AMERICAN INDIANS IN THE TRANS-MISSISSIPPI WEST

The westward expansion of ranching and farming after 1865 doomed the free range of the Plains Indians and the buffalo. In the 1830s, eastern tribes had been forced to preserves west of the Mississippi. Yet, in scarcely a decade, white settlers penetrated these lands. In the 1850s, when the Kansas and Nebraska territories opened to white settlement, the government forced a dozen tribes living there to cede 15 million acres, leaving them on reservations totaling less than 1.5 million acres. Thus began what historian Philip Weeks has called the "policy of concentration": No longer were Indians to be pushed ever westward. Instead, they were to be concentrated onto reservations a fraction of the size of where they had formerly hunted freely.

FOCUS QUESTION

How did the Indian peoples of the trans-Mississippi West respond to white settlement and U.S. government policies?

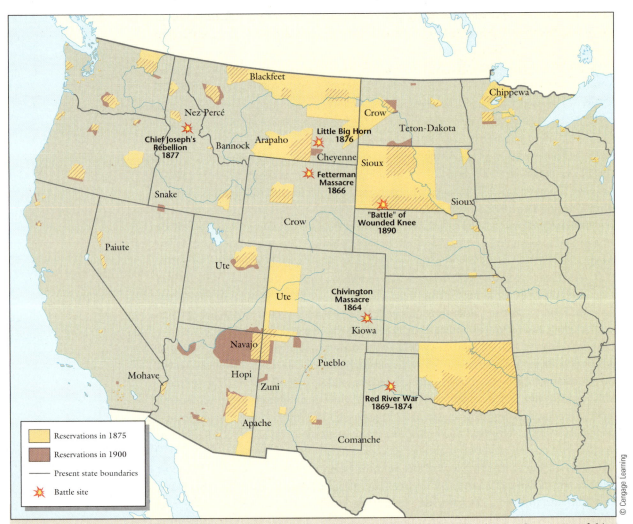

Map 18.2 Indian Reservations, 1875 and 1900. *Before the Civil War, Indians had hunted and trapped over most of this vast region. The shrinking areas on which they were confined by the reservation policy vividly illustrate that, for the first Americans, the story was not "the expansion of America" but "the contraction of America."*

In the aftermath of the Civil War, the process of concentrating Indian tribes on reservations accelerated. Chiefs of the five Civilized Tribes—Cherokees, Creeks, Choctaws, Chickasaws, and Seminoles—had signed treaties of alliance with the Confederacy. At that time, they were living in Indian Territory (most of present-day Oklahoma), where their economy was linked to the South. Many of them, especially members of the mixed-blood upper class, had slaves themselves. But siding with the Confederacy proved to be a costly mistake. Federal treaties with the five tribes in 1866 required them to grant tribal citizenship to their freed slaves and reduced tribal lands by half.

Conflict with the Sioux

The Civil War set in motion a generation of Indian warfare that was more violent and widespread than anything since the 17th century. Herded onto reservations along the Minnesota River by the Treaty of Traverse des Sioux in 1851, the Santee Sioux were angry in the summer of 1862 that annuity payments did not arrive, threatening starvation. Warriors began to speak openly of reclaiming ancestral hunting grounds. Then, on August 17, a robbery in which five white settlers were murdered seemed to open the floodgates. The warriors persuaded Chief Little Crow to take them on the warpath, and over the next few weeks at least 500 white Minnesotans were massacred.

Hastily mobilized militia and army units finally suppressed the uprising. A military court convicted 319 Indians of murder and atrocities and sentenced 303 of them to death. Appalled, Lincoln personally reviewed the trial transcripts and reduced the number of executions to 38, the largest act of executive clemency in American history. Even so, the hanging of 38 Sioux on December 26, 1862, was the largest mass execution the country has ever witnessed. The government evicted the remaining Sioux from Minnesota to Dakota Territory.

In the meantime, the army's pursuit of fleeing Santee Sioux provoked other Sioux tribes farther west. By 1864, and for a decade afterward, fighting flared between the army and the Sioux across the northern plains. It reached a climax in 1874 and 1875 after gold-seekers poured into the Black Hills of western Dakota, a sacred place to the Sioux. At the **Battle of Little Bighorn** in Montana Territory on June 25, 1876, Sioux warriors led by **Sitting Bull** and **Crazy Horse**, along with their Cheyenne allies, wiped out **George A. Custer** and the 225 men with him in the Seventh Cavalry. In retaliation, General Philip Sheridan carried out a winter campaign in which the Sioux and Cheyenne were crushed.

The largest and most warlike of the Plains tribes, the Sioux were confined to a reservation in Dakota Territory, where poverty, disease, apathy, and alcoholism reduced them to desperation.

Suppression of Other Plains Indians

Just as the Sioux uprising in Minnesota had triggered war on the northern plains in 1862, a massacre of Cheyennes in Colorado in 1864 sparked a decade of conflict on the southern plains. The discovery of gold near Pike's Peak set off a rush to Colorado in 1858–1859. The government responded by calling several Cheyenne and Arapaho chiefs to a council and persuading them to sign a treaty giving up all claims to land in this region in exchange for a reservation at Sand Creek in southeast Colorado.

In 1864, hunger and resentment prompted many warriors to return to their old hunting grounds and to raid white settlements. Skirmishes erupted into open warfare. In the fall, Cheyenne chief Black Kettle, believing that he had concluded peace with the Colorado settlers, returned to the reservation. There, at dawn on November 29, militia commanded by Colonel John Chivington surrounded and attacked Black Kettle's unsuspecting camp, killing 200 Indians, half of them women and children.

The Sand Creek massacre set a pattern for future attacks on Indian villages. Their purpose was to corral all of the Indians onto reservations that were being created throughout the West. In addition to subduing the Indians in battle, the army encouraged the extermination of the buffalo herds. Professional hunters slaughtered the animals by the millions for their hides, thus depriving Plains Indians of both physical and spiritual sustenance. When the buffalo became nearly extinct in 1883, the Plains Indians were left with no alternative but to come into the reservation, and by the 1880s nearly all of them did so. Chief Joseph of the Nez Percé pronounced the epitaph for their way of life when federal troops blocked the escape of his band from Montana to Canada in 1877: "I am tired of fighting. Our chiefs are killed. The old men are all dead. It is cold and we have no blankets . . . no food. . . . my heart is sick and sad. From where the sun now stands, I will fight no more forever."

Battle of Little Big Horn *A battle in eastern Montana Territory on the bluffs above Little Big Horn River on June 25, 1876.*

Sitting Bull *Hunkapapa Lakota (Sioux) chief and holy man who led warriors against the U.S. Army in Montana Territory in 1876, culminating in the Battle of Little Big Horn.*

Crazy Horse *War chief of the Oglala Lakota (Sioux) Indians who forged an alliance with Cheyenne chiefs to resist white expansion into the Black Hills in 1874–1875; led the attack on Custer's Seventh Cavalry at Little Big Horn.*

George A. Custer *Civil War hero and postwar Indian fighter who was killed at Little Big Horn in 1876.*

The "Peace Policy"

Many eastern reformers condemned America's suppression of the Indians. The most prominent was Helen Hunt Jackson, whose *A Century of Dishonor* (1881) was an indictment of anti-Indian violence, exploitation, and broken treaties. Yet as sympathetic as Jackson was to the Indians' plight, she believed, like other white Protestant reformers of her day, that Indians must be stripped of their culture in order to assimilate into American society.

In this she was in alignment with the government. In 1869 President Grant had announced a new "peace policy" toward Indians, urging "their civilization and ultimate citizenship." "Civilization" meant acceptance of white culture, including the English language, Christianity, and the individual ownership of property. "Citizenship" meant allegiance to the United States rather than to a tribe. In 1869, Grant established a Board of Indian Commissioners and staffed it with humanitarian reformers. In 1871, the century-long policy of negotiating treaties with Indian "nations" came to an end. Indians became "wards of the nation," to be civilized and prepared for citizenship, first on reservations and eventually on individually owned parcels of land that were carved out of the reservations. Most Indians acquiesced in the "reconstruction" that offered them citizenship by the 1880s—they had little choice.

The Dawes Severalty Act and Indian Boarding Schools

In order to further the goal of Indian ownership of private property, Protestant reformers in the 1880s found themselves in a strange alliance with land-hungry westerners, who greedily eyed the 155 million acres of land tied up in reservations. If part of that land could be allotted directly to individual ownership by Indian families, the remainder would become available for purchase by whites. The 1887 Dawes Severalty Act combined these impulses toward greed and reform. This landmark legislation called for the dissolution of Indian tribes as legal entities, offered Indians the opportunity to become citizens, and allotted each head of family 160 acres of farmland or 320 acres of grazing land as long as they were "severed" from their tribe.

For whites eager to seize reservation land, the Dawes Act brought a bonanza. At noon on April 22, 1889, the government threw open specified parts of the Indian Territory to "Boomers," who descended on the region like locusts and by nightfall had staked claim to nearly two million acres. Eventually, whites gained title to 108 million acres of former reservation land.

For Indians, the Dawes Severalty Act was a disaster. Private ownership of land was an alien concept to most tribes, and Indians received little training for a transition to farming, much less appropriate tools. Moreover, the poor quality of their land allotments made farming difficult, if not impossible. In an attempt to strip Indians of their culture, the Dawes Act forbade Indian religions and the telling of Indian myths and legends, as well as the practices of medicine men.

Indian boarding schools, established beginning in the late 1870s, also undermined Indian culture. Children were taken from their families to the Hampton Institute in Virginia and the Carlisle Institute in Pennsylvania, among other schools. There they were forbidden to speak Indian languages or wear Indian clothing. The writer Zitkala-Sa, a Yankton Sioux, later remembered her life in an Indian school: "The melancholy of those black days has left so long a shadow that it darkens the path of years that have since gone by."

Indian schools may have had assimilation into white culture as a goal, but they also had a very narrow vision of the place Indians would hold in a white world. Girls were educated for menial jobs as servants; many spent long hours

VISUAL LINK TO THE PAST

Indian Children at the Hampton Institute

At the Hampton Institute, Indian girls taken from reservations led a regimented life and learned domestic skills such as cooking and sewing. Yet the second photograph here shows girls apparently at leisure—playing checkers and reading—and a doll prominently displayed in the small chair. "Before-and-after" shots like these were used by a number of educational and charitable institutions in the late 19th century in fundraising efforts aimed at potential donors.

Q What messages do you think such "before-and-after" photographs were supposed to convey?

©2006 Harvard University, Peabody Museum Photo 2004.24.30439A

©2006 Harvard University, Peabody Museum Photo 2004.24.30440A

QUICK REVIEW

THE CONSEQUENCES OF WESTWARD EXPANSION FOR INDIANS

- Expansion led to a series of Indian wars

- Threatened the independent existence of western Indians, especially through the near extinction of the buffalo, the Peace Policy, and the Dawes Act

working in school laundries as virtual servants of the schools that were supposed to teach them. Students resisted as best they could by running away, often only to be caught and returned to school again. Many adults later resisted the training they had received by returning to Indian traditions. After graduation from a manual institute, Zitkala-Sa taught at the Carlisle School and became a much-praised writer in New York. But later she would compare herself to a "slender tree" that had been "uprooted from my mother, nature, and God"; she had "forgotten the healing in trees and brooks." Eventually she left New York, married a Sioux, and became an activist for Native American rights.

The Ghost Dance

At a time of despair for many Indians, a new visionary religious movement in 1890 offered a different kind of resistance to white domination. The Ghost Dance began with the visions of the Paiute shaman Wovoka, who counseled Indians that if they gave up alcohol, lived a simple life, and devoted themselves to prayer, white men would disappear from the earth, Indian lands would be restored, and dead Indians would rejoin the living. This message of hope was embodied in the Ghost Dance ritual, involving days of worship expressed in part through dance.

When the Ghost Dance religion spread to those Sioux led by Sitting Bull, and they began days of ecstatic dancing, Indian agents grew alarmed: As one agent telegraphed to authorities, "Indians are dancing in the snow and are wild and crazy. *We need protection and we need it now.*" The results were tragic. Sitting Bull and his grandson were killed in a skirmish with reservation authorities. A few days later, members of the Seventh Cavalry—Custer's old regiment—opened fire on a Sioux encampment at Wounded Knee in the Pine Ridge Reservation, killing 146 Indians, including 44 women and 18 children, as well as 25 soldiers. The massacre at Wounded Knee symbolized the death of 19th-century Plains Indian culture.

Sitting Bull and Buffalo Bill: Popular Myths of the West

Only a few years before he was killed, Sitting Bull had been one of the chief attractions in the entertainment extravaganza known as Buffalo Bill Cody's Wild West Show. Sitting Bull had been a canny negotiator of fees for his appearances in 1885; he required an interpreter, several attendants, and a salary that came to half the annual salary of the typical Indian agent. He also used press interviews while on the Wild West tour to ask the U.S. government to live up to its promises to Indians. If Sitting Bull was being used by Cody, he was certainly using Cody right back.

Having "real" Indians in his show was vital to Cody, who sought to satisfy the public's hunger for "authentic" entertainments in his Wild West shows. Cody was a mix of the new industrializing West, the frontier West, and the emergence of mass entertainment. Having begun his career as a soldier in the Civil War, Cody then worked for one of the transcontinental railroad lines (where he gained the nickname "Buffalo Bill" for slaughtering buffalo) before becoming a scout for the Fifth Cavalry. When Cody became the subject of a popular dime western novel, he decided to dramatize his own life in a series of theatrical entertainments. By the time Sitting Bull joined Buffalo Bill's Wild West Show, with its band of trick riders and sharpshooters, it required 18 railroad cars to transport performers (including a number of Indians), work crews, animals, and equipment.

The Wild West Show celebrated the white conquest of the West in a series of acts called "The Drama of Civilization," which showed scenes of an emigrant train crossing the prairie, Buffalo Bill rescuing a pioneer family from Indians, and a mining camp. Billed as "America's National Entertainment," these shows revealed just how tightly linked industrialization and conquest were in Americans' thinking—and even in their entertainment.

INDUSTRIALIZATION AND THE NEW SOUTH

Like the West, the South underwent a surge of industrialization in the last decades of the 19th century, with textiles leading the way to what some boosters envisioned as the "New South." In 1880, the South had only 5 percent of the country's textile-producing capacity; by 1900, it had 23 percent. Tobacco industrialized as well. Railroads and iron also saw a surge in growth. Between 1877 and 1900 the South built railroads faster than any other region in the country. In 1880 the former slave states produced only 9 percent of the nation's pig iron; by 1890, that proportion had doubled.

Not all the wealth from the new industries went into the pockets of southerners, though. Southern industry attracted more and more northern capital. At first, for instance, southerners supplied most of the capital in the expansion of the textile industry. But after 1893, an increasing amount came from the North, as New England mill owners relocated to the low-wage, nonunion South. In the tobacco industry, too, initial southern capital gave way to northern financing.

Heavy northern investment in southern industry meant that the South had less control over economic decisions that affected its welfare. Some historians have referred to the South's "colonial" relationship to the North in the late 19th century. Low wages meant that average southern per capita income remained only two-fifths of the average in the rest of the country well into the 20th century.

Race and Industrialization

Even those low wages were unequally distributed, as the politics of race influenced the structuring of industrial jobs. From Virginia to Alabama, new cotton mills sprang up for a white labor force drawn from farms on the worn-out red clay soil of the piedmont. About 40 percent of the workers were women, and 25 percent were children aged 16 and younger. Living in company towns, workers labored long hours for wages about half the level prevailing in New England. Their cheap labor gave mill owners a competitive advantage.

At first, African Americans assumed that there would be jobs for them in this new textile industry. Blacks had worked in mills before the Civil War, and they continued to work in tobacco factories in the postwar era, albeit in the lowest-paid jobs and performing the dirtiest work. But industrialization did not mean progress for blacks. Instead, it went hand in hand with segregation. To attract white workers, mill owners promised them segregated environments. The bargain offered was this: Mill workers might not earn very much, but they would gain what one historian has called the "wages of whiteness," a sense of racial superiority that could serve as compensation for their low economic status. Thus the emerging industrial economy of the New South was built around the politics of race. For most African Americans agricultural work was the only option.

FOCUS QUESTION

How did industrialization shape African American experience in the post-Reconstruction South?

Southern Agriculture

A major success story, however, was increasing black ownership of land in the post-Reconstruction period, with almost 200,000 farmers achieving that goal. Most black landowners in the South were in the upper South or coastal areas; others were in the trans-Mississippi West.

Still, most black were tenants rather than landowners, and many blacks and whites faced lives of grinding rural poverty. One-crop specialization, overproduction, declining prices, and an exploitative credit system all contributed to the problem. The basic institution of the southern rural economy was the **crop lien system** caused by the shortage of money and credit. Few banks survived the Civil War, and land values had plummeted, which left farmers unable to get a bank loan using their land as collateral. Instead, merchants provided farmers with supplies and groceries in return for a lien on their next crop.

This system might have worked well if merchants had charged reasonable interest rates and if cotton and tobacco prices had remained high enough for the farmer to pay off his debts after harvest with a little left over. But the country storekeeper charged a credit price 50 or 60 percent above the cash price, and crop prices, especially for cotton, were dropping steadily. As prices fell, farmers went deeper and deeper into debt to merchants. Sharecroppers and tenants incurred a double indebtedness: to the landowner, whose land they sharecropped or rented, and to the merchant, who furnished them supplies on credit.

One reason cotton prices fell was overproduction. Britain had encouraged the expansion of cotton growing in Egypt and India during the Civil War to make up for the loss of American cotton. After the war, southern growers had to face international competition. From 1878 to 1898, output doubled, and overproduction drove prices ever lower. To obtain credit, farmers had to plant every acre with the most marketable crop—cotton. This practice exhausted the soil, required increasing amounts of expensive fertilizer, and fed the cycle of overproduction and declining prices.

It also reduced the amount of land that could be used to grow food crops. By the 1890s, farmers had to import nearly half their food at a price 50 percent higher than it would have cost to grow their own. Many southerners recognized that only diversification could break this dependency, but the crop lien system locked them into dependency.

Exodusters and Emigrationists

Many rural African Americans dreamed of escaping these difficulties by leaving the South entirely. In the late 1870s, a movement called Exodus gained momentum among blacks who believed that they might have to "repeat the history of the Israelites" and "seek new homes beyond the reign and rule of Pharaoh." Most pinned their hopes on internal emigration to the West, although some explored the possibility of emigration to Liberia as well. In 1875, Benjamin Singleton, a former Tennessee slave, helped a group of African Americans to establish new lives in an agrarian colony in western Kansas; three years later, he circulated an advertisement picturing prairie abundance in the hopes of enticing a few hundred more settlers. Instead, in spring 1879, some 20,000 African Americans began an exodus to Kansas from all over the Southwest—drawn also by rumors that there was free land available as well as free supplies from the government. The rumors were false, but many Exodusters stayed on in Kansas anyway, although not as homesteaders amidst the prairie abundance but as domestics and laborers in Kansan towns, including some they founded, such as Nicodemus.

crop lien system *System of credit used in the poor rural South whereby merchants in small country stores provided necessary goods on credit in return for a lien on the crop. As the price of crops fell, small farmers, black and white, drifted deeper into debt.*

Race Relations in the New South

The desire to emigrate for better jobs, autonomy, and a place where African Americans could be truly free did not end with the Exodusters. There was a net loss of 537,000 African Americans in the South between 1880 and 1910. Economic reasons were important, but so too was the worsening world of white supremacy that arose in that period.

Adherence to the ideology behind the New South, with its emphasis on racial cooperation, was shallow at best among whites. They refused to let go of the legacy of the defeated plantation South. They celebrated the Lost Cause by organizing fraternal and sororal organizations such as the United Daughters of the Confederacy (UDC), whose members decorated the graves of Confederate soldiers, funded public statues of Confederate heroes, and preserved a romanticized vision of the slavery era. Several white southern authors became famous writing about this fabled South. Thomas Nelson Page's racist sentimental story "Marse Chan" created a national craze for southern literature in the 1880s. Published in a northern magazine, the story was written in what Page claimed to be authentic black dialect, with an aging freedman telling of the glorious days before the war when slaves supposedly had little work to do. Such stories cleansed the southern plantation of the horrors of slavery.

The national appeal of these stories made clear that white racism was not just a southern phenomenon. There was little northern reaction to the lynching of black men in the South in the 1890s. Lynchings rose to an all-time high, averaging 188 per year. At a time when middle-class blacks were gaining economically even as a downward spiral in the rural economy frustrated whites, lynchings were clear messages to entire black communities to keep their "place" in a white-dominated society. Lynchings were neither secret nor furtive events, but rather well-orchestrated community affairs, advertised in advance, sometimes including men, women, and children as spectators.

In 1892, three respected African American businessmen who owned a grocery store in Memphis, Tennessee, were taken from the jail where they awaited trial and lynched by a white mob. Their ostensible crime was attempted murder—firing on three white intruders who had burst into their store—but their real offense was challenging the dominance of a white grocery store in their area.

In response to the lynching, the African American journalist Ida B. Wells embarked on an extensive anti-lynching campaign involving an economic boycott as well as a series of editorials in her newspaper, *Free Speech*, that called into question the usual rationale for lynching: the supposed rape or molestation of a white woman. Exposing this common trumped-up charge as "the old racket," Wells ignited the wrath of white Memphis residents and was forced to flee to the North. Her anti-lynching campaign met with indifference from northerners until she traveled to England on a speaking tour. There, she received widespread publicity when she asked how civilized America could be if it tolerated a barbaric practice like lynching; she also touched a nerve back home. Upper-class white northerners who were indifferent to the murder of blacks but sensitive to English opinion finally began to take notice. Her English tour was a brilliant strategy to shake up northern complacency and challenge northern complicity in lynching.

The Emergence of an African American Middle Class

Wells was part of an extensive African American middle class that came of age in the 1880s and 1890s. These men and women, educated in the emerging black colleges, became teachers, doctors, lawyers, ministers, and business owners. They formed numerous civic organizations, such as the 1896 National Association of Colored Women, which was part of the women's club movement of the late

IDA B. WELLS. *A passionate crusader for justice, the renowned journalist Ida B. Wells received death threats after she began a campaign against lynching in her Memphis, Tennessee, newspaper,* Free Speech, *in 1892. Forced to leave Memphis, Wells moved to Chicago and continued her anti-lynching crusade in pamphlets, newspaper columns, and public lectures delivered both in the United States and in England. Together with Booker T. Washington, Wells was one of the most prominent African American leaders of the 1890s.*

© The Granger Collection, New York

19th century (see Chapter 19). Echoing the reform activities of middle-class white women, its president, Mary Church Terrell, called on middle-class black women to work with "the masses of our women" and to "uplift and claim them."

Such institution building, combined with increasing prosperity, gave middle-class blacks optimism that "racial uplift" might reduce or even eliminate racism in American society. Middle-class blacks believed that through education and self-improvement they could become "best men" and "best women," seen as equals by middle-class whites. These were not naïve hopes, as black entry into the middle class surged in the 1880s and early 1890s.

The Rise of Jim Crow

But these visible successes of middle-class African Americans enraged white supremacists, who denied any possibility of class solidarity across racial lines. Serious antiblack riots broke out at Wilmington, North Carolina, in 1898 and in Atlanta in 1906. Several states adopted new constitutions that disfranchised black voters by means of literacy or property qualifications (or both), poll taxes, and other clauses implicitly aimed at black voters. The new constitutions contained "understanding clauses" or "grandfather clauses" that enabled registrars to register white voters who were unable to meet the new requirements. In *Williams v. Mississippi* (1898), the U.S. Supreme Court upheld these disfranchisement clauses on the grounds that they did not discriminate "on their face" against blacks. State Democratic parties then established primary elections in which only whites could vote.

During these same years most southern states passed **Jim Crow laws** mandating racial segregation in public facilities of all kinds. In the landmark case *Plessy v. Ferguson* (1896), the Supreme Court sanctioned such laws as long as the separate facilities for blacks were equal to those for whites—which, in practice, they never were.

Jim Crow laws *Laws passed by southern states mandating racial segregation in public facilities of all kinds.*

At this "nadir" of the black experience in freedom, as one historian has called the 1890s, a new black leader emerged. **Booker T. Washington**, a 39-year-old educator who had founded Tuskegee Institute in Alabama, gave a speech at the 1895 Atlanta Exposition that made him famous. Speaking to a white audience, Washington in effect accepted segregation as a temporary accommodation between the races in return for white support of black efforts for education, social uplift, and economic progress. "In all things that are purely social we can be as separate as the fingers," said Washington, "yet one as the hand in all things essential to mutual progress."

Washington's listeners came away with very different impressions of his speech. Many African Americans applauded his appeal for black inclusion in the new industrial order; many white audience members simply took away the idea that Washington approved of segregation. An eloquent response to Washington came from the emerging African American leader **W. E. B. Du Bois** in his 1903 masterpiece, *The Souls of Black Folk*. Criticizing Washington for a policy of conciliation and submission, Du Bois reminded his audience that "only a firm adherence to their higher ideals and aspirations will ever keep those ideals within the realm of possibility."

Booker T. Washington
Founder of Tuskegee Institute and most famous for his controversial speech at the 1895 Atlanta Exposition.

W. E. B. Du Bois *An outspoken critic of Booker T. Washington and his accommodationist approach to race relations. He would become the leader of the NAACP.*

THE POLITICS OF STALEMATE

Between the Panic of 1873 and the Panic of 1893, serious economic and social issues beset the American polity. The strains of rapid industrialization, an inadequate monetary system, agricultural distress, and labor protest built up to potentially explosive force. The two mainstream political parties, however, seemed indifferent to these problems. Partisan memories of the Civil War mired Americans in the politics of the past. Paralysis gripped the national government.

FOCUS QUESTION

Why did politicians fail to address many of the most serious economic and social issues facing the nation in the post-Reconstruction world?

Knife-Edge Electoral Balance

The five presidential elections from 1876 through 1892, taken together, were the most closely contested elections in American history. No more than 1 percent separated the popular vote of the two major candidates in any of these contests except 1892, when the margin was 3 percent. The Democratic candidate won twice (Grover Cleveland in 1884 and 1892), and in two other elections carried a tiny plurality of popular votes (Tilden in 1876 and Cleveland in 1888) but lost narrowly in the Electoral College. During only 6 of those 20 years did the same party control the presidency and both houses, and then by thin margins.

Divided government and balance between the two major parties made for the political stalemate. Neither party had the power to enact a legislative program; both parties avoided taking firm stands on controversial issues. At election time, Republican candidates "waved the bloody shirt" to keep alive the memory of the Civil War. They castigated Democrats as former rebels who could not be trusted with the nation's destiny. Democrats, especially in the South, denounced racial equality and branded Republicans as the party of "Negro rule." From 1876 almost into the 20th century scarcely anyone but a Confederate veteran could be elected governor or senator in the South.

The solid Democratic South and the rather less solid Republican North gave each party a firm bloc of electoral votes in every election. But in three large northern states—New York, Ohio, and Indiana—the two parties were so closely balanced that the shift of a few thousand votes would determine the margin of victory for one or the other party in the state's electoral votes. These three states alone represented

74 electoral votes, fully one-third of the number necessary for victory. Of 20 nominees for president and vice president by the two parties in five elections, 16 were from these three states. Only once did each party nominate a presidential candidate from outside these states—both lost.

Civil Service Reform

The most salient issue of national politics in the early 1880s was civil service reform. The Republicans split into three factions known as Mugwumps (the reformers), Stalwarts (who opposed reform), and Half-Breeds (who supported halfway reforms). Mugwumps and Half-Breeds combined to nominate James A. Garfield for president in 1880. Stalwarts received a consolation prize with the nomination of Chester A. Arthur for vice president. Four months after Garfield took office, a man named Charles Guiteau approached the president at the railroad station in Washington and shot him. Garfield lingered for two months before dying on September 19, 1881. Described by psychiatrists as a paranoid schizophrenic, Guiteau had been a government clerk and a supporter of the Stalwart faction of the Republican Party. He had lost his job under the new administration. As he shot Garfield, he shouted, "I am a Stalwart and Arthur is president now!" This tragedy gave a final impetus to civil service reform.

In 1883, Congress passed the Pendleton Act, which established a category of civil service jobs to be filled by competitive examination. At first, only one-tenth of government positions fell within this category, but a succession of presidential orders gradually expanded the list to about half by 1897. State and local governments began to emulate federal civil service reform in the 1880s and 1890s.

Like the other vice presidents who had succeeded presidents who died in office (John Tyler, Millard Fillmore, and Andrew Johnson), Arthur failed to achieve nomination for president in his own right. The Republicans turned in 1884 instead to Speaker of the House James G. Blaine of Maine. Blaine had made enemies over the years, especially among Mugwumps, who felt that his cozy relationship with railroad lobbyists while Speaker disqualified him for the presidency.

The Mugwumps were small in number but large in influence. Many were editors, authors, lawyers, college professors, or clergymen. Concentrated in the Northeast, they admired the Democratic governor of New York, Grover Cleveland, who had gained a reputation as an advocate of reform and "good government." When Blaine won the Republican nomination, the Mugwumps defected to Cleveland.

In such a closely balanced state as New York, that shift could make a decisive difference, but Blaine hoped to neutralize it by appealing to the Irish vote. He made the most of his Irish ancestry on the maternal side, but that effort was rendered futile late in the campaign when a Protestant clergyman characterized the Democrats as the party of "Rum, Romanism, and Rebellion." Although Blaine was present when the Reverend Samuel Burchard made this remark, he failed to repudiate it. When the incident hit the newspapers, Blaine's hope for Irish support faded. Cleveland carried New York State by 1,149 votes (a margin of one-tenth of 1 percent) and thus became the first Democrat to be elected president in 28 years.

The Tariff Issue

Ignoring a rising tide of farmer and labor discontent, Cleveland decided to make or break his presidency on the tariff issue. In his December 1887 State of the Union

QUICK   REVIEW

POLITICAL STALEMATE

- Marked by persistence of Civil War political allegiances and balance of parties in national politics

- Except for civil service reform, Congress accomplished little

- Characterized by the politics of the tariff issue

message, he maintained that lower duties would help all Americans by reducing the cost of consumer goods and by expanding American exports. Republicans responded that low tariffs would flood the country with products from low-wage industries abroad, forcing American factories to close and throwing American workers out on the streets. The following year, the Republican nominee for president, Benjamin Harrison, pledged to retain the protective tariff. To reduce the budget surplus that had built up during the 1880s, the Republicans also promised more generous pensions for Union veterans.

The voters' response was ambiguous. Cleveland's popular-vote plurality actually increased from 29,000 in 1884 to 90,000 in 1888. But a shift of six-tenths of 1 percent put New York in the Republican column and Harrison in the White House. Republicans also gained control of both houses of Congress. They promptly passed legislation that almost doubled Union pensions and enacted the McKinley Tariff of 1890. Named for Congressman William McKinley of Ohio, this law raised duties on a large range of products to an average of almost 50 percent.

In the midterm congressional elections, the voters handed the Republicans a decisive defeat, and the Democrats took control of both houses of Congress. Nominated for a third time in 1892, Cleveland built on this momentum to win the presidency by the largest margin in 20 years, but this outcome was deceptive. On March 4, 1893, when Cleveland took the oath of office for the second time, he stood atop a social and economic volcano that would soon erupt.

Conclusion

In 1890 the superintendent of the U.S. Census made a sober announcement: "Up to and including 1880 the country had a frontier of settlement, but at present the unsettled area has been so broken into by isolated bodies of settlement that there can hardly be said to be a frontier line . . . any longer."

This statement prompted a young historian at the University of Wisconsin, Frederick Jackson Turner, to deliver a paper in 1893 that became the single most influential essay ever published by an American historian. For nearly 300 years, said Turner, the existence of a frontier of European–American settlement advancing relentlessly westward had shaped American character. To the frontier Americans owed their upward mobility, their high standard of living, and the rough equality of opportunity that made liberty and democracy possible. "American social development has been continually beginning over again on the frontier," declared Turner.

For decades, Turner's insight dominated Americans' perceptions of themselves and their history. Today, however, **Turner's "frontier thesis"** is discredited as failing to explain the experiences of the great majority of Americans who lived and worked in cities and towns or on farms and plantations hundreds of miles from any frontier, and whose culture and institutions were molded more by their place of origin than by a frontier. The concept of a frontier as uninhabited wilderness overlooked the tens of thousands of Indians who occupied the region. Furthermore, the Turner thesis ignored the environmental consequences of the westward movement.

For most Americans, however, the exploitation of the West was a matter for pride, not concern. The positive claims of the Turner thesis reflected beliefs shared widely among whites. They *believed* that liberty and equality were at least partly the product of the frontier, of the chance to go west and start a new life. And now that opportunity seemed to be ending. It seemed that a new and worrisome power was overtaking American life, threatening American liberty: the power of the corporation.

Turner's "frontier thesis"
Theory developed by historian Frederick Jackson Turner, who argued that the frontier had been central to the shaping of American character and the success of the U.S. economy and democracy.

CHAPTER REVIEW

Review Questions

1. How did the industrialization of the West change American lives?
2. How did the Indian peoples of the trans-Mississippi West respond to white settlement and U.S. government policies?
3. How did industrialization shape African American experience in the post-Reconstruction South?
4. Why did politicians fail to address many of the most serious economic and social issues facing the nation in the post-Reconstruction world?

Critical Thinking Questions

1. Both the South and the West industrialized in the late 19th century. What were the major differences in the industries that developed in each section, and why?
2. How were ordinary people's experiences of industrialization different in the two regions? Why? Assess the opportunities that were provided by industrialization as well as the drawbacks in the West and South.

Identifications

Review your understanding of the following key terms, people, and events for this chapter.

Anglo, p. 411
hydraulic mining, p. 411
longhorn, p. 412
railhead, p. 412
grangers, p. 412

soddies, p. 416
Battle of Little Bighorn, p. 419
Sitting Bull, p. 419
Crazy Horse, p. 419

George A. Custer, p. 419
crop lien system, p. 424
Jim Crow laws, p. 426
Booker T. Washington, p. 427

W. E. B. Du Bois, p. 427
Turner's "frontier thesis," p. 429

DISCOVERY

How did westward movement in the postwar period reshape the West?

In thinking about this question, begin by breaking it down into the components shown below. A discussion of the significance of each component should appear in your answer.

Geography

Look at the map on railroad expansion (page 410) and think about what you read in this chapter. What cities were accessible by rail in 1890 that had not been just two decades before? How did the expansion of railroads in the 1870s and 1880s affect the western cattle industry? How did railroads improve the lives of prairie farmers? In what other specific ways did the growth of railroads aid in westward expansion?

Economy and U.S. Indian Policy

Consider the following quote from Chief Joseph of the Nez Percé:

I am tired of fighting. Our chiefs are killed. The old men are all dead. It is cold and we have no blankets . . . no food. . . . The little children are freezing to death. . . . Hear me, my chiefs; I am tired; my heart is sick and sad. From where the sun now stands, I will fight no more forever.

How did the destruction of the bison contribute to the specific problems that Chief Joseph listed? Look at the photo. How does this image convey the magnitude of degradation of the natural environment and Plains Indian culture caused by excessive bison hunting? What role did the destruction of the buffalo play in the suppression of Plains Indians?

DESTRUCTION OF THE BUFFALO

© Cengage Learning

CourseMate

Visit the CourseMate website at www.cengagebrain.com for additional study tools and review materials for this chapter.

CHAPTER

19

THE RISE OF CORPORATE AMERICA, 1865–1914

A DYNAMIC CORPORATE ECONOMY
Engines of Economic Growth
Technological Innovation
The Rise of Big Business
Corporate Consolidation
Mass Production and Distribution
Revolution in Management

CORPORATIONS AND AMERICAN CULTURE
Standardized Time
A National Consumer Culture
Ideas of Wealth and Society
Sharpened Class Distinctions
Obsession with Physical and Racial Fitness

CHANGES IN MIDDLE-CLASS WOMEN'S LIVES
Middle-Class Women and Work
The Women's Club Movement
The "New Woman"
Higher Education and Professional Organizations

WORKERS' RESISTANCE TO CORPORATIONS
Industrial Conditions
The Great Railroad Strike of 1877
The Knights of Labor
Haymarket
The American Federation of Labor (AFL)
The Homestead Strike
Coxey's Army
The Pullman Strike

FARMERS' MOVEMENTS
Resistance to Railroads
The Greenback and Silver Movements
Grangers and the Farmers' Alliance

THE RISE AND FALL OF THE PEOPLE'S PARTY
The Silver Issue
The Election of 1896

"ROBBER BARONS" NO MORE

I n the summer of 1877, the same year that President Rutherford B. Hayes withdrew federal troops from the South and effectively ended Reconstruction, he called out the military to suppress the most serious labor uprising in the nation's history. The **Great Railroad Strike** ultimately involved hundreds of thousands of people across America, claimed at least 100 lives, resulted in injuries to hundreds more, and caused the destruction of millions of dollars of property. It also caught many onlookers by surprise: "Sudden as a thunderburst from a clear sky," one journalist wrote, "the crisis came upon the country."

But the strike was not so sudden as it seemed to middle-class observers. The end of the Civil War had inaugurated an era of rapid economic expansion, but industrialization left many workers as permanent wage earners, with little hope of the independence that had been a cherished part of antebellum free-labor ideology. As a roller-coaster economy also subjected employers to boom-and-bust cycles, many resorted to price-cutting and wage-cutting, even while demanding longer hours. The result was that capital and labor had never been more at odds with one another.

The Great Railroad Strike raised troubling questions that would continue to haunt Americans over the next few decades: Who held power in the emerging corporate order? How was liberty now defined, and whose liberty would the government uphold? Had America become a permanently unequal society?

Chapter 19

- 1880's move from agriculture to manufacturing
- Middle class ↑ working class ↓
- Railroad expansion = labor, need for iron, coal and <u>STEEL</u>
- Technological Innovation ⌐
  - Electricity
  - Steel Industry

- Jp Morgan - most powerful banker 19th Century.
- New York Stock Exchange.
- John D. Rockefeller Oil. ★
- Henry Ford - Model T
- Standardized Time - RailRoad Cause.
- Advertisment / Jell-O / Ivory Soap / Macy's new york.
- ★ Power Violence / 20 years Ivy leagues were nationall football powerhouses.
- Club Sorosis professional women writers.
- New Women - Independant, confident, young.
- 1866 National Labor Union 8hour day labor conditions
- Railroad strike 1877 - wage cut by 10%
- Knights of Labor 1877 - leader Terence Powerdly.
- May 3 Haymarket Square → May 4 anarchy attack.
- Coxey's Army - Unemployed Workers went to capital.
- Pullman Strike.
- Railroads charged high to transport goods in areas of no competition.
- Vertical integration - 2 or More stages of production
- Horizontal integration - monopoly.

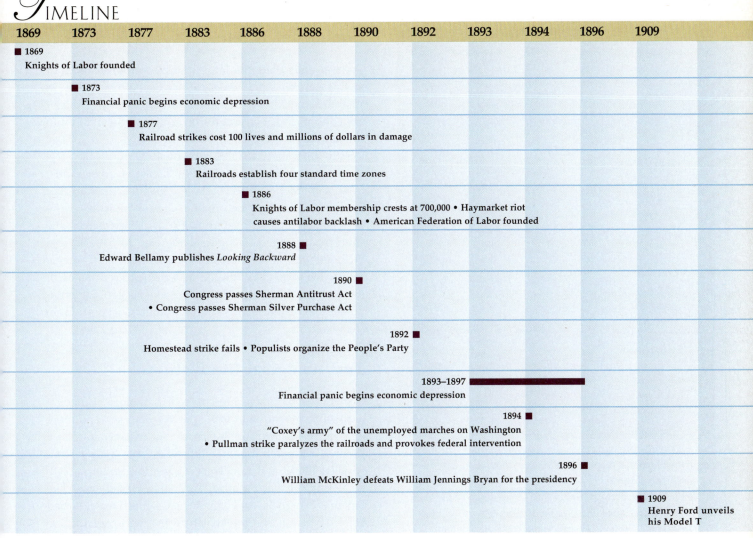

| 1869 | 1873 | 1877 | 1883 | 1886 | 1888 | 1890 | 1892 | 1893 | 1894 | 1896 | 1909 |

■ 1869
Knights of Labor founded

■ 1873
Financial panic begins economic depression

■ 1877
Railroad strikes cost 100 lives and millions of dollars in damage

■ 1883
Railroads establish four standard time zones

■ 1886
Knights of Labor membership crests at 700,000 • Haymarket riot causes antilabor backlash • American Federation of Labor founded

1888 ■
Edward Bellamy publishes *Looking Backward*

1890 ■
Congress passes Sherman Antitrust Act
• Congress passes Sherman Silver Purchase Act

1892 ■
Homestead strike fails • Populists organize the People's Party

1893–1897
Financial panic begins economic depression

1894 ■
"Coxey's army" of the unemployed marches on Washington
• Pullman strike paralyzes the railroads and provokes federal intervention

1896 ■
William McKinley defeats William Jennings Bryan for the presidency

■ 1909
Henry Ford unveils his Model T

© Cengage Learning

AᴅYNAMIC CORPORATE ECONOMY

The decades following the Civil War saw an unprecedented surge of economic growth. The gross national product was $9 billion for the five-year period from 1869–1873; it was $37 billion for the period from 1897–1901. In the 1880s, manufacturing began to outstrip agriculture as a source of new value added to the economy. America moved from fourth in the world in production in 1865 to first in 1900.

But this tremendous growth was accompanied by spectacular volatility. Cycles of overexpansion and overproduction were followed by inevitable contraction. Significant labor uprisings correlated with economic downturns, as employers and businesses sought to cut their losses by cutting wages or laying off workers. The Great Railroad Strike of 1877 occurred during an extended depression; 1886, another depression year, saw 1,400 strikes involving half a million workers.

Still, the growth of the economy in this period meant great opportunity and increased prosperity for many Americans. Titans of industry piled up previously unimaginable fortunes. A flourishing middle class achieved new power. But the working class shared unequally in this rising prosperity.

FOCUS QUESTION

What were the main engines of American economic growth in the late 19th and early 20th centuries?

Great Railroad Strike *Strike that occurred during a time of depression that caused employers to cut wages and lay off workers.*

THE GREAT RAILROAD STRIKE. *On August 11, 1877, the national magazine* Harper's Weekly *printed this illustration with the caption, "The Great Strike—the Sixth Maryland Regiment Fighting Its Way Through Baltimore." At first glance the illustration seems sympathetic to the strikers being fired upon in the foreground. The article accompanying this illustration, however, talked of the "reign of terror inaugurated by the railroad strikers" and "scenes of riot and bloodshed" such as "we have never before witnessed in the uprising of labor against capital."*

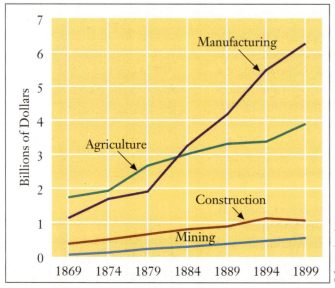

VALUE ADDED BY ECONOMIC SECTOR, 1869–1899 (IN 1879 PRICES).

Engines of Economic Growth

The railroads were the largest single employer of labor in this period. Track mileage increased from 30,000 in 1860 to some 200,000 in 1900. Railroad expansion meant a greater need for coal and iron, and later steel, to build cars and lay track; steel production soared from 732,000 tons in 1878 to 10,188,000 tons by 1900. Since the steel industry itself was a catalyst for a host of other industries, manufacturing as a whole expanded dramatically in this period. Just before the Civil War, there were 140,000 factories and manufacturing shops across the country; by 1899 this figure had risen to 512,000 and included the rise of industrial giants such as Carnegie Steel. This growth continued into the 20th century with the emergence of such businesses as Chicago's International Harvester factory and DuPont Corporation in Delaware.

Technological Innovation

Growth in manufacturing spurred technological innovation, while invention in turn spurred increased and more efficient manufacturing. Railroads, for instance, ran on a promise of reliability and efficiency, but poorly constructed tracks and rails were a significant hindrance to delivering on that promise. Technological advances like automatic signals and air brakes improved railroad efficiency; similarly, the switch from iron to steel tracks aided efficient production of tracks and promoted the growth of the new steel industry.

Scientists had long been fascinated by electricity, but only in the late 19th century did they find ways to make it practically useful. The work of Thomas Edison, George Westinghouse, and Nikola Tesla produced the incandescent bulb that brought electric lighting into homes and offices as well as the alternating current (AC) that made electric transmission possible over long distances. From 1890 to 1920, the proportion of American industry powered by electricity rose from virtually nil to almost one-third.

The Rise of Big Business

A host of other inventions in this period spurred economic growth: gasoline engines, Kodak cameras, the Otis elevator, and Alexander Graham Bell's telephone, to name a few. But technological breakthroughs alone do not fully explain the economic boom. New corporate structures and new management techniques created the conditions that powered economic growth. Railroad companies inaugurated a new era of big business that had profound effects on business practice. Many businesses now organized as corporations rather than single proprietorships: Corporations could raise capital through selling shares in a company directly to the public. They also used boards of directors as a management tool, allowing for shared responsibility and a new scale and complexity of enterprise.

Railroads were big business in every way, requiring huge tracts of land as well as enormous amounts of capital. In order to encourage railroad building, between 1862 and 1871 the government stepped in with extremely generous subsidies, signaling the beginning of a close relationship between government and business in the postwar period. Indeed, throughout the late 19th century and into the 20th century, government supported the rights of corporations rather than the rights of workers in a series of legal cases as well as major strikes.

Railroad companies stood to gain greatly if they built enough miles of track, but in order to build, they first needed often-staggering sums of money. In stepped financiers, bankers, and a wealthy elite—many of whom seized a golden opportunity to obtain power in the new industrial order. The savvy young banker **J. P. Morgan** helped finance the Albany & Susquehanna Railroad in upstate New York and joined its board in 1870. Morgan would become the most celebrated and powerful banker of the late 19th century, in large part through his shrewd investing in a variety of industries, including Edison's first electric power plant in 1882. Numerous other bankers would also gain new power through providing the finance capital needed by industry.

But there were financial losers as well as winners in the railroad-building frenzy of the post–Civil War era. Shaky financing and speculation characterized much of the railway boom. The most spectacular and far-reaching downfall of the postwar years was that of Jay Cooke, the legendary financial genius behind the sale of Union bonds during the Civil War. Cooke was undone by his attempts to finance the Northern Pacific Railroad: He ran out of capital in 1873 after selling risky bonds and mortgaging government property. When the Northern Pacific went into receivership, Cooke was forced to close his powerful Philadelphia banking house. Within hours, his closure triggered the crash of the New York Stock Exchange, which in turn began the Panic of 1873. In the severe depression that followed, 18,000 businesses went under.

Corporate Consolidation

Corporations began looking for ways to insulate themselves from downturns in the business cycle. Rather than engaging in ruinous rate wars, railroads took to sharing information on costs and profits, establishing standardized rates, and allocating discrete portions of the freight business among themselves. These cooperative arrangements rarely succeeded for long because they depended heavily on voluntary compliance. During difficult economic times, the temptation to lower rates and exceed one's market share could become too strong to resist.

Corporate efforts to restrain competition and inject order into the economic environment continued unabated, however. A number of corporate titans innovated with corporate organization, including **Andrew Carnegie**, the industrial leader who built giant Carnegie Steel after the Civil War. Carnegie steadily took control of all parts of the steelmaking process, starting with the mining of the raw material of iron ore and ending with the transportation and marketing of the final product. This vertical integration was a powerful new form of business organization that allowed for unprecedented consolidation and the building of business on a previously unimagined scale.

J. P. Morgan *Most celebrated and powerful banker of the late 19th century.*

Andrew Carnegie *A Scottish immigrant who became the most efficient entrepreneur in the U.S. steel industry and earned a great fortune.*

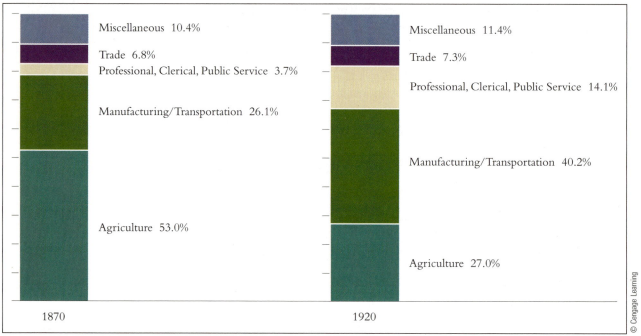

CHANGE IN DISTRIBUTION OF THE AMERICAN WORKFORCE, 1870–1920.

Source: Data from Alba Edwards, *Comparative Occupational Statistics for the United States 1870–1940*, U.S. Bureau of the Census, Sixteenth Census of the United States, 1940, Population (Washington, D.C., 1943).

John D. Rockefeller *Founder of the Standard Oil Company, whose aggressive practices drove many competitors out of business and made him one of the richest men in America.*

merger movement *Late 19th and early 20th century effort to integrate different enterprises into single, giant corporations able to eliminate competition and boost profits.*

Sherman Antitrust Act (1890) *Intended to declare any form of trade restraint illegal, but proved to be useless in prosecution of corporations.*

Another titan, the ruthless **John D. Rockefeller** of Standard Oil, either bought out or ruined his rivals through practices such as "predatory pricing" (selling below cost until he bankrupted a competitor) and demanding secret rebates from railroads that wanted his business. In the 1880s, he pioneered a new form of corporate structure, the trust. A vehicle for the creation of a monopoly, a trust was initially used by Rockefeller to gain control over the oil refining industry and create the horizontal integration of one aspect of his business. Soon, he engaged in vertical integration as well in order to gain control over every aspect of the oil industry, from extraction of crude oil to marketing. By the 1890s, Rockefeller controlled 90 percent of the oil business.

Mergers also emerged as an important instrument of corporate expansion and consolidation. Smoking tobacco manufacturer James Buchanan Duke led the way in 1890 when he and four competitors merged to form the American Tobacco Company. Over the next eight years, the quantity of cigarettes produced by Duke-controlled companies quadrupled, and American Tobacco used its powerful position in cigarette manufacture to achieve dominance in pipe tobacco, chewing tobacco, and snuff manufacture.

The **merger movement** only intensified as the depression of the 1890s lifted. Many of the corporations that would dominate American business throughout most of the 20th century acquired their modern form. The largest merger occurred in steel in 1901, when Andrew Carnegie and J. P. Morgan together fashioned the U.S. Steel Corporation from 200 separate iron and steel companies. U.S. Steel controlled 60 percent of the country's steelmaking capacity, and it dominated the procurement of raw materials and distribution of finished steel products.

A weak federal government and a conservative Supreme Court set few limits on corporations in this period, despite significant antitrust agitation in the 1880s and 1890s. By then, many Americans feared the power wielded by tycoons who had established monopolies or monopoly market shares. The **Sherman Antitrust Act** of 1890 was an attempt to declare any form of "restraint of trade" illegal, but it was so vague as to be almost useless in the actual prosecution of corporations. In 1895, the Supreme Court dealt a crippling blow to the already weak act when it ruled in *U.S. v. E.C. Knight Company* that the federal government did not have authority over manufacturing because it was not commerce—a form of semantic hair-splitting that revealed the conservative Court's unwillingness to curtail the power of big business.

mass production *High-speed and high-volume production.*

Mass Production and Distribution

In 1909, Henry Ford of Michigan unveiled his Model T: an unadorned, even homely, car, but reliable enough to travel hundreds of miles without servicing and cheap enough to be affordable to most working people. By the 1920s, Americans were buying his car by the millions. The stimulus this insatiable demand gave to the economy can scarcely be exaggerated. Millions of cars required millions of pounds of steel alloys, glass, rubber, petroleum, and other material. Millions of jobs in coal and iron-ore mining, oil refining and rubber manufacturing, steelmaking and machine tooling, road construction, and service stations came to depend on automobile manufacturing.

Ford innovated with **mass-production** techniques that increased production speed and lowered unit costs. Mass production often meant replacing skilled workers with machines that were coordinated to permit high-speed, uninterrupted production at every stage of the manufacturing process. But such production techniques were profitable only if large quantities of output could be sold. Although the domestic market offered a vast potential for sales, manufacturers often found distribution systems inadequate. This was the case with James Buchanan Duke. In 1885, at a time when relatively few Americans smoked, Duke invested in several Bonsack cigarette machines, each of which manufactured 120,000 cigarettes per day. To create a market for the millions of cigarettes he was producing, Duke advertised his product aggressively throughout the country. He also established regional sales offices so that his sales representatives could keep in touch with local jobbers and retailers. Over the course of the next 20 years, those corporations that integrated mass production and mass distribution, as Duke did in the 1880s and 1890s, came to define American "big business."

Revolution in Management

The growth in the number and size of corporations revolutionized corporate management. The ranks of managers mushroomed. Increasingly, senior managers took over from owners the responsibility for long-term planning. Day-to-day operations fell to middle managers who oversaw particular departments in corporate

From the General Negative Collection, North Carolina State Archives, Raleigh, NC.

CIGARETTE-MAKING MACHINE. *James Albert Bonsack's 1880 invention of a cigarette-making machine revolutionized the production of cigarettes. Skilled individual workers were able to produce around 200 cigarettes an hour. With the Bonsack machine, that rate soared to some 12,000 an hour.*

Map 19.1 Industrial America, 1900–1920. *This map shows that the Northeast, Midwest, and California dominated factory production in the United States from 1900 to 1920. It also reveals the state-by-state distribution of various industries— clothing in New York, automobiles in Michigan, petroleum refining in Texas and Oklahoma, and lumber in Oregon, Washington, and Idaho.*

headquarters, supervised regional sales offices, or directed particular factories. Middle managers also managed people—accountants, clerks, foremen, engineers, and salesmen. The expansion within corporate managerial ranks created a new middle class, loyal to its employers but at odds both with blue-collar workers and with the older middle class of shopkeepers, small businessmen, and independent craftsmen.

As management grew in importance, companies tried to make it more scientific. Firms introduced cost-accounting methods. Many corporations began requiring college or university training for entry into middle management. Corporations that had built their success on a profitable invention or discovery created research departments and hired professional scientists—those with doctorates from American or European universities—to come up with new technological and scientific breakthroughs.

CORPORATIONS AND AMERICAN CULTURE

New technological innovations changed urban dwellers' everyday relationship to physical space and even time. The world of mass-produced consumer goods also provided a new standardization of experience, and created a new national consumer culture.

FOCUS QUESTION

How did the rise of corporations reshape the everyday experiences of Americans?

Standardized Time

Before the post–Civil War boom in railroads, there was no such thing as "standard" time; instead, many localities and cities kept their own time, derived from the sun's meridian in each locality. If the clock read noon in Chicago, for instance, it read 11:50 in St. Louis, 11:38 in St. Paul, and 11:27 in Omaha. This situation played havoc with railroad timetables.

In a sign of corporations' power over American life, in 1883 a consortium of railroad companies agreed to standardize North American time with the creation of four different time zones—much as they exist today—in which all clocks would be set to exactly the same time. Some grumbling followed about the arrogance of railroad presidents changing "God's time." But "railroad time" was quickly adopted by people everywhere, although Congress did not officially sanction standard time zones until 1918.

A National Consumer Culture

Consumer goods also standardized experience as manufacturers produced national brands such as Ivory soap and Jell-O. Advertising firms began working hand in hand with manufacturers to create national marketing campaigns. Expenditures on advertising increased from some $50 million in 1867 to $500 million by 1900.

Advertisements became part of a shared national visual culture, as technological improvements in lithography and the half-tone process in the 1880s and 1890s allowed advertisers to create bright, colorful images that were distributed across the country. Technological breakthroughs in printing allowed new popular magazines and mass-circulation newspapers to reach hundreds of thousands of readers nationally, as well. The conservative *Ladies' Home Journal*, founded in 1893, soon reached over 500,000 readers. Newspapers responded to the demands of a growing population with the first color comics, women's pages, Sunday sections, society pages, and sports pages.

Advertising revenues from department stores fueled the growth of newspapers. These "palaces of consumption" dramatically changed the urban experience of buying consumer goods. In a major retailing innovation, stores such as Marshall Field & Co. in Chicago (1865) and R.H. Macy's in New York (1866) sold a wide variety of items—from perfume to shoes to household goods—all under one roof in different departments, instead of in different stores. Customers strolled down carpeted aisles, and ornate interiors with mirrors and lights added to a sensory experience of profusion, color, and excitement.

Outside of cities, men and women could participate in the new national culture of consumption through mail order. Mail-order catalogues were the brilliant idea of A. Montgomery Ward, who had worked at Marshall Field's firm in Chicago. Starting with a single price sheet of items in 1872, by 1884 Ward was producing a thick, 240-page catalogue that listed close to 1,000 items for sale—everything from women's underclothing to entire houses.

Ideas of Wealth and Society

A profusion of consumer goods reached a wide national audience in this period. But among the wealthy, some also practiced what the economist Thorstein Veblen described as "conspicuous consumption." They sent agents to Europe to buy paintings and tapestries from impoverished aristocrats. In their mansions on Fifth Avenue and their summer homes at Newport, Rhode Island, they entertained lavishly. The extravagant habits of a wealthy elite gave substance to Mark Twain's labeling of this era as the Gilded Age. The estimated number of *millionaires* (a word that came into use during this era) in 1860 was 300; by 1892, the number was 4,000.

Many among the wealthy, and eventually among a broader middle class as well, justified their right to wealth with an emerging post–Civil War vocabulary of **Social Darwinism.** In assuming that market forces were in fact laws of nature, Rockefeller, Carnegie, and other industrial titans drew upon the influential work of the English author Herbert Spencer, who had coined the phrase "survival of the fittest" in applying the evolutionary theories of Charles Darwin to human society. According to the tenets of Social Darwinism, human history could be understood in terms of an ongoing struggle among races, with the strongest and the fittest invariably triumphing. The wealth and power of the Anglo-Saxon race were ample testimony, in this view, to its superior fitness.

At first popular mostly among intellectuals (the social sciences took shape during these years), Social Darwinism was quickly adopted by a broader public, with "survival of the fittest" becoming a popular catchphrase. The theory provided a comfortable way of understanding the glaring social inequality of the era: Workers were doomed to be permanent wage laborers not because of some fault in the emerging corporate system, but because they were not "fit." The rich, meanwhile, were entitled to every dollar that came their way.

Sharpened Class Distinctions

The well-publicized activities of the wealthy sharpened a growing sense of class distinction in this era. Throughout the late 19th century, many Americans worried over the class distinctions they saw emerging around them as part of the corporate reordering of American life. The rise of corporations produced a need for salaried managers, professionals, office workers, and retail clerks—"white-collar" workers (a reference to detachable, starched white collars for shirts). Agricultural labor dropped from 53 percent of the gainfully employed in 1870, to 35 percent in 1900, and to 21 percent in 1930; clerical work in the same period rose from less than 1 percent to over 8 percent. The profession of engineer, directly related to the expansion of manufacturing, leapt by 586 percent between 1870 and 1900.

Many members of this new corporate middle class sought to distinguish themselves from the "lower classes" by moving to the suburbs. As early as 1873, *Scribner's* magazine noted that "the middle class, who cannot live among the rich, and will not live among the poor . . . go out of the city to find their houses." By the end of the 19th century, suburban communities of detached houses, surrounded by lawns, were markers of the middle-class status of businessmen and professionals who worked by day in cities and traveled back and forth by train or streetcar to their homes.

Social Darwinism *Set of beliefs explaining human history as an ongoing evolutionary struggle between different groups of people for survival and supremacy that was used to justify inequalities between races, classes, and nations.*

Theater, literature, and art were also arenas of class distinction. Before the Civil War, performances of Shakespeare had often been rowdy, participatory, cross-class events. By the end of the century, the middle class not only claimed Shakespeare as an icon of "high" culture, but also imposed new expectations of "genteel" silence during performances. In literary magazines, middle-class critics decried the vulgarity of dime novels and westerns. *Century* and *Harper's New Monthly* published serial novels by great authors and a variety of articles and "tasteful" fiction, including an emerging literature of nostalgia for slavery with virulently racist portrayals of blacks. A new art movement, American Impressionism, also expressed a middle-class desire for gentility. Artists such as William Merrit Chase and Childe Hassam painted light-flecked landscapes or flower-filled urban parks, recording middle-class pleasures in cities strikingly devoid of workers.

Yet increasingly over the late 19th century, mere gentility began to seem arid to some middle-class artists and writers. Painters such as Thomas Eakins and Thomas Anshutz pioneered a style that would develop into the "realism" of the early 20th century, with its grittier view of city life and less idealized vision of the human form. The dean of American letters, William Dean Howells, wrote novels exploring issues that had rarely been touched by American authors, including divorce, the moral bankruptcy of capitalism, and interracial marriage. Discouraged by the widening gulf between the classes, Edward Bellamy, in his 1888 utopian novel, *Looking Backward,* imagined a world in the year 2000 in which "labor troubles" and social inequities had been eradicated through a form of socialism. Bellamy's powerful fictional indictment of Gilded Age society resonated with half a million readers, making his novel one of the most popular of the 19th century.

Obsession with Physical and Racial Fitness

The fractious events of the 1890s induced many middle-class and wealthy Americans to engage in what Theodore Roosevelt dubbed "the strenuous life." In an 1899 essay with that title, Roosevelt exhorted Americans to live vigorously, to test their physical strength and endurance in competitive athletics, and to experience nature through hiking, hunting, and mountain climbing. Other writers, too, argued that through vigorous activity, men could find and express their virility.

In the country at large, the new enthusiasm for athletics and the outdoor life reflected a widespread dissatisfaction with the growing regimentation of industrial society. Millions of Americans, both women and men, began riding bicycles and eating healthier foods. Young women began to engage in organized sports. A passion for athletic competition also gripped American universities. The power and violence of football helped make it the sport of choice at the nation's elite campuses, and, for 20 years, Ivy League schools were the nation's football powerhouses.

Among middle-class and wealthy Americans, the quest for physical superiority reflected a deeper and more ambiguous anxiety: their *racial* fitness. Most of them were native-born Americans whose families had lived in the United States for several generations and whose ancestors had come from the British Isles or some other region of northwestern Europe. Having embraced the principles of Social Darwinism, they liked to attribute their success and good fortune to their "racial superiority." But events of the 1890s challenged the legitimacy of the elite's wealth and authority, and the ensuing depression mocked their ability to exert economic leadership. The immigrant masses laboring in factories, despite their poverty and alleged racial inferiority, seemed to possess a vitality that the "superior" Anglo-Saxons lacked.

QUICK REVIEW

CHANGES IN AMERICAN CULTURE

- Corporate culture led to the standardization of time and consumption

- Class distinctions sharpened

- Elites relied on theories of racial "fitness" to justify inequality

CHANGES IN MIDDLE-CLASS WOMEN'S LIVES

FOCUS QUESTION

What were the major changes in middle-class women's lives in the late 19th and early 20th centuries?

After the Civil War many middle-class women continued to adhere to the ideology of domesticity, assuming that their place was in the home. Yet an increasing number of women entered a wider sphere of life.

Middle-Class Women and Work

By 1900, 21 percent of all women—middle class and working class—were in the workforce, as opposed to 9.7 percent of women in 1860. After the Civil War, women moved into nursing and office work, while continuing to be a mainstay in teaching. By the end of the 19th century, middle-class women became editors, literary agents, and journalists in larger numbers, while also entering the professions of medicine and law in small numbers. Many college women moved to cities to take up work.

The increased interest in work was reflected in literature of the period. Louisa May Alcott's 1873 novel *Work* imagined an ideal cross-class, cross-race world of supportive female workers. Elizabeth Stuart Phelps spoke for many discontented middle-class women in her 1877 novel *The Story of Avis*, in which the despairing heroine gave up being an artist for her marriage. Writer and economist Charlotte Perkins Gilman's 1892 biting novella *The Yellow Wallpaper* spoke powerfully of a new domestic claustrophobia. In that brief work, the unnamed heroine desires to write after the birth of a child but is told by her husband and doctor that she must rest instead and is virtually imprisoned in her home.

Few middle-class observers—men or women—were able to imagine women combining work with family. And yet many women had to do so. For example, the nationally known journalist Jane Croly, who wrote columns under the name "Jenny June," supported her sick husband and four children as an editor and author during the 1880s before becoming the first female professor of journalism at Rutgers University.

The Women's Club Movement

In 1868, the New York Press Club decided to bar women journalists from a celebratory dinner for the great novelist Charles Dickens. Jane Croly was insulted and furious, but turned that fury toward a positive purpose: forming the women's club Sorosis (the name was chosen to suggest sisterhood). Composed primarily of professional women writers, Sorosis met regularly to discuss topics of the day and to exchange professional advice.

Sorosis inaugurated a movement of women's clubs across the nation. Distinct from antebellum moral reform societies, the new women's clubs were secular and had a variety of different purposes, from intellectual discussion to civic reform. They also provided a bridge to middle-class women's activism during the Progressive era. By the turn of the 20th century, the women's club movement was an important source of support for the revived suffrage movement (see Chapter 21). What's more, women had used the women's club movement to move into and even take over a variety of civic organizations—a way of practicing politics by other means in an era before women had the vote.

This was especially important in the Jim Crow South, where black men were disfranchised in the 1890s (see Chapter 21). Middle-class black women drew on their extensive experiences in church organizations and Republican aid societies to create effective new networks of public civic organizations. African American

VISUAL LINK TO THE PAST

The New Woman

John Singer Sargent's 1897 portrait of Mr. and Mrs. I. N. Phelps Stokes captures the vibrant, athletic independence of the emerging New Woman. Dressed in a shirtwaist and carrying a straw boater, Edith Minturn Stokes radiates an air of vitality and energy; her husband by contrast is very much in the background.

The New Woman was a much-discussed phenomenon of the late 19th century—the term variously described women who were entering the workforce in greater numbers, attending colleges or universities, playing such sports as golf and tennis, and sometimes living independently away from parents and family.

Although most New Women were middle-class whites, historians now recognize that there were also New Women among both working-class and African American women.

Many women writers celebrated the New Woman as a sign of women's progress in American life. But a number of conservative critics mounted a fierce counterattack on the New Woman, arguing that women were biologically unsuited both for work and higher education.

Q Why were some critics alarmed by the emergence of the New Woman? Why do you think the New Woman was controversial?

Image copyright © The Metropolitan Museum of Art/Art Resource, NY

women also joined the largest women's social organization of the late 19th century, the Woman's Christian Temperance Union (WCTU). Under the leadership of Frances Willard beginning in 1879, the WCTU engaged in a variety of social reform activities nationally and endorsed woman suffrage in 1884.

The "New Woman"

"New Woman" *1890s depiction of women as a public figure who was athletic, self-confident, young, and independent.*

The **"New Woman"** became a dominant figure of American popular culture in the 1890s. In cartoons, illustrations, paintings, short stories, and essays, the New Woman was a public figure who was athletic, self-confident, young, and independent: She wore the new, less confining fashion of shirtwaists and skirts; rode a bicycle; and even smoked in some images.

But to some observers, the New Woman threatened the sanctity of the home and traditional gender roles. A backlash against middle-class women's new roles was often rooted in new "scientific" expertise. Arguing against women's higher education, for instance, the Harvard Medical School professor Edward H. Clarke asserted in 1873 that intellectual work damaged women's reproductive organs. "A girl could study and learn," he warned, "but she could not do all this and retain uninjured health, and a future secure from neuralgia, uterine disease, hysteria, and other derangements of the nervous system."

The Comstock Law (1872) made it illegal to send reproductive literature or devices through the mails on the grounds that they were "obscene," eroding women's already-limited control of reproduction. During the bicycle craze of the 1890s, experts warned that it would be unhealthy for women to ride. Women actively resisted these attacks in articles, lectures, and through their own actions. Frances Willard took up bicycling at age 53 in part, she said, because she knew her example would "help women to a wider world."

Higher Education and Professional Organizations

QUICK REVIEW

NEW WOMEN

- Middle-class women entered the workforce in increasing numbers
- White and black women founded women's clubs to push for reform
- While more women attended college, they were often blocked from professional advancement

Women moved into higher education in large numbers in the late 19th century. In the Midwest and the West, universities began to admit women in the 1860s. In the East there were fewer coeducational institutions, but the founding of women's colleges—with Vassar leading the way in 1865—meant that by 1890, women were approximately 40 percent of all college graduates nationally.

This move into higher education did not translate into greater ease of access to professional education. Women had broken into medical training in 1849 with the admission of Elizabeth Blackwell to Geneva Medical College in upstate New York. But as separate medical colleges gave way to medical schools within universities in the late 19th century, women lost ground. Professional organizations often excluded women; at the turn of the 20th century, the American Medical Association, a gatekeeper to the profession, was an all-white, all-male organization, as were the American Bar Association, the American Historical Association, and the American Economic Association. Thus, while new professional organizations established much-needed uniform standards and training, they also closed ranks against women and minorities.

WORKERS' RESISTANCE TO CORPORATIONS

FOCUS QUESTION

How effective was workers' resistance to the new corporations? Why?

A national culture of consumption had grown up in the last decades of the 19th century, but not everyone had equal access to it. Wages that did not keep pace with the booming economy meant less money to spend, not to mention a struggle to put food on the table.

While some middle-class observers believed that all organizing workers were revolutionaries, most working people had more prosaic goals: fair wages and fair conditions in the workplace. They wanted equality in a system in which power had been systematically stripped from them, and liberty seemed to accrue more to corporations than to individuals. Broad-based workers' movements throughout the late 19th century attempted to rectify a situation in which equal opportunities no longer seemed to be available to all.

Industrial Conditions

One source of the rising tide of worker discontent was the dangerous conditions in the industrial workplace. The drive for even greater speed and productivity on railroads and in factories gave the United States the unhappy distinction of having the world's highest rate of industrial accidents. With little government regulation and no workmen's compensation, many families were impoverished by workplace accidents that killed or maimed their chief breadwinner. In the factories, new machinery took over tasks once performed by skilled workers, and managers, not the workers, made decisions about the procedures and pace of operations. Labor increasingly became a commodity bartered for wages rather than a craft whereby the worker sold the product of his labor rather than the labor itself. For the first time in American history, the census of 1870 reported that a majority of employed persons worked for wages paid by others rather than working for themselves.

Skilled artisans considered this loss of independence an alarming trend. In 1866, the leaders of several craft unions had formed the National Labor Union, which advocated for an eight-hour day at a time when many industries required workers to work for 10 or even 12 hours daily. Labor parties sprang up in several states; the Labor Reform candidate for governor of Massachusetts in 1870 won 13 percent of the vote.

The Great Railroad Strike of 1877

Yet the National Labor Union withered away in the depression of the 1870s, and industrial violence escalated. The worst labor violence in U.S. history up to that time, the Great Railroad Strike of 1877 underscored the deep discontent of workers nationwide. In July, the Baltimore and Ohio Railroad cut wages by 10 percent—its third recent wage reduction. When workers in Martinsburg, West Virginia, walked out in protest, workers up and down the B & O line joined them.

The strike touched a nerve nationally and spread rapidly; within a few days, what had begun as a local protest had traveled to Baltimore, Philadelphia, Pittsburgh, New York, Louisville, Chicago, St. Louis, Kansas City, and San Francisco. Women as well as men joined angry crowds in the streets, and workers from a variety of industries walked out in sympathy. Strikers and militia in a number of cities fired on each other, and workers set fire to railroad cars and depots.

Alarmed at the possibility of a "national insurrection," President Hayes called in the army, and the strike finally ended in early August. This spontaneous, unorganized labor upheaval did not produce solutions to workers' dilemmas. On the contrary, fears of a workers' "insurrection" led to a new cohesion in the middle class, which began to talk of a "war" between capital and labor.

The Knights of Labor

Many workers in the wake of 1877 looked to a new labor organization for inspiration. The **Knights of Labor** had been founded in 1869 in Philadelphia as a secret fraternal organization, one of many such artisan societies in eastern cities. Under the leadership of Terence Powderly, a machinist by trade, it became public in 1879 and expanded to become a potent national federation of unions, or "assemblies," as they

Knights of Labor *Secret fraternal organization that emerged into a potent national federation of unions.*

URBAN FORTRESSES. *In the 1880s and 1890s, numerous armories were built in cities across the country to protect against a perceived threat from the "dangerous classes"—workers and the poor. This immense, castle-like 1894 armory in Brooklyn, New York, was meant to inspire awe.*

were officially known. The Knights of Labor called for an eight-hour day, equal pay for women, public ownership of railroads, abolition of child labor, and a graduated income tax. Most of its assemblies were organized by industry rather than by craft, giving many unskilled and semiskilled workers union representation for the first time. Some admitted women; some also admitted blacks.

Most members of the Knights wanted to improve their lot within the existing system through higher wages, shorter hours, and better working conditions. This meant collective bargaining with employers; it also meant strikes. Powderly and the Knights' national leadership discouraged strikes, however, partly out of practicality: A losing strike often destroyed an assembly, as employers replaced strikes with strikebreakers, or "scabs." Another reason for Powderly's antistrike stance was philosophical: Strikes constituted a tacit recognition of the legitimacy of the wage system. In Powderly's view, wages siphoned off to capital a part of the wealth created by labor. He instead embraced a radical vision of the future, in which workers' cooperatives would own the means of production.

Despite Powderly's reservations, the Knights gained their greatest triumphs through strikes, not cooperatives. In 1884 and 1885, successful strikes against the Union Pacific and Missouri Pacific railroads won prestige and a rush of new members, which by 1886 totaled 700,000. But defeat in a second strike against the Missouri Pacific in spring 1886 was a serious blow. Then came the Haymarket bombing in Chicago.

Haymarket

Chicago, with an active number of socialists and anarchists, was a center of labor activism and radicalism. A national movement centered in that city called for a general strike on May 1, 1886, to achieve the eight-hour workday. Chicago police were notoriously hostile to labor organizers and strikers, so the scene was set for a violent confrontation.

The May 1 showdown coincided with a strike at Chicago's McCormick farm machinery plant. A fight outside the gates on May 3 brought a police attack on the strikers in which four people were killed. Anarchists then organized a protest meeting at Haymarket Square on May 4. Toward the end of the meeting, the police suddenly arrived in force. When someone threw a bomb into their midst, the police opened fire. When the wild melee ended, 50 people lay wounded and 10 dead, 6 of them policemen.

Haymarket set off a wave of hysteria against labor radicals. Chicago police rounded up hundreds of labor leaders. Eight anarchists went on trial for conspiracy to commit murder. Although no evidence turned up to prove that any of them had thrown the bomb, all eight were convicted. One of the men committed suicide; the governor commuted the sentences of two others to life imprisonment; the remaining four were hanged on November 11, 1887. The case bitterly divided the country. Many workers, civil libertarians, and middle-class citizens who were troubled by the events branded the verdicts judicial murder, but most Americans applauded the repression of radicalism they regarded as un-American.

The Knights of Labor were caught in this antilabor backlash. Although the Knights had nothing to do with the Haymarket affair, Powderly's opposition to the

Haymarket *Bombing at an Anarchist protest meeting at Haymarket Square in Chicago on May 4, 1886, resulting in 10 deaths, six of them policemen.*

wage system sounded suspiciously like socialism, perhaps even anarchism. Membership in the Knights plummeted from 700,000 in spring 1886 to fewer than 100,000 by 1890.

The American Federation of Labor (AFL)

As the Knights of Labor waned, a new national labor organization waxed. Founded in 1886, the American Federation of Labor (AFL) was a loosely affiliated association of unions organized by trade or craft: cigar-makers, machinists, carpenters, and so on. Most AFL members were skilled workers. The leader of the AFL, **Samuel F. Gompers**, was a onetime Marxist and cigarmaker who was reelected to the AFL presidency every year from 1896 until his death in 1924.

The AFL emerged in a hostile environment. Federal and state governments used military force to break strikes. The courts repeatedly found unions in violation of the Sherman Antitrust Act, even though that act had been intended to control corporations, not unions. Judges in most states usually granted employer requests for injunctions—court orders that barred striking workers from picketing their place of employment (and thus from obstructing employer efforts to hire replacement workers). In its *Lochner v. New York* (1805) ruling, the U.S. Supreme Court declared unconstitutional a seemingly innocent New York state law limiting bakery employees to a 10-hour day.

These challenges retarded the growth of unions and made the AFL, the major labor organization of those years, more timid and conservative than it had been before the depression of the 1890s. Very few AFL members were women and blacks. The AFL accepted capitalism and the wage system. Instead of agitating for governmental regulation of the economy and the workplace, it concentrated on better conditions, higher wages, shorter hours, and occupational safety within the system—"pure and simple unionism," as Gompers called it. In its early years the AFL showed considerable vitality under Gompers, with its membership quadrupling from less than a half million in 1897 to more than two million in 1904. But, concentrated among craft workers, it represented only a small portion of the industrial workforce.

The Homestead Strike

During the 1890s, strikes occurred with a frequency and a fierceness that made 1877 and 1886 look like mere preludes to the main event. The most dramatic confrontation took place in 1892 at the Homestead plant (near Pittsburgh) of the Carnegie Steel Company. Carnegie and his plant manager, Henry Clay Frick, were determined to break the power of the country's strongest union, the Amalgamated Association of Iron, Steel, and Tin Workers. Frick used a dispute over wages and work rules as an opportunity to close the plant (a "lockout"), preparatory to reopening it with non-union workers. When the union called a strike and refused to leave the plant, Frick called in 300 Pinkerton guards to oust them. A full-scale gun battle between strikers and Pinkertons erupted on July 6, leaving nine strikers and seven Pinkertons dead and scores wounded. Frick persuaded the governor to send in 8,000 militia to protect the strikebreakers, and the plant reopened. Public sympathy, much of it pro-union at first, shifted when the anarchist Alexander Berkman tried to murder Frick on July 23. The failed **Homestead Strike** crippled the Amalgamated Association.

Coxey's Army

Events after 1893 brought an escalation of conflict. The most serious economic crisis since the 1873–1878 depression was triggered by the Panic of 1893, a collapse of the stock market that plunged the economy into a severe four-year depression. By mid-1894, the unemployment rate had risen to more than 15 percent.

Samuel F. Gompers *America's most famous trade unionist while serving as president of the AFL (1896–1924). He achieved his greatest success in organizing skilled workers.*

Homestead Strike *Carnegie Steel closed its Homestead plant, planning to reopen with nonunion workers; the union went on strike, refusing to leave the building, which led to a gun battle and several deaths.*

An Ohio reformer named Jacob Coxey conceived the idea of sending Congress a "living petition" of unemployed workers to press for appropriations to put them to work on road building and other public works. "Coxey's army," as the press dubbed it, inspired other groups to travel to Washington during 1894. This descent of the unemployed on the capital provoked arrests by federal marshals and troops, and ended when Coxey and others were arrested for trespassing on the Capitol grounds. Coxey's idea for using public works to relieve unemployment turned out to be 40 years ahead of its time.

The Pullman Strike

The explosive tensions between capital and labor fueled the **Pullman Strike** of 1894. George M. Pullman had made a fortune in the manufacture of sleeping cars and other rolling stock for railroads. Workers in his large factory complex lived in the company town of Pullman just south of Chicago, with paved streets, clean parks, and decent houses rented from the company. But Pullman controlled many aspects of their lives, including banning liquor from the town and punishing workers whose behavior did not suit his ideas of decorum. When the Panic of 1893 caused a sharp drop in orders for Pullman cars, the company laid off one-third of its workforce and cut wages for the rest by 30 percent, but did not reduce company house rents or company store prices. Pullman refused to negotiate with a workers' committee, which called a strike and appealed to the American Railway Union (ARU) for help.

The ARU had been founded the year before by Eugene V. Debs, who was convinced that the conservative stance of the railroad unions was contrary to the best interests of labor. He formed the ARU to include all railroad workers in one union. When George Pullman refused the ARU's offer to arbitrate the strike of Pullman workers, Debs launched a boycott by which ARU members would refuse to run any trains that included Pullman cars. When the railroads attempted to fire the ARU sympathizers, whole train crews went on strike and paralyzed rail traffic.

Over the protests of Illinois governor John P. Altgeld, who sympathized with the strikers, President Grover Cleveland sent in federal troops. For a week in July 1894, the Chicago railroad yards resembled a war zone. Thirty-four people, mostly workers, were killed. Finally, 14,000 state militia and federal troops restored order and broke the strike. Debs went to jail for six months. The U.S. attorney general had obtained a federal injunction against him under the Sherman Antitrust Act on grounds that the boycott and the strike were a conspiracy in restraint of trade.

The Pullman Strike was only the most dramatic event of a year in which 750,000 workers went on strike and another three million were unemployed. But it was a surge of discontent from farmers that wrenched American politics off its foundations in the 1890s.

Pullman Strike *1894 labor strike that became the first nationwide workers' strike against the railroad.*

QUICK REVIEW

CONFLICT OF CAPITAL AND LABOR

- Railroad strikes of 1877

- Knights of Labor emerged as principal labor organization

- Haymarket affair of 1886

- The AFL discriminated against black workers and made little effort to organize unskilled workers

- Depression and strikes in the 1890s

FARMERS' MOVEMENTS

FOCUS QUESTION

What provoked the farmer protest movements in the last third of the 19th century?

Between 1870 and 1890, America's grain production increased three times as fast as the population. Only rising exports could sustain such expansion. But by the 1880s, the improved efficiency of large farms in eastern Europe brought intensifying competition, and prices on the world market for wheat and cotton fell about 60 percent from 1870 to 1895. Victims of a world market largely beyond their control, farmers lashed out at targets nearer home: railroads, banks, commission merchants, and the monetary system.

Resistance to Railroads

The power wielded by the railroad companies aroused hostility. Companies often charged less for long hauls than for short hauls in areas with little or no competition. They also formed "pools" by which they divided traffic and fixed their rates. Some of these practices made sound economic sense, but others appeared discriminatory and exploitative. Railroads kept rates higher in areas with no competition (most farmers lived in areas served by only one line) than in regions with competition. Grain elevators, many of which were owned by railroad companies, came under attack for cheating farmers.

Farmers responded by organizing cooperatives to sell crops and buy supplies. The umbrella organization for many of these cooperatives was the Patrons of Husbandry, known as the Grange, founded in 1867. Farmers organized "antimonopoly" parties and elected legislators who enacted "Granger laws" in several states. These laws established railroad commissions that fixed maximum freight rates and warehouse charges. Railroads challenged the laws, but the U.S. Supreme Court, in *Munn v. Illinois* (1877), ruled that states could regulate businesses clothed with a "public interest," including railroads.

In 1887, Congress issued new federal regulations with the Interstate Commerce Act. The act outlawed pools, discriminatory rates, long-haul versus short-haul differentials, and rebates to favored shippers. It required that freight and passenger rates must be "reasonable and just." What that meant was not entirely clear, but the law created the Interstate Commerce Commission (ICC) to define the requirement on a case-by-case basis. Because the ICC had minimal enforcement powers, however, federal courts frequently refused to issue the orders it requested. Nevertheless, the ICC had some effect on railroad practices, and freight rates continued to decline during this period as railroad operating efficiency improved.

The Greenback and Silver Movements

The long period of price deflation from 1865 to 1897, unique in American history, made credit even more costly for farmers. When crop prices declined, farmers had even less money to pay back loans. Thus it was not surprising that farmers who denounced banks or merchants for gouging them also attacked a monetary system that brought deflation.

After the Civil War, the Treasury moved to bring the greenback dollar to par with gold by reducing the amount of greenbacks in circulation. This limitation of the money supply produced deflationary pressures. Western farmers, who suffered from downward pressures on crop prices, were particularly vociferous in their protests against this situation, which introduced a new sectional conflict into politics—not North against South, but East against West.

Many farmers in 1876 and 1880 supported the Greenback Party, whose platform called for the issuance of more U.S. Treasury notes (greenbacks). Even more popular was the movement for **"free silver."** Until 1873, government mints had coined both silver and gold dollars at a ratio of 16 to 1 (16 ounces of silver were equal in value to 1 ounce of gold). However, when new discoveries of gold in the West after 1848 placed more gold in circulation relative to silver, that ratio undervalued silver, so that little was being sold for coinage.

Silver miners joined with farmers to demand a return to silver dollars, and pressure for "free silver"—that is, for government purchase of all silver offered for sale at a price of 16 to 1 and its coinage into silver dollars—continued during the 1880s. The admission of five new western states in 1889 and 1890 contributed to the passage of the Sherman Silver Purchase Act in 1890. That act increased the amount of silver coinage, but not at the 16-to-1 ratio. Even so, it went too far to suit "gold bugs," who wanted to keep the United States on the international gold standard. President Cleveland blamed the Panic of 1893 on the Sherman Silver Purchase Act, and he persuaded Congress to repeal it in 1893, setting the stage for the most bitter political contest in a generation.

free silver *Idea that the government would purchase all silver offered for sale and coin it into silver dollars at the preferred ratio between silver and gold of 16 to 1.*

Grangers and the Farmers' Alliance

Agrarian reformers supported the free silver movement, but many had additional grievances concerning credit, railroad rates, and the exploitation of workers and farmers by the "money power." Both the Grange and the Farmers' Alliance, a new farmers' organization that expanded rapidly in the 1880s, addressed these political concerns. Both also addressed farm families' social and cultural needs. The Grange sponsored picnics and cultural events, actively encouraging the participation of women. Local chapters were required to have female members, and women took up positions of leadership at the local level and attended national meetings.

Like the Grange, the Farmers' Alliance also provided a sense of community for farmers. Starting in Texas as the Southern Farmers' Alliance, by 1890, the movement had evolved into the National Farmers' Alliance and Industrial Union, which was affiliated with the Knights of Labor. It was also affiliated with a separate Colored Farmers' Alliance, formed by African Americans who recognized the utility of the Farmers' Alliance but were not welcome in the larger whites-only organization. Reaching out to two million farm families, the Farmers' Alliance set up marketing cooperatives to eliminate middlemen. It organized picnics and educational institutes in addition to camp meetings. The Alliance also bolstered farmers' pride to counter the image of "hick" and "hayseed."

The Farmers' Alliance developed a comprehensive political agenda. At a national convention in Ocala, Florida, in December 1890, it set forth these objectives: (1) a graduated income tax; (2) direct election of U.S. senators (instead of election by state legislatures); (3) free and unlimited coinage of silver at a ratio of 16 to 1; (4) effective government control and, if necessary, ownership of railroad, telegraph, and telephone companies; and (5) the establishment of "subtreasuries" (federal warehouses) for the storage of crops, with government loans at 2 percent interest on those crops. These were radical demands for the time, but most of them eventually became law: the income tax and the direct election of senators by constitutional amendments in 1913; government control of transportation and communications by various laws in the 20th century; and the subtreasuries in the form of the Commodity Credit Corporation in the 1930s.

Anticipating that the Republicans and the Democrats would resist these demands, many Alliancemen were eager to form a third party. In Kansas they had already done so, launching the People's Party, whose members were known as Populists, in summer 1890. White southerners, mostly Democrats, opposed the idea of a third party for fear that it might open the way for the return of the Republican Party, and African Americans, to power.

In 1890, farmers helped elect numerous state legislators and congressmen who pledged to support their cause, but the legislative results were thin. By 1892, many Alliance members were ready to take the third-party plunge.

THE RISE AND FALL OF THE PEOPLE'S PARTY

FOCUS QUESTION

Why did many Americans find Populism appealing in the 1890s?

The first nominating convention of the People's Party met at Omaha in July 1892. The preamble of their platform expressed the grim mood of delegates. "We meet in the midst of a nation brought to the verge of moral, political, and material ruin," it declared. "The fruits of the toil of millions are boldly stolen to build up colossal fortunes for a few." The platform called for the five demands issued at Ocala in 1890, as well as laws to protect labor unions against prosecution for strikes and boycotts. To ease the lingering tension between southern and western farmers, the party nominated Union veteran James B. Weaver of Iowa for president and Confederate veteran James G. Field of Virginia for vice president.

Despite winning 9 percent of the popular vote and 22 electoral votes, Populist leaders were shaken by the outcome. In the South, most of the black farmers who were allowed to vote stayed with the Republicans. Democratic bosses in several southern states kept white farmers in line for the party of white supremacy. Only in Alabama and Texas, among southern states, did the Populists get more than 20 percent of the vote. They did even worse in the older agricultural states of the Midwest, where their highest share of the vote was 11 percent in Minnesota. Only in distressed wheat states such as Kansas, Nebraska, and the Dakotas and in the silver states of the West did the Populists do well, carrying Kansas, Colorado, Idaho, and Nevada.

But the party remained alive, and the anguish caused by the Panic of 1893 seemed to boost its prospects. In several western states, Populists or a Populist-Democratic coalition controlled state governments for a time, and a Populist-Republican coalition won the state elections of 1894 in North Carolina. Women as well as men campaigned for the Populists: Mary Lease, one of the few women practicing law in Kansas, became famous for her impassioned speeches against corporate power.

The Silver Issue

In 1893, President Cleveland's success in getting the Sherman Silver Purchase Act repealed drove a wedge into the Democratic Party. Southern and western Democrats turned against Cleveland. The Democratic dissidents who stood poised to take over the party in 1896 adopted free silver as the centerpiece of their program. This stand raised possibilities for a fusion with the Populists. Meanwhile, out of the West came a new and charismatic figure, a silver-tongued orator named **William Jennings Bryan**. The one-term congressman from Nebraska came to the Democratic convention in 1896 as a young delegate—only 36 years old. Given the opportunity to make the closing speech in the debate on silver, Bryan brought the house to its feet in a frenzy of cheering with his peroration: "You shall not press down upon the brow of labor this crown of thorns, you shall not crucify mankind upon a cross of gold."

This speech catapulted Bryan into the presidential nomination. He ran on a platform that not only endorsed free silver but also embraced the idea of an income tax, condemned trusts, and opposed the use of injunctions against labor. Bryan's nomination created turmoil in the People's Party. Although some Populists wanted to continue as a third party, most of them saw fusion with silver Democrats as the road to victory. At the Populist convention, the fusionists got their way and endorsed Bryan's nomination. The Democratic whale had swallowed the Populist fish.

The Election of 1896

The Republicans nominated William McKinley, who would have preferred to campaign on his specialty, the tariff. Bryan made that impossible. Crisscrossing the

William Jennings Bryan
Democratic congressman from Nebraska who won the party's presidential nomination in 1896 after his "Cross of Gold" speech.

AN ANTI-BRYAN CARTOON, 1896. *This cartoon in* Judge *magazine, entitled "The Sacrilegious Candidate," charged William Jennings Bryan with blasphemy in his "Cross of Gold" speech at the Democratic national convention. Bryan grinds his Bible into the dust with his boot while waving a crown of thorns and holding a cross of gold. In the background, a bearded caricature of an anarchist dances amid the ruins of a church and other buildings.*

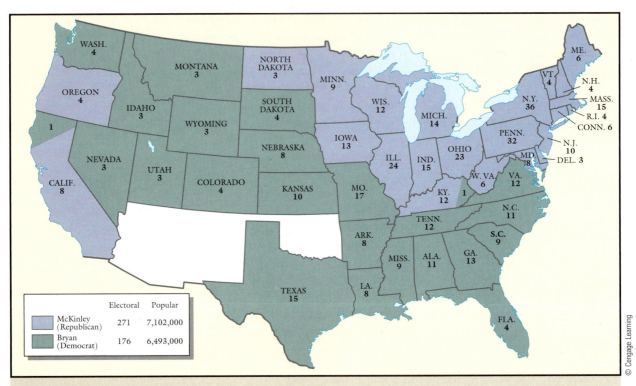

Map 19.2 **Presidential Election of 1896**. *Once again, note the continuity of voting patterns over the two generations from the 1850s to the 1890s by comparing this map with those on pages 322 and 341.*

	Electoral	Popular
McKinley (Republican)	271	7,102,000
Bryan (Democrat)	176	6,493,000

© Cengage Learning

QUICK REVIEW

FARMERS' MOVEMENTS AND POPULISM

- Postwar deflation fueled greenback and silver movements

- Farmers' Alliance and People's Party addressed farmers' plight

- Election of 1896 ushered in new era of Republican leadership, economic growth

country in an unprecedented whistle-stop campaign, Bryan gave as many as 30 speeches a day, focusing almost exclusively on the free silver issue. Republicans responded by denouncing the Democrats as irresponsible inflationists. Free silver, they said, would demolish the workingman's gains in real wages achieved over the preceding 30 years.

Under the skillful leadership of Ohio businessman Mark Hanna, chairman of the Republican National Committee, McKinley waged a "front-porch campaign" in which various delegations visited his home in Canton, Ohio, to hear carefully crafted speeches that were widely publicized in the mostly Republican press. Hanna sent out an army of speakers and printed pamphlets in more than a dozen languages to reach immigrant voters. His propaganda portrayed Bryan as a wild man from the prairie whose monetary schemes would further wreck an economy that had been plunged into depression during a Democratic administration. McKinley's election, by contrast, would maintain the gold standard, revive business confidence, and end the depression.

Many Americans believed that the fate of the nation hinged on the outcome of the 1896 election. The number of voters jumped by 15 percent over the 1892 election. Republicans won a substantial share of the urban, immigrant, and labor vote. McKinley rode to a convincing victory by carrying every state in the northeast quadrant of the country. Bryan carried most of the rest. Republicans won decisive control of Congress as well as the presidency. They would maintain control for the next 14 years. The election of 1896 marked a crucial turning point in American political history away from the stalemate of the preceding two decades.

Whether by luck or by design, McKinley did prove to be the advance agent of prosperity. The economy pulled out of the depression during his first year in office and entered into a long period of growth—not because of anything the new administration did (except perhaps to encourage a revival of confidence) but because of the mysterious workings of the business cycle. With the discovery of rich new goldfields in the Yukon, in Alaska, and in South Africa, the silver issue lost potency. The long deflationary trend since 1865 reversed itself in 1897. Farmers entered a new era of prosperity. Bryan ran against McKinley again in 1900 but lost even more emphatically. The nation seemed embarked on a placid sea of plenty. But below the surface, the currents of protest and reform still ran strong.

"ROBBER BARONS" NO MORE

The depression of the 1890s—along with the Populist movement and labor protests—shook the confidence of members of the industrial elite. Industrial titans were often called **"robber barons."** Seeking a more favorable image, some industrialists began to restrain their displays of wealth and use their private fortunes to advance the public welfare. As early as 1889, Andrew Carnegie had advocated a "gospel of wealth." The wealthy, he believed, should consider all income in excess of their needs as a "trust fund" for their communities. By the time he died in 1919, he had given away or entrusted to several Carnegie foundations 90 percent of his fortune. Among the projects he funded were New York's Carnegie Hall, Pittsburgh's Carnegie Institute (now Carnegie-Mellon University), and 2,500 public libraries throughout the country.

Other industrialists soon followed Carnegie's lead. In the wake of journalist Ida Tarbell's 1904 exposé of Standard Oil's business practices, and of the federal government's subsequent prosecution of Standard Oil for monopolistic practices in 1906, John D. Rockefeller transformed himself into a philanthropist. Between 1913 and 1919, his Rockefeller Foundation dispersed an estimated $500 million. His most significant gifts included money to establish the University of Chicago and the Rockefeller Institute for Medical Research (later renamed Rockefeller University). His charitable efforts did not escape criticism, however; many Americans interpreted them as an attempt to establish control over American universities, scientific research, and public policy.

FOCUS QUESTION

How and why did American elites seek to alter their "robber baron" image in the late 19th and early 20th centuries?

"robber barons" *Industrial leaders who began to restrain their displays of wealth and make philanthropic contributions.*

TABLE 19.1

LEADING INDUSTRIALIST PHILANTHROPIC FOUNDATIONS, 1905–1925		
Foundation	**Date of Origin**	**Original Endowment**
Carnegie Corporation of New York	1911	$125,000,000
Carnegie Endowment for International Peace	1910	$10,000,000
Carnegie Foundation for the Advancement of Teaching	1905	$10,000,000
Carnegie Institution of Washington	1902	$10,000,000
Duke Endowment	1924	$40,000,000
John Simon Guggenheim Memorial Foundation	1925	$3,000,000
Rockefeller Foundation	1913	$100,000,000
Rosenwald Fund	1917	$20,000,000
Russell Sage Foundation	1907	$10,000,000

Source: Joseph C. Kiger, *Operating Principles of the Larger Foundations* (New York: Russell Sage Foundation, 1957), p. 122.

Conclusion

For many Americans, the strikes and violence and third-party protests of the 1890s were a wake-up call. They realized that wrenching economic change threatened the liberty and equality they had long taken for granted as part of the American dream. Many middle-class Americans began to support greater government power to carry out progressive reforms that might cure the ills of an industrializing society.

The rise of corporate America created a fundamental paradox: On the one hand, the new industrial landscape denied workers independence and subjected them to harsh conditions, which they resisted as best they could in a series of strikes in the late 19th and early 20th century. Yet that same corporate world provided significant opportunities for a better life—opportunities that were especially embraced by the millions of immigrants who settled in American cities at the turn of the century. But opportunity did not necessarily translate into equality: The search for a more equal society was far from finished.

CHAPTER REVIEW

Review

1. What were the main engines of American economic growth in the late 19th and early 20th centuries?

2. How did the rise of corporations reshape the everyday experiences of Americans?

3. What were the major changes in middle-class women's lives in the late 19th and early 20th centuries?

4. How effective was workers' resistance to the new corporations? Why?

5. What provoked the farmer protest movements in the last third of the 19th century?

6. Why did many Americans find Populism appealing in the 1890s?

7. How and why did American elites seek to alter their "robber baron" image in the late 19th and early 20th centuries?

Critical Thinking

1. Some historians have argued that corporate power went virtually unchecked in the 19th century. Is this true? Why or why not?

2. How did the ongoing struggle between capital and labor reshape American society in the late 19th century?

Identifications

Review your understanding of the following key terms, people, and events for this chapter.

Great Railroad Strike, p. 432
J. P. Morgan, p. 435
Andrew Carnegie, p. 435
John D. Rockefeller, p. 436

merger movement, p. 436
Sherman Antitrust Act, p. 436
mass production, p. 437
Social Darwinism, p. 440

"New Woman," p. 444
Knights of Labor, p. 445
Haymarket, p. 446
Samuel F. Gompers, p. 447
Homestead Strike, p. 447

Pullman Strike, p. 448
free silver, p. 449
William Jennings Bryan, p. 451
"robber barons," p. 453

DISCOVERY

What impact did industrialization have on American society?

In thinking about this question, begin by breaking it down into the components shown below. A discussion of the significance of each component should appear in your answer.

Geography, Economy, and Technology

Study Map 19.1. Which industries generated the highest levels of factory output? In what regions and cities of the country were the highest levels of output achieved? In what regions were the lowest levels of output achieved? What conclusions can be drawn about the regions and cities in which industrialization had advanced the furthest by 1900–1920?

Now look at the graph on page 436. Compare the percentage of the workforce involved in agriculture, manufacturing, and professional jobs in 1870 and 1920. How did these changes transform the lives of workers? In which of these three economic sectors were jobs and skills in demand? In which of these three were jobs and skills in decline?

Map 19.1 Industrial America, 1900–1920

visit the CourseMate website at www.cengagebrain.com for additional study tools and review materials for this chapter.

20

CITIES, PEOPLES, CULTURES, 1890–1920

THE RISE OF THE CITY

IMMIGRATION
    European Immigration
    Chinese and Japanese Immigration
    Immigrant Labor
    Living Conditions

BUILDING ETHNIC COMMUNITIES
    A Network of Institutions

    The Emergence of an Ethnic Middle Class
    Political Machines and Organized Crime

AFRICAN AMERICAN LABOR AND COMMUNITY

WORKING-CLASS AND COMMERCIAL CULTURE
    Popular Literature

THE NEW SEXUALITY AND THE RISE OF FEMINISM

REIMAGINING AMERICAN NATIONALITY

America's cities grew rapidly in the late 19th and early 20th centuries, both to accommodate expanded production and trade and to house the working masses. The physical, social, and economic geography of the city changed as well. Running water, electric lighting and trolley lines, steel suspension bridges, skyscrapers, and elevators all appeared. Immigration soared to remedy severe labor shortfalls in manufacturing and construction; foreign languages and cultures, as a result, became an ever more noticeable feature of American urban life. At the same time, the new economic elites built mansions in posh residential districts either in the cities themselves or in tony suburbs. Urban elites were determined to uplift their cities through physical transformation and promotion of the arts, in part to counteract the urban distress and unruliness they associated with the masses.

Labor–capital conflict was one area in which the ideas of rich and poor clashed in late-19th century America; struggles over culture were another. A vigorous commercial culture took root in working-class and ethnic districts of the city, appearing in dance halls, **nickelodeons**, and amusement parks. Exuberance rather than refinement, adventure rather than education, defined these leisure pursuits. Young, working-class women pioneered a sexual revolution in the districts of this commercial culture, and immigrants began to emphasize both hybridity and diversity as signature features of American life. A new—and modern—America was taking shape in the country's cities, a development that aroused both hopes and fears.

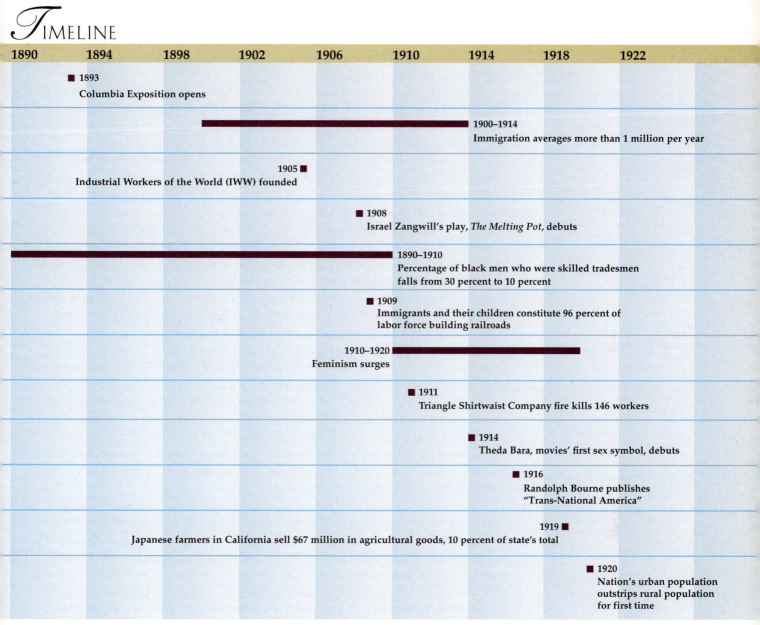

1890	1894	1898	1902	1906	1910	1914	1918	1922

■ 1893
Columbia Exposition opens

1900–1914
Immigration averages more than 1 million per year

1905 ■
Industrial Workers of the World (IWW) founded

■ 1908
Israel Zangwill's play, *The Melting Pot*, debuts

1890–1910
Percentage of black men who were skilled tradesmen falls from 30 percent to 10 percent

■ 1909
Immigrants and their children constitute 96 percent of labor force building railroads

1910–1920
Feminism surges

■ 1911
Triangle Shirtwaist Company fire kills 146 workers

■ 1914
Theda Bara, movies' first sex symbol, debuts

■ 1916
Randolph Bourne publishes "Trans-National America"

1919 ■
Japanese farmers in California sell $67 million in agricultural goods, 10 percent of state's total

■ 1920
Nation's urban population outstrips rural population for first time

© Cengage Learning

𝒯HE RISE OF THE CITY

By the late 19th century, cities were changing the face of America. Their populations, their physical size, and their capacity to transform the landscapes they inhabited dwarfed those of cities a mere 50 years earlier. The rate of urban growth was staggering. Chicago, for example, grew from 30,000 residents in 1850 to 500,000 in 1880 to 1,700,000 by 1900. New York City and Philadelphia also surpassed the million inhabitants mark, and the number of cities with more than 100,000 residents soared from 18 in 1870 to 38 in 1900.

A new kind of building, the skyscraper, came to symbolize the aspirations taking shape in these expanding urban milieus. These modern towers were made possible by the use of steel rather than stone frameworks and by the invention of electrically powered elevators. Impelled upward by rising real estate values, they were intended to evoke the same sense of grandeur as Europe's medieval cathedrals. But these monuments celebrated man, not God; material wealth, not spiritual riches; science, not faith. They were convincing embodiments of America's urban might.

FOCUS QUESTION

In what ways did urban elites seek to shape the physical and cultural character of their cities in the years between 1890 and 1910?

nickelodeons *Converted storefronts in working-class neighborhoods that showed early short silent films costing a nickel to view.*

If advances in construction made possible America's urban areas' vertical reach, technological advances encouraged horizontal expansion. Most important in this regard was the application of electricity to urban transportation systems. Between 1890 and 1920, virtually every major city built electric-powered transit systems to replace horse-drawn trolleys and carriages. In Boston, electricity made possible the construction of the first subways in 1897, and New York and Philadelphia soon followed suit.

As a result of these transportation improvements, urban dwellers could live miles away from where they worked. As recently as the 1870s, many of America's urban centers had been compact **walking cities**, with residential areas abutting work districts, and different income and ethnic groups living in close proximity to each other. By the 1890s, these walking cities had given way to metropolitan entities, with core areas of work and commerce—"downtowns"—now surrounded by expanding rings of residential areas offering inhabitants their own homes and gardens, and the promise of tree-lined streets. The intensifying congestion, dirt, poor air, and poverty of urban cores made these new residential areas into refuges of peace and quiet, and they drew those with ample economic resources. The old cores, meanwhile, increasingly became home to the poor, to immigrants, and to racial minorities.

These changes in the appearance of cities aboveground were matched by important changes below. None was more important than water and sewage systems. By 1900, American cities pumped 139 gallons a day for each of their inhabitants, dwarfing the 20 to 40 gallons per capita that British and German cities distributed to their residents. The scale and power of these water systems made flush toilets and bathtubs standard equipment in every American middle-class urban home by 1900. Such improvements came more slowly to the urban poor, but they still had far better access to running water than did their counterparts in Europe.

If measured by their ability to procure, pump, and carry away huge volumes of water, these American systems were unrivalled in the world. If measured by efforts to control costs, to ensure the safety of workers, and to enhance public health, they were less impressive. The construction and administration of these projects occurred within political systems that were often corrupt. City and state officials expected to receive kickbacks for awarding contracts. Some regarded the size of the kickback as a more important consideration in choosing a construction firm than the firm's competence or the prudent use of taxpayer monies. Those in charge of designing and building these systems often did not do enough to protect laborers from the hazards of working underground, to ensure that consumers used the water efficiently, or to protect local lakes, rivers, and oceans against contamination from sewage. Waterborne epidemics periodically struck.

By 1900, the problems caused by contaminated water had begun to yield to the insistence of urban reformers that cities improve water treatment. City governments were installing water filtration systems and were becoming more careful about sewage disposal. Newly paved roads lessened the dirt, mud, and stagnant pools of water on city streets and thus further curtailed the spread of disease. As a result, urban mortality rates began to fall.

Advances in water systems, in transportation, and in housing reflected the breadth of the commitment in America's urban centers to improving the lives of city dwellers. This commitment extended well beyond questions of physical well-being to those of education and morals. In the late 19th century, urban elites undertook one of the most intensive cultural improvement campaigns in all of American history. Symphonies, opera companies, museums, and libraries sprouted in countless cities. They were often interwoven with newly designed urban parks. Thus in New York City, the Metropolitan Museum of Art and the American Museum of Natural History each took shape in the 1870s alongside Central Park, the first

walking cities *Compact residential areas near working districts with different income and ethnic groups living in close proximity.*

landscaped public park in the United States. The park's principal designer, **Frederick Law Olmsted**, imagined his 50-block-long masterpiece with its five million plantings as a place where people "may stroll for an hour, seeing, hearing, and feeling nothing of the bustle and jar of the streets." If these same people took another hour to visit the museums, so much the better. Museums and parks were part of the same civic, civilizing, and regenerating enterprise.

Elites were constructing palatial institutions for posterity, imagining that the buildings and parks would stand as permanent monuments to their civic vision and influence. They were also proclaiming their concern not simply with their own private lives but with the public life and well-being of others. But the energy that they poured into these institutions also revealed anxieties about their own social status. For the newly wealthy in their ranks, museums, symphonies, operas, and the like offered a form of alchemy that converted their riches into cultural prestige and authority.

Elites worried, too, about plebeian resistance to their civilizing projects. What if the masses ignored or misused these institutions? Both the New York museums and Central Park were sites of conflict in the late 19th century between administrators and the people, the former laying down rules, the latter repeatedly declaring their intention to be left alone or demanding a role in shaping park and museum policies. In the 1880s, 100 labor organizations, representing 50,000 workers, presented petitions to the Metropolitan and Natural History museums asking that these institutions open their doors to the public on Sunday, the only day that was free of work for most of New York City's inhabitants. Religious groups and religious members of the boards of trustees brought intense pressure on these museums to keep their doors closed on the Sabbath. By 1892, however, both institutions decided to open on Sundays, handing a major victory to the city's labor movement.

Many of these urban trends coalesced in Chicago at the Columbia Exposition of 1893, a world's fair to celebrate the 400th anniversary of Columbus's discovery of America. At the heart of the fair was a monumental set of gleaming buildings called the **"White City,"** meant to evoke the classical grandeur of Greece and Rome and to trumpet the maturation of American civilization. The buildings inventoried America's achievements in various economic sectors and celebrated American women; the histories, cultures, and peoples of the individual states; and the contributions of foreign nations to the story of human progress. The Manufactures Building was the largest, covering more than twice as much area as the Great Pyramid of Egypt and being lit by 120,000 incandescent lamps. Exposition planners hoped that their work would endure as a design and influence if not as an actual urban space. A utopian dream of an ordered city and a triumphant industrial civilization, the White City embodied America's quest for and belief in perfection.

With paid admissions at 21,480,141 in a nation with a population of 63 million, the Columbia Exposition was the most successful fair in American history. The White City did fill many fairgoers with pride and inspiration, much as its planners desired. Yet visitors also found their attention drawn to another part of the fair, one that focused on amusement rather than education, and on the dissonances of modern life rather than its classical symmetry. The **Midway Plaisance** was a long strip located at some distance from the White City, full of concessions where one could buy food and drink, engage in games, line up for rides, and gaze upon the dime museums and freak shows. The chaotic variety of its sights and smells proved irresistible to the tourists.

Part of Midway's variety was deliberately ethnographic, as it housed numerous pavilions displaying life in areas of Africa and Asia. The accent was on the primitive and exotic: The pavilions did not display modernizing elites of these faraway places, or their achievements in manufacture or transportation, but rather native peoples barely touched by civilization. It was hard to miss the implication

QUICK REVIEW

THE RISE OF THE CITY

- Technological innovation facilitated the expansion of urban areas

- Elites attempted to shape the society and culture of their cities, but they often met resistance from working people

- The "White City" of the world's fair revealed the class and racial tensions embedded in urbanization

Frederick Law Olmsted *Principal designer of Central Park in New York City.*

White City *Monument created for the Columbia Exposition of 1893 in Chicago.*

Midway Plaisance *A section of the Columbia Exposition of 1893 that included concessions, games, rides, cultural pavilions, and freak shows.*

THE WHITE CITY. *This photograph captures the scale, grandeur, and classical lines of the Columbia Exposition's White City. The massive Agriculture building sits to the right of the Basin.*

Brooklyn Museum Archives, Goodyear Archival Collection. Visual material (6.1.016): World's Columbian Exposition lantern slides. Court of Honor, Chicago, United States (1893)

that civilization occurred in America and Europe, while primitivism belonged to people of color from Africa, the Middle East, and Asia.

The very structure of the fair thus posited the superiority of white, middle-class civilization. African Americans understood how much this hierarchy organized not only America's relationship to much of the world but also life within the United States itself. The anti-lynching crusader Ida B. Wells (see Chapter 18) published a pamphlet, with contributions from several black leaders, titled "The Reason Why the Colored American Is Not in the World's Columbian Exposition." Exploring the intertwined histories of American slavery and racism, it offered an accounting of the refusal of fair organizers to include African Americans: "Theoretically open to all Americans, the Exposition practically is, literally and figuratively, a 'White City.'" Try as it might, the world's fair of 1893 could not erase the question of race; nor could the White City erase the presence in Chicago and every other major American city of polyglot populations of diverse ethnic origins.

IMMIGRATION

FOCUS QUESTION

From which parts of the world did immigrants come in the years between 1880 and 1920? What caused them to migrate? What were their patterns of work and residence in the United States?

The United States had always been a nation of immigrants, but never had so many come in so short a time. Between 1880 and 1920, some 23 million immigrants came to a country that numbered only 76 million in 1900. From 1900 to 1914, an average of 1 million immigrants arrived each year. In many cities of the Northeast and Midwest, immigrants and their children constituted a majority of the population. Everywhere in the country, except in the South, the working class was overwhelmingly ethnic.

European immigration accounted for approximately three-fourths of the total. Some states received significant numbers of non-European immigrants—Chinese,

Japanese, and Filipinos in California; Mexicans in California and the Southwest; and French Canadians in New England. Although their presence profoundly affected regional economies, politics, and culture, their numbers, relative to the number of European immigrants, were small.

European Immigration

Most European immigrants who arrived between 1880 and 1914 came from eastern and southern Europe. Among them were three to four million Italians, two million Russian and Polish Jews, two million Hungarians, and an estimated five million Slavs and other peoples from eastern and southeastern Europe (Poles, Bohemians, Slovaks, Russians, Ukrainians, Lithuanians, Serbians, Croatians, Slovenians, Montenegrins, Bulgarians, Macedonians, and Greeks). Hundreds of thousands came as well from Turkey, Armenia, Lebanon, Syria, and other Near Eastern lands abutting the European continent.

These post-1880 arrivals were called "new immigrants" to underscore the cultural gap separating them from the "old immigrants," who had come from northwestern Europe—Great Britain, Scandinavia, and Germany. Old immigrants were regarded as racially fit, culturally sophisticated, and politically mature. The new immigrants were often regarded as racially inferior, culturally impoverished, and incapable of assimilating American values and traditions. This negative view of the new immigrants reflected in part a fear of their alien languages, religions, and economic backgrounds. Few spoke English, and most adhered to Catholicism, Orthodoxy, or Judaism rather than Protestantism. Most, with the exception of Jewish immigrants, were peasants, unaccustomed to urban industrial life.

In reality, the old and new European immigrants were more similar than different. Some immigrants left their homelands for political reasons, particularly Jews fleeing anti-Semitism in Russia. Many more were propelled by economic hardship. Europe's rural population was growing faster than the land could support. European factories absorbed some, but not all, of the rural surplus. As railroads penetrated rural areas, village artisans found themselves unable to compete with the cheap manufactured goods that arrived from city factories. These handicraftsmen were among the first to emigrate. Meanwhile, rising demand for food in the cities accelerated the growth of commercial agriculture in the hinterland. Some peasant families turned to producing crops for the market, only to discover that they could not compete with larger, more efficient producers. In addition, by the last third of the 19th century, peasants faced competition from North American farmers, and prices for agricultural commodities plummeted everywhere.

Many European peasants decided to try their luck in the New World. An individual's or family's decision to emigrate often depended on having a contact already established in an American city. This family member, relative, or fellow villager provided a destination, an inspiring success story, employment advice, and financial aid. Sometimes whole villages in southern Italy or western Russia—or at least all of the young men there—seemed to disappear, only to reappear in a certain section of Chicago, Pittsburgh, or New York.

Most immigrants viewed their trip to the United States as a temporary sojourn. They came in search of high wages that would improve their economic standing in their homeland. This attitude explains why, from 1899 to 1910,

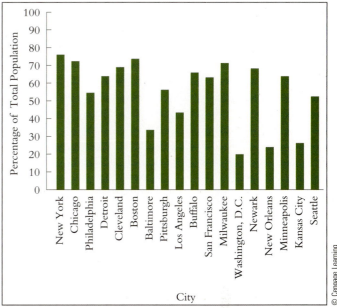

Immigrants and Their Children as a Percentage of the Population of Selected Cities, 1920.

Source: Data from U.S. Department of Commerce, Bureau of the Census, *Fourteenth Census of the United States, 1920, Population* (Washington, D.C.).

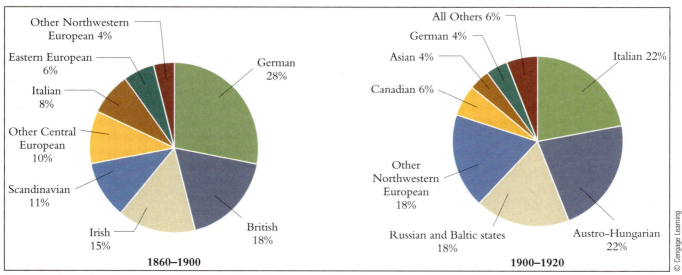

Sources of Immigration

Source: Data from *Historical Statistics of the United States, Colonial Times to 1970* (White Plains, NY: Kraus International, 1989), pp. 105–109.

three-fourths of the immigrants from southern and eastern Europe were adult men. Some had left wives and children behind; more were single. Most wanted merely to make enough money to buy a farm in their native land. True to their dream, many did return home. For every 100 Italian immigrants who arrived in the United States between 1907 and 1911, for example, 73 returned to Italy.

The rate of return was negligible among certain groups, however. Jews had little desire to return to the religious persecution they had fled, and only 5 percent returned to Europe. The rate of return was also low among the Irish, who saw few opportunities in their long-suffering (although much-loved) Emerald Isle. But in the early 20th century, such groups were exceptional.

Chinese and Japanese Immigration

The relatively small numbers of Chinese and Japanese immigrants who came to the United States in the late 19th and early 20th centuries reflected the efforts of native-born Americans and their allies to keep them out. As many as 300,000 Chinese immigrants arrived in the United States between 1851 and 1882, and more than 200,000 Japanese immigrants journeyed to Hawaii and the western continental United States between 1891 and 1907. They contributed in major ways to the development of two of the West's major industries: railroad building and commercial agriculture. These two immigrant groups might have formed two of America's largest, each numbering in the millions, but the U.S. government began to exclude Chinese immigrant laborers in 1882 (via the Chinese Exclusion Act) and Japanese immigrant laborers in 1907 (see Chapter 22). The government also interpreted a 1790 law to mean that Chinese, Japanese, and other East Asian immigrants were ineligible for citizenship. These exclusions remained in force until the 1940s and 1950s. They expressed the racial prejudice felt by most native-born white Americans toward nonwhite Asian immigrants and revealed how determined America was to remain a nation of European immigrants and their descendants.

The factors propelling Chinese and Japanese immigrants were similar to those motivating Europeans. The rural population was increasing faster than local economies could support. Many intended to move abroad just long enough

IMMIGRANT JAPANESE CHILDREN ARRIVE AT ANGEL ISLAND, SAN FRANCISCO HARBOR, 1905. *Beginning in 1907, as a result of the "gentlemen's agreement" between the United States and Japanese governments, it would no longer be possible for Japanese immigrants such as these children to come to the United States.*

© Bettmann/ CORBIS

to make enough money to establish themselves economically in their homelands. Most were men. They also tended to follow precise migratory paths—from one region or village in China or Japan to one city or region in the United States.

Conditions in China were more desperate than those in Japan, where industrialization had begun to generate new wealth and absorb some of the rural population. To get to the United States, many Chinese immigrants were forced to sign contracts with suppliers of overseas laborers that subjected them to slave-like conditions: They were herded onto boats for the transpacific voyage, bound to particular employers for years on end, thrust into dangerous working conditions, and paid paltry wages. The conditions of their labor in the western states where they tended to settle inflamed the sentiments of white working men, who saw the Asian migration as a threat to their own wages and livelihoods. White workers became leaders of the movements in the western states to keep these immigrants out.

Significant numbers of Chinese and Japanese immigrants continued to try to enter the United States during the period of Asian immigrant exclusion. Some were desperate to reunite with family members already living in the United States, while others were driven by economic circumstances. Many attempted to enter the United States with forged papers declaring them to be merchants (a permitted class of Chinese and Japanese immigrants), or to have been resident in the United States before the exclusion laws had gone into effect (and thus entitled to return). San Francisco was their principal port of entry, and Angel Island became the counterpart of Ellis Island in New York Harbor: the place where inspectors for the U.S. Bureau of Immigration interrogated them, scrutinized their documents, and, more often than not, sent them back to Asia.

Other East Asian immigrants attempted to enter the United States through Canada or Mexico, hoping to cross into the United States undetected. They became, in effect, America's first illegal aliens. That a certain percentage of East Asian immigrants were subject to deportation generated considerable fear among the

Asian immigrant populations resident in the United States, deepening tendencies within these communities to secrecy and to separation from mainstream American culture and society.

Immigrant Labor

In the first decade of the 20th century, immigrant men and their male children constituted 70 percent of the workforce in 15 of the 19 leading U.S. industries. They concentrated in industries where work was the most backbreaking. In 1909, first- and second-generation immigrants—especially Greeks, Italians, Japanese, and Mexicans—constituted more than 96 percent of the labor force that built and maintained the nation's railroads. Of the 750,000 Slovaks who arrived in America before 1913, at least 600,000 headed for the coal mines and steel mills of western Pennsylvania.

Immigrants also performed "lighter" but no less arduous work. Jews and Italians predominated in garment manufacturing. By 1920, California's rapidly growing agricultural industry depended primarily on Mexican and Filipino labor. In these industries, immigrant women and children, who worked for lower wages than men, formed a large part of the labor force. More than 25 percent of boys and 10 percent of girls aged 10 to 15 were "gainfully employed."

Those who worked in heavy industry, mining, or railroading were especially vulnerable to accident and injury. Between the years 1906 and 1911, for instance, almost one-quarter of the recent immigrants employed at the U.S. Steel Corporation's South Works (Pittsburgh) were injured or killed on the job. Lax attention to safety rendered even light industry hazardous. In 1911, a fire broke out on an upper floor of the **Triangle Shirtwaist Company**, a New York City garment factory. The building had no fire escapes, and the owners of the factory had locked the entrances to each floor as a way of keeping their employees at work. A total of 146 workers, mostly young Jewish and Italian women, perished in the fire or from desperate nine-story leaps to the pavement below.

Chronic fatigue and inadequate nourishment increased the risk of accident and injury. Workweeks averaged 60 hours—10 hours every day except Sunday. Steelworkers labored from 72 to 89 hours per week and were required to work one 24-hour shift every two weeks. Most workers had to labor long hours simply to eke out a meager living. In 1900, the earnings of American manufacturing workers averaged only $400 to $500 per year. Skilled jobs offered immigrants far more (as much as $1,500 to $2,000 per year), but most of them were held by Yankees and by Europeans from the old immigrant stream. Through their unions, these skilled workers also controlled access to new jobs that opened up and usually filled them with a son, relative, or fellow countryman. Consequently, relatively few of the new immigrants rose into the prosperous ranks of skilled labor.

Most working families required two or three wage earners to survive. If a mother could not go out to work because she had small children at home, she might rent rooms to some of the many single men who had recently immigrated. But

Triangle Shirtwaist Company
New York City site of a tragic 1911 industrial fire that killed 146 workers.

© Museum of the City of New York/ CORBIS

TRIANGLE SHIRTWAIST COMPANY FIRE. *In 1911, a fire at the Triangle Shirtwaist Company in New York City claimed the lives of 146 workers, most of them young Jewish and Italian women. Many died because they could not escape the flames. The building had no fire escapes, and the employer had locked the entrances to each floor to keep workers on the job. The tragedy spurred the growth of unions and the movement for factory reform in New York.*

economic security was difficult to attain. In his 1904 book, *Poverty,* social investigator Robert Hunter conservatively estimated that 20 percent of the industrial population of the North lived in poverty.

Living Conditions

Strained economic circumstances confined many working-class families to cramped and dilapidated living quarters. Many of them lived in two- or three-room apartments, with several people, often including boarders as well as family members, sleeping in each room. The lack of windows in city tenements allowed little light or air into these apartments. Overcrowding and poor sanitation resulted in high rates of infectious diseases, especially diphtheria, typhoid fever, and pneumonia. In the early years of the 20th century, improvements in the quality of housing and public health finally began to ease the dangers of urban life.

BUILDING ETHNIC COMMUNITIES

The immigrants may have been poor, but they were not helpless. Migration had required a good deal of resourcefulness, self-help, and mutual aid—assets that survived in American cities.

A Network of Institutions

Each ethnic group established a network of institutions that supplied a sense of community and multiplied sources of communal assistance. Some immigrants simply reproduced those institutions that had been important to them in the Old Country. The devout established churches and synagogues. Lithuanian, Jewish, and Italian radicals reestablished Old World socialist and anarchist organizations. Irish nationalists set up clandestine chapters of the Clan Na Gael to keep alive the struggle to free Ireland from the English. Germans felt at home in their traditional *Turnevereins* (athletic clubs) and musical societies.

Immigrants developed new institutions as well. In the larger cities, foreign-language newspapers disseminated news, advice, and culture. Each ethnic group created fraternal societies. Most of these societies provided members with a death benefit (ranging from a few hundred to a thousand dollars) that guaranteed the deceased a decent burial and the family a bit of cash. Some fraternal societies made small loans as well. Among those ethnic groups that prized home ownership, the fraternal societies also provided mortgage money. And all of them served as places to have a drink, play cards, or simply relax with fellow countrymen.

The Emergence of an Ethnic Middle Class

Within each ethnic group, a sizable minority directed their talents and ambitions toward economic gain. Some of these entrepreneurs first addressed their communities' needs for basic goods and services. Immigrants preferred to buy from fellow

FOCUS QUESTION

What were the ways in which immigrants sought economic success and social mobility? How successful were they in their efforts?

countrymen with whom they shared a language, a history, and presumably a bond of trust. Enterprising individuals responded by opening dry-goods stores, food shops, butcher shops, and saloons in their ethnic neighborhoods. Those who could not afford to rent a store hawked their wares from portable stands, wagons, or sacks carried on their backs. The work was endless and the competition tough. Although many of these small businesses failed, enough survived to give some immigrants and their children a toehold in the middle class.

Other immigrants turned to small industry, particularly garment manufacture, truck farming, and construction. A clothing manufacturer needed only a few sewing machines to become competitive. Many Jewish immigrants, having been tailors in Russia and Poland, opened such facilities, sometimes in their own apartments. Competition among these small manufacturers was fierce, and work environments were condemned by critics as "sweatshops." Workers suffered from inadequate lighting, heat, and ventilation; 12-hour workdays during peak seasons; and poor pay and no employment security, especially for the women and children who made up a large part of this labor force. Even at this level of exploitation, many small manufacturers failed, but over time, significant numbers of them managed to evolve into stable, responsible employers. Their success contributed to the emergence of a Jewish middle class.

In southern California, Japanese immigrants chose agriculture as their route to the middle class. Many acquired their own land in the early years of the 20th century. although altogether they owned only 1 percent of California's total farm acreage. Their specialization in fresh vegetables and fruits (particularly strawberries), combined with their family-labor-intensive agricultural methods, was yielding $67 million in annual revenues by 1919—one-tenth of the total California agriculture revenue that year. The success of Japanese farmers was all the more impressive given that the state of California had passed the Alien Land Law in 1913, prohibiting Japanese and other Asian aliens from owning property in the state. Japanese immigrant farmers thus depended on their native-born children or friendly whites to acquire land for them, arrangements that made them vulnerable to losing the land.

Each ethnic group created its own history of economic success and social mobility. From the emerging middle classes came leaders who would provide their ethnic groups with identity, legitimacy, and power and would lead the way toward Americanization and assimilation. Their children tended to do better in school than the children of working-class ethnics, and academic success served as a ticket to upward social mobility in a society that increasingly depended on university-trained professionals.

Political Machines and Organized Crime

The underside of this success story was the rise of government corruption and organized crime. Many ethnic entrepreneurs operated on the margins of economic failure and bankruptcy, and some accepted the help of those who promised financial assistance. Sometimes the help came from honest unions and upright government officials, but other times it did not. Unions were generally weak, and some government officials were susceptible to bribery. Economic necessity became a breeding ground for government corruption and greed. A contractor eager to win a city contract would find it advantageous to pay off government officials who could throw the contract his way. By 1900, such payments, referred to as "graft," had become essential to the day-to-day operation of government in most large cities. Graft, in turn, made local officeholding a source of economic gain. Politicians began building political organizations to guarantee their success in municipal elections. The "bosses" of these **political machines** won the loyalty of urban voters—especially immigrants—by providing poor neighborhoods with paved roads and sewer systems. They helped newly arrived immigrants find jobs (often on city payrolls) and occasionally provided food, fuel, or clothing to families in need.

But bosses served their own needs first. They saw to it that construction contracts went to those who offered the most graft, not to those who were likely to do the best job. They protected gamblers, pimps, and other purveyors of urban vice who contributed to their machine coffers. And they engaged in widespread election fraud by rounding up truckloads of immigrants and paying them to vote a certain way; having their supporters vote two or three times; and stuffing ballot boxes with the votes of phantom citizens.

Big-city machines, then, were both positive and negative forces in urban life. Reformers despised them for disregarding election laws and encouraging vice, but many immigrants valued them for providing social welfare services and for creating opportunities for upward mobility.

Underworld figures also influenced urban life. In the early years of the 20th century, gangsterism was a scourge of Italian neighborhoods, where Sicilian immigrants had established outposts of the notorious Mafia, and in Irish, Jewish, Chinese, and other ethnic communities as well. These gangsters often threatened small-scale manufacturers and contractors with violence and economic ruin if they did not pay a gang for "protection." Gangsters enforced their demands with physical force, beating up or killing those who failed to abide by the "rules." By the 1920s, petty extortion had escalated in urban areas, and underworld crime had become big business. Few immigrants, however, followed the criminal path to economic success.

political machines

Organizations that controlled local political parties and municipal governments through bribery, election fraud, and support of urban vice while providing some municipal services to the poor.

QUICK   REVIEW

IMMIGRANTS

- Twenty-three million arrived in the United States from 1880 to 1920

- Three-fourths came from Europe, most from eastern and southern Europe ("new immigrants")

- Worked in manufacturing, mining, and railroading for long hours and little pay

- Lived in cramped urban areas

- Rising middle class and new institutions provided leadership in ethnic communities

AFRICAN AMERICAN LABOR AND COMMUNITY

Unlike immigrants, African Americans remained a predominantly rural and southern people in the early 20th century. Most blacks were sharecroppers and tenant farmers. The markets for cotton and other southern crops had stabilized in the early 20th century, but black farmers remained vulnerable to exploitation. Landowners often forced sharecroppers to accept artificially low prices for their crops. At the same time, they charged high prices for seed, tools, and groceries at the local stores they controlled. Those sharecroppers who traveled elsewhere to sell their crops or purchase their necessities risked retaliation. Thus most remained beholden to their landowners, mired in poverty and debt.

Some African Americans sought a better life by migrating to industrial areas. In the South, they worked in iron and coal mines, in furniture and cigarette manufacture, as railroad track layers and longshoremen, and as laborers in the steel mills of Birmingham, Alabama. By the early 20th century, their presence was growing in the urban North as well, where they worked as janitors, elevator operators, teamsters, longshoremen, and servants of various kinds. Altogether, about 200,000 blacks left the South for the North and West between 1890 and 1910.

In southern industries, blacks were subjected to hardships and indignities that even the newest immigrants were not expected to endure. Railroad contractors in the South, for example, treated their black track layers like prisoners.

FOCUS   QUESTION

What were the similarities and differences between the African American and immigrant experiences in the early 20th century?

MUSICAL LINK TO THE PAST

Ragtime

Songwriter: Scott Joplin
Title: "Maple Leaf Rag" (probably written 1897; published 1899)

Upon writing the "Maple Leaf Rag," Scott Joplin proclaimed that the composition "will make me King of Ragtime Composers." With millions of worldwide sheet music sales stretching over two decades, and the continued popularity of the song over a century later, Joplin was prescient in his prediction.

Ragtime represented a popular amalgam of African American and Euro-American musical influences, combining a march-like bass foundation and syncopated melodic flourishes in the treble range. Its ecstatic, dance-inducing sound brought a welcome respite from sentimental Victorian "tear-jerker" ballads of the 19th century. Ragtime dominated the American music business between 1895 and 1910, providing a key source of inspiration for future songwriters Irving Berlin (see Chapter 23) and George Gershwin, among others.

Much like the waltz in the 1850s, and hip-hop in the 1980s, ragtime brought about heated controversy and numerous naysayers. Many viewed ragtime as a threat, sometimes for racist reasons. "Above all, as a black-originated music that was embraced by the youth of America, it was perceived as a negative influence that had to be confronted and eliminated," wrote Edward A. Berlin in his biography of Joplin.

John Stark, the white publisher who released "Maple Leaf Rag," promoted Joplin and other ragtime writers in a controversial way that flew in the face of ragtime's detractors. Stark proclaimed that rags, particularly Joplin's, were "the equal of classical music." One ad for the song proclaimed that it "has throttled and silenced those who oppose syncopations. It is played by the cultured of all nations, and is welcomed in the drawing rooms and boudoirs of good taste." Similar to marketing tactics used 30 years later for Duke Ellington (see Chapter 25), such advertising copy helped the process of overcoming bias against the artistic potential of blacks during a time of violent Jim Crow segregation, and widened the market for ragtime, bringing additional royalties to Stark and Joplin.

While rags were usually performed as solo piano pieces, there also existed a market for them as ensemble pieces. The expanded orchestration for "Maple Leaf Rag" and other compositions lent an even richer sound than usual to Joplin's familiar composition, proving irresistible to the crowds that gathered for ragtime performances on Sunday spring afternoons in municipal parks across the United States.

Q Can you think of other new genres in American popular music over the course of the 20th century that were looked upon suspiciously for having originated among African Americans or other minority groups?

Armed guards marched them to work in the morning and back at night. Track layers were paid only once a month and forced to purchase food at the company commissary, where the high prices claimed most of what they earned. Although not all southern employers of black workers engaged in labor practices as harsh as these, they still confined blacks to the dirtiest and most grueling jobs. The Jim Crow laws passed by every southern state legislature in the 1890s legalized this rigid racial separation (see Chapter 18).

The nation's worsening racial climate adversely affected southern blacks who came north, even though these migrants had moved to states that generally did not have Jim Crow laws. Industrialists typically refused to hire black migrants for manufacturing jobs, preferring the labor of European immigrants. Only when those immigrants went on strike did employers turn to African Americans. Employers hoped that the use of black strikebreakers would inflame racial tensions between white and black workers and undermine labor unity and strength.

African Americans who had long resided in northern urban areas also experienced intensifying discrimination in the late 19th and early 20th centuries. In 1870, about one-third of the black men in many northern cities had been skilled tradesmen: blacksmiths, painters, shoemakers, and carpenters. But by 1910 only 10 percent of black men made a living in this way. In many cities, the number of barber shops and food catering businesses owned by blacks also declined, as did black representation in the ranks of restaurant and hotel waiters. These barbers, food caterers, and waiters had formed a black middle class whose livelihood depended on the patronage of white clients. By the early 20th century, this middle class was the victim of growing racism, as whites turned to European immigrants for these services. The residential segregation of northern blacks also rose in these years, as whites excluded them from growing numbers of urban neighborhoods.

African Americans did not lack for resourcefulness. Urban blacks laced their communities with the same array of institutions—churches, fraternal insurance societies, political organizations—that solidified ethnic neighborhoods. A new black middle class arose, consisting of ministers, professionals, and businesspeople who serviced the needs of their racial group. Black-owned real estate agencies, funeral homes, doctors' offices, newspapers, groceries, restaurants, and bars opened for business in African American neighborhoods. Many businessmen had been inspired by the words of black educator Booker T. Washington, and specifically by his argument that blacks should devote themselves to self-help and self-sufficiency. **Madame C. J. Walker** offers one example of a black woman who built a lucrative business from the hair and skin lotions she devised and sold to black customers throughout the country.

Nevertheless, entrepreneurial success remained a tougher task among African Americans than among immigrants. Black communities were often smaller and poorer than white ethnic ones, and black businessmen found it difficult to cultivate customers outside of their core community. Meanwhile, blacks were so marginalized in politics that they had little opportunity to gain power or wealth through holding political office or controlling a political machine. Thus the African American middle class remained smaller and more precarious than did its counterpart in ethnic communities.

QUICK REVIEW

AFRICAN AMERICAN LIFE

- Predominantly rural and southern; most blacks worked as sharecroppers

- Migration to urban centers in the South and North began

- Intensifying segregation and discrimination in South and North

- Churches, fraternal societies, political organizations, and new black middle class forged bonds of community

Madame C. J. Walker *Black entrepreneur who built a lucrative business from the hair and skin lotions she devised and sold to black customers.*

WORKING-CLASS AND COMMERCIAL CULTURE

As much as the white elites and their middle-class allies attempted to impose a genteel order on urban life, the city's vitality escaped such bounds. Most workers shared in a new culture of commercial entertainment that included dance halls, music halls, vaudeville theatres, nickelodeons, amusement parks, and ballparks. Vaudeville shows, for instance, offered a variety of miscellaneous short acts for only a dime; a typical show might include sentimental ballads, acrobats, mind readers, blackface minstrelsy, sports stars, and dancing bears. Amusement parks such as Steeplechase Park at Coney Island, built in 1895, attracted a large working-class audience of men and women while soon also appealing to middle-class youth. Older middle-class commentators found the unchaperoned mingling of young men and women in an urban public space troubling, even shocking, but that loosening of restraint was what made Coney Island so pleasurable and exciting. Vaudeville also developed into a cross-class, national phenomenon.

FOCUS QUESTION

What kinds of commercial entertainment took root among urban workers in the late 19th and early 20th century? How did this commercial culture compare to the cultural initiatives undertaken by urban elites?

SURF AVENUE AND LUNA PARK, CONEY ISLAND, 1913. *With its one million lights, Surf Avenue in Brooklyn, New York, advertised itself as the most brilliantly lit thoroughfare in the world. The avenue included the entrance to Luna Park, one of Coney Island's most popular attractions.*

LUNA PARK, SURF AVENUE, BY NIGHT, CONEY ISLAND, N. Y.

© Lake County Museum/ CORBIS

Popular Literature

Urban workers read a wide variety of dime novels (paperbacks that sold for a dime; see Chapter 10) and newspapers. Beginning in the 1860s and 1870s, a flourishing cheap literature reflected the presence of working women in the new industrial order: The popular 1871 story "Bertha the Sewing Machine Girl; or, Death at the Wheel," inspired many imitators and was staged as a popular play in New York City. Its author, Laura Jane Libbey, published more than 60 novels in the 1880s. Working women read a variety of romances as well. Featuring wealthy heroines or working women who discovered that by birth they were actually aristocrats, these romantic tales offered fantasies that—in imagination, at least—closed the gulf between the classes. Dime novels appealing to working-class men often told heroic stories in which men overcame numerous obstacles to become the foremen or owners of factories. Such stories allowed a form of imagined compensation for the loss of independence men experienced as permanent wage earners.

If literature gestured toward the past, the movies pointed toward the future. Movies were well suited to poor city dwellers. Initially, they cost only a nickel. The nickelodeons where they were shown were usually in working-class neighborhoods. Movies did not require much leisure time because at first they lasted only 15 minutes on average. Viewers with more time on their hands could stay for a cycle of two or three films. And even non-English-speakers could understand what was happening on the "silent screen." By 1910, at least 20,000 nickelodeons dotted northern cities.

These early "moving pictures" were primitive by today's standards, but they were thrilling just the same. Moviegoers could transport themselves to parts of the world they would otherwise never see, encounter people they would otherwise never meet, and watch boxing matches they could otherwise not afford to attend. The darkened theater provided a setting in which secret desires, especially sexual ones, could be explored.

No easy generalizations are possible about the content of these early films, more than half of which came from France, Germany, and Italy. American-made films tended toward slapstick comedies, adventure stories, and romances such as

HISTORY THROUGH FILM

Coney Island (1917)

Directed by Roscoe "Fatty" Arbuckle (uncredited).
Starring Roscoe "Fatty" Arbuckle (Fatty), Buster Keaton
(Rival), Alice Mann (Love Interest), Agnes Neilson
(Fatty's Wife), and Al St. John (Old Friend).

Coney Island was one of the first silent films to feature a classic comedy duo: Roscoe "Fatty" Arbuckle and Buster Keaton. The two met through a mutual friend in New York City in 1917 and quickly struck up a silver-screen partnership. Arbuckle, already a silent movie star, and Keaton, a veteran of the vaudeville circuit, crafted a crude, slapstick tour de force of pratfalls, gags, and fights. It was the beginning of a popular style of comedy on film, the fat/skinny buddy pic, which would be recast in famous teams like Abbot and Costello, and, to an extent, the Three Stooges.

Coney Island opens to images of Luna Park at night, brightly lit towers, luminescent avenues, mechanized roller coasters. Highlighting these modern inventions, the film showcases the technological innovations of the late 19th and early 20th centuries. Coney Island itself—its state-of-the-art rides (The Witching Waves, Chutes), its street vendors hawking ice cream and candy, its carnival-like, consumer-driven atmosphere—is one of the most prominent "characters" in the film. It is cast as having irresistible allure. Like the Midway Plaisance and in contrast to the White City, Coney Island sought to fill urban dwellers' leisure time with adventure and fun rather than with moral improvement.

At the beginning of the film, Buster Keaton's character watches a parade with his girlfriend (Alice Mann) before the two decide to enter Luna Park. When Keaton comes up short on the entry fee, his lady friend drops him for a man who has the admission cash (Al St. John). Meanwhile, Fatty sits, bored, on the beach with his dowdy wife, but he eventually sneaks away from her after burying himself in the sand to hide. For the rest of the film, Keaton, Arbuckle, and St. John vie for Mann's attention, punching and pranking each other in the process. Keaton eventually wins back Mann's affection, and Fatty and St. John swear off women altogether, until they spy another young lady and run after her.

The raucous style of physical comedy that dominates this film offers us a glimpse of the values then coursing their way through working-class commercial culture. The cinematic displays of informal association between men and women, of adventure and sexuality, had themselves been inspired by behaviors that many young urban dwellers, including sizable numbers of immigrants, had themselves embraced. The film is notable, too, for the breadth of its attack on social conventions and authority figures. In the movie, no relationship is sacred (the primary narrative follows Fatty's attempts to cheat on his

Fatty Arbuckle (center) getting clobbered by Buster Keaton (right) in a scene from Coney Island. *Their love interest, played by Alice Mann, looks on.*

Courtesy of Everett Collection

wife), no authority figure powerful (the inadequate and often thickly mustachioed Keystone Kops all end up locked in jail, knocked out cold), and no gender line firm (Fatty cross-dresses to disguise himself from his wife). While the assault on authority in the movie is presented in a hilarious style, it carries a more serious message; namely, that working-class individuals were going to make their own way in the world. It is precisely these declarations of cultural independence that made urban elites and their middle-class allies so anxious about their ability to impose their own sense of order and morality on city life.

By the 1920s executives in the movie industry had taken steps to expunge Arbuckle-style antics from their films, and to make these art forms more suitable for refined middle-class audiences. Once decorum in the movies became the rule of the day, lords of cinematic anarchy, like Arbuckle, lost their footing. In fact, Arbuckle's career crashed in the twenties. In 1921, actress Virginia Rappe died four days after attending a bootleg liquor party at Fatty's San Francisco apartment. Arbuckle was accused of rape and was tried three times for manslaughter. Though eventually acquitted, his career as an actor never recovered. He died in 1933 of a heart attack at 46. Buster Keaton, however, went on to a successful acting career, sharing the Hollywood limelight with the likes of Charlie Chaplin.

THEDA BARA AS CLEOPATRA (1917). *Bara was the first movie actress to gain fame for her roles as a "vamp"—a woman whose irresistible sexual charm led men to ruin. Because little effort was made to censor movies before the early 1920s, movie directors were able to explore sexual themes and to film their female stars in erotic, and partially nude, poses.*

© Bettmann/ CORBIS

those generated by Buster Keaton and Fatty Arbuckle, two silent-screen stars (see the *History through Film* feature, p. 471). Producers did not yet shy away, as they soon would, from the lustier or seedier sides of American life. In 1914, the movies' first sex symbol, Theda Bara, debuted in a movie that showed her tempting an upstanding American ambassador into infidelity and ruin. She would be the first of the big screen's vamps, so-called because the characters they portrayed, like vampires, thrived on the blood (and death) of men.

THE NEW SEXUALITY AND THE RISE OF FEMINISM

FOCUS QUESTION

How did the early-20th-century movement toward sexual freedom contribute to the rise of feminism?

The appearance of the vamp was one sign that popular culture had become an arena in which Americans were beginning to experiment with more open expressions of sexuality. Another sign was the growing numbers of women who began insisting that they be accorded the same sexual freedom long enjoyed by men. This impulse was strongest among young, single, working-class women who were entering the workforce in large numbers and mixing at workplaces, in loosely supervised ways, with men their own age. The associations between young men and women that sprang up at work carried over into their leisure. Young people of both sexes flocked to the dance halls. They went to movies and to amusement parks together, and they engaged, far more than their parents had, in premarital sex. It is estimated that the proportion of women having sex before marriage rose from 10 percent to 25 percent in the generation that was coming of age between 1910 and 1920.

This movement toward sexual freedom was one expression of women's dissatisfaction with the restrictions that had been imposed on them by earlier generations. By the second decade of the 20th century, spokeswomen had emerged to make the case for full female freedom and equality. The author Charlotte Perkins Gilman called for the release of women from domestic chores through the collectivization of housekeeping. Social activist Margaret Sanger insisted, in her lectures on birth control, that women should be free to enjoy sexual relations without having to worry about unwanted motherhood. The anarchist Emma Goldman denounced marriage as a kind of prostitution and embraced the ideal of "free love" unburdened by contractual commitment. Alice Paul, founder of the National Women's Party, brought a new militancy to the campaign for woman suffrage (see Chapter 21).

These women were among the first to use the term **feminism** to describe their desire for complete equality with men. Some of them came together in **Greenwich Village**, a community of radical artists and writers in lower Manhattan. Crystal Eastman, a leader of the feminist Greenwich Village group called Heterodoxy, defined the feminist challenge as "how to arrange the world so that women can be human beings, with a chance to exercise their infinitely varied gifts in infinitely varied ways, instead of being destined by the accident of their sex to one field of activity."

The movement for sexual and gender equality aroused considerable anxiety. Parents worried about the promiscuity of their children. Conservatives were certain that sexual assertiveness among women would transform American cities into dens of iniquity. Vice commissions sprang up in major cities to clamp down on prostitution, drunkenness, and pornography. The campaign for prohibition—a ban on the sale of alcoholic beverages—gathered steam. Movie theater owners were pressured into excluding "indecent" films from their screens. Many believed the lurid tales of international vice lords scouring foreign lands for innocent girls who could be delivered to American brothel owners. This "white slave trade" inspired passage of the 1910 Mann Act, which made the transportation of women across state lines for immoral purposes a federal crime.

Nor did it escape the attention of conservatives that Greenwich Village was home not only to the exponents of "free love" but also to advocates of class warfare. William "Big Bill" Haywood, leader of a newly formed radical labor organization, the Industrial Workers of the World (IWW) (see Chapter 21) frequented Greenwich Village. So, too, did IWW organizer and Heterodoxy member Elizabeth Gurley Flynn. When Greenwich Village radicals began publishing an avant-garde artistic journal in 1914, they called it *The Masses;* its editor was Max Eastman, the brother of Crystal. This convergence of labor and feminist militancy intensified conservative feeling that the nation had strayed too far from its roots.

feminism *Desire for complete equality between men and women.*

Greenwich Village *Community of radical artists and writers in lower Manhattan.*

Reimagining American Nationality

The large presence of immigrants in America also alarmed conservatives. Among the native-born middle and upper classes, the prevailing view was that immigrants should shed their ethnic backgrounds and become thoroughly American in speech, dress, and culture, and in their commitment to the principles of liberty and democracy. A refusal or inability to do so was increasingly interpreted by these conservative sectors of the population as marking the inferiority of the immigrant group in question or their unfitness for life in America. Such interpretations of immigrant

FOCUS QUESTION

How did Israel Zangwill, Horace Kallen, and Randolph Bourne reimagine American nationality?

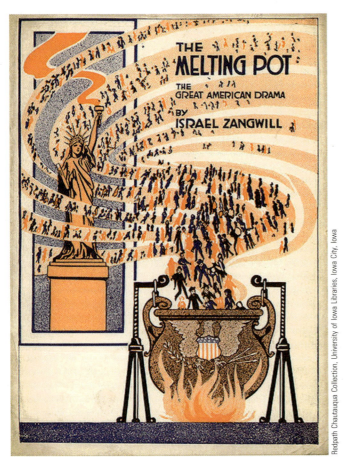

THE MELTING POT. *This program cover of a 1916 production of Zangwill's play visually recreates the process that unfolds in the drama itself: A swirl of diverse immigrants from many parts of the world is thrown into one great pot and fused into a strong, freedom-loving people.*

behavior generated support for coercive Americanization campaigns and for legislation that would extend the ban on "undesirable" immigrant groups from East Asians to eastern and southern Europeans, West Asians, and Africans.

As these pressures mounted, immigrants began to fight back, some insisting that all immigrants had the capacity to become fully American, others declaring that America would be a better place if it made room for at least some of the diversity that immigrants had brought to American culture. In 1908, Israel Zangwill, an Anglo-Jewish writer, debuted his play *The Melting Pot* on Broadway. The play's theme was that all immigrants, even those originating from eastern Europe, could become the most successful and best of Americans. The play's protagonist, David Quixano, a Russian Jew, survives an anti-Jewish riot and flees alone to New York City. A talented musician, he seizes the opportunity that America gives him, writes a successful American symphony, marries the Gentile girl of his dreams, and becomes a proud American.

It mattered greatly to Zangwill, the playwright, that David's success grew out of his willingness to abandon his ethnic and religious past and to embrace America. Zangwill imagined an America in which all immigrants, or at least all immigrants from Europe, would leave behind their old-world cultures (and grievances) and melt together to form a new and vigorous nationality.

Zangwill was criticized at the time and by subsequent writers for believing that the shedding of one's old-world culture was both possible and desirable. But his celebration of the **melting pot** should not be understood as a simpleminded call for conformity of the sort that conservatives desired. Zangwill believed that the core of American culture would change and become a different compound once immigrants had melted themselves and their cultures into it. Thus, even if the specific contributions of different immigrant cultures could not be precisely identified, they would nevertheless be present and influential in changing and refreshing American nationality.

Zangwill's views found support from prominent political figures who were beginning to identify themselves with reform. President Theodore Roosevelt wrote Zangwill in 1908, after watching a performance of *The Melting Pot*, that "I do not know when I have seen a play that stirred me as much." In 1915, President Woodrow Wilson credited immigrants for making America "the only country in the world" that experiences a "constant and repeated rebirth."

Other immigrant thinkers were discomfited by the kind of melting that Zangwill had advocated. Among them was Horace Kallen, a German-Jewish immigrant, philosopher, and social critic. While an undergraduate at Harvard University in the first years of the 20th century, Kallen, along with fellow student Alain Locke (see Chapter 24), developed the doctrine of **cultural pluralism**, which called on America to become home to many cultures, not one. It argued against coercive assimilation and the melting pot and for the celebration of ethnic difference. In a famous 1915 article, "Democracy versus the Melting Pot," Kallen imagined the American nation as an orchestra in which each ethnic group would have its own

melting pot *Term first used in the early 1900s that referred to the fusing of immigrants' culture with American culture as a continuous rebirth of the nation.*

cultural pluralism *Doctrine that celebrated ethnic diversity as the essence of American civilization.*

"theme and melody" and contribute a distinctive part to the "symphony of [American] civilization."

The following year, another critic, the native-born Randolph Bourne, wrote an essay, "Trans-National America," in which he picked up on Kallen's insistence that immigrants be given a role in shaping culture in the United States. Bourne located America's uniqueness in the encounters that occurred between immigrant cultures on the one hand and the nation's atmosphere of freedom and democracy on the other. This atmosphere permitted individuals from all kinds of groups, both immigrant and native-born, both to preserve their own cultures and to partake of others. Sharing cultures, Bourne argued, would increase cooperation and would make immigrants patriotic, able to believe that they "may have a hand in the destiny of America." Such integration, cooperation, and patriotism would create a nationality superior to any emerging from a "narrow 'Americanism' or forced chauvinism."

Bourne's ideal of American nationality, one he labeled **cosmopolitanism**, allowed for more variation and choice than did Kallen's, which viewed cultural expressions in America as arising almost exclusively from the traditions that immigrants had brought with them to the New World. For Bourne, the New World was much more about creating new cultural forms out of the mélange of peoples and cultures that inhabited America than it was about preserving old forms; unlike Zangwill, Bourne did not look forward to an America in which everyone had been melted into one shape.

Zangwill, Kallen, and Bourne all failed to grapple sufficiently with race and with the discrimination that America imposed on groups, especially African Americans, marked as racially different. Their writings did not address the perniciousness of Jim Crow, nor did they acknowledge the reality of Chinese and Japanese exclusion. Nevertheless, these thinkers were among the first to articulate in public forums arguments for diversity that were percolating among the masses of immigrants living in America. Today, Kallen and Bourne in particular are seen as early exponents of what late-20th-century Americans would call "multiculturalism."

Like feminism, calls for pluralism and cosmopolitanism generated anxiety in large stretches of America, especially in farming communities and small towns, and in the South, where industrialization and urbanization were proceeding at a slower rate. To these Americans, it seemed as though the cultures that immigrants were creating in cities were taking the nation too far from its Anglo-Saxon roots. Urban elites were also troubled. Many of their members, long frustrated by the apparent immigrant preference for movies, amusement parks, and saloons over the "civilizing forces" of museums, libraries, and lectures, were not predisposed to find virtue in immigrant cultures. Nevertheless, change was beginning to occur in these elite circles. Both Roosevelt and Wilson had begun to understand that American nationality might be strengthened by the infusion into it of new peoples and new cultures, and that the resulting melting-pot hybridity might be superior to an imagined Anglo-Saxon purity.

Conclusion

By 1920, America's urban population outstripped its rural population for the first time in the country's history. Despite a political system that was chronically vulnerable to corruption, urban leaders found ways to build housing and infrastructure that enabled cities to address the demands placed on them by rapid growth. Through the invention of skyscrapers, elevators, electrified railroad and trolley lines, and sophisticated water systems, cities became centers of technological innovation. Urban elites wanted to make their cities centers of culture, too, and embarked on grand projects of architectural and landscape renovation to spread civilization and refinement through the urban populations.

cosmopolitanism *Doctrine that celebrated the creation of new cultural forms out of the mélange of peoples and traditions present in the United States.*

The gap between the elites and the urban masses remained large, however. Enormous numbers of new workers, many of them foreign born, arrived in cities. Their working and living conditions were often poor. Groups defined as racially different—African Americans, Chinese and Japanese immigrants, and even groups of southern and eastern European immigrants—suffered from prejudice as well. Every group could point to examples of economic success among their ranks, and, by the second decade of the 20th century, solid middle classes had emerged within each. Yet, majorities came up short in their quest for equality and opportunity in America.

While economic success remained elusive, the new urban masses nevertheless demonstrated a spirit of creativity and independence that profoundly shaped an urban culture of adventure, liberty, and diversity. Working-class women discovered liberties in dress, employment, dating, and sex that they had not known and propelled feminism into being. Social critics began to imagine forms of American nationality that not only put immigrants on the same footing as the native born but that praised diversity as a central part of the American experience.

This association of the cities with newness and diversity only increased the cultural distance between them and countryside. Within the cities themselves the popular culture of the immigrant masses also troubled urban elites and their middle-class allies. These cultural tensions had already begun to spill over into politics, shaping a new and important movement called progressivism.

CHAPTER REVIEW

Review

1. In what ways did urban elites seek to shape the physical and cultural character of their cities in the years between 1890 and 1910?

2. From which parts of the world did immigrants come in the years between 1880 and 1920? What caused them to migrate? What were their patterns of work and residence in the United States?

3. What were the ways in which immigrants sought economic success and social mobility? How successful were they in their efforts?

4. What were the similarities and differences between the African American and immigrant experiences in the early 20th century?

5. What kinds of commercial entertainment took root among urban workers in the late 19th and early 20th century? How did this commercial culture compare to the cultural initiatives undertaken by urban elites?

6. How did the early-20th-century movement toward sexual freedom contribute to the rise of feminism?

7. How did Israel Zangwill, Horace Kallen, and Randolph Bourne reimagine American nationality?

Critical Thinking

1. Which group had a greater influence on urban life in the early 20th century: urban elites or immigrant masses?

2. Which philosophy, do you think, offered the best recipe for incorporating immigrants into American society in the early 20th century: melting-pot assimilation, cultural pluralism, or cosmopolitanism?

Identifications

Review your understanding of the following key terms, people, and events for this chapter.

nickelodeons, p. 456
walking cities, p. 458
Frederick Law Olmsted, p. 459

White City, p. 459
Midway Plaisance, p. 459
Triangle Shirtwaist Company, p. 464

political machine, p. 467
Madame C. J. Walker, p. 469
feminism, p. 473

Greenwich Village, p. 473
melting pot, p. 474
cultural pluralism, p. 474
cosmopolitanism, p. 475

DISCOVERY

America is a nation of immigrants. Why did so many immigrants come to America between 1860 and 1920?

In thinking about this question, begin by breaking it down into the components shown below. A discussion of the significance of each component should appear in your answer.

Culture and Society

Study the graph on Sources of Immigration. How did the ethnic makeup of the immigrant population change between 1860 and 1920? Did this change affect attitudes toward immigrants among native-born Americans? If so, how? How would you compare attitudes toward immigrants in the early 20th century to attitudes toward immigrants in the early 21st century?

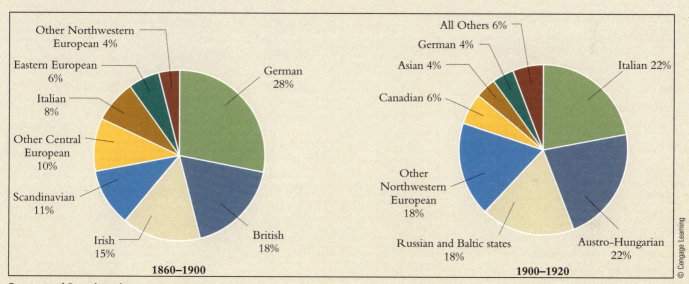

Sources of Immigration

Source: Data from *Historical Statistics of the United States, Colonial Times to 1970* (White Plains, NY: Kraus International, 1989), pp. 105–109.

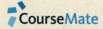

Visit the CourseMate website at www.cengagebrain.com for additional study tools and review materials for this chapter.

PROGRESSIVISM

PROGRESSIVISM AND THE PROTESTANT SPIRIT

MUCKRAKERS AND THE TURN TOWARD "REALISM"

SETTLEMENT HOUSES AND WOMEN'S ACTIVISM
Hull House
The Cultural Conservatism of Progressive Reformers
A Nation of Clubwomen

SOCIALISM
The Several Faces of Socialism
Socialists and Progressives

MUNICIPAL REFORM
The City Commission Plan
The City Manager Plan
The Costs of Reform

REFORM IN THE STATES
Restoring Sovereignty to "the People"
Creating a Virtuous Electorate
The Australian Ballot
Personal Registration Laws
Disfranchisement
Disillusionment with the Electorate
Woman Suffrage
Robert La Follette and Wisconsin Progressivism
Scientific Management on the Factory Floor

A CAMPAIGN FOR CIVIL RIGHTS
The Failure of Accommodationism
From the Niagara Movement to the NAACP

THE ROOSEVELT PRESIDENCY
Regulating the Trusts
Toward a "Square Deal"
Expanding Government Power: The Economy
Expanding Government Power: The Environment
Progressivism: A Movement for the People?
The Republicans: A Divided Party

THE TAFT PRESIDENCY: PROGRESSIVE
DISAPPOINTMENT AND RESURGENCE
Battling Congress
The Ballinger-Pinchot Controversy
Roosevelt's Return
The Bull Moose Campaign
The Rise of Woodrow Wilson
The Election of 1912

THE WILSON PRESIDENCY
Tariff Reform and a Progressive Income Tax
The Federal Reserve Act
From the New Freedom to the New Nationalism

Progressivism took its name from individuals who left the Republican Party in 1912 to join Theodore Roosevelt's new party, the Progressive Party. But the term *progressive* refers to an even larger and more varied group of reformers. Progressives wanted to cleanse politics of corruption and tame the power of the "trusts." They fought against prostitution, gambling, drinking, and vice. They first appeared in municipal politics, organizing to oust crooked mayors and break up local gas or streetcar monopolies. They then carried their fights to the states and finally to the nation.

Progressivism was popular among several groups with distinct, and often conflicting, aims, but most progressives agreed on the need for an activist government to right political, economic, and social wrongs. Some progressives wanted government to become active only long enough to clean up the political process, end drinking, upgrade the electorate, and break up trusts. But these problems were so difficult to solve that many other progressives came to see the federal government as the institution best equipped to solve social problems. They endorsed the notion of a permanently active government—with the power to tax income, regulate industry, protect consumers from fraud, safeguard the environment, and provide social welfare. Since Americans had long been suspicious of centralized government, progressives of all stripes had to build a new case for strong government as the protector of liberty and equality.

Timeline

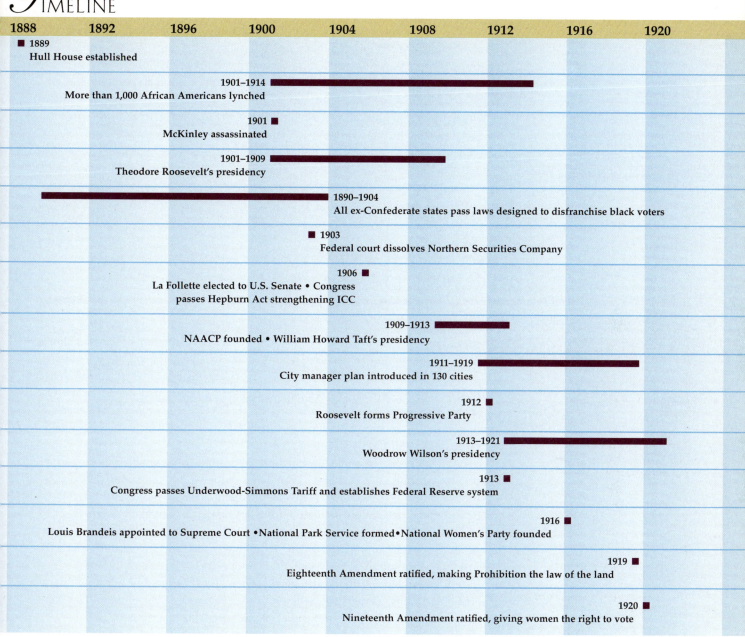

1888	1892	1896	1900	1904	1908	1912	1916	1920

1889
Hull House established

1901–1914
More than 1,000 African Americans lynched

1901
McKinley assassinated

1901–1909
Theodore Roosevelt's presidency

1890–1904
All ex-Confederate states pass laws designed to disfranchise black voters

1903
Federal court dissolves Northern Securities Company

1906
La Follette elected to U.S. Senate • Congress passes Hepburn Act strengthening ICC

1909–1913
NAACP founded • William Howard Taft's presidency

1911–1919
City manager plan introduced in 130 cities

1912
Roosevelt forms Progressive Party

1913–1921
Woodrow Wilson's presidency

1913
Congress passes Underwood-Simmons Tariff and establishes Federal Reserve system

1916
Louis Brandeis appointed to Supreme Court •National Park Service formed•National Women's Party founded

1919
Eighteenth Amendment ratified, making Prohibition the law of the land

1920
Nineteenth Amendment ratified, giving women the right to vote

© Cengage Learning

PROGRESSIVISM AND THE PROTESTANT SPIRIT

Progressivism emerged first and most strongly among young, mainly Protestant, middle-class Americans who felt alienated from society. Many had been raised in homes where religious conviction was a spur to social action. They were expected to become ministers or missionaries or to serve their church in some other way. They had abandoned this path, but they never lost their zeal for righting moral wrongs and for uplifting the human spirit. They were distressed by the immorality and corruption in American politics and by the gap that separated rich from poor.

FOCUS QUESTION

How did Protestantism influence reform?

Other Protestant reformers retained their faith. William Jennings Bryan, the former Populist leader, insisted that Christian piety and American democracy were integrally related. Billy Sunday, a former Major League Baseball player who became the most theatrical preacher of his day, elevated opposition to saloons and the "liquor trust" into a righteous crusade. And Walter Rauschenbusch led a movement known as the Social Gospel, which emphasized the duty of Christians to work for the social good.

Of the many groups of reformers that arose, three were of particular importance, especially in the early years: investigative journalists, who were called "**muckrakers**;" the founders and supporters of settlement houses; and socialists.

muckrakers *Investigative journalists who propelled progressivism by exposing corruption, economic monopoly, and moral decay in American society.*

MUCKRAKERS AND THE TURN TOWARD "REALISM"

FOCUS QUESTION

What was "realism" and how did it spur investigative reporting and reform?

The term *muckraker* was coined by Theodore Roosevelt, who had intended it as a criticism of reporters who wrote stories about scandalous situations. But it became a badge of honor among journalists who wanted to shock the public into taking action about the troublesome aspects of American life. Ida Tarbell revealed the shady practices by which John D. Rockefeller had transformed his Standard Oil Company into a monopoly. Lincoln Steffens unraveled the webs of bribery and corruption that were strangling local governments. George Kibbe Turner documented prostitution and family disintegration.

Two factors transformed investigative reporting into something of national importance during these years. First, newspaper and magazine circulation expanded. From 1870 to 1909, daily newspapers rose in number from 574 to 2,600, and their circulation increased from less than 3 million to more than 24 million. Cheap, 10-cent periodicals such as *McClure's Magazine* and *Ladies Home Journal,* with circulations of 400,000 to 1 million, displaced genteel and relatively expensive 35-cent publications such as *Harper's* and *The Atlantic Monthly.* The expanded readership brought journalists money and prestige and attracted many talented and ambitious men and women to the profession. It also made magazine publishers more receptive to stories that would appeal to the masses.

Second, the American middle class took a greater intellectual interest in **"realism."** "Realist" thinking prized detachment, objectivity, and skepticism. Many people, for example, felt that constitutional theory had little to do with the way government in the United States actually worked. What could one learn about bosses, machines, and graft from studying the Constitution? Others argued that the nation's glorification of the "self-made man" and of "individualism" prevented Americans from understanding how corporations, banks, and labor unions shaped the nation's economy and society.

By the first decade of the 20th century, intellectuals and artists were attempting to create truer, more realistic ways of representing and analyzing life in America. They exposed the captains of industry, the con artists, white slave traders, and corrupt policemen who thrived in the cities. Uneasy middle-class Americans applauded the muckrakers for telling these stories and became interested in reform. They pressured city and state governments to send crooked government officials to jail and to stamp out corruption and vice. Between 1902 and 1916, more than 100 cities launched investigations of the prostitution trade. The federal government, meanwhile, began to raise questions about "the trusts." Progressivism crystallized around the abuses that muckrakers exposed.

realism *Form of thinking, writing, and art that prized detachment, objectivity, and skepticism.*

"THE POVERTY AND GLOOM OF NEW YORK'S STREETS." *Jacob Riis published this picture in his book* How the Other Half Lives *(1890), a pioneering work in realist photography. The quoted words above are from Riis's text and reflect his efforts to rouse middle-class Americans from their complacency. This photograph depicts runaway boys who had no family and no home.*

© Bettmann/ CORBIS

SETTLEMENT HOUSES AND WOMEN'S ACTIVISM

Established by middle-class reformers, settlement houses were intended to help poor immigrant workers cope with the harsh conditions of city living. Much of the inspiration for settlement houses came from young, college-trained, Protestant women from middle-class homes. They rebelled against being relegated solely to the roles of wife and mother and sought to assert their independence and apply their talents in socially useful ways.

Hull House

Jane Addams and Ellen Gates Starr established the nation's first settlement house in Chicago in 1889. The two women had been inspired by a visit the year before to London's Toynbee Hall, where a group of middle-class men had been living and working with that city's poor since 1884. Addams and Starr bought a decaying mansion once owned by a prominent Chicagoan, Charles J. Hull, and now surrounded by factories, churches, saloons, and tenements inhabited by poor, largely foreign-born families.

Addams quickly emerged as the guiding spirit of **Hull House**. She moved into the building and demanded that all workers there do the same. She and Starr enlisted extraordinary women such as Florence Kelley, Alice Hamilton, and Julia Lathrop. They set up a nursery for the children of working mothers, a penny savings bank, and an employment bureau, soon followed by a baby clinic, a neighborhood playground, and social clubs. Determined to minister to cultural as well as economic needs, Hull House sponsored an orchestra, reading groups, and a lecture series. Members of Chicago's widening circle of reform-minded intellectuals, artists, and politicians contributed their energies to the enterprise.

FOCUS QUESTION

What contributions did associations of women reformers make to progressivism?

Hull House *First American settlement house, established in Chicago in 1889 by Jane Addams and Ellen Gates Starr.*

Brown Brothers

JANE ADDAMS. *The founder of the settlement house movement, Addams was the most famous woman reformer of the progressive era. This photograph dates from the 1890s or 1900s, Hull House's formative period.*

Soon Hull House leaders themselves gained significant political influence. In 1893, Illinois Governor John P. Altgeld named Florence Kelley as the state's chief factory inspector. Kelley's investigations led to Illinois's first factory law, which prohibited child labor, limited the employment of women to eight hours a day, and authorized the state to hire inspectors to enforce the law. Julia Lathrop used her appointment to the State Board of Charities to agitate for improvements in the care of the poor, the handicapped, and the delinquent. And although Hull House leaders did not command the instant fame accorded the muckrakers, they inspired thousands of women across the country to build their own settlement houses. By 1910, Jane Addams was one of the nation's most famous women.

The Cultural Conservatism of Progressive Reformers

In general, settlement house workers were more sympathetic toward the poor, the illiterate, and the downtrodden than the muckrakers were. Although she disapproved of machine politics, Jane Addams saw firsthand the benefits machine politicians delivered to their constituents. Yet even Addams, who respected the cultural inheritance of the immigrant poor and admired their resourcefulness, disapproved of the new working-class entertainments that gave adolescents opportunities for intimate association. She was also troubled by the emerging sexual revolution (see Chapter 20). Addams tended to equate female sexuality with prostitution, and she joined many other women reformers in a campaign to suppress both.

The cultural conservatism evident in the attitudes of Addams and others on female sexuality also emerged in their attitudes toward alcohol. Drinking was a serious problem in poor, working-class areas.

TABLE 21.1

WOMEN ENROLLED IN INSTITUTIONS OF HIGHER EDUCATION, 1870–1930				
Year	Women's Colleges (thousands of students)	Coed Institutions (thousands of students)	Total (thousands of students)	Percentage of All Students Enrolled
1870	6.5	4.6	11.1	21.0%
1880	15.7	23.9	39.6	33.4%
1890	16.8	39.5	56.3	35.9%
1900	24.4	61.0	85.4	36.8%
1910	34.1	106.5	140.6	39.6%
1920	52.9	230.0	282.9	47.3%
1930	82.1	398.7	480.8	

Source: From Mabel Newcomer, *A Century of Higher Education for American Women* (New York: Harper and Row, 1959), p. 46.

for legislation to shut down saloons. Progressives joined forces with the Woman's Christian Temperance Union and the Anti-Saloon League. By 1916, their collective efforts had won prohibition of the sale and manufacture of alcoholic beverages in 16 states. In 1919, their crowning achievement was the Eighteenth Amendment to the U.S. Constitution, making prohibition the law of the land (see Chapter 23).

In depicting alcohol and saloons as evils, however, the prohibition movement ignored the role saloons played in working-class communities. On Chicago's South Side, for example, saloons provided thousands of packinghouse workers with the only decent place to eat lunch. Some saloons catered to particular ethnic groups: They served traditional foods and drinks, provided meeting space for fraternal organizations, and offered camaraderie to men longing to speak in their native tongue. Saloonkeepers sometimes functioned as informal bankers, cashing checks and making small loans. Not surprisingly, many immigrants shunned the prohibition movement.

A Nation of Clubwomen

Settlement house workers comprised only one part of a vast network of female reformers. Hundreds of thousands of women belonged to local women's clubs. Conceived as self-help organizations in which women would be encouraged to sharpen their minds, refine their domestic skills, and strengthen their moral faculties, these clubs embraced social reform. Clubwomen focused their energies on improving schools, building libraries and playgrounds, expanding educational and vocational opportunities for girls, and securing fire and sanitation codes for tenement houses. They transformed traditional female concerns—education and the home—into questions of public policy.

Clubwomen rose to prominence in black communities, too. In the Jim Crow South, where whites had stripped black men of their civil rights, many black female activists persevered in the face of white threats, determined to provide leadership in their communities and voice their people's concerns.

SOCIALISM

In the early 20th century, **socialism** stood for the transfer of big businesses from the capitalists who owned them to the laboring masses who worked in them. Socialists believed that such a transfer, usually defined in terms of government ownership of corporations, would make it impossible for wealthy elites to control society.

The Socialist Party of America, founded in 1901, became a political force, and socialist ideas influenced progressivism. In 1912, at the peak of its influence, the party's presidential candidate, Eugene V. Debs, attracted almost one million votes—6 percent of the total. In that same year, 1,200 Socialists held elective office in 340 different municipalities (see Map 21.1). More than 300 newspapers and periodicals spread the socialist gospel. In 1905, the socialist publication *Appeal to Reason* published, in serial form, a novel by an obscure muckraker named Upton Sinclair, which depicted scandalous working conditions in Chicago's meatpacking industry. When it was published as a book in 1906, *The Jungle* created a popular outcry.

QUICK REVIEW

PROGRESSIVISM

- Embraced an activist government to right political, economic, and social wrongs

- Led by middle-class reformers often inspired by Protestant values and fearing more radical critiques of capitalism such as those rooted in socialism

- Intellectual roots in realism

- Conservative undertones most evident in morality crusades over sexuality, temperance, and racial control

FOCUS QUESTION

What was the relationship of socialism to progressivism?

socialism *Political movement that called for the transfer of industry from private to public control, and the transfer of political power from elites to the laboring masses.*

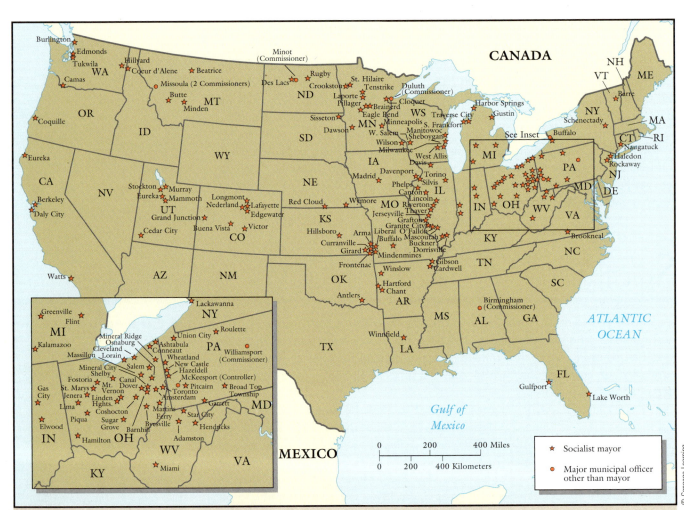

EUGENE V. DEBS. *This photograph captures the energy and charisma of Debs as he addresses a working-class audience in New York during his 1912 presidential campaign.*

Map 21.1 Cities and Towns Electing Socialists as Mayors or as Other Major Municipal Officers, 1911–1920. *This map reveals the strength of socialist electoral support in some unexpected areas: western Pennsylvania; Ohio; Illinois; Minnesota; a cluster of towns where Oklahoma, Missouri, and Kansas meet; Colorado; and Utah.*

The Several Faces of Socialism

Socialists came in several varieties: German working-class immigrants and their descendants in midwestern cities; Jewish immigrants from eastern Europe in New York and other Eastern Seaboard cities; disgruntled farmers and former Populists in the Southwest; and western miners, timber cutters, and other laborers who joined the Industrial Workers of the World (IWW).

Socialists differed not only in their occupations and ethnic origins but also in their politics. The IWW was the most radical socialist group. Those who followed Debs shared the IWW's commitment to revolution but saw themselves working within, rather than outside, American political, cultural, and religious traditions. They hoped to redeem the American republic by electing Debs president. Evolutionary socialists, led by Victor Berger of Milwaukee, abandoned talk of revolution altogether and chose instead an aggressive brand of reform politics. They were dubbed "gas and water socialists" because of their interest in improving city services.

Socialists and Progressives

Debs both attracted and unsettled progressives. On the one hand, he addressed the economic threats that concerned progressives. His confidence that strong government could regulate the economic system mirrored the progressives' own faith in the positive uses of government. Progressives and socialists often cooperated to win economic and political reforms, especially at the municipal and state levels. Prominent intellectuals—including John Dewey, Richard Ely, and Thorstein Veblen—and reformers traveled back and forth between the socialist and progressive camps. So did Helen Keller, the country's leading spokesperson for the disabled.

On the other hand, Debs's talk of revolution scared progressives, as did his efforts to organize a working-class political movement independent of middle-class control. Although progressives wanted to tame capitalism, they did not want to eliminate it. They wanted to improve conditions for the masses but not cede political control to them. The progressives hoped to offer just enough socialist elements to counter the appeal of Debs's more radical movement. In this, they were successful.

MUNICIPAL REFORM

Progressive-era reform battles first erupted over control of city transportation networks and utilities. Private corporations typically owned and operated street railways and electrical and gas systems. By bribing city officials who belonged to political machines, these corporations won the right to charge exorbitant rates and achieved generous reductions in real estate taxes.

The assault on private utilities and their protectors in city government gained momentum in the mid-1890s. In Detroit, reform-minded Mayor Hazen S. Pingree led successful fights to control the city's gas, telephone, and trolley companies. In Cleveland, reformer Tom Johnson won election as mayor in 1901, curbed the power of the streetcar interests, and brought honest and efficient government to the city.

Occasionally, a reform politician of Johnson's caliber would rise to power through one of the regular political parties. But this path to power was difficult, especially in cities where the political parties were controlled by machines. Consequently, progressives worked for reforms that could strip the parties of their power. Two of their favorite reforms were the city commission and the city manager forms of government.

FOCUS QUESTION

What were the benefits and costs of municipal reform?

The City Commission Plan

First introduced in Galveston, Texas, in 1900, in the wake of a devastating tidal wave, the city commission shifted municipal power from the mayor and his aldermen to five city commissioners, each responsible for a different department of city government. The impetus for this reform came from civic-minded businessmen determined to rebuild government on the principles of efficiency and scientific management. The results were often impressive. The Galveston commissioners restored the city's credit, improved its harbor, and built a massive seawall, all on budgets that had been cut by one-third. By 1913, more than 300 cities had adopted the city commission plan.

The City Manager Plan

Sometimes city commissioners rewarded supporters with jobs and contracts and sought undue power and prestige for their respective departments. The city manager plan sought to overcome such problems. Under this plan, the commissioners continued to set policy, but the implementation of policy now rested with a "chief executive." This official, who was appointed by the commissioners, would curtail rivalries between commissioners and ensure that no outside influences interfered with the businesslike management of the city. The job of city manager was explicitly modeled after that of a corporation executive. First introduced in Sumter, South Carolina, in 1911 and then in Dayton, Ohio, in 1913, by 1919 the city manager plan had been adopted in 130 cities.[4]

QUICK REVIEW

MUNICIPAL REFORM

- Shifted local transportation networks and utilities to public control

- Applied principles of business efficiency and scientific management to local government

- Diluted working-class power through nonpartisan and expensive nature of citywide elections

The Costs of Reform

Although these reforms limited corruption and improved services, they reduced the political influence of poor and minority voters. Previously, candidates for municipal office (other than the mayor) competed in ward elections rather than in citywide elections. Voters in working-class wards commonly elected workingmen to represent them, and voters in immigrant wards made sure that fellow ethnics represented their interests on city councils. Citywide elections diluted the strength of these constituencies. Candidates from poor districts often lacked the money needed to mount a citywide campaign, and they were further hampered by the nonpartisan nature of such elections. Denied the support of a political party or platform, they had to make themselves personally known to voters throughout the city. That was a much easier task for "leading citizens"—manufacturers, merchants, and lawyers—than it was for workingmen.

REFORM IN THE STATES

FOCUS QUESTION

What were the results of progressive efforts to create a "responsible" and "virtuous" electorate?

As at the local level, political parties at the state level were often dominated by corrupt politicians who did the bidding of powerful private lobbies. In New Jersey in 1903, for example, industrial and financial interests, working through the Republican Party machine, controlled the chief justice of the state supreme court, the attorney general, and the commissioner of banking and insurance.

Restoring Sovereignty to "the People"

Progressives introduced reforms designed to undermine the power of party bosses, restore sovereignty to "the people," and encourage honest, talented individuals to enter politics. The direct primary enabled voters themselves, rather than party bosses, to choose party candidates. By 1916, all but three states had adopted this reform. Closely related was a movement to strip state legislatures of their power to choose U.S. senators. State after state enacted legislation that permitted voters to choose Senate candidates in primary elections. In 1912, a reluctant U.S. Senate was obliged to approve the Seventeenth Amendment to the Constitution, mandating the direct election of senators.

A total of 18 states followed the example of Oregon after 1902 by adopting two other reforms, the initiative and the referendum. The initiative allowed reformers to put legislative proposals before voters in general elections without having to wait for state legislatures to act. The referendum gave voters the right in general elections to repeal an act that a state legislature had passed. Less widely adopted was the recall, a device that allowed voters to remove from office a public servant who had betrayed their trust. Numerous states also enacted laws that regulated corporate campaign contributions and restricted lobbying activities in state legislatures. These laws did not eliminate corporate privilege or destroy the power of machine politicians, but they made politics more honest and strengthened the influence of ordinary voters.

Creating a Virtuous Electorate

Progressive reformers focused as well on creating an electorate that recognized the importance of the vote and resisted efforts to manipulate elections. To create this ideal electorate, reformers had to see to it that all of those citizens who were deemed virtuous could cast their votes free of coercion and intimidation. At the same time, reformers sought to disfranchise citizens who were considered irresponsible and corruptible. In pursuing these goals, progressives enlarged the electorate by extending the right to vote to women, but they also supported laws that barred large numbers of minority and poor voters from the polls.

The Australian Ballot

Government regulation of voting had begun in the 1890s when virtually every state adopted the **Australian, or secret, ballot.** This reform required voters to vote in private rather than in public. It also required the government, rather than political parties, to print the ballots and supervise the voting. Before this time, each political party had printed its own ballot with only its candidates listed. At election time, each party mobilized its loyal supporters. Party workers offered liquor, free meals, and other bribes to get voters to the polls and to "persuade" them to cast the right ballot. Because the ballots were cast in public, few voters dared to cross watchful party officials.

The Australian ballot solved these problems. Although it predated progressivism, it embodied the progressives' determination to use government power to encourage citizens to cast their votes responsibly and wisely.

Personal Registration Laws

That same determination was apparent in the progressives' support for the personal registration laws that virtually every state passed between 1890 and 1920. These

---

initiative *Reform that gave voters the right to propose and pass a law independently of their state legislature.*

referendum *Reform that gave voters the right to repeal an unpopular act passed by their state legislature.*

recall *Reform that gave voters the right to remove from office a public servant who had betrayed the voters' trust.*

Australian ballot (secret ballot) *Practice that required citizens to vote in private rather than in public, and required the government (rather than political parties) to supervise the voting process.*

laws allowed prospective voters to register to vote only if they appeared at a designated government office with proper identification. Frequently, the laws also mandated a certain period of residence in the state prior to registration and a certain interval between registration and actual voting.

Personal registration laws were meant to disfranchise citizens who showed no interest in voting until Election Day, when party workers offered them money and free rides to the polls. But they also excluded many poor people who wanted to vote but failed to register, either because their work schedules made it impossible or because they were intimidated. The laws were particularly frustrating for immigrants who knew little English.

Disfranchisement

Progressives also promoted election laws expressly designed to keep noncitizen immigrants from voting. In the 1880s, 18 states had passed laws allowing immigrants to vote without first becoming citizens. Progressives reversed this trend. At the same time, the newly formed Bureau of Immigration and Naturalization (1906) made it more difficult to become a citizen. Applicants for citizenship now had to appear before a judge who interrogated them in English on American history and civics. Progressives defended this new process. U.S. citizenship, they believed, was not to be bestowed lightly.

Progressives in the North excluded immigrants on the grounds that they were unfit to handle the responsibilities of voting; progressives in the South saw African Americans in the same light. Between 1890 and 1904, every ex-Confederate state passed laws designed to strip black citizens of their right to vote. Because laws explicitly barring blacks from voting would have violated the Fifteenth Amendment, their **disfranchisement** was accomplished indirectly through literacy tests, property qualifications, and poll taxes. Any citizen who failed a reading test, could not sign his name, did not own a minimum amount of property, or could not pay a poll tax lost his right to vote. The citizens who failed these tests most frequently were blacks, who formed the poorest and least educated segment of the southern population, but a large portion of the region's poor whites also failed the tests.

Disillusionment with the Electorate

In the process of identifying those "unfit" to hold the franchise, some progressives soured on the electoral process altogether. The more they looked for rational and virtuous voters, the fewer they found. The growing disillusionment with the electorate, in combination with intensifying restrictions on the franchise, created an environment in which fewer and fewer Americans went to the polls. Voting participation rates fell from 79 percent in 1896 to only 49 percent in 1920.

Woman Suffrage

The major exception to this trend was the enfranchisement of women. Launched in 1848 at the famous Seneca Falls convention (see Chapter 12), the women's rights movement had floundered in the 1870s and 1880s. In 1890, suffragists came together in a new organization, the **National American Woman Suffrage Association** (NAWSA). Thousands of young, college-educated women campaigned door-to-door, held impromptu rallies, and pressured state legislators.

Wyoming, which attained statehood in 1890, became the first state to grant women the right to vote, followed in 1893 by Colorado and in 1896 by Idaho

---

disfranchisement *Process of barring groups of adult citizens from voting.*

National American Woman Suffrage Association *Organization established in 1890 to promote woman suffrage; stressed that women's special virtue made them indispensable to politics.*

Handwritten margin notes:
Identification to Vote
Voting rules
Stopped people that just wanted to vote for money
1880's 18 states allowed immigrants to vote
Progressivism stopped that.
Disfranchisement.
laws to strip blacks of rights to vote.

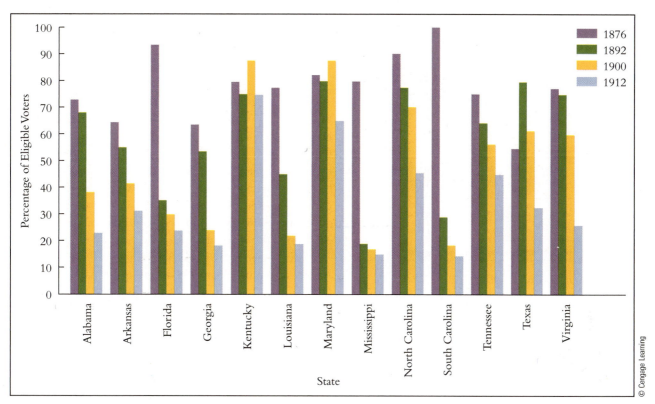

Voter Participation in 13 Southern States, 1876, 1892, 1900, 1912

Source: Data from *Historical Statistics of the United States, Colonial Times to 1970* (White Plains, NY: Kraus International, 1989).

WOMAN SUFFRAGE. *The confident, torch-bearing suffragist striding across the continent in this 1915 cartoon conveys the conviction of woman suffragists everywhere that their most cherished goal, gaining the vote for women, was within reach. The cartoon also reveals the interesting split among the states: Western states had already granted women the vote, whereas eastern states had not.*

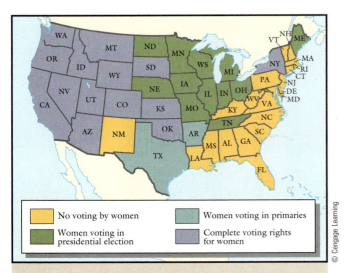

Map 21.2 Woman Suffrage before 1920. *This map illustrates how woman suffrage prior to 1920 had advanced furthest in the West.*

West first to allow women to vote.

and Utah. The main reason for success in these sparsely populated western states was not egalitarianism but rather the conviction that women's supposedly gentler and more nurturing nature would tame and civilize the men of the frontier (see Map 21.2).

Earlier generations had insisted that women were fundamentally equal to men, but many of the new suffragists argued that women were different from men. Women, they stressed, possessed a moral sense and a nurturing quality that men lacked. Their experience as mothers and household managers, they argued, would enable them to guide local and state governments in efforts to improve education, sanitation, and the condition of women and children in the workforce.

Suffragists were slow to ally themselves with blacks, Asians, and other disfranchised groups. In fact, many suffragists, especially those in the South and West, opposed the franchise for Americans of color. They, like their male counterparts, believed that members of these groups lacked political virtue and thus did not deserve the vote.

Washington, California, Kansas, Oregon, and Arizona followed the lead of the other western states by enfranchising women in the years from 1910 to 1912. After a series of setbacks in eastern and midwestern states, the movement regained momentum under the leadership of Carrie Chapman Catt, who became president of NAWSA in 1915. Equally important was the radical Alice Paul, who founded the Congressional Union in 1913 and later renamed it the National Woman's Party. Paul and her supporters picketed the White House 24 hours a day, daring the police to arrest them. Several suffrage demonstrators were jailed, where they continued their protests with hunger strikes. Aided by a heightened enthusiasm for democracy generated by America's participation in the First World War (see Chapter 23), the suffragists achieved their goal of universal woman suffrage with the ratification of the Nineteenth Amendment in 1920.

Robert La Follette and Wisconsin Progressivism

In some states, progressive reform extended well beyond political parties and the electorate. Progressives also wanted to limit the power of corporations, strengthen organized labor, and offer social welfare protection to the weak. State governments were pressured into passing such legislation by progressive alliances of middle-class and working-class reformers and by dynamic state governors.

Nowhere did the progressives' campaign for social reform flourish as it did in Wisconsin, where Robert La Follette emerged into prominence. La Follette entered politics as a Republican in the 1880s and embraced reform in the late 1890s. Elected governor in 1900, he secured for Wisconsin both a direct primary and a law that stripped the railroad corporations of tax exemptions. In 1905, he pushed through a civil service law mandating that every state employee meet a certain level of competence.

A tireless campaigner and vigorous speaker, "Fighting Bob" won election to the U.S. Senate in 1906. Meanwhile, Wisconsin's advancing labor and socialist movements persuaded progressive reformers to focus their legislative efforts on issues of corporate greed and social welfare. By 1910, reformers had passed state laws that regulated railroad and utility rates, instituted the nation's first state income tax, and provided workers with compensation for injuries, limitations on work hours, restrictions on child labor, and minimum wages for women.

QUICK REVIEW

POLITICAL REFORM IN THE STATES

- Attempted to eliminate corruption from voting and politics

- Australian (secret) ballot freed voters from coercion and intimidation

- Disfranchisement of many minorities and immigrants deemed "unworthy of the ballot"

- Enfranchisement of women

LINK TO THE PAST

Humor and the Woman Suffrage Movement

The length and difficulty of the struggle for woman suffrage have left many Americans with an image of suffragists as a rather serious and humorless group. But the poem reproduced below, from a book by suffragist Alice Duer Miller, *Are Women People? A Book of Rhymes for Suffrage Times* (New York: George H. Doran Company, 1915), suggests that we need to rethink this image. The poems in this book make the case for woman suffrage and attack antisuffragists (known at the time simply as "antis") in a humorous, lighthearted way. The poem below ridicules a "consistent anti," meaning someone opposed to woman suffrage. The poem imagines this anti to be a mother anguished by the knowledge that her son, Willie, who has just turned 21 (then the voting age), must soon confront the "danger" of the polls, those "dark and dreadful places where many lose their souls." By making the fear of voting seem ludicrous, the poem attempts to discredit those who dreaded the consequences of extending the franchise to women.

A Consistent Anti to Her Son

You're twenty-one to-day, Willie,
And a danger lurks at the door,
I've known about it always,
But I never spoke before;
When you were only a baby
It seemed so very remote,
But you're twenty-one to-day, Willie,
And old enough to vote.
You must not go to the polls, Willie,
Never go to the polls,

They're dark and dreadful places
Where many lose their souls;
They smirch, degrade and coarsen,
Terrible things they do
To quiet, elderly women—
What would they do to you!
If you've a boyish fancy
For any measure or man,
Tell me, and I'll tell Father,
He'll vote for it, if he can.
He casts my vote, and Louisa's,
And Sarah, and dear Aunt Clo;
Wouldn't you let him vote for you?
Father, who loves you so?
I've guarded you always, Willie,
Body and soul from harm;
I'll guard your faith and honor,
Your innocence and charm
From the polls and their evil spirits,
Politics, rum and pelf;
Do you think I'd send my only son
Where I would not go myself?

Q What does this poem reveal about the arguments of the antis (those who opposed woman suffrage)?

Q Is the poem successful in its effort to poke fun at (and thus to undermine) these arguments?

Source: from Alice Duer Mill, *Are Women People? A Book of Rhymes for Suffrage Times*, New York (George H. Doran Company, 1915), pp. 11–12.

In the first decade of the 20th century, John R. Commons, a University of Wisconsin economist, drafted Wisconsin's civil service and public utilities laws. In 1911, Commons designed and won legislative approval for the Wisconsin Industrial Commission, which brought together employers, trade unionists, and professionals and gave them broad powers to investigate and regulate relations between industry and labor in the state. For the first time, the rights of labor would be treated with the same respect as the rights of industry.

The "Wisconsin idea" quickly spread to Ohio, Indiana, New York, and Colorado. In 1913, the federal government established its own Industrial Relations Commission and hired Commons to direct its investigative staff. In other areas, too, reformers urged state and federal governments to shift the policy-making initiative away from political parties and toward administrative agencies staffed by nonelected professionals.

Scientific Management on the Factory Floor

Progressivism also drew support from businessmen who sought to use the principles of **scientific management** to create more efficient, productive, and harmonious workplaces. The leader of this movement was Frederick Winslow Taylor who, as chief engineer at Philadelphia's Midvale Steel Company in the 1880s, had examined every task and movement involved in a production-process. In "time-and-motion studies," he recorded every distinct movement of the worker, how long it took, and how often it was performed. He hoped to identify and eliminate wasted effort and make human labor emulate the smooth, automatic operation of a machine.

Taylor achieved his greatest popularity during the first two decades of the 20th century, and his 1911 book, *The Principles of Scientific Management,* drew the interest of countless corporate managers and engineers. By then, Taylor himself had been influenced by the spirit of progressive reform, and he offered his program as a way of achieving industrial peace. Scientific management, Taylor claimed, would allow each worker to be matched with his perfect job. Efficiency and wages would rise; so, too, would worker satisfaction. Workplace antagonisms would then dissolve.

Henry Ford, the pioneer in automobile manufacturing, was one of Taylor's disciples. By 1910, Ford's engineers had broken down the production of its main car, the "Model T," into a series of simple, sequential tasks. Each worker performed only one task, such as adding a carburetor to an engine or inserting a windshield. Then, in 1913, Ford's engineers introduced the first moving assembly line. This innovation eliminated precious time previously wasted in transporting car parts by crane or truck from one work area to another. It also limited the time available to workers to perform their assigned tasks.

By 1913, the continuous assembly line made Ford Motor Company's new Highland Park plant the most tightly integrated and continuously moving production system in American industry. A thousand Model Ts began rolling off the assembly line each day. This striking pace enabled Ford to slash the price of a Model T from $950 in 1909 to only $295 in 1923. The assembly line quickly became the most admired symbol of American mass production.

Problems immediately beset the system, however. Repeating a single motion all day induced mental stupor, and speeding up the line produced physical exhaustion—both of which increased errors and injuries. By 1913, employee turnover at Highland Park had reached the astounding rate of 370 percent per year. In response, Ford raised assembly-line wages to $5 per day, double the average manufacturing wage in 1914. Workers, especially young and single men, flocked to Detroit.

Ford recognized that workers were more complex than Taylor had allowed, and his innovations went well beyond what Taylor himself had contemplated. Ford set up a sociology department, forerunner of the personnel department, to collect job, family, and other information about his employees. He sent social workers into workers' homes to inquire into (and "improve") their personal lives. For the foreign born, he instituted Americanization classes. He offered his employees housing subsidies, medical care, and other benefits. But it would take another generation or two for significant sectors of the corporate world to follow his lead, and American industry remained more the target than the ally of progressive reform.

scientific management
Attempt to break down each factory job into its smallest components to increase efficiency, eliminate waste, and promote worker satisfaction.

A CAMPAIGN FOR CIVIL RIGHTS

The reform energy unleashed by progressivism inspired a new generation of African American activists to insist that the nation grapple anew with issues of racial inequality.

The Failure of Accommodationism

Booker T. Washington's message—that blacks should accept segregation and disfranchisement as unavoidable and focus their energies instead on self-help and self-improvement—faced increasing criticism from black activists such as W. E. B. Du Bois, Ida B. Wells, and Monroe Trotter. Washington's accommodationist leadership (see Chapter 18), in their eyes, had brought blacks in the South no reprieve from racism. More than 100 blacks had been lynched in 1900 alone; between 1901 and 1914 at least 1,000 others would be hanged. Increasingly, rumors of black assaults on whites became pretexts for white mobs to destroy black neighborhoods. In 1908, a mob in Springfield, Illinois, attacked black businesses and individuals; a force of 5,000 state militia was required to restore order. The troops were too late, however, to stop the lynching of two innocent black men.

Washington had long believed that blacks who educated themselves or who succeeded in business would be accepted as equals by whites. But, as Washington's critics observed, white rioters in Illinois made no distinction between rich blacks and poor, or between solid citizens and petty criminals. All that had seemed to matter was the color of their skin.

From the Niagara Movement to the NAACP

Seeing no future in accommodation, Du Bois and other young activists, mostly black, came together at Niagara Falls in 1905 to fashion a new political agenda. They demanded that African Americans be allowed to exercise their constitutional right to vote; that segregation be abolished; and that barriers to black advancement be removed. They declared their commitment to freedom of speech, the brotherhood of all peoples, and respect for the workingman.

The 1908 Springfield riot had shaken whites. Some, especially those already involved in social reform, now joined in common cause with the Niagara movement. The following February, distinguished progressives, black and white, came together to found the **National Association for the Advancement of Colored People (NAACP)**, an organization dedicated to fighting racial discrimination and prejudice.

The formation of the NAACP marked the beginning of the modern civil rights movement. The organization published a magazine, *The Crisis*, edited by Du Bois, to publicize and protest lynchings, riots, and other abuses directed against blacks. Equally important was the Legal Redress Committee, which initiated lawsuits against city and state governments for violating the constitutional rights of African Americans. The committee scored its first major success in 1915, when the U.S. Supreme Court ruled that the so-called grandfather clauses of the Oklahoma and Maryland constitutions violated the Fifteenth Amendment. (These clauses allowed poor, uneducated whites—but not blacks—to vote, even if they failed to pay their state's poll tax or to pass its literacy test, by exempting from those provisions the descendants of men who had voted prior to 1867.)

FOCUS QUESTION

How did W. E. B. Du Bois's approach to reform for African Americans differ from that of Booker T. Washington?

QUICK REVIEW

ECONOMIC AND SOCIAL REFORM IN THE STATES

- Progressive alliances of middle-class reformers, working-class activists, and dynamic governors pioneered government regulation of the economy

- States regulated railroads and utilities, restricted child labor, and established state income taxes, minimum wages, and workmen's compensation

- "Wisconsin idea" brought together employers, trade unionists, and professionals to solve industrial problems

- Henry Ford used the principles of scientific management to great success in automobile manufacturing

- Modern civil rights movement was born with the founding of the NAACP in 1909

National Association for the Advancement of Colored People (NAACP) *Organization founded in 1909 to fight racial discrimination and prejudice and to promote civil rights for blacks.*

By 1914, the NAACP had enrolled thousands of members in scores of branches throughout the United States. The organization's success generated other civil rights groups. The National Urban League, founded in 1911, pressured urban employers to hire blacks, distributed lists of available jobs and housing in African American urban communities, and developed social programs to ease the adjustment of rural black migrants to city life.

Attacking segregation and discrimination through lawsuits was a slow strategy that would take decades to complete. The NAACP, although growing rapidly, was not large enough to qualify as a mass movement, and its interracial character made the organization seem dangerously radical to many whites. White NAACP leaders responded to this hostility by limiting the number and power of African Americans who worked for the organization. This policy angered black militants, who argued that no civil rights organization should be in the business of appeasing white racists. Despite such limitations, the NAACP, more than any other organization, helped resurrect the issue of racial equality at a time when most white Americans accepted racial segregation and discrimination as normal.

THE ROOSEVELT PRESIDENCY

FOCUS QUESTION

What would you identify as Roosevelt's three most important contributions to progressivism?

Progressives sought to increase their influence in national politics. State regulations seemed inadequate to the task of curtailing the power of the trusts, protecting workers, or monitoring the quality of consumer goods. The courts repeatedly struck down laws regulating working hours or setting minimum wages, on the grounds that they impinged on the freedom of contract and trade. A national progressive movement could force the passage of laws less vulnerable to judicial veto or elect a president who could overhaul the federal judiciary with progressive-minded judges.

National progressive leadership came from the executive branch, and from one president in particular. Upon McKinley's assassination in September 1901, Theodore Roosevelt, age 42, became the youngest chief executive in the nation's history. Although born to an aristocratic New York family, Roosevelt developed an uncommon affection for "the people." Asthmatic, sickly, and nearsighted as a boy, he remade himself into a vigorous adult. While Roosevelt indulged his appetite for high-risk adventure, he was also a voracious reader and an accomplished writer. Aggressive and swaggering in his public rhetoric, he was in private a skilled negotiator. A believer in the superiority of English-speaking peoples, he nevertheless assembled an administration that was diverse by the standards of the time. Rarely has a president's personality so enthralled the American public.

Regulating the Trusts

Roosevelt quickly revealed his flair for the dramatic. In 1902, he ordered the Justice Department to prosecute the Northern Securities Company, a $400 million monopoly that controlled railroad lines between Chicago and Washington State. In 1903, a federal court ordered

THEODORE ROOSEVELT. *The youthful and animated president addresses a crowd in Evanston, Illinois (a suburb of Chicago), in 1903.*

Northern Securities dissolved, and the U.S. Supreme Court upheld the decision the next year. Roosevelt was hailed as the nation's "trust-buster."

But Roosevelt did not want to break up all, or even most, large corporations. Industrial concentration, he believed, brought the United States wealth, productivity, and a rising standard of living. The role of government should be to regulate these industrial giants and to punish those that used their power improperly. This new role would require the federal government to expand its powers.

Toward a "Square Deal"

Roosevelt displayed his willingness to use government power to protect the economically weak in a 1902 coal miners' strike. Miners in the anthracite fields of eastern Pennsylvania wanted recognition for their union, the United Mine Workers (UMW). They also wanted a 10 percent to 20 percent increase in wages and an eight-hour day. When their employers, led by George F. Baer of the Reading Railroad, refused to negotiate, they went on strike. In October, the fifth month of the strike, Roosevelt summoned the mine owners and John Mitchell, the UMW president, to the White House. Baer expected Roosevelt to threaten the striking workers with arrest by federal troops if they failed to return to work. Instead, Roosevelt supported Mitchell's request for arbitration and warned the mine owners that if they refused to go along, 10,000 federal troops would seize their property. Stunned, the mine owners agreed to submit the dispute to arbitrators, who awarded the unionists a 10 percent wage increase and a nine-hour day.

Roosevelt enjoyed a surge of support from ordinary Americans following his intervention in the coal miners' strike. He also raised the hopes of African Americans when, only a month into his presidency, he dined with Booker T. Washington at the White House. In his 1904 election campaign, Roosevelt promised that, if reelected, he would offer every American a "Square Deal." The slogan resonated with voters and helped carry Roosevelt to a victory over the conservative Democrat nominee, Alton B. Parker.

Expanding Government Power: The Economy

Emboldened by his victory, Roosevelt intensified his efforts to extend government regulation of economic affairs. His most important proposal was to give the government power to set railroad shipping rates and thereby to eliminate the industry's discriminatory marketing practices. The government, in theory, already possessed this power through the Interstate Commerce Commission (ICC), but the courts had so weakened ICC oversight as to render it virtually powerless. In 1906, Congress passed the Hepburn Act, which increased the ICC's powers of rate review and enforcement. Roosevelt supported the Pure Food and Drug Act, passed by Congress that same year, which protected the public from fraudulently marketed foods and medications. He also campaigned for the Meat Inspection Act (1906), which obligated the government to monitor the quality and safety of meat being sold to American consumers.

Expanding Government Power: The Environment

Roosevelt did more than any previous president to extend federal control over the nation's physical environment. He oversaw the creation of 5 new national parks, 16 national monuments, and 53 wildlife reserves. The work of his administration led directly to the formation of the National Park Service in 1916.

Roosevelt also emerged a supporter of **conservation.** Conservationists cared little for national parks or grand canyons. They wanted to manage the environment to ensure the most efficient use of the nation's resources for economic development. Roosevelt shared the conservationists' belief that the plundering of western timberlands, grazing areas, water resources, and minerals had reached crisis proportions. He appointed a Public Lands Commission in 1903 to survey public lands, inventory them, and establish permit systems to regulate their use. Soon after, the Departments of Interior and Agriculture decreed that certain western lands rich in natural resources and waterpower could not be used for agricultural purposes. When political favoritism within the Departments of the Interior and Agriculture threatened these efforts at regulation, Roosevelt authorized the hiring of university-trained experts to replace state and local politicians. Scientific expertise, rather than political connections, would now determine the distribution and use of western lands.

Gifford Pinchot, a specialist in forestry management, led the drive for scientific management of natural resources. In 1905, he persuaded Roosevelt to relocate jurisdiction for the national forests from the Department of the Interior to the Department of Agriculture. The newly created National Forest Service quickly instituted a system of competitive bidding for the right to harvest timber on national forest lands. Pinchot and his expanding staff of college-educated foresters also exacted user fees from ranchers who had previously used national forest grazing lands for free. Armed with new legislation and bureaucratic authority, Pinchot and fellow conservationists in the Roosevelt administration declared vast stretches of federal land in the West off-limits to mining and dam construction.

The Republican Old Guard disliked these initiatives, and congressional conservatives struck back in 1907 with legislation that curtailed the president's power to create new government land reserves. Roosevelt responded by seizing another 17 million acres for national forest reserves before the new law went into effect. To his opponents, flouting the will of Congress with a 17-million-acre land grab violated the constitutional separation of powers. Yet, to millions of voters, Roosevelt's willingness to defy cattle barons, mining tycoons, and other "malefactors of great wealth" added to his popularity.

Progressivism: A Movement for the People?

Historians have long debated how much Roosevelt's economic and environmental reforms altered the balance of power between the "interests" and the people. Some have demonstrated that many corporations were eager for federal government regulation—that railroad corporations wanted relief from price wars that were driving them to bankruptcy, for example, and that the larger meatpackers believed that the costs of government food inspections would drive smaller meatpackers out of business. According to this view, government regulation benefited the corporations more than it benefited workers, consumers, and small businessmen.

Indeed, these early reforms often curtailed corporate power only to a limited extent. But in 1907, the progressive program was still evolving. Popular anger over the power of the corporations and over political corruption remained a driving force. The presence in the Senate of La Follette, Albert Beveridge of Indiana, and other anticorporate Republicans gave that anger a national voice. Whether the corporations or the people would benefit most remained unclear.[4]

The Republicans: A Divided Party

The financial panic of 1907 further strained relations between Roosevelt reformers and Old Guard conservatives. A failed effort by several New York banks to corner the

conservation *Movement that called for managing the environment to ensure the careful and efficient use of the nation's natural resources.*

QUICK REVIEW

ROOSEVELT'S EFFORTS AT NATIONAL REFORM

- Regulated large corporations in the interests of prosperity and the general welfare

- Supported organized labor and ordinary Americans in their dealings with corporations (the "Square Deal")

- Used government to protect the environment and promote conservation

- Left Republican Party in 1912 to found Progressive Party as an instrument of reform; labeled reform program the "New Nationalism"

copper market triggered a run on banks, a severe dip in industrial production, and widespread layoffs. Everywhere, people worried that a devastating depression was in the offing. Only the timely decision of J. P. Morgan and his fellow bankers to pour private cash into the collapsing banks saved the nation from an economic crisis.

The panic prompted Roosevelt to call for an overhaul of the banking system and for regulation of the stock market. The Republican Old Guard, meanwhile, was more determined than ever to run the "radical" Roosevelt out of the White House. Sensing that he might fail to win his party's nomination, and mindful of a rash promise he had made in 1904 not to run again in 1908, Roosevelt decided not to seek reelection. It was a decision that he would soon regret.

THE TAFT PRESIDENCY: PROGRESSIVE DISAPPOINTMENT AND RESURGENCE

Roosevelt thought he had found in **William Howard Taft**, his secretary of war, an ideal successor. Roosevelt believed Taft possessed both the ideas and the skills to complete the Republican reform program.

To reach that conclusion, however, Roosevelt had to ignore some obvious differences between Taft and himself. Taft was not particularly adept at politics. With the exception of a judgeship in an Ohio superior court, he had never held elective office. He was a cautious and conservative man. As Roosevelt's anointed successor, Taft won the election of 1908, defeating the Democrat William Jennings Bryan with 52 percent of the vote. But his conservatism soon revealed itself in his choice of corporation lawyers, rather than reformers, for cabinet positions.

Battling Congress

Taft's troubles began when he appeared to side against progressives in a congressional battle over tariff legislation. Progressives had long desired tariff reduction, believing that competition from foreign manufacturers would benefit American consumers and check the economic power of American manufacturers. Taft had raised expectations for tariff reduction when he called Congress into special session to consider a reform bill that called for a modest reduction of tariffs and an inheritance tax. The bill passed the House but was gutted in the Senate, and the Payne-Aldrich Tariff that Taft signed into law in 1909 did little to reduce tariffs. Progressive Republicans, bitterly disappointed, criticized Taft for not standing up to the Old Guard.

The Ballinger-Pinchot Controversy

A bruising fight over Taft's conservation policies brought relations between Taft and the progressive Republicans to the breaking point. Richard A. Ballinger, secretary of the interior, had aroused progressives' suspicions by reopening for private commercial use one million acres of land that the Roosevelt administration had previously brought under federal protection. Gifford Pinchot, still head of the National Forest Service, obtained information implicating Ballinger in the sale of Alaskan coal deposits to a private syndicate. Pinchot shared the information with Taft, who defended Ballinger. Pinchot went public with his charges and a congressional investigation ensued. Whatever hope Taft may have had of escaping political

William Howard Taft
Roosevelt's successor as president (1909–1913) who tried but failed to mediate between reformers and conservatives in the Republican Party.

damage disappeared when Roosevelt, returning from an African hunting trip by way of Europe in the spring of 1910, staged a public rendezvous with Pinchot in England. In signaling his support for his old friend Pinchot, Roosevelt was expressing displeasure with Taft.

Roosevelt's Return

Roosevelt had barely returned to the United States in summer 1910 when he dove back into politics. In September, Roosevelt embarked on a speaking tour, the high point of which was his elaboration at Osawatomie, Kansas, of his **New Nationalism**, a reform program that called for the federal government to stabilize the economy, protect the weak, and restore social harmony.

The 1910 congressional elections confirmed the popularity of Roosevelt's positions. Insurgent Republicans trounced conservative Republicans in primary after primary, and the Democrats' embrace of reform brought them a majority in the House of Representatives. In 1912, Roosevelt announced that he would challenge Taft for the Republican presidential nomination. In the 13 states sponsoring preferential primaries, Roosevelt won nearly 75 percent of the delegates, but the party's national leadership remained in the hands of the Old Guard, and they were determined to deny Roosevelt the nomination. At the Republican convention in Chicago, Taft won renomination on the first ballot.

The Bull Moose Campaign

Roosevelt had expected this outcome. He and his supporters withdrew from the Republican Party and soon reassembled as the new **Progressive Party.** This party nominated Roosevelt for president and California governor Hiram W. Johnson for vice president while hammering out an ambitious reform platform: sweeping regulation of the corporations, extensive protections for workers, a sharply graduated income tax, and woman suffrage. "I am as strong as a bull moose," Roosevelt roared to his supporters; his proud followers took to calling themselves **"Bull Moosers."**

Some of them, probably including Roosevelt, knew that their mission was futile. Too many Republicans who had supported Roosevelt in the primaries now refused to abandon the GOP. Consequently, the Republican vote would be split between Roosevelt and Taft, making them both vulnerable to the Democrats' candidate, Woodrow Wilson.

The Rise of Woodrow Wilson

The son of a Presbyterian minister from Virginia, Woodrow Wilson had practiced law for a short time after graduating from Princeton in 1879 before settling on an academic career. Earning his doctorate in political science from Johns Hopkins in 1886, he taught history and political science at Bryn Mawr and Wesleyan (Connecticut) before returning to Princeton in 1890. He became president of Princeton in 1902, a post he held until he ran for the governorship of New Jersey in 1910.

Identifying himself with the anti-Bryan wing of the Democratic Party, Wilson attracted the attention of wealthy conservatives. They convinced the bosses of the New Jersey Democratic machine to nominate Wilson for governor in 1910. Wilson accepted the nomination and won the governorship handily. He then shocked his conservative backers by declaring his independence from the state's Democratic machine and moving New Jersey into the forefront of reform.

New Nationalism *Roosevelt's reform program between 1910 and 1912, which called for establishing a strong federal government to regulate corporations, stabilize the economy, protect the weak, and restore social harmony.*

Progressive Party *Political party formed by Theodore Roosevelt in 1912 when the Republicans refused to nominate him for president. The party adopted a sweeping reform program.*

Bull Moosers *Followers of Theodore Roosevelt in the 1912 election.*

WOODROW WILSON. *The Democratic presidential candidate campaigning from the back of a train in 1912, pledging to fulfill progressivism's promise.*

The Election of 1912

At the Democratic convention of 1912, Wilson defeated House Speaker Champ Clark of Missouri on the fourth day and the 46th ballot to win the nomination. Given the split in Republican ranks, Democrats had their best chance in 20 years of regaining the White House. A Wilson victory, moreover, would give the country its first southern-born president in almost 50 years. Finally, whatever its outcome, the election promised to deliver a hefty vote for reform. Both Roosevelt and Wilson were running on reform platforms, and the Socialist Party candidate, Eugene V. Debs, was attracting large crowds and enthusiasm. Taft was so certain of defeat that he barely campaigned.

Debate among the candidates focused on the trusts. All three reform candidates agreed that corporations had acquired too much economic power. Debs argued that the only way to ensure popular control of that power was for the federal government to assume ownership of the trusts. Roosevelt called for the establishment of a strong government that would regulate and, if necessary, curb the power of the trusts—the essence of his New Nationalism.

Rather than regulate the trusts, Wilson wanted to break them up. He wanted to reverse the tendency toward economic concentration and thus restore opportunity to the people. This philosophy, which Wilson labeled the **"New Freedom,"** called for a temporary concentration of governmental power in order to dismantle the trusts. But once that was accomplished, Wilson promised, the government would relinquish its power.

New Freedom *Wilson's reform program of 1912 that called for temporarily concentrating government power so as to dismantle the trusts and return America to 19th-century conditions of competitive capitalism.*

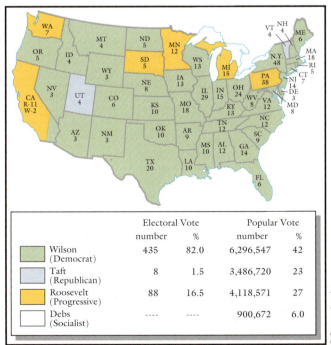

		Electoral Vote		Popular Vote	
		number	%	number	%
	Wilson (Democrat)	435	82.0	6,296,547	42
	Taft (Republican)	8	1.5	3,486,720	23
	Roosevelt (Progressive)	88	16.5	4,118,571	27
	Debs (Socialist)	----	----	900,672	6.0

***Map 21.3* Presidential Election, 1912.** *Taft and Roosevelt split the Republican vote, allowing Wilson to win with a plurality of the popular vote (42 percent) and a big majority (82 percent) of the electoral vote.*

Wilson won the November election with 42 percent of the popular vote to Roosevelt's 27 percent and Taft's 23 percent; Debs garnered 6 percent, the largest in his party's history (see Map 21.3).

THE WILSON PRESIDENCY

Wilson assembled a cabinet of talented men who could be counted on for wise counsel, loyalty, and influence over vital Democratic constituencies. He cultivated a public image of himself as a president firmly in charge of his party and as a faithful tribune of the people.

Tariff Reform and a Progressive Income Tax

Like Taft, Wilson first turned his attention to tariff reform. The House passed a tariff reduction bill within a month, and Wilson used his leadership skills to push the bill through a reluctant Senate. The resulting Underwood-Simmons Tariff of 1913 reduced tariff barriers from approximately 40 percent to 25 percent. To make up for revenue lost to tariff reduction, Congress then passed the first income tax law. It required the wealthy to pay taxes on a greater percentage of their income than the poor.

The Federal Reserve Act

> **Federal Reserve Act** *Act that brought private banks and public authority together to regulate and strengthen the nation's financial system.*

Wilson then asked Congress to overhaul the nation's financial system. The banking interests and their congressional supporters wanted the government to give the authority to regulate credit and currency flows either to a single bank or to several regional banks. Progressives opposed the vesting of so much financial power in private hands and insisted that any reformed financial system must be publicly controlled. Wilson worked out a compromise plan that included both private and public controls and marshaled the votes to push it through Congress. By the end of 1913 Wilson had signed the **Federal Reserve Act**, the most important law passed in his first administration.

The Federal Reserve Act established 12 regional banks, each controlled by the private banks in its region. Every private bank in the country was required to deposit an average of 6 percent of its assets in its regional Federal Reserve bank. The reserve would be used to make loans to member banks and to issue paper currency (Federal Reserve notes) to facilitate financial transactions. The regional banks would also use their funds to shore up member banks in distress and respond to sudden changes in credit demands by easing or tightening the flow of credit. A Federal Reserve Board appointed by the president and responsible to the public rather than to private bankers would set policy and oversee activities within the 12 reserve banks.

The Federal Reserve System strengthened the nation's financial structure, but in its final form revealed that Wilson was retreating from his New Freedom pledge. The Federal Reserve Board was a less powerful and less centralized federal authority than a national bank would have been. The bill authorizing the system made no attempt to break up private

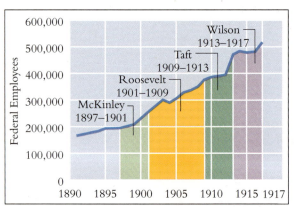

GROWTH IN FEDERAL EMPLOYMENT, 1891–1917

Source: Reprinted by permission from *The Federal Government Service*, ed. W. S. Sayre (Englewood Cliffs, NJ: Prentice-Hall, 1965), p. 41.

financial institutions that had grown too powerful. Because it sought to work with large banks rather than to break them up, the Federal Reserve System seemed more consonant with the principles of Roosevelt's New Nationalism than with those of Wilson's New Freedom.

From the New Freedom to the New Nationalism

Wilson's failure to mount a vigorous antitrust campaign confirmed his drift toward the New Nationalism. For example, in 1914 Wilson supported the Federal Trade Commission Act, which created a government agency by that name to regulate business practices. The FTC might have attacked trusts for "unfair trade practices," but the Senate stripped the FTC Act's companion legislation, the Clayton Antitrust Act, of virtually all provisions that would have allowed the government to prosecute the trusts. Wilson supported this weakening of the Clayton Act, having decided that the breakup of large-scale industry was no longer practical or preferable. In accepting the existing structure of business and in seeking to regulate its behavior, Wilson had become, in effect, a New Nationalist.

At first, Wilson's New Nationalism led him to support business interests. But in late 1915 Wilson moved to the left, in part because he feared losing his reelection in 1916. The Bull Moosers of 1912 were retreating back to the Republican Party. To halt the progressives' rapprochement with the GOP, Wilson bid for their support by nominating Louis Brandeis to the Supreme Court. Not only was Brandeis a respected progressive, he was also the first Jew nominated to serve on the country's highest court. Congressional conservatives did everything they could to block the confirmation of a man they considered dangerously radical, but Wilson was better organized, and by June his forces in the Senate had emerged victorious.

Wilson followed up this victory by pushing through Congress the first federal workmen's compensation law (the Kern-McGillicuddy Act, which covered federal employees), the first federal law outlawing child labor (the Keating-Owen Act), and the first federal law guaranteeing workers an eight-hour day (the Adamson Act, which covered the nation's 400,000 railway workers). Although the number of Americans affected by these acts was relatively small, Wilson had reoriented the Democratic Party to a New Nationalism that cared as much about the interests of the powerless as the interests of the powerful.

Trade unionists flocked to Wilson, as did most of the prominent progressives who had followed the Bull Moose in 1912. Meanwhile, Wilson had appealed to the supporters of William Jennings Bryan by supporting legislation that made federal credit available to farmers in need. He had put together a reform coalition capable of winning a majority at the polls. From 1916 on, the Democrats, rather than the Republicans, became the chief guardians of America's reform tradition.

QUICK REVIEW

WILSON'S EFFORTS AT NATIONAL REFORM

- Claimed he would break up corporate trusts ("New Freedom"), but ended up similar to Roosevelt in his efforts to regulate them

- Most important laws overhauled financial system, reduced tariffs, instituted national income tax, and offered some groups of workers protection at workplace

- Appointed Louis Brandeis to Supreme Court

Conclusion

By 1916, the progressives had accomplished a great deal. They exposed and curbed some of the worst abuses of the American political system. They enfranchised some women and took steps to protect the environment. They broke the hold of laissez-faire economic policies on national politics and replaced it with the idea of a strong federal government committed to economic regulation and social justice. They enlarged the executive branch by establishing new commissions and agencies charged with administering government policies.

The progressives, in short, had presided over the emergence of a new national state, one in which power increasingly flowed away from municipalities and states and toward the federal government. This reorientation followed a compelling logic: A national government stood a better chance of solving the problems of economic inequality, mismanagement of natural resources, and consumer fraud than did local and state governments.

The promise of effective federal government intervention, however, also brought the possibility that government administrators might use their power to fashion themselves into a new bureaucratic elite. Some progressive reformers were doing as much to advance their own interests or those of their corporate allies as they were helping to improve the welfare of ordinary Americans. But these elitist tendencies did not go unchallenged. The democratic movements of the progressive era—those involving workers, women, minorities, consumers, and environmentalists—were determined to hold both elected and appointed government officials accountable to the popular will. The struggle between the contrasting progressive impulses toward democracy and elitism would manifest itself not simply in domestic politics but also in foreign affairs, where the United States was seeking to balance its interest in spreading liberty with the protection of its international economic interests.

CHAPTER REVIEW

Review

1. How did Protestantism influence reform?
2. What was "realism" and how did it spur investigative reporting and reform?
3. What contributions did associations of women reformers make to progressivism?
4. What was the relationship of socialism to progressivism?
5. What were the benefits and costs of municipal reform?
6. What were the results of progressive efforts to create a "responsible" and "virtuous" electorate?
7. How did W. E. B. Du Bois's approach to reform for African Americans differ from that of Booker T. Washington?
8. What would you identify as Roosevelt's three most important contributions to progressive reform?

Critical Thinking

1. Progressivism sought to reform all of American society—its politics, its economy, and culture. What were the most important reforms in each of these realms? Were these reforms successful in achieving their aims?
2. When the progressive reform movement peaked during the first Wilson administration (1913–1917), did it bring Americans greater liberty and equality than they had known in 1900?

Identifications

Review your understanding of the following key terms, people, and events for this chapter.

muckrakers, p. 480
realism, p. 480
Hull House, p. 481
socialism, p. 483
initiative, p. 487
referendum, p. 487
recall, p. 487

Australian ballot (secret ballot), p. 487
disfranchisement, p. 488
National American Woman Suffrage Association, p. 488
scientific management, p. 492

National Association for the Advancement of Colored People (NAACP), p. 493
conservation, p. 496
William Howard Taft, p. 497

New Nationalism, p. 498
Progressive Party, p. 498
Bull Moosers, p. 498
New Freedom, p. 499
Federal Reserve Act, p. 500

DISCOVERY

Was progressivism successful in reforming politics and culture in America?

In thinking about this question, begin by breaking it down into the components shown below. A discussion of the significance of each component should appear in your answer.

Government and Law

Examine the graph on voter participation. Compare the percentage of voter participation in 1876 to that of 1912, noting the significant decrease. What factors account for the drop over these elections? Why did the greatest decline in voting occur in the southern states? Is this decline in voting attributable to changes wrought by the progressive movement, or is it more the result of resistance to progressivism?

Culture and Society

Study the table on women and higher education on page 482. How did women's activism and education help them achieve electoral power? What role did women like Jane Addams (page 482) play in both the progressive and women's movements? Did women achieve significant, long-lasting reforms? What reforms did they consider the most important? What methods did they use to achieve them? Have women today achieved all that the progressive reformers hoped to achieve?

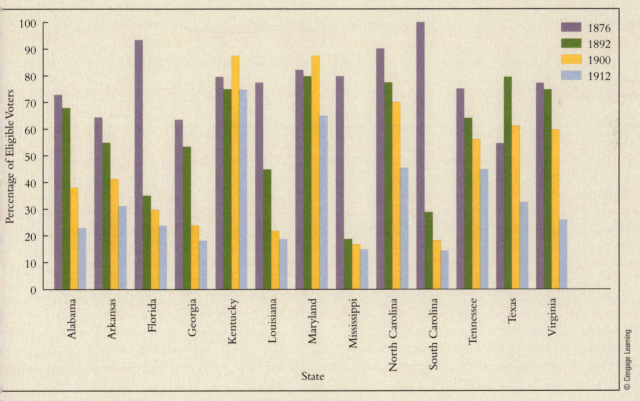

© Cengage Learning

VOTER PARTICIPATION IN 13 SOUTHERN STATES, 1876, 1892, 1900, 1912.

CourseMate

Visit the CourseMate website at www.cengagebrain.com for additional study tools and review materials for this chapter.

BECOMING A WORLD POWER, 1898–1917

THE UNITED STATES LOOKS ABROAD
  Protestant Missionaries
  Businessmen
  Imperialists

THE SPANISH–AMERICAN WAR
  "A Splendid Little War"

THE UNITED STATES BECOMES A WORLD POWER
  The Debate over the Treaty of Paris
  The American–Filipino War

Controlling Cuba and Puerto Rico
China and the "Open Door"

THEODORE ROOSEVELT, GEOPOLITICIAN
  The Roosevelt Corollary
  The Panama Canal
  Keeping the Peace in East Asia

WILLIAM HOWARD TAFT, DOLLAR DIPLOMAT

WOODROW WILSON, STRUGGLING IDEALIST

For much of the 19th century, most Americans were preoccupied by continental expansion. The nation's rapid industrial growth toward the end of that century forced a turn away from such continentalism. Technological advances, especially the laying of transoceanic cables and the introduction of steamship travel, diminished America's physical isolation. The babble of languages one could hear in American cities testified to how much the Old World had penetrated the New. Then, too, Americans watched anxiously as England, Germany, Russia, Japan, and other industrial powers intensified their competition for overseas markets and colonies. Some believed America needed to enter this contest.

War with Spain in 1898 gave the United States an opportunity to upgrade its military and acquire colonies and influence in the Western Hemisphere and Asia. Not all Americans supported this imperial project, and many protested the subjugation of the peoples of Cuba, Puerto Rico, and the Philippines. In the eyes of these anti-imperialists, the United States seemed to be becoming the kind of nation that many Americans had long despised—one that valued power more than liberty.

Exercising imperial power did not trouble President Theodore Roosevelt, who wanted to create an international system in which a handful of industrial nations pursued their global economic interests, dominated world trade, and kept the world at peace. It did concern Woodrow Wilson, who sought to devise a policy toward post-revolutionary Mexico that restrained American might and respected Mexican desires for liberty. It was a worthy ambition but one that proved exceedingly difficult to achieve.

TIMELINE

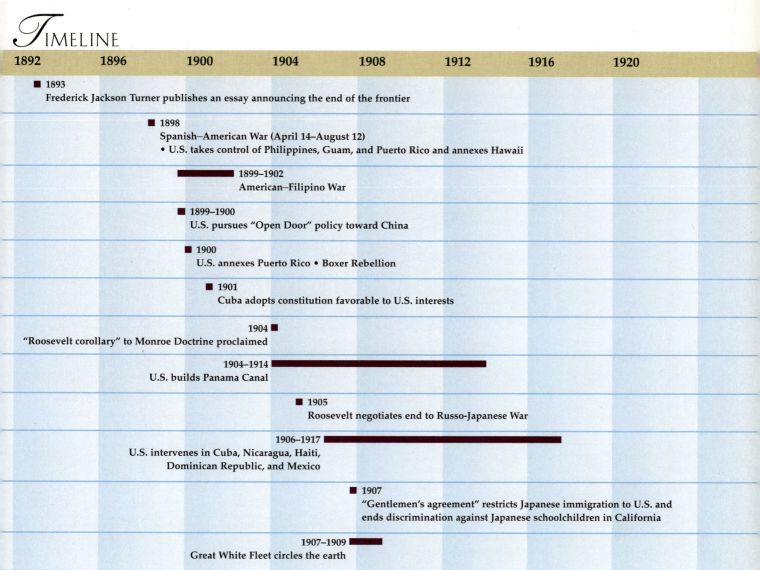

| 1892 | 1896 | 1900 | 1904 | 1908 | 1912 | 1916 | 1920 |

■ 1893
Frederick Jackson Turner publishes an essay announcing the end of the frontier

■ 1898
Spanish–American War (April 14–August 12)
• U.S. takes control of Philippines, Guam, and Puerto Rico and annexes Hawaii

1899–1902
American–Filipino War

■ 1899–1900
U.S. pursues "Open Door" policy toward China

■ 1900
U.S. annexes Puerto Rico • Boxer Rebellion

■ 1901
Cuba adopts constitution favorable to U.S. interests

1904 ■
"Roosevelt corollary" to Monroe Doctrine proclaimed

1904–1914
U.S. builds Panama Canal

■ 1905
Roosevelt negotiates end to Russo-Japanese War

1906–1917
U.S. intervenes in Cuba, Nicaragua, Haiti,
Dominican Republic, and Mexico

■ 1907
"Gentlemen's agreement" restricts Japanese immigration to U.S. and
ends discrimination against Japanese schoolchildren in California

1907–1909
Great White Fleet circles the earth

1909–1913
William Howard Taft conducts "dollar diplomacy"

THE UNITED STATES LOOKS ABROAD

By the late 19th century, many Americans had become interested in extending their country's influence abroad. The most important groups were Protestant missionaries, businessmen, and imperialists.

Protestant Missionaries

Protestant missionary activity grew quickly between 1870 and 1900, most of it directed toward China. Convinced of the superiority of the Anglo-Saxon race, these missionaries considered it their Christian duty to teach the gospel to the "ignorant" Asian masses and save their souls. Missionaries also believed that their efforts would free those masses from their racial destiny, enabling them to become "civilized."

FOCUS QUESTION

Which groups in American society were most interested in expanding U.S. influence abroad?

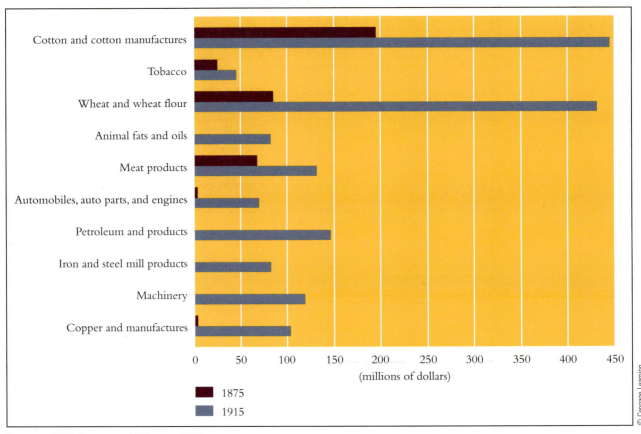

LEADING U.S. EXPORTS, 1875 AND 1915

Source: Data from *Historical Statistics of the United States, Colonial Times to 1970* (White Plains, N.Y.: Kraus International, 1989).

Businessmen

Financial gains in foreign lands.

Industrialists, traders, and investors also began to look overseas, sensing that they could make fortunes in foreign lands. Exports of American manufactured goods rose substantially after 1880. By 1914, American foreign investment equaled 7 percent of the nation's gross national product. Companies such as Eastman Kodak, Singer Sewing Machine, Standard Oil, American Tobacco, and International Harvester had become multinational corporations with overseas branch offices.

Frederick Jackson Turner's frontier thesis intensified the appeal of foreign markets among many white Americans (see Chapter 18). For them, as for Turner, concern about the disappearing frontier expressed a fear that the increasingly urbanized and industrialized nation had lost its way. Turner's essay appeared just as the country was entering the deepest, longest, and most conflict-ridden depression in its history (see Chapter 19). Overseas markets offered new frontiers that would allow the republic to regain its economic prosperity and political stability.

Imperialists

Army power to expand

A group of politicians, intellectuals, and military strategists viewed overseas economic expansion as essential to the pursuit of world power. They believed that the United States should build a strong navy, solidify a sphere of influence in the Caribbean, and extend markets into Asia. Their desire to control ports and territories beyond the continental borders of their own country made them imperialists.

Perhaps the most influential imperialist was Admiral Alfred Thayer Mahan. In a widely read book, *The Influence of Sea Power upon History, 1660–1783* (1890),

TABLE 22.1

THE U.S. NAVY, 1890–1914: EXPENDITURES AND BATTLESHIP SIZE				
Fiscal Year	Total Federal Expenditures	Naval Expenditures	Naval Expenditures as Percent of Total Federal Expenditures	Size of Battleships (average tons displaced)
1890	$318,040,711	$ 22,006,206	6.9%	11,000
1900	520,860,847	55,953,078	10.7	12,000
1901	524,616,925	60,506,978	11.5	16,000
1905	657,278,914	117,550,308	20.7	16,000
1909	693,743,885	115,546,011	16.7	27,000 (1910)
1914	735,081,431	139,682,186	19.0	32,000

Sources: (for expenditures) E. B. Potter, *Sea Power: A Naval History* (Annapolis: Naval Institute Press, 1982), p. 187; (for size of ships) Harold Sprout, *Toward a New Order of Sea Power* (New York: Greenwood Press, 1976), p. 52.

Mahan argued that all past empires, beginning with Rome, had relied on their capacity to control the seas. He called for the construction of a U.S. navy with enough ships and firepower to make its presence felt across the world. To be effective, that global fleet would require a canal across Central America and a string of far-flung service bases. Mahan recommended that the U.S. government take possession of Hawaii and other strategically located Pacific islands with superior harbor facilities.

Presidents William McKinley and Theodore Roosevelt would eventually make almost the whole of Mahan's vision a reality, but, in the early 1890s, Mahan doubted that Americans would accept the responsibility and costs of empire. Many Americans still insisted that the United States should not aspire to world power by acquiring overseas bases and colonizing foreign peoples.

Mahan underestimated the government's alarm over the scramble of Europeans to extend their imperial control. Every administration from the 1880s on committed itself to a "big navy" policy (see Table 22.1). Already in 1878, the United States had secured rights to Pago Pago, a superb deepwater harbor in Samoa (a collection of islands in the southwest Pacific inhabited by Polynesians), and in 1885, it had leased Pearl Harbor from the Hawaiians. Both harbors were expected to serve as fueling stations for the growing U.S. fleet.

These attempts to project U.S. power overseas had already deepened the U.S. government's involvement in the affairs of distant lands. In 1889, the United States established a protectorate over part of Samoa. In the early 1890s, President Grover Cleveland's administration was increasingly drawn into Hawaiian affairs, as tensions between American sugar plantation owners and native Hawaiians upset the islands' economic and political stability. In 1891, plantation owners managed to depose the Hawaiian king and put into power Queen Liliuokalani. When Liliuokalani strove to establish her independence, the planters, assisted by U.S. sailors, overthrew her too. Cleveland declared Hawaii a protectorate in 1893, but he resisted the imperialists in Congress who wanted to annex the islands.

Still, imperialist sentiment in Congress and throughout the nation continued to grow, fueled by "jingoism." Jingoists were nationalists who thought that a swaggering foreign policy and a willingness to go to war would enhance their nation's glory. Spain's behavior in Cuba in the 1890s gave jingoists the war they sought.

[handwritten marginal note:] Alfred Thayer Mahan. "The Influence of Sea Power Upon History" – idea of canal in central america (see Panama Canal)

QUICK REVIEW

ROOTS OF AMERICAN EXPANSION

- Protestant missionaries spread the gospel to "less civilized" people

- Businessmen pursued overseas markets

- Imperialists pushed the United States to become a world power with a big navy and control of foreign ports and territory

THE SPANISH–AMERICAN WAR

FOCUS QUESTION

In going to war against Spain in 1898, was the United States impelled more by imperialist or anti-imperialist motives?

[handwritten margin notes: U.S. helping Cubans from Spanish. General Valeriano "Butcher" Weyler]

yellow journalism *Newspaper stories embellished with sensational or titillating details when the true reports did not seem dramatic enough.*

QUICK REVIEW

THE SPANISH–AMERICAN WAR, 1898

- Cuban efforts to gain independence from Spain drew U.S. sympathy. The 1898 sinking of the *Maine* in Havana harbor prompted United States to declare war

- United States victorious in five months, chiefly as a result of naval superiority and lack of Spanish will to fight

- Treaty of Paris (December 10, 1898) granted United States formal control over the Philippines, Guam, and Puerto Rico and informal control over Cuba

Relations between the Cubans and their Spanish rulers had long been deteriorating. The Spanish had taken 10 years to subdue a revolt begun in 1868. In 1895, the Cubans staged another revolt. Cuban forces destroyed large areas of the island to render it uninhabitable by the Spanish. The Spanish army, led by General Valeriano Weyler, responded in kind, forcing large numbers of Cubans into concentration camps. Denied adequate food, shelter, and sanitation, an estimated 200,000 Cubans—one-eighth of the island's population—died of starvation and disease.

Many Americans sympathized with the Cubans, who seemed to be fighting the kind of anticolonial war Americans had waged more than 100 years earlier. They stayed informed about Cuban-Spanish struggles by reading the *New York Journal,* owned by William Randolph Hearst, and the *New York World,* owned by Joseph Pulitzer. To boost circulation, Hearst and Pulitzer sought out sensational and shocking stories and described them in lurid detail. They were accused of engaging in **"yellow journalism"**—embellishing stories with titillating details when the true reports did not seem dramatic enough.

The sensationalism of the yellow press and its frequently jingoistic accounts were not sufficient to bring about American intervention in Cuba, however. In the final days of his administration, President Cleveland resisted mounting pressure to intervene. William McKinley, who succeeded him in 1897, denounced the Spanish, with the aim of forcing Spain into concessions that would satisfy the Cuban rebels and end the conflict. Initially, this strategy seemed to be working: Spain relieved "Butcher" Weyler of his command, began releasing incarcerated Cubans from concentration camps, and granted Cuba limited autonomy. But the Spaniards living on the island refused the authority of a Cuban government, and Cuban rebels continued to demand full independence. Late in 1897, when riots broke out in Havana, McKinley ordered the battleship *Maine* into Havana harbor to protect U.S. citizens and their property.

Two unexpected events then set off a war. The first was the February 9, 1898, publication in Hearst's *New York Journal* of a letter stolen from Enrique Depuy de Lôme, the Spanish minister to Washington, in which he described McKinley as "a cheap politician" and a "bidder for the admiration of the crowd." The de Lôme letter also implied that the Spanish cared little about resolving the Cuban crisis through negotiation and reform. The news embarrassed Spanish officials and outraged the United States. Then, only six days later, the *Maine* exploded in Havana harbor, killing 260 American sailors. Although subsequent investigations revealed that the most probable cause of the explosion was a malfunctioning boiler, Americans were certain that it had been the work of Spanish agents. "Remember the *Maine*!" screamed the headlines in the yellow press.

On March 8, Congress responded to the clamor for war by authorizing $50 million to mobilize U.S. forces. In the meantime, McKinley notified Spain of his conditions for avoiding war: Spain would pay an indemnity for the *Maine,* abandon its concentration camps, end the fighting with the rebels, and commit itself to Cuban independence. On April 9, Spain accepted all the demands but the last; on April 11, McKinley asked Congress for authority to go to war. Three days later Congress approved a war resolution, which included a declaration (spelled out in the Teller Amendment) that the United States would not use the

Chicago History Museum

"REMEMBER THE MAINE!" *The explosion of the battleship* Maine *in Havana harbor on February 15, 1898, killed 260 American sailors and helped drive the United States into war with Spain.*

war as an opportunity to acquire territory in Cuba. On April 24, Spain responded with a formal declaration of war against the United States.

"A Splendid Little War"

Secretary of State John Hay called the fight with Spain "a splendid little war." Begun in April, it ended in August. More than one million men volunteered to fight, and fewer than 500 were killed or wounded in combat. The American victory over Spain was complete, not just in Cuba but in the neighboring island of Puerto Rico and in the Philippines, Spain's strategic possession in the Pacific.

Actually, the war was more complicated than it seemed. The main reason for the easy victory was U.S. naval superiority. In the war's first major battle, a naval engagement in Manila harbor in the Philippines on May 1, a U.S. fleet commanded by Commodore George Dewey destroyed an entire Spanish fleet and lost only one sailor (to heatstroke). On land, the story was different. On the eve of war, the U.S. Army consisted of only 26,000 troops. A force of 80,000 Spanish regulars awaited them in Cuba. Congress immediately increased the army to 62,000 and called for an additional 125,000 volunteers. The response to this call was astounding, but outfitting, training, and transporting the new recruits overwhelmed the army's capacities. Its blue flannel uniforms proved too heavy for fighting in Cuba. Most of the volunteers had to make do with old Civil War rifles. The army was unprepared for the effects of malaria and other tropical diseases.

[handwritten margin notes: April to August. US won due to navy size. Spanish had advantage on land army) (causing the U.S. to send reinforcements.]

That the Cuban revolutionaries were predominantly black also came as a shock to the U.S. forces. In their attempts to arouse support for the Cuban cause, U.S. newspapers had portrayed the Cuban rebels as fundamentally similar to white Americans, with an "Anglo-Saxon tenacity of purpose." The Spanish oppressors, by contrast, were depicted as dark complexioned and as possessing the characteristics of their "dark race": barbarism, cruelty, and indolence. The U.S. troops' first encounters with Cuban and Spanish forces challenged these stereotypes. Their Cuban allies appeared poorly outfitted, rough mannered, and primarily black skinned. The Spanish soldiers appeared well disciplined, tough in battle, and light complexioned.

The Cuban rebels were skilled guerrilla fighters, but racial prejudice prevented most U.S. soldiers and reporters from crediting their military expertise. Instead, they judged the Cubans as primitive, savage, and incapable of self-control or self-government. White U.S. troops preferred not to fight alongside the Cubans; increasingly, they refused to coordinate strategy with them.

At first, the U.S. Army's logistical unpreparedness and its racial misconceptions did little to diminish the soldiers' hunger for a good fight. No one was more eager for battle than Theodore Roosevelt who, along with Colonel Leonard Wood, led a volunteer cavalry unit composed of Ivy League gentlemen, western cowboys, sheriffs, prospectors, Indians, and a small number of Hispanics and ethnic European Americans. Roosevelt's **Rough Riders**, as the unit came to be known, landed with the invasion force and played an active role in the three battles fought in the hills surrounding Santiago (see inset of Map 22.1).

Rough Riders *Much-decorated volunteer cavalry unit organized by Theodore Roosevelt and Leonard Wood to fight in Cuba in 1898.*

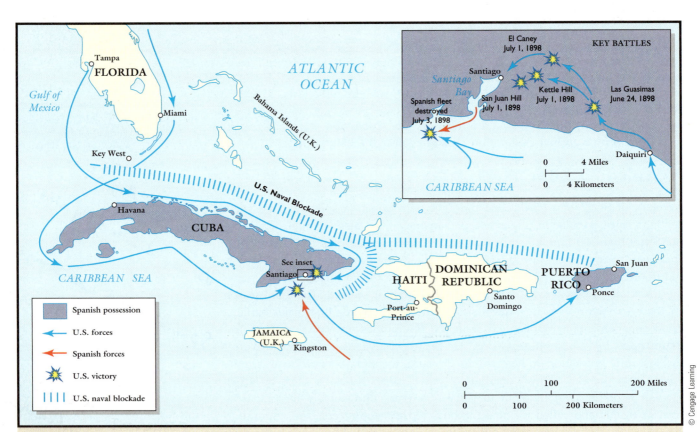

Map 22.1 Spanish–American War in Cuba, 1898. *This map shows the following: the routes taken by U.S. ships transporting troops from Florida to Cuba; the concentration of troop landings and battles around Santiago, Cuba; and a U.S. naval blockade, stretching hundreds of miles from Puerto Rico to Cuba, that attempted to keep the Spanish troops in Cuba and Puerto Rico from being reinforced.*

Their most famous action was a furious charge up Kettle Hill into the teeth of Spanish defenses. Roosevelt's bravery was stunning, though his judgment was faulty. Nearly 100 men were killed or wounded.

Reports of Roosevelt's bravery overshadowed the equally brave performance of black troops, notably the **9th and 10th Negro Cavalries**, which played a pivotal role in clearing away Spanish fortifications on Kettle Hill. One Rough Rider commented: "If it had not been for the Negro cavalry, the Rough Riders would have been exterminated." The 24th and 25th Negro Infantry Regiments performed equally vital tasks in the U.S. Army's conquest of the adjacent San Juan Hill.

African American soldiers risked their lives despite the segregationist policies that confined them to all-black regiments. Yet the fury of the fighting so scrambled the white and black regiments that they became racially intermixed. The black troops, Roosevelt declared, were "an excellent breed of Yankee," and no "Rough Rider will ever forget," he added, "the tie that binds us to the Ninth and Tenth Cavalry." But soon after returning home, Roosevelt downplayed the role of black troops and questioned their ability to fight. The attack on black fighting abilities would become so widespread that by the start of the First World War, the U.S. military had largely excluded black troops from combat roles. Thus, an episode that had demonstrated the possibility of interracial cooperation ended in the hardening of racial boundaries.

The taking of Kettle Hill, San Juan Hill, and other high ground surrounding Santiago gave the U.S. forces a substantial advantage over the Spanish defenders. Nevertheless, the troops were short of food, ammunition, and medical facilities. Their ranks were devastated by malaria, typhoid, and dysentery; more than 5,000 soldiers died from disease. Fortunately, the Spanish had lost the will to fight. On July 3, Spain's Atlantic fleet tried to retreat from Santiago harbor and was promptly destroyed by a U. S. fleet. The Spanish army in Santiago surrendered on July 16; on July 18 the Spanish government asked for peace. While negotiations for an armistice proceeded, U.S. forces overran the neighboring island of Puerto Rico. On August 12, the U.S. and Spanish governments agreed to an armistice. But before the news could reach the Philippines, the United States had captured Manila and had taken prisoner 13,000 Spanish soldiers.

The armistice required Spain to relinquish its claim to Cuba, cede Puerto Rico and the Pacific island of Guam to the United States, and tolerate the American occupation of Manila until a peace conference could be convened in Paris on October 1, 1898. At that conference, American diplomats startled their Spanish counterparts by demanding that Spain also cede the Philippines to the United States. After two months of stalling, the Spanish government agreed to relinquish its coveted Pacific colony for $20 million, and the transaction was sealed by the Treaty of Paris on December 10, 1898.

ROUGH RIDERS AND 10TH CAVALRY. *Roosevelt stands with his Rough Riders (top image) while members of the 10th Cavalry pose in the bottom image. Both groups played pivotal roles in the battles of San Juan Hill and Kettle Hill, but America would celebrate only the Rough Riders, not the black cavalrymen.*

9th and 10th Negro Cavalries
African American army units that played pivotal roles in the Spanish–American war.

THE UNITED STATES BECOMES A WORLD POWER

FOCUS QUESTION

What different mechanisms of control did the United States use to achieve its aims in Hawaii, Cuba, the Philippines, Puerto Rico, and China?

America's initial war aim, to oust the Spanish from Cuba, was supported by both imperialists and anti-imperialists, but for different reasons. Imperialists hoped to incorporate Cuba into a new American empire; anti-imperialists hoped to see the Cubans gain their independence. But only the imperialists condoned the U.S. acquisition of Puerto Rico, Guam, and the Philippines, and, soon after the war began, President McKinley had cast his lot with them. First, he annexed Hawaii, giving the United States permanent control of Pearl Harbor. Next, he established a U.S. naval base at Manila. Never before had the United States sought such a large military presence outside the Western Hemisphere (see Map 22.2).

In a departure of equal importance, McKinley announced his intent to administer much of this newly acquired territory as U.S. colonies. Virtually all the territory previously gained by the United States had been settled by Americans, who had eventually petitioned for statehood. Of these new territories, however, only Hawaii would be allowed to follow this traditional path. There, the powerful American sugar plantation owners prevailed on Congress to pass an act in 1900 extending U.S. citizenship to all Hawaiian citizens. No such influential group of Americans resided in the Philippines. The country was made a U.S. colony to prevent other powers, such as Japan and Germany, from gaining a foothold in the 400-island archipelago and launching attacks on the American naval base in Manila.

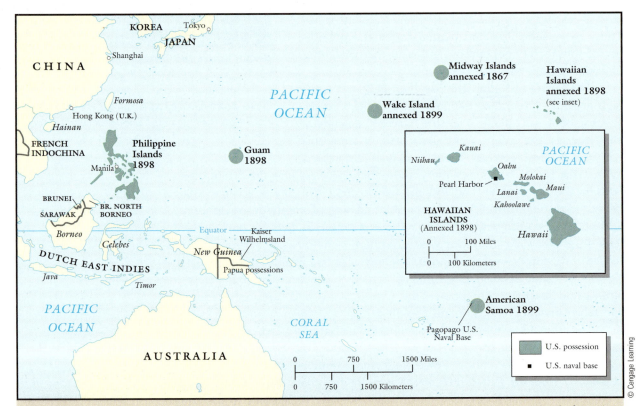

Map 22.2 American South Pacific Empire, 1900. *By 1900, the American South Pacific empire consisted of a series of strategically located islands with superior harbor facilities, stretching from the Hawaiian Islands and Samoa in the middle of the Pacific to the Philippines on the ocean's western edge.*

The McKinley administration might have negotiated an arrangement with **Emilio Aguinaldo**, a Filipino anticolonial leader, that would have given the Philippines independence in exchange for a U.S. naval base at Manila. Alternatively, the United States might have annexed the Philippines outright and offered Filipinos U.S. citizenship as the first step toward statehood. But McKinley and his supporters believed that self-government was beyond the capacity of the "inferior" Filipino people. The United States would undertake a solemn mission to "civilize" the Filipinos and thereby prepare them for independence. Until that mission was complete, the Philippines would be ruled by American governors appointed by the president.

The Debate over the Treaty of Paris

The proposed acquisition of the Philippines aroused opposition both in the United States and in the Philippines. The Anti-Imperialist League enlisted the support of several elder statesmen in McKinley's own party, as well as former Democratic president Grover Cleveland, industrialist Andrew Carnegie, and labor leader Samuel Gompers. William Jennings Bryan, meanwhile, marshaled protest among Democrats in the South and West. Some anti-imperialists believed that the subjugation of the Filipinos would violate the nation's most precious principle: the right of all people to independence and self-government.

Other anti-imperialists were motivated more by self-interest than by democratic ideals. U.S. sugar producers feared competition from Filipino producers. Trade unionists worried that poor Filipino workers would flood the U.S. labor market and depress wages. Some businessmen warned that the costs of maintaining an imperial outpost would exceed any economic benefits. Still other anti-imperialists feared the contaminating effects of contact with "inferior" Asian races.

The anti-imperialists almost dealt McKinley and his fellow imperialists a defeat in the U.S. Senate. On February 6, 1899, the Senate voted 57 to 27 in favor of the Treaty of Paris, only one vote beyond the minimum two-thirds majority required for ratification. Two last-minute developments may have brought victory. First, William Jennings Bryan, in the days just before the vote, abandoned his opposition and announced his support for the treaty. Second, on the eve of the vote, Filipinos rose in revolt against the U.S. army of occupation. With another war looming and the lives of American soldiers imperiled, a few senators who had been reluctant to vote for the treaty may have felt obligated to support the president.

The American–Filipino War

The acquisition of the Philippines immediately embroiled the United States in a brutal war to subdue the Filipino rebels. In four years of fighting, more than 120,000 American soldiers served in the Philippines, and more than 4,200 died. The war brought Americans face to face with an unpleasant truth: that U.S. actions in the Philippines were virtually indistinguishable from Spain's actions in Cuba. Like Spain, the United States refused to acknowledge a people's aspiration for self-rule. Like "Butcher" Weyler, American generals permitted their soldiers to drive whole communities into concentration camps and destroy their houses, farms, and livestock. American soldiers executed so many Filipino rebels that the ratio of Filipino dead to wounded reached 15 to 1. Estimates of total Filipino deaths from gunfire, starvation, and disease range from 50,000 to 200,000.

Emilio Aguinaldo *Anticolonial leader who fought for independence of the Philippines, first from Spain and then from the United States.*

THE "WATER CURE" IN THE PHILIPPINES. *This extraordinary photograph shows U.S. soldiers forcing water into the mouth of a Filipino guerrilla to the point where it would overflow his esophagus and pour into his breathing channels, creating the sensation of drowning. The image reveals U.S. forces using brutal tactics to break down the resistance of their Filipino opponents.*

"A Philippine Album: American Era Photographs" by Jonathan Best. (Bookmark, Manila 1998)

Platt Amendment *Clause that the United States forced Cuba to insert into its constitution, giving it broad <u>control over Cuba's foreign and domestic policies.</u>*

The United States finally gained the upper hand after General Arthur MacArthur (father of Douglas) was appointed commander of the islands in 1900. MacArthur did not lessen the war's ferocity, but he understood that it could not be won by guns alone. He offered amnesty to Filipino guerrillas who agreed to surrender, and he cultivated close relations with the islands' economic elites. McKinley supported this effort to build a Filipino constituency sympathetic to the U.S. presence. He sent William Howard Taft to the islands in 1900 to establish a civilian government. In 1901, Taft became the colony's first "governor-general." He transferred many governmental functions to Filipino control and launched a program of public works. By 1902, this dual strategy of ruthless war against those who had taken up arms and concessions to those who were willing to live under benevolent American rule had crushed the revolt, though sporadic fighting continued until 1913.

Controlling Cuba and Puerto Rico

Helping the Cubans achieve independence had been a major rationalization for the war against Spain. Even so, in 1900, when General Leonard Wood, now commander of U.S. forces in Cuba, authorized a constitutional convention to write the laws for a Cuban republic, the McKinley administration made clear it would not easily relinquish control of the island. At McKinley's urging, the U.S. Congress attached to a 1901 army appropriations bill the **Platt Amendment**, delineating three conditions for Cuban independence. First, Cuba would not be permitted to make treaties with foreign powers. Second, the United States would have broad authority to intervene in Cuban political and economic affairs. Third, Cuba would sell or lease land to the United States for naval stations. The delegates to Cuba's constitutional convention were outraged, but the dependence of Cuba's vital sugar industry on the U.S. market and the continuing presence of a U.S. army rendered resistance futile. By a vote of 15 to 11, the delegates reluctantly wrote the Platt conditions into their constitution.

Cuba's status differed little from that of the Philippines. Both were politically subordinate to the United States. In the case of Cuba, economic dependence closely

MUSICAL LINK TO THE PAST

Music for Patriots

Composers: John Philip Sousa
Title: "Stars and Stripes Forever" (circa 1895)

In the five years following the writing of "Stars and Stripes Forever," John Philip Sousa was probably the most famous musician in America. When he and his band arrived in town, a holiday atmosphere ensued: Flags flew, schools closed, and businesses released their workers for the day. International respect for American music grew as Sousa helped dispel the pervasive stereotype that the United States could not produce high-culture musical works and performers. Most famous composers had built their reputations on symphonies. For Sousa, symphonies were pretentious, full of padding, and dawdled before they reached their most crowd-pleasing sections. Sousa favored short, snappy, and often patriotic three-minute pieces such as "Stars and Stripes Forever."

Sousa viewed music as entertainment: He insisted on giving audiences what they wanted, and plenty of it. He did not mandate what audiences should hear, as most classical conductors did; instead, he allowed them to render their choices democratically, with applause. He mixed highbrow and lowbrow material, classical themes with march music, and frequently used humor in his arrangements, purposely avoiding what he regarded as the stuffiness of classical concerts. If audiences wished to hear "Stars and Stripes Forever" as an encore over and over (and they consistently did, until he died in 1932), then Sousa and his men would service them, with no withering of enthusiasm.

Besides his own works, Sousa championed the works of young and struggling American composers, but he demanded to know the stories behind their compositions. Musical inspiration, in Sousa's opinion, needed to be generated from "glorious events"; he avoided material from "atheistic composers" or those "crazily in love" because such works would not produce the appropriate nationalist feelings that he wished to cultivate in his audiences. "This was my mission. The point was to move all of America, while busied in its everyday pursuits, by the power of direct and simple music," he proclaimed in 1910. "I wanted to make a music for the people, a music to be grasped at once."

It was hardly an accident that Sousa's period of greatest popularity coincided with the wave of patriotic feeling that swept over America during the second half of the 1890s. The economy was recovering from the depression, and America was successfully flexing its muscles in a war with Spain. Many Americans wanted to wave the stars and stripes. They found special inspiration in Sousa's music.

Q Does music, even instrumental music such as Sousa's, have the power to generate a patriotic mood?

Q Have recent years in America—from 1896 until 2012—produced music that has influenced Americans in a manner similar to that of Sousa's in the 1890s?

 Listen to an audio recording of this music on the Musical Links to the Past CD.

followed political subjugation. Between 1898 and 1914, U.S. trade with Cuba increased more than tenfold, while investments more than quadrupled. The United States intervened in Cuban political affairs five times between 1906 and 1921 to protect its economic interests and those of an indigenous ruling class with which it had become closely allied. The economic, political, and military control that the United States imposed on Cuba would fuel anti-American sentiment there for years to come.

Puerto Rico received somewhat different treatment. The United States annexed the island outright with the Foraker Act (1900). This act contained no provision for making the inhabitants citizens of the United States. Puerto Rico was designated an "unincorporated" territory, which meant that Congress would dictate the island's government and specify the rights of its inhabitants. Puerto Ricans

UNCLE SAM GETS COCKY, 1901. *From 1898 to 1917, the United States broadened its influence in world affairs and especially sought to establish its dominance in Latin America. This cartoon illustrates that dominance through the figure of a giant Uncle Sam rooster that dwarfs both the European chickens (gamely protesting, "you're not the only rooster in South America") and the diminutive Latin American republics.*

were allowed no role in designing their government, nor was their consent requested. In some respects Puerto Rico fared better than "independent" Cuba: Puerto Ricans were granted U.S. citizenship in 1917 and won the right to elect their own governor in 1947. Still, Puerto Ricans enjoyed fewer political rights than Americans in the 48 states, and they endured a poverty rate far exceeding that of the mainland.

The subjugation of Cuba and the annexation of Puerto Rico troubled Americans far less than the U.S. takeover in the Philippines. Since the first articulation of the Monroe Doctrine in 1823, many Americans believed the United States possessed the right to act unilaterally to protect its interests in the Western Hemisphere. Before 1900, most of its actions (with the exception of the Mexican War) had been designed to limit the influence of European powers. After 1900, it assumed a more aggressive role, seizing land, overturning governments it did not like, and forcing its economic and political policies on weaker neighbors.

China and the "Open Door"

Except for Hawaii, the Philippines, and Guam, the United States made no effort to take control of Pacific islands or Asian territory. Such a policy might well have triggered war with other world powers already well established in the area. The United States opted for a diplomatic rather than a military strategy to achieve its foreign policy objectives. For China, in 1899 and 1900, it proposed the policy of the "open door."

The United States feared that the actions of the other world powers in China would block its own efforts to open up China's markets to American goods. Britain, Germany, Japan, Russia, and France each coveted its own chunk of China, where it

HISTORY THROUGH FILM

Tarzan, The Ape Man (1932)

Directed by W. S. Van Dyke; starring Johnny Weismuller (Tarzan), Maureen O'Sullivan (Jane Parker), Neil Hamilton (Harry Holt), C. Aubrey Smith (James Parker), and Cheeta the Chimp

Tarzan was one of the most popular screen figures of the 1930s, 1940s, and 1950s. Based on the best-selling novels of Edgar Rice Burroughs, this Tarzan movie, like the ones that followed, was meant to puncture the civilized complacency in which Americans and other westernized, imperial peoples had enveloped themselves. The movie opens with an American woman, Jane Parker, arriving in Africa to join her father, James, and his crew as they search for a mythic elephant graveyard said to contain untold riches in ivory tusks. Jane is depicted as bright, energetic, and attractive; she defies conventional expectations for women. The white male adventurers, however, are portrayed as greedy, haughty, contemptuous of the African environment, and ignorant. The Africans who act as their servants and guides are presented as primitive and superstitious, more like animals than humans. This expedition in search of ivory is destined for disaster. Its members succumb to attacks by the wild animals and "wild humans" who inhabit this "dark continent." During one such attack by hippos and pygmies, Tarzan, played by handsome Olympic swimming champion Johnny Weismuller, comes to the rescue, scaring off the attackers by mobilizing a stampede of elephants with a piercing, high-pitched, and unforgettable jungle cry. He takes Jane, who has become separated from the group, to his tree house. Thus begins one of the more unusual screen romances.

Tarzan's origins are not explained, though one infers that he was abandoned by whites as a baby and raised by apes. He has none of the refining features of civilization—decent clothes, language, manners—but he possesses strength, honesty, and virtue. As Jane falls in love with Tarzan and decides to share a jungle life with him, we, the viewers, are asked to contemplate, with Jane, the benefits of peeling off the stultifying features of civilized life (which seem to drop away

JOHNNY WEISMULLER AND MAUREEN O'SULLIVAN AS TARZAN AND JANE.

from Jane along with many of her clothes) and returning to a simpler, more wholesome, and more natural form of existence.

Although the movie critiques and lampoons the imperial pretensions and smugness of the West, it never asks viewers to see the indigenous African peoples as anything other than savage. Tarzan may be ignorant of civilized customs, but he is white and, as such, equipped with the "native" intelligence and character of his race. The African characters in the movie show no such intelligence or character. They are presented as weak and superstitious or as brutally aggressive and indifferent to human life. Thus Tarzan, the Ape Man manages to critique the West without asking Western viewers to challenge the racism that justified the West's domination of non-Western peoples and territories.

could monopolize trade, exploit cheap labor, and establish military bases. By the 1890s, each of these powers was building a sphere of influence, either by wringing economic and territorial concessions from the weak Chinese government or by seizing outright the land and trading privileges it desired.

To prevent China's breakup and to preserve U.S. economic access to the whole of China, McKinley's secretary of state, John Hay, sent **"Open Door" notes** to the major world powers. The notes asked each power to open its Chinese sphere of influence to the merchants of other nations. Hay also asked each nation to respect China's sovereignty by enforcing Chinese tariff duties in the territory it controlled. While none of the world powers outright embraced Hay's requests, he nevertheless declared that they had agreed to observe his Open Door principles and that he regarded their assent as "final and definitive."

The first challenge to Hay's policy came from the Chinese. In May 1900, a Chinese organization, colloquially known as the **Boxers**, sparked an uprising to rid China of all "foreign devils" and foreign influences. Hundreds of Europeans were killed, as were many Chinese men and women who had converted to Christianity. When the Boxers laid siege to the foreign legations in Beijing and cut off communication between that city and the outside world, the imperial powers raised an expeditionary force to rescue the diplomats and punish the Chinese rebels. The force, which included 5,000 U.S. soldiers, broke the Beijing siege in August and ended the Boxer Rebellion soon thereafter.

Hay now sent out a second round of Open Door notes, asking each power to respect China's political independence and territorial integrity, in addition to guaranteeing unrestricted access to its markets. Worried that Chinese rebels might strike again, the imperialist rivals responded more favorably. Significantly, when the imperial powers decided that the Chinese government should pay them reparations for their property and personnel losses during the Boxer Rebellion, Hay convinced them to accept payment in cash rather than in territory. By keeping China intact and open to free trade, the United States had achieved a major foreign policy victory.

Open Door notes (1899–1900) *Foreign policy tactic in which the United States asked European powers to respect China's independence and to open their spheres of influence to merchants from other nations.*

Boxers *Chinese nationalist organization that instigated an uprising in 1900 to rid China of foreigners and foreign influence.*

THEODORE ROOSEVELT, GEOPOLITICIAN

FOCUS QUESTION

What were the similarities and differences between Theodore Roosevelt's foreign policies in Latin America and East Asia? What explains the differences?

As assistant secretary of the navy, as a military hero, as a speaker and writer, and then as vice president, Roosevelt worked tirelessly during the McKinley administration to remake the country into one of the world's great powers. He believed that Americans were a racially superior people destined for supremacy in economic and political affairs. He did not assume, however, that international supremacy would automatically accrue to the United States. A nation, like an individual, had to strive for greatness. It had to build a military force that could convincingly project power overseas—and it had to be prepared to fight.

Roosevelt's appetite for a good fight caused many people to rue the ascension of this "cowboy" to the White House after McKinley's assassination in 1901. But behind his blustery exterior lay a shrewd analyst of international relations. As much as he craved power for himself and the nation, he understood that the United States could not rule every portion of the globe through military or economic means. Consequently, he sought a balance of power among the great industrial nations through negotiation rather than war. Such a balance would enable each imperial power to safeguard its key interests and contribute to world peace and progress.

Absent from Roosevelt's geopolitical thinking was concern for the interests of less powerful nations. Roosevelt had little patience with the claims to sovereignty of small countries or the human rights of weak peoples. In his eyes, the peoples of Latin America, Asia (with the exception of Japan), and Africa were racially inferior and thus incapable of self-government or industrial progress.

Map 22.3 **U.S. Presence in Latin America, 1895–1934.** *The United States possessed few colonies in Latin America but intervened (often repeatedly) in Mexico, Cuba, Nicaragua, Panama, Haiti, the Dominican Republic, and Venezuela to secure its economic and political interests.*

The Roosevelt Corollary

Ensuring U.S. dominance in the Western Hemisphere ranked high on Roosevelt's list of foreign policy objectives. In 1904 he issued a "corollary" to the Monroe Doctrine, which had asserted the right of the United States to keep European powers from meddling in hemispheric affairs. In his corollary Roosevelt declared that the United States also possessed the right to intervene in the domestic affairs of hemispheric nations to quell disorder and forestall European intervention. The **Roosevelt corollary** formalized a policy that the United States had already deployed against Cuba and Puerto Rico in 1900 and 1901. Subsequent events in Venezuela and the Dominican Republic had further convinced Roosevelt of the need to expand the scope of U.S. intervention.

[handwritten: Allowed U.S to become a world power and intervine on a world stage.]

Both Venezuela and the Dominican Republic were controlled by dictators who had defaulted on debts owed to European banks. Their delinquency prompted a German-led European naval blockade and bombardment of Venezuela in 1902 and a threatened invasion of the Dominican Republic by Italy and France in 1903. The United States forced the German navy to retreat in 1903. In the Dominican Republic, after a revolution had chased the dictator from power, the United States assumed control of the nation's customs collections in 1905 and refinanced the Dominican national debt through U.S. bankers.

The willingness of European bankers to loan money to Latin America's corrupt regimes had created the possibility that the countries ruled by these regimes would suffer bankruptcy, social turmoil, and foreign intervention. The United States, under Roosevelt, did not hesitate to intervene to make sure that loans were repaid and social stability was restored. But it did not show a willingness to help the people who had suffered under these regimes to establish democratic

> **Roosevelt corollary** *1904 corollary to the Monroe Doctrine, stating that the United States had the right to intervene in domestic affairs of hemispheric nations to quell disorder and forestall European intervention.*

institutions or achieve social justice. When Cubans seeking genuine national independence rebelled against their puppet government in 1906, the United States sent in the Marines to silence them.

The Panama Canal

Panama Canal *An engineering marvel completed in 1914 across the new Central American nation of Panama. Connecting the Atlantic and Pacific oceans, it shortened ship travel between New York and San Francisco by 8,000 miles.*

Roosevelt's interest in Latin America also engendered the building of the **Panama Canal** across Central America. Central America's narrow width, especially in its southern half, made it the logical place to build a canal. The French had tried and failed to build a canal across Panama, then a province of Colombia. Roosevelt was determined to succeed where the French had not. He first presided over the signing of the Hay-Pauncefote Treaty with Great Britain in 1901, releasing the United States from an 1850 agreement that prohibited either country from building a Central American canal without the other's participation. He then instructed his advisers to develop plans for a longer canal across Nicaragua, since the French company that possessed the rights to the unfinished Panamanian canal wanted $109 million for it. But in 1902, the company reduced the price to $40 million, a sum that Congress approved.

Secretary of State Hay quickly negotiated an agreement with Tomas Herran, the Colombian chargé d'affaires in Washington, stipulating that the United States would pay Colombia a onetime $10 million payment and annual rent of $250,000 for the rights to a six-mile-wide strip across Panama, the same land that the failed French canal had been intended to traverse. The Colombian legislature, however, rejected the proposed fee as insufficient and sent a new ambassador to the United States with instructions to ask for a onetime payment of $20 million and a share of the $40 million being paid to the French company. Actually, the Colombians were hoping to stall negotiations until 1904, when they would regain the rights to the canal zone and consequently to the $40 million payment promised to the French company.

As negotiations failed to deliver the result he desired, Roosevelt encouraged the Panamanians to revolt against Colombian rule. Panamanians had staged several rebellions in the previous 25 years, all of which had failed. But, with the backing of American naval forces, the 1903 rebellion succeeded. The United States formally recognized Panama as a sovereign state only two days after the rebellion against Colombia began.

Philippe Bunau-Varilla, a director of the French company from which the United States had bought the rights to the canal, declared himself the new state's diplomatic representative. Before the duly appointed Panamanian delegation even reached the United States to negotiate a canal deal, Bunau-Varilla and Secretary of State Hay signed the Hay–Bunau-Varilla Treaty (1903). It granted the United States a 10-mile-wide canal zone in return for $10 million down and $250,000 annually.

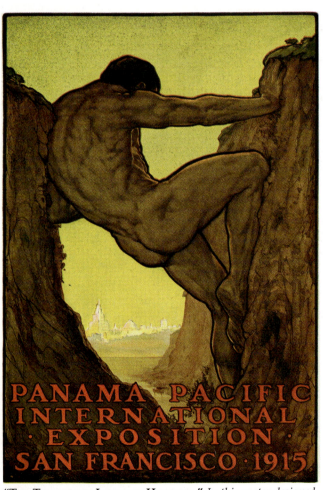

"THE THIRTEENTH LABOR OF HERCULES." *In this poster designed by Perham W. Nahl for the 1915 Panama Pacific International Exposition in San Francisco, the building of the Panama Canal is celebrated as a work on the scale of Hercules, among the greatest— and the strongest—of Greek-Roman heroes.*

The Thirteenth Labor of Hercules poster, 1915, paper, 18 3/16 x 12 inches, on view at the 1915 Panama-Pacific Exposition, San Francisco; courtesy Hagley Museum and Library.

Roosevelt turned the building of the canal into a test of American ingenuity and willpower. Engineers overcame every obstacle; doctors developed drugs to combat malaria and yellow fever; armies of construction workers "made the dirt fly." The canal remains a testament to the labor of some 30,000 workers, imported mainly from the West Indies, who, over a 10-year period, labored 10 hours a day, six days a week, for 10 cents an hour. Completed in 1914, the canal shortened the voyage from San Francisco to New York by more than 8,000 miles and significantly enhanced the international prestige of the United States (see Map 22.4).

In 1921, the United States paid the Colombian government $25 million as compensation for its loss of Panama. Panama waited more than 70 years, however, to regain control of the land. President Jimmy Carter signed a treaty in 1977 providing for the reintegration of the Canal Zone into Panama, and the canal itself was transferred to Panama in 2000.

Keeping the Peace in East Asia

Roosevelt strove to preserve the Open Door policy in China and the balance of power in East Asia. The chief threats came from Russia and Japan. At first, Russian expansion into Manchuria and Korea prompted Roosevelt to support Japan's 1904 attack on the Russian Pacific

Map 22.4 Panama Canal Zone, 1914. *This map shows the route of the completed canal through Panama and the 10-mile-wide zone surrounding it that the United States controlled. The inset map locates the Canal Zone in the context of Central and South America.*

fleet anchored at Port Arthur, China. But once the ruinous effects of the war on Russia became clear, Roosevelt entered into secret negotiations to arrange a peace. He invited representatives of Japan and Russia to Portsmouth, New Hampshire, and prevailed on them to negotiate a compromise. The settlement favored Japan by perpetuating its control over most of the territories it had won during the brief **Russo-Japanese War**. Its chief prize was Korea, which became a protectorate of Japan, but Japan also acquired the southern part of Sakhalin Island, Port Arthur, and the South Manchurian Railroad. Russia avoided paying Japan a large indemnity and it retained Siberia, thus preserving its role as an East Asian power. Finally, Roosevelt protected China's territorial integrity by inducing the armies of both Russia and Japan to leave Manchuria. Roosevelt's success in ending the Russo-Japanese War won him the Nobel Prize for Peace in 1906.

Although Roosevelt succeeded in negotiating a peace between these two world powers, he generally ignored, and sometimes encouraged, challenges to the sovereignty of weaker Asian nations. In a secret agreement with Japan (the Taft-Katsura Agreement of 1905), for example, the United States agreed that Japan could dominate Korea in return for a Japanese promise not to attack the Philippines. And in the Root-Takahira Agreement of 1908, the United States recognized Japanese expansion into southern Manchuria.

In Roosevelt's eyes, the overriding need to maintain peace with Japan justified ignoring the claims of Korea and, increasingly, of China. The task of American diplomacy, he believed, was first to allow the Japanese to build a secure sphere of influence in East Asia and second to encourage them to join the United States in pursuing peace rather than war. This was a delicate diplomatic task, especially when anti-Japanese agitation broke out in California in 1906.

Russia and Japan territory conflict.

Russo-Japanese War *Territorial conflict between imperial Japan and Russia mediated by Theodore Roosevelt at Portsmouth, New Hampshire. The peace agreement gave Korea and other territory to Japan, ensured Russia's continuing control over Siberia, and protected China's territorial integrity.*

White Californians had pressured Congress into passing the Chinese Exclusion Act of 1882, which ended most Chinese immigration to the United States (see Chapter 18). They next turned their racism on Japanese immigrants. In 1906, the San Francisco school board ordered the segregation of Asian schoolchildren so that they would not "contaminate" white children. In 1907, the California legislature debated a law to end Japanese immigration to the state. Anti-Asian riots erupted in San Francisco and Los Angeles.

gentlemen's agreement (1907)
Agreement by which the Japanese government promised to halt the immigration of its adult male laborers to the United States in return for President Theodore Roosevelt's pledge to end anti-Japanese discrimination in California.

Militarists in Japan began talking of a possible war with the United States. Roosevelt assured the Japanese government that he too was appalled by the white Californians' behavior. In 1907, he reached a **"gentlemen's agreement"** by which the Tokyo government promised to halt the immigration of Japanese adult male laborers to the United States in return for Roosevelt's pledge to end anti-Japanese discrimination in California. Roosevelt did his part by persuading the San Francisco school board to rescind its segregation ordinance.

At the same time, Roosevelt worried that the Tokyo government would interpret his sensitivity to Japanese honor as weakness. He ordered the main part of the U.S. fleet to embark on a 45,000-mile world tour, including a stop in Tokyo Bay. Many Americans deplored the cost of the tour and feared that the appearance of the U.S. Navy in a Japanese port would provoke military retaliation. Roosevelt brushed his critics aside, and, true to his prediction, the Japanese were impressed by the **Great White Fleet's** show of strength. Their response seemed to lend validity to the African proverb Roosevelt often invoked: "Speak softly and carry a big stick." Roosevelt's policies lessened the prospect of a war with Japan while preserving a strong U.S. presence in East Asia.

Great White Fleet *Naval ships sent on a 45,000-mile world tour by President Roosevelt (1907–1909) to showcase American military power.*

WILLIAM HOWARD TAFT, DOLLAR DIPLOMAT

FOCUS QUESTION

What was "dollar diplomacy," and how effective was it as a foreign policy tool for the United States under William Howard Taft?

Having served as the first governor-general of the Philippines and as Roosevelt's secretary of war, William Howard Taft brought impressive foreign policy credentials to the job of president. Yet he lacked Roosevelt's grasp of balance-of-power politics and capacity for leadership in foreign affairs. Further, Taft's secretary of state, Philander C. Knox, a corporation lawyer from Pittsburgh, lacked diplomatic expertise. Knox's conduct of foreign policy seemed to be directed almost entirely toward expanding opportunities for corporate investment overseas, prompting critics to deride his policies as **"dollar diplomacy."** Taft and Knox believed that U.S. investments would effectively substitute "dollars for bullets," and thus offer a more peaceful and less coercive way of maintaining stability and order.

The inability of Taft and Knox to grasp the complexities of power politics led to a diplomatic reversal in East Asia. Knox sought to expand American economic activities throughout China—even in Manchuria, where they encroached on the Japanese sphere of influence. In 1911, Knox proposed that a syndicate of European and American bankers buy the South Manchurian Railroad to open up north China to international trade. Japan reacted by signing a friendship treaty with Russia, its former enemy, which signaled their joint determination to exclude American, British, and French goods from Manchurian markets. Knox's plan to purchase the railroad fell apart. His further efforts to increase American trade with Central and South China triggered additional hostile responses from the Japanese and the Russians and contributed to the collapse of the Chinese government and the onset of the Chinese Revolution in 1911.

dollar diplomacy *Diplomatic strategy formulated under President Taft that focused on expanding American investments abroad, especially in Latin America and East Asia.*

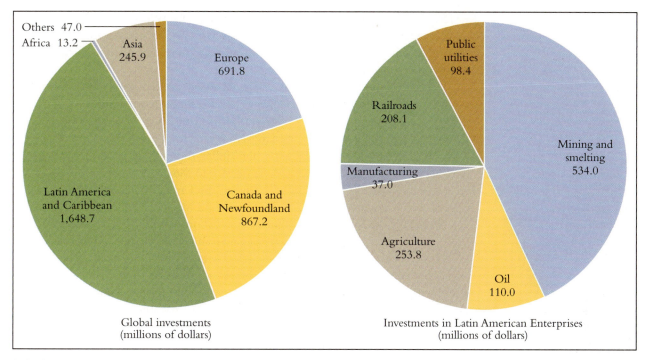

U.S. GLOBAL INVESTMENTS AND INVESTMENTS IN LATIN AMERICA, 1914

Source: From Cleona Lewis, *America's Stake in International Investments* (Washington, D.C.: The Brookings Institute, 1938), pp. 576–606.

Dollar diplomacy worked better in the Caribbean, where no major power contested U.S. policy. Knox encouraged American investment. Companies such as United Fruit of Boston, which established extensive banana plantations in Costa Rica and Honduras, grew so powerful that they were able to influence both the economies and the governments of Central American countries. When political turmoil threatened their investments, the United States simply sent in its troops. Thus the United States toppled the regime of Nicaraguan dictator José Santos Zelaya in 1910 after he reportedly began negotiating with a European country to build a second trans-Isthmian canal in 1910.

WOODROW WILSON, STRUGGLING IDEALIST

Woodrow Wilson's foreign policy in Latin America initially appeared no different from that of his Republican predecessors. In 1915, the United States sent troops to Haiti to put down a revolution; they remained as an army of occupation for 21 years. In 1916, when the people of the Dominican Republic refused to accept a treaty making them more or less a protectorate of the United States, Wilson forced a U.S. military government upon them. When German influence in the Danish West Indies began to expand, Wilson purchased the islands from Denmark, renamed them the Virgin Islands, and added them to the U.S. Caribbean empire (see Map 22.3).

Still, Wilson's relationship with Mexico in the wake of its revolution reveals that he was troubled by a foreign policy that ignored a less powerful nation's right to determine its own future. Yet while Wilson wanted U.S. foreign policy to advance democratic ideals and institutions in Mexico, he also feared that political unrest there could lead to violence, social disorder, and revolutionary governments hostile to U.S. economic interests. With a U.S.-style democratic government in

FOCUS QUESTION

What does Woodrow Wilson's policy toward Mexico reveal about his underlying approach to foreign policy? How similar or different was his approach to the one favored by Theodore Roosevelt?

Mexico, Wilson believed, property rights would be respected and U.S. investments would remain secure. Wilson's desire both to encourage democracy and to limit the extent of social change made it difficult to devise a consistent foreign policy toward Mexico.

The Mexican Revolution broke out in 1910 when dictator Porfirio Diaz was overthrown by democratic forces led by Francisco Madero. Madero's talk of democratic reform frightened many foreign investors. Thus, when Madero himself was overthrown early in 1913 by Victoriano Huerta, a conservative general who promised to protect foreign investments, the dollar diplomatists breathed a sigh of relief. Henry Lane Wilson, the U.S. ambassador to Mexico, had helped to engineer Huerta's coup. Before close relations between the United States and Huerta could be worked out, however, Huerta's men murdered Madero.

Woodrow Wilson, who became president shortly after Madero's assassination in 1913, refused to recognize Huerta's "government of butchers" and demanded that Mexico hold democratic elections. Wilson favored Venustiano Carranza and Francisco ("Pancho") Villa, two enemies of Huerta who commanded rebel armies and who claimed to be democrats. In April 1914, Wilson seized upon the arrest of several U.S. sailors by Huerta's troops to send a fleet into Mexican waters. He ordered the U.S. Marines to occupy the Mexican port city of Veracruz and to prevent a German ship there from unloading munitions meant for Huerta's army. In the resulting confrontation between U.S. and Mexican forces, 19 Americans and 126 Mexicans were killed. The battle brought the two countries dangerously close to war. American control over Veracruz, however, weakened Huerta's regime to the point where Carranza was able to take power.

Carranza did not behave as Wilson had expected. Rejecting Wilson's efforts to shape a new Mexican government, he announced an extensive land reform program. If the program went into effect, U.S. petroleum companies would lose control of their Mexican properties, a loss that Wilson deemed unacceptable. Wilson now threw his support to Pancho Villa, who seemed more willing to protect American oil interests. When Carranza's forces defeated Villa's forces in 1915, Wilson reluctantly withdrew his support of Villa and prepared to recognize the Carranza government.

Furious that Wilson had abandoned him, Villa and his soldiers pulled 18 U.S. citizens from a train in northern Mexico and murdered them, along with another 17 in an attack on Columbus, New Mexico. Wilson obtained permission from Carranza to send a U.S. expeditionary force under General John J. Pershing into Mexico, once again bringing the countries to the brink of war. Because the United States was about to enter the First World War, Wilson could not afford a fight with Mexico. So, in 1917, he quietly ordered Pershing's troops home and grudgingly recognized the Carranza government.

Although his policies toward Mexico in the years from 1913 to 1917 seemed to have produced few concrete results, Wilson in fact recognized something that Roosevelt and Taft had not: that more and more peoples of the world were determined to control their own destinies. Somehow the United States had to find a way to support their democratic aspirations while also safeguarding its own economic interests.

Conclusion

The United States after 1898 achieved its major objectives in world affairs: It tightened its control over the Western Hemisphere and projected its military and economic power into Asia. It did so while sacrificing relatively few American lives and while constraining the jingoistic appetite for truly extensive military adventure

---

QUICK REVIEW

U.S. POLICY TOWARD REVOLUTIONARY MEXICO, 1913–1917

- President Wilson was torn between supporting Mexico's right to be self-governing and protecting U.S. investments

- Wilson reacted angrily to the 1913 assassination of Francisco Madero, a popular democrat; United States maneuvered to put Venustiano Carranza, another democrat, in power

- Carranza threatened U.S. oil interests, and Wilson switched his support to rebel leader Francisco "Pancho" Villa

- When Carranza defeated Villa in 1915, Wilson reluctantly recognized Carranza's government

- Villa's soldiers murdered U.S. citizens, and Wilson sent U.S. troops into Mexico to capture Villa

and conquest. McKinley, Roosevelt, Taft, and Wilson all placed limits on U.S. expansion and avoided, until 1917, far-reaching foreign entanglements and wars.

If measured against the standard of America's own democratic ideals, however, U.S. foreign policy after 1898 must be judged more harshly. It demeaned the peoples of the Philippines, Puerto Rico, Guam, Cuba, and Colombia as inferior and primitive and denied them the right to govern themselves. In choosing to behave like the imperialist powers of Europe, the United States abandoned its longstanding claim that it was a nation that valued liberty more than power.

Many Americans of the time thus faced a dilemma. On the one hand, they believed that the size, economic strength, and honor of the United States required it to accept the role of world power and policeman. On the other hand, they continued to believe they had a mission to spread the values of 1776 to the farthest reaches of the earth. The Mexico example demonstrates how hard it was for the United States to reconcile these two very different approaches to world affairs.

CHAPTER REVIEW

Review Questions

1. Which groups in American society were most interested in expanding U.S. influence abroad?

2. In going to war against Spain in 1898, was the United States impelled more by imperialist or anti-imperialist motives?

3. What different mechanisms of control did the United States use to achieve its aims in Hawaii, Cuba, the Philippines, Puerto Rico, and China?

4. What were the similarities and differences between Theodore Roosevelt's foreign policies in Latin America and East Asia? What explains the differences?

5. What was "dollar diplomacy," and how effective was it as a foreign policy tool for the United States under William Howard Taft?

6. What does Woodrow Wilson's policy toward Mexico reveal about his underlying approach to foreign policy? How similar or different was his approach to the one favored by Theodore Roosevelt?

Critical Thinking

1. What is the appropriate standard for judging the 1898 turn in U.S. foreign policy: the policies of rival world powers or America's own democratic ideals?

2. If you had been president, secretary of state, or a leading senator in the period 1898–1917, with the power to alter U.S. foreign policy, what, if anything would you have changed? What leads you to believe that your change of policy would not only have been desirable but successful?

Identifications

Review your understanding of the following key terms, people, and events for this chapter.

yellow journalism, p. 508
Rough Riders, p. 510
9th and 10th Negro
   Cavalries, p. 511
Emilio Aguinaldo, p. 513

Platt Amendment, p. 514
Open Door notes
   (1899–1900), p. 518
Boxers, p. 518
Roosevelt corollary, p. 519

Panama Canal, p. 520
Russo-Japanese War,
   p. 521
gentlemen's agreement
   (1907), p. 522

Great White Fleet,
   p. 522
dollar diplomacy,
   p. 522

DISCOVERY

Was American foreign policy imperialist or anti-imperialist? Did it spread liberty?

In thinking about this question, begin by breaking it down into the components shown below. A discussion of the significance of each component should appear in your answer.

Geography and Foreign Policy

Examine Map 22.1 (below) and compare it to Map 22.2 on page 512. What areas did the United States seek to influence or come to control during these years? What propelled the country to exercise its influence abroad? How successful was it in its aims? In which of these areas does the United States still exercise control or influence?

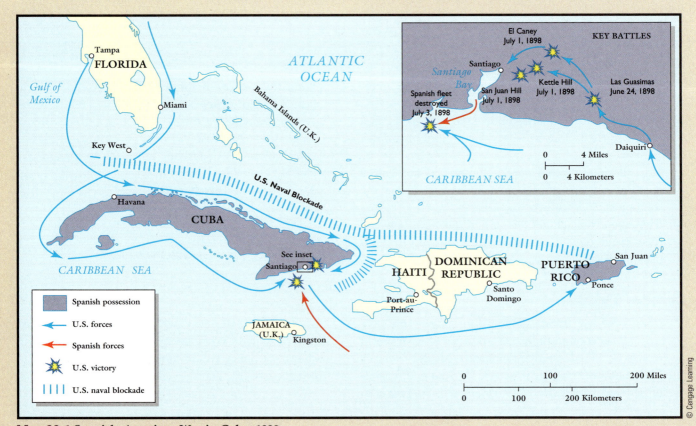

Map 22.1 Spanish–American War in Cuba, 1898

Visit the CourseMate website at www.cengagebrain.com for additional study tools and review materials for this chapter.

23

WAR AND SOCIETY, 1914–1920

EUROPE'S DESCENT INTO WAR

AMERICAN NEUTRALITY
    Submarine Warfare
    The Peace Movement
    Wilson's Vision: "Peace without Victory"
    German Escalation

AMERICAN INTERVENTION

MOBILIZING FOR "TOTAL" WAR
    Organizing Industry
    Securing Workers, Keeping Labor Peace
    Raising An Army
    Paying the Bills

Arousing Patriotic Ardor
Wartime Repression

THE FAILURE OF THE INTERNATIONAL PEACE
    The Paris Peace Conference and the Treaty of
        Versailles
    The League of Nations
    Wilson versus Lodge: The Fight over Ratification
    The Treaty's Final Defeat

THE POSTWAR PERIOD: A SOCIETY IN
CONVULSION
    Labor–Capital Conflict
    Radicals and the Red Scare
    Racial Conflict and the Rise of Black Nationalism

The First World War broke out in Europe in August 1914. The **Triple Alliance** of Germany, Austria-Hungary, and the Ottoman Empire squared off against the **Triple Entente** of Great Britain, France, and Russia. The United States entered the war on the side of the Entente (the Allies, or Allied Powers, as they came to be called) in 1917. Over the next year and a half, the United States converted its large, sprawling economy into a disciplined war production machine, raised a five-million-man army, and provided both the war matériel and troops that helped propel the Allies to victory.

But the war also convulsed American society more deeply than any event since the Civil War. The U.S. government pursued a degree of industrial control and social regimentation unprecedented in American history. Significant numbers of Americans from a variety of constituencies opposed the war. Disadvantaged groups stirred up trouble by declaring that American society had failed to live up to its democratic and egalitarian ideals. Wilson supported repressive policies to silence these rebels and to enforce unity and conformity on the American people. In the process, he tarnished the ideals for which America had been fighting. And in the end, Wilson needed England's and France's support to deliver his idealistic goal of **"peace without victory."** This support never came.

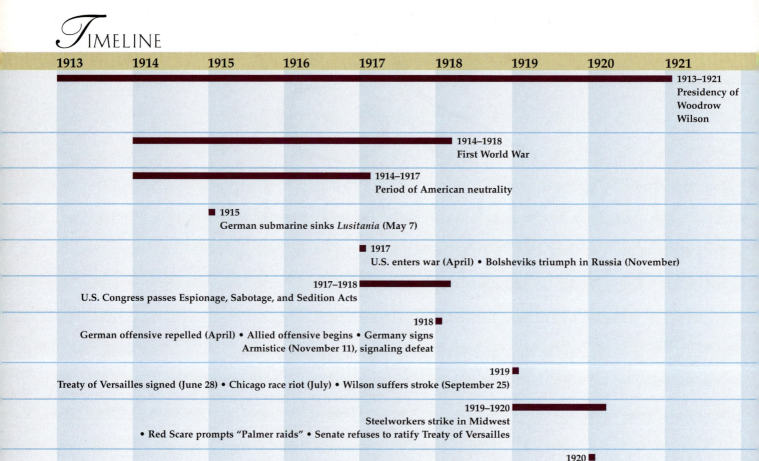

TIMELINE

1913	1914	1915	1916	1917	1918	1919	1920	1921

1913–1921
Presidency of Woodrow Wilson

1914–1918
First World War

1914–1917
Period of American neutrality

1915
German submarine sinks *Lusitania* (May 7)

1917
U.S. enters war (April) • Bolsheviks triumph in Russia (November)

1917–1918
U.S. Congress passes Espionage, Sabotage, and Sedition Acts

1918
German offensive repelled (April) • Allied offensive begins • Germany signs Armistice (November 11), signaling defeat

1919
Treaty of Versailles signed (June 28) • Chicago race riot (July) • Wilson suffers stroke (September 25)

1919–1920
Steelworkers strike in Midwest • Red Scare prompts "Palmer raids" • Senate refuses to ratify Treaty of Versailles

1920
Anarchists Sacco and Vanzetti convicted of murder

© Cengage Learning

EUROPE'S DESCENT INTO WAR

FOCUS QUESTION

What caused Europe's descent into war?

Triple Alliance *One set of combatants in the First World War, consisting of Germany, Austria-Hungary, and Italy. When Italy left the alliance, this side became known as the Central Powers.*

Triple Entente *One set of combatants in the First World War, consisting of Britain, France, and Russia. As the war went on, this side came to be known as the Allies or Allied Powers.*

On June 28, 1914, in Sarajevo, Bosnia, a Bosnian nationalist assassinated Archduke Franz Ferdinand, heir to the Austro-Hungarian throne. This act was meant to protest the Austro-Hungarian imperial presence in the Balkans and to encourage the Bosnians, Croatians, and other Balkan peoples to join the Serbs in establishing independent nations. Austria-Hungary responded to this provocation on July 28 by declaring war on Serbia, holding it responsible for the archduke's murder.

The conflict might have remained local if a series of treaties had not divided Europe into two hostile camps. Germany, Austria-Hungary, and Italy, the so-called **Triple Alliance**, had promised to come to each other's aid if attacked. Italy would soon leave this alliance, to be replaced by the Ottoman Empire. Arrayed against the nations of the Triple Alliance were Britain, France, and Russia in the **Triple Entente**. Russia was obligated by another treaty to defend Serbia against Austria-Hungary, and consequently on July 30 it mobilized its armed forces to go to Serbia's aid. That brought Germany into the conflict to protect Austria-Hungary from Russian attack. On August 3, German troops struck not at Russia but at France, Russia's western ally. To reach France, German troops had marched through neutral Belgium. On August 4, Britain reacted by declaring war on Germany.

Complicated alliances and defense treaties of the European nations hastened the rush toward war. But equally important was the competition among the major

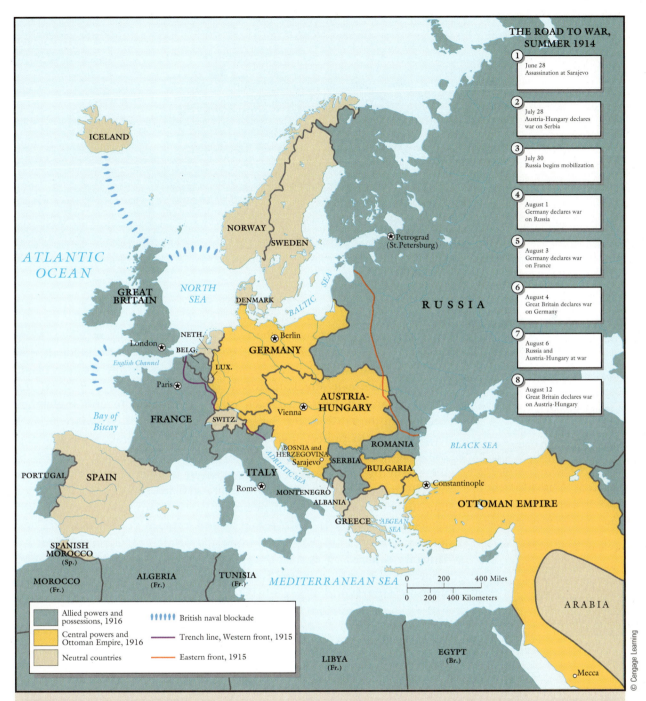

THE ROAD TO WAR, SUMMER 1914

1. June 28
Assassination at Sarajevo

2. July 28
Austria-Hungary declares war on Serbia

3. July 30
Russia begins mobilization

4. August 1
Germany declares war on Russia

5. August 3
Germany declares war on France

6. August 4
Great Britain declares war on Germany

7. August 6
Russia and Austria-Hungary at war

8. August 12
Great Britain declares war on Austria-Hungary

Allied powers and possessions, 1916

Central powers and Ottoman Empire, 1916

Neutral countries

British naval blockade

Trench line, Western front, 1915

Eastern front, 1915

Map 23.1 **Europe Goes to War.** *In the First World War, Great Britain, France, and Russia squared off against Germany, Austria-Hungary, and the Ottoman Empire. Most of the fighting occurred in Europe along the western front in France (purple line) or the eastern front in Russia (red line). This map also shows Britain's blockade of German ports. British armies based in Egypt (then a British colony) clashed with Ottoman armies in Arabia and other parts of the Ottoman Empire.*

powers to build the strongest economies, the largest armies and navies, and the grandest colonial empires. Britain and Germany, in particular, struggled for European and world supremacy. Historians believe that several advisers close to the German emperor, Kaiser Wilhelm II, urged going to war against Russia and France. They expected that a European war would be swift and decisive—in Germany's favor.

peace without victory
Woodrow Wilson's 1917 pledge to work for a peace settlement that did not favor one side over the other but ensured an equality among combatants.

GASSED, BY JOHN SINGER SARGENT. *An artist renders the horror of a poison gas attack in the First World War. The Germans were the first to use this new and brutal weapon, which contributed greatly to the terror of war.*

QUICK REVIEW

CAUSES OF FIRST WORLD WAR

- Competition among European nations to build strongest economies, largest navies, and grandest empires created international friction and instability

- Assassination of Archduke Franz Ferdinand prompted Austria-Hungary to declare war on Serbia

- Intricate series of treaties compelled Russia, England, and France to go to war with Serbia, and Germany to support Austria-Hungary

Victory was not swift. The two camps were evenly matched. Moreover, the first wartime use of machine guns and barbed wire made it easier to defend against attack than to go on the offensive. On the western front, after the initial German attack narrowly failed to take Paris in 1914, the two opposing armies confronted each other along a battle line stretching from Belgium in the north to the Swiss border in the south (see Map 23.1). Troops dug trenches to protect themselves from artillery bombardment and poison gas attacks. Commanders on both sides mounted suicidal ground assaults on the enemy by sending tens of thousands of infantry out of the trenches and directly into enemy fire. Enemy artillery and machine guns cut down appalling numbers of men caught in barbed wire. Many who were not killed in combat succumbed to disease that spread rapidly in the cold, wet, and rat-infested trenches. In Eastern Europe the armies of Germany and Austria-Hungary squared off against those of Russia and Serbia. Although the eastern front did not employ trench warfare, the combat was no less lethal. By the time the First World War ended, total casualties, both military and civilian, had reached 37 million.

AMERICAN NEUTRALITY

FOCUS QUESTION

Why did the U.S. policy of neutrality fail, and why did the United States get drawn into war?

neutrality *U.S. foreign policy from 1914 to 1917 that called for staying out of war but maintaining normal economic relations with both sides.*

Soon after the fighting began, Woodrow Wilson told Americans that this was a European war; neither side was threatening a vital U.S. interest. The United States would therefore proclaim its **neutrality**—and continue trading with both sides while seeking to secure peace. Most Americans applauded Wilson's determination to keep the country out of war.

Neutrality was easier to proclaim than achieve, however. Many Americans identified more with the English, with whom they shared a language, ancestry, and a commitment to liberty. Germany's acceptance of monarchical rule, the prominence of militarists in German politics, and the weakness of democratic traditions offended U.S. officials.

The United States had strong economic ties to Great Britain as well. In 1914 the United States exported more than $800 million in goods to Britain and its allies, compared with $170 million to Germany and Austria-Hungary (which came to be known as the Central Powers). Once war began, the British and then the French turned to the United States for food, clothing, munitions, and other war supplies. Bankers began to issue loans to the Allied Powers, further knitting together the U.S. and British economies and giving American investors a direct stake in an Allied victory. The British navy also blockaded German ports, which raised another barrier against U.S. trade with Germany.

The Wilson administration protested the British navy's search and occasional seizure of American merchant ships, but it never retaliated by suspending loans or exports to Great Britain. To do so would have plunged the U.S. economy into a recession. In failing to protect its right to trade with Germany, the United States compromised its neutrality and allowed itself to be drawn into war.

Submarine Warfare

To combat British control of the seas, Germany unveiled a terrifying new weapon, the *Unterseeboot,* or U-boat, the first militarily effective submarine. On May 7, 1915, without warning, a German U-boat torpedoed the British passenger liner ***Lusitania,*** en route from New York to London. The attack killed 1,198 men, women, and children, 128 of them U.S. citizens. The Germans claimed that the *Lusitania* was secretly carrying a large store of munitions to Great Britain (a charge later proved true). But this did not stop Wilson from denouncing the sinking of the *Lusitania* and demanding that Germany pledge never to launch another attack on the citizens of neutral nations, even when they were traveling in British or French ships. Germany acquiesced to Wilson's demand.

In early 1916, the Allies began to arm their merchant vessels with guns and depth charges capable of destroying German U-boats. Considering this a provocation, Germany renewed surprise submarine attacks. In March 1916, a German submarine torpedoed the French passenger liner *Sussex,* causing a heavy loss of life and injuring several Americans. Again Wilson demanded that Germany spare civilians from attack. In the so-called *Sussex* pledge, Germany once again relented but warned that it might resume unrestricted submarine warfare if the United States did not prevail upon Great Britain to permit neutral ships to pass through the blockade.

The German submarine attacks strengthened the hand of Theodore Roosevelt and others who had been arguing that war with Germany was inevitable. No longer able to ignore these critics, Wilson sought and won congressional approval for bills to increase the size of the army and navy. But, to forestall the necessity of American military involvement, he dispatched Colonel Edward M. House to London in January 1916 to draw up a peace plan with the British foreign secretary, Lord Grey. In the House-Grey memorandum of February 22, 1916, Britain agreed to ask the United States to negotiate a settlement between the Allies and the Central Powers. The British were furious, however, when Wilson revealed that he wanted an impartial, honestly negotiated peace that respected the claims of the Allies and Central Powers.

Lusitania British passenger liner sunk by a German U-boat on May 7, 1915, killing more than 1,000 men, women, and children.

THE HORROR OF WAR. *This cover of the* United Mine Workers Journal *(1916) presents the Great War in the bleakest possible terms: as giving the Grim Reaper license to claim the bodies and souls of Europe's young men. Progressive labor unions were part of the broad coalition in the United States opposed to America's entry into war.*

Britain now rejected U.S. peace overtures, and relations between the two countries grew tense.

The Peace Movement

Underlying Wilson's 1916 peace initiative was a vision of a new world order in which relations between nations would be governed by negotiation rather than war and in which justice would replace power as the fundamental principle of diplomacy. On May 27, 1916, Wilson formally declared his support for what he would later call the League of Nations, an international parliament dedicated to the pursuit of peace, security, and justice for all the world's peoples.

Many Americans supported Wilson's efforts to promote international peace rather than conquest and to keep the United States out of war. Carrie Chapman Catt, president of the National American Woman Suffrage Association, and Jane Addams, founder of the Women's Peace Party, actively opposed U.S. involvement in the war. A substantial pacifist group emerged among the nation's Protestant clergy. In April 1916, progressives and socialists formed the American Union Against Militarism to pressure Wilson to continue pursuing peace. The country's Irish and German ethnic populations, who wanted to block a formal military alliance with Great Britain, also supported Wilson's peace campaign.

Wilson's Vision: "Peace without Victory"

The 1916 presidential election revealed the breadth of peace sentiment. Wilson ran as the "peace president" who had "kept us out of war." Combining the promise of peace with a pledge to push ahead with progressive reform, Wilson won a narrow victory over the pro-war Republican, Charles Evan Hughes.

Wilson appeared before the Senate on January 22, 1917, to outline his plans for peace. He reaffirmed his commitment to the League of Nations, but for such a league to succeed, Wilson argued, it would have to be handed a sturdy peace settlement. Only a peace without victory, one that did not crown a victor or humiliate a loser, would last. Wilson listed the crucial principles of a lasting peace: freedom of the seas; disarmament; and the right of every people to self-determination, democratic self-government, and security against aggression. Wilson's new world order would allow all the earth's peoples, regardless of their size or strength, to achieve political independence and to participate as equals in world affairs.

German Escalation

The German military responded to Wilson's entreaties for peace by preparing to unleash its submarines to attack all vessels heading for British ports. Germany knew that this action would compel the United States to enter the war, but it gambled on being able to strangle the British economy and leave France isolated before significant numbers of American troops could arrive.

Wilson continued to hope for a negotiated settlement until February 25, when the British intercepted and passed on to the president a telegram from Germany's foreign secretary, Arthur Zimmermann, to the German minister in Mexico. The **Zimmermann telegram** instructed the minister to ask the Mexican government to attack the United States in the event of war between Germany and the United States. In return, Germany would pay the Mexicans a large fee and regain for them the "lost provinces" of Texas, New Mexico, and Arizona. Wilson, Congress, and the American public were outraged.

In March, news arrived that Tsar Nicholas II's autocratic regime in Russia had collapsed and been replaced by a liberal-democratic government. As long as the tsar

Zimmermann telegram

Telegram from Germany's foreign secretary instructing the German minister in Mexico to ask that country's government to attack the United States in return for German assistance in regaining Texas, New Mexico, and Arizona.

ruled Russia and stood to benefit from the Central Powers' defeat, Wilson could not honestly claim that America's going to war against Germany would bring democracy to Europe. Russia's fledgling democratic government's need for assistance gave Wilson the rationale to justify American intervention.

Appearing before a joint session of Congress on April 2, Wilson declared that the United States must enter the war because "the world must be made safe for democracy." On April 6, Congress voted to declare war by a vote of 373 to 50 in the House and 82 to 6 in the Senate. The United States thus embarked on a grand experiment to reshape the world.

AMERICAN INTERVENTION

The entry of the United States into the war gave the Allies the muscle they needed to defeat the Central Powers, but it almost came too late. The French and British armies had bled themselves white by taking the offensive in 1916 and 1917 and had scarcely budged the trench lines. The Germans had been content simply to hold their trench position in the West because they were engaged in a huge offensive against the Russians in the East. But a second Russian revolution in November 1917 had brought to power a socialist government under Vladimir Lenin and his Bolshevik Party, which pulled Russia out of the war.

Russia's exit hurt the Allies. Not only did the French and British now have to cope with a much larger German force, but they also had to weather the political storm unleashed by Lenin's decision to publish the texts of secret Allied treaties showing that Britain and France, like Germany, had plotted to enlarge their nations and empires through war. The revelation that the Allies were fighting for land and riches rather than democratic principles outraged people in France and Great Britain, demoralized Allied troops, and threw the French and British governments into disarray. The treaties also embarrassed Wilson, who had brought America into the war to fight for democracy, not territory. Wilson sought to restore the Allies' credibility by unveiling, in January 1918, a concrete program for peace. His **Fourteen Points** (discussed later in this chapter) rejected territorial aggrandizement as a legitimate war aim.

In March and April 1918, Germany launched its offensive against British and French positions, sending Allied troops reeling. German troops advanced 10 miles a day until they reached the Marne River, within striking distance of Paris. The French government prepared to evacuate the city. At this perilous moment, a large American army arrived to reinforce what remained of the French lines.

In fact, these American troops, part of the American Expeditionary Force (AEF) commanded by General **John J. Pershing**, had begun landing in France almost a year earlier. During the intervening months, the United States had had to create a modern army from scratch. Men had to be drafted, trained, and supplied with food and equipment. In France, Pershing put his troops through additional training before committing them to battle. He was determined that the American soldiers—or "doughboys," as they were called—should acquit themselves well on the battlefield. The army he ordered into battle to counter the German spring offensive of 1918 fought well. Many American soldiers fell, but Paris was saved, and Germany's best chance for victory slipped away.

Buttressed by this show of AEF strength, the Allied troops staged a major offensive of their own in late September. Millions of Allied troops advanced across

FOCUS QUESTION

What contribution did the United States make to the Allied Powers' victory?

QUICK REVIEW

PATH TO U.S. INTERVENTION

- Economic and cultural ties with Great Britain compromised American neutrality

- U-boat attacks on British and French shipping made Germany an easy target for U.S. condemnation

- Wilson quieted antiwar movement by promising "peace without victory"

- Zimmermann telegram in February 1917 outraged U.S. public opinion

- Overthrow of Russian tsar Nicholas II in March 1917 enabled Wilson to declare that America was fighting a "war for democracy"

Fourteen Points *Plan laid out by Woodrow Wilson in January 1918 to give concrete form to his dream of a "peace without victory" and a new world order.*

John J. Pershing *Commander of the American Expeditionary Force that began landing in Europe in 1917 and that entered battle in the spring and summer of 1918.*

the 200-mile-wide Argonne forest in France, cutting German supply lines. By late October, they had reached the German border. German leaders asked for an armistice, to be followed by peace negotiations based on Wilson's Fourteen Points. Having forced the Germans to agree to numerous concessions, the Allies ended the war on November 11, 1918.

MOBILIZING FOR "TOTAL" WAR

FOCUS QUESTION

What problems did the United States encounter in mobilizing for total war, and how successfully were those problems overcome?

Compared to Europe, the United States suffered little from the war. The deaths of 112,000 American soldiers paled in comparison to European losses: 900,000 by Great Britain, 1.2 million by Austria-Hungary, 1.4 million by France, 1.7 million by Russia, and 2 million by Germany. The U.S. civilian population was also spared the destruction of homes and industries and the shortages of food and medicine that afflicted millions of Europeans. Only the flu epidemic that swept across the Atlantic from Europe in 1918 and 1919 to claim approximately 500,000 American lives caused wholesale suffering and death.

Still, the war had a profound effect on American society. Every military engagement the United States had fought since the Civil War had been limited in scope. The First World War was a **"total" war** to which every combatant nation had committed virtually all its resources. The scale of the effort for the United States became apparent early in 1917 when Wilson asked Congress for a conscription law that would permit the federal government to raise a multimillion-man army. The United States would also have to devote much of its agricultural, transportation, industrial, and population resources to the war effort if it wished to end the European stalemate.

Organizing Industry

At first Wilson pursued a decentralized approach to mobilization, delegating tasks to local defense councils throughout the country. When that effort failed, Wilson created several federal agencies, each charged with supervising nation-wide activity in its assigned economic sector. The success of these agencies varied. The Food Administration, headed by mining engineer Herbert Hoover, increased production of basic foodstuffs and delivered food to millions of troops and European civilians. At the other extreme, the Aircraft Production Board and Emergency Fleet Corporation did a poor job of supplying the Allies with combat aircraft and merchant vessels.

Most of the new government war agencies were more powerful on paper than in fact. Consider, for example, the **War Industries Board** (WIB), the agency responsible for mobilizing American industry for war production. The WIB floundered for its first nine months, lacking the authority to force manufacturers and the military to adopt its plans. Only the appointment of Wall Street investment banker Bernard Baruch as WIB chairman in March 1918 turned the agency around. Rather than attempting to force manufacturers to do the government's bidding, Baruch permitted industrialists to charge high prices for their products. He won exemptions from antitrust laws for corporations that complied with his requests. Under Baruch's forceful leadership, production increased substantially, and manufacturers discovered the financial benefits of cooperation between the public and private sectors. But Baruch's favoritism toward large corporations hurt smaller competitors, and the cozy relationship between government and corporate America violated the progressive pledge to protect the people against the "interests."

total war *New kind of war requiring every combatant to devote virtually all its economic and political resources to the fight.*

War Industries Board *U.S. government agency responsible for mobilizing American industry for war production.*

LINK TO THE PAST

"A Storm of Our People toward the North"

When jobs became available in the North during the First World War, African Americans from the South began journeying north in record numbers. Between 1916 and 1920, 500,000 made the journey, a population movement so large it became known as the Great Migration. That so many went north in such a brief period demonstrates how tough life was in the South for most African Americans and how ready they were to seize an opportunity to improve their situation. Many of the migrants were rural folk—tenant farmers, sharecroppers, and agricultural laborers—whose skills were not easily transferable to the urban and industrial economies of northern cities. They thus had to enter northern labor forces at the bottom—as unskilled industrial or service employees. But the Great Migration also counted educated African Americans in its ranks, as this excerpt from a letter sent to the *Chicago Defender*, a prominent black newspaper, demonstrates. The four letter writers were educated women from Florida who had been teachers in black schools and were now looking for jobs as domestic servants with well-off Chicago families. We do not know whether the *Chicago Defender* responded to this particular letter, but we do know that in general the newspaper played a key role in facilitating migration by providing important information to southern migrants and northern employers.

We have several times read your noted newspaper and we are delighted with the same because it is a thorough Negro paper. There is a storm of our people toward the North and especially to your city. We have watched your want ad regularly and we are anxious for location with good families (white) where we can be cared for and do domestic work. We want to engage as cook, nurse, and maid. We have had some educational advantages, as we have taught in rural schools for few years but our pay so poor we could not continue. We can furnish testimonial of our honesty and integrity and moral standing. Will you please assist us in securing places as we are anxious to come but want jobs before we leave. Our chance here is so poor.

Q What, if anything, can we learn about these four potential migrants from this letter excerpt? In particular, how desperate were they to leave the South?

Q What steps had they taken to prepare for going north?

Q What risks were they willing to endure for the sake of gaining an opportunity for a better life?

Source: *The Journal of Negro History*, Vol. IV, ed. Carter G. Woodson, Lancaster, PA (The Association for the Study of Negro Life and History, Inc., 1919), pp. 318–319.

Securing Workers, Keeping Labor Peace

The government worried as much about labor's cooperation as about industry's compliance. War increased the demand for industrial labor while cutting the supply. European immigrants had stopped coming, and millions of workers already in American were conscripted into the military and thus lost to industry.

Manufacturers responded to the labor shortage by recruiting new sources of labor from the rural South; 500,000 African Americans migrated to northern cities between 1916 and 1920. Another half-million white southerners followed the same path during that period. Hundreds of thousands of Mexicans left their homeland for jobs in the Southwest and Midwest. Approximately 40,000 northern women found work as streetcar conductors, railroad workers, munitions makers, and in other jobs customarily reserved for men. The number of female clerical workers doubled between 1910 and 1920, with many of these women finding work in government war bureaucracies.

These workers alleviated but did not eliminate the nation's labor shortage. Quick to recognize the benefits to be won from the tight labor market, workers quit jobs they did not like and took part in strikes and other collective actions in large numbers. Union membership almost doubled, from 2.6 million in 1915 to 5.1 million in 1920. Workers sought higher wages and shorter hours through strikes and unionization. They also struck in response to managerial attempts to speed up production and tighten discipline. As time passed, increasing numbers of workers began to wonder why the war for democracy in Europe had no counterpart in their factories at home. "Industrial democracy" became the battle cry of an awakened labor movement.

Wilson's willingness to include labor in his 1916 progressive coalition reflected his awareness of labor's potential power. In 1918, he bestowed prestige on the newly formed **National War Labor Board** (NWLB) by appointing former president William Howard Taft to be co-chair alongside Samuel Gompers of the AFL. The NWLB brought together representatives of labor, industry, and the public to resolve labor disputes.

Raising An Army

The Selective Service Act of May 1917 empowered the administration to raise an army through conscription. By war's end, local Selective Service boards had registered 24 million young men age 18 and older and had drafted nearly 3 million of them into the military. Another 2 million volunteered for service.

Relatively few men resisted the draft, even among recent immigrants. Foreign-born men constituted 18 percent of the armed forces—a percentage greater than their share of the total population. Almost 400,000 African Americans served, representing approximately 10 percent of armed forces, the same as the percentage of African Americans in the total population.

The U.S. Army, under the command of Chief of Staff Peyton March and General John J. Pershing, had to fashion these diverse millions into a professional fighting force. Rather than teaching the raw recruits to put aside their prejudices, Pershing and March segregated black soldiers from white. Most African Americans were assigned to all-black units and barred from combat. Being stripped of a combat role was particularly galling to blacks, who, in previous wars, had proven themselves to be among the best American fighters.

But some African Americans did demonstrate their valor on the battlefield. One of the most decorated units was **New York's 369th Regiment,** a black unit recruited in Harlem. Bowing to pressure from civil rights groups to allow some black troops to fight, Pershing had offered the 369th to the French army. The 369th entered the French front line and scored one major success after another. In gratitude for its service, the French government decorated the entire unit with one of its highest honors—the *Croix de Guerre.*

Paying the Bills

As chief purchaser of supplies for the U.S. military, the government incurred huge debts. To help pay its bills, it sharply increased tax rates. The richest were slapped with a 67 percent income tax and a 25 percent inheritance tax. Corporations were ordered to pay an "excess profits" tax. Tax revenues, however, provided only about one-third of the $33 billion the government ultimately spent on the war. The rest came from the sale of **Liberty Bonds**, 30-year bonds the government sold to individuals with a return of 3.5 percent in annual interest. The government offered

National War Labor Board
U.S. government agency during World War I that brought together representatives of labor, industry, and the public to resolve labor disputes.

New York's 369th Regiment
Black army unit recruited in Harlem that served under French command and was decorated with the Croix de Guerre *for its valor.*

Liberty Bonds *Thirty-year government bonds with an annual interest rate of 3.5 percent sold to fund the war effort.*

THE 369TH RETURNS TO NEW YORK. *Denied the opportunity to fight in the U.S. Army, this unit fought for the French. For the length and distinction of its service in the front lines, this entire unit was awarded the Croix de Guerre (War Cross) by the French government.*

five bond issues between 1917 and 1920, and all were quickly sold out, thanks, in no small measure, to a high-powered sales pitch that equated bond purchases with patriotic duty.

Arousing Patriotic Ardor

The Treasury's bond campaign was only one aspect of an extraordinary government effort to arouse public support for the war. In 1917, Wilson set up a new agency, the **Committee on Public Information** (CPI), to popularize the war. Under the chairmanship of George Creel, a Midwestern progressive and a muckraker, the CPI distributed 75 million copies of pamphlets explaining U.S. war aims in several languages. It trained a force of 75,000 "Four-Minute Men" to deliver succinct, uplifting war speeches. It papered the walls of countless public institutions (and many private ones) with posters, placed advertisements in magazines, sponsored exhibitions, and issued thousands of press releases on the progress of the war. Through CPI materials, Americans everywhere learned that the United States had entered the war "to make the world safe for democracy."

This uplifting message imparted to many a deep love of country. Among others, particularly those experiencing poverty and discrimination, it sparked a new spirit of protest. Workers rallied to the cry of "industrial democracy." Women seized upon the democratic fervor to bring their fight for suffrage to a successful conclusion (see Chapter 21). African Americans began to dream that the war might deliver them from second-class citizenship. European ethnics believed that Wilson's support of their countrymen's rights abroad would improve their own chances for success in the United States.

Wartime Repression

Although the CPI had helped to unleash it, this new democratic enthusiasm troubled Creel and others in the Wilson administration. They had not anticipated that the promotion of democratic ideals at home would exacerbate, rather than lessen, existing social and cultural conflicts. As a result, the CPI's campaign became

Committee on Public Information *U.S. government agency established in 1917 to arouse support for the war and, later, to generate suspicion of war dissenters.*

WOMEN DOING "MEN'S WORK." *Labor shortages during the war allowed thousands of women to take industrial jobs customarily reserved for men. Here women operate pneumatic hammers at the Midvale Steel and Ordnance Company, Nicetown, Pennsylvania, 1918.*

National Archives

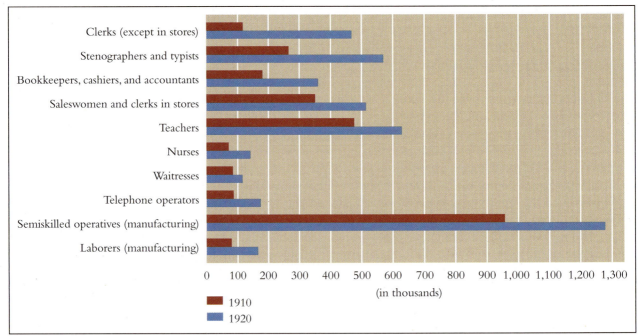

OCCUPATIONS WITH LARGEST INCREASE IN WOMEN, 1910–1920

Source: Joseph A. Hill, *Women in Gainful Occupations, 1870–1920*, U.S. Bureau of the Census, Monograph no. 9 (Washington, D.C.: Government Printing Office, 1929), p. 33.

more coercive by early 1918. Inflammatory advertisements called on patriots to report on neighbors, coworkers, and ethnics whom they suspected of subverting the war effort. Propagandists called on immigrants to repudiate ties to their homeland. The CPI spread lurid tales of German atrocities and encouraged the public to see movies like *The Prussian Cur* and *The Beast of Berlin*. The Justice Department arrested thousands of German and Austrian immigrants whom it suspected of subversive activities. Congress passed the Trading with the Enemy Act, which required foreign-language publications to submit all war-related stories to post office censors for approval.

- June 28 Bosnian nationalists Archduke
Ferdinand assasinated

- Italy left Triple Alliance in the beginning.
- Britian blocked out U.S trade withe Germany
drawing the US. into the war.
- Britian had control of Seas so Germany created
a U-boat (submarine)
- Woodrow Wilson = Peace during war.
- Charles EVan Hughes = War.
- April 6th US declares War.
- During WWI was the first time the
government took away the "freedom of speech"

- Paris Conferece - Treaty of Versailles
- Discuss peace treaty / 14 points.

- 1921, Germany pays victors 33 billion
and were force to admit responsibility of war
- Fourteen Points created by League of Nations.
- Henry Cabot Lodge - reject treaty, led
- 1919 steel Strike
- diffrent ethnicities got together
- Were rejected on strike
- Workers walked off.

German Americans became the objects of popular hatred, and American patriots sought to expunge every trace of German influence from American culture. Libraries removed works of German literature from their shelves, while Theodore Roosevelt and others urged school districts to prohibit the teaching of the German language. Some school boards burned German books (see Table 23.1).

German Americans risked being fired from work, losing their businesses, and being assaulted on the street. A St. Louis mob lynched an innocent German immigrant whom they suspected of subversion. After only 25 minutes of deliberation, a jury acquitted the mob leaders, who had defended their crime as an act of patriotism. German Americans began hiding their ethnic identity, changing their names, speaking German only in the privacy of their homes, and celebrating their holidays only with trusted friends.

The anti-German campaign escalated into a general anti-immigrant crusade. Congress passed the **Immigration Restriction Act of 1917,** which declared that all adult immigrants who failed a reading test would be denied admission to the United States. The act also banned the immigration of laborers from India, Indochina, Afghanistan, Arabia, the East Indies, and several other countries within an "Asiatic Barred Zone." Congress also passed the Eighteenth Amendment to the Constitution, which prohibited the manufacture and distribution of alcoholic beverages. The crusade for prohibition was not new, but anti-immigrant feelings gave it added impetus. Prohibitionists pictured the nation's urban ethnic ghettos as scenes of drunkenness, immorality, and disloyalty.

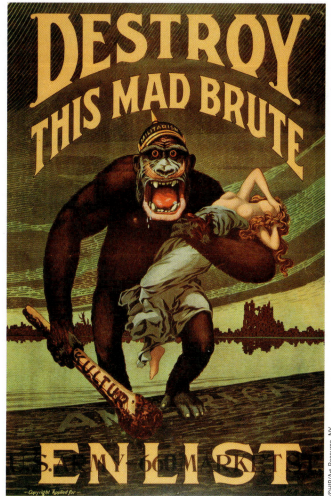

THE CAMPAIGN OF FEAR. *By 1918, the government's appeal to Americans' best aspirations—to spread liberty and democracy—had been replaced by a determination to arouse fear of subversion and conquest. Here the German enemy is depicted as a terrifying brute who violates Lady Liberty and uses his kultur club to destroy civilization.*

©HIP/Art Resource, NY

TABLE 23.1

RENAMED GERMAN AMERICAN WORDS	
Original	**"Patriotic" Name**
hamburger	Salisbury steak, liberty steak, liberty sandwich
sauerkraut	liberty cabbage
Hamburg Avenue, Brooklyn, New York	Wilson Avenue, Brooklyn, New York
Germantown, Nebraska	Garland, Nebraska
East Germantown, Indiana	Pershing, Indiana
Berlin, Iowa	Lincoln, Iowa
pinochle	liberty
German shepherd	Alsatian shepherd
Deutsches Haus of Indianapolis	Athenaeum of Indiana
Germania Maennerchor of Chicago	Lincoln Club
Kaiser Street	Maine Way

Source: From La Vern J. Rippley, *The German Americans* (Boston: Twayne, 1976), p. 186; and Robert H. Ferrell, *Woodrow Wilson and World War I, 1917–1921* (New York: Harper and Row, 1985), pp. 205–206.

Immigration Restriction Act of 1917 *Measure that denied any adult immigrant who failed a reading test entry into the United States, and banned immigration from the "Asiatic Barred Zone."*

Espionage, Sabotage, and Sedition Acts *Laws passed in 1917 and 1918 that gave the federal government sweeping powers to silence and even imprison dissenters.*

In the **Espionage, Sabotage, and Sedition Acts** passed in 1917 and 1918, Congress gave the administration sweeping powers to silence and imprison dissenters. These acts went far beyond outlawing spying, sabotaging war production, and calling for the enemy's victory. By making it illegal to write or utter any statement that could be construed as profaning the flag, the Constitution, or the military, they constituted the most drastic restriction of free speech at the national level since the Alien and Sedition Acts of 1798 (see Chapter 7).

Government repression fell most heavily on the Industrial Workers of the World (IWW) and the Socialist Party. Both groups had opposed intervention. Although they subsequently muted their opposition, they continued to insist that the true enemies of American workers were to be found in the ranks of American employers, not in Germany or Austria-Hungary. The government responded by banning many socialist materials from the mails and by disrupting socialist and IWW meetings. By spring 1918, government agents had arrested 2,000 IWW members, including the organization's entire executive board. Many of those arrested would be sentenced to long jail terms. Eugene V. Debs, the head of the Socialist Party, received a 10-year jail term for making an antiwar speech in Canton, Ohio, in summer 1918.

Private citizens also organized groups to enforce patriotism. The largest of these, the American Protective League, spied on fellow workers and neighbors, and opened the mail and tapped the phones of those suspected of disloyalty. Attorney General Thomas Gregory publicly endorsed the group and sought federal funds to support its "police" work. The spirit of coercion even infected institutions that had long prided themselves on tolerance. In July 1917, Columbia University fired two professors for speaking out against U.S. intervention in the war.

Wilson did attempt to block some repressive legislation. He vetoed both the Immigration Restriction Act and the Volstead Act (the act passed by Congress to enforce Prohibition), only to be overridden by Congress. But Wilson did little to halt the prosecution of radicals or the campaign to exclude Socialist Party publications from the mail. He ignored pleas from progressives that he intervene in the Debs case. His acquiescence in these matters cost him dearly among progressives and socialists. Wilson believed, however, that once the Allies won the war and arranged a just peace in accordance with the Fourteen Points, his administration's wartime actions would be forgiven and the progressive coalition would be restored.

THE FAILURE OF THE INTERNATIONAL PEACE

FOCUS QUESTION

What were Woodrow Wilson's peace proposals, and how did they fare?

In the Fourteen Points, Wilson had translated his principles for a new world order into specific proposals for international peace and justice. The first group of points called for all nations to abide by a code of conduct that embraced free trade, freedom of the seas, open diplomacy, disarmament, and the resolution of disputes through mediation. A second group, based on the principle of self-determination, proposed redrawing the map of Europe to give the subjugated peoples of the Austro-Hungarian, Ottoman, and Russian empires national sovereignty. The last point called for establishing a League of Nations, an assembly in which all nations would be represented and in which all international disputes would be given a fair hearing and an opportunity for peaceful solutions.

The Paris Peace Conference and the Treaty of Versailles

To capitalize on his international prestige, Wilson broke with diplomatic precedent and decided to head the American delegation to the Paris Peace Conference. Although representatives of 27 nations began meeting in Paris on January 12, 1919, to discuss the Fourteen Points, negotiations were controlled by the "Big Four": the United States, Great Britain, France, and Italy. When Italy quit the conference after a dispute with Wilson, the Big Four became the Big Three. Wilson quickly learned that his negotiating partners' support for the Fourteen Points was much weaker than he had believed. France and England refused to include most of Wilson's points in the peace treaty. The points having to do with freedom of the seas and free trade were omitted, as were the proposals for open diplomacy and Allied disarmament. Wilson won partial endorsement of the principle of self-determination: Belgian sovereignty was restored, Poland's status as a nation was affirmed, and the new nations of Czechoslovakia, Yugoslavia, Finland, Lithuania, Latvia, and Estonia were created. Some lands of the former Ottoman Empire— Armenia, Palestine, Mesopotamia, and Syria—were to be placed under League of Nations' trusteeships with the understanding that they would someday gain their independence. But Wilson failed in his efforts to block a British plan to transfer former German colonies in Asia to Japanese control, an Italian plan to annex territory inhabited by 200,000 Austrians, and a French plan to take from Germany its valuable Saar coal mines (see Map 23.2).

Nor could Wilson blunt the drive to punish Germany for its wartime aggression. In addition to awarding the Saar basin to France, the Allies gave portions of northern Germany to Denmark and portions of eastern Germany to Poland and Czechoslovakia. Germany was stripped of virtually its entire navy and air force, and forbidden to place soldiers or fortifications in western Germany along the Rhine. In addition, Germany was forced to admit its responsibility for the war, in effect agreeing to compensate the victors in cash ("reparations") for the pain and suffering it had inflicted on them.

On June 28, 1919, Great Britain, France, the United States, Germany, and other European nations signed the Treaty of Versailles. In 1921, an Allied commission notified Germany that it was to pay the victors $33 billion, a sum well beyond the resources of the defeated nation.

The League of Nations

The Allies' single-minded pursuit of self-interest disillusioned many liberals and socialists in the United States, but Wilson seemed undismayed. He had won approval of the most important of his Fourteen Points—that which called for the creation of the League of Nations. The League, whose structure and responsibilities were set forth in a Covenant attached to the peace treaty, would function as an international parliament and judiciary, establishing rules of international behavior and resolving disputes between nations through rational and peaceful means.

Wilson believed that the League would redeem the failures of the Paris Peace Conference. Under its auspices, free trade and freedom of the seas would be achieved, reparations against Germany would be reduced or eliminated, disarmament of the Allies would proceed, and the principle of self-determination would be extended to peoples outside Europe. Moreover, the League would have the power to punish aggressor nations through economic isolation and military retaliation.

Map 23.2 Europe and the Near East after the First World War. *The First World War and the Treaty of Versailles changed the geography of Europe and the Near East. Nine nations in Europe, stretching from Yugoslavia in the south to Finland in the north, were created (or re-formed) out of the defeated Austro-Hungarian and Ottoman empires. In the Near East, meanwhile, Syria, Lebanon, Palestine, Transjordan, and Iraq were carved out of the Ottoman Empire, placed under British or French control, and promised eventual independence.*

Wilson versus Lodge: The Fight over Ratification

The League's success, however, depended on Wilson's ability to convince the U.S. Senate to ratify the Treaty of Versailles. The Republicans had gained a majority in 1918, and two groups within their ranks were determined to frustrate Wilson's ambitions. One group was a caucus of 14 Midwesterners and westerners known as the "irreconcilables." Most of them were conservative isolationists, but a few were prominent progressives who had voted against the declaration of war in 1917. The self-interest displayed by England and France at the peace conference convinced this group that the Europeans were incapable of decent behavior in international matters.

Senator **Henry Cabot Lodge** of Massachusetts led the second opposition group. Its members subscribed to Theodore Roosevelt's vision of a world controlled by a few great nations, each militarily strong, secure in its own sphere of influence, and determined to avoid war through a carefully negotiated balance of power. These Republicans preferred to let Europe return to the power politics that had prevailed before the war rather than experiment with a new world order that might constrain and compromise U.S. power and autonomy.

Lodge and his supporters raised important questions about **Article X of the Covenant**, which gave the League the right to undertake military actions against aggressor nations. Did Americans want to authorize an international organization to decide when the United States would go to war? Was this not a violation of the Constitution, which vested war-making power solely in Congress? How could the United States ensure that it would not be forced into a military action that might damage its national interest?

It soon became clear, however, that several Republicans, including Lodge, were as interested in humiliating Wilson as in developing an alternative approach to foreign policy. They accused Wilson of promoting socialism through his wartime expansion of government power. They were angry that he had failed to include any distinguished Republicans in the Paris peace delegation. And they were bitter about the 1918 congressional elections, when Wilson had argued that a Republican victory would embarrass the nation abroad.

WILSON IN PARIS, 1919. *This photograph shows President Wilson (on right), recently arrived in Paris to negotiate the Treaty of Versailles, striding confidently and comfortably alongside his two allies, British Prime Minister Lloyd George (on left) and French Premier Clemenceau (in center). In the negotiations themselves, Lloyd George and Clemenceau would prove to be as much adversaries as allies to Wilson.*

©Bettmann/ CORBIS

When the Senate Foreign Relations Committee, chaired by Lodge and packed with opponents of the treaty, finally reported the treaty to the full Senate, it came encumbered with nearly 50 amendments whose adoption Lodge made a precondition of his support. Some of the amendments expressed reasonable concerns—namely, that participation in the League not diminish the role of Congress in determining foreign policy or compromise the sovereignty of the nation. But many were meant only to complicate the task of ratification.

Despite Lodge's obstructionism, the treaty's chances for ratification by the required two-thirds majority of the Senate remained good. Many Republicans were prepared to vote for ratification if Wilson indicated a willingness to accept some of the proposed amendments. But Wilson refused to compromise and announced that he would carry his case to the people. In September 1919, he undertook a whirlwind cross-country tour in which he addressed as many crowds as he could reach, sometimes speaking for an hour at a time, four times a day.

On September 25, after giving a speech at Pueblo, Colorado, Wilson suffered excruciating headaches throughout the night. His physician ordered him back to Washington, where on October 2 he suffered a near-fatal stroke. Wilson hovered near death for two weeks and remained seriously disabled for another six. His condition improved somewhat in November, but his left side remained paralyzed, his speech was slurred, his energy level low, and his emotions unstable. Wilson's wife, Edith Bolling Wilson, and his doctor isolated him from Congress and the press, withholding news they thought might upset him and preventing the public from learning how much his body and mind had deteriorated.

Henry Cabot Lodge *Republican senator from Massachusetts who led the campaign to reject the Treaty of Versailles.*

Article X of the Covenant *Addendum to the Treaty of Versailles that empowered the League of Nations to undertake military actions against aggressor nations.*

QUICK REVIEW

THE TREATY OF VERSAILLES (1919)

- The treaty formally ended World War I and punished Germany with territorial loss and reparations for its "war guilt"

- Wilson largely failed to make his Fourteen Points the basis of this treaty and a new world order (see Table 23.2)

- Covenant to the treaty brought Wilson a temporary victory by calling for the establishment of the League of Nations

- U.S. Senate, however, refused to ratify the treaty, making it impossible for America to join the League of Nations

Many historians believe that the stroke impaired Wilson's political judgment. He refused to consider any of the Republican amendments to the treaty, even after it had become clear that compromise offered the only chance of winning U.S. participation in the League. When Lodge presented an amended treaty for a ratification vote on November 19, Wilson ordered Senate Democrats to vote against it; 42 (of 47) Democratic senators complied, and with the aid of 13 Republican irreconcilables, the Lodge version was defeated. Only moments later, the unamended version of the treaty—Wilson's version—received only 38 votes.

The Treaty's Final Defeat

Supporters of the League in Congress, the nation, and the world urged the Senate and the president to reconsider. Wilson would not budge. A bipartisan group of senators tried to work out a compromise without consulting him. When that effort failed, the Senate put to a vote, one more time, the Lodge version of the treaty. Because 23 Democrats, most of them southerners, still refused to break with Wilson, this last-ditch effort at ratification failed on March 8, 1920, by a margin of seven votes.

Many believe that the flawed treaty and the failure of the League contributed to Adolf Hitler's rise and the outbreak of a second world war more devastating than the first. Would American participation in the League have significantly altered the course of world history?

The mere fact of U.S. membership in the League would not have magically solved Europe's postwar problems. The U.S. government was inexperienced in diplomacy and prone to mistakes. Its freedom to negotiate solutions to international disputes would have been limited by the large number of American voters who remained strongly opposed to U.S. entanglement in European affairs. Even if such opposition could have been overcome, the United States would still have confronted European countries determined to go their own way.

Nevertheless, one thing is clear: No stable international order could have arisen after the First World War without the full involvement of the United States.

TABLE 23.2

WOODROW WILSON'S FOURTEEN POINTS, 1918: RECORD OF IMPLEMENTATION	
1. Open covenants of peace openly arrived at	Not fulfilled
2. Absolute freedom of navigation upon the seas in peace and war	Not fulfilled
3. Removal of all economic barriers to the equality of trade among nations	Not fulfilled
4. Reduction of armaments to the level needed only for domestic safety	Not fulfilled
5. Impartial adjustments of colonial claims	Not fulfilled
6. Evacuation of all Russian territory; Russia to be welcomed into the society of free nations	Not fulfilled
7. Evacuation and restoration of Belgium	Fulfilled
8. Evacuation and restoration of all French lands; return of Alsace-Lorraine to France	Fulfilled
9. Readjustment of Italy's frontiers along lines of Italian nationality	Compromised
10. Self-determination for the former subjects of the Austro-Hungarian Empire	Compromised
11. Evacuation of Romania, Serbia, and Montenegro; free access to the sea for Serbia	Compromised
12. Self-determination for the former subjects of the Ottoman Empire; secure sovereignty for Turkish portion	Compromised
13. Establishment of an independent Poland with free and secure access to the sea	Fulfilled
14. Establishment of a League of Nations affording mutual guarantees of independence and territorial integrity	Compromised

Source: From G. M. Gathorne-Hardy, *The Fourteen Points and the Treaty of Versailles*, Oxford Pamphlets on World Affairs, no. 6 (1939), pp. 8–34; and Thomas G. Paterson et al., *American Foreign Policy: A History*, 2nd ed. (Lexington, Mass.: D. C. Heath, 1983), vol. 2, pp. 282–293.

The League of Nations required American authority and prestige in order to operate effectively as an international parliament. We cannot know whether the League, with American involvement, would have offered the Germans a less humiliating peace, nor whether an American-led League would have stopped Hitler's expansionism. Still, it seems fair to suggest that American participation would have strengthened the League and improved its ability to bring a lasting peace to Europe.

THE POSTWAR PERIOD: A SOCIETY IN CONVULSION

The end of the war brought no respite from the forces convulsing American society. Workers wanted to regain the purchasing power they had lost to inflation. Employers wanted to halt or reverse the wartime gains labor had made. Radicals saw in this conflict between capital and labor the possibility of a socialist revolution. Conservatives were certain that the revolution had already begun. Returning white servicemen were nervous about regaining their civilian jobs and looked with hostility on the black, Mexican, and female workers who had been recruited to take their places. Black veterans were in no mood to return to segregation and subordination.

FOCUS QUESTION

What issues convulsed American society in the immediate aftermath of war, and how were they resolved?

Labor–Capital Conflict

In 1919, four million workers—one-fifth of the nation's manufacturing workforce—went on strike. That January, a general strike paralyzed the city of Seattle. By August, walkouts had been staged by 400,000 eastern and Midwestern coal miners, 120,000 New England textile workers, and 50,000 New York City garment workers. Then came two strikes that turned public opinion sharply against labor. In September, Boston policemen walked off their jobs after the police commissioner refused to negotiate with their newly formed union. Rioting and looting soon broke out. Massachusetts governor Calvin Coolidge refused to negotiate with the policemen, called out the National Guard to restore order, and fired the entire police force.

Hard on the heels of the policemen's strike came a strike by more than 300,000 steelworkers in the Midwest. No union had established a footing in the steel industry since the 1890s, when Andrew Carnegie had ousted the ironworkers' union from his Homestead, Pennsylvania, mills. Most steelworkers labored long hours (the 12-hour shift was still standard) for low wages in dangerous workplaces. The organizers of the **1919 steel strike** had somehow managed to persuade steelworkers with varied skill levels and ethnic backgrounds to put aside their differences and demand an eight-hour day and union recognition. When the employers rejected those demands, the workers walked off their jobs. Employers responded by procuring armed guards to beat up the strikers and by hiring nonunion labor to keep the plants running. In many areas, local and state police prohibited union meetings, ran strikers out of town, and opened fire on those who disobeyed orders. The strike collapsed in January 1920.

Radicals and the Red Scare

The steel companies succeeded in putting down the strike by fanning the public's fear that revolutionary sentiment was spreading among workers. Radical sentiment was indeed on the rise. Mine workers and railroad workers had begun calling for the permanent nationalization of coal mines and railroads. Socialist trade unionists

1919 steel strike *Walkout by 300,000 steelworkers in the Midwest demanding union recognition and an eight-hour day. It was defeated by employers and local and state police forces, who sometimes resorted to violence.*

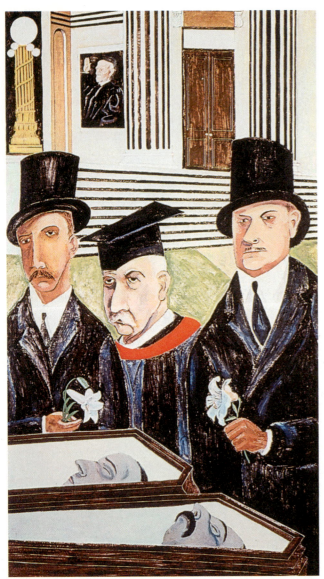

THE PASSION OF SACCO AND VANZETTI, BY BEN SHAHN. The 1920 trial and 1927 execution of Nicola Sacco and Bartolomeo Vanzetti became the passion of many immigrants, liberal intellectuals, and artists (such as Ben Shahn), who were convinced that the two anarchists had been unfairly tried and convicted.

Ben Shahn 1898-1969, The Passion of Sacco and Vanzetti, 1931-1932 Sacco-Vanzetti series. Tempera on canvas, Unframed: 84 1/2 x 48in. (214.6 x 121.9cm) Framed: 85 1/2 x 50x 4 in. (10.2 x 217.2 x 127cm). Whitney Museum of American Art, New York; Gift of Edith and Milton Lowenthal in memory of Juliana Force 49.22. Art ©Estate of Ben Shahn/Licensed by VAGA, New York, NY.

Red Scare *Widespread fear in 1919–1920 that radicals had coalesced to establish a communist government on American soil. In response, the U.S. government and private citizens undertook a campaign to identify, silence, and, in some cases, imprison radicals.*

mounted the most serious challenge to Samuel Gompers's control of the American Federation of Labor (AFL) in 25 years. In 1920, nearly a million Americans voted for the Socialist presidential candidate Debs, who ran his campaign from jail.

This radical surge did not mean, however, that leftists had fashioned themselves into a single movement or political party. On the contrary, the Russian Revolution had split the American Socialist Party. One faction, which would keep the name Socialist and would continue under Debs's leadership, insisted that radicals follow a democratic path to socialism. The other group, which would take the name Communist, wanted to establish a Lenin-style "dictatorship of the proletariat." Small groups of anarchists represented a third radical tendency.

Most Americans nevertheless continued to assume that radicalism was a single, coordinated movement bent on establishing a communist government on American soil. Beginning in 1919, this perceived **"Red Scare"** prompted government officials and private citizens to embark on yet another campaign of repression. Thirty states passed sedition laws to punish those who advocated revolution. Numerous public and private groups intensified Americanization campaigns designed to strip foreigners of their subversive ways and remake them into loyal citizens. A newly formed veterans' organization, the American Legion, took on the American Protective League's role of identifying seditious individuals and organizations and ensuring the public's devotion to "100 percent Americanism."

The Red Scare reached its climax on New Year's Day 1920, when federal agents broke into the homes and meeting places of thousands of suspected revolutionaries in 33 cities. Directed by Attorney General A. Mitchell Palmer, these widely publicized "Palmer raids" were meant to expose the extent of revolutionary activity. Although Palmer's agents uncovered only three pistols, no rifles, and no explosives, they arrested more than 4,000 people and kept many of them in jail for weeks without formally charging them with a crime. Finally, those who were not citizens (approximately 600) were deported and the rest were released.

Palmer next alleged that revolutionaries were planning a series of assaults on government officials and government buildings for May 1, 1920. When nothing happened on that date, many Americans began to wonder whether Palmer had exaggerated the threat of dissent and subversion.

But the political atmosphere remained hostile to radicals, as the **Sacco and Vanzetti case** revealed. In May 1920, two Italian-born anarchists, Nicola Sacco and Bartolomeo Vanzetti, were arrested in Brockton, Massachusetts, and charged with armed robbery and murder. Both men proclaimed their innocence and insisted they were being punished for their political beliefs. Their foreign accents and their espousal of anarchist doctrines in the courtroom inclined many Americans, including the judge who presided at their trial, to view them harshly. Despite the weak case against them, they were convicted of first-degree murder and sentenced to death. Their lawyers attempted numerous appeals, all of which failed. Protests from Italian Americans, radicals, and liberal intellectuals compelled the governor of Massachusetts to appoint a commission to review the case, but no new trial was ordered. On August 23, 1927, Sacco and Vanzetti were executed, still insisting that they were innocent.

Racial Conflict and the Rise of Black Nationalism

The more than 400,000 blacks who served in the armed forces believed that a victory for democracy abroad would help them achieve democracy for their people at home. Thus the discrimination they experienced after the war was difficult to endure. Many blacks who had found jobs in the North were fired to make way for returning white veterans. Returning black servicemen had to scrounge for poorly paid jobs as unskilled laborers. In the South, lynch mobs targeted black veterans who refused to tolerate the usual insults and indignities.

The worst antiblack violence after the war occurred in the North. In Chicago, in July 1919, a black teenager who had been swimming in Lake Michigan was killed by whites after coming too close to a whites-only beach. Rioting soon broke out, with white mobs invading black neighborhoods, torching homes and stores, and attacking innocent residents. Led by war veterans, some of whom were armed, blacks fought back. The five days of fighting left 38 dead (23 black, 15 white) and more than 500 injured. Race rioting in other cities pushed the death total to 120 before summer's end.

The riots made it clear to blacks that the North was not the Promised Land. The NAACP carried on its campaign for civil rights and racial equality, but many blacks no longer shared its belief that they would one day be accepted as first-class citizens. They turned instead to a leader from Jamaica, **Marcus Garvey**. Garvey called on blacks to give up their hopes for integration and to set about forging a separate black nation. He reminded blacks that they possessed a rich culture stretching back over the centuries that would enable them to achieve greatness. Garvey's ambition was to build a black nation in Africa that would bring together all the world's people of African descent. In the short term, he wanted to help American and Caribbean blacks achieve economic and cultural independence.

Garvey's call for black separatism and self-sufficiency—black nationalism, as it came to be called—elicited a favorable response among African Americans. In the early 1920s, the Universal Negro Improvement Association (UNIA), which Garvey had founded, enrolled millions of members. His newspaper, the *Negro World*, reached a circulation of 200,000. Garvey's most visible economic venture was the Black Star Line, a shipping company with three ships flying the UNIA flag from their masts.

This black nationalist movement did not endure for long. Garvey entered into bitter disputes with other black leaders, including W. E. B. Du Bois, who regarded him as a flamboyant, self-serving demagogue. Garvey sometimes showed poor judgment, as when he expressed support for the Ku Klux Klan on the grounds that it shared his pessimism about the possibility of racial integration. Garvey also squandered UNIA money on ill-conceived business ventures. In 1923, he was convicted of mail fraud involving the sale of Black Star Line stock and was sentenced to five years in jail. In 1927, he was deported to Jamaica and the UNIA folded. But Garvey's philosophy of black nationalism endured.

Sacco and Vanzetti case (1920) *Controversial conviction of two Italian-born anarchists accused of armed robbery and murder.*

Marcus Garvey *Jamaican-born black nationalist who attracted millions of African Americans in the early 1920s to a movement calling for black separatism and self-sufficiency.*

QUICK REVIEW

POSTWAR SOCIAL DISORDER

- Labor strikes surged in 1919; most were defeated

- Bolshevik Revolution in Russia (1917) generated fears of communist uprising in the United States (the "Red Scare"), prompting widespread repression

- Black migration north increased racial tensions and triggered urban race riots in 1919

- Disillusionment among African Americans led many to support Marcus Garvey's black nationalist movement

MARCUS GARVEY, BLACK NATIONALIST. *This portrait was taken in 1924, after Garvey's conviction on mail fraud charges.*

Library of Congress, Prints and Photographs Division

Conclusion

The resurgence of racism in 1919 and the consequent turn to black nationalism among African Americans were signs of how the high hopes of the war years had been dashed. Industrial workers, immigrants, and radicals also found their pursuit of liberty and equality interrupted by the fear, intolerance, and repression unleashed by the war. Woman suffragists had gained the right to vote. For feminists, however, suffrage did not fully compensate for the collapse of the progressive movement and, with it, their program of achieving equal rights for women across the board.

A similar disappointment engulfed those who had embraced and fought for Wilson's dream of creating a new and democratic world order. The world in 1919 appeared as volatile as it had been in 1914. More and more Americans—perhaps even a majority—were coming to believe that U.S. intervention had been a mistake.

Economically, the United States benefited a great deal from the war. The war had accelerated technological and managerial innovation. By 1919, the American economy was by far the world's strongest, poised for a decade of remarkable growth. But the prosperity of the 1920s growth would not be enough to dissolve the class, ethnic, and racial tensions that the war had exposed. And the failure of the peace process added to Europe's problems, delayed the emergence of the United States as a leader in world affairs, and created the preconditions for another world war.

CHAPTER REVIEW

Review

1. What caused Europe's descent into war?
2. Why did the U.S. policy of neutrality fail, and why did the United States get drawn into war?
3. What contribution did the United States make to the Allied Powers' victory?
4. What problems did the United States encounter in mobilizing for total war, and how successfully were those problems overcome?
5. What were Woodrow Wilson's peace proposals, and how did they fare?
6. What issues convulsed American society in the immediate aftermath of war, and how were they resolved?

Critical Thinking

1. Did the First World War do more to enhance or interrupt the pursuit of liberty and equality on the home front?
2. Do you think that the chances of a second world war breaking out in Europe in the late 1930s would have been substantially lessened had Woodrow Wilson prevailed on the U.S. Senate to ratify the Treaty of Versailles in 1919, thereby bringing the United States into the League of Nations?

Identifications

Review your understanding of the following key terms, people, and events for this chapter.

Triple Alliance, p. 527
Triple Entente, p. 527
"peace without victory," p. 527
neutrality, p. 530
Lusitania, p. 531
Zimmermann telegram, p. 532
Fourteen Points, p. 533

John J. Pershing, p. 533
total war, p. 534
War Industries Board, p. 534
National War Labor Board, p. 536
New York's 369th Regiment, p. 536
Liberty Bonds, p. 536

Committee on Public Information, p. 537
Immigration Restriction Act of 1917, p. 539
Espionage, Sabotage, and Sedition Acts, p. 540
Henry Cabot Lodge, p. 543
Article X of the Covenant, p. 543

1919 steel strike, p. 545
Red Scare, p. 546
Sacco and Vanzetti case (1920), p. 546
Marcus Garvey, p. 547

DISCOVERY

What role did nationalism play in the war and on the home front in World War I?

In thinking about this question, begin by breaking it down into the components shown below. A discussion of the significance of each component should appear in your answer.

Geography

Study Map 23.1 on page 529 and Map 23.2 on page 542. Which nations and empires lost the most territory following World War I? What new countries emerged following the war? How many "empires" existed in Europe and the Middle East after World War I? How were League of Nations trusteeships different from colonies? Did the collapse of empires, the emergence of new nations, and the shifting borders of existing nations weaken or intensify expressions of nationalism among Europe's peoples? What were the consequences of this development?

War and Society

Read through the renamed German American words in Table 23.1. In what ways do the new words express an American nationalism? How do you think you would react if you were a German American living at that time? Does this kind of erasure of foreign culture still occur during wartime or international disputes? If so, can you think of a recent example?

TABLE 23.1

RENAMED GERMAN AMERICAN WORDS	
Original	**"Patriotic" Name**
hamburger	Salisbury steak, liberty steak, liberty sandwich
sauerkraut	liberty cabbage
Hamburg Avenue, Brooklyn, New York	Wilson Avenue, Brooklyn, New York
Germantown, Nebraska	Garland, Nebraska
East Germantown, Indiana	Pershing, Indiana
Berlin, Iowa	Lincoln, Iowa
pinochle	liberty
German shepherd	Alsatian shepherd
Deutsches Haus of Indianapolis	Athenaeum of Indiana
Germania Maennerchor of Chicago	Lincoln Club
Kaiser Street	Maine Way

Source: From La Vern J. Rippley, *The German Americans* (Boston: Twayne, 1976), p. 186; and Robert H. Ferrell, *Woodrow Wilson and World War I, 1917–1921* (New York: Harper and Row, 1985), pp. 205–206.

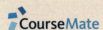

Visit the CourseMate website at www.cengagebrain.com for additional study tools and review materials for this chapter.

24

THE 1920s

PROSPERITY
    A Consumer Society
    A People's Capitalism
    The Rise of Advertising and Mass
       Marketing
    Changing Attitudes toward Marriage
       and Sexuality
    An Age of Celebrity
    Celebrating a Business Civilization
    Industrial Workers
    Women and Work
    The Women's Movement Adrift

THE POLITICS OF BUSINESS
    Harding and the Politics of Personal Gain
    Coolidge and Laissez-Faire Politics
    Hoover and the Politics of Associationalism
    The Politics of Business Abroad

FARMERS, SMALL-TOWN PROTESTANTS, AND
MORAL TRADITIONALISTS
    Agricultural Depression and Cultural Dislocation
    Prohibition
    The Ku Klux Klan
    Immigration Restriction
    Fundamentalism versus Liberal Protestantism
    The Scopes Trial

ETHNIC AND RACIAL COMMUNITIES
    European American Ethnics
    African Americans
    The Harlem Renaissance
    Mexican Americans

THE "LOST GENERATION" AND DISILLUSIONED
INTELLECTUALS
    Democracy on the Defensive

To many Americans, the 1920s was a decade of fun rather than reform, of good times rather than high ideals. It was, in the words of novelist F. Scott Fitzgerald, the "Jazz Age," a time when the quest for personal gratification seemed to replace the quest for public welfare.

Despite President Warren G. Harding's call for a "return to normalcy," America seemed to be rushing headlong into the future. The word *modern* began appearing everywhere, and, although it was rarely defined, it connoted certain beliefs: that science was a better guide to life than religion; that people should be free to choose their own lifestyles; that sex should be a source of pleasure for women as well as men; that women and minorities should be equal to white men and enjoy the same rights.

Many Americans, however, reaffirmed their belief that God's word transcended science; that people should obey the moral code set forth in the Bible; that women were not equal to men; and that blacks, Mexicans, and eastern European immigrants were inferior to Anglo-Saxon whites. They made their voices heard in a resurgent Ku Klux Klan and the fundamentalist movement, and on issues such as evolution and immigration.

Modernists and traditionalists confronted each other in party politics, in legislatures, in courtrooms, and in the press. Their battles belie the vision of the 1920s merely as a time for the pursuit of leisure.

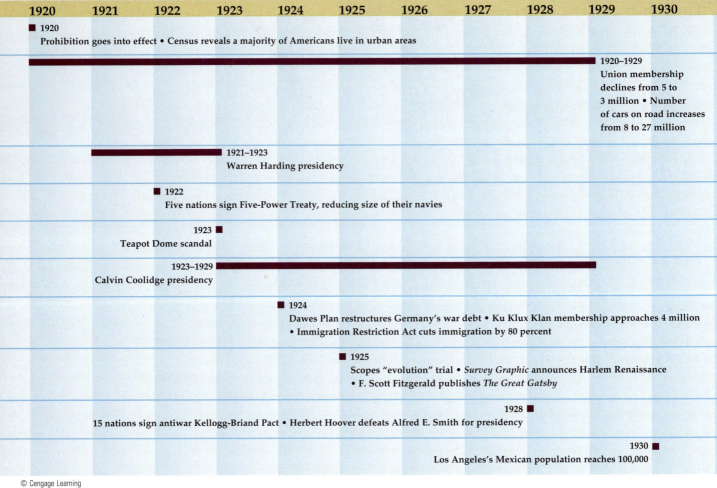

| 1920 | 1921 | 1922 | 1923 | 1924 | 1925 | 1926 | 1927 | 1928 | 1929 | 1930 |

■ **1920**
Prohibition goes into effect • Census reveals a majority of Americans live in urban areas

1920–1929
Union membership declines from 5 to 3 million • Number of cars on road increases from 8 to 27 million

1921–1923
Warren Harding presidency

■ **1922**
Five nations sign Five-Power Treaty, reducing size of their navies

1923 ■
Teapot Dome scandal

1923–1929
Calvin Coolidge presidency

■ **1924**
Dawes Plan restructures Germany's war debt • Ku Klux Klan membership approaches 4 million • Immigration Restriction Act cuts immigration by 80 percent

■ **1925**
Scopes "evolution" trial • *Survey Graphic* announces Harlem Renaissance • F. Scott Fitzgerald publishes *The Great Gatsby*

1928 ■
15 nations sign antiwar Kellogg-Briand Pact • Herbert Hoover defeats Alfred E. Smith for presidency

1930 ■
Los Angeles's Mexican population reaches 100,000

© Cengage Learning

PROSPERITY

From 1919 to 1921, the economy faltered as the country struggled to redirect industry from wartime to civilian production. But, from 1922 to 1929, the gross national product grew at an annual rate of 5.5 percent. The unemployment rate never exceeded 5 percent, and real wages rose about 15 percent.

A Consumer Society

In the 19th century, economic growth had rested primarily on the production of capital goods, such as factory machinery and railroad tracks. In the 1920s, growth rested more on consumer goods. Some products, such as cars and telephones, had been available since the early 1900s, but in the 1920s their sales reached new levels. In 1920, just 12 years after Ford introduced the Model T, 8 million cars were on the road. By 1929, there were 27 million—one for every five Americans. Other consumer goods became available for the first time: tractors, washing machines, refrigerators, radios, and vacuum cleaners. The term "consumer durable" was coined to describe such goods, which, unlike food, clothing, and other perishables, were meant to last. Yet even perishables took on new allure, as improvements in refrigeration and in packaging made it possible to transport fresh produce long distances and to extend its shelf life in grocery stores.

The public responded to these innovations with excitement. American industry had made fresh food and stylish clothes available to the masses. Refrigerators, vacuum cleaners, and washing machines would spare women the drudgery of housework. Radios would expand the public's cultural horizons. Cars, service stations, hot dog stands, "tourist cabins" (the forerunners of motels), and traffic lights seemed to herald a wholly new automobile civilization. The country had a network of paved roads by the middle of the decade. Suburbs proliferated. Young men and women everywhere discovered that cars were a place where they could "make out," and even make love, without fear of reproach by prudish parents or prying neighbors.

In the 1920s, Americans also discovered the benefits of owning stock. The number of stockholders in AT&T, the nation's largest corporation, rose from 140,000 to 568,000. By 1929, as many as seven million Americans owned stock, most of them people of middle-class or upper-class means.

A People's Capitalism

Capitalists boasted that they had created a **"people's capitalism"** in which virtually all Americans could have a share of luxuries and amenities. Poverty, they claimed, was banished, and the gap between rich and poor all but closed.

Actually, although wages were rising, millions of Americans still earned too little to partake fully of the marketplace. Social scientists Robert and Helen Lynd discovered, in their classic study of Muncie, Indiana, that working-class families who bought a car often lacked money for other goods. One housewife admitted, "The car is the only pleasure we have." But many industrialists resisted pressure to increase wages, and workers lacked the organizational strength to force them to pay more.

One solution came with the introduction of consumer credit. Car dealers, home appliance salesmen, and other merchants began to offer installment plans that enabled consumers to make a down payment and promise to pay the rest in installments. By 1930, 15 percent of all purchases were made on the installment plan. Even so, few poor Americans benefited from the consumer revolution. Middle-class Americans bought most of the consumer durables, fresh vegetables, and stocks.

The Rise of Advertising and Mass Marketing

Even middle-class consumers had to be wooed. How could they be persuaded to buy another car only a few years after they had bought their first one? General Motors had the answer. In 1926, it introduced the annual model change, giving its cars a new look and new features every year. GM leaped past Ford and became the world's largest car manufacturer.

Henry Ford reluctantly introduced his Model A in 1927 to provide customers with a colorful alternative to the drab Model T. Having spent decades selling a product renowned for its utility and reliability, Ford did not believe that sales could be increased by appealing to the intangible hopes and fears of consumers. He was wrong. The desire to be sexually attractive; to exercise power; to demonstrate success; to escape anonymity; to experience pleasure—all such desires, once activated, could motivate a consumer to buy a new car even when the old one was still serviceable, or to spend money on goods that might have once seemed frivolous.

To stoke Americans' desires for new products, campaigns by professional advertising firms played upon the emotions and vulnerabilities of their target audiences. A perfume manufacturer's ad pronounced: "The first duty of woman is to attract. . . . It does not matter how clever or independent you may be, if you fail to influence the men you meet, consciously or unconsciously, you are not fulfilling

people's capitalism *An egalitarian capitalism in which all Americans could participate and enjoy the consumer goods that U.S. industry had made available.*

THE ART OF SELLING CARS. *The creators of this dazzling advertisement mixed female sexuality, bold colors, and the power and speed of lightning bolts to generate consumer interest in the "New Morris-Oxford Six" automobile.*

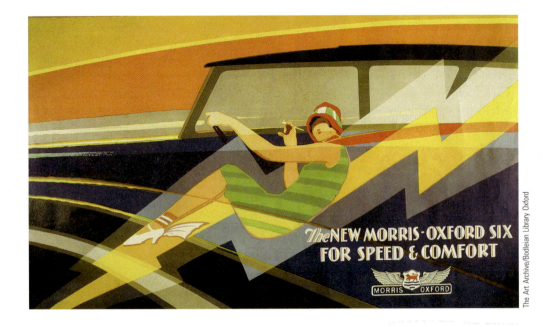

The Art Archive/Bodleian Library Oxford

your fundamental duty as a woman." A tobacco ad matter-of-factly declared: "Men at the top are apt to be pipe-smokers. . . . A pipe is back of most big ideas."

Advertising professionals believed they were helping people to manage their lives in ways that would increase their satisfaction and pleasure. American consumers, especially in the middle class, responded enthusiastically. Many were newcomers to middle-class ranks, searching for ways to affirm—or even create—their new identity. Men new to middle-class jobs in offices and banks needed reassurance, as did their stay-at-home wives. Vacuum cleaners and washing machines would make homemakers more efficient. Cosmetics would aid wives in their "first duty"—to be beautiful to their men.

Changing Attitudes toward Marriage and Sexuality

That husbands and wives were encouraged to pursue sexual satisfaction together was one sign of how prescriptions for married life had changed since the 19th century, when women were thought to lack sexual passion and men were tacitly expected to satisfy their drives through extramarital liaisons. Modern husbands and wives were expected to share other leisure activities as well—dining out, going to the movies, and discussing the latest selection from the newly formed Book-of-the-Month Club.

The public pursuit of pleasure was also noticeable among young and single middle-class women. The so-called **flappers** of the 1920s donned short dresses, rolled their stockings down, wore red lipstick, and smoked in public. Flappers were signaling their desire for independence and equality, but they did not intend to achieve those goals through politics, as had their predecessors in the woman suffrage movement. Rather, they aimed to create a new female personality endowed with self-reliance, outspokenness, and a new appreciation for the pleasures of life.

An Age of Celebrity

The pursuit of pleasure became both an individual and a group endeavor. Mass marketers began to understand the money that could be made by staging mega-events that tens of thousands would attend and that radio announcers would

flappers *Rebellious middle-class young women who signaled their desire for independence and equality through style and personality rather than through politics.*

[handwritten margin note: Expressed desire for independance & equality]

MUSICAL LINK TO THE PAST

Women Singers and the Birth of Modern Country Music

Composer: A.P. Carter (credited as writer but probably was not)
Title: "Single Girl, Married Girl" (1927)
Performers: The Carter Family

Plaintive and never preachy, "Single Girl, Married Girl" explores women's roles and marriage in ways rarely seen in the country music of the 1920s. As she did throughout her career, Sara Carter, a country music pioneer, sang simply and passionately about the lives of common people, in this case women: "Single girl, single girl, she goes to the store and buys . . . Married girl, married girl, she rocks the cradle and cries . . . Single girl, single girl, she's going where she please . . . Married girl, married girl, baby on her knees." Is Sara sad or angry about the plight of this "married girl" tied down by her baby, or is she just plainly stating how women's lives change when children arrive? In either case, Sara Carter, in this song, offers us a glimpse of how country women of the 1920s, often thought to be conservative in outlook, were themselves struggling to producing hit recordings that sold throughout the United States, England, and South Africa, among other places. The group consisted of Sara, who played autoharp and contributed lead vocals; her sister-in-law Maybelle on guitar; and her husband A.P., who occasionally sang with them, but whose most important job was traveling in search of material for the group, for which he often took unwarranted credit (a common practice at the time). Ralph Peer, Victor Records talent scout, discovered them at an open talent audition held in Bristol, Tennessee, on August 2, 1927. This recording, made at those sessions, provides us with a historic glimpse of the birth of modern country music.

The Carter women were relegated to the background in publicity for the group. Posters promised a "morally good" program in which a man (A.P.) appeared onstage, an important promise because women who performed popular music independently were considered morally suspect. Also, despite general agreement that Sara had a major hand in writing and arranging Carter Family material, her name rarely surfaced in the credits, where A.P.'s name typically dominated. Despite such caveats, the Carter Family represented an important example of the trend of women claiming new kinds of identities and expression in the modern mass media. Sara seemed to be an innovator in her personal life as well—her relatives described her as "very liberated" for a southern woman in the 1920s and 1930s, wearing slacks, shooting big game, writing and arranging music, openly smoking, and divorcing A.P. in 1938.

Maybelle, A.P., and Sara Carter posing for a photograph in Poor Valley, Virginia.

© Michael Ochs Archives/CORBIS

balance traditional female responsibilities (in this case, motherhood) with the freedoms that modern society seemed to be offering young women.

The national commercialization of country and blues music in the 1920s opened up new, but still limited, roles for women in the mass media. The Carter Family was by far the most successful of the initial female country groups,

Q Why do you think women performing music independently were frowned on and viewed by many as morally suspect during this period?

  Listen to an audio recording of this music on the Musical Links to the Past CD.

[handwritten: fly across Atlantic "Spirit of St. Louis"]

CHARLES A. LINDBERGH AND THE *SPIRIT OF ST. LOUIS.* *Lindbergh poses before the plane that will carry him from Long Island to Paris in the first solo flight across the Atlantic.*

[handwritten: Yankee Stadium 1923]

[handwritten: The Man that nobody knows]

Charles A. Lindbergh *First individual to fly solo across the Atlantic (1927) and the greatest celebrity of the 1920s.*

broadcast to millions. Newspapers and word of mouth ensured that these events would be discussed for days, even months. This trend became most pronounced in sports, particularly baseball and boxing. When Yankee Stadium opened in 1923, its size dwarfed every other sport amphitheater in the country. To succeed in such a venue, sports required not just stirring athletic competitions but individual athletes who seemed larger than life, such as baseball star George Herman "Babe" Ruth and boxer Jack Dempsey.

Americans also found celebrities in the movies, among stars such as comedian Charlie Chaplin and the exotically handsome Rudolph Valentino. Movie stars became so familiar that fans longed for news about their private lives as well, an interest that the movie industry was eager to exploit.

Perhaps no single individual achieved more fame and adoration, however, than **Charles A. Lindbergh**, the young pilot who, in 1927, became the first person to cross the Atlantic in a solo flight. Piloting his single-engine monoplane, *The Spirit of St. Louis*, Lindbergh flew nonstop (and without sleep) for 34 hours from the time he took off from Long Island until he landed at Le Bourget Airport in Paris. Thousands of Parisians were waiting for him at the airfield. When he returned to New York, an estimated four million fans lined the parade route.

This fame could not have happened without the new machinery of celebrity culture—aggressive journalists, radio commentators, promoters, and others who understood how fame could yield a profit. It mattered, too, that Lindbergh performed his feat in an airplane, one of the era's exciting innovations. But Lindbergh's celebrity involved more than hype and technology: He accomplished what others said could not be done, and he did it on his own. In an industrialized, bureaucratized world, Lindbergh demonstrated that an individual could still make a difference.

Celebrating a Business Civilization

Industrialists, advertisers, and merchandisers in the 1920s began to claim that their accomplishments lay at the heart of American civilization. In 1924, President Calvin Coolidge declared that "the business of America is business." Even religion became a business. Bruce Barton, in his best seller *The Man That Nobody Knows* (1925), depicted Jesus as an executive "who picked up twelve men from the bottom ranks of business and forged them into an organization that conquered the world."

Some employers adopted benevolent attitudes toward their employees. They set up workplace cafeterias, staffed on-site medical clinics, and engaged psychologists to counsel troubled workers. They built ball fields. They gave awards to employees who did their jobs well and with good spirit. The real purpose of these measures—collectively known as welfare capitalism—was to encourage loyalty to the firm and to convince employees that capitalism could work in their interests.

[vertical text: Library of Congress, Prints and Photographs Division]

Industrial Workers

While skilled craftsmen in the older industries of construction, railroad transportation, and printing enjoyed rising wages, steady income, and good benefits, semi-skilled and unskilled industrial workers had to contend with a labor surplus throughout the decade. As employers replaced workers with machines, the demand for industrial labor increased at a lower rate than it had in the preceding 20 years. As rural whites, blacks, and Mexicans continued their migration to the cities, stiffening the competition for factory jobs, employers could hire and fire as they saw fit and therefore keep wage increases lagging behind productivity increases. An estimated 40 percent of workers lived in poverty.

The million or more workers who labored in the nation's two largest industries, coal and textiles, suffered the most during the 1920s. Both industries experienced severe overcapacity. By 1926, only half of the coal mined each year was being sold. Unemployment in New England textile cities sometimes approached 50 percent. One reason was that many textile industrialists had opened factories in the South, where taxes and wages were lower. But the southern textile industry also suffered from excess capacity, and prices and wages continued to fall. Plant managers pressured their workers to speed up production. Workers loathed the frequent "speed-ups" of machines and the "stretch-outs" in the number of spinning or weaving machines each worker was expected to tend. By the late 1920s, labor strife and calls for unionization were rising in both the South and the North.

Most unions, however, lost ground in the 1920s as business and government remained hostile to labor organization. A conservative Supreme Court whittled away at labor's legal protections. In 1921, it ruled that lower courts could issue injunctions against union members, prohibiting them from striking or picketing an employer. State courts also enforced what union members called **"yellow dog" contracts**, written pledges by employees not to join a union while they were employed. Any employee who violated that pledge was subject to immediate dismissal.

These measures crippled efforts to organize trade unions. Membership fell from a high of five million in 1920 to fewer than three million in 1929, a mere 10 percent of the nation's industrial workforce. Other forces contributed to the decline, too. Many workers, especially those benefiting from welfare capitalist programs, decided they no longer needed trade unions. And the labor movement hurt itself by moving too slowly to open its ranks to semiskilled and unskilled factory workers.

Women and Work

Women workers experienced the same hardships as men in the industrial workforce and fewer of the benefits. They were largely excluded from the ranks of skilled craftsmen and thus missed out on the substantial wage increases that men in those positions enjoyed. Where women held the same jobs as men, they usually earned less. A female trimmer in a meatpacking plant, for example, typically made 37 cents an hour, only two-thirds what a male trimmer earned.

White-collar work established itself, in the 1920s, as a magnet for women. Discrimination prevented women from becoming managers, accountants, or supervisors, but they did dominate the ranks of secretaries, typists, filing clerks, bank tellers, and department store clerks. By the 1930s two million women, or 20 percent of the female workforce, labored in these and related occupations. Initially, these positions had a glamour that factory work lacked. Work environments were cleaner and brighter, and women had the opportunity—indeed were expected—to dress

Competition for factory jobs increase.

yellow dog contracts *Written pledges by employees promising not to join a union while they were employed.*

AMELIA EARHART, AVIATOR. *In 1932 Earhart became the first female aviator to fly solo across the Atlantic, matching the feat that Charles Lindbergh had accomplished in 1927. In 1935 Earhart became the first individual, male or female, to fly nonstop from Hawaii to California.*

© Hulton-Deutsch Collection/CORBIS

well and fashionably. Still, wages were low, managerial authority was absolute, and unions had virtually no presence.

Women with ambitious work aspirations usually pursued the "female" professions, such as teaching, nursing, social work, and librarianship. Opportunities in several of these fields were growing, and women responded by enrolling in college in large numbers. The number of female college students increased by 50 percent during the 1920s. Some of these college graduates used their skills in new fields, such as writing for women's magazines. A few, drawing strength from their feminist forebears during the progressive era, managed to crack such male bastions of work as mainstream journalism and university research and teaching.

In every field of endeavor, women demonstrated that the female sex possessed the talent and drive to match or exceed what men had done, but these women who broke the gender line remained, by and large, solitary figures. In 1932, Amelia Earhart matched Charles Lindbergh by flying the Atlantic solo, but her feat failed to improve opportunities for women who wanted to work as pilots. In the airline industry, as in most lines of work, gender prejudices remained too entrenched.

The Women's Movement Adrift

Many supporters of the Nineteenth Amendment to the Constitution, which, in 1920, gave women the right to vote, expected it to transform American politics. Women voters would reverse the decline in voter participation, cleanse politics of corruption, and launch reform initiatives. This female-inspired transformation failed to materialize. The women's movement seemed to succumb to the same exhaustion and frustration as had the more general progressive movement from which it had emerged 20 years earlier. Younger women searching for independence and equality (such as the flappers) often turned away from reform altogether, preferring a lifestyle that emphasized private achievement and personal freedom. Those who continued to agitate for reform found progress more difficult to achieve once the conservative Republican administrations of Harding and Coolidge took office.

Nevertheless, female reformers made significant strides. In 1921, one group succeeded in getting Congress to pass the **Sheppard-Towner Act**, a social welfare program that provided federal funds for prenatal and child health care centers throughout the United States. It remained in effect until 1929. In 1923, Alice Paul and the National Women's Party (see Chapter 21) prevailed on Congress to consider an Equal Rights Amendment (ERA) to the Constitution, phrased as follows: "Men and women shall have equal rights throughout the United States and every place subject to its jurisdiction." And the National American Woman Suffrage Association, the major force behind the struggle for suffrage, transformed itself in 1920 into the **League of Women Voters** (LWV) and worked to encourage women to run for elective office, to educate voters, and to improve the condition of those Americans—the poor, female and child laborers, the mentally ill—who needed assistance.

Sometimes the women's movement was stymied not just by external opposition but also by internal division—as it was over the ERA. Supporters insisted that there could be no compromise with the proposition that women were the equals of men. The LWV countered that child rearing and mothering duties did render women different from men in key respects and thus, in some instances, in need of special treatment by Congress and other lawmaking bodies.

The question of female difference crystallized around the issue of protective labor legislation for women. Over the years, a series of state and federal laws had given women protections at the workplace—limitations on the hours of labor, prohibitions on overnight work, and other such measures—that men did not have. Many reformers considered these measures vital to protecting the masses of women workers from the worst forms of exploitation and thus enabling them to have enough time and energy to perform their roles as mothers and wives. Fearing that the ERA would render this protective legislation unconstitutional, the LWV and its allies opposed it. Alice Paul and her allies argued, on the other hand, that female protective laws did not really benefit women. Instead, employers used them as an excuse to segregate women in stereotyped jobs that were mostly low status and low paying. Women activists' inability to speak with a single voice on this complicated matter weakened their cause during the 1920s.

Sheppard-Towner Act *Major social welfare program providing federal funds for prenatal and child health care, 1921–1929.*

League of Women Voters *Successor to National American Woman Suffrage Association, it promoted women's role in politics and dedicated itself to educating voters.*

THE POLITICS OF BUSINESS

Republican presidents governed the country from 1921 to 1933. In some respects, their administrations resembled those of the Gilded Age, when corruption was rampant and the government's chief objective was to remove obstacles to capitalist development. But in other respects, the state-building tradition of Theodore Roosevelt lived on, albeit in a somewhat altered form.

Harding and the Politics of Personal Gain

Republican Party bosses believed that almost anyone they nominated in 1920 could defeat the Democratic candidate, James M. Cox. They chose Senator Warren Gamaliel Harding of Ohio because they could control him. Harding's good looks and geniality made him a favorite with voters, and he swept into office with 61 percent of the popular vote.

FOCUS QUESTION

What were the similarities and differences in the politics of Harding, Coolidge, and Hoover?

Republicans from 1921 to 1933

Harding included talented men in his cabinet, such as Secretary of Commerce Herbert Hoover, but he lacked the will to alter his ingrained political habits. He had built his political career on a willingness to please the lobbyists who came to his Senate office asking for favors and deals. As president he continued to placate his friends, and, as a result, scandal plagued his administration. Harding's old friends, the "Ohio gang," got rich selling government appointments, judicial pardons, and police protection to bootleggers. In what became known as the **Teapot Dome scandal**, Secretary of the Interior Albert Fall secretly leased government oil reserves at Teapot Dome, Wyoming, and Elk Hills, California, to two oil tycoons, who then paid him almost $400,000. Fall spent a year in jail, and he was not the only Harding appointee to do so. Charles R. Forbes, head of the Veterans' Bureau, would go to Leavenworth Prison for swindling the government out of $200 million in hospital supplies.

Harding initially kept himself blind to this widespread use of public office for private gain but grew depressed when he finally realized what had been going on. In summer 1923, in poor spirits, he left Washington for a West Coast tour. He died from a heart attack in San Francisco.

Coolidge and Laissez-Faire Politics

Harding's successor, Vice President Calvin Coolidge, never socialized with the "boys," nor was he tempted by corruption. He believed that the best government was the government that governed least, and that the welfare of the country hinged not on politicians but on the people—their willingness to work hard, to be honest, to live within their means.

Coolidge gained national visibility in September 1919, when as governor of Massachusetts he stood firm against Boston's striking policemen (see Chapter 23). His reputation for battling labor radicals earned him a place on the 1920 national Republican ticket. His image as an ordinary man helped convince voters that the Republican Party would return the country to its commonsensical ways after a decade or more of progressive reform. Coolidge won his party's presidential nomination handily in 1924 and easily defeated his Democratic opponent, John W. Davis.

Coolidge took greatest pride in those measures that reduced the government's control over the economy. The Revenue Act of 1926 slashed the high income and estate taxes that progressives had pushed through Congress during the First World War. Coolidge curtailed the power of the Federal Trade Commission to regulate business affairs and endorsed Supreme Court decisions invalidating progressive era labor laws.

Hoover and the Politics of Associationalism

Republicans in the 1920s did more than simply remove government restraints and regulations from the economy. Some, led by Secretary of Commerce Herbert Hoover, conceived of government as a dynamic, even progressive, economic force. Hoover did not want government to control industry, but he did want government to persuade private corporations to abandon their wasteful, selfish ways and turn to cooperation and public service. Hoover envisioned an economy built on an approach that historian Ellis Hawley has called "**associationalism**." Industrialists, wholesalers, retailers, operators of railroad and shipping lines, small businessmen, farmers, workers, doctors—each of these groups would form a trade association whose members would share economic information, discuss problems of production and distribution, and seek ways of achieving greater efficiency and profit.

Teapot Dome scandal
Secretary of Interior Albert Fall allowed oil tycoons access to government oil reserves in exchange for $400,000 in bribes.

associationalism *Herbert Hoover's approach to managing the economy. Firms and organizations in each economic sector would be asked to cooperate with each other in the pursuit of efficiency, profit, and the public good.*

[Handwritten margin note: Best government didn't govern]

Hoover believed that associationalism would convince participants of the superiority of cooperation over competition, of negotiation over conflict, of public service over selfishness.

To this end, Hoover achieved some notable successes. He persuaded farmers to join together in marketing cooperatives, steel executives to abandon the 12-hour day for their employees, and some groups of bankers in the South to organize their institutions into regional associations. His dynamic conception of government did not endear him to Coolidge, who declared in 1927: "That man has offered me unsolicited advice for six years, all of it bad."

The Politics of Business Abroad

As secretary of commerce, Hoover intended to apply associationalism to international relations. He wanted the world's leading nations to meet regularly in conferences, to limit military buildups, and to foster an international environment in which capitalism could flourish. Aware that the United States must help create such an environment, Hoover hoped to persuade American bankers to adopt investment and loan policies that would aid European recovery. If they refused to do so, he was prepared to urge the government to take an activist, supervisory role in foreign investment.

In 1921 and 1922, Hoover helped design the Washington Conference on the Limitation of Armaments. He supplied Secretary of State Charles Evans Hughes's team with a wealth of economic information that became the basis for bold, detailed proposals for disarmament. Those proposals helped U.S. negotiators win a stunning accord, the **Five-Power Treaty**, by which the United States, Britain, Japan, France, and Italy agreed to scrap more than two million tons of their warships.

This triumph redounded to Hughes's credit but not to Hoover's. Hughes's reputation continued to grow when he solved a crisis in Franco-German relations. The victorious Allies had imposed on Germany an obligation to pay $33 billion in war reparations (see Chapter 23). When the impoverished German government suspended its payments in 1923, France sent troops to occupy the Ruhr valley, whose industry was vital to the German economy. German workers retaliated by going on strike. The crisis threatened to undermine Europe's precarious economic recovery. Hughes responded by compelling the French to attend a U.S.-sponsored conference in 1924 to restructure Germany's debt obligation.

The conference produced the **Dawes Plan** (after the Chicago banker and chief negotiator, Charles G. Dawes), which reduced German reparations payments from $542 million to $250 million annually and called on U.S. and foreign banks to stimulate the German economy with $200 million in loans. Within a matter of days, banker J. P. Morgan, Jr., raised more than $1 billion from American investors. Money poured into German financial markets, and the German economy appeared to stabilize.

The Dawes Plan won applause on both sides of the Atlantic, but soon the U.S. money flooding into Germany created new problems. American investors were so eager to lend to Germany that their investments became speculative and unsound. A stronger effort by the U.S. government to direct loans to solid investments, a strategy that Hoover would have supported, might have helped. But Hughes, his successor as secretary of state, Frank Kellogg, and other prominent Republicans were now content to leave investment decisions in the hands of private bankers.

Republican initiatives to ensure world peace continued, however. Secretary of State Kellogg drew up a treaty with Aristide Briand, the French foreign minister, outlawing war as a tool of national policy. In 1928, representatives of the United States, France, and 13 other nations met in Paris to sign the Kellogg-Briand Pact, an

QUICK REVIEW

REPUBLICAN PRESIDENCIES, 1921–1933

- Struggle between laissez-faire and associationalism shaped policy debates

- Warren G. Harding (1921–1923) guided by political lobbyists and cronies

- Calvin Coolidge (1923–1929) driven by the ideal that the best government was a government that governed least

- Herbert Hoover (1929–1933) promoted the idea that government should persuade private corporations to abandon their wasteful, selfish ways and embrace cooperation and public service

Five-Power Treaty *1922 treaty in which the United States, Britain, Japan, France, and Italy agreed to scrap more than two million tons of their warships.*

Dawes Plan *1924 U.S.-backed agreement to reduce German reparation payments by more than half. The plan also called on banks to invest $200 million in the German economy.*

agreement that soon attracted the support of 48 other nations. Coolidge viewed Kellogg-Briand as an opportunity to scale back the military and further reduce the size of the U.S. government. Unfortunately, the pact contained no enforcement mechanism and was therefore ineffective.

Republican administrations did attempt initially to curtail American military involvement in the Caribbean and Central America. The Coolidge administration pulled U.S. troops out of the Dominican Republic in 1924 and Nicaragua in 1925. But Coolidge sent U.S. Marines back to Nicaragua in 1926 to end a war between liberals and conservatives there and to protect American property; this time they stayed until 1934. U.S. troops, meanwhile, occupied Haiti continuously between 1919 and 1934, keeping in power governments friendly to U.S. interests.

FARMERS, SMALL-TOWN PROTESTANTS, AND MORAL TRADITIONALISTS

FOCUS QUESTION

What concerned farmers and conservative white Protestants in the 1920s, and what policies did they support?

Although many Americans benefited from the prosperity of the 1920s, others did not. Overproduction impoverished substantial numbers of farmers. Beyond these economic hardships, many white Protestants, especially those in rural areas and small towns, protested the new economy and new culture that was taking shape in the cities.

Agricultural Depression and Cultural Dislocation

The 1920s brought hard times to the nation's farmers. European agriculture, disrupted by the war, quickly restored itself. Foreign demand for American foodstuffs fell precipitously, as did prices. Tractors increased productivity, leading to further drops in prices. By 1929, the annual per capita income of rural Americans was only $223, one-quarter that of the nonfarm population. Hundreds of thousands had to sell their farms.

A sense of cultural dislocation further demoralized farmers, most of whom were white, Protestant, and of northwest European descent. They had long perceived themselves as the backbone of the nation—hardworking, honest, democratic, liberty loving, and God fearing. The 1920 census challenged the validity of that view. For the first time, a majority of Americans now lived in urban areas (see Map 24.1). Industry, the chief engine of prosperity, was an urban phenomenon. Amusement parks, department stores, professional sports, and movies had emerged in cities; so had flashy fashions and open sexuality. Catholics, Jews, and African Americans together outnumbered white Protestants in many cities. Cities also were the home of secular intellectuals who had embraced science over scripture and God.

Throughout the progressive era, rural white Americans had believed that the cities could be redeemed and that the Protestant values of rural America would triumph. War had replaced that confidence with the fear that urban masses and secular culture would ruin America. These fears grew even more intense as the consumer culture of the city—movies, radios, cars, magazines—penetrated the countryside. Rural white Americans' determination to protect their imperiled way of life was manifested by their support of **Prohibition**, the Ku Klux Klan, immigration restriction, and religious fundamentalism.

Prohibition *Constitutional ban on the manufacture and sale of alcohol in the United States (1920–1933).*

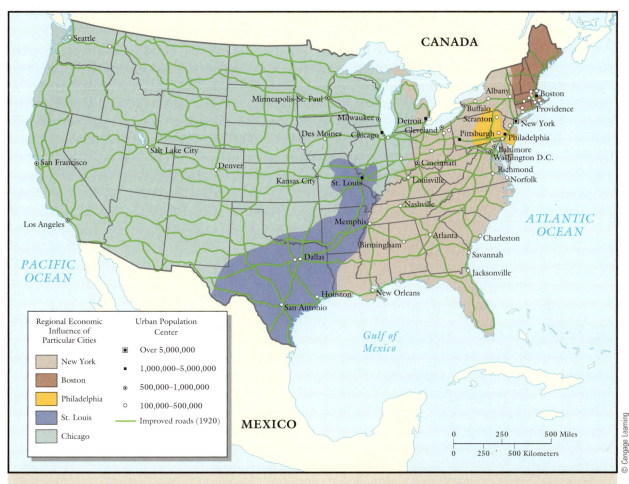

Map 24.1 Urbanization, 1920. *By 1920 New York City had surpassed 5 million people, and Boston, Philadelphia, Pittsburgh, Detroit, Chicago, and St. Louis had surpassed 1 million. Another 10 cities, from Los Angeles, California, to Buffalo, New York, had surpassed 500,000. This color-coded map also shows the regions in which the country's five largest cities exercised economic influence.*

Prohibition

The Eighteenth Amendment to the Constitution, which prohibited the manufacture and sale of alcohol, went into effect in January 1920. It soon became apparent that Prohibition was doing as much to encourage lawbreaking as abstinence. With only 1,500 federal agents to enforce the law, the government could not possibly police the drinking habits of 110 million people. With little fear of punishment, those who wanted to drink did so, either brewing liquor at home or buying it from speakeasies, smugglers, and bootleggers. Because the law prevented legitimate businesses from manufacturing liquor, organized crime simply added alcohol to its portfolio. Al Capone's Chicago-based mob alone employed 1,000 men to protect its liquor trafficking.

These unexpected consequences caused many early advocates of Prohibition, especially in the cities, to withdraw their support. To Prohibition's rural, Protestant supporters, however, the violence spawned by illegal liquor trafficking confirmed their view of alcohol as evil. The high-profile participation of Italian, Irish, and Jewish gangsters in the bootleg trade reinforced their belief that Catholics and Jews threatened law and morality. Many rural Protestants became more, not less, determined to rid the country of liquor once and for all; some resolved to rid the country of Jews and Catholics as well.

1860's South
1915

The Ku Klux Klan

The original Ku Klux Klan, formed in the South in the late 1860s, had died out with the defeat of Reconstruction and the reestablishment of white supremacy (see Chapter 17). The new Klan was created in 1915 by William Simmons, a white southerner who had been inspired by D. W. Griffith's racist film, *Birth of a Nation*, in which the early Klan was depicted as having saved the nation from predatory blacks. By the 1920s, control of the Klan had passed to a Texas dentist, Hiram Evans, and its ideological focus had expanded from a loathing of blacks to a hatred of Jews and Catholics as well. Evans's Klan propagated a nativist message that the country should contain—or better yet, eliminate—the influence of Jews and Catholics and restore "Anglo-Saxon" racial purity, Protestant supremacy, and traditional morality to national life. This message swelled Klan ranks and expanded its visibility and influence in the North and South alike. By 1924, as many as four million Americans are thought to have belonged to the Klan, including the half-million members of its female auxiliary, Women of the Ku Klux Klan.

In some respects, the Klan resembled other fraternal organizations. It offered members friendship networks and social services. Its rituals, regalia, and mock-medieval language (the Imperial Wizard, Exalted Cyclops, Grand Dragons) gave initiates a sense of superiority, valor, and mystery. But the Klan's determination to stir up hate toward blacks, Catholics, and Jews marked it as different and dangerous.

Immigration Restriction

Although most white Protestants never joined the Klan, by the early 1920s most Americans did believe that the country could no longer accommodate the million immigrants who had been arriving each year before the war and the more than 800,000 who arrived in 1921. Industrialists did not need unskilled European laborers, their places having been taken either by machines or by African American, Mexican, or Filipino workers. Most labor movement leaders were convinced that the influx of workers unfamiliar with English and with trade unions weakened labor solidarity. Progressive reformers no longer believed that immigrants could be easily Americanized. Congress responded to constituents' concerns by passing an immigration restriction act in 1921. Then, in 1924, the more comprehensive **Immigration Restriction Act (Johnson-Reed Act)** imposed a yearly quota of 165,000 immigrants from countries outside the Western Hemisphere.

The sponsors of the 1924 act believed that certain groups—British, Germans, and Scandinavians, in particular—were racially superior and that these groups should be allowed to enter the United States in greater numbers. Because the Constitution prohibited the enactment of explicitly racist laws, Congress had to achieve this racist aim through subterfuge. Lawmakers established a formula to determine the annual immigrant quota for each foreign country, which was to be computed at 2 percent of the total number of immigrants from

---

Immigration Restriction Act of 1924 (Johnson-Reed Act) *Limited immigration to the United States to 165,000 a year, shrank immigration from southern and eastern Europe to insignificance, and banned immigration from East and South Asia.*

© The Granger Collection, New York

"Spoiling the Broth" *This anti-immigrant cartoon, appearing in 1921, shows America's fabled melting pot being forced to take in far more immigrants from Europe and Asia than it could possibly handle. The result was hundreds of thousands, even millions, of immigrants being disgorged from the pot as "unassimilated aliens."*

TABLE 24.1

ANNUAL IMMIGRANT QUOTAS UNDER THE JOHNSON-REED ACT, 1925–1927

Northwest Europe and Scandinavia		Eastern and Southern Europe		Other Countries	
Country	Quota	Country	Quota	Country	Quota
Germany	51,227	Poland	5,982	Africa (other than Egypt)	1,100
Great Britain and Northern Ireland	34,007	Italy	3,845	Armenia	124
Irish Free State (Ireland)	28,567	Czechoslovakia	3,073	Australia	121
Sweden	9,561	Russia	2,248	Palestine	100
Norway	6,453	Yugoslavia	671	Syria	100
France	3,954	Romania	603	Turkey	100
Denmark	2,789	Portugal	503	New Zealand and Pacific Islands	100
Switzerland	2,081	Hungary	473	All others	1,900
Netherlands	1,648	Lithuania	344		
Austria	785	Latvia	142		
Belgium	512	Spain	131		
Finland	471	Estonia	124		
Free City of Danzig	228	Albania	100		
Iceland	100	Bulgaria	100		
Luxembourg	100	Greece	100		
Total (number)	142,483	Total (number)	18,439	Total (number)	3,745
Total (%)	86.5%	Total (%)	11.2%	Total (%)	2.3%

Note: Total annual immigrant quota was 164,667.

Source: From *Statistical Abstract of the United States* (Washington, D.C.: Government Printing Office, 1929), p. 100.

that country already resident in the United States in the year 1890—a year in which immigrant ranks had been dominated by the British, Germans, and Scandinavians (see Table 24.1). Immigrant groups that were poorly represented in the 1890 population —Italians, Greeks, Poles, Slavs, and Eastern European Jews—were effectively locked out.

The Johnson-Reed Act also reaffirmed the longstanding policy of excluding Chinese immigrants, and it added Japanese and other East and South Asians to the list of groups that were altogether barred from entry. The act did not officially limit immigration from nations in the Western Hemisphere, chiefly because agribusiness interests in Texas and California had convinced Congress that they required cheap Mexican laborers. Still, the establishment of a border patrol along the U.S.-Mexican border and the imposition of a $10 head tax on all prospective Mexican immigrants made entry into the United States more difficult.

The Johnson-Reed Act accomplished Congress's underlying goal. Annual immigration from transoceanic nations fell by 80 percent. A "national origins" system put in place in 1927 further reduced the total annual quota to 150,000, and reserved more than 120,000 of these slots for immigrants from northwestern Europe. Remarkably few Americans, outside of the ethnic groups that were being discriminated against, objected to these laws at the time they were passed—an indication of how broadly acceptable racism and nativism had become.

Fundamentalism versus Liberal Protestantism

Of all the movements protesting against modern urban life, Protestant fundamentalism was perhaps the most enduring. **Fundamentalists** regard the Bible as God's word and thus the source of all "fundamental" truth. They believe that

Fundamentalists *Those who regarded the Bible as God's word and thus the source of all fundamental truth. Its followers believed that every event depicted in the Bible happened just as the Bible described it.*

every event depicted in the Bible, from the creation of the world in six days to the resurrection of Christ, happened exactly as the Bible describes it. For fundamentalists, God was a deity who intervened directly in the lives of individuals and communities.

The rise of the fundamentalist movement from the 1870s through the 1920s roughly paralleled the rise of urban-industrial society. Fundamentalists recoiled from what they perceived as the poverty, moral degeneracy, irreligion, and crass materialism of the city. Fundamentalism took shape in reaction against two additional aspects of urban society: the growth of liberal Protestantism and the revelations of science.

Liberal Protestants believed that religion had to be adapted to the skeptical and scientific temper of the modern age. The Bible was to be mined for its ethical values rather than for its literal truth. Liberal Protestants refashioned God into a distant and benign deity who watches over the world but does not intervene to punish or to redeem. They turned religion away from the quest for salvation and toward the pursuit of good deeds, social conscience, and love for one's neighbor. Fundamentalism arose in part to counter these "heretical" ideas.

Liberal Protestants and fundamentalists both believed that science posed the greatest challenge to Christianity. Scientists endorsed rational inquiry over prayer and revelation, and they even challenged the ideas that God had created the world and had fashioned mankind in his own image. These were assertions that many religious peoples, particularly fundamentalists, simply could not accept. Conflict was inevitable. It came in 1925, in Dayton, Tennessee.

The Scopes Trial

No aspect of science aroused more anger among fundamentalists than Charles Darwin's theory of evolution. There was no greater blasphemy than to suggest that man emerged from lower forms of life instead of being created by God. In Tennessee in 1925, fundamentalists succeeded in passing a law forbidding the teaching of "any theory that denies the story of the divine creation of man as taught in the Bible."

For Americans who accepted the authority of science, denying the truth of evolution was ludicrous. They ridiculed the fundamentalists, but they worried that passage of the Tennessee law might signal the onset of a campaign to undermine First Amendment guarantees of free speech. The American Civil Liberties Union began searching for a teacher who would be willing to challenge the constitutionality of the Tennessee law. They found their man in John T. Scopes, a 24-year-old biology teacher in Dayton. After confessing that he had taught evolution to his students, Scopes was arrested. The case quickly attracted national attention. William Jennings Bryan announced that he would help to prosecute Scopes, and the famous liberal trial lawyer Clarence Darrow led Scopes's defense. A small army of journalists, led by H. L. Mencken, descended on Dayton.

Most observers expected Scopes to be convicted. He was, but the hearing took an unexpected turn when Darrow persuaded the judge to let Bryan testify as an "expert on the Bible." Darrow knew that Bryan's testimony would have no bearing on the question of Scopes's innocence or guilt. His aim was to expose Bryan as a fool for believing that the Bible was a source of literal truth and thus to embarrass the fundamentalists. In a riveting confrontation, Darrow made Bryan's defense of the Bible look problematic and led Bryan to admit that the "truth" of the Bible was not always easy to determine. But Darrow could not shake Bryan's belief that the Bible was God's word and thus the source of all truth.

liberal Protestants *Those who believed that religion had to be adapted to science and that the Bible was to be mined for ethical values rather than for its literal truth.*

QUICK REVIEW

CULTURAL CONSERVATISM AND MORAL TRADITIONALISM

- Rural Americans feared dominance of cities, industry, immigrants, and mass culture

- Immigrants targeted through Prohibition (1920) and immigration restriction (1921, 1924)

- Ku Klux Klan gained support as racist and nativist protector of Anglo-Saxon purity

- Fundamentalism surged; Scopes Trial (about evolution) became rallying point

In his account of the trial, Mencken portrayed Bryan as a pathetic figure who had been devastated by his humiliating experience on the witness stand. When Bryan died only a week after the trial ended, Mencken claimed that the trial had broken Bryan's heart. Bryan deserved a better epitaph. Diabetes caused his death, not a broken heart. Nor was Bryan the innocent fool that Mencken made him out to be. His rejection of Darwinism evidenced his democratic faith that all human beings were creatures of God and thus capable of striving for perfection and equality.

The public ridicule attendant on the Scopes trial took its toll on fundamentalists. Many retreated from politics and refocused their attention on purging sin from their own hearts rather than from the hearts of others. In the end, the fundamentalists prevailed on three more states to prohibit the teaching of evolution, but the controversy had even more far-reaching effects. Worried about losing sales, publishers quietly removed references to Darwin from their science textbooks, a policy that would remain in force until the 1960s.

ETHNIC AND RACIAL COMMUNITIES

Some ethnic and racial minorities benefited from the prosperity of the 1920s; others created and sustained vibrant subcultures. All, however, experienced a surge in discrimination.

European American Ethnics

European American ethnics were concentrated in the cities of the Northeast and Midwest. Many were semiskilled and unskilled industrial laborers who suffered economic insecurity. In addition, they faced cultural discrimination. Catholics and Jews were targets of the Klan. Catholics generally opposed Prohibition, viewing it as an attempt by Protestants to control their behavior. Southern and Eastern Europeans, particularly Jews and Italians, resented immigration restriction and the implication that they were inferior to Anglo-Saxon whites. Many Italians were outraged by the execution of Nicola Sacco and Bartolomeo Vanzetti in 1927 (see Chapter 23). Had the two men been native-born Protestants, Italians argued, their lives would have been spared.

Southern and Eastern Europeans endured intensive Americanization campaigns, and they responded to these insults by strengthening the very institutions and customs Americanizers sought to undermine. Ethnic associations flourished in the 1920s. Children learned their native languages and customs at home and at church since they weren't taught them at school, and they joined with their parents to celebrate their ethnic heritage.

But these immigrants and their children also flocked to movies and amusement parks, to baseball games and boxing matches. Children usually entered more enthusiastically into the world of American mass culture than did their immigrant parents, a behavior that often set off family conflicts. But many ethnics found it possible to reconcile their own culture with American culture.

European American ethnics also resolved to develop the political muscle needed to defeat the forces of nativism and to turn government policy in a more favorable direction. The number of immigrants who became U.S. citizens rose sharply. Armed with the vote, ethnics turned out on Election Day to defeat unsympathetic public officials. Their growing national strength first became

FOCUS QUESTION

How were the experiences of ethnic and racial groups in 1920s America similar and how were they different?

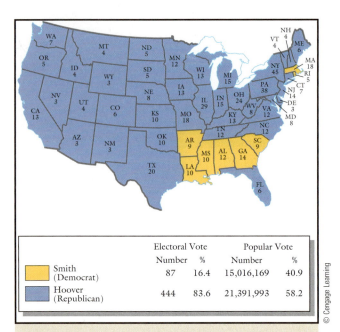

Map 24.2 **Presidential Election, 1928.** *This map shows Hoover's landslide victory in 1928, as he carried all but eight states and won almost 84 percent of the electoral vote.*

	Electoral Vote		Popular Vote	
	Number	%	Number	%
Smith (Democrat)	87	16.4	15,016,169	40.9
Hoover (Republican)	444	83.6	21,391,993	58.2

© Cengage Learning

apparent at the Democratic national convention of 1924, when urban-ethnic delegates almost won approval of planks calling for the repeal of Prohibition and condemnation of the Klan. After denying the presidential nomination to the presumed favorite, William G. McAdoo, they nearly secured it for their candidate, **Alfred E. Smith**, the Catholic Irish American governor of New York. McAdoo represented the rural and southern constituencies of the Democratic Party. His forces ended up battling Smith's urban-ethnic forces for 103 ballots, until both men gave up and supporters from each camp switched their votes to a compromise candidate, the corporate lawyer John W. Davis, who lost to Calvin Coolidge.

Although the nomination fight damaged the Democratic Party in the short term, it also marked an important milestone in the bid by European American ethnics for political power. They would achieve a second milestone at the Democratic national convention of 1928 when, after another bitter struggle, they secured the presidential nomination for Al Smith. Never before had a major political party put forward a Catholic for the presidency. Herbert Hoover crushed Smith in the general election, as nativists stirred up anti-Catholic prejudice and large numbers of southern Democrats either stayed home or voted Republican (see Map 24.2). But Smith did beat Hoover in the nation's 12 largest cities.

African Americans

Despite the urban race riots of 1919 (see Chapter 23), African Americans continued to leave their rural homes for the industrial centers of the South and the North. In major areas of settlement, such as New York City and Chicago, complex societies emerged consisting of workers, businessmen, professionals, intellectuals, artists, and entertainers. Social differentiation intensified as various groups—long-resident northerners and newly arrived southerners, religious conservatives and cultural radicals, African Americans and African Caribbeans—found reason to disapprove of one another's ways. Still, the diversity and complexity of urban black America were thrilling, nowhere more so than in Harlem, the "Negro capital."

Yet not even the glamour of Harlem could erase the reality of racial discrimination. Most African Americans could find work only in New York City's least-desired and lowest-paying jobs. Because they could rent apartments only in areas that real estate agents and banks had designated as "colored," African Americans suffered the highest rate of residential segregation of any minority group. Harlem became a black ghetto, an area set apart from the rest of the city by the skin color of its inhabitants, by its higher population density and poverty rate, by its higher incidence of infectious diseases, and by the lower life expectancy of its people (see Table 24.2).

Many African Americans grew pessimistic about achieving racial equality. After Marcus Garvey's black nationalist movement collapsed in the mid-1920s (see Chapter 23), no comparable organization arose to take its place. The

Alfred E. Smith *Irish American, Democratic governor of New York who became in 1928 the first Catholic ever nominated for the presidency by a major party.*

TABLE 24.2

DEATH RATES FROM SELECTED CAUSES FOR NEW YORK CITY RESIDENTS, 1925		
Cause of Death	Total Population	African American Population
General death rate (per 1,000 population)	11.4	16.5
Pneumonia	132.8	282.4
Pulmonary tuberculosis	75.5	258.4
Infant mortality (per 1,000 live births)	64.6	118.4
Maternal mortality (per 1,000 total births)	5.3	10.2
Stillbirths (per 1,000 births)	47.6	82.7
Homicide	5.3	19.5
Suicide	14.8	9.7

Note: Rate is per 100,000 population, unless noted.
Source: Cheryl Lynn Greenberg, *"Or Does It Explode?" Black Harlem in the Great Depression* (New York: Oxford University Press, 1991), p. 32.

NAACP continued to fight racial discrimination, and the Urban League carried on quiet negotiations with industrial elites to open up jobs to African Americans. Black socialists led by A. Philip Randolph built a strong all-black union, the Brotherhood of Sleeping Car Porters, but the victories were small, and white allies were scarce.

In terms of black culture, however, the 1920s were vigorous and productive. Black musicians coming north to Chicago and New York brought with them their distinctive musical styles, most notably the blues and ragtime. Influenced by the harmonies and techniques of European classical music, these southern styles metamorphosed into jazz. Urban audiences, first black and then white, found this new music irresistible. In Chicago, Detroit, New York, New Orleans, and elsewhere, jazz musicians came together in cramped apartments, cabarets, and nightclubs to jam, compete, and entertain. Jazz seemed to express something quintessentially modern. Musicians broke free of convention, improvised, and produced new sounds that gave rise to new sensations. Both blacks and whites found in jazz an escape from the routine of their everyday lives.

The Harlem Renaissance

Paralleling the emergence of jazz was a black literary and artistic awakening known as the **Harlem Renaissance**. Black novelists, poets, painters, sculptors, and playwrights created works rooted in their own culture instead of imitating the styles of whites. The movement had begun during the war, when blacks sensed that they might at last be advancing to full equality. It was symbolized by the image of the "New Negro," who would no longer be deferential to whites but who would display his or her independence through talent and determination. Langston Hughes, a young black poet, said of the Harlem Renaissance: "We younger Negro artists who create now intend to express our individual dark-skinned selves without fear or shame. If white people are pleased, we are glad. If they are not, it doesn't matter. We know we are beautiful. And ugly, too." In 1925, *Survey Graphic*, a white liberal magazine, enlisted Howard University sociologist Alain Locke to edit an entire issue devoted to "Harlem—the Mecca of the New Negro."

These cultural advances did not escape white prejudice. The most popular jazz nightclubs in Harlem, most of which were owned and operated by whites,

Harlem Renaissance *1920s African American literary and artistic awakening that sought to create works rooted in black culture instead of imitating white styles.*

HISTORY THROUGH FILM

The Jazz Singer (1927)

Directed by Alan Crosland
Starring Al Jolson (Jake Rabinowitz/Jack Robin), May McAvoy (Mary Dale),
and Warner Oland (Cantor Rabinowitz)

The Jazz Singer was a sensation when it opened because it was the first movie to use sound (although relatively few words of dialogue were actually spoken). It also starred Al Jolson, the era's most popular Broadway entertainer, and bravely explored an issue that the film industry usually avoided—the religious culture and generational dynamics of a "new immigrant" family.

The movie focuses on Jake Rabinowitz and his immigrant parents, who are Jewish and devout. Jake's father is a fifth-generation cantor whose job it is to fill his New York City synagogue with ancient and uplifting melodies on the Sabbath and Jewish holidays. Cantor Rabinowitz looks upon his work as sacred, and he expects Jake to take his place one day. But Jake has other ideas. He loves music but is drawn to the new rhythmic ragtime and sensual jazz melodies emerging from his American surroundings. In an early scene, we encounter Jake at a dance hall, absorbed in playing and singing ragtime tunes and forgetting that he should be at home preparing for Yom Kippur, the holiest day in the Jewish calendar. His distraught father finds him and whips him, and Jake, in anger and pain, runs away. These early scenes allow us to glimpse an important theme in the immigrant experience of the early 20th century: the deep attraction among the children of immigrants to the energy and vitality of American popular culture and the strains that this attraction often caused between these children and parents desperate to maintain the traditions they had brought with them from Europe.

Jake's estrangement from his family and community gives him the space to reinvent himself as Jack Robin, the jazz singer. His love relationship with a prominent (and non-Jewish) stage actress, Mary Dale, brings him the big break he needs, a starring role in a Broadway show. Jack hopes to use his return to New York to reconcile with his father. This eventually happens when Jake, on the eve of Yom Kippur once again, agrees to skip his show's premiere in order to take his ailing father's place as cantor in the synagogue. Jake's melodies soar and reach his bedridden father who, thinking that his son has succeeded him as cantor and thus fulfilled his (the father's) deepest wish, peacefully dies.

His father is deceived, for Jake returns to his Broadway show as soon as Yom Kippur ends to deliver an outstanding performance as the "Jazz Singer." His future lies with Broadway, rather than with a synagogue, and with the gentile Mary. The movie, however, makes it seem as though everything will work out: Jake's mother is in the audience for the Broadway show, enjoying her son's success and in effect blessing him for the career and woman he has chosen. That this resolution requires misleading the father reminds us, however, that the strains between immigrant parents and their American-born children could be deep and sometimes not resolvable.

The movie also allows us to ask questions about the relationship between immigrants and African Americans. As part of his Broadway performance, Jake does a blackface routine, using burnt cork to turn his face and neck black and thus to appear to audiences as a "black" entertainer. From the early 19th to the early 20th centuries, "blacking up" was a performance style popular among white entertainers who wanted to appropriate and ridicule expressive aspects of black culture. What did it mean for a child of Jewish immigrants, himself vulnerable to being stigmatized as an outsider in America, to "black up"? Jake may have been expressing in part his desire to draw closer to rich elements in black musical culture. But Jake may also have been signaling his desire to distance himself from African Americans by participating in a tradition popular among white American entertainers. Ironically, "blacking up" may have been a way for an entertainer to embrace not black but white America, and for someone like Jake to be accepted by non-Jewish white Americans as one of them.

A billboard in New York City advertising The Jazz Singer. Al Jolson is shown in blackface.

© Bettmann/CORBIS

frequently refused to admit black customers. Moreover, black musicians often had to play what the white patrons wanted to hear. Duke Ellington, for example, featured "jungle music," which for whites revealed the "true" African soul—sensual, innocent, primitive. Such pressures curtailed the artistic freedom of black musicians and reinforced racist stereotypes of African Americans as inferior people who were closer to nature than the "more civilized" white audiences. Writers experienced similar pressures. Many of them depended for their sustenance on the support of wealthy white patrons. Those patrons were generous, but they wanted a return on their investment. Charlotte Mason, the New York City matron who supported Hughes and another black writer, Zora Neale Hurston, for example, expected them to entertain her friends by demonstrating "authentic Negritude."

Mexican Americans

After the Johnson-Reed Act of 1924, Mexicans became the country's chief source of immigrant labor. A total of 500,000 Mexicans entered the United States in the 1920s. Most settled in the Southwest. In Texas 3 of every 4 construction workers and 8 of every 10 migrant farmworkers were Mexicans. In California, Mexican immigrants made up 75 percent of the state's agricultural workforce.

Mexican farm laborers in Texas worked long hours for little money. They were usually barred from skilled positions. Forced to follow the crops, they had little opportunity to develop settled homes and communities. Because farm owners rarely required the services of Mexican workers for more than several days or weeks, few were willing to spend the money required to provide decent homes and schools. Houses typically lacked wooden floors or indoor plumbing. Mexican laborers found it difficult to protest these conditions because their knowledge of English was limited. Many were in debt to employers who had advanced them money and who threatened them with jail if they failed to fulfill the terms of their contract. Others feared deportation; they lacked visas, having slipped into the United States illegally rather than pay the immigrant tax or endure harassment from the border patrol.

Increasing numbers of Mexican immigrants managed to find their way to California. Some escaped agricultural labor altogether for construction and manufacturing jobs. Many Mexican men in Los Angeles, for example, worked in the city's large railroad yards, at the city's numerous construction sites, and as unskilled workers in local factories. Mexican women labored in garment shops, fish canneries, and food processing plants.

The Los Angeles Mexican American community increased in complexity as it grew in size. By the mid-1920s, it included a growing professional class, a proud group of *californios* (Spanish speakers who had been resident in California for generations), many musicians and entertainers, a small but energetic band of entrepreneurs and businessmen, conservative clerics and intellectuals who had fled or been expelled from revolutionary Mexico, and Mexican government officials who had been sent to counter the influence of the conservative

californios Spanish-speaking people whose families had resided in California for generations.

MEXICAN AMERICAN WOMEN WORKERS, 1920s. *These women were employed at a tortilla factory in Los Angeles.*

Security Pacific Colleciton/Los Angeles Public Library

exiles and strengthen the ties of the immigrants to their homeland. This diverse mix created internal conflict, but it also generated cultural vitality. Los Angeles became the same kind of magnet for Mexican Americans that Harlem had become for African Americans.

This flowering of Mexican American culture in Los Angeles could not erase the hardships Mexicans faced; nor did it encourage Mexicans to mobilize themselves as a political force. Unlike European immigrants, Mexican immigrants showed little interest at this time in becoming American citizens and acquiring the vote. Yet the cultural vibrancy of the Mexican immigrant community did sustain many individuals who were struggling to survive in a strange, and often hostile, environment.

THE "LOST GENERATION" AND DISILLUSIONED INTELLECTUALS

FOCUS QUESTION

To whom did the phrase "Lost Generation" refer and what caused these individuals to become disillusioned?

Many native-born white artists and intellectuals also felt uneasy in America in the 1920s. Their unease arose not from poverty or discrimination but from alienation. They despaired of American culture and regarded the average American as anti-intellectual, small-minded, materialistic, and puritanical.

Before the First World War intellectuals and artists had been deeply engaged with "the people." Although they were critical of many aspects of American society, they believed they could help bring about a new politics and improve social conditions. Some of them joined the war effort before the United States had officially intervened. Ernest Hemingway, John Dos Passos, and e. e. cummings, among others, sailed to Europe and volunteered their services, usually as ambulance drivers carrying wounded soldiers from the front.

America's intellectuals were shaken by the war's effect on American society. The wartime push for consensus created intolerance of radicals, immigrants, and blacks. Not only had many Americans embraced conformity for themselves, but they seemed determined to force conformity on others. The young critic Harold Stearns wrote in 1921 that "the most moving and pathetic fact in the social life of America today is emotional and aesthetic starvation." Before these words were published, Stearns had sailed for France. So many alienated young men like Stearns showed up in Paris that Gertrude Stein, an American writer whose Paris apartment became a gathering place for them, took to calling them the **"Lost Generation."**

These writers and intellectuals managed to convert their disillusionment into a rich literary sensibility. The finest works of the decade focused on the psychological toll of living in what the poet T. S. Eliot referred to as *The Waste Land* (1922). F. Scott Fitzgerald's novel *The Great Gatsby* (1925) told of a man destroyed by his desire to be accepted into a world of wealth, fancy cars, and fast women. In the novel *A Farewell to Arms* (1929), Ernest Hemingway wrote of an American soldier overwhelmed by the senselessness and brutality of war who deserts the army for the company of a woman he loves. The playwright Eugene O'Neill created characters haunted by despair, loneliness, and unfulfilled longing. Writers innovated in style as well as in content. Sherwood Anderson, in his novel *Winesburg, Ohio* (1919), blended fiction and autobiography. John Dos Passos, in *Manhattan Transfer* (1925), mixed journalism with more traditional literary methods. In the South, white writers such as William Faulkner found a tragic sensibility surviving from the

Lost Generation *Term used by Gertrude Stein to describe U.S. writers and artists who fled to Paris in the 1920s after becoming disillusioned with America.*

South's defeat in the Civil War that spoke to their own loss of hope. One group of southern writers, calling themselves "the Agrarians," argued that the enduring agricultural character of their region offered a more hopeful path to the future than did the mass-production and mass-consumption regime that had overtaken the North.

Democracy on the Defensive

Disdain for the masses led some intellectuals to question democracy. Walter Lippmann, a former radical and progressive, declared that modern society had rendered democracy obsolete. In his view, average citizens, buffeted by propaganda emanating from powerful opinion makers, could no longer make the kind of informed, rational judgments needed to make democracy work. Lippmann's solution, and that of many other political commentators, was to shift government power from the people to educated elites. Those elites, who would be appointed rather than elected, would conduct foreign and domestic policy in an informed, intelligent way.

These antidemocratic views did not go uncontested. The philosopher **John Dewey** was the most articulate spokesman for the "pro-democracy" position. He acknowledged that the concentration of power in a few giant organizations had eroded the authority of political institutions, but democracy, he insisted, was not doomed. People could reclaim their freedom by making big business subject to government control. Government could use its power to democratize corporations and regulate the communications industry to ensure that every citizen had access to the facts needed to make reasonable, informed political decisions.

Dewey's views attracted the support of a wide range of liberal intellectuals and reformers, including Robert and Helen Lynd; Rexford Tugwell, professor of economics at Columbia; and Felix Frankfurter, a rising star at Harvard Law School. But these reformers were without power, except in a few states, and they took little comfort in the presidential election of 1928. Hoover's smashing victory suggested that the dominance of the Republicans would continue unabated.

Conclusion

Signs abounded in the 1920s that the American economy had become more prosperous, more consumer oriented, even somewhat more egalitarian. Moves to greater equality within marriage and to enhanced liberty for single women suggested that economic change was propelling social change as well.

But many working-class and rural Americans benefited little from the decade's prosperity. Changes in social life aroused resistance, especially from farmers and small-town Americans who feared that the growth of cities was rendering their white, Protestant America unrecognizable. Ethnic and racial minorities, as a result, experienced discrimination. As the decade ended, many of the issues that had divided the traditionalists and modernists—whether science should supplant religion; whether the federal government had the authority to enforce morality on individual citizens (as it was doing with Prohibition); and whether Americans who were not white Protestants should be first-class citizens—remained unresolved.

John Dewey *Philosopher who believed that American technological and industrial power could be made to serve the people and democracy.*

CHAPTER REVIEW

Review Questions

1. What were the achievements and limitations of "people's capitalism" in the 1920s?
2. What were the similarities and differences in the politics of Harding, Coolidge, and Hoover?
3. What concerned farmers and conservative white Protestants in the 1920s, and what policies did they support?
4. How were the experiences of ethnic and racial groups in 1920s America similar, and how were they different?
5. To whom did the phrase "Lost Generation" refer, and what caused these individuals to become disillusioned?

Critical Thinking Questions

1. Can the deep cultural differences that divided America in the 1920s best be explained by where people lived (country versus city), where they were born (in the United States or abroad), their race (white or not), their wealth or poverty, or something else?

2. A Great Depression was the furthest thing from Americans' minds in the 1920s. Reviewing carefully what you have learned about the economy in those years, can you spot areas of economic trouble that contemporaries may have overlooked?

Identifications

Review your understanding of the following key terms, people, and events for this chapter.

people's capitalism, p. 553
flappers, p. 554
Charles A. Lindbergh, p. 556
yellow dog contracts, p. 557
Sheppard-Towner Act, p. 559

League of Women Voters, p. 559
Teapot Dome scandal, p. 560
associationalism, p. 560
Five-Power Treaty, p. 561
Dawes Plan, p. 561

Prohibition, p. 562
Immigration Restriction Act of 1924 (Johnson-Reed Act), p. 564
fundamentalists, p. 565
liberal Protestants, p. 566
Alfred E. Smith, p. 568

Harlem Renaissance, p. 569
californios, p. 571
Lost Generation, p. 572
John Dewey, p. 573

DISCOVERY

How did the disillusionment that followed World War I shape social and cultural conflict in the 1920s?

In thinking about this question, begin by breaking it down into the components shown below. A discussion of the significance of each component should appear in your answer.

Culture and Society

The image below illustrates many characteristics of American life in the 1920s. What does it suggest about the general mood of the country and activities of daily life? How does it convey changes that had taken place in the previous decade for women? What does it say about the new consumer society?

Immigration and Society

Examine Table 24.1 on page 565 and the textual analysis in the section on immigration restriction on pages 564 and 565. The table identifies the countries that were given large annual immigrant quotas by the Immigration Restriction Act of 1924 (also known as the Johnson-Reed Act) and those that were given small annual quotas. Which countries received the largest quotas? Which countries received the smallest quotas? How were these quotas determined? What did Congress hope to accomplish with this legislation? Was the legislation successful?

The Art Archive/Bodleian Library Oxford

THE ART OF SELLING CARS

Visit the CourseMate website at www.cengagebrain.com for additional study tools and review materials for this chapter.

THE GREAT DEPRESSION AND THE NEW DEAL, 1929–1939

CAUSES OF THE GREAT DEPRESSION
    Stock Market Speculation
    Ineffective Federal Policies
    A Maldistribution of Wealth

HOOVER: THE FALL OF A SELF-MADE MAN
    Hoover's Program
    The Bonus Army

A CULTURE IN CRISIS

THE DEMOCRATIC ROOSEVELT
    An Early Life of Privilege
    Roosevelt Liberalism

THE FIRST NEW DEAL, 1933–1935
    Saving the Banks
    Economic Relief
    Agricultural Reform
    Industrial Reform
    Rebuilding the Nation's Infrastructure
    The TVA Alternative
    The New Deal and Western Development

POLITICAL MOBILIZATION, POLITICAL UNREST, 1934–1935
    Populist Critics of the New Deal

Labor Protests
Anger at the Polls
Radical Third Parties

THE SECOND NEW DEAL, 1935–1937
    Philosophical Underpinnings
    Legislation
    Victory in 1936: The New Democratic Coalition
    Rhetoric versus Reality
    Men, Women, and Reform
    Labor in Politics and Culture

AMERICA'S MINORITIES AND THE NEW DEAL
    Eastern and Southern European Ethnics
    African Americans
    Mexican Americans
    American Indians

THE NEW DEAL ABROAD

STALEMATE, 1937–1940
    The Court-Packing Fiasco
    The Recession of 1937–1938

The **Great Depression** began on October 29, 1929 (Black Tuesday) with a spectacular stock market crash. On that one day, the value of stocks plummeted $14 billion. By the end of that year, stock prices had fallen 50 percent from their September highs. By 1932, the worst year of the Depression, they had fallen another 30 percent. The unemployment rate soared to 25 percent, and scenes of misery unfolded across the nation. In cities, the poor meekly awaited their turn at ill-funded soup kitchens. Scavengers poked through garbage cans for food. Hundreds of thousands of Americans built makeshift shelters out of cardboard and scrap metal. They called their towns "Hoovervilles," after the president they despised for his apparent refusal to help them.

The gloom broke in early 1933 when **Franklin Delano Roosevelt** became president and unleashed the power of government to regulate capitalist enterprises, to restore the economy, and to ensure the social welfare of Americans unable to help themselves. Roosevelt called his pro-government program a "new deal for the American people." In the short term, the New Deal failed to restore prosperity to America, but the "liberalism" it championed found acceptance among millions, who agreed with Roosevelt that only a large and powerful government could guarantee Americans their liberty.

ᴛIMELINE

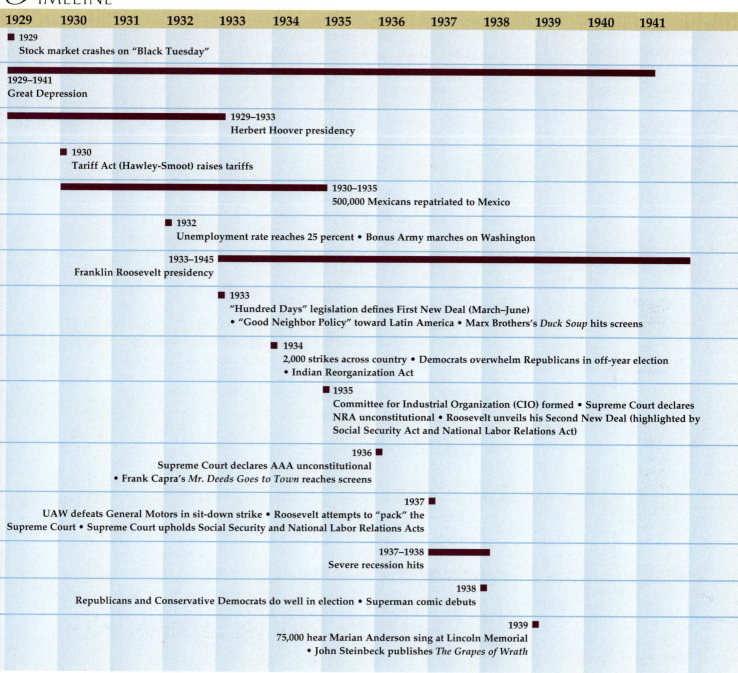

1929	1930	1931	1932	1933	1934	1935	1936	1937	1938	1939	1940	1941

1929
Stock market crashes on "Black Tuesday"

1929–1941
Great Depression

1929–1933
Herbert Hoover presidency

1930
Tariff Act (Hawley-Smoot) raises tariffs

1930–1935
500,000 Mexicans repatriated to Mexico

1932
Unemployment rate reaches 25 percent • Bonus Army marches on Washington

1933–1945
Franklin Roosevelt presidency

1933
"Hundred Days" legislation defines First New Deal (March–June)
• "Good Neighbor Policy" toward Latin America • Marx Brothers's *Duck Soup* hits screens

1934
2,000 strikes across country • Democrats overwhelm Republicans in off-year election
• Indian Reorganization Act

1935
Committee for Industrial Organization (CIO) formed • Supreme Court declares
NRA unconstitutional • Roosevelt unveils his Second New Deal (highlighted by
Social Security Act and National Labor Relations Act)

1936
Supreme Court declares AAA unconstitutional
• Frank Capra's *Mr. Deeds Goes to Town* reaches screens

1937
UAW defeats General Motors in sit-down strike • Roosevelt attempts to "pack" the
Supreme Court • Supreme Court upholds Social Security and National Labor Relations Acts

1937–1938
Severe recession hits

1938
Republicans and Conservative Democrats do well in election • Superman comic debuts

1939
75,000 hear Marian Anderson sing at Lincoln Memorial
• John Steinbeck publishes *The Grapes of Wrath*

ᴄAUSES OF THE GREAT DEPRESSION

America had experienced other depressions, or "panics," but no one was prepared for the economic catastrophe of the 1930s.

Stock Market Speculation

In 1928 and 1929, the New York Stock Exchange had undergone a remarkable run-up in prices. Money had poured into the market, but many investors were buying on a 10 percent "margin," putting up only 10 percent of the price of a stock and

FOCUS QUESTION

What caused the crash of 1929, and why did the ensuing Depression last so long?

Great Depression *Economic downturn triggered by the stock market crash in October 1929 and lasting until 1941.*

Franklin Delano Roosevelt *President from 1933 to 1945, and the creator of the New Deal.*

borrowing the rest from brokers or banks. They expected to resell their shares within a few months at dramatically higher prices, pay back their loans, and still clear a handsome profit. This worked for a while, but money soon flowed into risky enterprises, and speculation became rampant. The stock market spiraled upward, out of control. When, in October 1929, confidence in future earnings faltered, creditors began demanding that investors who had bought stocks on margin repay their loans. They could not, and the market crashed from its dizzying heights.

Ineffective Federal Policies

Still, the crash, by itself, fails to explain why the Great Depression lasted as long as it did. Poor decisions made by the federal government worsened the collapse. In 1930 and 1931, the Federal Reserve curtailed the amount of money in circulation and raised interest rates, thereby making credit more difficult for the public to secure. This action plunged an economy starved for credit deeper into depression.

Additionally, the Tariff Act of 1930, also known as the Hawley-Smoot Tariff, accelerated economic decline abroad and at home. It raised tariffs to protect American industry, but angry foreign governments retaliated by raising their own tariff rates to keep out American goods. International trade, already weakened by the tight credit policies of the Federal Reserve, declined even further.

A Maldistribution of Wealth

A maldistribution in the nation's wealth that had developed in the 1920s also stymied economic recovery. Between 1918 and 1929, the share of the national income that went to the wealthiest 20 percent of the population rose by more

UNEMPLOYED MEN IN NEW YORK CITY, **1931.** *The thousands of men waiting to register at the Emergency Unemployment Relief office became so frustrated that they rioted. Police reserves arrived to restore order.*

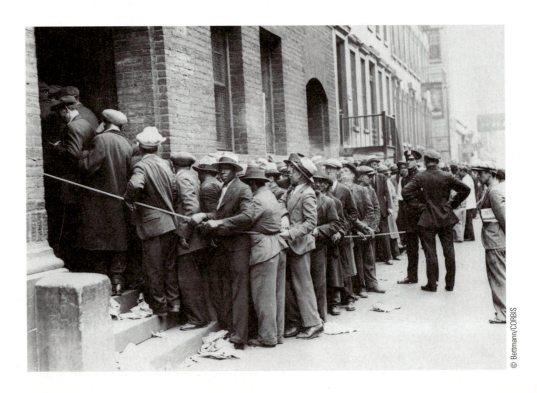

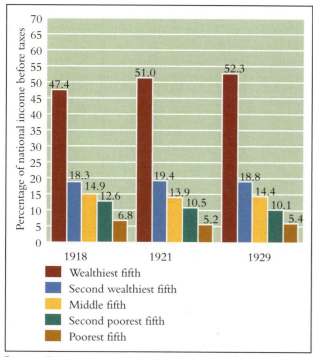

INCOME DISTRIBUTION BEFORE THE GREAT DEPRESSION

Source: From Gabriel Kolko, *Wealth and Power in America: An Analysis of Social Class and Income Distribution* (New York: Praeger, 1962), p. 14.

than 10 percent, while the share that went to the poorest 60 percent fell by almost 13 percent. (See chart above.) The Coolidge administration contributed to this maldistribution by lowering taxes on the wealthy. Putting more of the total increase in national income into the pockets of average Americans would have steadied the demand for consumer goods and strengthened the newer consumer industries. Such an economy might have recovered more quickly from the stock market crash of 1929. Instead, recovery from the Great Depression lagged until 1941.

QUICK REVIEW

CAUSES OF THE GREAT DEPRESSION

• Speculation fueled unsound stock market, leading to crash

• Federal Reserve Board worsened crash by curtailing money in circulation and raising interest rates

• Hawley-Smoot Tariff accelerated economic decline by damaging foreign trade

• Deepening inequality of income distribution depressed consumer demand and slowed recovery

HOOVER: THE FALL OF A SELF-MADE MAN

Herbert Hoover won an international reputation during the First World War for his success in feeding millions of European soldiers and civilians. In the 1920s, he was an active and influential secretary of commerce (see Chapter 24). As the decade wound down, no American seemed better qualified to become president of the United States, an office that Hoover assumed in March 1929. "We in America today are nearer to the final triumph over poverty than ever before in the history of any land," he had declared in August 1928. A little more than a year later, the Great Depression struck.

FOCUS QUESTION

Why did Hoover lose his popularity?

Hoover's Program

To cope with the crisis, Hoover first turned to the associational principles he had followed as secretary of commerce. He encouraged organizations of farmers,

Bonus Army *Army veterans who marched on Washington, D.C., in 1932 to lobby for economic relief but who were rebuffed by Hoover.*

THE BONUS ARMY'S ENCAMPMENT SET ABLAZE. *U.S. troops under the command of General Douglas MacArthur burned the tents and shacks that housed thousands of First World War veterans who had come to Washington to demand financial assistance from the government.*

industrialists, and bankers to share information, bolster one another's spirits, and devise policies to aid recovery. Hoover also secured a one-year moratorium on loan payments that European governments owed American banks. To ease the crisis at home, he created the Reconstruction Finance Corporation (RFC) in 1932 to make $2 billion available in loans to ailing banks and to corporations willing to build low-cost housing, bridges, and other public works.

Despite this new activism, Hoover was uncomfortable with the idea that the government was responsible for restoring the nation's economic welfare. When RFC projects in 1932 created the largest peacetime deficit in U.S. history, Hoover tried to balance the budget. He also insisted that the RFC issue loans only to healthy institutions that could repay them and that it favor public works, such as toll bridges, that were likely to become self-financing. As a result of these constraints, the RFC spent considerably less than Congress had authorized.

Hoover was especially reluctant to engage the government in providing relief to unemployed and homeless Americans. To give money to the poor, he insisted, would destroy their desire to work and undermine their sense of self-worth.

The Bonus Army

In spring 1932, a group of army veterans challenged Hoover's policies. In 1924, Congress had authorized a $1,000 bonus for First World War veterans in the form of compensation certificates that would mature in 1945. Now the veterans were demanding that the government pay the bonus immediately. A group of Portland, Oregon, veterans, calling themselves the Bonus Expeditionary Force, hopped onto empty boxcars of freight trains heading east, determined to march on Washington. By the time it reached the capital, this "army" had swelled to 20,000. The so-called **Bonus Army** set up camp near the Capitol and petitioned Congress for early payment of the bonus. The House of Representatives agreed, but the Senate turned them down. Hoover refused to meet with them. In July, federal troops attacked the veterans' encampment, set the tents and shacks ablaze, and dispersed the protesters. More than 100 veterans were wounded, and one infant died.

News that veterans and their families had been attacked in the nation's capital hardened anti-Hoover opinion. In the 1932 elections, Hoover received only 39.6 percent of the popular vote and just 59 (of 531) electoral votes.

A CULTURE IN CRISIS

The economic crisis of the early 1930s expressed itself not just in politics but also in culture, especially literature and cinema. Edmund Wilson traveled the country in 1930 and 1931 writing essays about how Americans had lost their way and knew not where to turn. A sense of aimlessness and hopelessness characterized the Studs Lonigan trilogy (1932–1935) by James T. Farrell. In another decade, Farrell might have cast his scrappy Irish American protagonist, Studs, as an American hero whose pluck and guile enable him to achieve success. But Studs dies poor and alone, not yet 30.

One can detect parallel themes of despair in the period's cinema. In *Fugitive from a Chain Gang* (1932), an industrious and honorable man, James Allen, returns from Europe a war hero, only to sink into vagabondage, serve jail time for a crime he did not commit, and live the rest of his life on the run after a daring escape. This powerful, bleak film won an Academy Award for Best Picture. Less grim but still sobering were gangster movies, especially *Little Caesar* (1930) and *The Public Enemy* (1931). Moviegoers were gripped by the intensity, suspense, and violence of gangster films, but they were drawn, too, to the gangsters themselves, modern-day outlaws who demonstrated how it might be necessary to break the rules to succeed in America.

Lawlessness also surfaced in the wild comedy of Groucho, Chico, Harpo, and Zeppo Marx. The Marx Brothers ridiculed authority figures, broke every rule of etiquette, smacked around their antagonists (and each other), and mangled the English language. They offered moviegoers 90-minute escapes from the harsh realities of their daily lives, although some Marx Brothers films were more serious. *Duck Soup* (1933) delivers the dispiriting message that people cannot hope to better themselves through politics, for politics has been emptied of all meaning and honesty. This cinematic sentiment echoed the conviction of many Americans in 1932 and early 1933 that their own politicians, especially Hoover and the Republicans, had failed them.

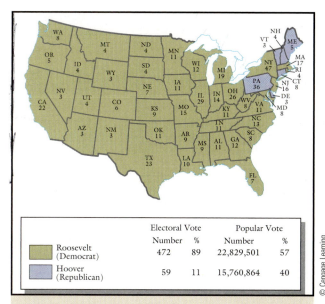

Map 25.1 Presidential Election, 1932. *The trauma of the Great Depression can be gauged by the shifting fortunes of President Herbert Hoover. In 1928, he had won 444 electoral votes and carried all but eight states (see Map 24.2, p. 568). In 1932, by contrast, he won only 59 electoral votes and carried only seven states. His Democratic opponent, Franklin D. Roosevelt, was the big winner.*

	Electoral Vote		Popular Vote	
	Number	%	Number	%
Roosevelt (Democrat)	472	89	22,829,501	57
Hoover (Republican)	59	11	15,760,864	40

THE DEMOCRATIC ROOSEVELT

Between 1933 and 1935, the country's mood shifted sharply, and politics would, once again, generate hope rather than despair. This change was largely attributable to the personality and politics of Hoover's successor, Franklin D. Roosevelt.

An Early Life of Privilege

Roosevelt was born in 1882 into a patrician family, descended on his father's side from Dutch gentry. His mother's family—the Delanos—traced its ancestors back to the *Mayflower*. His education at Groton, Harvard College, and Columbia Law School was typical of the path followed by the sons of America's elite. He had not distinguished himself either at school or at law. He owed his political ascent more to his famous name—Theodore Roosevelt was his older cousin—than to actual accomplishments. He was charming, gregarious, and popular among his associates in the New York Democratic Party. He enjoyed a good time and the company of women other than his wife, **Eleanor Roosevelt.**

Then, in 1921, at age 39, Roosevelt was stricken by polio and permanently lost the use of his legs. The polio attack changed him, and he seemed to acquire a new determination and seriousness. He developed a compassion for those suffering misfortune that would later enable him to reach out to the millions caught in the Great Depression. His physical debilitation also transformed his relationship with

© Cengage Learning

FOCUS QUESTION

What events transformed Franklin D. Roosevelt into a focused politician? What beliefs defined his liberalism?

Eleanor Roosevelt *A politically engaged and effective First Lady and an architect of American liberalism.*

elected 1932

Eleanor, whose dedication to nursing him back to health forged a new bond between them. More conscious of his dependence on others, he now welcomed her as a partner in his career. Eleanor soon displayed a talent for political organization and public speaking. She would become an active, eloquent First Lady and an architect of American liberalism.

Roosevelt Liberalism

As governor of New York (1929–1933), Roosevelt had initiated various reform programs, and his success made him the front-runner for the 1932 Democratic presidential nomination. Even so, he had little assurance that he would be the party's choice. Since 1924, the Democrats had been divided between southern and midwestern agrarians on the one hand and northeastern ethnics on the other. The agrarians favored government regulation—both of the nation's economy and of the private affairs of its citizens. By contrast, urban ethnics opposed Prohibition and other forms of government interference in their private lives. Urban ethnics were divided over whether the government should regulate the economy, with former New York governor Al Smith increasingly committed to a laissez-faire policy and Senator Robert Wagner of New York and others supporting more federal control.

Roosevelt sought to carve out a middle ground. He surrounded himself with men and women who embraced a new reform movement called **liberalism**. Liberals shared with the agrarians and Wagner's supporters a desire to regulate capitalism, but agreed with Al Smith that the government had no business telling people how to live their private lives. Roosevelt united the party behind him at the 1932 Democratic Party convention, where he declared: "Ours must be the party of liberal thought, of planned action, of enlightened international outlook, and of the greatest good for the greatest number of citizens." He promised "a new deal for the American people."

Roosevelt liberalism *New reform movement that sought to regulate capitalism but not the morals of private citizens. This reform liberalism overcame divisions between southern agrarians and northeastern ethnics.*

THE FIRST NEW DEAL, 1933–1935

FOCUS QUESTION

What do you consider to be the three or four most important pieces of legislation in the First New Deal? Why?

By the time Roosevelt assumed office, the economy lay in shambles. From 1929 to 1932, industrial production fell by 50 percent. The nation's banking system was on the verge of collapse. Unemployment soared.

In his first Hundred Days, from early March through early June 1933, Roosevelt persuaded Congress to repeal Prohibition and to pass 15 major pieces of legislation to help bankers, farmers, industrialists, workers, homeowners, the unemployed, and the hungry (see Table 25.1). Although not all the new laws relieved distress and promoted recovery, Roosevelt had brought energy and hope to the nation. He was confident, decisive, and defiantly cheery. "The only thing we have to fear is fear itself," he declared.

On the second Sunday after his inaugural address, Roosevelt launched a series of radio addresses known as "fireside chats," speaking in a plain, friendly, and direct voice to the forlorn and discouraged. To hear the president speaking warmly and conversationally—as though he were actually there in the room—riveted Americans. On the radio and elsewhere, Roosevelt's political rhetoric sometimes promised more than he was prepared to deliver. Yet the bond that he developed with average people became a political force in its own right.

TABLE 25.1

LEGISLATION ENACTED DURING THE "HUNDRED DAYS," MARCH 9–JUNE 16, 1933		
Date	Legislation	Purpose
March 9	Emergency Banking Act	Provide federal loans to private bankers
March 20	Economy Act	Balance the federal budget
March 22	Beer-Wine Revenue Act	Repeal Prohibition
March 31	Unemployment Relief Act	Create the Civilian Conservation Corps
May 12	Agricultural Adjustment Act	Establish a national agricultural policy
May 12	Emergency Farm Mortgage Act	Provide refinancing of farm mortgages
May 12	Federal Emergency Relief Act	Establish a national relief system, including the Civil Works Administration
May 18	Tennessee Valley Authority Act	Promote economic development of the Tennessee Valley
May 27	Securities Act	Regulate the purchase and sale of new securities
June 5	Gold Repeal Joint Resolution	Cancel the gold clause in public and private contracts
June 13	Home Owners Loan Act	Provide refinancing of home mortgages
June 16	National Industrial Recovery Act	Set up a national system of industrial self-government and establish the Public Works Administration
June 16	Glass-Steagall Banking Act	Create Federal Deposit Insurance Corporation; separate commercial and investment banking
June 16	Farm Credit Act	Reorganize agricultural credit programs
June 16	Railroad Coordination Act	Appoint federal coordinator of transportation

Source: Arthur M. Schlesinger Jr., *The Coming of the New Deal* (Boston: Houghton Mifflin, 1959), pp. 20–21.

© Bettmann/CORBIS

CONNECTING WITH ORDINARY AMERICANS. *In 1933, FDR began broadcasting "Fireside Chats," frank and accessible radio addresses about the problems confronting the nation and how Americans might solve them. Millions listened to these chats in their homes, gathered around the radio as though it were a hearth.*

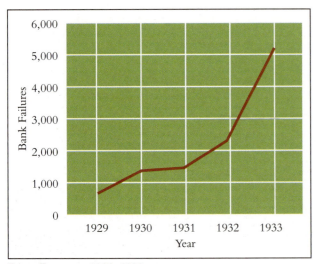

BANK FAILURES, 1929–1933

Source: From C. D. Bremer, *American Bank Failures* (New York: Columbia University Press, 1935), p. 42.

Saving the Banks

By inauguration day, many of the nation's banks had shut their doors. Roosevelt immediately ordered all banks closed—a bold move he brazenly called a "bank holiday." At his request, Congress rushed through the Emergency Banking Act, which made federal loans available to private bankers, and the Economy Act, which committed the government to balancing the budget. Both were fiscally conservative reforms that Hoover had proposed.

As the financial crisis eased, Roosevelt turned to the structural reform of banking. The Glass-Steagall Act (1933) separated commercial banking from investment banking. It also created the Federal Deposit Insurance Corporation (FDIC), which assured depositors that the government would protect up to $5,000 of their savings. The Securities Act (1933) and the Securities Exchange Act (1934) regulated the New York Stock Exchange by reining in buying on margin and by establishing the Securities and Exchange Commission to enforce federal law.

Economic Relief

Roosevelt understood the need to temper financial prudence with compassion. Congress responded swiftly in 1933 to Roosevelt's request to establish the Federal Emergency Relief Administration (FERA), granting it $500 million for relief to the poor. Roosevelt then won congressional approval for the Civilian Conservation Corps (CCC), which put more than two million single young men to work planting trees, halting erosion, and otherwise improving the environment. The Civil Works Administration (CWA), begun the following winter, hired four million unemployed people at $15 a week and put them to work on 400,000 government projects. The Homeowners' Loan Corporation (1933) refinanced mortgages for Americans threatened with the loss of their homes.

Agricultural Reform

In 1933, Roosevelt expected economic recovery to come not from relief but through agricultural and industrial cooperation. His policies were based on the idea that curtailing production would trigger economic recovery. As demand for scarce goods exceeded supply, Roosevelt's economists reasoned, prices would rise and revenues would climb. Farmers and industrialists would then hire more workers.

To curtail farm production, the **Agricultural Adjustment Administration (AAA),** set up by the Agricultural Adjustment Act of May 1933, began paying farmers to keep a portion of their land out of cultivation and to reduce the size of their herds. The AAA had made little provision, however, for the tenant farmers and farm laborers who would be thrown out of work by the reduction in acreage. In the South, the victims were disproportionately black. AAA programs also proved inadequate to Great Plains farmers, whose economic problems had been compounded by drought. The land, stripped of its native grasses by decades of plowing, dried up and turned to dust. And then the dust began to blow, sometimes traveling 1,000 miles across open prairie. Dust became a fixed feature of daily life on the plains (which soon became known as the Dust Bowl), covering furniture, floors, and stoves, and accumulating in people's hair and lungs.

Agricultural Adjustment Administration (AAA) *1933 attempt to promote economic recovery by reducing supply of crops, dairy, and meat produced by American farmers.*

By 1935, nearly 1 million sharecroppers and tenant farmers had left their homes, and another 2.5 million would leave after 1935. Most headed west, piling their belongings onto their jalopies, snaking along Route 66 until they reached California. They became known as Okies, because many, although not all, had come from Oklahoma.

In 1936, the Supreme Court ruled that AAA-mandated limits on farm production constituted illegal restraints of trade. Congress responded by passing the Soil Conservation and Domestic Allotment Act, which justified the removal of land from cultivation for reasons of conservation rather than economics. It also called upon landowners to share their government subsidies with sharecroppers and tenant farmers, although many land-owners refused to comply.

Industrial Reform

American industry was so vast that Roosevelt's administration never contemplated paying individual manufacturers direct subsidies to reduce, or even halt, production. Instead, the government decided to limit production through persuasion and association. The first task of the **National Recovery Administration (NRA)**, authorized under the National Industrial Recovery Act (NIRA) of June 1933, was to convince industrialists and business owners to raise employee wages to a minimum of 30 to 40 cents an hour and to limit employee hours to a maximum of 30 to 40 hours a week. The intent was to reduce the quantity of goods that any factory or business could produce.

The NRA also brought together the largest producers in every sector of manufacturing and asked each group (or conference) to limit competition and to develop a code of fair competition to govern prices, wages, and hours in their industry. In the summer and fall of 1933, the NRA codes seemed to be working. The economy improved, and hard times seemed to be easing. But in winter and spring 1934, economic indicators plunged downward once again, and manufacturers began to evade the codes. By fall 1934, it was clear that the NRA had failed. When the Supreme Court declared the NRA codes unconstitutional in May 1935, the Roosevelt administration allowed the agency to die.

Rebuilding the Nation's Infrastructure

The National Industrial Recovery Act also launched the Public Works Administration (PWA) to strengthen the nation's infrastructure of roads, bridges, sewage systems, hospitals, airports, and schools. The PWA authorized the building of major dams in the West and funded the construction of the Triborough Bridge in New York City and the 100-mile causeway linking Florida to Key West. It also appropriated money to construct thousands of new schools.

The TVA Alternative

In contrast to the NIRA, the Tennessee Valley Authority Act (1933) called for the government—rather than private corporations—to promote economic development

SEARCHING FOR A BETTER LIFE. *Scenes like this one were common in the 1930s as farm families in Oklahoma and Texas who had lost their land began heading to California. Here a family's entire belongings are packed onto a truck, and the mother tends to her baby on an isolated road. The woman's fur collar suggests that this family had once known better times.*

FDR Library

National Recovery Administration (NRA) *1933 attempt to promote economic recovery by persuading private groups of industrialists to decrease production, limit hours of work per employee, and standardize minimum wages.*

Tennessee Valley Authority (TVA) *Ambitious and successful use of government resources and power to promote economic development throughout the Tennessee Valley.*

throughout the Tennessee Valley, which encompassed parts of Kentucky, Tennessee, Mississippi, Alabama, Georgia, and North Carolina. The **Tennessee Valley Authority (TVA)** built, completed, or improved more than 20 dams. It constructed hydroelectric generators and soon became the nation's largest producer of electricity. Its low electric rates compelled private utility companies to reduce their rates as well. The TVA also redirected waterways to bypass nonnavigable stretches of the river, reduced the danger of flooding, and taught farmers how to prevent soil erosion and use fertilizers.

Although the TVA was one of the New Deal's most celebrated successes, it generated little support for other experiments in national planning. For the government to have assumed control of established industries and banks would have been quite a different matter from bringing prosperity to an impoverished region. Like Roosevelt, few members of Congress or the public favored the radical growth of governmental power such programs would have entailed.

The New Deal and Western Development

The West benefited most from the New Deal. Between 1933 and 1939, per capita payments for public works projects, welfare, and federal loans in the Rocky Mountain and Pacific Coast states outstripped those of any other region.

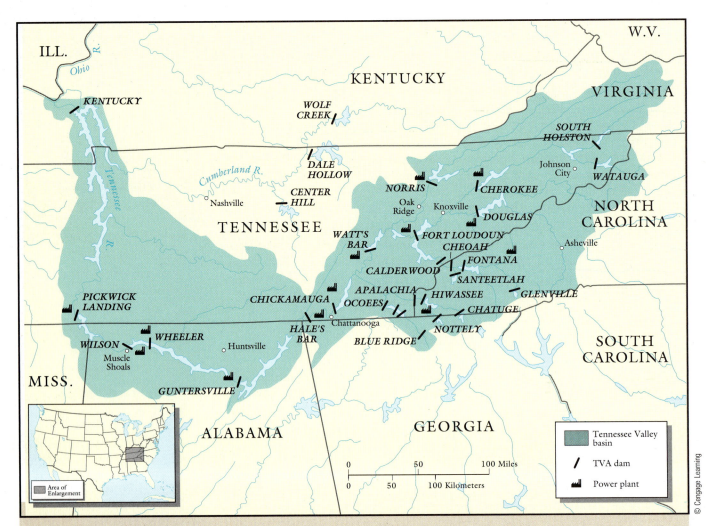

Map 25.2 **Tennessee Valley Authority.** *This map shows the vast scale of the TVA and pinpoints the locations of 29 dams and 13 power plants that emerged from this project.*

Dam building was central to this western focus. Western real estate and agricultural interests wanted to dam major rivers to provide water and electricity for urban and agricultural development. They found a government ally in the Bureau of Reclamation, which became, under the New Deal, a prime dispenser of infrastructural funds. Drawing on PWA monies, the bureau oversaw the building of the Boulder Dam (later renamed Hoover Dam), Grand Coulee Dam, and other dams that provided drinking water, irrigation water, and electricity to westerners.

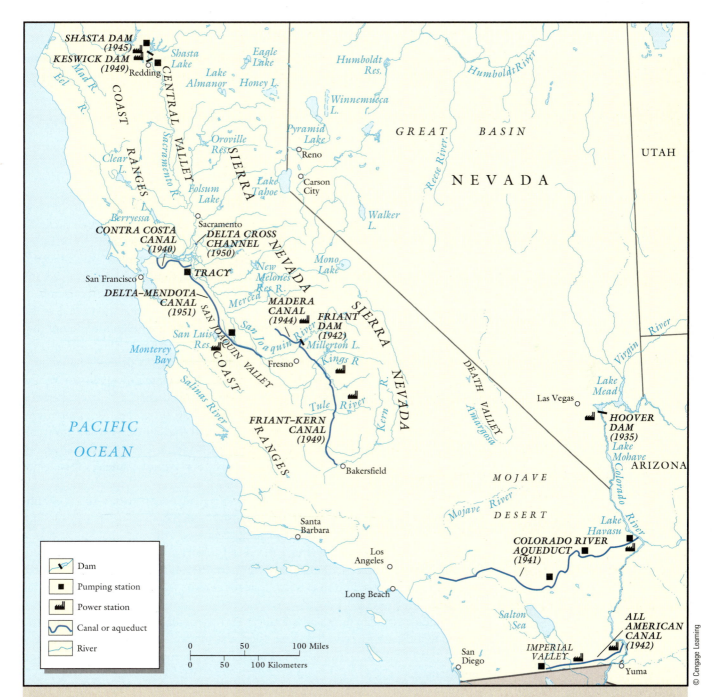

Map 25.3 Federal Water Projects in California Built or Funded by the New Deal. *This map demonstrates how much California cities and agriculture benefited from water projects—dams, canals, aqueducts, pumping stations, and power plants—begun under the New Deal. The projects extended from the Shasta Dam in the northern part of the state to the All-American Canal that traversed the Imperial Valley south of San Diego, and included the Colorado River Aqueduct that would bring drinking water to Los Angeles.*

Unlike the TVA, the Bureau of Reclamation hired private contractors to do the work, and the benefits of these dams were intended to flow first to large agricultural and real estate interests, not to the poor. In political terms, dam building in the West was more conservative than it was in the Tennessee Valley; it was intended to aid private enterprise rather than to supplant it.

POLITICAL MOBILIZATION, POLITICAL UNREST, 1934–1935

FOCUS QUESTION

What forms did political unrest take in 1934 and 1935?

Although Roosevelt and the New Dealers dismantled the NRA in 1935, they could not stop the political forces it had set it in motion. Ordinary Americans now believed that they could make a difference. If the New Dealers could not achieve economic recovery, the people would find others who could.

Populist Critics of the New Deal

Some critics were disturbed by what they perceived as the conservatism of New Deal programs. In the South and Midwest, millions listened to the radio addresses of Louisiana Senator **Huey Long**, a former governor of that state and a compelling orator. He criticized the New Deal for failing "to relieve the masses" and offered a simple alternative: "Break up the swollen fortunes of America and … spread the wealth among all our people." Long's rhetoric inspired hundreds of thousands of Americans to join Share the Wealth clubs. By 1935, Roosevelt regarded Long as the man most likely to unseat him in the presidential election of 1936. But before that campaign began, Long was assassinated.

In the Midwest, **Father Charles Coughlin,** the "radio priest," delivered a message similar to Long's. Coughlin appealed to anxious middle-class Americans and to once-privileged groups of workers who believed that middle-class status was slipping from their grasp. A former Roosevelt supporter, Coughlin now claimed that the New Deal was run by bankers, and that the NRA was a program to resuscitate corporate profits. He founded the National Union of Social Justice (NUSJ) in 1934 as a precursor to a political party that would challenge the Democrats in 1936.

As Coughlin's disillusionment with the New Deal deepened, a strain of anti-Semitism appeared in his radio talks; he accused Jewish bankers of masterminding a world conspiracy to dispossess the toiling masses. Although Coughlin was a powerful speaker, he failed to build the NUSJ into an effective force. Embittered, Coughlin moved further to the political right. By 1939, his denunciations of democracy and Jews had become so extreme that some radio stations refused to carry his addresses.

Another popular figure was Francis E. Townsend, a California doctor who claimed that the way to end the Depression was to give every senior citizen $200 a month. The Townsend Plan briefly garnered the support of an estimated 20 million Americans.

Huey Long *Democratic senator and former governor of Louisiana who used the radio to attack the New Deal as too conservative. FDR regarded him as a major rival.*

Father Charles Coughlin *The "radio priest" from the Midwest who alleged that the New Deal was being run by bankers. His growing anti-Semitism discredited him by 1939.*

Labor Protests

The attacks by Long, Coughlin, and Townsend on New Deal programs deepened popular discontent and helped to legitimate other insurgent movements. The most important was the labor movement. Workers began joining unions in response to the 1933 National Industrial Recovery Act, and especially its clause granting them the right to join labor organizations of their own choosing and obligating employers to bargain with them in good faith. Union members' demands were modest at first: They wanted to be treated fairly, and they wanted employers to observe the provisions of the NRA codes and to recognize their unions. But many employers ignored the NRA's wage and hour guidelines and even used their influence with NRA code authorities to get worker requests for wage increases and union recognition rejected.

Workers flooded Washington with protest letters and then began to take matters into their own hands. In 1934 they staged 2,000 strikes in virtually every industry and region of the country. A few of those strikes escalated into armed confrontations that shocked the nation. Two strikers were killed in an exchange of gunfire at the Electric Auto-Lite plant in Toledo in May. In San Francisco in July, skirmishes between longshoremen and employers killed two and wounded scores of strikers. In September, 400,000 textile workers at mills from Maine to Alabama walked off their jobs. Attempts by employers to bring in replacement workers triggered additional violence.

Anger at the Polls

In the fall of 1934, workers took their anger to the polls. Democrats won 70 percent of the contested seats in the Senate and House, increasing their majorities. Although no sitting president's party had ever done so well in an off-year election, the victory was not an unqualified one for Roosevelt. The 74th Congress would include the largest contingent of radicals ever sent to Washington. Their support for the New Deal depended on whether Roosevelt delivered more relief, more income security, and more political power to farmers, workers, the unemployed, and the poor.

Radical Third Parties

Radicals also made an impressive showing in state politics in 1934 and 1936. In Wisconsin, Philip La Follette, the son of Robert La Follette (see Chapter 21), was elected governor in 1934 and 1936 as the candidate of the radical Wisconsin Progressive Party. The new Minnesota Farmer-Labor Party elected its candidate to the governorship. And in California, the socialist and novelist Upton Sinclair and his organization, End Poverty in California (EPIC), came close to winning the governorship.

The growing appeal of the Communist Party offered further evidence of voter volatility. The American Communist Party (CP) had emerged in the early 1920s with the support of radicals who wanted to adopt the Soviet Union's path to socialism. In the early 1930s, CP organizers spread out among the poorest and most vulnerable populations in America—homeless urban blacks in the North, black and white sharecroppers in the South, Chicano and Filipino agricultural workers in the West—and mobilized them in unions and unemployment leagues. CP members also played significant roles in strikes, and they were influential in the Minnesota Farmer-Labor Party. Once they stopped preaching world revolution in 1935 and began calling instead for a "popular front" of democratic forces against fascism, their ranks grew even more. By 1938, approximately 80,000 Americans are thought to have been members of the CP.

The party never became large or strong enough to gain power for itself. Its chief role in 1930s politics was to channel popular discontent into unions and political parties that would force New Dealers to respond to the demands of the poor.

THE SECOND NEW DEAL, 1935–1937

FOCUS QUESTION

What was "underconsumptionism," and how did it inform the legislation of the Second New Deal? How was the Second New Deal different from the first?

For a time, Roosevelt kept his distance from protesters, but in spring 1935, with the 1936 presidential election looming, he decided to place himself at their head. He attacked the wealthy for their profligate ways and called for new programs to aid the poor and downtrodden. Rather than becoming a socialist, as his critics charged, Roosevelt sought to reinvigorate his appeal among poorer Americans and turn them away from radical solutions.

Philosophical Underpinnings

To point the New Deal in a more populist direction, Roosevelt turned to a relatively new economic theory, **underconsumptionism**. Advocates held that a chronic weakness in consumer demand had caused the Great Depression. The path to recovery lay, therefore, not in restricting production, as the architects of the First New Deal had tried to do, but in boosting consumer expenditures through government support for labor unions (to force up wages), social welfare expenditures (to put more money in the hands of the poor), and public works projects (to create new jobs).

Underconsumptionists did not worry that new programs might strain the federal budget. If the government found itself short of revenue, it could always borrow additional funds from private sources. These reformers, in fact, viewed government borrowing as a useful antidepression tool. Those who lent the government money would receive a return on their investment; those who received government assistance would have income to spend on consumer goods; and manufacturers would profit from consumer spending. This fiscal policy, a reversal of the conventional wisdom that government should always balance its budget, would in the 1940s come to be known as Keynesianism, after John Maynard Keynes, the British economist who had been its advocate.

As the nation entered its sixth year of the Depression, Roosevelt was willing to give the new ideas a try. Reform-minded members of the 1934 Congress were eager for new legislation directed more to the needs of ordinary Americans than to the needs of big business.

Legislation

Congress passed much of that legislation in January to June 1935—a period that came to be known as the Second New Deal. The **Social Security Act** required the states to set up welfare funds from which money would be disbursed to the elderly poor, the unemployed, unmarried mothers with dependent children, and the disabled. It also enrolled a majority of working Americans in a pension program that guaranteed them a steady income upon retirement. A federal system of employer and employee taxation was set up to fund the pensions.

Equally historic was the passage of the National Labor Relations Act (NLRA). This act delivered what the NRA had only promised: the right of every worker to join a union of his or her choosing and the obligation of employers to bargain with that union in good faith. The **NLRA**, also called the **Wagner Act** after its Senate sponsor, Robert Wagner of New York, set up a National Labor Relations Board (NLRB) to supervise union elections, to

underconsumptionism *Theory that underconsumption, or a chronic weakness in consumer demand, had caused the Depression. This theory guided the Second New Deal, leading to the passage of laws designed to stimulate consumer demand.*

Social Security Act *Centerpiece of the welfare state (1935) that instituted the first federal pension system and that required state governments to set up funds to take care of groups (such as the disabled and unmarried mothers with children) unable to support themselves.*

Wagner Act (NLRA) *Named after its sponsor, Senator Robert Wagner (D-NY), this 1935 act gave every worker the right to join a union and compelled employers to bargain with unions in good faith.*

investigate claims of unfair labor practices, and to impose fines on employers who violated the law.

Congress also passed the Holding Company Act to break up the 13 utility companies that controlled 75 percent of the nation's electric power. It passed the Wealth Tax Act, which increased tax rates on wealthy individuals to 75 percent and on corporations to 15 percent. It created the Rural Electrification Administration (REA) to bring electric power to rural households. Finally, it passed the $5 billion Emergency Relief Appropriation Act. Roosevelt funneled part of this sum to create the National Youth Administration (NYA), which provided work and guidance to the nation's youth.

Roosevelt directed most of the new relief money, however, to the **Works Progress Administration (WPA)**. The WPA built or improved thousands of schools, playgrounds, airports, and hospitals. WPA crews raked leaves, cleaned streets, and landscaped cities. In the process, the WPA provided jobs to approximately 30 percent of the nation's jobless.

It also funded a program of public art, supporting the work of thousands of painters, architects, writers, playwrights, actors, and intellectuals. It fostered the creation of art that spoke to the concerns of ordinary Americans, adorned public buildings with colorful murals, and boosted public morale (see Table 25.2).

Works Progress Administration (WPA) *Federal relief agency established in 1935 that disbursed billions to pay for infrastructure improvements and funded a vast program of public art.*

Photo © Smithsonian American Art Museum, Washington, DC/Art Resource, NY. Art © Estate of Moses Soyer/Licensed by VAGA, New York, NY

WPA Artists at Work. *This 1935 painting by Moses Soyer shows painters hired by the WPA at work on their art, much of it commissioned by local and state governments to be hung in post offices, schools, city halls, train stations, and other public buildings.*

TABLE 25.2

SELECTED WPA PROJECTS IN NEW YORK CITY, 1938		
Construction and Renovation	**Education, Health, and Art**	**Research and Records**
East River Drive	Adult education: homemaking, trade and technical skills, and art and culture	Sewage treatment, community health, labor relations, and employment trends surveys
Henry Hudson Parkway	Children's education: remedial reading, lip reading, and field trips	Museum and library catalogs and exhibits
Bronx sewers	Prisoners' vocational training, recreation, and nutrition	Municipal office clerical support
Glendale and Queens public libraries	Dental clinics	Government forms standardization
King's County Hospital	Tuberculosis examination clinics	
Williamsburg Housing Project	Syphilis and gonorrhea treatment clinics	
School buildings, prisons, and firehouses	City hospital kitchen help, orderlies, laboratory technicians, nurses, doctors	
Coney Island and Brighton Beach boardwalks	Subsistence gardens	
Orchard Beach	Sewing rooms	
Swimming pools, playgrounds, parks, drinking fountains	Central Park sculpture shop	

Source: John David Millet, *The Works Progress Administration in New York City* (Chicago: Public Administration Service, 1938), pp. 95–126.

Victory in 1936: The New Democratic Coalition

Roosevelt described his Second New Deal as a program to limit the power and privilege of the wealthy few and to increase the security and welfare of ordinary citizens. American voters responded by handing Roosevelt a landslide victory. He received 61 percent of the popular vote; Alf Landon of Kansas, his Republican opponent, received only 37 percent (see Map 25.4).

Rhetoric versus Reality

Roosevelt's 1935–1936 anticorporate rhetoric was more radical than the laws he supported. The Wealth Tax Act took less out of wealthy incomes and estates than was advertised, and the utility companies that the Holding Company Act should have broken up remained largely intact. Roosevelt also promised more than he delivered to the nation's poor. Farmworkers, for example, were not covered by the Social Security Act or by the National Labor Relations Act. Consequently, thousands of African American sharecroppers in the South, along with substantial numbers of Chicano and Filipino farmworkers in the Southwest, were excluded from these acts' protections and benefits. The sharecroppers were shut out because southern Democrats would not have voted for an act they saw as benefiting southern blacks. For the same reason, the New Deal made little effort to restore voting rights to southern blacks or to demand that their other civil rights be respected.

Roosevelt's populist stance also obscured the support that capitalists—construction firms, real estate developers, mass merchandisers, clothing manufacturers—were giving the Second New Deal. These firms, in turn, had financial connections with investment and consumer-oriented banks. They tolerated strong labor unions, welfare programs, and high levels of government spending

QUICK REVIEW

THE SECOND NEW DEAL (1935–1938)

- Prompted by failure of First New Deal and widespread political unrest

- Wanted to boost consumer demand through support for labor unions, social welfare, and public works

- Social Security, Wagner Act, and emergency relief appropriations were most important acts

- Democrats and FDR rode Second New Deal to electoral victory in 1936

- Anticorporate rhetoric was more powerful than the reality of the laws

in the belief that these developments would strengthen consumer spending, but they would not surrender their wealth or power. The conflicting interests of the masses on one hand and big business on the other would create tensions within the Democratic Party throughout the years of its domination.

Men, Women, and Reform

The years 1936 and 1937 were exciting ones for the dedicated and idealistic academics, policy-makers, and bureaucrats who designed and administered New Deal programs and agencies. They won congressional approval for the Farm Security Administration (FSA), an agency designed to improve the economic lot of tenant farmers, sharecroppers, and farm laborers. They passed laws that outlawed child labor, set minimum wages and maximum hours for adult workers, and committed the federal government to building low-cost housing. They tried to regulate concentrations of corporate power.

Who were these reformers? Many of the men among them had earned advanced degrees in law and economics at elite universities. Not all had been raised among wealth and privilege, however. To his credit, Franklin Roosevelt was the first president since his cousin Theodore Roosevelt to welcome Jews and Catholics into his administration. These men had struggled to make their way, first on the streets and then in school and at work. They brought to the New Deal intellectual aggressiveness, quick minds, and mental toughness.

The profile of New Deal women was different. They tended to be a generation older than their male colleagues and were more likely to be Protestant than Catholic or Jewish. Although there were exceptions—notably Eleanor Roosevelt and Secretary of Labor Frances Perkins—many of the female New Dealers worked in relative obscurity, in agencies like the Women's Bureau or the Children's Bureau (both in the Department of Labor). And women who worked on major legislation or directed major programs received less credit than men in comparable positions.

Demands for greater economic opportunity, sexual freedom, and full equality for women and men were heard less often in the 1930s than they had been in the preceding two decades. One reason was that the women's movement had fragmented after achieving suffrage. Another was that prominent New Deal women concentrated on protective legislation. Those who insisted that women needed special protections could not easily argue that women were the equal of men in all respects.

Feminism was also constricted by a male hostility that the Depression had only intensified. The loss of work made men feel inadequate, and male vulnerability

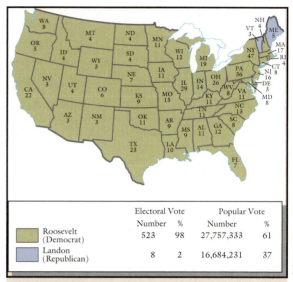

© Cengage Learning

Map 25.4 Presidential Election, 1936. *In 1936, Franklin D. Roosevelt's reelection numbers were overwhelming: 98 percent of the electoral vote, and more than 60 percent of the popular vote. No previous election in American history had been so one-sided.*

The 1936 election won the Democratic Party its reputation as the party of reform and the party of the "forgotten American." Of the six million Americans who went to the polls for the first time, five million voted for Roosevelt. Among the poorest Americans, Roosevelt received 80 percent of the vote. Black voters in the North deserted the Republican Party. Roosevelt also did well among white middle-class voters, many of whom stood to benefit from the Social Security Act. These constituencies would constitute the "Roosevelt coalition" for most of the next 40 years.

AP Images

An Activist First Lady. *No woman was more prominent in the 1930s than Eleanor Roosevelt. During the decade, she met with many different groups of Americans, including the miners depicted in this photo, seeking to learn more about their condition and the ways in which the New Deal could assist them.*

CIO *The Congress for Industrial Organizations, founded in 1935 to organize the unskilled and semiskilled workers ignored by the AFL. The CIO reinvigorated the labor movement.*

TABLE 25.3

RATES OF UNEMPLOYMENT IN SELECTED MALE AND FEMALE OCCUPATIONS, 1930		
Male Occupations	**Percentage Male**	**Percentage Unemployed**
Iron and steel	96%	13%
Forestry and fishing	99	10
Mining	99	18
Heavy manufacturing	86	13
Carpentry	100	19
Laborers (road and street)	100	13
Female Occupations	**Percentage Female**	**Percentage Unemployed**
Stenographers and typists	96%	5%
Laundresses	99	3
Trained nurses	98	4
Housekeepers	92	3
Telephone operators	95	3
Dressmakers	100	4

Source: U.S. Department of Commerce, Bureau of the Census, *Fifteenth Census of the United States, 1930, Population* (Washington, D.C.: Government Printing Office, 1931).

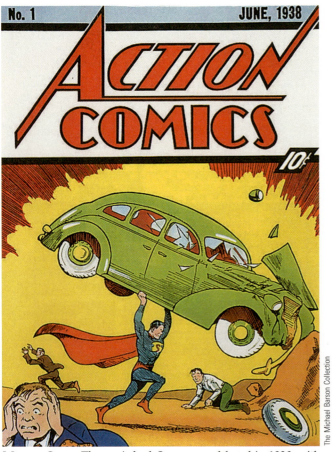

The Michael Barson Collection

MAN OF STEEL. *The comic book* Superman *debuted in 1938, with the cover that appears in this reproduction. The character* Superman *partook of the New Deal's commitment to help ordinary Americans in need while offering men a fantasy about unconquerable male power.*

increased as the unemployment rates of men rose higher than those of women (see Table 25.3). This male anxiety had consequences. Several states passed laws outlawing the hiring of married women. The labor movement made the protection of the male wage earner one of its principal goals. The Social Security pension system did not cover waitresses, domestic servants, and other largely female occupations. Artists introduced a strident masculinism into their painting and sculpture. Boys and male adolescents found a new hero in Superman, the "man-of-steel" comic-book figure who debuted in 1938. Superman's strength, unlike that of so many men in the 1930s, could not be taken away—except by Kryptonite and Lois Lane, that dangerous working woman.

Labor in Politics and Culture

In 1935, John L. Lewis of the United Mine Workers, Sidney Hillman of the Amalgamated Clothing Workers, and the leaders of six other unions that had seceded from the American Federation of Labor (AFL) cobbled together a new labor organization. The Committee for Industrial Organization (**CIO**—later renamed the Congress of Industrial Organizations) aspired to organize millions of unskilled and semiskilled workers whom the AFL had largely ignored. In 1936, Lewis and

Hillman created Labor's Non-Partisan League (LNPL) to channel labor's money, energy, and talent into Roosevelt's reelection campaign. Roosevelt welcomed the league's help, and labor became a key constituency of the new Democratic coalition. The passage of the Wagner Act and the creation of the NLRB in 1935 enhanced the labor movement's status and credibility. Membership in labor unions climbed, and union members began flexing their muscles in politics.

In late 1936, the United Auto Workers (UAW) took on General Motors, widely regarded as the mightiest corporation in the world. Workers occupied key GM factories in Flint, Michigan, declaring that their **sit-down strike** would continue until GM agreed to recognize the UAW and negotiate a collective-bargaining agreement. Frank Murphy, the pro-labor governor of Michigan, refused to use National Guardsmen to evict the strikers, and Roosevelt declined to send federal troops. GM capitulated after a month of resistance. Soon, the U.S. Steel Corporation, which had defeated unionists in the bloody strike of 1919 (see Chapter 23), announced that it would negotiate a contract with the newly formed CIO steelworkers union.

The labor movement's public stature grew along with its size. Many writers and artists, funded through the WPA, depicted the labor movement as the voice of the people and the embodiment of the nation's values. For example, Broadway's most celebrated play in 1935 was Clifford Odets's *Waiting for Lefty*, a raw drama about taxi drivers who confront their bosses and organize an honest union.

Many of the most popular novels and movies of the 1930s celebrated the decency, honesty, and patriotism of ordinary Americans. In *Mr. Deeds Goes to Town* (1936) and *Mr. Smith Goes to Washington* (1939), Frank Capra delighted movie audiences with fables about simple men who vanquish the evil forces of wealth and decadence. John Steinbeck's 1939 best seller, *The Grapes of Wrath*, told an epic tale of an Oklahoma family's fortitude in surviving eviction from their land, migrating westward, and suffering exploitation in the "promised land" of California.

The Okie migrants to California included a writer and musician named Woody Guthrie, who found a radio audience among the many Texas and Oklahoma transplants in California. He developed a broader appeal by casting himself as the bard of ordinary Americans everywhere. He loved America for the beauty of its landscape and its people, sentiments he expressed in "This Land Is Your Land," written in 1940 in response to Irving Berlin's "God Bless America" (a song Guthrie disliked because he thought it encouraged a false sense of complacency). As Guthrie traveled extensively in the 1930s and learned about the hardships of individual Americans, he drew closer to the labor movement and to the Communist Party. Increasingly, his writings and songs criticized industrialists, financiers, and their political agents. Guthrie hoped that the working people of America, united, could take back their land—the message he meant to convey with "This Land Is Your Land"— and restore its greatness. In his focus on ordinary working Americans, in his hope for the future, and in his fusion of dissent and patriotism, Guthrie was emblematic of the dominant stream of culture and politics in the late 1930s.

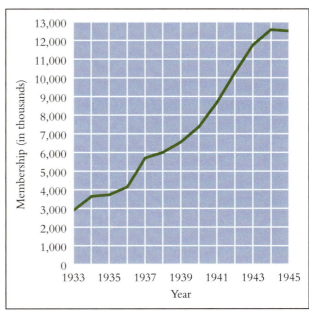

LABOR UNION MEMBERSHIP, 1933–1945

Source: From Christopher Tomlins, "AFL Unions in the 1930s," in Melvyn Dubofsky and Stephen Burwood, eds., *Labor* (New York: Garland, 1990), p. 1023.

sit-down strike *Labor strike strategy in which workers occupied their factory and refused to do any work until the employer agreed to recognize the workers' union.*

AMERICA'S MINORITIES AND THE NEW DEAL

FOCUS QUESTION

Which minority groups in American society benefited most from the New Deal and which benefited least?

Reformers in the 1930s generally believed that economic issues outweighed problems of racial and ethnic discrimination. Because they were disproportionately poor, most minority groups did profit from New Deal reforms, but the gains were distributed unevenly.

Eastern and Southern European Ethnics

Eastern and southern European immigrants and their children had begun mobilizing politically in the 1920s in response to religious and racial discrimination (see Chapter 24). By the early 1930s, they had made themselves into a political force in the Democratic Party. Roosevelt understood their importance as voters and as members of labor organizations and made sure that a significant portion of New Deal monies reached the urban areas where most European ethnics lived. As a result, Jewish and Catholic Americans voted for Roosevelt in large numbers. The New Deal did not eliminate anti-Semitism and anti-Catholicism from American society, but it did allow millions of European ethnics to believe that they would overcome the second-class status they had long endured.

African Americans

The New Deal did more to reproduce patterns of racial discrimination than to advance the cause of racial equality. African Americans who belonged to CIO unions or who lived in northern cities benefited from New Deal programs, but most blacks lived in rural areas of the South, where they were barred from voting, largely excluded from AAA programs, and denied federal protection in their efforts to form agricultural unions. The TVA hired few blacks. Those enrolled in work-relief programs were often paid less than whites doing the same jobs. Roosevelt consistently refused to support legislation to make lynching a federal crime.

This failure to push a strong civil rights agenda did not mean that New Dealers were oblivious to concerns about race. Eleanor Roosevelt spoke out frequently against racial injustice. In 1939, she resigned from the Daughters of the American Revolution when the organization refused to allow black opera singer **Marian Anderson** to perform in its concert hall. She then pressured the federal government into granting Anderson permission to sing from the steps of the Lincoln Memorial. On Easter Sunday, 75,000 people gathered to hear Anderson and to demonstrate their support for racial equality.

Franklin Roosevelt did eliminate segregationist practices in the federal government that had been in place since Woodrow Wilson's presidency. He appointed Mary McLeod Bethune, Robert Weaver, William Hastie, and other African Americans to important second-level posts in his administration. Working together in what came to be known as the Black Cabinet, these officials fought hard against discrimination in New Deal programs. Roosevelt, however, refused to support the Black Cabinet and civil rights measures if it meant alienating white southern voters and the white southern senators who controlled key congressional committees. African Americans and their supporters were not yet strong enough as an electoral constituency or as a reform movement to compel Roosevelt to support a civil rights agenda.

Marian Anderson *Black opera singer who broke a color barrier in 1939 when she sang to an interracial audience of 75,000 from the steps of the Lincoln Memorial.*

MUSICAL LINK TO THE PAST

An African American Rhapsody

Songwriter: Duke Ellington
Title: "Creole Rhapsody Parts One and Two" (1931—the second recording)
Performers: Duke Ellington and His Orchestra

By 1931, Duke Ellington was the premier African American bandleader, his hit songs airing nightly through a live national radio hookup (the first for any black act) from Harlem's Cotton Club. But Ellington was not satisfied with mere popularity and fame. "I have always been a firm believer in musical experimentation," he proclaimed. "To stand still musically is equivalent to losing ground." Ellington was a serious artist and composer, and "Creole Rhapsody" represented one of his first major bids to cultivate this image. Most pop records seldom broke the three-minute barrier, but "Creole" lasted nine minutes, spanning two sides of a 78-RPM record. While jazz and blues artists generally composed within 8-, 12-, and 16-bar forms, Ellington experimented with different phrase lengths. In an era when blacks were primarily associated with "torrid" dance records, the shifting tempos of "Creole" marked it as a record for concentrated listening. Ellington also composed the solos to ensure that they jelled with his elaborate arrangement, which did away with musical improvisation, a trademark of jazz and blues performances. Ellington was more involved with recording technique than most artists, sometimes placing microphones far away from his players to achieve a more evocative sound.

"Creole Rhapsody" reached only minor hit status, but Ellington and his manager Irving Mills took advantage of the event of this unprecedented recording to bolster Ellington's image as a serious artist, a status that no other African American had achieved in the segregated and white-dominated popular music marketplace of the period. In contrast to the denigrating stereotypes that accompanied the appearance of most blacks in the mass media, Ellington was respectfully portrayed in the manner of a classical conductor, usually clad in a tuxedo and tails, baton in his hand.

Not all contemporary observers endorsed the idea of Ellington as a major composer. The English critic Constant Lambert wrote in 1934 that "Ellington is definitely a petit maitre," a "small master" incapable of extended composition. Many music lovers, however, embraced "Creole Rhapsody." The New York School of Music named it the best composition of the year because "it portrayed Negro life as no other piece had." Ellington kept the critics, both the laudatory and castigating ones, at a distance and continued to search for musical innovation. He almost never took a formal political stand or made a speech demanding civil rights for blacks during the 1930s, choosing to let his music and his reputation as an innovative bandleader speak for themselves.

Q From listening to "Creole Rhapsody," can you discern what the New York School of Music meant when it celebrated this composition as a unique portrait of Negro life?

 Listen to an audio recording of this music on the Musical Links to the Past CD.

Mexican Americans

The Mexican American experience during the Great Depression was particularly harsh. In 1931, Hoover's secretary of labor, William N. Doak, announced a plan for repatriating illegal aliens (returning them to their land of origin) and giving their jobs to American citizens. The federal campaign quickly focused on Mexican repatriation in California and the Southwest. The U.S. Immigration Service rounded up large numbers of Mexicans and Mexican Americans and demanded that each detainee prove his or her legal status. Those who failed to produce the necessary documentation were deported. Local governments pressured many more into leaving. The combined efforts of federal, state, and local governments created a climate of fear in Mexican communities. By 1935, 500,000 had returned to Mexico, the same

[handwritten margin note: William N. Doak plan to deport Mexican]

number as had come to the United States in the 1920s. Among these were legal immigrants unable to produce their immigration papers, the American-born children of illegals, and some Mexican Americans who had lived in the Southwest for generations.

The New Deal eased but did not eliminate pressure on Chicano communities. Mexican Americans who worked in urban, blue-collar industries joined unions in large numbers. Like African Americans, however, most Chicanos lived in rural areas and labored in agricultural jobs, and the New Deal offered them little help. Where Mexicans gained access to relief rolls, they received payments lower than those given to "Anglos" (whites). New Dealers also did little to dissuade local officials from continuing their campaign to deport Mexican immigrants.

American Indians

From the 1880s until the early 1930s, federal policy had contributed to the elimination of American Indians as a distinctive population. The Dawes Act of 1887 (see Chapter 18) had called for tribal lands to be broken up and allotted to individual owners in the hope that Indians would adopt the work habits of white farmers. But American Indians had proved loyal to their languages, religions, and cultures. Few of them succeeded as farmers, and many lost land to white speculators.

The shrinking land base in combination with a growing population deepened American Indian poverty. Assimilationist pressures, meanwhile, reached a climax in the 1920s when the Bureau of Indian Affairs (BIA) outlawed Indian religious ceremonies, forced children from tribal communities into federal boarding schools, banned polygamy, and imposed limits on the length of men's hair.

Government officials working in the Hoover administration began to question this assimilationist policy, but its reversal had to await the New Deal and Roosevelt's appointment of **John Collier** as BIA commissioner. Collier pressured New Deal agencies to employ Indians on projects that improved reservation land and trained Indians in land conservation methods. He prevailed on Congress to pass the Pueblo Relief Act of 1933, which compensated Pueblos for land taken from them in the 1920s, and the Johnson-O'Malley Act of 1934, which provided funds to states for Indian health care, welfare, and education. He also took steps to abolish federal boarding schools and insisted that American Indians be allowed to practice their traditional religions.

The centerpiece of Collier's reform strategy was the Indian Reorganization Act (IRA, also known as the Wheeler-Howard Act) of 1934, which revoked the allotment provisions of the Dawes Act. This landmark act recognized the rights of Native American tribes to chart their own political, cultural, and economic futures. It reflected Collier's commitment to "cultural pluralism," a doctrine that celebrated and protected the diversity of peoples and cultures in American society. The IRA restored land to tribes, granted Indians the right to establish constitutions and bylaws for self-government, and provided support for new tribal corporations that would regulate the use of communal lands.

Collier encountered opposition everywhere: among assimilationist Protestant missionaries and cultural conservatives; land-hungry white farmers and business owners; and even a sizable number of Indians, some of whom had embraced assimilation while others viewed the IRA as one more attempt by the federal government to impose "the white man's will" on the Indian peoples. Although a vocal minority of Indians continued to oppose the act even after its passage, most tribes began to organize new governments under the IRA.

John Collier *Activist head of the Bureau of Indian Affairs who improved U.S. policy toward Native Americans and guided the landmark Indian Reorganization Act through Congress.*

QUICK REVIEW

MINORITIES AND THE NEW DEAL

- Eastern and southern Europeans benefited because of growing power in Democratic Party and in organized labor

- African Americans supported New Deal but FDR never made civil rights a priority

- Government pressured 500,000 Mexicans to return to Mexico

- New Deal reversed harsh policy toward Native Americans through Indian Reorganization Act

THE NEW DEAL ABROAD

When he entered office, Roosevelt believed that the United States should pursue foreign policies to benefit its domestic affairs, without regard for the effects of those policies on world trade and international stability. By late 1933, however, Roosevelt put the United States on a more internationalist course. That November, he became the first president to establish diplomatic ties with the Soviet Union. In December, he inaugurated a **Good Neighbor Policy** toward Latin America by formally renouncing the right of the United States to intervene in the affairs of Latin American nations. To back up his pledge, Roosevelt ordered home the Marines stationed in Haiti and Nicaragua, scuttled the Platt Amendment that had given the United States control over the Cuban government since 1901, and granted Panama more political autonomy and a greater administrative role in operating the Panama Canal. While the United States did not give up its influence over Latin America, it did exercise restraint while remaining the dominant force in hemispheric affairs.

The Roosevelt administration's internationalism also reflected its interest in stimulating trade. American businessmen wanted access to the Soviet Union's market. Latin America was already a major market for the United States, but one in need of greater stability. Roosevelt expressed his commitment to international trade through his support for the Reciprocal Trade Agreement, passed by Congress in 1934. This act allowed the United States to lower tariffs by as much as 50 percent in exchange for similar reductions by other nations. By the end of 1935, the United States had negotiated reciprocal trade agreements with 14 countries.

FOCUS QUESTION

What were the achievements and limitations of the New Deal's turn toward internationalism?

Good Neighbor Policy
Roosevelt's foreign policy initiative that formally renounced the right of the United States to intervene in Latin American affairs, leading to improved relations between the United States and Latin American countries.

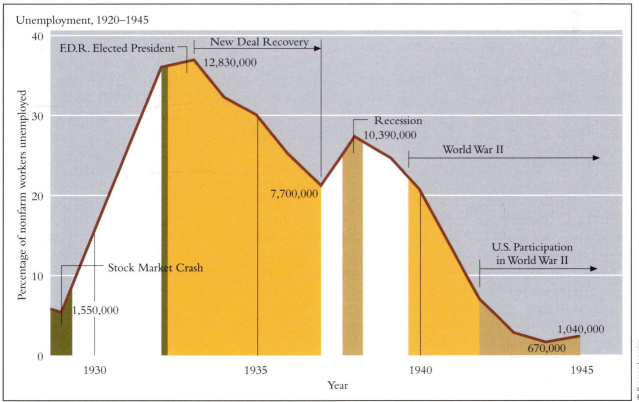

UNEMPLOYMENT IN THE NONFARM LABOR FORCE, 1929–1945

Source: Data from *Historical Statistics of the United States, Colonial Times to 1970* (White Plains, NY: Kraus International, 1989), p. 126.

Actually increasing the volume of international trade was more difficult than passing legislation to encourage it. In Germany and Italy, Adolf Hitler and Benito Mussolini told their people that the solution to their ills lay not in trade but in military strength and conquest. Throughout the world, similar appeals to national pride proved more popular than calls for tariff reductions and international trade.

STALEMATE, 1937–1940

FOCUS QUESTION

Why did the New Deal lose momentum in 1937 and 1938?

By 1937 and 1938 the New Deal had begun to lose momentum, as Roosevelt's decisions aroused opposition from Republicans and conservative Democrats.

The Court-Packing Fiasco

On February 5, 1937, Roosevelt asked Congress to give him the power to appoint one new Supreme Court justice for every member of the Court who was older than age 70 and had served for at least 10 years. His stated reason was that the current justices were too feeble to handle the large volume of cases coming before them, but his real purpose was to prevent the conservative justices on the court from dismantling his New Deal. His proposal would have given him the authority to appoint six additional justices, thereby securing a pro–New Deal majority.

The president seemed genuinely surprised by the outrage that greeted his **"court-packing" plan**. Although working-class support remained strong, many middle-class voters turned away from the New Deal. In 1937 and 1938, a conservative opposition took shape, uniting Republicans and conservative Democrats who believed the New Deal had gone too far.

Ironically, Roosevelt's court-packing scheme was probably unnecessary. In March 1937, Supreme Court Justice Owen J. Roberts, a former opponent of New Deal programs, decided to support them. In April and May, the Court upheld the constitutionality of the Wagner Act and Social Security Act, both by a 5-to-4 margin. Roosevelt allowed his court-reform proposal to die in Congress that summer. Within three years, five of the aging justices had retired, giving Roosevelt the opportunity to fashion a court more to his liking. Nonetheless, Roosevelt's reputation had suffered.

The Recession of 1937–1938

A sharp recession struck the country in late 1937 and 1938. The New Deal programs of 1935 had stimulated the economy, prompting Roosevelt to scale back relief programs. Meanwhile, new payroll taxes took $2 billion from wage earners' salaries to finance the Social Security pension fund even though the government did not intend to begin paying benefits until 1941. Thus, the government substantially shrunk the volume of dollars it was putting into circulation. Starved for money, the economy and stock market crashed once again. Unemployment, which had fallen to 14 percent, shot back up to 20 percent. In the 1938 elections, voters elected many conservative Democrats and Republicans who opposed the New Deal. These conservatives could not dismantle the New Deal reforms already in place, but they did block the passage of new ones.

Conclusion

Some Americans feared that Roosevelt aspired to autocratic rule, but nothing of the sort happened. The New Dealers inspired millions of Americans who had never

court-packing plan *1937 attempt by Roosevelt to appoint one new Supreme Court justice for every sitting justice over the age of 70 who had served for at least 10 years. Roosevelt's purpose was to prevent conservative justices from dismantling the New Deal, but the plan died in Congress and inflamed opponents of the New Deal.*

before voted to go to the polls. Groups that had been marginalized now felt that their political activism could make a difference.

Northern factory workers, farm owners, European ethnics, and middle-class consumers were among the groups that benefited most from the broadening of American democracy. In contrast, the socialist and communist elements of the labor movement failed to achieve their radical aims. Unionization proceeded far more slowly among southern industrial workers, black and white. Sizable occupational groups, such as farm laborers and domestic servants, were denied Social Security benefits. Feminists made no headway. African Americans and Mexican Americans gained meager influence over public policy.

New Deal reforms might not have mattered to any group if the Second World War had not rescued the New Deal economic program. With government war orders flooding factories from 1941 on, prosperity finally returned. The architects of the Second New Deal, who had argued that large government expenditures would stimulate consumer demand and trigger economic recovery, were vindicated.

The war also solidified the political reforms of the 1930s: an increased role for the government in regulating the economy and in ensuring the social welfare of those unable to help themselves; strong state support for unionization, agricultural subsidies, and progressive tax policies; and the use of government power and money to develop the West and Southwest. Voters returned Roosevelt to office for unprecedented third and fourth terms, and these same voters remained wedded for the next 40 years to Roosevelt's central idea: that a powerful state would enhance the pursuit of liberty and equality.

— Mirian Anderson   — restored prosperity
                                              False

— expanded money supply
            true

— Herbert Hoover anxious
        false

— Black Tuesday

— Elanoor Roosevelt
        false

CHAPTER REVIEW

Review Questions

1. What caused the crash of 1929, and why did the ensuing Depression last so long?
2. Why did Hoover lose his popularity?
3. In what ways did the political pessimism of the early 1930s influence American culture?
4. What events transformed Franklin D. Roosevelt into a focused politician? What beliefs defined his liberalism?
5. What do you consider to be the three or four most important pieces of legislation in the First New Deal? Why?
6. What forms did political unrest take in 1934 and 1935?
7. What was "underconsumptionism," and how did it inform the legislation of the Second New Deal? How was the Second New Deal different from the first?
8. Which minority groups in American society benefited most from the New Deal and which benefited least?
9. What were the achievements and limitations of the New Deal's turn toward internationalism?
10. Why did the New Deal lose momentum in 1937 and 1938?

Critical Thinking Questions

1. How did the Great Depression and New Deal shape the literature and art of the 1930s?
2. Why did the New Deal prove so popular given that, in the 1930s, it failed to solve the problem of unemployment?

Identifications

Review your understanding of the following key terms, people, and events for this chapter.

Great Depression, p. 576
Franklin Delano Roosevelt, p. 576
Bonus Army, p. 580
Eleanor Roosevelt, p. 581
Roosevelt liberalism, p. 582
Agricultural Adjustment Administration (AAA), p. 584

National Recovery Administration (NRA), p. 585
Tennessee Valley Authority (TVA), p. 586
Huey Long, p. 588
Father Charles Coughlin, p. 588
underconsumptionism, p. 590

Social Security Act, p. 590
Wagner Act (NLRA), p. 590
Works Progress Administration (WPA), p. 591
CIO, p. 594
sit-down strike, p. 595

Marian Anderson, p. 596
John Collier, p. 598
Good Neighbor Policy, p. 599
court-packing plan, p. 600

DISCOVERY

Why did the New Deal prove so popular even though it did not immediately solve the problem of unemployment?

In thinking about this question, begin by breaking it down into the components shown below. A discussion of the significance of each component should appear in your answer.

Government and Law

Think about what you read in this chapter and study the information in Table 25.1 below. The legislation of the First Hundred Days was numerous and varied, as it attempted to repair the economic damage suffered by various sectors of the economy: banks, farmers, business owners, and the unemployed. Which of the programs established by this legislation were most successful in repairing the economy? Which programs were least successful? Was this legislation successful in remedying the Great Depression? Roosevelt's popularity increased between 1932 and 1936. Was this the result of the legislation of the First Hundred Days or legislation passed in subsequent years? Or both?

Economics and Technology

The New Deal placed major emphasis on harnessing water to generate electricity, irrigate fields, and supply drinking water to urban areas. Two of the major areas in which the New Deal underwrote these projects were the Tennessee Valley and central and southern California. Study Maps 25.2 and 25.3 on pages 586 and 587. How successful were these projects? In what ways were the projects in the Tennessee Valley and California similar? In what ways were they different? How do you explain the differences in approach? Which of the two projects brought more lasting support and credit to the New Deal?

TABLE 25.1

LEGISLATION ENACTED DURING THE "HUNDRED DAYS," MARCH 9–JUNE 16, 1933		
Date	Legislation	Purpose
March 9	Emergency Banking Act	Provide federal loans to private bankers
March 20	Economy Act	Balance the federal budget
March 22	Beer-Wine Revenue Act	Repeal Prohibition
March 31	Unemployment Relief Act	Create the Civilian Conservation Corps
May 12	Agricultural Adjustment Act	Establish a national agricultural policy
May 12	Emergency Farm Mortgage Act	Provide refinancing of farm mortgages
May 12	Federal Emergency Relief Act	Establish a national relief system, including the Civil Works Administration
May 18	Tennessee Valley Authority Act	Promote economic development of the Tennessee Valley
May 27	Securities Act	Regulate the purchase and sale of new securities
June 5	Gold Repeal Joint Resolution	Cancel the gold clause in public and private contracts
June 13	Home Owners Loan Act	Provide refinancing of home mortgages
June 16	National Industrial Recovery Act	Set up a national system of industrial self-government and establish the Public Works Administration
June 16	Glass-Steagall Banking Act	Create Federal Deposit Insurance Corporation; separate commercial and investment banking
June 16	Farm Credit Act	Reorganize agricultural credit programs
June 16	Railroad Coordination Act	Appoint federal coordinator of transportation

Source: Arthur M. Schlesinger Jr., *The Coming of the New Deal* (Boston: Houghton Mifflin, 1959), pp. 20–21.

CourseMate

Visit the CourseMate website at www.cengagebrain.com for additional study tools and review materials for this chapter.

AMERICA DURING THE SECOND WORLD WAR

THE ROAD TO WAR: AGGRESSION AND RESPONSE

The Rise of Aggressor States
U.S. Neutrality
The Mounting Crisis
The Outbreak of War in Europe
The U.S. Response to War in Europe
An "Arsenal of Democracy"
Pearl Harbor

FIGHTING THE WAR IN EUROPE AND THE PACIFIC

Campaigns in North Africa and Italy
Operation OVERLORD
Seizing the Offensive in the Pacific
China Policy
U.S. Strategy in the Pacific
A New President, the Atomic Bomb, and Japan's
    Surrender

THE WAR AT HOME: THE ECONOMY

Government's Role in the Economy
Business and Finance
The Workforce
The Labor Front
A New Role for Government?

THE WAR AT HOME: SOCIAL ISSUES

Selling the War
Gender Issues
Racial Issues
Internment of Japanese Americans
Challenging Racial Inequality

SHAPING THE PEACE

International Organizations
Spheres of Interest and Postwar Settlements

T he Second World War vastly changed American life. The United States abandoned isolationism, moved toward military engagement on the side of the Allies, and emerged triumphant in a global war. The nation's productive capacity dwarfed that of all other nations and provided the economic basis for military victory. The mobilization for war finally lifted the economy out of the Great Depression.

The war also raised questions about the meanings of liberty and equality in America. How would the nation, while striving for victory, reorder its economy, its politics, and the cultural and social patterns that had shaped racial, ethnic, and gender relationships during the 1930s? What processes of reconstruction, at home and abroad, might be required to build a prosperous and lasting peace?

1913 Gonzalo Mendez born in Mexico

Westminster Main School X all white

Plesey V Fergeson 1896

14th Amendment no state shall deny to any
person equal protection - ratified 1868

David Marcus attorney
James Kent Thesis used as evidence.
Judge Paul McCormick unified schools.
Governor Earl Warren ending school segregation.

Silvia Mendez
Feb 15 2011 - Presidental medal of Freedom.

Brown Vs. Court of Education

Draft Legislation for African Americans.
- southern postal men hid black mens draft
cards so they could get arrested.

- Segregation in Army.
-

- Harlem Hell Fighters.
Deportation — by Herbert Hoover because of the
California   Great Depression.
Texas
Colorado   San Fernando, La Placita, and El
                    Monte Raids.

Raymond Rodriguez
Francisco Balderrama

Decade of Betrayal.

1929 Immigration Law
1934 warrants

Jim Crow laws. - Blacks, Mexicans, and Native Americans.
Cart War — Cart merchants
Salt War — Salt Mine in El Paso
Summer 1912 Guerilla
John Garner Brownsville
Wet Bag 1950's

- May 18 1917 — Draft

- Latinos in WWI
  ~ lack of records, but did make an impact.

- Language Barrier.
  - United States largely unprepared for war.
  - Most new recruits did not speak english.
- David B. Barkely
  - ~~son~~ swam across Meuse River to get
  behind german lines
  - recieved medal of honor.
- Marcelino Serna
  - was denied Medal of Honor for not knowing
  much english and being a "buck private"
- Nicolas Lucero
-

- Latinos in the States.
  - first asimilation
- African Americans in WWI
  - wanted to serve for the army

- Regiments
  7 and 10th cavalry.
  24th and 25th cavalry

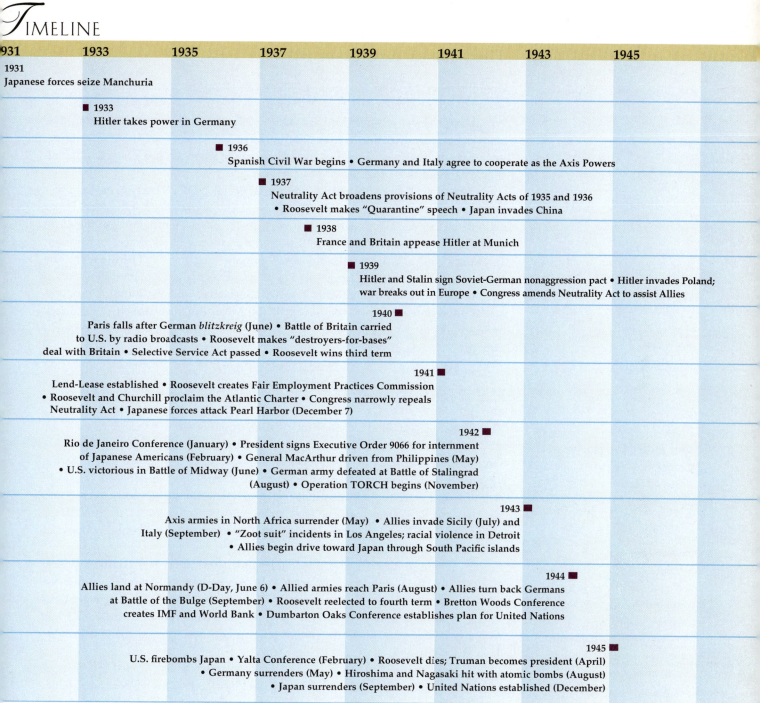

| 931 | 1933 | 1935 | 1937 | 1939 | 1941 | 1943 | 1945 |

1931
Japanese forces seize Manchuria

■ **1933**
Hitler takes power in Germany

■ **1936**
Spanish Civil War begins • Germany and Italy agree to cooperate as the Axis Powers

■ **1937**
Neutrality Act broadens provisions of Neutrality Acts of 1935 and 1936
• Roosevelt makes "Quarantine" speech • Japan invades China

■ **1938**
France and Britain appease Hitler at Munich

■ **1939**
Hitler and Stalin sign Soviet-German nonaggression pact • Hitler invades Poland;
war breaks out in Europe • Congress amends Neutrality Act to assist Allies

1940 ■
Paris falls after German *blitzkreig* (June) • Battle of Britain carried
to U.S. by radio broadcasts • Roosevelt makes "destroyers-for-bases"
deal with Britain • Selective Service Act passed • Roosevelt wins third term

1941 ■
Lend-Lease established • Roosevelt creates Fair Employment Practices Commission
• Roosevelt and Churchill proclaim the Atlantic Charter • Congress narrowly repeals
Neutrality Act • Japanese forces attack Pearl Harbor (December 7)

1942 ■
Rio de Janeiro Conference (January) • President signs Executive Order 9066 for internment
of Japanese Americans (February) • General MacArthur driven from Philippines (May)
• U.S. victorious in Battle of Midway (June) • German army defeated at Battle of Stalingrad
(August) • Operation TORCH begins (November)

1943 ■
Axis armies in North Africa surrender (May) • Allies invade Sicily (July) and
Italy (September) • "Zoot suit" incidents in Los Angeles; racial violence in Detroit
• Allies begin drive toward Japan through South Pacific islands

1944 ■
Allies land at Normandy (D-Day, June 6) • Allied armies reach Paris (August) • Allies turn back Germans
at Battle of the Bulge (September) • Roosevelt reelected to fourth term • Bretton Woods Conference
creates IMF and World Bank • Dumbarton Oaks Conference establishes plan for United Nations

1945 ■
U.S. firebombs Japan • Yalta Conference (February) • Roosevelt dies; Truman becomes president (April)
• Germany surrenders (May) • Hiroshima and Nagasaki hit with atomic bombs (August)
• Japan surrenders (September) • United Nations established (December)

*T*HE ROAD TO WAR: AGGRESSION AND RESPONSE

The road to the Second World War began at least a decade before U.S. entry in 1941. In Japan, Italy, and Germany, economic stagnation created political conditions that nurtured ultranationalist movements. Elsewhere in Europe and in the United States, economic problems led governments to concentrate on domestic recovery and avoid foreign entanglements.

FOCUS QUESTION

How did events in Asia and in Europe affect debate within the United States over whether or not to embrace more interventionist policies overseas?

The Rise of Aggressor States

On September 18, 1931, Japanese military forces seized Manchuria and created Manchukuo, a puppet state. This action violated the League of Nations charter, the Washington naval treaties, and the Kellogg-Briand Pact (see Chapter 24). The Hoover-Stimson Doctrine (1931) announced a U.S. policy of "nonrecognition" toward Manchukuo, and the League of Nations condemned Japan's action. Japan simply ignored these rebukes.

Two years later, **Adolf Hitler's** National Socialist (Nazi) Party came to power in Germany and instituted a **fascist** regime, a one-party dictatorial state. Hitler denounced the Versailles peace settlement of 1919, blamed Germany's problems on a Jewish conspiracy, claimed a genetic superiority for the "Aryan race" of German-speaking peoples, and promised a new Germanic empire, the **Third Reich**. The regime withdrew from the League of Nations in 1933 and, in a blatant violation of the Versailles treaty, dramatically boosted Germany's military budget. Another fascist government in Italy, headed by Benito Mussolini, also launched a military buildup and dreamed of empire. In October 1935, Mussolini's armies took over Ethiopia.

U.S. Neutrality

Many Americans wished to isolate their nation from these foreign troubles. Antiwar movies, such as *All Quiet on the Western Front* (1931), implicitly portrayed the First World War as a power game played by business and governmental elites. During the mid-1930s, a Senate investigating committee headed by Republican Gerald P. Nye of North Dakota concluded that the United States had been maneuvered into the First World War to preserve the profits of American bankers and munitions makers. By 1935, opinion polls suggested that Americans overwhelmingly opposed involvement in foreign conflicts.

In response, Congress enacted neutrality legislation. The **Neutrality Acts of 1935 and 1936** mandated an arms embargo against belligerents, prohibited loans to them, and curtailed travel by Americans on ships belonging to nations at war. The Neutrality Act of 1937 extended the embargo to include all trade with any belligerent, unless the nation paid in cash and carried the goods away in its own ships.

Critics charged that foreswearing U.S. intervention actively aided expansionist powers. In March 1936, Nazi troops seized the Rhineland. A few months later, Hitler and Mussolini began assisting General Francisco Franco, a fellow fascist seeking to overthrow Spain's republican government. Republicans in Spain appealed to non-fascist nations for assistance, but only the Soviet Union responded.

Although the United States remained officially aloof, the Spanish Civil War precipitated a major debate. Conservative groups generally hailed Franco as a staunch anticommunist who supported religion and social stability in Spain. In contrast, the political left championed republican Spain and denounced fascism. Cadres of Americans, including the famed "Abraham Lincoln Brigade," crossed the Atlantic to fight alongside republican forces in Spain. American peace groups splintered: Some continued to advocate neutrality and isolation, but others argued for intervention against the spread of fascism.

In October 1937, Roosevelt called for international cooperation to "quarantine" aggressor nations. Still suspicious of foreign entanglements, a majority in Congress refused to budge, even if this meant a victory by Franco in Spain's civil war.

Adolf Hitler *German fascist dictator whose aggressive policies touched off the Second World War in Europe.*

fascism *Type of highly centralized government that used terror and violence to suppress opposition. Its rigid social and economic controls often incorporated strong nationalism and racism. Fascist governments were dominated by strong authority figures or dictators.*

Third Reich *New empire Adolf Hitler promised the German people would bring glory and unity to the nation.*

Neutrality Acts of 1935 and 1936 *Legislation that restricted loans, trade, and travel with belligerent nations in an attempt to avoid the entanglements that had brought the United States into the First World War.*

The Mounting Crisis

As Americans debated how to deal with foreign aggression, Japan invaded China. In summer 1937, Japan captured Shanghai, Nanjing, Shandong, and Beijing and demanded that China become subservient to Tokyo. It also proposed an East Asian Co-Prosperity Sphere that would supposedly liberate Asian nations from Western colonialism and create a self-sufficient economic zone under Japanese leadership. Later that year, Japanese planes sank the American gunboat *Panay* as it evacuated Americans from Nanjing. Japan's quick apology defused a potential crisis, but the *Panay* incident and Japan's brutality in occupying Nanjing, where perhaps 300,000 Chinese civilians were killed, alarmed Roosevelt.

In Europe, Germany continued on the march. In March 1938, Hitler annexed Austria to the Third Reich and announced his intention to seize the Sudetenland, a portion of Czechoslovakia inhabited by 3.5 million people of German descent. In May, FDR began a program of naval rearmament. French and British leaders, still hoping to avoid war, met with Hitler in Munich in September. They acquiesced to Germany's seizure of the Sudetenland in return for Hitler's promise to seek no more territory. Hailed by Britain's prime minister as a guarantee of "peace in our time," the arrangement soon became a symbol of what interventionists called the "appeasement" of aggression.

In March 1939, Germans marched into Prague and, within a few months, annexed the rest of Czechoslovakia. In August, Hitler signed a nonaggression pact with the Soviet Union. In a secret protocol, Hitler and Soviet leader **Joseph Stalin** agreed on a plan to divide up Poland and the Baltic States.

The Outbreak of War in Europe

When Hitler's armies stormed into Poland on September 1, 1939, the Second World War officially began. Britain and France declared war but could not mobilize in time to help Poland, which fell within weeks. Then an eerie calm settled over Europe during the winter.

In April 1940, a full-scale German *blitzkrieg*, or "lightning war," began moving swiftly, shocking Allied leaders and overrunning Denmark, Norway, the Netherlands, Belgium, Luxembourg, and France. Early in June, Italy joined Germany by declaring war on the Allies. Later in June, France fell, and Hitler installed a pro-Nazi government at Vichy in southern France. In only six weeks, Hitler's army had seized complete control of Europe's Atlantic coastline, from the North Sea south to Spain, where Franco remained officially neutral but decidedly pro-Axis. The Axis powers gained another member in September 1940, when Japan joined Germany and Italy in a Tripartite Pact.

The U.S. Response to War in Europe

Alarmed at the Nazi surge, Roosevelt pressured Congress to modify its neutrality legislation and called for other measures, "short of war," to help Britain and France. Late in 1939, Congress lifted the ban on selling military armaments and substituted a **cash-and-carry** provision that permitted arms sales to belligerents who could pay cash and use their own ships for transport. Because its naval forces dominated the Atlantic sea lanes, Britain primarily benefited from this policy. Congress passed the Selective Training and Service Act of 1940, the first peacetime draft in U.S. history. Abandoning any pretense of neutrality, the United States also facilitated Britain's direct acquisition of U.S. "surplus" war materiel.

Joseph Stalin *Soviet communist dictator.*

blitzkrieg *A "lightning war"; a coordinated and massive military strike by German army and air forces.*

cash and carry *U.S. foreign policy prior to American entry into World War II that required belligerents to pay cash and carry products away in their own ships. This arrangement minimized risks to American exports, loans, and shipping.*

Map 26.1 German Expansion at Its Height. *This map shows the expansion of German power from 1938 through 1942. Which countries fell to German control? Why might Americans have differed over whether these moves by Germany represented a strategic threat to the United States?*

Meanwhile, from August through October 1940, Germany's *Luftwaffe* (air force) conducted daily raids on British air bases and nearly knocked out its Royal Air Force (RAF). On the verge of a KO, however, Hitler suddenly changed strategy and ordered, instead, the bombing of London and other cities. The use of airpower against civilians in the Battle of Britain, as it was called, aroused sympathy among Americans, who heard of events during dramatic radio broadcasts from London.

In September 1940, Roosevelt agreed to transfer 50 First World War–era naval destroyers to the British navy. In return, the United States gained the right to build eight naval bases in British territories in the Western Hemisphere. This "destroyers-for-bases" deal infuriated those who favored staying out of the war.

Isolationists opposed American involvement in the war for various reasons. Some pacifists opposed all wars as immoral. Some political progressives disliked fascism but feared even more the centralization of governmental power that conducting a war would require. And some conservatives sympathized with the anti-communism of fascist states.

A current of anti-Jewish sentiment also existed in the United States. In 1939, congressional leaders had quashed the Wagner-Rogers bill, which would have boosted immigration quotas in order to allow for the entry of 20,000 Jewish children otherwise slated for Hitler's concentration camps. Bowing to anti-Semitic prejudices, the United States adopted a restrictive refugee policy. The consequences of these policies became especially grave after June 1941, when Hitler established the death camps that would systematically exterminate millions of Jews, gypsies, homosexuals, and anyone else whom the Nazis deemed unfit for life in the Third Reich.

Presidential electoral politics in 1940 forced Roosevelt, nominated for a third term, to tone down his pro-Allied rhetoric. The Republicans nominated Wendell Willkie, a lawyer and business executive with ties to the party's liberal, internationalist wing. To differentiate his policies from Willkie's, the president promised not to send American troops to fight in "foreign wars." Once he had won an unprecedented third term, however, Roosevelt unveiled his most ambitious plan yet to support Britain's war effort.

An "Arsenal of Democracy"

Britain was nearly out of money, so the president proposed that the United States would now "lend-lease," or loan rather than sell, munitions to the Allies. Making the United States a "great arsenal of democracy," FDR claimed, would "keep war away from our country and our people." After bitter congressional debate, the **Lend-Lease Act** passed on March 11, 1941. When Germany turned its attention away from Britain and suddenly attacked its recent ally, the Soviet Union, in June, Roosevelt extended lend-lease assistance to the communist regime of Joseph Stalin.

Roosevelt next began coordinating military strategy with Britain. He secretly pledged to follow a Europe-first approach if the United States was drawn into a two-front war against both Germany and Japan. Publicly, Roosevelt and British Prime Minister Winston Churchill met in August 1941 off the coast of Newfoundland to work toward a formal wartime alliance. They agreed to an eight-point Atlantic Charter that disavowed territorial expansion, endorsed protection of human rights and self-determination, and pledged the postwar creation of a new world organization that would ensure "general security."

By this time Roosevelt and his advisers believed that defeating Hitler would require U.S. entry into the war, but public support still lagged. Privately, the president likely hoped that Germany would commit some provocative act in the North Atlantic that would jar public opinion. The October 1941 sinking of the U.S. destroyer *Reuben James* led Congress to repeal the Neutrality Act, but the vote was so close and debate so bitter that Roosevelt knew he could not yet seek a formal declaration of war.

Pearl Harbor

As it turned out, Japan, rather than Germany, sparked America's involvement. In response to Japan's 1937 invasion of China, the United States extended economic credits to China and curtailed sales of equipment to Japan. In 1939, the United States abrogated its Treaty of Commerce and Navigation with Japan, an action that further restricted U.S. exports to the island nation. A 1940 ban on the sale of aviation fuel and high-grade scrap iron was also intended to slow Japan's military advances.

QUICK REVIEW

THE SECOND WORLD WAR APPROACHES

- Germany occupied Czechoslovakia and invaded Poland

- Britain and France declared war on Germany and appealed for U.S. aid

- Japan invaded Manchuria and China, and bombed Pearl Harbor

- U.S. gradually terminated neutrality for "measures short of war" and ultimately entered war

Lend-Lease Act *A 1941 act by which the United States "loaned" munitions to the Allies, hoping to avoid war by becoming an "arsenal" for the Allied cause.*

These measures did not halt Japanese expansion. Japanese militarists hoped to grab Europe's Asian colonies and incorporate them into their country's East Asian Co-Prosperity Sphere. Japan therefore pushed deep into French Indochina, seeking the raw materials it could no longer buy from the United States, and prepared to launch attacks on Singapore, the Netherlands East Indies (Indonesia), and the Philippines.

Roosevelt expanded the trade embargo against Japan, promised further assistance to China, accelerated the American military buildup in the Pacific, and, in mid-1941, froze all Japanese assets in the United States. Yet Japanese leaders still did not reassess their plan to create an East Asian empire. Instead, they began planning a preemptive attack on the United States. With limited supplies of raw materials, especially oil, Japan had little hope of winning a prolonged war. Japanese military strategists gambled that a surprise, crippling blow would force concessions.

On December 7, 1941, Japanese bombers swooped down on **Pearl Harbor**, Hawaii, and destroyed much of the U.S. Pacific Fleet. Altogether, 19 ships were sunk or severely damaged; nearly 200 aircraft were destroyed or disabled; and 2,200 Americans were killed. The attack could have been worse. U.S. aircraft carriers, out to sea at the time, were spared, as were the base's fuel storage tanks and repair facilities. In a dramatic message broadcast by radio on December 8, Roosevelt decried the attack and labeled December 7 as "a date which will live in infamy," a phrase that served as a battle cry throughout the war. Japan had rallied Americans, not brought them to terms.

On December 8, 1941, Congress declared war against Japan. Japan's allies, Germany and Italy, declared war on the United States three days later. Hitler mistakenly assumed that the fight against Japan would keep the United States preoccupied in the Pacific. The three Axis Powers drastically underestimated America's ability to mobilize swiftly and effectively.

Pearl Harbor *Japan's December 7, 1941, attack on this U.S. base in Hawaii brought the United States into the Second World War.*

FIGHTING THE WAR IN EUROPE AND THE PACIFIC

FOCUS QUESTION

What military strategies did the United States and the Allies ultimately adopt when fighting in both the European and Asian theaters of the Second World War?

The United States had been unprepared for war, but new bureaucracies and technologies quickly guided a crash program for mobilization. The newly formed Joint Chiefs of Staff, consisting of representatives from each of the armed services, guided Roosevelt's strategy. The War Department's Pentagon complex, a giant, five-story, five-sided building, was completed in January 1943. In 1942, aircraft equipped with radar, a new technology developed in collaboration with Britain, proved effective against submarines. Perhaps most critical, a massive Allied codebreaking operation perfected decryption machines. Throughout the war, Germans never discovered that many of their decoded radio communications were being forwarded to Allied commanders—sometimes even before they had reached their German recipients.

Campaigns in North Africa and Italy

The Soviet Union pleaded with Roosevelt and Churchill to open a second front in Western Europe by way of an invasion across the English Channel into France, to relieve pressure on the USSR. Many of Roosevelt's advisers agreed: If German troops succeeded in knocking the Soviet Union out of the war, Hitler could turn his full attention toward Britain. Churchill urged instead the invasion of French North Africa, which German forces controlled, in order to nibble away at the edges of enemy power.

At a meeting in Casablanca, Morocco, in January 1943, Roosevelt sided with Churchill. To assuage Stalin's fear that his two allies might sign a separate peace with Hitler, Roosevelt and Churchill promised to remain in the fight until Germany agreed to an "unconditional surrender."

The North African operation, code-named TORCH, began with Anglo-American landings in Morocco and Algeria in November 1942. As TORCH progressed, the Soviets turned the tide of battle on the eastern front with a decisive victory at Stalingrad.

Hitler poured reinforcements into North Africa but could stop neither TORCH nor the British drive westward from Egypt. In summer 1943, the Allies followed up their successful North African campaign by overrunning the island of Sicily and then fighting their way, slowly, northward through Italy's mountains.

Some U.S officials worried about the postwar implications of wartime strategy. Secretary of War Henry Stimson warned that the Allied campaigns through Africa and Italy might leave the Soviets dominant in most of Europe. Acting on their advice, Roosevelt finally agreed to set a date for the cross-Channel invasion that Stalin had long been promised.

Operation OVERLORD

Operation OVERLORD, directed by General **Dwight D. Eisenhower**, began on June 6, 1944, D-Day. During the preceding months, probably the largest invasion force in history had assembled in England. Disinformation and diversionary tactics fooled the Germans into expecting a landing at the narrowest part of the English Channel rather than in the Normandy region. After several weather-related delays, nervous commanders finally ordered the daring plan to begin. The night before, as naval guns pounded the Normandy shore, three divisions of paratroopers dropped behind enemy lines to disrupt German communications. Then, at dawn, more than 4,000 Allied ships landed troops and supplies on Normandy's beaches. The first American forces to come ashore at Omaha Beach took enormous casualties, but the waves of invading troops continued. Only three weeks after D-Day, more than a million Allied personnel controlled the French coast and opened the long-awaited Second Front.

Just as the 1943 Battle of Stalingrad had reversed the course of the war in the East, so OVERLORD changed the momentum in the West. Within three months, U.S., British, and Free French troops entered Paris. After repulsing a desperate German counteroffensive in Belgium, at the Battle of the Bulge in December and January, Allied armies swept eastward, crossing the Rhine, and headed toward Berlin to meet up with westward-advancing Soviet troops.

As the war in Europe drew to a close, the horrors perpetrated by the Third Reich became fully visible to the world. Hitler's campaign of extermination, now called the Holocaust, killed more than 5 million Jews out of Europe's prewar population of 10 million. Hundreds of thousands more from various other groups were also murdered, especially gypsies, homosexuals, intellectuals, communists, and the physically and mentally challenged. Although only a military victory put an end to German death camps, the Allies might have saved thousands of Jews by helping them escape and emigrate. But Allied leaders worried about how to deal with large numbers of Jewish refugees, and they also claimed they could not spare scarce ships to transport them to sanctuary. The Allies would, in 1945 and 1946,

Dwight D. Eisenhower
Supreme Commander of the Allied Forces in Europe, orchestrator of the Normandy invasion, and president of the United States (1953–1961).

HISTORY THROUGH FILM

Saving Private Ryan (1998)

Directed by Steven Spielberg
Starring Tom Hanks (Captain John Miller), Matt Damon (Private James Ryan), Harve Presnell (General George Marshall)

Hollywood marked the 50th anniversary of the Allied effort in the Second World War with a series of films about "the good war." Although *Saving Private Ryan* invited comparison with *The Longest Day* (1962) because of its depiction of the D-Day invasion of Normandy, Steven Spielberg's battlefield sequences represented a considerable advance in the art of waging war on film. His production team employed sophisticated computer graphics and nearly deafening Dolby sound to mount battle scenes so realistic that reviewers cautioned veterans susceptible to posttraumatic stress syndrome about watching the film.

The film also suggested the kind of family-centered melodrama that Spielberg had grafted onto the sci-fi genre in *E.T.: The Extra-Terrestrial* (1982). A heroic squad led by Captain John Miller is trying to locate a single U.S. soldier, Private James Ryan, whose mother has already lost her three other sons to the war. The film poses the question of whether such a family-related mission legitimates and sanctifies the sacrifices of the Second World War. *Saving Private Ryan* answers "yes" to this question.

The major body of the film carefully justifies the rescue mission. Although Captain Miller wonders if his dangerous assignment is simply a public relations stunt, he quickly drops this idea and pursues his mission with the gallantry required of a Hollywood-commissioned officer. Later, his platoon members debate the morality of risking eight lives to save one, but the cause of Ryan's mother always seems overriding. General George Marshall cuts off debate over the appropriateness of the Ryan mission by invoking an earlier war leader, Abraham Lincoln, who once faced a similar dilemma. When Miller's troops finally locate Private Ryan, the film's audience discovers that he is the kind of clean-cut Iowa farm boy who will stay with his would-be saviors rather than retreat to safety. Ryan survives, although most of his comrades perish. Captain Miller, dying, implores young Ryan to lead a "good" life to justify the sacrifice of so many others.

The film *Saving Private Ryan*, in contrast to its characters, takes few risks. It secures its emotional investment in the rescue effort by bracketing the Second World War segments with two brief framing sequences in which an aging Ryan, along with his own family, returns to Normandy and visits the grave of Captain Miller. In the final segment, Ryan's wife provides the final reassurance that the trauma of the Second World War served a good cause, because Private Ryan's own family life has justified Miller's sacrifice. "Tell me I've led a good life. Tell me I'm a good man," he implores his wife. After nearly three hours of this Spielberg epic, the question is rhetorical.

SAVING PRIVATE RYAN, *which garnered four Academy Award nominations, celebrated the heroism of what popular historians called America's "greatest generation."*

bring 24 German high officials to trial at Nuremberg for "crimes against humanity." Large quantities of money, gold, and jewelry that Nazi leaders stole from victims of the Holocaust and deposited in Swiss banks, however, remained concealed for more than 50 years. Not until 1997 did Jewish groups and the U.S. government force an investigation of the Swiss banking industry's holdings of stolen "Nazi gold," an inquiry that finally prompted some restitution for victims' families.

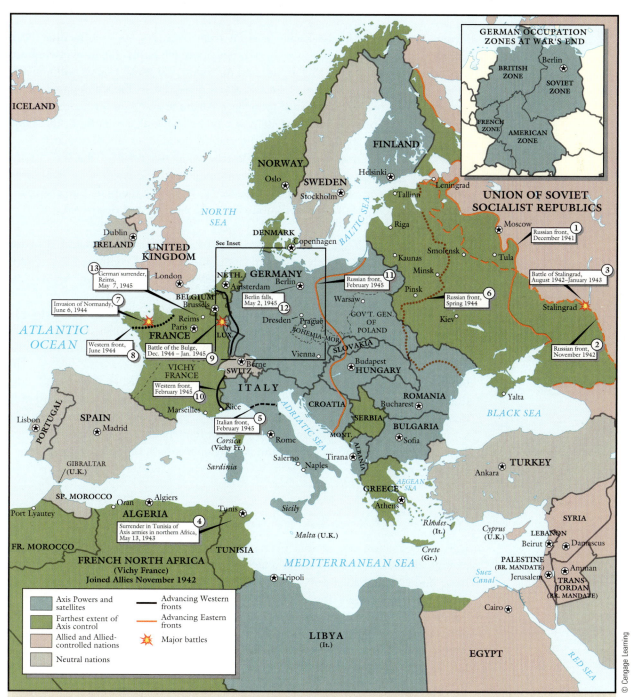

Map 26.2 **Allied Advances and Collapse of German Power.** *This map depicts the final Allied advances and the end of the war in Germany. Through what countries did Soviet armies advance, and how might their advance have affected the postwar situation? How was Germany divided by occupying powers, and how might that division have affected postwar politics?*

With Hitler's suicide in April and Germany's surrender on May 8, 1945, the military foundations for peace in Europe were complete. Soviet armies controlled Eastern Europe; British and U.S. forces predominated in Italy and the rest of the Mediterranean; Germany and Austria fell under divided occupation. Governmental leaders now needed to work out a plan for transforming these military arrangements into a comprehensive political settlement for the postwar era.

Seizing the Offensive in the Pacific

Meanwhile, the war in the Pacific was far from over. For six months after Pearl Harbor, Japan's forces steadily advanced. Singapore fell easily. Japan overwhelmed U.S. naval garrisons in the Philippines and on Guam and Wake islands. Filipino and American troops surrendered at Bataan and Corregidor in the Philippines. Other Japanese forces headed southward to menace Australia and New Zealand.

When Japan finally suffered its first naval setback at the Battle of the Coral Sea in May 1942, Japanese naval commanders decided to hit back hard. They amassed 200 ships and 600 planes to destroy what remained of the U.S. Pacific Fleet and to take Midway Island. U.S. Naval Intelligence, however, was monitoring Japanese codes and warned Admiral Chester W. Nimitz of the plan. Surprising the Japanese armada, U.S. planes sank four Japanese carriers and destroyed a total of 322 planes.

Two months later, American forces splashed ashore at Guadalcanal in the Solomon Islands. The bloody engagements in the Solomons continued for months on both land and sea, but they accomplished one major objective: seizing the military initiative in the Pacific.

The bloody Pacific engagements reinforced racial prejudices and brutality on both sides. Japanese leaders hoped the war would confirm the superiority of their "divine" Yamato race. Prisoners taken by the Japanese, particularly on the Asian mainland, were brutalized in almost unimaginable ways. The Japanese army's Unit 731 tested bacteriological weapons in China and conducted horrifying medical experiments on live subjects. American propaganda images played on themes of racial superiority, portraying the Japanese people as animalistic subhumans. American troops often rivaled Japan's forces in their disrespect for the enemy dead and sometimes killed the enemy rather than take prisoners.

China Policy

U.S. policy-makers hoped that China would fight effectively against Japan and emerge after the war as a strong, united nation. But China was beset by civil war. Jiang Jieshi's Nationalist government was incompetent and unpopular. It avoided engaging the Japanese invaders and still made extravagant demands for U.S. assistance. A growing communist movement led by Mao Zedong fought more effectively, but U.S. policy continued to support Jiang as China's future leader. All the while, Japan's advance continued, and in 1944 its forces captured seven key U.S. air bases in China.

U.S. Strategy in the Pacific

In contrast to the European theater, no unified command guided the war in the Pacific, and military actions often emerged from compromise. General Douglas

NAVAJO SIGNAL CORPS. *Sending messages in their native language, which neither the Japanese nor the Germans could decipher, Navajo Indians in the Signal Corps made a unique contribution to preserving the secrecy of U.S. intelligence.*

National Archives #127-N-69559-A

MacArthur, commander of the army in the South Pacific, favored an offensive launched from his headquarters in Australia through New Guinea and the Philippines and on to Japan. After Japan had driven him out of the Philippines in May 1942, he promised to return. Admiral Nimitz disagreed. He favored an advance across the smaller islands of the central Pacific, bypassing the Philippines. Unable to decide between the two strategies, the Joint Chiefs of Staff authorized both. MacArthur took New Guinea, and Nimitz's forces liberated the Marshall Islands and the Marianas in 1943 and 1944. An effective radio communication system conducted by a Marine platoon of Navajo Indians, the **Navajo Signal Corps**, made a unique contribution to success. Navajo, a language unfamiliar to Japanese intelligence officers, provided a secure medium for sensitive communications.

In late 1944, the fall of Saipan brought American bombers within range of Japan. The capture of the islands of Iwo Jima and Okinawa during spring 1945 further shortened that distance. Okinawa illustrated the ferocity of the campaigns: An estimated 120,000 Japanese and 48,000 American soldiers died.

Given these numbers, U.S. military planners dreaded the prospect of invading Japan's home islands, and airpower looked more and more enticing. In February 1944, General Henry Harley ("Hap") Arnold devised a plan for firebombing major Japanese cities. Bombers added to the horror of war, Arnold conceded, but when used "with the proper degree of understanding" could become "the most humane of all weapons" by shortening the war. Arnold's air campaign, operating from China, turned out to be cumbersome. It was

Navajo Signal Corps *Navajo Indians who conveyed military intelligence in their native language to preserve its secrecy.*

replaced by a more effective and lethal operation run by General Curtis LeMay from Saipan.

LeMay summarized his strategy: "Bomb and burn them until they quit." The official position on the incendiary raids against Japanese cities was that they constituted "precision" rather than "area" bombing. In actuality, the success of a mission was measured by the number of square miles it left scorched. The number of Japanese civilians killed in the raids is estimated to have been greater than the number of Japanese soldiers killed in battle. Air attacks on Tokyo during the night of March 9, 1945, leveled nearly a quarter of the city and incinerated more than 100,000 people.

By the winter of 1944–1945, a combined sea and air strategy had emerged: The United States sought "unconditional surrender" by blockading Japan's seaports, bombarding its cities from the air, and invading if necessary. American leaders believed that victory would only come through massive destruction.

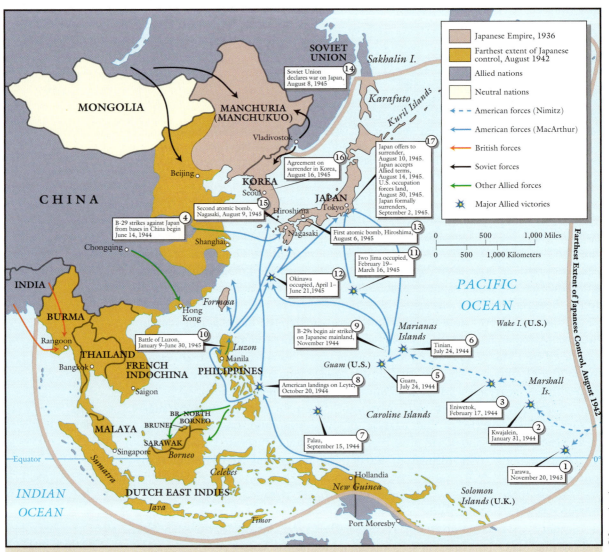

Map 26.3 **Pacific Theater Offensive Strategy and Final Assault Against Japan.** *This map suggests the complicated nature of devising a war strategy in the vast Pacific region. What tactics did the United States use to advance upon and finally prevail over the island nation of Japan?*

© Cengage Learning

A New President, the Atomic Bomb, and Japan's Surrender

On April 12, 1945, Franklin Roosevelt died of a cerebral hemorrhage. Sorrow and shock spread through the armed forces, where many young men and women had hardly known any other president. Through diplomatic conference halls, Roosevelt's personal magnetism had often brought unity, if not always clarity. To be sure, he had accumulated a host of critics and enemies, and he had defeated Republican Thomas E. Dewey in the 1944 presidential election by the smallest popular-vote margin in nearly 30 years. But among his supporters, he had symbolized optimism and unity through depression and war.

Emerging from Roosevelt's shadow, the new president, **Harry S Truman,** seemed an unimposing presence. Born on a farm near Independence, Missouri, Truman served in France during the First World War, became a U.S. senator in 1934, and was tabbed as Roosevelt's running mate in 1944. Roosevelt offered an upper-class image of well-practiced and worldly charm. In contrast, Truman knew little about international affairs or about any informal understandings that Roosevelt may have had with foreign leaders.

Only after succeeding Roosevelt did Truman learn about events at Los Alamos, New Mexico. There, since the late 1930s, scientists from all across the world had been secretly working on a new weapon. Advances in theoretical physics had suggested that splitting the atom (fission) would release a tremendous amount of energy. Fearful that Germany was racing ahead of the United States in this research, Albert Einstein, a Jewish refugee from Germany, had urged Roosevelt to launch a secret program to build an atomic bomb. The government enlisted top scientists in the Manhattan Project, a huge, secret military operation. On July 16, 1945, the first atomic weapon was successfully tested at Trinity Site, near Alamogordo, New Mexico.

Truman and his top policy-makers assumed that the weapon would be put to immediate use. They were eager to end the war, both because a possible land invasion of Japan might prove so costly in American lives and because the Soviet Union was planning to enter the Pacific theater, where Truman wished to limit Soviet power. Churchill called the bomb a "miracle of deliverance." Truman later publicly claimed that he had never lost a night's sleep over its use.

Privately, there was disagreement over where and how the bomb should be deployed. A commission of atomic scientists recommended a "demonstration" that would impress Japan with the bomb's power yet cause no loss of life. General George C. Marshall suggested using it on purely military installations or only on manufacturing sites, after first warning away Japanese workers. Ultimately, the Truman administration discarded these options. The bomb, Secretary of War Henry Stimson said, had to make "a profound psychological impression on as many inhabitants as possible."

In one sense, the atomic bombs dropped on the previously unbombed cities of **Hiroshima** and Nagasaki on August 6 and 9, 1945 could be regarded as merely bigger, more effective firebombs. In another sense, however, atomic weapons produced an unprecedented level of violence. Teams of U.S. observers who entered Hiroshima and Nagasaki in the aftermath were stunned at the instantaneous incineration of both human beings and manmade structures and shocked to contemplate the longer-lasting horror of radiation disease.

QUICK REVIEW

MAJOR CAMPAIGNS AND STRATEGIES

- Invasion of Northwest Africa as peripheral strategy (TORCH)
- Opening of second front in France (OVERLORD)
- Bombing of cities in Germany and firebombing in Japan
- Dropping of atomic bomb on two Japanese cities

Harry S Truman *Franklin Roosevelt's vice president, who became president when Roosevelt died on April 12, 1945.*

Hiroshima *Japanese city destroyed by atomic bomb on August 6, 1945.*

TOTAL WAR: DRESDEN AND HIROSHIMA. *The effects of "total war" are graphically illustrated in these photographs—of the devastation of Dresden, Germany (top), by the British Bomber Command and the U.S. 8th Air Force on February 13 and 14, 1945, and that of Hiroshima, Japan (bottom), by the U.S. 509th Composite Group on August 6, 1945. In the initial attack on Dresden, 786 aircraft dropped 5,824,000 pounds (2,600 long tons) of bombs on the city, killing an estimated 60,000 people and injuring another 30,000. An area of more than 2.5 square miles in the city center was demolished, and some 37,000 buildings were destroyed. To critics, the bombing of Dresden, a target that many argued was of little strategic value, exemplified the excessive use of airpower.*

In sobering comparison, Hiroshima was devastated by one bomb weighing only 10,000 pounds (4.4 long tons)—an atomic bomb—dropped from one aircraft. The single U-235 bomb killed 68,000 people outright, injured another 30,000, and left 10,000 missing. (These figures do not include those who later developed diseases from deadly gamma rays.) The bomb obliterated almost five square miles of the city's center and destroyed 40,653 buildings. Truman reported the strike as "an overwhelming success." Many hailed the atomic bomb as a necessary step toward military victory; others worried about the dawn of the "nuclear age."

© Bettmann/CORBIS

© Bettmann/CORBIS

V-J Day *August 15, 1945; day on which the Allies won the war in the Pacific.*

The mushroom clouds over Hiroshima and Nagasaki inaugurated a new "atomic age" in which dreams of peace mingled with nightmares of global destruction. But in those late summer days of 1945, most Americans sighed with relief. News reports of August 15 proclaimed Japan's surrender, **V-J Day.**

THE WAR AT HOME: THE ECONOMY

The success of the U.S. military effort depended on economic mobilization at home. Mobilization ultimately brought the Great Depression to an end and transformed the nation's government, its business and financial institutions, and its labor force.

Government's Role in the Economy

The federal bureaucracy nearly quadrupled in size during the war. New economic agencies proliferated. The most powerful of these, the War Production Board, oversaw the conversion and expansion of factories, allocated resources, and enforced production priorities and schedules. The War Labor Board adjudicated labor-management disputes. The Office of Price Administration regulated prices to control inflation and rationed such scarce commodities as gasoline, rubber, steel, shoes, coffee, sugar, and meat. Although most of the controls were abandoned after the war, the concept of greater governmental oversight of the economy survived.

From 1940 to 1945, the U.S. economy expanded rapidly, and the gross national product (GNP) rose, year-by-year, by 15 percent or more. When Roosevelt called for the production of 60,000 planes shortly after Pearl Harbor, skeptics jeered. Yet within a few years the nation produced nearly 300,000 planes. A once stagnant economy spewed out prodigious quantities of other supplies, including 2.5 million trucks and 50 million pairs of shoes.

Striving to increase production, industry entered into a close relationship with government to promote scientific and technological research and development. Government money subsidized new industries, such as electronics, and transformed others, such as rubber and chemicals. Eventually, an Office of Scientific Research and Development contracted with universities and scientists. Radar and penicillin (both British discoveries), rocket engines, and other new products were perfected for wartime use. Refugees from Nazi tyranny contributed significantly to this scientific innovation.

Business and Finance

To finance the war effort, government spending rose from $9 billion in 1940 to $98 billion in 1944. In 1941, the national debt stood at $48 billion; by V-J Day it was $280 billion. As production shifted from autos to tanks, and from refrigerators to guns, consumer goods became scarce. With few goods to buy, Americans invested in war bonds. Essentials such as food, fabrics, and gasoline were rationed and, consequently, were shared more equitably than before the war. Higher taxes on wealthier Americans redistributed income and narrowed the gap in wealth. War bonds, rationing, and progressive taxation encouraged a sense of shared sacrifice and helped ease the class tensions of the 1930s.

The war fostered personal savings and lessened income inequality, but it also facilitated the dismantling of some New Deal agencies most concerned with the poor. A Republican surge in the off-year elections of 1942 helped strengthen an anti–New Deal coalition in Congress. In 1943, legislators abolished the job-creation programs of the Works Progress Administration (WPA), the Civilian Conservation Corps (CCC), and the National Youth Administration (NYA) (see Chapter 25). They also shut down the Rural Electrification Administration (REA) and Farm Security Administration (FSA), agencies that had assisted impoverished rural areas.

FOCUS QUESTION

How did mobilizing for war transform the American economy, its labor force, and the role of government?

WOMEN JOIN THE WAR EFFORT. *Women employees at the Convair Company in California use a rivet gun and bucking bar, tools traditionally used only by men.*

The Roosevelt administration adopted a relatively cooperative stance toward big business, and those businesses considered essential to wartime victory flourished under governmental subsidies. What was essential became a matter of definition. Coca-Cola and Wrigley's chewing gum won precious sugar allotments by arguing that GIs overseas "needed" to enjoy these products. The Kaiser Corporation, whose spectacular growth during the 1930s had been spurred by federal dam contracts, now turned its attention to building ships, aircraft, and military vehicles. Federal subsidies and tax breaks enabled factories to expand and retool.

The war concentrated power in the largest corporations. Roosevelt ordered his justice department to postpone enforcement of antitrust laws. Congressional efforts to investigate possible collusion in the awarding of large government contracts and to increase assistance to small businesses made little headway. The top 100 companies, which had provided 30 percent of the nation's total manufacturing output in 1940, provided 70 percent by 1943.

The Workforce

During the early years of the military buildup, people who had scrounged for jobs during the Great Depression found work. Employment in heavy industry invariably went to men, and most of the skilled jobs went to whites. But as military service depleted the ranks of white males, both private employers and public officials began encouraging women to go to work, southern African Americans to move to northern industrial cities, and Mexicans to enter the United States under the *bracero* guest farmworker program.

Hired for jobs never before open to them, women became welders, shipbuilders, lumberjacks, and miners. They won places in prestigious symphony orchestras, and one Major League Baseball owner financed the creation of a women's league to give new life to the national pastime. Many employers hired married women, who before the war would have been lucky to obtain a position even in traditionally female occupations such as teaching. Minority women moved into clerical and sales jobs, where they had not previously been welcome. Most workplaces, however, continued to be segregated by sex.

The scope of unpaid labor, long provided primarily by women, also expanded. Volunteer activities such as Red Cross projects, civil defense work, and recycling drives claimed the time of women, children, and older people. Government publications exhorted homemakers: "Wear it out, use it up, make it do, or do without." Both in the home and in the workplace, women's responsibilities and workloads increased.

The new labor market improved the general economic position of African Americans. By executive order in June 1942, Roosevelt created the Fair Employment Practices Commission (FEPC), which aimed to ban discrimination in hiring. In 1943, the government announced that it would not recognize as collective bargaining agents any unions that discriminated on the basis of race. The War Labor Board outlawed the practice of paying different wages to whites and nonwhites doing the same job. Before the war, the African American population had been mainly southern, rural, and agricultural; within a few years, a substantial percentage of African

braceros **Guest workers from Mexico allowed into the United States because of labor shortages from 1942 to 1964.**

Americans had become northern, urban, and industrial. Although employment discrimination was hardly eliminated, twice as many African Americans held skilled jobs at the end of the war as at the beginning.

The Labor Front

The scarcity of labor during the war strengthened the union movement. Union membership rose by 50 percent. Although women and workers of color joined unions in unprecedented numbers, the main beneficiaries of labor's new clout were the white males who still comprised the bulk of union workers.

Especially on the national level, the commitment of organized labor to female workers was weak. Not a single woman served on the executive boards of either the American Federation of Labor (AFL) or the Congress of Industrial Organizations (CIO). Unions did fight for contracts stipulating equal pay for men and women who worked in the same job, but these benefited women only as long as they held "male" jobs. The unions' primary purpose in advocating equal pay was to maintain wage levels for the men who would return to their jobs after the war. During the first year of peace, as employers trimmed their workforces, both businesses and unions gave special preference to returning veterans and eased women and minority workers out of their wartime positions. Unions based their policies on seniority and their wage demands on the goal of securing male workers a "family wage," one sufficient to support an entire family.

Some union leaders feared that hiring traditionally lower-paid workers (women and minorities) would jeopardize the wage gains and recognition that unions had won during the 1930s. As growing numbers of African Americans were hired, racial tensions in the workplace increased. At some plants, white workers walked off the job to protest the hiring of blacks, fearing that management might use the war as an excuse to erode union power.

The labor militancy of the 1930s, although muted by a wartime no-strike pledge, persisted into the 1940s. Wildcat strikes erupted among St. Louis bus drivers, Detroit assembly-line workers, and Philadelphia streetcar conductors. The United Mine Workers called a walkout in the bituminous coal fields in 1943. When the War Labor Board took a hard line against the union's demands, the strike was prolonged. The increasingly conservative Congress responded with the Smith-Connally Act of 1943, which empowered the president to seize plants or mines if strikes interrupted war production. Even so, the war helped to strengthen organized labor's place in American life.

A New Role for Government?

The growth of governmental power during the war years prompted debates over the role of government in a postwar world. As military victory began to seem likely, President Roosevelt and his advisers talked of harnessing the national government's power behind expanded efforts to enhance security in everyday life. Some dreamed of extending wartime health-care and day-care programs into a more comprehensive social welfare system.

In 1944, Roosevelt introduced a "Second Bill of Rights" calling for measures to ensure that Americans could enjoy the "right" to regular employment, adequate food and shelter, appropriate educational opportunities, and guaranteed health care. Translating this vision into reality, its proponents generally assumed, would require the government to continue the kind of economic and social planning it was doing in wartime.

Large insurance companies and some private businesses, recognizing the popularity of security-focused proposals, came forward with private alternatives to governmental programs. Insurers expanded earlier efforts to market individual policies that would pay in cases of sickness, disability, and unexpected death. At the same time, insurance companies worked with large corporations to develop group insurance plans as substitutes, and also as supplements, for the governmental programs already provided by the New Deal and imagined in the controversial Second Bill of Rights.

THE WAR AT HOME: SOCIAL ISSUES

FOCUS QUESTION

How did the war propel movements for greater equality in American life?

The war demanded sacrifice from all, and most Americans willingly obliged. Yet, for many, the war unsettled established patterns, and wartime ideals spotlighted everyday inequalities.

Selling the War

Hollywood studios and directors eagerly answered the government's call to mobilize the country for war. The film factory produced both commercial movies with military themes, such as *Destination Tokyo* (1943), and documentaries, such as the *Why We Fight* series, directed by Frank Capra. Capra contrasted images of wholesome and diverse Americans with harrowing portrayals of the tightly regimented lifestyles in the dictatorships of Germany, Italy, and Japan. Hollywood personalities sold war bonds, entertained the troops, and worked on documentaries for the army's Pictorial Division.

The advertising industry also contributed. Roosevelt encouraged advertisers to sell the benefits of freedom. "Freedom" often appeared in the form of new washing machines, streamlined automobiles, a wider range of lipstick hues, and other consumer products. As soon as the fighting ended, wartime ads promised, technological know-how would transform the United States into a consumer's paradise.

In spring 1942, Roosevelt created the Office of War Information (OWI) to coordinate propaganda and censorship. Many New Deal Democrats viewed the OWI as catering to advertisers who preferred imagery extolling the future joys of consumerism to ones promoting broader visions of liberty and equality. Republicans blasted the agency for cranking out crass political appeals for causes favored by New Dealers. Despite such criticism, the OWI established branch offices throughout the world, published a magazine called *Victory*, and produced hundreds of films, posters, and radio broadcasts.

Office of War Information, 1943. Courtesy, the American Legion Poster Collection

"FOOD IS A WEAPON." *This 1943 poster shows the Office of War Information skillfully extending its major theme: that people at home could assist the war by watching what they ate. The poster's final directive suggests how the war made better nutrition both a personal and patriotic goal.*

Gender Issues

The wartime United States called on women to serve their country as more than wives and mothers. Some 350,000 women volunteered for military duty during the war, and more than a thousand became pilots for the Women's Airforce Service Pilots (WASPs). Not everyone approved, but most in Congress supported a women's corps in each branch of the military.

Even as the war narrowed gender differences in employment, widespread imagery frequently portrayed women's expanded participation in the workplace as a temporary sacrifice intended, ultimately, to preserve and protect their "natural" sphere in the home. Stereotypes abounded. A typical ad suggesting that women take on farm work declared: "A woman can do anything if she knows she looks beautiful doing it."

In some ways, the war may have even widened the symbolic gap between notions of femininity and masculinity. Military culture fostered a "pinup" mentality toward women. Tanks and planes were decorated with images of female sexuality, and the home-front entertainment industry promoted its glamorous female stars as anxious to "please" their "boys" in the military. Wartime popular culture sometimes associated masculinity with misogyny. After the war, tough-guy fiction, on display in Mickey Spillane's "Mike Hammer" series of detective novels, portrayed female sexuality as both alluring and threatening to men.

Public policy-making sometimes worked to reinforce gender divisions. The military assigned most of the women who joined the armed services to stateside clerical and supply jobs. Day-care programs for mothers working outside their homes received reluctant and inadequate funding, and they swiftly shut down after the war. Social scientists oftentimes blamed mothers for an apparent spike in rates of juvenile delinquency and divorce during the war years.

Racial Issues

Messages about race were as ambiguous as those related to gender. President Roosevelt refused to abandon the policy of segregation in the armed forces, despite pressure from the NAACP and others. Although the army integrated Latino and American Indian soldiers, along with those from various European ethnic groups, into its combat units, military leaders did not do the same for people of African and Japanese ancestry. The army even adopted the scientifically absurd practice of segregating donated blood into separate stores of "white" and "black" plasma. African Americans were relegated to inferior jobs and excluded from combat duty. Toward the end of the war, when troop shortages forced the administration to put African American units into combat, they performed with distinction.

© Bettmann/CORBIS

A SEGREGATED MILITARY. *This photo of an African American regiment eating in a mess hall during the Second World War illustrates racial segregation in the armed forces.*

On the home front, volatile social issues continued to simmer. As the wartime production system created more jobs, vast numbers of people from the rural South, including several hundred thousand African Americans, moved to cities such as Los Angeles and Detroit. People already living in these areas often chafed at the influx of newcomers, who competed with them for jobs and housing and placed greater demands on public services.

Social strains sometimes flared into violence. This escalation most often occurred in overcrowded urban spaces, where diverse populations and cultures already competed and clashed. In Detroit, in June 1943, conflict between white and black youth at an amusement park rapidly spiraled into a multiple-day riot. The violence left nearly 40 people, most of them African American, dead, injured hundreds, and inflicted millions of dollars' worth of damage to property.

Racial disturbances were not restricted to confrontations between whites and blacks. In Los Angeles, the "Zoot Suit Riots" of 1943 erupted when soldiers and sailors from nearby military bases attacked young Mexican American and African American men wearing **zoot suits**—flamboyant outfits featuring oversized coats and trousers. Violence only escalated as the city's police force entered the fray, often beating and arresting Mexican Americans. A military order restricting servicemen to their bases finally helped quell the disorder.

Even when wartime tensions did not produce the kind of violence seen in Detroit and Los Angeles, the Second World War highlighted longstanding social divisions. For many Native Americans, for instance, the wartime years increased the pressures associated with longer-term patterns of migration and assimilation. Approximately 25,000 Indian men and several hundred Indian women served in the armed forces. Tens of thousands of other Indian men and women, many leaving their reservations for the first time, found wartime work in urban areas. Many Indians moved back and forth between city and reservation, seeking to live in two significantly different worlds.

Internment of Japanese Americans

People of Japanese descent faced a unique situation. Shortly after the attack on Pearl Harbor, fear of sabotage by pro-Japanese residents engulfed West Coast communities. One military report claimed that a "large, unassimilated, tightly knit racial group, bound to an enemy nation by strong ties of race, culture, custom, and religion . . . constituted a menace" that justified extraordinary action.

Although lacking evidence of disloyalty, the president in February 1942 issued Executive Order 9066, directing the relocation and **internment** of first- and second-generation Japanese Americans (called Issei and Nisei, respectively) at inland camps. Significantly, in Hawaii, where the presumed danger of subversion might have been much greater, no such internment took place. There, people of Japanese ancestry constituted nearly 40 percent of the population and were essential to the economy. The government also closely watched foreign-born Germans and Italians who lived in the United States and detained roughly 10,000 Germans and several hundred Italians.

Forced to abandon their possessions or sell them for a pittance, nearly 130,000 Japanese Americans were confined in flimsy barracks, enclosed by barbed wire and under armed guard. Two-thirds of the detainees were native-born U.S. citizens. Many left behind thriving agricultural enterprises vital to wartime production. In December 1944, a divided U.S. Supreme Court upheld the constitutionality of Japanese relocation in *Korematsu v. United States*. In 1988, Congress officially apologized for the internment, revealed that military investigators at the time had

zoot suits *Flamboyant outfits that featured oversized trousers, commonly worn by young Mexican American men as a symbol of ethnic and cultural rebellion.*

internment *Removal of first- and second-generation Japanese Americans into secured camps, a 1942 action then justified as a security measure but since deemed unjustified by evidence.*

INTERNMENT OF JAPANESE AMERICANS. *Taken by the famous photographer Ansel Adams, this image shows internees walking in the snow at a remote relocation camp.*

reported no cases of subversion, and authorized a cash indemnity for anyone who had been confined in the camps.

Challenging Racial Inequality

The global fight against fascism proved helpful to movements working for social change in America. Nazism, based on the idea of racial inequality, exposed the racist underpinnings of older social-science research. The view that racial difference was not the result of biology but of culture gained wider acceptance during the war. The idea that a democracy could bridge racial differences provided a basis for the postwar struggle against racial discrimination.

The *Amsterdam News,* a Harlem newspaper, called for a "Double V" campaign—victory at home as well as abroad. In January 1941, the labor leader A. Philip Randolph promised to lead tens of thousands of black workers in a march on Washington to demand more defense jobs and integration of the military forces. President Roosevelt feared the event would embarrass his administration and urged that it be canceled. Randolph's persistence ultimately forced Roosevelt to create the FEPC. Although this new agency gained little effective power, its very existence helped advance the ideal of nondiscrimination.

Northward migration of African Americans accelerated demands for equality. Drawn by the promise of wartime jobs, nearly 750,000 African Americans relocated to northern cities, where many sensed the possibility of political power for the first time in their lives. They found an outspoken advocate of civil rights in First Lady

LINK TO THE PAST

Civil Liberties in Wartime: *Korematsu v. United States*

Fred Korematsu, an American of Japanese background, was born in Oakland and had been a law-abiding citizen. In his early twenties, when the order to relocate Japanese Americans to internment camps was announced, he challenged the legality of the measure. The case was ultimately heard by the Supreme Court. In a controversial decision in December 1944, a divided court upheld the constitutionality of internment. The following selections suggest some of the arguments made in both the majority and minority opinions. Nearly 45 years later, after an examination of military records, Congress took a stand on the issue. Officially apologizing for internment, Congress stated that it was "not justified by military necessity, and . . . not driven by analysis of military conditions."

Exclusion of those of Japanese origin was deemed necessary because of the presence of an unascertained number of disloyal members of the group, most of whom we have no doubt were loyal to this country. It was because we could not reject the finding of the military authorities that it was impossible to bring about an immediate segregation of the disloyal from the loyal. . . .

Compulsory exclusion of large groups of citizens from their homes, except under circumstances of direct emergency and peril, is inconsistent with our basic governmental institutions. But when under conditions of modern warfare our shores are threatened by hostile forces, the power to protect must be commensurate with the threatened danger. . . . To cast this case into outlines of racial prejudice, without reference to the real military dangers which were presented, merely confuses the issue.

JUSTICE HUGO BLACK
from the majority opinion of the Supreme Court in *Korematsu v. United States* (1944), upholding the constitutionality of Executive Order 9066

We must accord great respect and consideration to the judgments of the military authorities who are on the scene and who have full knowledge of the military facts. . . . At the same time, however, it is essential that there be definite limits to military discretion, especially where martial law has not been declared. Individuals must not be left impoverished of their constitutional rights on a plea of military necessity that has neither substance nor support. . . .

In support of this blanket condemnation of all persons of Japanese descent, however, no reliable evidence is cited to show that such individuals were generally disloyal, or had . . . furnished reasonable ground for their exclusion as a group. . . . No adequate reason is given for the failure to treat these Japanese Americans on an individual basis by holding investigations and hearings to separate the loyal from the disloyal, as was done in the case of persons of German and Italian ancestry. . . . I dissent, therefore, from this legalization of racism.

JUSTICE FRANK MURPHY
from the dissenting opinion in *Korematsu v. United States*

Q Are there conditions that would constitutionally permit detention of citizens on the basis of their nationality or ethnic background?

Q What might explain Congress's later decision to issue an apology?

Eleanor Roosevelt, who repeatedly antagonized southern Democrats and members of her husband's administration by her advocacy of civil rights and her participation in integrated social functions. These urban areas also saw the formation of new civil rights groups, like the interracial Committee (later, Congress) on Racial Equality (CORE), which staged sit-ins to integrate restaurants, theaters, and other public facilities.

In California and throughout the Southwest during the war years, Latino organizations, too, highlighted the irony of fighting overseas for a nation that denied equality at home. They challenged the United States to live up to its democratic rhetoric.

Approximately 500,000 Mexican Americans served, often with great distinction, in the military. Not wishing to anger this constituency, the Roosevelt administration also feared discrimination might harm the credibility of its Good Neighbor Policy in Latin America (see Chapter 25). The president's coordinator of Inter-American affairs allocated federal money to train Spanish-speaking workers for wartime employment, improve education in barrios, and provide high school graduates with new opportunities to enter college. Organizations such as the League of United Latin American Citizens (LULAC) mounted several drives against discrimination.

People of Japanese descent, despite the internment, also laid the basis for postwar campaigns for equality. The courage and sacrifice of Japanese American soldiers became legendary. The 100th Battalion and the 442nd Regimental Combat Team, segregated units, suffered stunning casualties, often while undertaking extremely dangerous combat missions in Europe. In the Pacific theater, 6,000 members of the Military Intelligence Service provided invaluable service.

In the face of divisive issues and calls for greater equality, wartime propaganda stressed national unity and contrasted America's "melting pot" ethos with German and Japanese obsessions about racial "purity." Movies, plays, radio dramas, and music fostered a sense of national community by expressing pride in cultural diversity. As members of each of America's racial and ethnic groups distinguished themselves in the military, the claim of equality took on greater moral force. Imagery extolling social solidarity and freedom provided a foundation for the antidiscrimination movements of the decades ahead.

SHAPING THE PEACE

Even before the war ended, U.S. policy-makers began considering postwar peace arrangements. The Truman administration built on Roosevelt's wartime conferences and agreements to shape the framework of international relations for the next half-century.

International Organizations

In the Atlantic Charter of 1941, and at a conference in Moscow in October 1943, the Allied Powers had pledged to create a replacement for the defunct League of Nations. Internationalist-minded Americans hoped the new United Nations (UN) would offer a more realistic version of Woodrow Wilson's vision for a world body that could deter aggressor nations and promote peaceful political change. At the Dumbarton Oaks Conference in Washington in August 1944, and at a subsequent meeting in San Francisco in April 1945, the Allies worked out the UN's organizational structure. It included a General Assembly, in which each member nation would be represented and cast one vote. A smaller body, the Security Council, would include five permanent members from the Allied Coalition—the United States, Great Britain, the Soviet Union, France, and Nationalist China—and six rotating members. The Security Council would have primary responsibility for maintaining peace, but permanent members could veto any council decision. A UN Secretariat, headed by a secretary general, would handle day-to-day business, and an Economic and Social Council would sponsor measures to improve living conditions throughout the world.

The U.S. Senate, with only two dissenting votes, approved joining the UN in July 1945. Opponents of Wilson's dream had worried that internationalist policies

FOCUS QUESTION

What major institutions and policies did the United States and the Allies adopt in their effort to shape the reconstruction of the postwar world?

QUICK   REVIEW

WAR BROUGHT CHANGES TO AMERICAN LIFE

- Government increased controls over the economy

- War production ended Great Depression

- New job opportunities emerged for women and minorities

- African Americans migrated from the South to northern cities

- United States embraced new international organizations

might limit the ability of the United States to pursue its own interests, but following the Second World War, a newly powerful United States appeared able to dominate international organizations such as the UN. In addition, most U.S. leaders recognized that the war had partly resulted from the lack of a coordinated, international response to aggression during the 1930s.

Eleanor Roosevelt played a prominent role in building the new postwar internationalist ethos. A delegate to the first meeting of the UN's General Assembly, she chaired its Commission on Human Rights and guided the drafting of a Universal Declaration of Human Rights, adopted by the UN in 1948. The document set forth "inalienable" human rights and freedoms as cornerstones of international law.

Economic agreements also illustrated a growing acceptance of international organizations. At the Bretton Woods (New Hampshire) Conference of 1944, assembled nations created the International Monetary Fund (IMF), which was designed to maintain stable exchange by ensuring that each nation's currency could be converted into any other national currency at a fixed rate. The International Bank for Reconstruction and Development, later renamed the World Bank, was also created to provide loans to war-battered countries and promote the resumption of world trade. In 1948, the General Agreement on Tariffs and Trade (GATT) established the institutional groundwork for breaking up closed trading blocs and implementing free and fair trade agreements.

Spheres of Interest and Postwar Settlements

In wartime negotiations, Stalin, Churchill, and Roosevelt had assumed that powerful nations—their own—would enjoy special "spheres of influence" in the postwar world. As early as January 1942, the Soviet ambassador to the United States reported to Stalin that Roosevelt had tacitly assented to Soviet postwar control over the Baltic states of Lithuania, Latvia, and Estonia. In 1944, Stalin and Churchill agreed, informally and secretly, that Britain would continue its sway over Greece and that the Soviets could control Romania and Bulgaria. U.S. leaders assumed that Latin America would remain within their sphere of influence. Roosevelt expressed contradictory positions on the Soviet Union. He sometimes seemed to imply that he accepted Stalin's goal of having states friendly to the USSR on his vulnerable western border, but at the Tehran Conference of November 1943 he also told Stalin that U.S. voters of Eastern European descent expected their homelands to be independent after the war. After Roosevelt's death, the Soviets' powerful position in Eastern Europe became a focus of bipolar tensions.

Early in the war, both the United States and the Soviet Union had urged the dismemberment and deindustrialization of a defeated Nazi Germany. At a conference held at Yalta, in Ukraine, in February 1945, the three Allied powers agreed to divide Germany into four zones of occupation (with France as the fourth occupying force). Later, as relations among the victors worsened, this temporary division of Germany hardened into a Soviet-dominated zone in the east and the other three zones to its west. Berlin, the German capital, also was divided, even though the city itself lay totally within the Soviet zone.

The future of Poland also posed difficult issues. At Yalta, the Soviets agreed to permit free elections in postwar Poland, but Stalin believed that the other Allied leaders had tacitly accepted Soviet dominance over Poland. The agreement at Yalta was ambiguous at best; the war was still at a critical stage, and the western Allies chose to sacrifice clarity in order to encourage cooperation with the Soviets. After Yalta, the Soviets assumed that Poland would be in their sphere of influence, but many Americans charged the Soviets with bad faith for failing to hold free elections and for not relinquishing control.

In Asia, military realities likewise influenced postwar settlements. The first U.S. atomic bomb fell on Hiroshima just one day before the Soviets were to enter the Pacific theater of the war, and the United States assumed total charge of the occupation and postwar reorganization of Japan. The Soviet Union and the United States divided Korea, which had been controlled by Japan, into separate zones of occupation. Here, as in Germany, these zones would later emerge as two antagonistic states (see Chapter 27).

The fate of the European colonies seized by Japan in Southeast Asia was another contentious issue. Most U.S. officials preferred to see the former British and French colonies become independent nations, but they also worried about the left-leaning politics of many anticolonial nationalist movements. As the United States developed an anticommunist foreign policy after the war, it moved to support British and French efforts to reassemble their colonial empires.

In the Philippines, the United States honored its longstanding pledge to grant independence. A friendly government that agreed to respect American economic interests and military bases took power in 1946 and enlisted American advisers to help suppress leftist rebels. In 1947 the United Nations designated the Mariana, Caroline, and Marshall Islands as the "Trust Territories of the Pacific" and authorized the United States to administer their affairs.

Wartime conferences avoided clear decisions about creating a Jewish homeland in the Middle East. The Second World War prompted survivors of the Holocaust and Jews from around the world to take direct action. **Zionism**, the movement to found a Jewish state in Palestine, which Jews claimed to be an ancient homeland, attracted thousands of Jews. They began to carve out, against the wishes of Palestinians and other Arab people, the new nation of Israel.

Conclusion

The world changed dramatically during the Second World War. For the United States, wartime mobilization ended the Great Depression and focused most of the government's attention on international concerns. A more powerful national government, concerned with preserving national security, assumed nearly complete power over the economy. Government, business, and scientific researchers worked together to provide the seemingly miraculous growth in productivity that ultimately won the war. The 1940s also sharpened debates over liberty and equality. Many Americans saw the Second World War as a struggle to protect and preserve the liberties they already enjoyed. Others, inspired by a struggle against racism and injustice abroad, insisted that a war for freedom abroad should help secure equal rights at home.

The war brought victory over dictatorial, expansionist regimes, and the United States emerged as the world's preeminent power. Still, Americans remained uncertain about postwar reconstruction policies and about future relations with their wartime ally, the Soviet Union. And the nation now faced the future without the charismatic leadership of Franklin D. Roosevelt.

Zionism *Movement to establish a Jewish state in Palestine.*

CHAPTER REVIEW

Review Questions

1. How did events in Asia and in Europe affect debate within the United States over whether or not to embrace more interventionist policies overseas?

2. What military strategies did the United States and the Allies ultimately adopt when fighting in both the European and Asian theaters of the Second World War?

3. How did mobilizing for war transform the American economy, its labor force, and the role of government?

4. How did the war propel movements for greater equality in American life?

5. What major institutions and policies did the United States and the Allies adopt in their effort to shape the reconstruction of the postwar world?

Critical Thinking Questions

1. In what ways had the United States already moved, even before the attack on Pearl Harbor, toward intervention in the Second World War?

2. How did Franklin Roosevelt's domestic policies during the Second World War both fulfill and retreat from the aspirations of his New Deal?

Identifications

Review your understanding of the following key terms, people, and events for this chapter.

Adolf Hitler, p. 606
fascism, p. 606
Third Reich, p. 606
Neutrality Acts of 1935 and 1936, p. 606
Joseph Stalin, p. 607

blitzkrieg, p. 607
cash and carry, p. 607
Lend-Lease Act, p. 609
Pearl Harbor, p. 610
Dwight D. Eisenhower, p. 611

Navajo Signal Corps, p. 615
Harry S Truman, p. 617
Hiroshima, p. 617
V-J Day, p. 618

braceros, p. 620
zoot suits, p. 624
internment, p. 624
Zionism, p. 629

DISCOVERY

How did World War II affect citizens both in America and elsewhere, thus making it a true "total" war?

In thinking about this question, begin by breaking it down into the components shown below. A discussion of the significance of each component should appear in your answer.

Warfare

Examine the destruction to the cities of Dresden and Hiroshima shown in these photos. Were these areas densely populated? From your examination of these photos and your reading in this chapter, what observations can you make about how World War II impacted civilians? Do you think civilians had become a bigger target in the Second World War than they had been in the First? If so, why?

Total War: Dresden and Hiroshima

CourseMate

Visit the CourseMate website at www.cengagebrain.com for additional study tools and review materials for this chapter.

CHAPTER

27

THE AGE OF CONTAINMENT, 1946–1953

CREATING A NATIONAL SECURITY STATE,
1945–1949
  Onset of the Cold War
  The Truman Doctrine and Containment Abroad
  Truman's Loyalty Program and Containment
    at Home
  The National Security Act, the Marshall Plan, and the
    Berlin Crisis
  The Election of 1948

THE ERA OF THE KOREAN WAR, 1949–1952
  NATO, China, and the Bomb
  NSC-68 and the Korean War
  Korea and Containment

PURSUING NATIONAL SECURITY AT HOME
  Anticommunism and the U.S. Labor Movement
  Containing Communism at Home
  Targeting Difference

The "Great Fear"
Joseph McCarthy
The National Security Constitution and the Structure
  of Governance

POSTWAR SOCIAL-ECONOMIC POLICY-MAKING
  The Employment Act of 1946 and Economic Growth
  Truman's Fair Deal
  Civil Rights

SIGNS OF A CHANGING CULTURE
  The Baseball "Color Line"
  The New Suburbia
  Postwar Hollywood

THE ELECTION OF 1952
  Continuing Containment
  A Soldier–Politician

As the Second World War gave way to a **Cold War** between the United States and the Soviet Union, U.S. leaders overhauled military strategy. They claimed broad powers for the executive branch and called for a global stand against communism. The effort to shore up "national security" soon translated into an ever-larger military establishment and an economic system that could supply its needs.

At home, debate over the use of governmental power generated controversy. How might Washington help organize a postwar economy that satisfied household as well as military consumption? Should a more powerful and active federal government assist movements seeking greater equality? Could such a government contain security threats at home without endangering liberty?

IMELINE

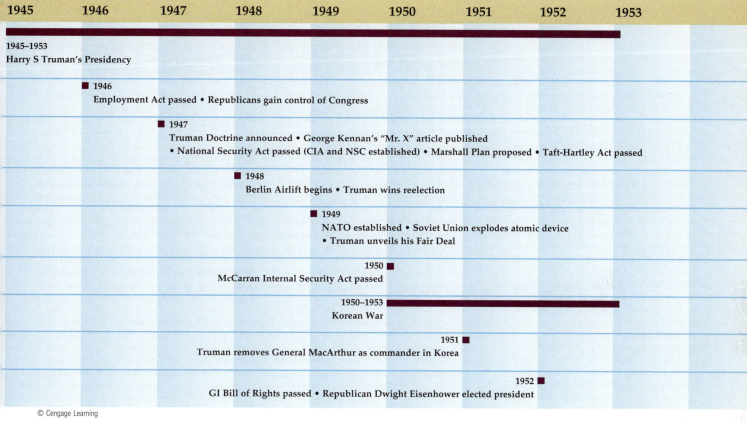

1945	1946	1947	1948	1949	1950	1951	1952	1953

1945–1953
Harry S Truman's Presidency

■ **1946**
Employment Act passed • Republicans gain control of Congress

■ **1947**
Truman Doctrine announced • George Kennan's "Mr. X" article published
• National Security Act passed (CIA and NSC established) • Marshall Plan proposed • Taft-Hartley Act passed

■ **1948**
Berlin Airlift begins • Truman wins reelection

■ **1949**
NATO established • Soviet Union explodes atomic device
• Truman unveils his Fair Deal

1950 ■
McCarran Internal Security Act passed

1950–1953
Korean War

1951 ■
Truman removes General MacArthur as commander in Korea

1952 ■
GI Bill of Rights passed • Republican Dwight Eisenhower elected president

© Cengage Learning

CREATING A NATIONAL SECURITY STATE, 1945–1949

Defeating the Axis had forced the United States and the Soviet Union to cooperate, but their collaboration began unraveling even before war's end. Relations deteriorated into a Cold War of mutual suspicions and massive military buildups but few direct confrontations between the two superpowers themselves.

Onset of the Cold War

Historians have dissected the beginning of the Cold War from different perspectives. A familiar view focuses on Soviet expansionism, stressing a historically rooted appetite for new territory, an ideological zeal to spread communism, or some interplay between the two. According to this view, the United States needed to adopt firm, anti-Soviet policies. Other historians—generally called revisionists—see the Soviet Union's obsession with securing its borders as an understandable response to the invasion of its territory during both world wars. The United States, in this view, should have pursued conciliatory policies instead of ones that intensified Soviet fears. Still other scholars maintain that assigning blame obscures the inevitability of postwar tensions between the two culturally and politically divergent superpowers.

In almost every view, President Harry Truman's role was central. Truman initially hoped to bargain with Soviet Premier Joseph Stalin, but when differences

FOCUS QUESTION

What major conflicts between the United States and the Soviet Union shaped the Cold War and prompted a U.S. foreign policy focused on containment of communism?

Cold War *The political, military, cultural, and economic rivalry between the United States and the Soviet Union that developed after the Second World War and lasted until the disintegration of the Soviet state after 1989.*

between the former allies emerged, Truman came to distrust Stalin and listen to hard-line, anti-Soviet advisers.

The atomic bomb became an important source of friction. At the Potsdam Conference of July 1945, Truman had casually told Stalin, without mentioning the atomic bomb, about a new U.S. weapon of "unusual destructive force." Well informed by Soviet intelligence operations about the Manhattan Project, Stalin ordered Soviet scientists to intensify their nuclear weapons program. Truman likely hoped that the bomb would scare the Soviets—and it did. Historians debate whether it frightened the Soviets into more cautious behavior or made them more aggressive.

As atomic warfare against Japan gave way to atomic diplomacy with the Soviet Union, U.S. leaders differed over how to proceed. One group, recognizing that the Soviets would soon possess atomic weapons, urged Truman to share technology with the USSR in hopes of forestalling an arms race. Hard-liners, fearing Soviet intentions and underestimating their nuclear knowledge, rejected this approach.

In 1946, Truman authorized Bernard Baruch, his special representative at the United Nations, to explore ways of controlling atomic power. The Baruch Plan proposed that the United States would abandon its nuclear weapons if the USSR agreed to outside monitoring of its weapons program and surrendered veto power in the UN on atomic issues. Soviet leaders, rejecting the Baruch Plan, counterproposed that the United States destroy its atomic weapons as the first step toward any bargain. The United States rejected this idea. Both nations used the deadlock to justify a stepped-up arms race.

Other sources of friction involved U.S. loan policies and Soviet domination of Eastern Europe. Truman ended lend-lease assistance to the Soviet Union at the end of the war and linked future reconstruction loans to Soviet cooperation with the United States over the future of Europe. This linkage strategy failed. Lack of capital and suspicions about the intentions of the United States and its allies provided the Soviets with excuses for their own hard-line stance. A repressive Soviet sphere of influence, which Stalin called defensive and Truman labeled expansionist, spread over Eastern Europe.

Truman pledged to stop the campaign of communist expansionism he claimed Moscow directed. His anticommunist initiatives, in both foreign and domestic affairs, extended the reach and power of the executive branch.

The Truman Doctrine and Containment Abroad

In March 1947, the president announced what became known as the Truman Doctrine when speaking to Congress about a civil war in Greece, where communist-led insurgents threatened to topple a pro-Western government. Truman's advisers feared a leftist victory in Greece would expose Turkey, a nation considered critical to the U.S. strategic position, to Soviet expansionism. In publicly justifying U.S. aid to Greece and Turkey, Truman asserted that U.S. security interests now spanned the globe and that the fate of "free peoples" everywhere hung in the balance. Unless the United States aided people "resisting attempted subversion by armed minorities or by outside pressures," totalitarian communism would spread and, ultimately, threaten the United States itself.

 The Truman Doctrine's global vision of national security encountered some skepticism. Henry Wallace, the most visible Democratic critic, chided Truman for exaggerating the Soviet threat. Conservative Republicans were suspicious of the increase of executive power and the vast expenditures the Truman Doctrine seemed to imply. If Truman wanted to win support for his position, Republican Senator Arthur Vandenberg had already advised, he should "scare hell" out of people, something Truman proved quite willing to do. With votes from Republicans and Democrats, the president gained congressional approval for $400 million in assistance to Greece and Turkey, most of it for military aid, in the spring of 1947. This vote signaled broad, bipartisan support for a national security policy that came to be called **containment.**

The term *containment* first appeared in a 1947 article in the journal *Foreign Affairs* by George Kennan, the State Department's premier Soviet expert. Writing under the pseudonym "X," Kennan argued that the "main element" in any U.S. policy "must be that of a long-term, patient but firm and vigilant containment of Russian expansive tendencies."

Containment thus became a catchphrase for a global, anticommunist national security policy. As popularly articulated, containment linked all leftist insurgencies, wherever they occurred, to a totalitarian movement controlled from Moscow that threatened American security. Even a small gain for the Soviets in one part of the world could encourage communist aggression elsewhere. Although foreign policy debates included disagreements over how to pursue containment, most American leaders came to support a global and activist foreign policy.

Truman's Loyalty Program and Containment at Home

Nine days after proclaiming the Truman Doctrine, the president issued Executive Order 9835. It authorized a system of government loyalty boards empowered to determine if there were "reasonable grounds" for concluding that a federal employee belonged to a subversive organization or espoused ideas that might endanger national security. People found to pose a "security risk" would lose their jobs. The Loyalty Program also empowered the Justice Department to identify political organizations it deemed subversive and place them on a new attorney general's list.

The Truman administration thus embarked on what became a controversial approach to containing communism at home. Although few people ever doubted that Soviets were conducting spy operations in the United States, there has long been disagreement over their scope and effectiveness. Recently declassified evidence from Soviet and U.S. surveillance files reveals that both nations conducted a wide range of intelligence activity. By 1943, the U.S Army had begun intercepting transmissions between Moscow and the United States. Called the VENONA files and finally released in 1995, these messages show that the Soviet Union had helped finance America's Communist Party; placed informants in governmental agencies; and obtained secret information about U.S. atomic work. Still, historians remain divided over the significance and reliability of specific pieces of the VENONA evidence.

Truman claimed that the harmful potential from a relatively few security risks demanded a response unprecedented in peacetime. His position, however, angered both fervent anticommunists, who accused the president of doing too little to fight communist activities at home, and civil libertarians, who charged him with whipping up fears that far exceeded any actual threat.

The National Security Act, the Marshall Plan, and the Berlin Crisis

Shaking off criticism, the Truman administration extended its containment initiative. The **National Security Act of 1947** created several new bureaucracies. The old Navy and War Departments were transformed, by 1949, into the Department of Defense. An entirely new addition to the executive branch, the National Security Council, obtained broad authority over planning containment policy. The air force became a separate service equal to the army and navy.

The act also created the Central Intelligence Agency (CIA) to gather information and conduct covert activities. The CIA quickly became the most flexible arm of

containment *Label used to describe the global anticommunist national security policies adopted by the United States.*

National Security Act of 1947 *Reorganized the U.S. military forces within a new Department of Defense, and established the National Security Council and the Central Intelligence Agency.*

CONTAINMENT POLICY

- Recommended by State Department's Soviet expert George Kennan in 1947

- Adapted and extended by the Truman Doctrine, Marshall Plan, Berlin Airlift, NSC-68, and the Korean War

- Encouraged the global buildup of U.S. economic, psychological, and military resources

Marshall Plan *Plan of U.S. aid to Europe that aimed to contain communism by fostering postwar economic recovery. Proposed by Secretary of State George C. Marshall in 1947, it was known formally as the European Recovery Program.*

the new national security apparatus. Shrouded from public scrutiny, its secret operations crisscrossed the globe. The CIA cultivated ties with anti-Soviet groups in Eastern Europe and within the Soviet Union. It helped finance pro-U.S. labor unions in Western Europe. It orchestrated covert campaigns to bolster anticommunist parties in Italy, France, Japan, and elsewhere.

The Truman administration also linked its economic initiatives in Western Europe to its overall containment policy. Fearing that Europe's economic problems might benefit communist movements, Secretary of State George C. Marshall sought to strengthen the region's economies. Under his 1947 proposal, known as the European Recovery Program or simply the **Marshall Plan**, U.S. funds would allow governments in Western Europe to coordinate programs of economic reconstruction. Between 1946 and 1951, the United States provided nearly $13 billion in assistance to 17 Western European nations. Industrial production in Western Europe rebounded, and improved standards of living enhanced political stability and helped undercut the appeal of leftist movements.

U.S. policy-makers viewed the future of postwar Germany, initially divided into four zones of occupation, as crucial to the security of Western Europe. In June 1948, the United States, Great Britain, and France announced a currency-reform program as the first step toward integrating their separate sectors into the Federal Republic of Germany or West Germany. Having been invaded by German forces in both world wars, the Soviet Union worried about Germany again becoming an economic power. Hoping to sidetrack Western plans, the Soviets cut off all highways, railroads, and water routes into West Berlin, which was located within their zone of military occupation.

This Berlin Blockade failed. American and British pilots, in what became known as the Berlin Airlift, delivered virtually all of the items West Berliners needed to continue their daily routines. Truman, hinting at a military response, sent two squadrons of B-29 bombers to Britain. Stalin abandoned the blockade in May 1949, and the Soviets then created the German Democratic Republic, or East Germany, out of their sector. West Berlin survived as an anticommunist enclave inside East Germany.

The Election of 1948

National security issues helped Harry Truman win the 1948 election. Truman had been losing the support of those Democrats, led by his secretary of commerce, Henry Wallace, who considered his containment policies overly confrontational. When Wallace had continued to criticize these initiatives, Truman had ousted him from the cabinet. Two months later, in the off-year national elections of November 1946, voters had given the Republicans control of Congress for the first time since 1928.

Challenged from the left by a new Progressive Party, which nominated Wallace, and from the right by both Thomas E. Dewey, the Republican nominee, and Strom Thurmond, the pro-segregationist candidate of the new States' Rights Party, or Dixiecrats, Truman waged a vigorous campaign. He called the GOP-controlled Congress into special session, presented it with domestic policy proposals abhorrent to most Republicans, and then denounced "that do-nothing, good-for-nothing, worst Congress."

Truman's victory now seems less surprising to historians than it had to analysts in 1948. Despite GOP

AP Images/ Byron Rollins

DEWEY DEFEATS TRUMAN? *U.S. President Harry S Truman holds up an Election Day edition of the* Chicago Daily Tribune, *which mistakenly announced "Dewey Defeats Truman" in the 1948 presidential election. The president told well-wishers, "That is one for the books!"*

victories in the 1946 congressional elections, the Democratic Party was hardly enfeebled. Democratic candidates identifying with the legacy of Franklin Roosevelt, rather than with the presidency of his successor, generally polled a higher percentage of the vote in their districts than did Truman. Loyalty to the memory of Roosevelt and his New Deal coalition helped bring the Democrats their victory in 1948.

After Truman endorsed his party's call for new civil rights measures, the president survived the revolt of the Dixiecrats, whose candidate, Strom Thurmond, denounced Truman for backing a "civil wrongs" program and charged that "radicals, subversives, and reds" now controlled the Democratic Party. Although the Dixiecrat movement portended a political shift among southern whites, Truman carried all but four states of the old Confederacy in 1948.

Truman's staunch anticommunism helped bury Henry Wallace. Hampered by his Progressive Party's refusal to reject support from the U.S. Communist Party, Wallace received less than 3 percent of the popular tally and no electoral votes. The 1948 election suggested a blueprint for winning elections to come: Successful presidential candidates must never appear "soft" on national security issues.

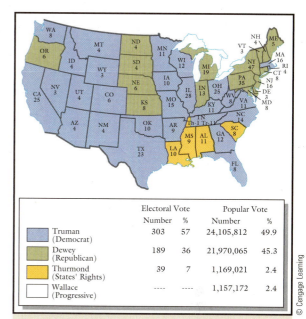

© Cengage Learning

Map 27.1 **Presidential Election, 1948.** *This electoral map shows how, in this close election, Truman won the presidency despite gaining less than 50 percent of the popular vote.*

THE ERA OF THE KOREAN WAR, 1949–1952

To implement his containment policy, Truman marshaled the nation's economic and military resources. A series of Cold War crises in 1949 and the outbreak of war on the Korean peninsula in 1950 heightened anticommunist fervor and provided support for funding an expanded national security state.

FOCUS QUESTION

How did the Korean War help reinforce and militarize the policy of containment?

NATO, China, and the Bomb

In April 1949, the United States, Canada, and 10 European nations formed the **North Atlantic Treaty Organization (NATO)**. They pledged that an attack against one nation would automatically be treated as a strike against all. Republican Senator Robert Taft called NATO a provocation to the Soviet Union, an "entangling alliance" that violated traditional U.S. foreign policy, and a threat to Congress's constitutional power to declare war. Still, the NATO concept prevailed, and the United States would continue to pursue containment through this "mutual defense" pact.

Meanwhile, events in China heightened Cold War tensions. Although the United States had extended Jiang Jieshi's incompetent Nationalist government billions in military aid and economic assistance, Jiang had steadily lost ground to Mao Zedong's communist movement. Experienced U.S. diplomats privately predicted Jiang's downfall, but the Truman administration continued publicly to portray Jiang as the respected leader of "free China."

In 1949, when Mao's armies forced Jiang off the mainland to the nearby island of Formosa (Taiwan), many Americans wondered how communist forces could

North Atlantic Treaty Organization (NATO)
Established by treaty in 1949 to provide for the collective defense of noncommunist European and North American nations against possible aggression from the Soviet Union and to encourage political, economic, and social cooperation.

have triumphed. Financed by conservative business leaders, the powerful "China lobby" blamed Truman and his new secretary of state, Dean Acheson, for having "lost" China to communism. This political pressure and new international tensions convinced the Truman administration to embrace Jiang's regime on Taiwan and to refuse diplomatic recognition for Mao's "Red China."

The communist threat grew more alarming when, in 1949, the Soviets exploded a crude atomic device, marking the end of the U.S. monopoly. Besieged by critics who saw recent history marked by Soviet gains and U.S. losses, Truman authorized the development of a new and far more deadly weapon, the hydrogen bomb.

The cold war split Europe into two opposing alliances. Germany was divided into two countries: The Federal Republic of Germany (West Germany) and the German Democratic Republic (East Germany). Berlin, the former capital of Germany, was also divided. In 1949 NATO was formed, and in 1955 the Warsaw Pact came into existence.

THE DIVISION OF BERLIN

American Zone
British Zone
French Zone
Soviet Zone

(The American, British, and French zones were consolidated as West Berlin)

NATO Countries
Warsaw Pact Countries
Nonaligned Countries

© Cengage Learning

Map 27.2 Divided Germany and the Nato Alliance. *This map shows the geopolitics of the Cold War. Which countries aligned with the United States through NATO? Which aligned with the Soviet Union through the Warsaw Pact? Note how Berlin became a divided city, although it was located within East Germany.*

NSC-68 and the Korean War

The Truman administration also reviewed its core foreign policy assumptions. Hard-liner Paul Nitze produced a top-secret policy paper, **NSC-68** (National Security Council Document 68). It opened with a dramatic account of a global clash between "freedom," spread by U.S. power, and "slavery," promoted by the Soviet Union. Despairing of fruitful negotiations with the Soviets, NSC-68 urged a dramatic upgrade of U.S. national security capabilities. It endorsed covert action, economic pressure, propaganda campaigns, and a massive military buildup. Because Americans might oppose larger military spending and budget deficits, the report cautioned, U.S. actions should be labeled as "defensive" and presented as a stimulus to the economy rather than as a drain on national resources.

The alarmist tone of NSC-68 seemed to be confirmed in June 1950 when communist North Korea invaded South Korea. Truman characterized the invasion as a simple case of Soviet-inspired aggression, but the Korean situation defied such one-dimensional analysis. Japanese military forces had occupied Korea between 1905 and 1945, and after Japan's defeat in the Second World War, Koreans had expected to reemerge as one independent nation. Instead, the Soviet and U.S. zones of occupation became two states, split at the 38th parallel. The Soviet Union supported North Korea's communist government, headed by the dictatorial Kim Il-sung. The United States backed Syngman Rhee, the leader of an unsteady and autocratic, but anticommunist, government in South Korea.

NSC-68 *National Security Council Document number 68 (1950), which provided the rationale and comprehensive strategic vision for U.S. policy during the Cold War.*

Courtesy of the Truman Library

KOREAN REFUGEES MOVE SOUTH. *The Korean War disrupted life throughout the peninsula. Here, refugees flee their homes after receiving orders from the South Korean army to evacuate.*

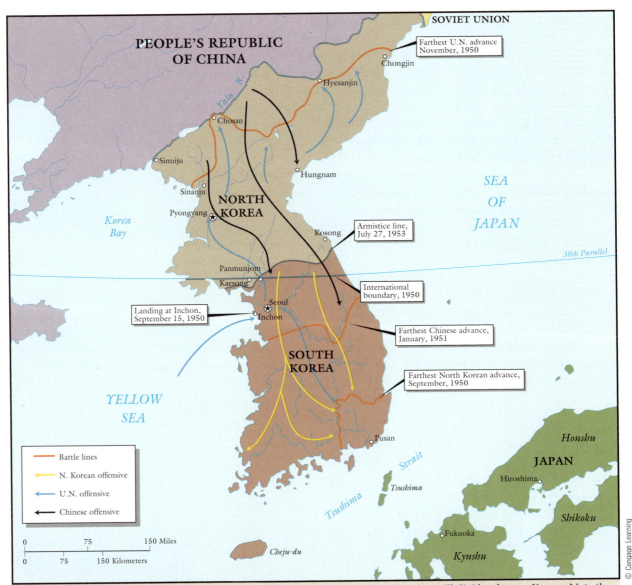

Map 27.3 Korean War. *This map shows the lines of battle and the armistice line that still divides the two Koreas. Note the advances made first by North Korea and then by UN (U.S.-led) troops.*

On June 25, 1950, Kim made a bid for reunification, after receiving general support from Soviet and Chinese leaders. He moved troops across the 38th parallel. Rhee appealed to the United States for military assistance, and Truman responded without consulting Congress. The Soviets, unaware of the specific details of Kim's plans, were boycotting the UN when the invasion began and could not veto a U.S. proposal to send a UN peacekeeping force to Korea. Acting under UN auspices, the United States rushed assistance to Rhee, who moved to quell dissent in the South as well as to repel the armies of the North.

The United States confronted critical foreign policy questions in Korea. Should it seek to contain communism by driving North Korea's forces back over the 38th parallel? Or should it try to reunify Korea under Rhee's leadership? This option seemed somewhat fanciful when, within three months, North Korean forces took Seoul, the capital of South Korea, and approached the southern tip of the Korean Peninsula. American firepower, however, gradually took its toll on North Korea's elite troops and on the untrained recruits sent to replace them.

General Douglas MacArthur then launched a controversial but ultimately successful amphibious landing behind enemy lines. On September 15, 1950, Marines landed at Inchon, suffered minimal casualties, and quickly recaptured Seoul.

The shifting tide of battle devastated Korea. The **Korean War** is called a "limited" war because it never spread off the Korean Peninsula or involved nuclear weapons, but intense bombing preceded every military move, and neither side seemed concerned about civilian casualties. The number of estimated dead and wounded reached perhaps one-tenth of Korea's total population. Seoul became rubble, with only the capitol building and a train station left standing.

As MacArthur's troops drove northward, Truman faced another crucial decision. Emboldened by success, MacArthur urged moving beyond containment to attempt a rollback of communism in Korea with an all-out war of "liberation" and reunification. Other advisers warned that China would retaliate if U.S. forces approached its border. Truman allowed MacArthur to carry the war into the North but cautioned against provoking China.

When MacArthur pushed near to the Chinese–Korean border, China sent at least 400,000 troops into North Korea and forced MacArthur back across the 38th parallel. With China now in the war, Truman pondered his options. When MacArthur's troops regained the initiative, Truman ordered the general to negotiate a truce at the 38th parallel. MacArthur, challenging the president, argued for a victory over North Korea—and over China, too. Truman thereupon relieved MacArthur of his command in April 1951, declaring that the Constitution made military officers subordinate to the president, the nation's commander in chief.

MacArthur returned home a war hero, and Truman's approval ratings dipped under 30 percent. Nevertheless, the president set out to arrange a peace settlement, but negotiations stalled. Truman would leave office in 1953 without formally ending the Korean War.

Korea and Containment

The Korean War, by seeming to justify a global anticommunist stance, helped the Truman administration implement the broad vision of NSC-68. The White House formulated plans to rearm West Germany, scarcely five years after the defeat of the Third Reich, and to increase NATO's military forces. Its proposal for direct military aid to Latin American governments, which had been rejected in the past, slid through Congress. In the Philippines, the United States stepped up military assistance to suppress the leftist Huk rebels. In 1951, Washington signed a formal peace treaty with Japan and a security pact that granted the United States a military base on Okinawa. The United States acquired similar bases in the Middle East. The ANZUS mutual defense pact of 1952 linked the United States strategically to Australia and New Zealand. And Truman began assisting the efforts of France to retain its colonial possession in Indochina against the challenge from communist Ho Chi Minh's Democratic Republic of Vietnam. Warning of potential communist gains, U.S. policy-makers opposed any movement that seemed to lean toward the political left.

This fear led the United States to ally with South Africa. In 1949, the all-white (and militantly anticommunist) Nationalist Party instituted a legal-social system, called **apartheid**, based on elaborate rules of racial separation and subordination of blacks. Some State Department officials warned that any pact with South Africa, by implying support for apartheid, would damage U.S. prestige, but the Truman administration nonetheless supported South Africa's white supremacist regime.

The containment crusade of the Korean War era featured the military buildup proposed in NSC-68. Truman's national security policies produced what the

General Douglas MacArthur *Supreme commander of Allied forces in the southwest Pacific during the Second World War; leader of the occupation forces in the reconstruction of Japan; and head of UN forces during the Korean War.*

Korean War *Conflict lasting from 1950 to 1953 between communist North Korea, aided by China, and South Korea, aided by UN forces consisting primarily of U.S. troops.*

apartheid *Legal system practiced in South Africa and based on elaborate rules of racial separation and subordination of blacks.*

historian Michael Sherry has called "the militarization of American life." By 1951, two-thirds of the federal budget went for military-related spending. By early 1953, U.S. military production totaled seven times what it had been before the North Korean attack.

Containment also included, again in line with NSC-68, economic pressure, CIA covert activities, and propaganda campaigns to advance anticommunist objectives. Truman's global "Campaign of Truth" used mass media imagery and cultural exchanges to counter Soviet propaganda. A rhetoric of "national defense" took hold: The Defense Department replaced the War Department; when policy-makers discussed America's role in the world, the phrase *national security* replaced the older, more limited, phrase *national interest*.

PURSUING NATIONAL SECURITY AT HOME

FOCUS QUESTION

How did the foreign policy of containment affect domestic policy-making and American culture?

Although containment abroad generally gained bipartisan support, Truman's programs for containing subversive influences at home encountered bitter, sustained opposition. Civil libertarians complained about "witch hunts" against people who were merely dissenting from prevailing policies. As militant anticommunists leveled increasingly alarming allegations about internal communist subversion, even dedicated anticommunists began to worry that exaggerated charges harmed the effort to identify authentic Soviet agents.

Anticommunism and the U.S. Labor Movement

The politics of anticommunism helped unsettle the U.S. labor movement. After the end of the Second World War, workers had struck for increased wages and a greater voice in workplace routines and production decisions. Strikes had brought both the auto and the electronics industries to a standstill. In Stamford, Connecticut, and Lancaster, Pennsylvania, general strikes had led to massive work stoppages that later spread to other large cities. After Truman threatened to seize mines and railroads shut down by work stoppages and to order strikers back to work, labor militancy began to subside.

In 1947, a Republican-controlled Congress tapped anticommunist sentiment to pass the Labor-Management Relations Act, popularly known as the Taft-Hartley Act. The law negated some gains made by organized labor during the 1930s by limiting a union's power to conduct boycotts, to compel employers to accept "closed shops" in which only union members could be hired, and to continue a strike that the president judged harmful to national security. In addition, the measure required union officials to sign affidavits stating that they did not belong to the Communist Party or any other "subversive" organization. Truman vetoed Taft-Hartley, but Congress overrode him. By the end of the Truman era, some type of loyalty-security check had been conducted on about 20 percent of the U.S. workforce, more than 13 million people.

Anticommunism also affected internal union politics. Some union members feared that communist organizers could damage unionization efforts. Differences over whether to support the Democratic Party or Henry Wallace's Progressive Party effort in 1948 had also splintered a number of unions. In the years following Truman's victory, the Congress of Industrial Organizations (CIO) expelled 13 unions—a full third of its membership.

INSTRUCTORS ON STRIKE, 1947. *Employees of an Arthur Murray Dance Studio in New York City demonstrate the conga, a popular Latin American dance—and their determination to form a union affiliated with the United Office and Professional Workers of America. In the immediate postwar period, in response to unionization campaigns, workers in a wide range of occupations used labor strikes to secure higher wages, better working conditions, and greater job security.*

Containing Communism at Home

Anticommunists targeted the entertainment industry with special zeal. In 1947, the **House Un-American Activities Committee (HUAC)** opened hearings into communist influences in Hollywood. Basking in the glare of newsreel cameras, committee members seized on the refusal of ten screenwriters, producers, and directors—all current or former members of the American Communist Party—to testify about political allegiances within the film community. "The Hollywood Ten" claimed that the First Amendment barred HUAC from scrutinizing their political activities. The federal courts upheld HUAC's investigative powers, however, and the Hollywood Ten eventually went to prison for contempt of Congress.

Studio heads and leaders in television responded to the anticommunist fervor by drawing up a **"blacklist"** of alleged subversives whom they agreed not to hire as performers or as technical and support workers. Soon, many people were unable to find jobs unless they agreed to appear as "friendly witnesses" before HUAC or a similar investigative body to provide the names of people they had seen at some "communist meeting" sometime in the increasingly distant past. Some of those called to testify, such as the screenwriter Lillian Hellman, refused to answer any questions. Others, such as the director Elia Kazan, cooperated. Decisions over whether or not to "name names" would divide people in the entertainment industry for decades.

The search for subversives also created anticommunist celebrities. Ronald Reagan, who was president of the Screen Actors Guild *and* a secret informant for the FBI (identified as "T-10"), testified about communist influence in Hollywood. Richard Nixon, then an obscure member of Congress from California, began his political ascent in 1948 when Whittaker Chambers, a journalist formerly active in communist circles, came before HUAC to charge prominent Democrat **Alger Hiss** with passing classified information to Soviet agents during the late 1930s. Hiss portrayed himself as the victim of a frame-up. Although legal technicalities prevented his indictment for espionage, he was charged with lying to Congress and spent nearly four years in prison. To Nixon and his supporters, the case of Alger

House Un-American Activities Committee (HUAC) *Congressional committee (1938–1975) that zealously investigated suspected Nazi and communist sympathizers.*

blacklist *In the postwar years, a list of people who could no longer work in the entertainment industry because of alleged contacts with communists.*

Alger Hiss *High-level State Department official who was accused, in a controversial case, of being a communist and a Soviet spy.*

VISUAL LINK TO THE PAST

It's Okay—We're Hunting Communists

Herbert Block (1909–2001), who published editorial cartoons under the name "Herblock," favored an active role for the national government in both domestic and foreign policy. He thus editorialized on behalf of anticommunist Cold War policies such as the Marshall Plan. At the same time, Block also saw the more extreme anticommunism of Richard Nixon, Joseph McCarthy, and the House Un-American Activities Committee (HUAC) as a threat to constitutionally protected civil liberties.

Q Is this 1947 cartoon for the *Washington Post*, which addresses HUAC's approach to investigating communist subversion, critical of the overall effort to contain communism at home? What, specifically, does "Herblock" find objectionable in HUAC's brand of anticommunism?

Library of Congress, Prints and Photographs Division

Hiss, who had advised Franklin Roosevelt during the Yalta Conference (see Chapter 26), demonstrated how deeply rooted communist subversion had become and how only new leadership could uncover it.

During the mid-1990s, the availability of long-classified documents revived the Hiss controversy. A few scholars continued to see the Hiss case, as that of the Hollywood Ten, as more hype than substance, but the vast majority concluded that Hiss (along with several other high-ranking government officials) had likely passed some information to the Soviets during the 1930s and 1940s.

Pursuing its own anticommunist course, the Truman administration dismissed hundreds of federal employees under its loyalty program. Truman's attorney general secretly authorized J. Edgar Hoover, head of the FBI, to compile a covert list of alleged subversives whom the government could then detain, without any legal hearing, during a time of national emergency.

Fears that subversives might immigrate to the United States helped shape the McCarran-Walter Act of 1952. This congressional statute authorized denying immigrant status to anyone who might endanger national security by bringing dangerous ideas into the country. It also allowed the deportation of immigrants, even U.S. citizens, who belonged to organizations on the attorney general's list.

At the same time, Hoover's FBI compiled its own confidential dossiers on a wide range of artists and intellectuals, including some, such as Ernest Hemingway and John Steinbeck, with no ties to the Communist Party. The FBI often singled out prominent African Americans. Its agents kept close tabs on civil rights activist Bayard Rustin. W. E. B. Du Bois, Richard Wright (author of the acclaimed novel *Native Son*), and Paul Robeson (a well-known entertainer-activist) encountered trouble from the State Department and immigration officials. Their association with the U.S. Communist Party and their identification with anti-imperialist and antiracist organizations throughout the world threatened their ability to travel overseas. In addition, suspicions of homosexuality could make people, including the nominally closeted Rustin, into targets for governmental surveillance and discrimination.

Targeting Difference

Public signs of homosexual behavior increased during the postwar era. During the Second World War, visible gay and lesbian subcultures had emerged, particularly in larger cities such as New York and San Francisco. After the war, Dr. Alfred Kinsey's research on sexual behavior claimed that homosexual behavior could be found throughout American life and that people pursued a wide range of sexual behaviors, from exclusively heterosexual to exclusively homosexual.

Soon a small "homophile" movement, which challenged the most egregious forms of discrimination, appeared. Gay men formed the Mattachine Society (in 1950), and lesbians later founded the Daughters of Bilitis, organizations that began to advocate rights for people who were homosexual. They condemned police departments for singling out businesses catering to gays and lesbians when making raids for "disorderly conduct" and the U.S. Post Office for banning homosexual publications on the basis of "decency" requirements.

This homophile movement, however, confronted aggressive new efforts to contain signs of homosexuality. The Kinsey Report's implicit claim that homosexuality was simply another form of sexuality, alongside the emergence of new gay and lesbian organizations, helped fuel this campaign. The fact that several founders of the Mattachine Society had also been members of the Communist Party, coupled with the claim that Soviet agents could blackmail homosexuals more easily than heterosexuals, helped link homosexuality with threats to national security. "One homosexual can pollute a Government office," a Senate report claimed.

Today, historians of sexuality see a "Lavender Scare" about homosexuality accompanying the "Red Scare" about communism. Popular imagery portrayed both homosexuality and communism as subversive "diseases" that inwardly "sick" people, who seemed outwardly little different than other Americans, could spread throughout the body politic. Suspicion of "sexual deviance" became an acceptable basis for subjecting government employees to loyalty board hearings and, ultimately, denying them the same legal and constitutional protections enjoyed by heterosexuals.

The "Great Fear"

The postwar search for subversion unfolded within an atmosphere of anxiety that some cultural historians call the "Great Fear." Genuine threats, such as the atomic program of the Soviets, heightened the impact of spurious claims about communist agents roaming military bases or about gay subversives shaping foreign policy. A growing sense of insecurity, in turn, intensified efforts to safeguard national security.

As this fear was settling over U.S. politics, the Justice Department arrested, in 1950, several members of an alleged spy ring. Julius and Ethel Rosenberg, the parents of two young children and members of the American Communist Party, became the central characters in a Cold War melodrama. Their trial, the verdicts of guilty, the sentences of death, the numerous legal appeals, the worldwide protests, and their 1953 executions at Sing Sing Prison captured media attention. To their supporters, the Rosenbergs (who died maintaining their innocence) had fallen victim to anticommunist hysteria. To others, solid evidence showed they had channeled information to the Soviets. Documents released after the fall of the Soviet Union in 1989 now clearly confirm Julius Rosenberg's spying activities. Ethel Rosenberg had apparently known about his work, but the evidence of her direct involvement in passing along "vital information" to the Soviets remains lacking.

The courts' response to the Great Fear became a matter for sustained debate. During a 1949 prosecution of leaders of the American Communist Party, the trial judge accepted the Justice Department's plea that the 11 defendants be considered participants in an international conspiracy. Their Marxist ideas and publications, even without any proof of subversive acts, could justify convicting them of the crime of sedition. Civil libertarians insisted that the government never showed how Communist Party publications and speeches, by themselves, posed a "clear and present danger" to national security. In this view, *political expression* should enjoy the protection of the First Amendment and only *illegal activity* could be put on trial. In *Dennis v. United States* (1951), the Supreme Court upheld the convictions of the Communist Party leaders. The Soviet threat was so serious, the Court ruled, that pro-communist expression, in the absence of any overt criminal activity, could constitute sedition.

Even the Truman administration itself began to incur the ire of more zealous red-hunters. In Congress, Republicans and conservative Democrats denounced Truman's anticommunist initiatives as too limited and passed the Subversive Activities Control Act of 1950. It created the Subversive Activities Control Board (SACB) to oversee the registration of groups allegedly controlled or infiltrated by communists. It barred communists from working in the defense industry, holding a labor union office, and acquiring a passport.

Joseph McCarthy

Republican Senator Joseph McCarthy of Wisconsin became Truman's prime accuser. He claimed during a 1950 speech in Wheeling, West Virginia, to have compiled a list of 205 communists then working in the State Department. The number of subversives immediately shrank to 57, but McCarthy expanded his attacks to include Secretary of State Dean Acheson and his predecessor, General George C. Marshall.

Adept at using political imagery and sexual innuendo, McCarthy linked the Lavender and Red Scares. He portrayed anticommunists in Truman's administration as both overly privileged and insufficiently manly. People such as Acheson, who had been "born with silver spoons in their mouths," represented effete "enemies from within." McCarthy derided Acheson as the "Red Dean of fashion" and as the leader of the "lace handkerchief crowd."

Initially, McCarthy seemed unstoppable, even though he substantiated none of his more sensational claims. Influential people tolerated, even encouraged, him. Conservative anticommunist leaders of the Roman Catholic Church embraced

Q U I C K   R E V I E W

MCCARTHYISM

- Named after Republican senator Joseph McCarthy of Wisconsin

- Targeted Truman's State Department, Democrats, and alleged subversives

- Term came to connote any demagogic use of exaggerated and unsubstantiated charges against one's political opponents

McCarthy, himself a Catholic. Leading Republicans welcomed McCarthy's assaults on their Democratic rivals. In contrast, historically minded opponents saw the senator as the early 1950s personification of an old form of demagogic "attack politics," which would soon become known as **"McCarthyism."**

The National Security Constitution and the Structure of Governance

Focusing on the theatrics of McCarthyism can obscure fundamental constitutional changes that generated relatively little controversy. Except for the Twenty-second Amendment (1951), which barred future presidents from being elected to more than two terms, the written Constitution was not modified during the era of the Great Fear. But congressional legislation and several executive orders by the office of the president significantly altered the nation's structure of governance. Scholars now see a National Security Constitution taking shape during the early postwar years. The view that the presidency possessed only limited powers gave way to the idea that protecting national security justified greatly extending the power of the executive branch. Most obviously, Truman encountered no constitutional roadblocks when taking the United States into an undeclared war in Korea.

The specter of constitutional limitations on presidential power did arise in 1952, however, when Truman ordered his commerce secretary to seize control of the U.S. steel industry in order to prevent a threatened strike. Although Truman could have invoked a 60-day "cooling off" period under the Taft-Hartley Act, he sought to justify this action with a more fundamental, novel, and controversial constitutional claim: The president, as commander in chief, possessed extraordinary power whenever emergency action was required to safeguard national security.

The steel companies challenged this assertion in court. When *Youngstown Sheet & Tube Company v. Sawyer* (1952) reached the Supreme Court, three justices who had been nominated by Truman supported his broad claim of executive power. Six others, for differing reasons, rejected Truman's position in this particular instance, but all supported a relatively expansive view of presidential authority whenever national security seemed more clearly at stake. Constitutional scholars would come to see this case as a short-term defeat for Truman but a long-term victory for the National Security Constitution.

McCarthyism *Public accusations of disloyalty made with little or no regard for actual evidence. Named after Senator Joseph McCarthy, these accusations and the scandal and harm they caused came to symbolize the most virulent form of anticommunism.*

Postwar social-economic policy-making

Truman embraced Franklin Roosevelt's domestic agenda, and many supporters of FDR's New Deal still championed his Second Bill of Rights of 1944 (see Chapter 26). But proposals for government planning and for new social welfare measures stalled during Truman's presidency. Any attempt to build on the New Deal and wartime arrangements, insisted most Republicans and some Democrats, would cause unconstitutional intrusions into people's liberties and undermine individual initiative and responsibility. Dixiecrat Democrats joined conservative Republicans to block any legislation that they believed might dismantle white supremacy in the South. The National Association of Manufacturers (NAM) denounced the Truman administration as a menace to the nation's free-enterprise system.

FOCUS QUESTION

What assumptions dominated postwar policy-making, especially in Truman's Fair Deal? What major initiatives seemed most likely to gain approval from Congress? Which proposals seemed likely to stall there?

The Employment Act of 1946 and Economic Growth

The 1946 debate over the Full Employment Bill provided a new template for domestic policy-making. This measure, as conceived, would have empowered Washington to ensure employment for all citizens seeking work. To the bill's opponents, the phrase "full employment" implied a step toward a European style of welfare state, even socialism.

As the effort to enact this measure stalled, a scaled-back approach emerged. The law that Congress finally passed, the Employment Act of 1946, called for "maximum" (rather than full) employment and specifically declared that private enterprise, not government, bore primary responsibility for economic decision making. The measure nonetheless created a new executive branch body, the Council of Economic Advisers, to formulate long-range policy recommendations, and it signaled that government would assume considerable responsibility for the performance of the economy.

The Employment Act of 1946 also showed a growing faith that *advice* to public officials from economic experts, as an alternative to government *planning*, could guarantee a constantly expanding economy. An influential group of economists, disciples of Britain's John Maynard Keynes, insisted that their expertise could temper boom-and-bust cycles.

The promise of economic expansion dazzled postwar leaders. Using the relatively new measure of gross national product (GNP)—defined as the total dollar value of all goods and services produced in the nation during a given year—economists could calculate the nation's growing economic bounty. Corporate executives, who had feared that the end of the war would bring long-term labor unrest and trigger a deep recession, viewed a rising GNP as a guarantor of social stability. The Truman administration welcomed the prospect of an expanding economy, which would increase federal tax revenues and, in turn, finance governmental programs at home and abroad.

Truman and his advisers spread the gospel of economic growth. This new faith nicely dovetailed with their national security plans. Spending for the Cold War could serve as a "pump primer" for the U.S. economy. Sharp increases in military rearmament signaled a tilt in economic policy that critical observers began calling "military Keynesianism." Moreover, Cold War assistance programs such as the Marshall Plan could create markets and investment opportunities overseas. Economic growth at home was linked to development in the world at large—and to the all-pervasive concern with national security.

Truman's Fair Deal

In 1949, Truman unveiled his "Fair Deal." He proposed extending popular New Deal programs such as Social Security and minimum wage laws; enacting legislation dealing with civil rights, national health care, and federal aid for education; and repealing the Taft-Hartley Act. The Fair Deal also envisioned substantial spending on public housing projects and a complicated plan to support farm prices. The Fair Deal's core assumption—that sustained economic growth could finance new government programs—came to focus the Truman administration's policy planning.

Two prominent programs illustrate the emerging approach to domestic social policy. The **GI Bill** (officially titled the Serviceman's Readjustment Act of 1944) provided comprehensive benefits for those who had served in the armed forces. The bill provided veterans with financial assistance for college and job-training programs. By 1947, the year of peak enrollment, roughly half of the students enrolled at colleges

GI Bill *Officially called the Serviceman's Readjustment Act of 1944, it provided veterans with college and job-training assistance, preferential treatment in hiring, and subsidized home loans, and was extended to Korean War veterans in 1952.*

and universities were receiving aid under the GI Bill. Veterans also received preferential treatment when applying for government jobs; favorable financial terms when purchasing homes or businesses; and, eventually, comprehensive medical care in veterans' hospitals. The Veterans Readjustment Assistance Act of 1952, popularly known as the "GI Bill of Rights," extended these programs to veterans of the Korean War. Although the Truman administration never enacted FDR's Second Bill of Rights, the GI Bill did extend some of its key provisions to veterans.

The Social Security program also expanded. Rebutting attacks from conservatives, Social Security's supporters defended its provisions for the disabled and the blind and argued that older people had earned the "income security" through years of work and monetary contributions withheld from their paychecks. Under the Social Security Act of 1950, the level of benefits increased significantly; the retirement portions of the program expanded; and coverage was extended to more than 10 million people, including agricultural workers.

More expansive (and expensive) Fair Deal proposals, however, either failed or were scaled back. For instance, Truman's plan for a comprehensive national health insurance program faced opposition from several different quarters. Consumer groups and labor unions, intent on creating nonprofit community-run health plans, feared that a centralized system would unnecessarily bureaucratize medical care. The American Medical Association (AMA) and the American Hospital Association (AHA) opposed any governmental intervention in the traditional fee-for-service medical system. Large insurance companies, which were continuing to push their own private plans, also opposed the Truman initiative. Opinion polls suggested that many voters found Truman's health proposals confusing.

The Fair Deal's housing proposals made some headway. Continued shortage of affordable housing in urban areas stirred support for home-building programs. Even some conservatives supported the Housing Act of 1949. This law authorized construction of 810,000 public housing units and provided federal funds for "urban renewal" zones, areas to be cleared of rundown dwellings and rebuilt with new construction. The Housing Act proclaimed ambitious goals but provided relatively modest funding, especially for its public-housing component. Private construction firms and real estate agents welcomed funding for federal home loan guarantee programs—such as those established under the GI Bill—but they lobbied effectively against publicly financed housing projects.

Fair Deal policy-making ultimately focused on specific groups, such as veterans and older Americans, rather than on more extensive programs such as national health care or an extensive housing program. With opponents of the Fair Deal charging that it would move the United States toward a European-style "welfare state," the White House found it easier to defend more narrowly targeted programs that it could present as economic security measures for specific recipients who deserved government assistance.

Civil Rights

The Truman administration also struggled to place the national government's power behind a growing civil rights movement. After returning home, veterans of African, Latino, and American Indian descent increasingly refused to remain passive bystanders when laws and discriminatory practices reduced them to second-class citizens. Moreover, the people of color who had moved to cities seeking wartime employment wanted to build on the social and economic gains they had made. Drives to translate the visions of liberty and equality into reality animated grassroots activists in the postwar period.

During his 1948 presidential campaign, Truman endorsed the proposals of a civil rights committee he had established in 1946. Its report, entitled "To Secure These Rights," called for federal legislation against lynching; a special civil rights division within the Department of Justice; antidiscrimination initiatives in employment, housing, and public facilities; and desegregation of the military. These proposals helped prompt the Dixiecrat revolt of 1948, but they also gained Truman significant support from activist groups.

Civil rights became an increasingly important political issue. After successive Congresses failed to enact any civil rights legislation—including a law against lynching and a ban on poll taxes—leaders of the movement turned to the White House and to the federal courts. A plan by labor leader A. Philip Randolph to organize a protest campaign prompted Truman to issue Executive Order 9981 (1948), which called for gradual desegregation of the armed forces. Truman understood how segregation tarnished America's image in a Cold War world "which is 90 percent colored." Although Cold War politics could help justify harassment of African American leaders allegedly linked to subversive causes, the crusade against communism on behalf of the "free world" also made racial discrimination into a foreign policy liability.

Truman's Justice Department thus appeared in court to support litigants who contested government-backed "restrictive covenants" (legal agreements that prevented racial or religious minorities from acquiring real estate) and segregated education. In 1946, the Supreme Court declared restrictive covenants unconstitutional and began chipping away at the "separate-but-equal" principle used since *Plessy v. Ferguson* (1896) to justify segregated schools. A federal court in California, ruling on a case brought the previous year in Orange County by a coalition of Mexican American and African American activists, held that segregating students of Mexican descent in separate, and unequal, schools violated their constitutional rights. In 1948, a second federal court—with the case now entitled *Westminster School District v. Mendez*—agreed with the first. In 1950, the Supreme Court ruled that, under the Fourteenth Amendment, racial segregation in state-financed graduate and law schools was unconstitutional. The familiar arguments used to legitimize racial segregation in public education seemed ripe for a successful challenge.

QUICK REVIEW

TRUMAN'S FAIR DEAL

- Marked by faith that postwar economic growth could fund new governmental social welfare programs

- Major initiatives aimed at creating "maximum" employment opportunities, extending Social Security and GI Bill benefits, easing the housing shortage, and providing national health insurance

- Also included Truman's endorsement of a number of civil rights measures, including anti-lynching legislation and integration of the military

SIGNS OF A CHANGING CULTURE

FOCUS QUESTION

How did a resurgent civil rights movement and a new suburban culture help signal important cultural changes during the immediate postwar era?

The pace of cultural change accelerated during the postwar years. Encouraged by the advertising industry, Americans seemed, in one sense, to view anything new as "progress." Yet, in another, the speed and scope of change accentuated feelings of uneasiness and anxiety.

The Baseball "Color Line"

Jackie Robinson *African American whose addition to the Brooklyn Dodgers in 1947 began the lengthy process of integrating Major League Baseball.*

The interplay between celebrating and containing change could be seen in the integration of organized baseball during the 1940s and early 1950s. In 1947, **Jackie Robinson** finally cracked Major League Baseball's policy of racial segregation. Robinson had played in the Negro National Baseball League before joining the Brooklyn Dodgers. Some ballplayers, including several on Robinson's own club, considered a boycott. Baseball's leadership, seeking new sources of players and seeing a steady stream of African American fans coming through the turnstiles, threatened to suspend any player who would not play with or against Robinson.

Officially, Major League Baseball became desegregated. The Cleveland Indians signed center fielder Larry Doby, and other top-flight players abandoned the Negro leagues for clubs in the American and National circuits. Eventually, the skills of Robinson—named Rookie of the Year in 1947 and the National League's Most Valuable Player in 1949—and other players of African descent carried the day. Although light-skinned Latinos had long passed through the racial barrier, Orestes ("Minnie") Minoso, a Cuban-born veteran of the Negro circuits, became the first Afro-Latino to break into the big leagues in 1949. Major League teams began fielding greater numbers of African American and Latino players, and some began recruiting in Mexico and the Caribbean.

Yet baseball's leadership had unofficially limited its own desegregation effort. Several teams waited years before integrating their rosters, claiming that they could find no talented African American or Latino prospects. More commonly, clubs restricted the number of nonwhite players they would take on and kept their managers, coaches, and front-office personnel solidly white.

The African American and Latino players who followed in Robinson's footsteps confronted continuing obstacles. They often encountered overt, off-the-field discrimination during spring training in the South and Southwest and in small towns elsewhere when playing in the minor leagues. Spanish-speaking players struggled to convince managers, sportswriters, and team-mates that they could "understand" the subtleties of either baseball or North American culture.

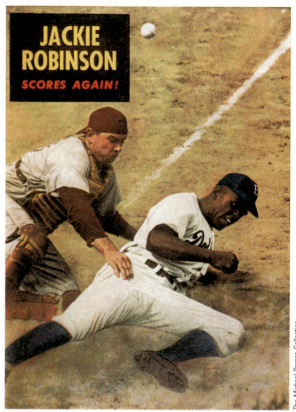

JACKIE ROBINSON. *In 1947 Jackie Robinson joined the Brooklyn Dodgers and became the first African American since the 19th century to play Major League Baseball. He had served as a lieutenant in the army during the Second World War. Racial integration of the national pastime of baseball became a powerful symbol of progress in race relations.*

The Michael Barson Collection

The New Suburbia

In suburbia, too, change was simultaneously celebrated and feared. Suburban living had long been a feature of the "American dream." The new Long Island town of Levittown, New York, which welcomed its first residents in October 1947, seemed to make that dream an affordable reality for middle-income families.

Nearly everything about Levittown appeared unprecedented. Levitt & Sons, a construction company that had mass-produced military barracks during the Second World War, claimed to be completing a five-room bungalow every 15 minutes. Architectural critics sneered at these "little boxes," but potential buyers stood in long lines for the chance to purchase one. By 1950, Levittown contained more than 10,000 homes and 40,000 residents, and bulldozers and construction crews were sweeping through other suburban developments across the country.

To assist potential buyers, the government offered an extensive set of programs. The Federal Housing Administration (FHA), established during the New Deal, helped underwrite an elaborate lending system. Typically, people who bought FHA-financed homes needed only 5 percent of the purchase price as a down payment; they could finance the rest with a long-term, government-insured mortgage. Veterans enjoyed even more favorable terms under the GI loan program. These government programs made it cheaper to purchase a suburban house than to rent an apartment in most cities.

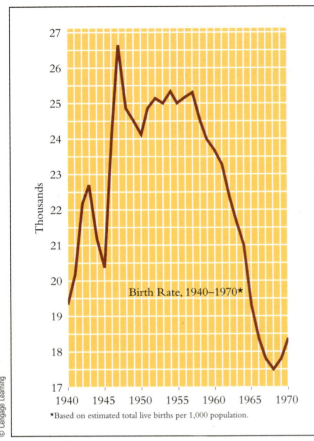

*Based on estimated total live births per 1,000 population.

© Cengage Learning

THE BABY BOOM

Homeowners could also deduct the interest payments on their mortgages from their federal income tax.

The new suburbs gained a reputation for being ideal places to raise children. Toward the end of the war, a number of factors, including earlier marriages and rising incomes, fueled a **baby boom** that would last until the mid-1960s. With houses occupying only about 15 percent of suburban lots, large lawns served as private playgrounds. Suburban schools were as new as the homes, and their well-appointed facilities attracted both skilled, enthusiastic teachers and baby-boom children. Suburbia symbolized new possibilities, confidence in the future, and acceptance of change.

As contemporary observers noted, however, it also appeared to offer a material and psychological refuge. Buying a suburban home seemed a way of containing the impact of the social and cultural changes of the Cold War era. As African American families migrated to northern and western cities in search of jobs and greater opportunity, some whites began to see moving to the new suburbs as a way to avoid living in integrated communities. Governmental policies contributed to this trend through the financial incentives provided to homebuyers. After the Supreme Court declared restrictive covenants unconstitutional, local officials rarely enforced the decision. Various informal and extralegal arrangements prevented, until well into the 1960s, any African American from buying a home in Levittown.

Other policies and practices helped to segregate the new postwar suburbs. Local governments vetoed public housing projects in their communities. Although land and building costs would have been cheaper in the suburbs, public housing projects remained concentrated on relatively expensive, high-density urban sites. At the same time, the lending industry channeled government-guaranteed loans away from most urban neighborhoods, and private lenders routinely denied credit to African Americans and Latinos seeking to buy new suburban housing. All the while, leaders of the postwar housing industry, including William Levitt, denied any discriminatory intent.

Similarly, the architects of this new suburbia saw nothing problematic with postwar gender patterns. The private financial industry extended the vast majority of its loan guarantees to white men. Only rarely could single women, from any ethnic background, obtain loans. The FHA, a governmental agency, justified a similar policy on the grounds that men were the family breadwinners and that women seldom made enough money to qualify as good credit risks. Analogous justifications often kept men from non-European backgrounds from obtaining loans for housing in the new suburbs.

Postwar Hollywood

baby boom *Dramatic increase in births during the years after World War II, 1946–1964.*

Hollywood turned out powerful symbols of the Cold War era's fascination with—and containment of—cultural change. The motion picture industry expected to cheer the nation through the Cold War much as it had through the Depression and the Second World War. The familiar musical genre, filled with lively stars, upbeat tunes, and flashy dance sequences, provided a ready formula for expressing postwar optimism.

But Hollywood's fortunes were changing. Attendance figures—along with profits—began to plummet in 1949. A year before, the Supreme Court had ruled that antitrust laws required the major studios to give up their highly profitable ownership of local movie theaters. This decision rocked Hollywood just as it faced labor strife, internal conflict over blacklisting, and soaring production costs. The rise of television delivered another blow to an industry already reeling backward.

Meanwhile, Hollywood released a cycle of motion pictures that came to be called *film noir*, or "dark cinema." Almost always filmed in black and white and generally set in large cities, *film noir* peeked into the dark corners of postwar America. Noir characters still pursued their dreams and hopes but with little chance of ever succeeding. Failure and loss seemed to be the rule rather than the exception.

Film noir featured alluring *femmes fatales*, beautiful but dangerous women who challenged the prevailing order, particularly its gender relationships. The *femme fatale* disdained the confinement that came with being a faithful, nurturing wife and mother. Usually unmarried and childless, she threatened both men and women. The postwar era's most prominent female stars—including Barbara Stanwyck, Joan Crawford, Rita Hayworth, and Lana Turner—achieved both popular and critical acclaim playing *femmes fatales*.

DEADLY IS THE FEMALE. *Also called* Gun Crazy *(1949), this film noir played on fears of social breakdown and inspired the later movie* Bonnie and Clyde *(1967).*

THE ELECTION OF 1952

Harry Truman, with his approval rating ultimately falling to nearly 20 percent, declined to run for another term in 1952. His presidency had put his Democratic Party on the defensive, while denunciations of communism and of Truman's outgoing administration animated Republican campaign efforts.

Continuing Containment

Both major parties embraced the policy of containment in 1952. Adlai Stevenson of Illinois, the Democratic presidential candidate, warned that "Soviet secret agents and their dupes" had "burrowed like moles" into governments throughout the world. "We cannot let our guard drop for even a moment," he claimed. A solidly anticommunist stance, however, could not save Stevenson or his party. The Republicans linked Stevenson to the unpopular Truman presidency and highlighted several scandals that featured administration figures receiving kickbacks for granting government contracts. The GOP's vice presidential nominee, Senator Richard Nixon of California, called Stevenson "Adlai the appeaser." The Republican formula for electoral victory could be expressed in a simple equation, "K1C2": "Korea, corruption, and communism."

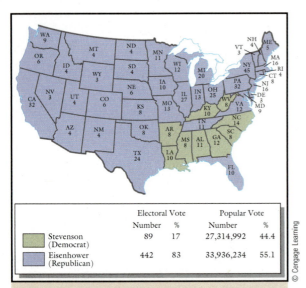

	Electoral Vote		Popular Vote	
	Number	%	Number	%
Stevenson (Democrat)	89	17	27,314,992	44.4
Eisenhower (Republican)	442	83	33,936,234	55.1

© Cengage Learning

Map 27.4 Presidential Election, 1952. *In this overwhelming victory for Eisenhower, Stevenson carried only a few states. Note that the so-called "solid South" remained largely Democratic. This trend would shift substantially over the next two decades.*

A Soldier–Politician

For their presidential candidate, Republicans turned to a hero of the Second World War, General Dwight David Eisenhower, popularly known as "Ike." After directing the Normandy invasion of 1944 as Supreme Allied Commander, Eisenhower served as Army Chief of Staff from 1945 to 1948 and, after an interim period as president of Columbia University, became the commander of NATO, a post he held until resigning to run for president. Eisenhower had never before sought elective office, but a half-century of military service had honed his political instincts.

Eisenhower's personal appeal dazzled political insiders, media commentators, and ordinary voters. Marketed as a middle-of-the-road candidate, Ike appeared ready to direct the nation through a cold war as skillfully as he had led it through a hot one. He promised to end the increasingly unpopular, stalemated Korean conflict. The Republican effort in 1952, the first to feature televised appeals, downplayed Eisenhower's uncertain grasp of complicated policy issues in favor of highlighting his winning personality. A GOP campaign button simply announced "I Like IKE!"

The first military leader to gain the presidency since Ulysses S. Grant (1869–1877), Eisenhower could claim a great personal victory. The Eisenhower–Nixon ticket rolled up almost seven million more popular votes than the Democrats and carried the Electoral College by a nearly five-to-one margin. Yet the Republican Party itself made only modest gains. It managed a single-vote majority in the Senate and an eight-vote edge in the House of Representatives. The New Deal political coalition still survived but showed increasing signs of fraying in the South. There, some of the white southern votes that had gone to the Dixiecrats in 1948 began moving toward the Republicans, and Eisenhower carried four states in the Democratic Party's once "Solid South."

Conclusion

An emphasis on safeguarding national security helped reshape national life during the years that followed the Second World War. As worsening relations between the United States and the Soviet Union produced a Cold War, the Truman administration pursued policies that expanded the power of the government, particularly the executive branch. The militarization of foreign policy intensified when the United States, after going to war in Korea in 1950, began implementing the assumptions laid out in NSC-68.

Americans also debated how best to protect national security and calm cultural anxieties on the home front. The New Deal vision faded, but Truman's Fair Deal promised that new economic wisdom would guarantee economic growth and thereby provide the tax revenues to expand domestic programs. The Truman administration also expressed support, even when it alienated many white southerners, for a civil rights agenda. Although the 1952 election of Dwight Eisenhower gave the Republicans the presidency for the first time in two decades, Eisenhower's personal appeal did not signal an end to the power of the Democratic coalition that had held sway since the 1930s.

CHAPTER REVIEW

Review Questions

1. What major conflicts between the United States and the Soviet Union shaped the Cold War and prompted a U.S. foreign policy focused on containment of communism?

2. How did the Korean War help reinforce and militarize the policy of containment?

3. How did the foreign policy of containment affect domestic policy and American life?

4. What assumptions dominated postwar policy-making, especially in Truman's Fair Deal? What major initiatives seemed most likely to gain approval from Congress? Which proposals seemed likely to stall there?

5. How did a resurgent civil rights movement and a new suburban culture help signal important cultural changes during the immediate postwar era?

Critical Thinking Questions

1. In what ways did U.S. foreign policy after the Second World War prompt important changes in the nation's system of constitutional governance? How did U.S. intervention in Korea help to underscore these changes?

2. How did postwar policy-making at home follow—and also depart from—the vision of Franklin Roosevelt's New Deal?

Identifications

Review your understanding of the following key terms, people, and events for this chapter.

Cold War, p. 632
containment, p. 635
National Security Act of 1947, p. 635
Marshall Plan, p. 636

North Atlantic Treaty Organization (NATO), p. 637
NSC-68, p. 639
General Douglas MacArthur, p. 641

Korean War, p. 641
apartheid, p. 641
House Un-American Activities Committee (HUAC), p. 643
blacklist, p. 643

Alger Hiss, p. 643
McCarthyism, p. 647
GI Bill, p. 648
Jackie Robinson, p. 650
baby boom, p. 652

DISCOVERY

How did the Cold War affect American politics and culture?

In thinking about this question, begin by breaking it down into the components shown below. A discussion of the significance of each component should appear in your answer.

Government and Law

Examine the cartoon "It's Okay—We're Hunting Communists." Who are the people in the street who have been run over? Who is driving the car? What was the House Un-American Activities Committee and what was it attempting to do in early Cold War America? Why did it claim that its actions were justified? Does the cartoonist think that the actions of this committee were legitimate? From reading this chapter, how do you assess the threat that communists posed to America during these years and the work of the Un-American Activities Committee, and then Senator McCarthy, in containing this threat?

Culture and Society

Look at the *film noir* poster on page 653 in light of the material in this chapter. What is suggested by the woman's dress, pose, expression, and size compared to the man? What was the social significance of the *femme fatale*? How was this image of women seen to threaten both men and women and represent social breakdown? How might these movies have both challenged the conformity of the late 1940s and 1950s and underscored the threats posed by those who broke the law or stepped outside traditional roles?

Library of Congress, Prints and Photographs Division

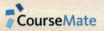

**Visit the CourseMate website at
www.cengagebrain.com for
additional study tools and review
materials for this chapter.**

28

AFFLUENCE AND ITS DISCONTENTS, 1953–1963

REORIENTING CONTAINMENT, 1953–1960
    Eisenhower Takes Command
    The New Look, Global Alliances, and Summitry
    Covert Action and Economic Leverage

THE THIRD WORLD

AFFLUENCE—A "PEOPLE OF PLENTY"
    Economic Growth
    Labor–Management Accord
    Political Pluralism
    A Religious People

DISCONTENTS OF AFFLUENCE
    Conformity in an Affluent Society
    Restive Youth
    The Critique of Mass Culture

DEBATING THE ROLE OF GOVERNMENT
    The New Conservatism
    The Case for a More Active Government

NEW FRONTIERS, 1960–1963
    The Election of 1960
    Foreign Policy

    Cuba and Berlin
    Southeast Asia and Flexible Response

DOMESTIC POLICY-MAKING

THE POLITICS OF GENDER
    The New Suburbs and Gender Politics
    Signs of Women's Changing Roles
    A New Women's Movement

THE EXPANDING CIVIL RIGHTS MOVEMENTS, 1953–1963
    The *Brown* Cases, 1954–1955
    The Montgomery Bus Boycott
    The Politics of Civil Rights: From the Local to the
       Global
    The Politics of American Indian Policy
    Spanish-Speaking Communities and Civil Rights
    Urban-Suburban Issues
    New Forms of Direct Action, 1960–1963

NOVEMBER 1963
    Policy Choices
    The Assassination of John F. Kennedy

Containment of communism continued to dominate American foreign policy between 1953 and 1963. Republican President Dwight David Eisenhower modulated the pitch of the anticommunist rhetoric coming from the White House, but both he and his Democratic successor, John F. Kennedy, supported the national security bureaucracy's plans for new ways to fight the Cold War.

On the domestic front, Ike and JFK supported, with differing degrees of enthusiasm, social and economic programs initiated during the 1930s and 1940s. Sustained economic growth during the late 1950s and early 1960s encouraged talk about an age of "affluence." It also generated discontent, particularly over conformity, restive young people, and commercial mass culture. At the same time, economic disparities and racial discrimination sparked debate over greater use of governmental power—and the meanings of liberty and equality.

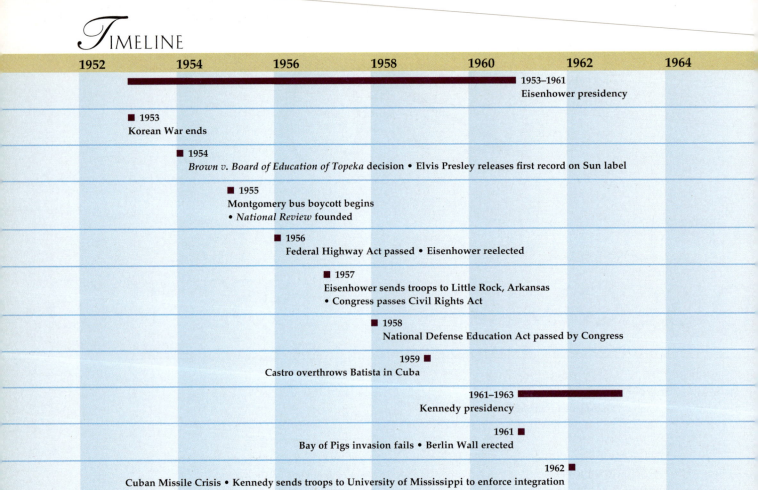

| 1952 | 1954 | 1956 | 1958 | 1960 | 1962 | 1964 |

1953–1961
Eisenhower presidency

■ **1953**
Korean War ends

■ **1954**
Brown v. Board of Education of Topeka decision • Elvis Presley releases first record on Sun label

■ **1955**
Montgomery bus boycott begins
• *National Review* founded

■ **1956**
Federal Highway Act passed • Eisenhower reelected

■ **1957**
Eisenhower sends troops to Little Rock, Arkansas
• Congress passes Civil Rights Act

■ **1958**
National Defense Education Act passed by Congress

1959 ■
Castro overthrows Batista in Cuba

1961–1963
Kennedy presidency

1961 ■
Bay of Pigs invasion fails • Berlin Wall erected

1962 ■
Cuban Missile Crisis • Kennedy sends troops to University of Mississippi to enforce integration

1963 ■
Civil rights activists undertake march on Washington • Kennedy assassinated

© Cengage Learning

REORIENTING CONTAINMENT, 1953–1960

FOCUS QUESTION

In what ways did the Eisenhower administration retain but also reorient the foreign policy of containment that it inherited from the immediate postwar period?

Third World *Less economically developed areas of the world, primarily the Middle East, Asia, Latin America, and Africa.*

The U.S. strategy for containing communism shifted during the 1950s. Bipolar confrontation between the United States and the Soviet Union over European issues gave way to greater reliance on nuclear weaponry and on subtle power plays in the **Third World:** the Middle East, Asia, Latin America, and Africa.

Eisenhower Takes Command

Eisenhower honored his campaign pledge to travel to Korea to end U.S. military involvement there. On July 27, 1953, both sides signed a truce, and a conflict that claimed the lives of more than two million Asians, mostly noncombatants, and 53,000 Americans finally ended. Still, a formal peace treaty remained unsigned, and the 38th parallel became one of the most heavily militarized borders in the world.

At home, Ike patiently wrested control of the national security issue from more militant anticommunists. Congress exceeded the wishes of the Eisenhower administration when it passed the Communist Control Act of 1954, which barred the American Communist Party from running candidates in elections and extended the 1950 Subversive Activities Control Act. With a GOP president in the White House, however, most Republicans began turning away from the confrontational styles of anticommunist politics associated with Joe McCarthy.

When a Senate committee investigated his sensational charges about subversives in the U.S. Army, McCarthy finally careened out of control. Under the glare of TV lights, McCarthy appeared as a crude bully who hurled wild slanders in every direction. In late 1954, the Senate voted to "condemn" him for "unbecoming" conduct. Eisenhower's decision to allow McCarthy to self-destruct, rather than to confront him head-on, seemed vindicated. Indeed, presidential historians now generally see Eisenhower as a president who could skillfully employ the full power of his office, often working behind the scenes.

The New Look, Global Alliances, and Summitry

Eisenhower collaborated with his national security advisers to reinforce executive branch leadership in foreign policy. He allowed Secretary of State John Foster Dulles to warn, repeatedly, that Washington would consider adopting measures to "roll back," rather than simply to contain, communism. Eisenhower also extended Truman's earlier programs of domestic surveillance and continued a secret program to develop new aerial surveillance capabilities using U-2 spy planes.

The Eisenhower administration also secretly reviewed overall military policy. It initially decided to rein in the military budget by introducing a New Look, which emphasized nuclear weaponry and airpower as a way to halt spiraling expenditures. The New Look became associated with the doctrine of **massive retaliation**—the theory that the threat of U.S. nuclear weaponry would check Soviet expansion.

Additionally, the Eisenhower administration elevated psychological warfare and "informational" programs into major Cold War weapons. The government-run Voice of America extended its global radio broadcasts. Washington secretly funded Radio Free Europe, Radio Liberty (beamed to the Soviet Union), and Radio Asia. In 1953, Eisenhower persuaded Congress to create the United States Information Agency (USIA) to coordinate anticommunist propaganda campaigns.

The United States and the USSR, hoping to improve relations, began holding high-level "summit meetings" in 1955. In May, U.S. and Soviet leaders agreed to end the military occupation of Austria and to transform it into a neutral nation. Two months later, the United States, the Soviet Union, Britain, and France met in Geneva, Switzerland, and inaugurated cultural exchanges. Despite the Soviet Union's brutal suppression of a revolt against its rule in Hungary in 1956, meetings between the superpowers continued. In fall 1959, Khrushchev toured the United States, visiting a farm in Iowa and Disneyland in California. Although a 1960 Paris summit meeting fell apart after the Soviets shot down a U-2 spy plane over their territory, the tone of Cold War rhetoric seemed to become less strident during Eisenhower's presidency. The superpowers even slowed aboveground nuclear testing and discussed a broader test-ban agreement.

Covert Action and Economic Leverage

The U.S. campaign to contain communism shifted toward the Third World, with covert action and economic pressure as primary tools. The CIA, headed by

QUICK REVIEW

EISENHOWER'S FOREIGN POLICY

- Negotiated truce in Korean War

- Provided surveillance of Soviet military capabilities with U-2 spy planes

- Emphasized airpower and nuclear capabilities in his New Look military posture

- Used covert action, economic pressure, and informational diplomacy as techniques of containment

- Lowered Cold War tensions at summit meetings and atomic test-ban talks

massive retaliation *Assertion by the Eisenhower administration that the threat of U.S. atomic weaponry would hold communist powers in check.*

Allen Dulles, brother of the secretary of state, played a key role in U.S. policy. In 1953, the CIA helped elect an anticommunist, U.S.-friendly government in the Philippines and facilitated a coup against an elected government in Iran to replace it with one more friendly to Western oil interests. The following year, the agency secretly helped topple an elected government in Guatemala that threatened the landholdings of an American fruit company. Impressed by these covert operations, the National Security Council widened the CIA's mandate, and by 1961 the CIA deployed approximately 15,000 agents around the world.

Eisenhower also employed economic strategies—trade and aid—to contain communism and win allies. Governmental initiatives sought to open new opportunities for U.S. enterprises overseas, discourage other countries from adopting state-directed economic systems, and encourage expanded trade ties. Military aid to Third World nations rose sharply as well. This buildup of armaments provided the United States with stronger anticommunist allies but also contributed to the development of military dictatorships.

THE THIRD WORLD

In Latin America, the White House gravitated toward dictatorial regimes that welcomed U.S. economic investment and opposed leftist movements. Such policies encouraged anti-American sentiment, and events in Cuba dramatized the growing hostility. In late 1959, a revolutionary movement led by Fidel Castro toppled dictator Fulgencio Batista's pro-U.S. regime and pledged to reduce Cuba's dependence on the United States. The Eisenhower administration responded with an economic boycott. Castro turned to the Soviet Union, openly embraced communism, squashed dissent at home, and pledged to support Cuban-style insurgencies throughout Latin America. The CIA pondered how best to hamstring, and then eliminate, Castro.

In the Middle East, distrust of nationalism and neutralism shaped U.S. policy. In 1954, when Colonel Gamal Abdel Nasser led a successful military coup in Egypt against a corrupt monarchy, he promised to rescue other Arab nations from European domination and guide them toward "positive neutralism" in the Cold War. Nasser denounced Israel; boosted Egypt's economic and military power; extended diplomatic recognition to the People's Republic of China; and purchased advanced weapons from communist Czechoslovakia.

The Eisenhower administration viewed these policies as neither positive nor neutral. It cancelled loans for the Aswan Dam, a project designed to improve agriculture along the Nile River and provide power for new Egyptian industries. Nasser responded, in July 1956, by seizing the British-controlled Suez Canal. British forces, joined by those of France and Israel, attacked Egypt in October and took back the canal.

Eisenhower distrusted Nasser but also opposed Britain's blatant attempt to retain its imperial position. Denouncing the Anglo-French-Israeli action, he threatened to destabilize Britain's currency unless the invasion ended. Eventually, a plan supported by the United States and the UN gave Egypt control over the Suez Canal, but U.S. influence in the area suffered as the Soviet Union underwrote construction of the Aswan Dam.

The Eisenhower administration feared the spread of "Nasserism" throughout the energy-rich Middle East. In spring 1957, the **Eisenhower Doctrine** pledged to

Eisenhower Doctrine *Policy that stated that the United States would use armed force to respond to imminent or actual communist aggression in the Middle East.*

defend Middle Eastern countries "against overt armed aggression from any nation controlled by international communism." When governments in Lebanon and Jordan faced revolts by domestic forces friendly to Nasser, Eisenhower dispatched U.S. Marines to Lebanon, and Britain helped Jordan's King Hussein retain his throne.

Eisenhower's effort to thwart communism and neutralism in the Third World set the stage for the most substantial U.S. commitment—in Indochina. During the Korean War, the Truman administration had increased economic aid for France's war to retain its colony in Indochina against a communist-nationalist movement led by Ho Chi Minh (see Chapter 27). Eisenhower continued Truman's policy.

During the early spring of 1954, Ho's forces surrounded French forces in the valley of Dien Bien Phu. France surrendered and abandoned the colony it had created in 1887. The Geneva Peace Accords of 1954, which the Eisenhower administration refused to sign, divided French Indochina into three new nations: Laos, Cambodia, and Vietnam. The accords temporarily split Vietnam, at the 17th parallel, into two jurisdictions—North Vietnam and South Vietnam—until a subsequent election could unify the country under a single government. Ho Chi Minh and his communist allies in China and the Soviet Union accepted this settlement, confident that Ho would win the political contest, scheduled for 1956.

Eisenhower's advisers feared that a communist electoral victory in Vietnam might set off a geopolitical chain reaction that could "endanger the stability and security" of noncommunist nations throughout Asia, a formulation known as the "domino theory." After Ho Chi Minh's communist government consolidated control over the Democratic Republic of Vietnam (North Vietnam), Eisenhower ordered covert operations and economic programs to forestall Ho from assuming control of a unified Vietnam. The CIA staged a rigged 1955 election that installed Ngo Dinh Diem as the first president of the Republic of Vietnam (South Vietnam).

An anticommunist Catholic, Ngo Dinh Diem renounced the Geneva Peace Accords and the election intended to create a unified government. He consolidated his political support, augmented his military forces, and cracked down on his opponents. Diem's policies cost him support inside South Vietnam, especially among the sizable Buddhist population, and he became increasingly dependent on the United States. Although Eisenhower feared that direct U.S. military involvement in South Vietnam would be a "tragedy," he increased aid and tied America's policy to Diem's shaky political fortunes.

AFFLUENCE—A "PEOPLE OF PLENTY"

In his farewell address of 1961, Eisenhower warned that the greatest danger to the United States was not communism but the nation's own "military-industrial complex." This complex, the former general said, threatened to so accelerate the costs of containment that the burden of military expenditures would eventually harm the U.S. domestic economy.

The speech contained several ironies. Eisenhower's administration had failed to prevent ever-larger sums from flowing to the military. His selection of businessmen to head the Department of Defense seemingly dramatized the same linkage he decried. And his warnings about possible dangers came after eight

FOCUS QUESTION

How did economic growth change American life during the post-1953 decade?

LINK TO THE PAST

A Warning about the Future: President Dwight Eisenhower's Farewell Address, 1961

Eisenhower raised the stakes in the Cold War arms race with the Soviet Union: new missiles for the delivery of increasingly powerful nuclear bombs, new aerial surveillance techniques, and vast tracking centers to coordinate the nation's defenses. Yet he left office warning Americans about the growth in what he called the "military-industrial complex."

We annually spend on military security more than the net income of all United States corporations. This conjunction of an immense military establishment and a large arms industry is new in the American experience. The total influence—economic, political, even spiritual—is felt in every city, every State house, every office of the Federal government. We recognize the imperative need for this development. Yet we must not fail to comprehend its grave implications. . . .

In the councils of government, we must guard against the acquisition of unwarranted influence, *whether sought or unsought, by the military-industrial complex. The potential for the disastrous rise of misplaced power exists and will persist.*

We must never let the weight of this combination endanger our liberties or democratic pro-cesses. . . . I confess that I lay down my official responsibilities in this field with a definite sense of disappointment.

PRESIDENT DWIGHT D. EISENHOWER
   farewell address, 1961

Q What did Eisenhower mean by the "military-industrial complex"?

Q Why did he think it threatened American democracy?

Q How might his warnings be evaluated today?

years during which his White House had praised the nation's continued economic growth. By 1960, the United States could claim a GNP more than five times that of Great Britain and roughly 10 times that of Japan. National security policies facilitated U.S. access to raw materials and energy. Government spending for these same policies, what economists called "military Keynesianism," also pumped money into economic growth.

Economic Growth

The post-1953 decade, despite three brief recessions, would mark the midpoint of a period of steady economic growth that continued until the early 1970s. Corporations turned out vast quantities of consumer goods and enjoyed rising profits. The rise of the suburbs and widespread ownership of kitchen appliances, television sets, and automobiles supported the claim of historian David Potter that Americans were a "people of plenty."

In 1958, Harvard economist John Kenneth Galbraith reached the best-seller lists with his book *The Affluent Society.* The ideal of affluence fit with the dominant vision that celebrated constant economic growth and steady improvement of living standards as a uniquely American way of life. The gulf between rich and poor no longer seemed to be between people with cars and those without them, but between people with Cadillacs and those with Fords. Keynesian economists such as Galbraith argued that greater government expenditures would generate even faster growth. But Eisenhower feared that increased spending would fuel inflation, and his administration remained committed to balanced budgets.

Eisenhower did, however, endorse several costly new programs. Most significantly, he supported the **Highway Act of 1956**, citing national security considerations. Financed largely by a national tax on gasoline, the act funded a national system of limited-access expressways. Touted as the largest public works project in world history, this interstate highway program delighted the oil, concrete, and tire industries; provided steady work for construction firms and labor unions; and boosted the interstate trucking business.

The White House also supported expensive water-diversion projects in the West. The Army Corps of Engineers and the Bureau of Reclamation spent billions of dollars on dams, irrigation canals, and reservoirs. Irrigation turned desert into cropland, and elaborate pumping systems even forced rivers to flow uphill. Although these measures often introduced ecological problems, by 1960 much of the West had access to trillions of gallons of water per year, and governmental expenditures laid the basis for new economic growth in Texas, California, and Arizona.

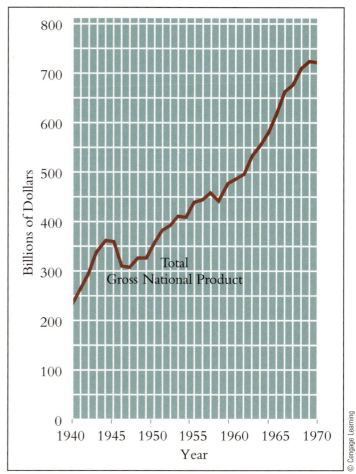

STEADY GROWTH OF GROSS NATIONAL PRODUCT, 1940–1970

Labor–Management Accord

During the 1950s and early 1960s real wages (what workers make after adjusting their paychecks for inflation) rose steadily; jobs were plentiful; benefits and living standards improved; and union leaders recognized that closer cooperation with corporate management could guarantee employment stability and political influence. Labor agreed to bargain aggressively on issues that immediately affected worker paychecks and benefits but to abide by its contracts with management and disavow aggressive tactics such as wildcat strikes. To police this new labor–management détente, both sides looked to the federal government's National Labor Relations Board (NLRB). Meanwhile, in 1955, the American Federation of Labor (AFL) and the Congress of Industrial Organizations (CIO), long at odds, merged.

Labor activists expressed concern. Nearly two-thirds of all unionized workers lived in only 10 states. Worse, companies in some areas of union strength, such as the Northeast, were moving jobs to states in the South, where the union movement lacked strong roots. Business leaders, on the other hand, applauded the new direction in labor–management relations. Some nonunionized businesses voluntarily expanded benefits for their workers in hopes of reducing the appeal of both unionization and governmental welfare measures.

Political Pluralism

Economic growth also gained credit for producing political stability. After the Great Depression, the Second World War, and the Great Fear of the early Cold War

Highway Act of 1956 *Act that appropriated $25 billion for the construction of more than 40,000 miles of interstate highways over a 10-year period.*

THE QUEEN OF ABUNDANCE. *The double-store, frost-free refrigerator offered consumers an elegant display case for the new prepackaged and frozen food products that became available during the 1950s. Advertisements such as this one proclaimed that Americans had become a "people of plenty."*

period, the 1950s seemed an era of relative tranquility. Political life in America exhibited more stability than that in any other part of the Cold War world. An increasingly prosperous nation, most observers agreed, would mute social conflict and eventually solve major problems.

According to the dominant viewpoint, which political scientists called "pluralism" (or "interest-group pluralism"), U.S. politics featured a roughly equal bargaining process among well-organized interest groups. John Kenneth Galbraith coined the term "countervailing power" when claiming that labor unions, consumer lobbies, farm organizations, and other groups could check the desires of giant corporations. No single group could dictate terms to the others, celebrants of pluralism claimed, because so many interests felt securely empowered. Short-term conflicts over specific issues would never disappear, but supporters of the pluralist vision insisted that affluence could moderate political passions and point warring interests toward agreement. Pluralists shrugged off declining voting numbers by arguing that voter apathy actually reflected widespread satisfaction with how well the process of political pluralism worked.

A Religious People

Many observers expressed an analogous faith in religious pluralism. Congress, as part of the crusade against "atheistic communism," constructed a nondenominational prayer room on Capitol Hill; added the phrase "under God" to the Pledge of Allegiance; and declared the phrase "In God We Trust" the official national motto. Many Americans claimed that differing religious allegiances no longer divided people as much as in the past. President Eisenhower declared that "our government makes no sense unless it is founded in a deeply felt religious faith—and I don't care what it is."

Religious leaders echoed the theme of pluralism. Will Herberg's *Protestant-Catholic-Jew* (1955) argued that these three faiths were really "saying the same thing." The rabbi who headed the Jewish Chaplains Organization reassured Protestants and Catholics that they and their Jewish neighbors shared "the same rich heritage of the Old Testament." A 1954 survey claimed that more than 95 percent of the population identified with one of the three major faiths, and religious commentators praised the "Judeo-Christian tradition."

This tradition could also produce religious celebrities such as Baptist evangelist Billy Graham, who achieved superstar status during the 1950s. And while famous evangelists often identified their religious ideals with conservative causes, an emphasis on religious faith could be found across the political spectrum. For example, religious leaders provided very visible support for civil rights efforts.

DISCONTENTS OF AFFLUENCE

Critics challenged the celebrations of economic growth, political pluralism, and religious faith. They warned about the threat of conformity, the problems of young people, the dangers of mass culture, the evil of discrimination, and the effects of economic inequality.

Conformity in an Affluent Society

In *The Organization Man* (1956), sociologist William H. Whyte, Jr., indicted corporate culture for contributing to an unwanted by-product of affluence: conformity. Whyte saw ordinary corporate employees deferring to their bosses at the expense of their own wishes and values. Journalist Vance Packard's best seller *The Hidden Persuaders* (1957) criticized the advertising industry for encouraging conformist behavior. In *The Lonely Crowd* (1950), sociologist David Riesman wrote of a shift from an "inner-directed" culture, in which people looked to themselves and their families for their sense of identity and

FOCUS QUESTION

What kinds of social criticism did the general economic prosperity of the post-1953 decade help to highlight?

Betty Friedan *Author of* The Feminine Mystique *(1963) and founder of the National Organization for Women (1966).*

SPLIT-LEVEL LIVING.

SPLIT-LEVEL LIVING. *This 1960 cartoon, by the* Washington Post's *"Herblock" (Herbert Block), illustrates the growing critique of Eisenhower-era social policy. While suburbanites enjoy new affluence in a split-level home, public services and distressed people remain underfunded.*

QUICK REVIEW

CHARACTERISTICS OF THE "AGE OF AFFLUENCE" IN THE 1950S

- New consumer products, youth culture, and expanded mass culture

- Rising wages, benefits, and living standards, and steady employment for most male workers

- New system of interstate highways

- New lands for development opened by massive government-funded irrigation projects

- Emphasis on political and religious "pluralism"

- New concerns about conformity, restive youth, and mass culture

self-worth, to an "other-directed" one, in which people looked to others for approval. Riesman pointed to *Tootle, the Engine,* a popular children's book, to show how mass culture taught baby boomers conformist values. After Tootle shows a preference for jumping the rails, peer pressure from his community gets him "back on the tracks." If he follows lines laid down by others, Tootle learns, a bright future seems assured.

Critics such as Whyte, Packard, and Riesman invariably highlighted signs of conformity supposedly evident among middle-class men. **Betty Friedan** warned about a corresponding malaise among middle-class women who found themselves entrapped in a stultifying sphere of domestic obligations. A conformist "feminine mystique," Friedan wrote, stifled women's individuality and power.

Restive Youth

Another body of critical analysis targeted the culture of young people. The *Seduction of the Innocent* (1954), by the psychologist Frederick Wertham, blamed comic books featuring images of sex and violence for "mass-conditioning" children and stimulating social unrest. Responding to legislation by some U.S. cities and to calls for federal regulations, the comic book industry embraced self-censorship, and the "great comic book scare" faded away.

Other worrisome signs persisted. In 1954 Elvis Presley, a former truck driver from Memphis, rocked the pop music establishment with a string of "rock 'n' roll" hits on the tiny Sun record label. Presley's sensual, electric stage presence thrilled his young admirers and outraged critics. Presley and other youthful exponents of Fifties rock— including Buddy Holly from West Texas, Richard Valenzuela (Richie Valens) from East Los Angeles, Frankie Lymon from Spanish Harlem, and "Little Richard" (Penniman) from Georgia—leaped over cultural and ethnic barriers and shaped new musical forms from older ones, especially African American rhythm and blues and the "hillbilly" music of southern whites.

Guardians of more genteel cultural forms denounced rock 'n' roll as an assault on the very idea of music. Even its name brazenly appealed to raging teenage hormones. Religious groups denounced rock as the "Devil's music;" anticommunists detected a covert Red strategy to corrupt youth; and segregationists saw it as part of a plot to encourage "race-mixing." But rock 'n' rollers spoke to the concerns of their millions of young fans. The satirical "Charlie Brown" contrasted pieties about staying in school with the bleak educational opportunities open to many students. Chuck Berry sang of a terminally bored teenager riding around "with no particular place to go." This kind of implied social criticism anticipated the more overtly rebellious music of the 1960s.

At the same time, rock music and the larger youth culture of the 1950s could also merge into that era's general affluence. Record companies and Top-40 radio stations saw middle-class teenagers as a market segment worth targeting. They promoted performers who exalted the pursuit of "fun, fun, fun," which apparently required the latest clothes, automobiles, and records.

The Critique of Mass Culture

Concern about social conformity and youth culture merged into the wider mass culture critique of the 1950s. Cosmopolitan critics worried that "bad" art—such as comics and rock 'n' roll—would soon purge anything "good" from the cultural marketplace. They further warned that superficial imagery manufactured for a national audience could wipe out more vibrant local traditions.

Television, dominated by three large corporations (NBC, CBS, and ABC) and sustained by advertising revenue, provided a prominent target for this critique. Network television, critics argued, encouraged millions of passive viewers to retreat into unrealities such as a mythical Old West or the fake competition of TV quiz shows. They also disliked how "the boob tube" changed the fabric of everyday life. Architects rearranged living space so that the TV set could become the focal point of family gatherings. New products—the frozen TV dinner, the TV tray, *TV Guide* magazine—became extensions of television culture.

The mass culture that critics decried, however, was embedded within the economic system and pluralist political process they celebrated. If, for example, Congress legislated against "dangerous" comic books, its censorship might end up curtailing free expression. If local communities were to step in, the results might be even worse. The prospect of southern segregationists censoring civil rights literature hardly appealed to the cosmopolitan critics of mass culture. Their extensive critique seemed short on solutions and did nothing to halt the flood of products and programs aimed at an ever-expanding audience.

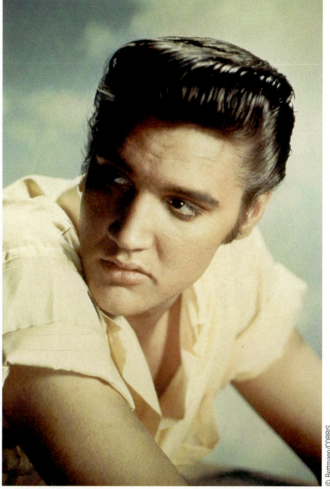

ELVIS PRESLEY. *A former truck driver from Memphis, "Elvis the Pelvis" drew upon blues, gospel, hillbilly, and pop music traditions to become the premier rock 'n' roll star of the 1950s.*

DEBATING THE ROLE OF GOVERNMENT

Although Eisenhower sometimes hinted that he favored rolling back the New and Fair Deals, he actually presided over a modest expansion of earlier initiatives: a broader Social Security system, a higher minimum wage, better unemployment benefits, and a new Department of Health, Education, and Welfare (HEW). Eisenhower liked to call his approach "modern Republicanism."

The New Conservatism

Eisenhower's brand of Republicanism angered members of a political movement eventually called the "new conservatism." This movement drew much of its energy from Republicans who conceded Eisenhower's popularity but questioned his commitment to conservative GOP principles.

FOCUS QUESTION

How did the post-1953 decade help to focus competing views of the role of government? What did the new conservatism advocate? What did advocates of more active government hope to accomplish?

Arizona Senator Barry Goldwater emerged as the key political spokesperson for the new conservatism. *The Conscience of a Conservative* (1960) summarized Goldwater's critique. By refusing to take stronger military measures against the Soviet Union and by not making "victory the goal" of U.S. policy, Eisenhower was likely endangering national security. Goldwater portrayed almost all domestic programs, including federal civil rights legislation, as grave threats to individual liberty and steps toward national bankruptcy. His conservatism proved especially appealing to the fiercely anticommunist "suburban warriors" from the Sunbelt states who focused on making sure that "outside" authorities could not infringe on local institutions and practices.

While Goldwater was pressing the GOP to reject Eisenhower's modern Republicanism, the author-publisher William F. Buckley, Jr., was framing a broad ideological platform for the new conservatism. In 1955, Buckley helped found the *National Review*, which avoided the anti-Semitism of some old-line conservatives and adopted an organizational strategy for the long run. To this end, conservatives established Young Americans for Freedom (YAF) in 1960, several years before similar college-based political organizations emerged on the political left.

Buckley's group adopted another long-term approach to building a conservative movement, "fusionism." The *National Review* fused three broad constituencies: "traditionalist" conservatives, who insisted that social stability depended on the educated, talented few, such as themselves, dominating the nation's institutions; "libertarians," who favored reducing the power of government; and staunch anticommunists, who endorsed unleashing U.S. military power against the Soviets.

The Case for a More Active Government

While a new conservatism argued for scaling back the domestic role of government, social activists criticized Eisenhower's reluctance to use the power of his office more forcefully. When unemployment rose during an economic downturn in 1958–1959, Keynesian economists ridiculed the president's commitment to a balanced budget. Other critics, while avoiding the rhetoric of conservatives such as Goldwater, still criticized Eisenhower's national security policies for their timidity. The 1957 Gaither Report, prepared by foreign policy analysts with ties to the defense industry, urged an immediate increase of about 25 percent in the Pentagon's budget.

Concerns about national security and calls for greater government spending also affected U.S. educational policies. Critics argued that American students were not keeping up with their Soviet counterparts and pressed for more funding for public schools. Simultaneously, the nation's leading universities sought greater federal aid for higher education, and prominent scientists implored the Defense Department to expand its support for scientific research. The case for increased spending suddenly became more compelling when, in October 1957, the Soviets launched the world's first artificial satellite—the 22-inch sphere, *Sputnik*.

After *Sputnik*, phrases such as "national security" and "national defense" cleared the way for federal money to flow more freely. The National Defense Education Act of 1958 funneled aid to college-level programs in science, engineering, foreign languages, and the social sciences. This act marked a milestone in overcoming congressional opposition to federal funding of education, especially from southerners who feared that federal aid could increase pressure for racial integration. Fear that the Soviets had gained superiority in satellite technology fueled a research and development effort overseen by a new National Aeronautics and Space Administration (NASA).

Sputnik First Soviet satellite sent into orbit around the earth in 1957.

Many hoped that domestic social welfare programs would become similar beneficiaries of increased federal spending. Michael Harrington wrote passionate essays about economic inequality. At least one-third of the nation's people—living in rural areas, small towns, and cities—barely subsisted in a land of supposed abundance. Avoiding detailed economic analysis, Harrington crafted dramatic stories about how a culture of poverty ravaged the health and spirit of people whose lives had been largely untouched by the economic growth of the post-Depression era.

NEW FRONTIERS, 1960–1963

By 1960, the time for translating some of the calls for a more active federal government into congressional legislation and executive orders seemed at hand. The off-year election of 1958 had not only deposed some conservative Republican stalwarts but also emboldened public officials sympathetic to more energetic government. One of these was **John Fitzgerald Kennedy (JFK)**.

The Election of 1960

A wealthy, politically ambitious father had groomed John F. Kennedy for the White House. The young Kennedy graduated from Harvard, won military honors as a naval officer during the Second World War, became a representative from Massachusetts in 1946, and captured a Senate seat in 1952. Kennedy became better known for his social life than his command of legislative details, but he parlayed charm and youthful good looks into political stardom. His 1953 marriage to Jacqueline Bouvier added another dash of glamour. A favorite of the media herself, Jackie won plaudits for her good taste, stylish dress, and use of several languages.

After John Kennedy narrowly missed winning the vice presidential nomination in 1956, he took aim at the top spot on the 1960 Democratic ticket. Skilled campaigning, along with a talented staff and his family's vast wealth, helped Kennedy overwhelm his Democratic challengers, Senators Hubert Humphrey of Minnesota and Lyndon Johnson of Texas. By pledging to separate his Catholic religion from his politics and by confronting those who appealed to anti-Catholic prejudice, Kennedy defused the religious issue that had doomed the candidacy of Al Smith in 1928 (see Chapter 24).

Vice President Richard Nixon, running for the Republicans, spent much of the 1960 presidential campaign on the defensive. He seemed off-balance during the first of several televised debates in which a relaxed, tanned Kennedy emerged, according to surveys of TV viewers, with a clear victory over a pale, nervous Nixon. (Radio listeners awarded Nixon no worse than a draw.) Despite chronic and severe health problems which his entourage concealed, Kennedy projected vigor and energy, if not experience.

Kennedy's 1960 campaign highlighted issues from the 1950s that, taken together, became the agenda for his New Frontier. Although Senator Kennedy's civil rights record had been mixed, candidate Kennedy declared support for new legislation and, in an important symbolic act, dispatched aides to Georgia to assist Martin Luther King, Jr., who was facing jail time for a minor traffic violation. He also endorsed new social programs to rebuild rural communities, increase educational opportunities, and improve urban conditions.

FOCUS QUESTION

How did the foreign and domestic policies championed by the administration of John F. Kennedy both accept and reject those embraced by the Eisenhower administration during the 1950s? What policy changes did the early 1960s bring?

John F. Kennedy (JFK)
President from 1961 to 1963; noted for youthful charm and vigor, and his "New Frontier" vision for America.

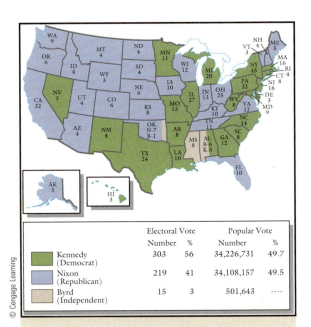

© Cengage Learning

		Electoral Vote		Popular Vote	
		Number	%	Number	%
(green)	Kennedy (Democrat)	303	56	34,226,731	49.7
(blue)	Nixon (Republican)	219	41	34,108,157	49.5
(tan)	Byrd (Independent)	15	3	501,643	----

Map 28.1 Presidential Election, 1960. *In one of the closest elections in American history in terms of the popular vote, Kennedy narrowly outpolled Nixon. Kennedy's more commanding victory in the electoral vote produced some discussion about the consequences if the Electoral College one day produced a president who had failed to carry the popular vote—a situation that did indeed occur in the election of 2000.*

flexible response *Kennedy's approach to the Cold War that aimed to provide a wide variety of military and nonmilitary methods to confront communist movements.*

Bay of Pigs *Site of an ill-fated 1961 invasion of Cuba by a U.S.-trained force that attempted to overthrow the government of Fidel Castro.*

Kennedy's New Frontier included two other central issues rooted in the critical culture of the 1950s: promoting greater economic growth and conducting a more aggressive foreign policy. Kennedy suggested using tax cuts and deficit spending to juice the economy. He criticized Eisenhower for failing to rid the hemisphere of Castro and for allowing a "missile gap" to develop in the arms race with the Soviet Union. By spending more on national security, Kennedy claimed, he could create a **"flexible response"** against communism, especially in the Third World.

Kennedy defeated Nixon by only about 100,000 popular votes, and his victory in the Electoral College rested on razor-thin margins in several states. JFK's triumph owed a great debt to his vice presidential running mate, Lyndon Baines Johnson, whose regional appeal helped the Democratic ticket carry the Deep South and his home state of Texas.

Supporters of the new president forgot about the closeness of his election as JFK and Jackie, already first-name celebrities, riveted media attention on the White House. Kennedy's inaugural featured designer clothing, a poignant appearance by the aged poet Robert Frost, and an oft-quoted speech in which JFK challenged people to "ask not what your country can do for you; ask what you can do for your country."

Foreign Policy

Implementing flexible response gained the new president's immediate attention. Although Secretary of Defense Robert McNamara quickly found that the alleged missile gap never existed, the Kennedy administration boosted the defense budget anyway. It supported military assistance programs, propaganda agencies, and covert-action plans. In one of his most popular initiatives, the president created the Peace Corps, a volunteer program that sent Americans, especially young people, to nations around the world to work on development projects that might undercut communism's appeal.

Eisenhower's effort to reorient U.S. Latin American policy away from dictators and toward socioeconomic programs was repackaged as Kennedy's "Alliance for Progress." Unveiled in spring 1961 in hopes of checking the spread of Castro-like insurgencies, the Alliance promised $20 billion in loans over a 10-year period to Latin American countries that would undertake land reform and economic development measures. Most Latin Americans judged Kennedy's Alliance, which underestimated obstacles to social and economic change, as more symbolic than substantive.

Cuba and Berlin

The worst fiasco of the Kennedy presidency, an ill-conceived 1961 CIA mission against Cuba, also had its roots in the Eisenhower administration. The CIA had been planning a secret invasion to oust Castro, and Kennedy, overriding the doubts of key advisers, agreed to go forward. On April 17, 1961, however, when U.S.-trained forces (mainly anticommunist Cuban exiles) landed at the Bahia de Cochinas (**Bay of Pigs**) on the southern coast of Cuba, the expected popular uprising failed to materialize. Instead, forces loyal to Castro quickly captured the invaders. Kennedy rejected any additional steps, including the air strikes the Cuban exiles had expected, and, initially, denied any U.S. involvement in the Bay of Pigs invasion. But the CIA's role quickly became public knowledge, and anti-U.S sentiment swept across much of Latin America. Castro tightened his grip over Cuban life and strengthened his ties to the Soviet Union. Kennedy responded by calling the Bay of Pigs invasion a mistake—and by devising a new covert program, "Operation Mongoose," to destabilize Cuba's economy and, in concert with organized crime figures, to kill the Cuban leader.

Tensions between the United States and the Soviet Union increased as well. After Kennedy refused a proposal from Khrushchev to abandon West Berlin, the communist regime in East Germany, in August 1961, began to erect first a barbed-wire fence and then a concrete barrier to separate East from West Berlin. This "Berlin Wall" became a powerful symbol of communist repression.

Superpower confrontation escalated to a potentially lethal level during the **Cuban Missile Crisis** of October 1962. The Soviet Union, responding to pleas from Castro, sent armaments to Cuba. After U-2 spy planes revealed missile-launching sites in Cuba, the Kennedy administration declared it would never allow the Soviet Union to place nuclear warheads so close to U.S. soil. It demanded that the Soviets dismantle the missile silos and turn back supply ships heading for Cuba. Kennedy ordered the navy to "quarantine" Cuba, and the Strategic Air Command went on full alert for a possible nuclear conflict. Both sides also began frantic, secret diplomatic maneuvers to forestall such a catastrophe.

The showdown ended after 13 anxious days. On October 28, 1962, Khrushchev ordered the Soviet missiles in Cuba dismantled and the supply ships brought home; Kennedy promised not to invade Cuba and secretly assured Khrushchev that he would complete a previously ordered withdrawal of U.S. missiles from Turkey. When Soviet archives opened in the mid-1990s, Americans learned that the confrontation had been even more dangerous than imagined. Unknown to the Kennedy administration in 1962, the Soviets had already placed tactical nuclear weapons, which could have reached U.S. targets, in Cuba.

The Cuban Missile Crisis underscored the risk of nuclear conflict and made the superpowers more cautious. To prevent a future confrontation or an accident, they established a direct telephone "hotline" between Moscow and Washington, D.C.

Southeast Asia and Flexible Response

In Southeast Asia, Kennedy continued the effort to preserve a noncommunist state in South Vietnam, but the odds against keeping a pro-U.S. government there only seemed to grow longer over time. Opposition to the regime of Ngo Dinh Diem had coalesced in the National Liberation Front (NLF). Formed in December 1960, the NLF included noncommunist groups that resented Diem's dependence on the United States; communists who demanded more extensive land reform; political leaders fed up with Diem's corruption and cronyism; and groups beholden to Ho Chi Minh's communist government in the North. North Vietnam began sending supplies and troops to the South to support the NLF.

The Kennedy administration saw Vietnam as the crucial test case for flexible response. It dispatched elite U.S. troops, the Green Berets, who were trained in "counterinsurgency" tactics. It also sent teams of social scientists, charged with "nation building," to consult on economic reforms and internal security. Finally, JFK sent U.S. combat troops. These forces, numbering nearly 24,000 by late 1963, would supposedly only advise, rather than actively fight alongside, South Vietnam's forces.

QUICK REVIEW

KENNEDY AND THE COLD WAR

- Emphasized foreign affairs over domestic issues
- Projected image of a young and vigorous new leader
- Authorized ill-fated Bay of Pigs invasion
- Steered careful diplomatic responses during Cuban Missile Crisis
- Developed "flexible response" as new way of fighting communism abroad
- Entangled the United States in South Vietnam

Cuban Missile Crisis *Serious Cold War confrontation between the United States and the Soviet Union in October 1962 over the installation of Soviet missiles in Cuba.*

South Vietnam still lacked a credible government. Diem's decision, in May 1963, to fire on Buddhist demonstrators in the city of Hue prompted a series of protests. Several Buddhist priests committed suicide by setting fire to their robes. The Kennedy administration recognized these self-immolations as a sign of the deep-seated opposition to Diem—and as a public relations disaster. It signaled to South Vietnam's military that U.S. support for Diem was nearing its end.

DOMESTIC POLICY-MAKING

Kennedy hesitated to follow up on his campaign promise to increase federal spending to speed economic growth. He feared that budget deficits might alienate fiscal conservatives and business leaders. In 1962, however, the White House asked Congress to lower tax rates as a means of promoting economic growth. The economy had continued its rebound from its downturn of 1957–1958, but Kennedy argued that lower tax rates for everyone, along with special deductions for businesses that invested in new plants and equipment, would further boost growth. Despite opposition from Democrats who thought the proposal favored corporations and the wealthy, the tax bill slowly moved through Congress.

On social welfare issues, the Kennedy administration proposed a higher minimum wage and new urban rebuilding programs. It also supported the Area Redevelopment Bill of 1961, which called for directing federal grants and loans to impoverished areas such as Appalachia, the 13-state region running along the Appalachian Mountain chain, from southern New York to northern Mississippi.

THE POLITICS OF GENDER

The 1950s and early 1960s saw significant changes in how and where people lived and worked. This era produced especially important changes in everyday gender politics.

The New Suburbs and Gender Politics

In middle-class homes, especially in the new suburbs, women discovered just how "liberating" consumer technology might be. The time that women spent on domestic duties was not reduced so much as shifted to new activities requiring new household gadgets like automatic clothes washers and more powerful vacuum cleaners. Life in the new suburbs was structured by a broad pattern of "separate spheres": a public sphere of work and politics dominated by men, and a private sphere of housework and child care reserved for women. With few employment opportunities in the new suburbs, mothers spent considerable time tending to their baby-boomer children. Without mothers or grandmothers living close by, young suburban mothers turned, of necessity, to child-care manuals for advice. **Dr. Benjamin Spock**'s *Baby and Child Care,* first published in 1946, sold millions of copies. Like earlier advice books, Spock's assigned virtually all child-care duties to women and implied that the family and the nation itself depended on how well mothers performed.

Dr. Benjamin Spock
Pediatrician who wrote Baby and Child Care *(1946), the most widely used child-rearing book during the baby-boom years.*

Women who sought careers outside of the home and marriage risked being labeled as maladjusted and deviant. Versions of this message appeared nearly everywhere. Even the nation's prestigious women's colleges assumed their graduates would pursue men and marriage. Popular magazines, psychology literature, and pop-culture imagery suggested that wives and mothers held the keys to social stability. Women who desired alternative arrangements, either in their work or their sexual preferences, needed to be pressured, much as Tootle the Engine, to return to the straight and narrow.

Competing portraits painted a more complicated picture of gender arrangements. Most men told researchers that they preferred an "active partner" to a "submissive, stay-at-home" wife. Popular TV shows, such as *Father Knows Best* and *Leave It to Beaver*, suggested that fathers should be more engaged in family life than they seemed to be. Parenting literature emphasized "family togetherness," partly in response to what cultural historians have seen as an incipient "male revolt" against the "male breadwinner role." Hugh Hefner's *Playboy* magazine, which debuted in 1953, ridiculed men who neglected their own happiness in order to support a wife and children as suckers rather than saints.

Signs of Women's Changing Roles

Despite media images of homebound wives and mothers, female employment, even among married women, rose steadily as jobs expanded in the clerical and service sectors. In 1948, about 25 percent of married mothers held jobs outside the home; at the end of the 1950s nearly 40 percent did. With the 1960 introduction of a new method of oral contraception, the birth control pill, women could exercise greater control over family planning and career decisions—and over decisions about their own sexual behavior. By 1964, one-quarter of the couples who used contraception relied on "The Pill." At the same time, activists began to press for an end to anti-abortion laws that restricted the ability of women to find legal and relatively safe ways to terminate pregnancies.

Employment opportunities still remained circumscribed. Virtually all of the nation's nurses, telephone operators, secretaries, and elementary school teachers were women. Historically, pay scales in these areas lagged behind those for men in comparable fields. Jobs for women in unionized sectors remained rare, and as the number of low-paid jobs for women expanded during the 1950s, better-paid professional opportunities actually narrowed. Medical, law, and other professional schools admitted lower percentages of women than in the past. When Sandra Day (who would later become U.S. Supreme Court Justice Sandra Day O'Connor) graduated with honors from a prestigious law school during the 1950s, not a single private firm offered her a job.

Although employers still invoked the "family wage" to justify higher pay for men, more women were trying to support a family on their own paychecks. This was especially true for women of color. Recognizing that images of domesticity hardly fit the lives of many African American women, *Ebony* magazine celebrated black women who combined success in parenting and at work.

A New Women's Movement

The seeds of a resurgent women's movement were also being sown between 1953 and 1963. All across the political spectrum, women began speaking out on contemporary issues. The energy of women such as Phyllis Schlafly helped fuel the new conservatism. African American activists such as Bernice Johnson

Reagon (whose work with the Freedom Singers combined music and social activism) and Fannie Lou Hamer (who spearheaded the organization of a racially integrated Freedom Democratic Party in Mississippi) fought discrimination based on both race and gender. Women union leaders pushed for greater employment opportunities and more equitable work environments. Chicana farmworkers became key figures in union-organizing efforts in California. Women also played a central role in protests, through the Committee for a Sane Nuclear Policy (SANE) and the Women's Strike for Peace, against the U.S.–Soviet arms race. During Kennedy's final year in office, Betty Friedan published *The Feminine Mystique*. Widely credited with helping to revive organized feminist activity in the United States, Friedan's book drew on her own social criticism from the late 1950s and articulated the dissatisfactions that many middle-class women felt about the narrow confines of domestic life and the lack of public roles available to them.

To address women's concerns, Kennedy appointed a Presidential Commission on the Status of Women, chaired by Eleanor Roosevelt. The commission issued a report that documented discrimination against women in employment and wages, and Kennedy responded with a presidential order to eliminate gender discrimination within the federal civil service. He also supported the Equal Pay Act of 1963, which made it a federal crime for employers to pay lower wages to women who did the same work as men.

THE EXPANDING CIVIL RIGHTS MOVEMENTS, 1953–1963

FOCUS QUESTION

How did expanding civil rights movements raise new political issues and visions during the 1950s and early 1960s? How did the nation's political and social institutions respond?

When Dwight Eisenhower took office in 1953, the Supreme Court was preparing to rehear a legal challenge to racially segregated educational systems. The NAACP and its chief legal strategist, Thurgood Marshall, spearheaded the case. Before the rehearing took place, Eisenhower appointed Earl Warren, a former Republican governor of California, as chief justice.

The *Brown* Cases, 1954–1955

The Supreme Court case popularly known as "the *Brown* decision" actually included a series of constitutional rulings, the *Brown* cases. In 1954, Chief Justice Warren wrote a unanimous opinion (in *Brown v. Board of Education* of *Topeka*) declaring that state-mandated segregation of public schools violated the constitutional right of African American students to equal protection of the law. A companion case decided the same day (*Bolling v. Sharpe*) outlawed segregated schools in the District of Columbia. Although these decisions technically applied only to schools, they suggested that other segregated public facilities could no longer survive constitutional challenge. In 1955, though, yet another Supreme Court decision, known as "*Brown II*," decreed that school desegregation should not go into effect immediately; it could, instead, move forward "with all deliberate speed."

Implementing the *Brown* cases challenged the nation's political, social, and cultural institutions. The politics of civil rights sometimes seemed focused on the South, but demographic changes helped make the civil rights movement much more than a regional phenomenon.

Brown v. Board of Education *1954 case in which the U.S. Supreme Court unanimously overruled the "separate but equal" doctrine and held that segregation in the public schools violated the principle of equal protection under the law.*

During the 1950s the South became more like the rest of the country. Network television penetrated the region. Machines were displacing predominantly black field workers. The absence of strong labor unions and the presence of favorable tax laws attracted national chain stores and northern-based businesses.

Meanwhile, the racial composition of cities in the West, Midwest, and Northeast became more like that of the South. In 1940, more than three-quarters of the nation's African Americans lived in the South. After the Second World War, many African Americans left the rural South and became important political constituencies in northern urban areas, where Democrats and Republicans generally supported efforts to end racial discrimination. As more African Americans voted Democratic, however, the GOP gained ground among white voters in the South and in the new suburban neighborhoods, especially in the Middle and Far West.

A relatively broad movement to end segregation and racial discrimination emerged, especially among African Americans, in virtually every northern and western city. These urban-based movements employed a variety of tactics, such as "shop where you can work" campaigns, which urged consumers to patronize only businesses that would employ them. They also tried to bring more black workers into the union movement and the public-service sector.

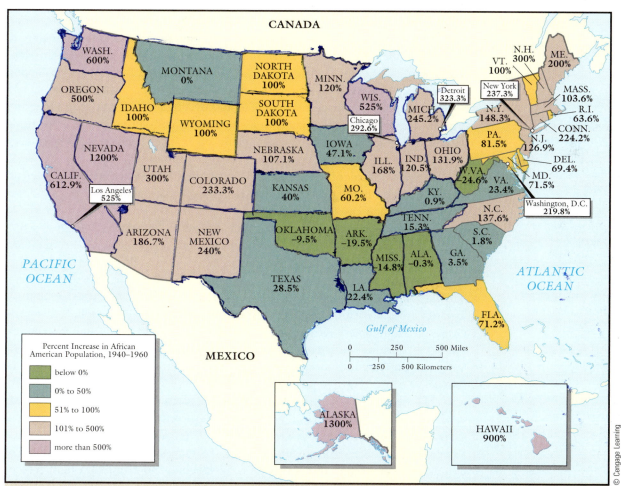

Map 28.2 Shifts in African American Population Patterns, 1940–1960. *During and after the Second World War, large numbers of African Americans left the rural South and migrated to new locations. Which states had the largest percentage of outmigration? Which saw the greatest percentage of population increase? How might this migration have affected American life?*

As African Americans mounted new attacks on segregation and discrimination in the South, white segregationists pledged "massive resistance" to the *Brown* decisions. One hundred members of Congress signed a "Southern Manifesto" in 1956 that condemned the desegregation rulings as a "clear abuse of judicial power" and offered support for any state that intended "to resist forced integration by any lawful means."

Defiance went beyond the courtroom. White vigilantes unfurled the banners of the Ku Klux Klan and formed new racist organizations, such as the White Citizens Council. People who worked in the civil rights cause constantly risked injury and death. Racial tensions escalated. In August 1955, two white Mississippians murdered 14-year-old Emmett Till, a visitor from Chicago, because they thought he had acted "disrespectful" toward a white woman. Mamie Till Bradley insisted that her son's death not remain a private incident. She demanded that his maimed corpse be displayed for "the whole world to see" and that his killers be punished. When their case came to trial, an all-white Mississippi jury quickly found the two men—who would subsequently confess their crime to a magazine reporter—not guilty.

The Montgomery Bus Boycott

The southern civil rights movement increasingly supplemented legal maneuvering with direct action. Following an earlier, partially successful 1953 campaign to desegregate the transportation system in Baton Rouge, Louisiana, activists in Montgomery, Alabama, raised their sights. After police arrested **Rosa Parks** for defying an ordinance that required segregated seating on municipal buses, Montgomery's black community demanded desegregation, boycotted public transportation, and organized carpools as alternative transit. Joining with Rosa Parks, a longtime bastion of the local NAACP chapter, many other black women in Montgomery helped coordinate the complicated, months-long boycott.

After a campaign lasting more than a year, the **Montgomery bus boycott** succeeded. The Supreme Court declared segregation of public buses to be unconstitutional, forcing city officials, saddled with financial losses and legal defeats, to end Montgomery's separatist transit policy. Events in Montgomery suggested that black activists could effectively mobilize—and then organize—community resources to fight against racial discrimination.

The bus boycott also vaulted **Dr. Martin Luther King, Jr.,** one of its leaders, into the national spotlight. Born and educated in Atlanta, with a doctorate in theology from Boston University, King and other black ministers followed up the victory in Montgomery by forming the Southern Christian Leadership Conference (SCLC). In addition to demanding desegregated public facilities, the SCLC sought to organize an ongoing social-political movement that would work for permanent change.

The young, male ministers in SCLC sought assistance across generational and gender divides, enlisting tactical advice from Bayard Rustin and the organizational skills of Ella Baker, another veteran organizer. They also incurred the unwelcome attention of J. Edgar Hoover and the FBI. To monitor King's activities, the FBI illegally recorded many of his private conversations and clamped a tight web of surveillance around his every move.

King and the SCLC relied on civil disobedience to obtain change. According to Dr. King, nonviolent direct action would dramatize, through both word and deed, the evil of racial discrimination. King's powerful presence and religiously rooted rhetoric carried the message of civil rights to the nation—and the world.

Rosa Parks *African American seamstress in Montgomery, Alabama, who, after refusing to give up her bus seat to a white man, was arrested and fined. Her protest sparked a bus boycott that broadened national support for the civil rights cause.*

Montgomery bus boycott *Political protest campaign mounted in 1955 to oppose the city's policy of racial segregation on its public transit system. The Supreme Court ultimately declared segregation on public transit unconstitutional.*

Dr. Martin Luther King, Jr. *African American clergyman who advocated nonviolent social change and shaped the civil rights movement of the 1950s and 1960s.*

The Politics of Civil Rights: From the Local to the Global

All across the country, civil rights activities went forward. Shortly after the conclusion of the Montgomery bus boycott, New York City passed the nation's first "open housing" ordinance, a model for other local and state measures aimed at ending racial discrimination in the sale and rental of homes and apartments. (White homeowners in those urban and older suburban neighborhoods where African Americans or Latinos might hope to buy or rent instead adopted the same exclusionary strategies used so effectively by their counterparts in the new suburbs.) Outside the South, civil rights groups won legislation to outlaw discrimination in hiring. In 1958, for example, a labor–civil rights coalition in California, joining under slogans such as "Fight Sharecropper Wages," defeated an anti-union right-to-work proposal they said threatened to drive down pay for all workers.

Political institutions in Washington, D.C., felt similar pressure to act on civil rights. With southern segregationists, all members of the Democratic majority, holding key posts on Capitol Hill, antidiscrimination measures faced formidable obstacles. Nevertheless, Congress did pass its first civil rights measure in more than 80 years. The **Civil Rights Act of 1957** expedited lawsuits by African Americans who claimed abridgement of their right to vote. It also created a Commission on Civil Rights, an advisory body empowered to study alleged violations and recommend remedies. In 1960, with the crucial support of Senator Lyndon Johnson, a second civil rights act added more procedures to safeguard voting rights. These measures became law against fierce opposition from southern Democrats and conservative Republicans such as Barry Goldwater.

President Eisenhower initially hesitated to use his executive power to aid the civil rights movement. Although he supported the Civil Rights Act of 1957, he saw the fight against segregation as a slow process, and he doubted that federal power could change the attitudes of people opposed to integration. In 1957, however, events in Little Rock, Arkansas, forced Eisenhower to enforce a federal court decree ordering the desegregation of the city's Central High School. Orval Faubus, the state's segregationist governor, promised to prevent black students from entering the school building and deployed the National Guard to block them. Confronting this direct challenge to national authority, Eisenhower took command of the National Guard and augmented it with members of the U.S. Army. Black students, escorted by armed troops, finally entered Central High. The primary issue at stake, Eisenhower insisted, was a state's defiance of federal law rather than school desegregation.

The confrontation in Little Rock underscored the international, Cold War dimension of civil rights politics in the United States. Washington often found itself on the defensive when foreign critics pointed to the U.S. record on civil rights. The Soviet Union delighted in telling people, particularly in the Third World, how racial discrimination showed "the façade of the so-called 'American democracy.'" When the U.S. Supreme Court, in *Cooper v. Aaron* (1958), unanimously invalidated an Arkansas law intended to block integration, the Eisenhower administration's global informational campaign stressed America's support for liberty and equality.

The Politics of American Indian Policy

The Eisenhower administration also struggled with its policy toward American Indians. It attempted to implement two programs, **Termination and Relocation**, already under way before it took office. Termination called for an end to the status of Indians as "wards of the United States" and a grant of all the "rights

Civil Rights Act of 1957 *First civil rights act since Reconstruction; aimed at securing voting rights for African Americans in the South.*

Termination and Relocation *Policies designed to assimilate American Indians by terminating tribal status and relocating individuals to cities removed from their reservations.*

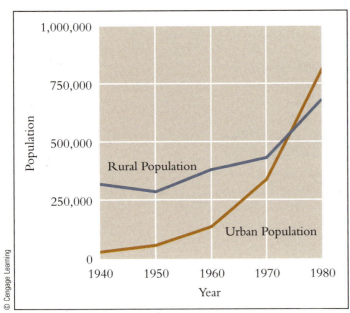

TOTAL URBAN AND RURAL INDIAN POPULATION IN THE UNITED STATES, 1940–1980

© Cengage Learning

and privileges pertaining to American citizenship." It sought to abolish reservations, liquidate tribal assets, and curtail the social services offered by the Bureau of Indian Affairs (BIA). Under the Relocation program, which had begun in 1951, Indians were encouraged to leave rural reservations and seek jobs in urban areas. Proponents of Termination and Relocation insisted that American Indians could easily be assimilated into the mainstream of U.S. life.

The initiatives quickly failed. As several tribes were terminated during the 1950s almost 12,000 people lost their status as tribal members, and the bonds of communal life for many Indians grew weaker. Land once held by tribes fell into the hands of commercial developers. Indians from terminated tribes lost both their exemption from state taxation and social services provided by the BIA. They gained little in return. Relocation went no better. Most relocated Indians found only low-paying, dead-end jobs and discrimination.

American Indian activists and their supporters mobilized against Termination and Relocation. By 1957, their efforts forced the government to scale back the initial timetable, which had called for liquidating every tribe within five years. In 1960, the party platforms of both the Republicans and Democrats repudiated Termination, and in 1962 the policy was stopped. But the Relocation program continued, and by 1967 almost half of the nation's Indians lived in relocation cities. This policy neither touched the deep-rooted problems that many Indians confronted, including a life expectancy only two-thirds that of whites, nor provided significantly better employment or education opportunities.

Spanish-Speaking Communities and Civil Rights

Millions of Spanish-speaking people, many recently arrived in the United States, also mobilized in order to realize the nation's rhetorical commitment to liberty and equality. Puerto Ricans began moving in larger numbers from their island commonwealth to the mainland in the 1950s. New York City's Puerto Rican population, for example, was nearly 100 times greater by the early 1960s than it had been before the Second World War. Officially U.S. citizens, Puerto Ricans organized against the discrimination they faced in housing and jobs. The Puerto Rican–Hispanic Leadership Forum, organized in 1957, presaged the emergence of groups that looked more to social and economic conditions—and, ultimately, greater political clout—in the United States than to cultural affinities with Puerto Rico.

Spanish-speaking people from Mexico continued to move to California and the Southwest. In 1940, Mexican Americans had been the most rural of all the major ethnic groups; by 1950, more than 65 percent of Mexican Americans lived in urban areas, a figure that would climb to 85 percent during the 1960s. Mexican Americans were becoming an important political force in many southwestern cities.

Beginning in 1942 and continuing until 1967, the U.S. government sponsored the *bracero* (or farmhand) program, which brought nearly five million Mexicans northward to fill agricultural jobs. Many *braceros* and their families remained in the United States after their work contracts expired. Legal immigrants from Mexico joined them, as did undocumented immigrants, who became targets of a government dragnet called "Operation Wetback." ("Wetback" was a term of derision, implying a swim across the Rio Grande River to reach the United States.) During a five-year period the government claimed to have rounded up and deported to Mexico nearly four million undocumented immigrants. This operation, critics charged, helped stigmatize even U.S. citizens of Mexican heritage and justify discriminatory treatment.

As a result, civil rights groups representing Mexican Americans intensified earlier mobilization efforts. Labor organizers sought higher wages and better working conditions, even as the FBI labeled their efforts "communist inspired." Civil rights organizations such as the League of United Latin American Citizens (LULAC) and the Unity League sought to desegregate schools and other public facilities. Lawyers for these groups faced a strategic dilemma, since most states classified persons whose ancestors came from Mexico as legally "white." As earlier cases such as *Westminster* had shown (see Chapter 27), school officials in states such as California and Texas segregated students of Mexican descent on the basis of real and alleged "language deficiencies" rather than on "race." The "other white" legal status of Mexican Americans complicated the ability of organizations to frame court challenges based on precedents involving "white-against-black" discrimination.

Urban-Suburban Issues

The growth of suburbia during the 1950s helped to highlight urban issues, many of them related to changing racial patterns. Adopting a policy called **redlining**, many banks and loan institutions denied funds for homebuyers and businesses in areas that were labeled "decaying" or "marginal" because they contained aging buildings, dense populations, and growing numbers of people of non-European descent. The Federal Housing Administration (FHA) and other governmental agencies channeled most lending toward the newer suburbs. "Urban renewal" programs, authorized by the Housing Act of 1949 (see Chapter 27), often seemed aimed at "urban removal." Although the law called for "a feasible method for the temporary relocation" of persons displaced, developers generally ignored the requirement.

Plans for federally built public housing also faltered, as suburban homeowners used their political clout and zoning laws to freeze out government-sponsored housing projects. Private housing interests lobbied to limit the number of public units actually constructed in urban areas. Originally conceived as short-term alternatives for families who would soon move to their own homes, publicly built facilities became stigmatized as "the projects," permanent housing of last resort for people with chronically low incomes.

New Forms of Direct Action, 1960–1963

In early 1960, African American students at North Carolina A&T College in Greensboro sat down at a drugstore lunch counter and politely asked to be served in the same manner as white customers. This was the beginning of the **sit-in movement,** a new phase of civil rights activism. In both the South and the North, young demonstrators staged nonviolent sit-ins at restaurants, bus and train stations, and other public facilities. Singing anthems such as "We Shall Overcome" to inspire solidarity, the sit-in movement encouraged further activism. In 1961, interracial activists from CORE and the **Student Nonviolent Coordinating Committee (SNCC),** a student group that emerged from the sit-in movement, risked racist retaliation by reviving a form of direct action that CORE had first tried in the 1940s: "freedom

redlining *Refusal by banks and loan associations to grant loans for homebuying and business expansion in neighborhoods that contained aging buildings, dense populations, and growing numbers of nonwhites.*

sit-in movement *Activity that challenged legal segregation by demanding that blacks have the same access to public facilities as whites. These nonviolent demonstrations were staged at restaurants, bus and train stations, and other public places.*

Student Nonviolent Coordinating Committee (SNCC) *Interracial civil rights organization formed by young people involved in the sit-in movement that later adopted a direct-action approach to fighting segregation.*

rides" across the South. The **freedom riders** challenged the Kennedy administration to enforce federal court decisions that had declared state laws requiring segregation on interstate buses (and in bus stations) to be unconstitutional.

Although Kennedy had talked about new civil rights legislation, he initially tried to placate the segregationist wing of his Democratic Party. Grassroots activism forced his administration into action. It dispatched U.S. marshals and National Guard troops to protect the freedom riders and to help integrate educational institutions in the Deep South, including the Universities of Mississippi and Alabama. In November 1962, Kennedy issued the long-promised executive order that banned racial discrimination in federally financed housing. The following February he sent Congress a civil rights bill that called for speedier trials in cases involving challenges to racial discrimination in voting.

Events in the South grew still more violent. In 1963, racial conflict convulsed Birmingham, Alabama. White police officers unleashed dogs and turned high-pressure water hoses on African Americans, including young children, who were seeking to desegregate public facilities. Four young girls were later murdered (and 20 people injured) when white supremacists bombed Birmingham's Sixteenth Street Baptist Church, a center of the local civil rights campaign. After thousands of African Americans rallied in protest—and two more children were killed, this time by police officers—the Kennedy administration moved to staunch the bloodletting.

The determination of civil rights activists created a real-life drama that played to the entire world on television—and made the United States look bad in the process. The president insisted that racial violence was "weakening the respect with which the rest of the world regards us," but the White House still hoped it might influence the direction and pace of change. It crafted legislation designed to dampen the enthusiasm for civil rights demonstrations, calling for a ban against racial discrimination in public facilities and for new measures to protect the voting rights of African Americans in the South. When the administration recognized that its legislative proposals would not derail a March on Washington for Jobs and Freedom sponsored by a coalition of civil rights and labor organizations planned for the late summer of 1963, it belatedly endorsed the event.

freedom riders *Members of interracial groups who traveled the South on buses to test a series of federal court decisions declaring segregation on buses and in waiting rooms to be unconstitutional.*

RACIAL CONFLICT IN BIRMINGHAM. *Images such as this 1963 photograph of a confrontation in Birmingham, Alabama, in which segregationists turned dogs on youthful demonstrators, helped rally public support for civil rights legislation. Events in Birmingham, however, also presaged the increasingly violent clashes that would punctuate the efforts to end racial discrimination.*

AP Images/Bill Hudson

On August 28, 1963, an integrated group of more than 200,000 people marched through the nation's capital to the Lincoln Memorial. There, Martin Luther King, Jr., delivered his famous "I Have a Dream" speech. Speakers generally applauded Kennedy's latest initiatives but urged a broader agenda, including a higher minimum wage and a federal program to guarantee new jobs. Well-organized and smoothly run, the event received overwhelmingly favorable coverage from the national media and put even greater political pressure on the White House and Congress to lend a hand to the movement.

NOVEMBER 1963

As fall turned to winter in 1963, the United States confronted major policy issues. They had deep historical roots but now carried special urgency.

Policy Choices

The Kennedy administration continued to puzzle over how to recast Eisenhower's containment policy and execute its own flexible-response approach in Vietnam. U.S. officials gave disgruntled South Vietnamese military officers the green light to orchestrate the overthrow of Diem's regime. On November 2, 1963, Diem was routed from his presidential palace and—despite assurances to the contrary from the coup's leaders—murdered. This coup, which brought a military regime to power in Saigon, bred even greater political instability.

There were also domestic political dilemmas. Kennedy's tax bill was languishing in Congress. On the civil rights front, the administration renewed efforts to mobilize its political resources on behalf of long-promised congressional legislation. Recognizing that provisions to lessen discrimination in housing would never pass, White House strategists pondered how best to use federal power to eliminate state-sanctioned segregation in the South and to advance a "fair employment" agenda everywhere.

The Assassination of John F. Kennedy

On November 22, 1963, the president was shot dead as his presidential motorcade moved through Dallas, Texas. Vice President Lyndon Johnson, who had accompanied Kennedy to Texas, took the oath of office and rushed back to Washington. Equally quickly, the Dallas police arrested Lee Harvey Oswald and pegged him as JFK's assassin. Oswald had vague ties to organized crime; had once lived in the Soviet Union; and had a bizarre set of political affiliations, including shadowy ones with groups interested in Cuba. He declared his innocence but never faced trial. Jack Ruby, a Dallas nightclub owner, killed Oswald on national television, while the alleged gunman was in police custody. An investigation by a special commission headed by Chief Justice Earl Warren concluded that both Oswald and Ruby had acted alone.

Kennedy's life and presidency remain topics of historical debate and tabloid-style speculation. His assassination still provokes conspiracy theories and controversies. Researchers have provided new details about his poor health, reliance on exotic medications, and dalliances with women—all of which were kept from the public at the time. Historians continue to debate what JFK might have done in Vietnam and on the domestic front had he won the 1964 presidential election.

FOCUS QUESTION

What were the most important issues left unsettled at Kennedy's death?

HISTORY THROUGH FILM

JFK (1991)

Directed by Oliver Stone; starring Kevin Costner (Jim Garrison), Tommy Lee Jones (Clay Shaw), Donald Sutherland ("Mr. X"), and Joe Pesci (David Ferrie)

JFK addressed two questions that have intrigued the historical profession and the general public: Did John F. Kennedy fall victim to a lone assassin or a larger conspiracy? How might the course of U.S. history, including the nation's involvement in Vietnam, have been different if Kennedy's presidency had not ended in November 1963?

This movie restages the 1967 criminal prosecution by Jim Garrison, then the district attorney of New Orleans, against Clay Shaw, a local business leader. This real-life court case provides the vehicle for speculating that a shadowy conspiracy—involving government officials, military officers, and business executives— killed Kennedy because of fears he would end the U.S. commitment in South Vietnam.

To dramatize its claims, *JFK* employs numerous cinematic techniques. When showing the famous "Zapruder film," the home movie that provides the most important visual record of Kennedy's shooting, *JFK* inserts simulated, black-and-white images of sharpshooters catching the president in a deadly cross fire. Later, the movie shows a mysterious figure planting the "magic bullet," a nearly pristine projectile the Warren Commission insisted came from the rifle of Lee Harvey Oswald and passed through Kennedy's body, on a hospital gurney.

JFK is vintage Oliver Stone. This controversial filmmaker-historian delights in disrupting dominant narratives about the past. His most successful historical movies—*JFK, Platoon* (1986), *Born on the Fourth of July* (1989), *The Doors* (1991), and *Nixon* (1995)—all feature disjuncture and uncertainty. When the Garrison character in *JFK* decides to challenge the official story of the Kennedy assassination, he warns his staff that "we're through the looking glass . . . white is black, and black is white."

Resembling Stone's equally controversial *Natural Born Killers* (1994), *JFK* focuses less on telling a coherent tale than on using the film format to suggest tangled relationships between visual imagery and popular perception. The opening sequence of his Kennedy movie bombards the screen with quick-moving, seemingly disconnected imagery. Viewers, as if they themselves are passing "through the looking glass," immediately must struggle to connect the disjointed visual pieces contained in the cinematic puzzle that is *JFK*.

The movie, in this sense, seems more interested in posing, rather than settling, historical questions. Viewers might compare and contrast, for example, how *JFK* uses two very differently composed sequences, featuring performances by two very different character actors (Donald Sutherland and Joe Pesci), to speculate about Kennedy's death. Sutherland's "Mr. X," an entirely fictive employee in the national security bureaucracy, sees Kennedy's assassination as only one in a long line of "dirty tricks" orchestrated by a military-industrial complex. During a scene shot against the iconography of the nation's capital, Sutherland calmly offers Garrison (and film viewers) a logically ordered, tightly packaged account of Kennedy's assassination. In contrast, the brief sequence featuring Joe Pesci's frenetic David Ferrie—a foot soldier in organized crime and Cuban-exile circles—lacks any coherent center. This real-life character, in contrast to Sutherland's fictional one, warns Garrison that he will never puzzle out Kennedy's death.

JFK, the movie, prompted a massive, congressionally ordered project to safeguard any evidence that might relate to Kennedy's assassination. Will the preservation of these sources ever bring historians any closer to solving, beyond reasonable doubts, Kennedy's assassination? Or, as Joe Pesci's character warns in *JFK*, will historians still confront "a mystery, inside a riddle, wrapped in an enigma"?

Kevin Costner portrays New Orleans District Attorney Jim Garrison in JFK.

WARNER BROS./THE KOBAL COLLECTION

Conclusion

Tensions with the Soviet Union, which brought the superpowers to the brink of nuclear war during the Cuban Missile Crisis of 1962, dominated national security calculations between 1953 and 1963. The United States stockpiled nuclear weapons, employed new forms of economic pressure, and expanded covert activities. Left-leaning movements in the Third World, particularly in Cuba and Southeast Asia, became of growing concern to policy-makers.

At home, the post-1953 decade brought economic growth. New consumer products encouraged talk about an age of affluence but also produced apprehension about conformity, unruly youth, and mass culture. At the same time, the millions of people whom economic prosperity bypassed, and those who faced racial and ethnic discrimination, saw their causes move to the center of public debates over the role of government. Critics charged the Eisenhower administration with failing to use governmental power to support civil rights and to promote faster, more equitably distributed economic growth. Although Kennedy also hesitated, the press of domestic events, particularly those associated with civil rights movements, forced him to consider how best to advance the issues of liberty and equality at home. More quietly, a new conservative movement with ideas different from those of Kennedy, and even Eisenhower, was also taking shape.

The years that immediately followed Kennedy's assassination would continue to highlight questions about liberty, equality, and power at home and abroad during "America's longest war."

CHAPTER REVIEW

Review Questions

1. In what ways did the Eisenhower administration retain but also reorient the foreign policy of containment that it inherited from the immediate postwar period?

2. How did economic growth change American life during the post-1953 decade?

3. What kinds of social criticism did the general economic prosperity of the post-1953 decade help to highlight?

4. How did the post-1953 decade help to focus competing views of the role of government? What did the new conservatism advocate? What did advocates of more active government hope to accomplish?

5. How did the foreign and domestic policies championed by the administration of John F. Kennedy both accept and reject those embraced by the Eisenhower administration during the 1950s? What policy changes did the early 1960s bring?

6. How did expanding civil rights movements raise new political issues and visions during the 1950s and early 1960s? How did the nation's political and social institutions respond?

7. What were the most important issues left unsettled at Kennedy's death?

Critical Thinking Questions

1. How did the policies of the Eisenhower and the Kennedy administrations toward the Cold War, discrimination, and economic growth show both differences and similarities?

2. Why does the relatively brief presidency of JFK loom so large in popular memory?

Identifications

Review your understanding of the following key terms, people, and events for this chapter.

Third World, p. 658
massive retaliation, p. 659
Eisenhower Doctrine, p. 660
Highway Act of 1956, p. 663
Betty Friedan, p. 666
Sputnik, p. 668
John Fitzgerald Kennedy (JFK), p. 669

flexible response, p. 670
Bay of Pigs, p. 670
Cuban Missile Crisis, p. 671
Dr. Benjamin Spock, p. 672
Brown v. Board of Education, p. 674
Rosa Parks, p. 676

Montgomery bus boycott, p. 676
Dr. Martin Luther King, Jr., p. 676
Civil Rights Act of 1957, p. 677
Termination and Relocation, p. 677

redlining, p. 679
sit-in movement, p. 679
Student Nonviolent Coordinating Committee (SNCC), p. 679
freedom riders, p. 680

DISCOVERY

How did images of America as an "affluent society" generate a critique of conformity and focus attention on the situation of African Americans in the 1950s and 1960s?

In thinking about this question, begin by breaking it down into the components shown below. A discussion of the significance of each component should appear in your answer.

Economics and Technology

How does the advertisement below represent the growing "affluent society" of the 1950s? What evidence can you point to in the picture that the country's economic growth and improvements in transportation and technology had major effects on the everyday life of ordinary people? How broadly accessible were consumer items such as refrigerators in 1950s America? Did their accessibility shape perceptions about equality in America and the gap separating rich from poor? If so, how? What connections, if any, can be drawn between the "affluent society" of the 1950s and the protest movements that emerged in the 1960s?

Culture and Society

Look at Map 28.2 on page 675 and reflect on what you read in this chapter about racial discrimination and the civil rights movement. Which areas of the country gained the largest African American population between 1940 and 1960? Which areas lost the most? What do you think were the main causes for these shifts?

THE QUEEN OF ABUNDANCE

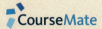

AMERICA DURING ITS LONGEST WAR, 1963–1974

THE GREAT SOCIETY
    Closing the New Frontier
    The Election of 1964
    Lyndon Johnson's Great Society
    Evaluating the Great Society

ESCALATION IN VIETNAM
    The Gulf of Tonkin Resolution
    The War Continues to Widen
    The Media and the War

THE WAR AT HOME
    The Movement of Movements
    A New Left
    The Counterculture
    Civil Rights and Black Power
    The Antiwar Movement

1968
    Turmoil in Vietnam
    Turmoil at Home
    The Election of 1968

CONTINUED POLARIZATION, 1969–1974
    Lawbreaking, Violence, and a New President
    Social Policy
    Environmentalism
    Controversies over Rights
    The Economy

FOREIGN POLICY IN A TIME OF TURMOIL, 1969–1974
    Détente
    Vietnamization and the Nixon Doctrine
    The United States Leaves Vietnam
    Expanding the Nixon Doctrine

A CRISIS OF GOVERNANCE, 1972–1974
    The Election of 1972
    The Watergate Investigations
    Nixon's Resignation

L yndon Baines Johnson (LBJ) promised to finish what John F. Kennedy (JFK) had begun. At home, Johnson hoped to mobilize the power of government to promote liberty and advance equality. In Southeast Asia, however, Johnson saw no obvious route to follow. His decisions bout Vietnam generated discord at home, and controversy also overtook his initially popular domestic moves. By 1968, polarization embittered national politics.

This polarization only grew worse during the years that followed. By the end of America's longest war and the Watergate crisis that brought President Richard Nixon's resignation, the nation's political culture and social fabric looked very different from how they had appeared in 1963.

*T*IMELINE

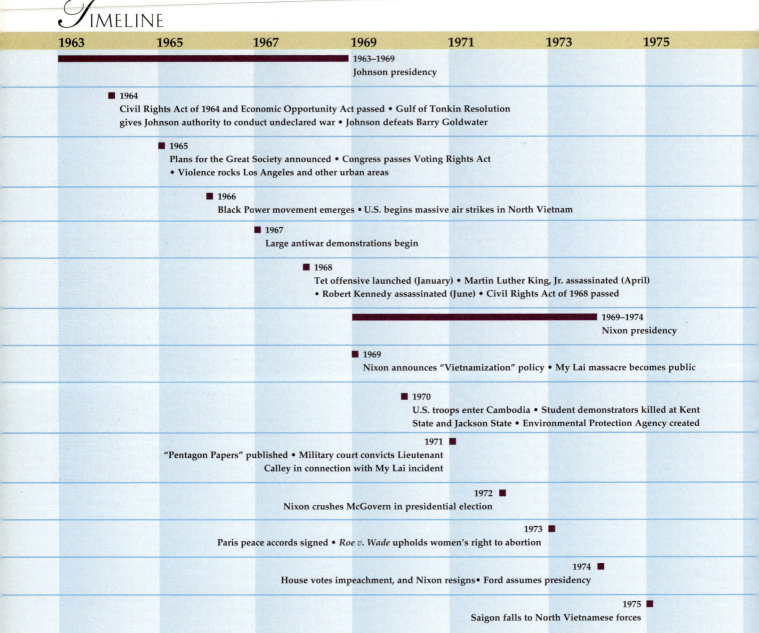

1963	1965	1967	1969	1971	1973	1975

1963–1969
Johnson presidency

1964
Civil Rights Act of 1964 and Economic Opportunity Act passed • Gulf of Tonkin Resolution gives Johnson authority to conduct undeclared war • Johnson defeats Barry Goldwater

1965
Plans for the Great Society announced • Congress passes Voting Rights Act • Violence rocks Los Angeles and other urban areas

1966
Black Power movement emerges • U.S. begins massive air strikes in North Vietnam

1967
Large antiwar demonstrations begin

1968
Tet offensive launched (January) • Martin Luther King, Jr. assassinated (April) • Robert Kennedy assassinated (June) • Civil Rights Act of 1968 passed

1969–1974
Nixon presidency

1969
Nixon announces "Vietnamization" policy • My Lai massacre becomes public

1970
U.S. troops enter Cambodia • Student demonstrators killed at Kent State and Jackson State • Environmental Protection Agency created

1971
"Pentagon Papers" published • Military court convicts Lieutenant Calley in connection with My Lai incident

1972
Nixon crushes McGovern in presidential election

1973
Paris peace accords signed • *Roe v. Wade* upholds women's right to abortion

1974
House votes impeachment, and Nixon resigns • Ford assumes presidency

1975
Saigon falls to North Vietnamese forces

© Cengage Learning

*T*HE GREAT SOCIETY

FOCUS QUESTION

How did the Johnson administration define its domestic goals, and how did it approach problem solving? Why did Johnson's "Great Society" produce so much controversy?

Johnson lacked Kennedy's charisma, but he had mastered the art of interest-group horse trading during his long career in Congress. Johnson flattered, cajoled, or threatened people until they lent him their support. Although eager to enact a bold social-economic agenda, Johnson began cautiously. He asked Congress to honor JFK's memory by addressing three legislative issues proposed by Kennedy's administration: tax cutting, economic inequality, and civil rights.

Closing the New Frontier

Working behind the scenes, Johnson easily secured passage of the Kennedy tax cut. Although analysts still differ on its contribution to the economic boom of the mid-1960s, the tax measure appeared to work. GNP rose 7 percent in 1964 and 8 percent the following year, unemployment dropped, and inflation remained low.

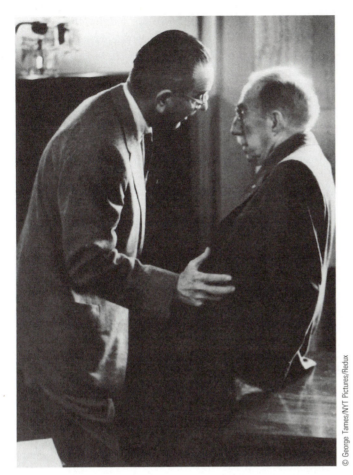

THE PRESENCE OF LYNDON B. JOHNSON. *As both senator and president, Lyndon Johnson employed body language—the "Johnson treatment"—as one means of lining up support for his policies.*

In his January 1964 State of the Union address, Johnson called for "an unconditional war on poverty in America." Relentlessly prodded by the White House, Congress soon passed The Economic Opportunity Act of 1964. It created the Office of Economic Opportunity (OEO) to eliminate "the paradox of poverty in the midst of plenty." The act also mandated loans for rural and small-business development; established a work-training program called the Jobs Corps; created Volunteers in Service to America (VISTA), a domestic version of the Peace Corps; provided low-wage, public service jobs for young people; began a "work-study program" to assist college students; and created a Community Action Program (CAP) that would plan federally funded social programs in concert with local community groups.

Johnson also helped push an expanded version of Kennedy's civil rights proposal through Congress. Although championing the measure as a memorial to JFK, LBJ knew that southern Democrats would still try to block it. Consequently, he successfully sought Republican support. The **Civil Rights Act of 1964**, passed in July, strengthened federal remedies, monitored by a new Equal Employment Opportunity Commission (EEOC), against racially inspired job discrimination. The act also prohibited racial discrimination in all public accommodations connected to interstate commerce, such as motels and restaurants. Title VII, a provision added during congressional debate, barred discrimination based on "sex" and became important to the reviving women's movement.

Civil Rights Act of 1964
Bipartisan measure that denied federal funding to segregated schools and barred discrimination by race and sex in employment, public accommodations, and labor unions.

That same summer, a coalition of civil rights groups led by the Student Nonviolent Coordinating Committee (SNCC) recruited nearly a thousand young volunteers for **Freedom Summer**, a campaign to register African American voters in Mississippi. During the tension-filled summer, at least six civil rights workers met violent deaths. In the most notorious incident, a conspiracy among KKK leaders and law-enforcement officers from Neshoba County was responsible for brutally murdering three volunteers—James Chaney, Michael Schwerner, and Andrew Goodman. No one was convicted of the crime until 2005, when a Mississippi jury found a former KKK leader, by then in his 80s, guilty of manslaughter.

Supporters of Freedom Summer pressed forward, only to see the national Democratic Party reject their grassroots political work. Pressured by LBJ, the 1964 Democratic convention voted to seat Mississippi's "regular" all-white delegates rather than members of a new, racially diverse Mississippi Freedom Democratic Party (MFDP). The regulars had made clear their intention to support the GOP's presidential candidate, but Johnson declined to support the MFDP in hopes of keeping some other southern states in the Democratic camp in the fall election. LBJ's rebuff of the MFDP prompted its leaders, such as Fannie Lou Hamer, to question the president's commitment to their cause.

The Election of 1964

The Republicans nominated Senator Barry Goldwater of Arizona, hero of the new conservatism, to challenge Johnson. Goldwater denounced Johnson's foreign policy for tolerating communist expansion and attacked his domestic agenda, including civil rights, for overextending the power of the national government. Democrats countered by savaging Goldwater's policies, his grasp of issues, and even his mental stability. Goldwater's proclamation at the 1964 Republican convention that "extremism in the pursuit of liberty is no vice" and "moderation in the pursuit of justice is no virtue" fed Democratic claims that "extremist" forces on the "radical right" would dominate a Goldwater presidency.

Many moderate Republicans deserted Goldwater, who led the GOP to a spectacular defeat in November. Johnson carried 44 states and won more than 60 percent of the popular vote; Democrats also gained 38 seats in Congress.

Although the 1964 election boosted Lyndon Johnson's agenda, it also foreshadowed deeply rooted, long-term political changes. Indeed, during the Democratic primaries of 1964, Alabama's segregationist governor, George Wallace, had run strongly against the president in several states by denouncing any "meddling" by Washington in local affairs. The 1964 election proved the last, until that of 2008, in which the Democratic Party would capture the White House by proposing an expansion in the power of the national government.

Goldwater's defeat invigorated rather than discouraged supporters of the new conservatism. His staff pioneered innovative campaign tactics, such as direct-mail fundraising. By refining these techniques during future campaigns, conservative strategists helped make 1964 the beginning, not the end, of the Republican Party's movement to the right. Goldwater's victories in five southern states—along with Wallace's earlier appeal to "white backlash" voters—suggested that opposition to additional civil rights measures could woo southern whites away from the Democratic Party.

The Goldwater campaign also introduced a new corps of conservative activists, many of them from the Sunbelt, to national politics. Ronald Reagan championed the new conservatism so effectively that Goldwater Republicans in California began grooming the former movie and TV actor for a political career.

Freedom Summer *Summer 1964 campaign in which black and white activists worked in Mississippi on voter registration and other civil rights projects.*

Younger conservatives, such as William Rehnquist and Newt Gingrich, entered the national arena. Historians now credit the Goldwater campaign for spearheading the overhaul of American conservatism—and the Republican Party.

Lyndon Johnson's Great Society

Lyndon Johnson rushed to capitalize on his electoral victory. Enjoying broad support in Congress, Johnson unveiled plans for a **Great Society,** an array of federal programs designed to "enrich and elevate our national life." Many of the Great Society's proposals rested on the midcentury "affluence" that the Johnson administration expected to continue. Ongoing economic growth could provide the tax dollars to underwrite a bold expansion of national power without any overhaul of fundamental political and economic arrangements.

Some Great Society programs fulfilled the dreams of Johnson's Democratic predecessors. Nationally funded medical coverage for the elderly (Medicare) and for low-income citizens (Medicaid) grew out of health-care proposals from the New Deal and Fair Deal eras. Great Society legislation also addressed discrimination. The **Voting Rights Act of 1965** gave the Justice Department broadly defined authority to monitor electoral procedures in jurisdictions with a history of discriminating against African American voters. The **Immigration and Nationality Act of 1965** finally abolished the discriminatory "national origins" quota system established in 1924 (see Chapter 24).

The array of Great Society initiatives that rolled through Congress during the mid-1960s heartened LBJ's supporters and appalled his critics. The Model Cities Program (1966) offered smaller-scale alternatives to urban renewal efforts. Rent supplements and an expanded food stamp program assisted low-income families. The Head Start Program (1965) provided help for children considered educationally unprepared for kindergarten. These measures and others were meant to help people fight their own way out of distress. The Great Society, Johnson insisted, would give people a "hand up" rather than a "handout."

Evaluating the Great Society

How did the Great Society become so controversial? Most obviously, the extension of Washington's reach rekindled old debates about the use of the power of the national government. In addition, Johnson announced ambitious long-term objectives, such as an "unconditional" victory over poverty, that failed to survive the short-term rhythms of partisan politics. Republicans picked up 47 seats in Congress in the midterm elections of 1966. Finally, worsening economic conditions, exacerbated by the escalating cost of the war in Vietnam, made social welfare measures politically vulnerable. Facing financial worries of their own, people who had initially supported the Great Society became receptive to the claim, first championed by George Wallace and the Goldwater campaign in 1964, that bureaucrats in Washington would waste their hard-earned tax dollars on flawed social experiments, especially those involving local community groups financed through the CAP initiative.

Historians disagree about the impact of Johnson's programs. Charles Murray's *Losing Ground* (1984) charged the Great Society with encouraging too many people, lured by welfare payments, to abandon the goals of marrying, settling down, and seeking jobs. Money spent on Johnson's programs, moreover, created government deficits that slowed economic growth.

Other analysts rejected this view, including the claim that most people preferred welfare to work. Funds spent on Great Society programs neither matched

Great Society *Series of domestic initiatives announced in 1964 by President Lyndon Johnson to end poverty and racial injustice.*

Voting Rights Act of 1965 *Law that provided new federal mechanisms to help guarantee African Americans the right to vote.*

Immigration and Nationality Act of 1965 *Law eliminating the national origins quota system for immigration and substituting preferences for people with certain skills or with relatives in the United States.*

Johnson's promises nor reached the levels claimed by the new conservatism. The charge that government expenditures choked off growth ignored the systemic economic problems that emerged in the early 1970s. In addition, poverty rates fell from 19 percent in 1962 to 10 percent in 1969.

Even so, many antipoverty activists faulted the Johnson administration for failing to challenge the prevailing distribution of political and economic power. In their view, the assumption that economic growth would fund the Great Society had precluded any serious attempt, such as a revised tax code, to redistribute income and wealth.

Despite disagreements over how to interpret the Great Society, historians concur over its impact on the federal budget. Washington's financial outlay for domestic programs increased more than 10 percent during every year of LBJ's presidency.

From the perspective of political viability, however, the Great Society proved a failure. LBJ's domestic policies, based on extending national power, inflamed partisan passions, giving energy to conservatives and dividing Democrats. Calls for limiting the reach of Washington increasingly dominated political discussion and reshaped American political culture.

ESCALATION IN VIETNAM

Johnson's divisive crusade to build a Great Society at home found its counterpart abroad in Vietnam. His policy there diminished the nation's international standing, further polarized its domestic politics, and strained its economy.

The Gulf of Tonkin Resolution

Although Johnson had resisted additional support for South Vietnam immediately after Kennedy's assassination, his fears of appearing "soft" on communism soon led him to side with those advisers who recommended air strikes against North Vietnam. Johnson prepared a congressional resolution authorizing this escalation of hostilities.

Events in the Gulf of Tonkin, off the coast of North Vietnam, provided the rationale for taking the resolution to Capitol Hill. On August 1, 1964, the U.S. destroyer *Maddox,* while on an intelligence-gathering mission, exchanged gunfire with North Vietnamese ships. Three days later, the *Maddox* reported what seemed to be signs of a failed torpedo attack. Although the *Maddox*'s commander advised further analysis, Johnson immediately denounced "unprovoked aggression" by North Vietnam against the United States. (A later study concluded that there had never been any North Vietnamese attack.) With only two dissenting votes in the Senate, Congress passed the **Gulf of Tonkin Resolution**, which authorized Johnson to take "all necessary measures to repel armed attack."

Johnson immediately began bombing strikes against North Vietnam and used the Gulf of Tonkin Resolution as tantamount to a congressional declaration of war. The resolution also helped Johnson position himself as a cautious moderate during the presidential campaign of 1964. Barry Goldwater demanded stronger measures against North Vietnam and even hinted at possible use of tactical nuclear weapons. Johnson, by contrast, seemingly promised not to commit U.S. troops to any land war in Southeast Asia.

Gulf of Tonkin Resolution
Measure passed by Congress in August 1964 that provided authorization for an air war against North Vietnam after U.S. destroyers were allegedly attacked by North Vietnamese torpedoes. Johnson invoked it as authority for expanding the Vietnam War.

Soon after the election, however, Johnson faced a complicated decision. More than a year after the 1963 coup against Diem (see Chapter 28), South Vietnam still faced political disarray, and South Vietnamese troops were deserting at an alarming rate. By the beginning of 1965, the National Liberation Front (NLF) controlled much of the countryside. In January, another Saigon regime collapsed.

National Security Adviser McGeorge Bundy predicted Saigon's defeat unless the United States greatly increased its military role. By contrast, Undersecretary of

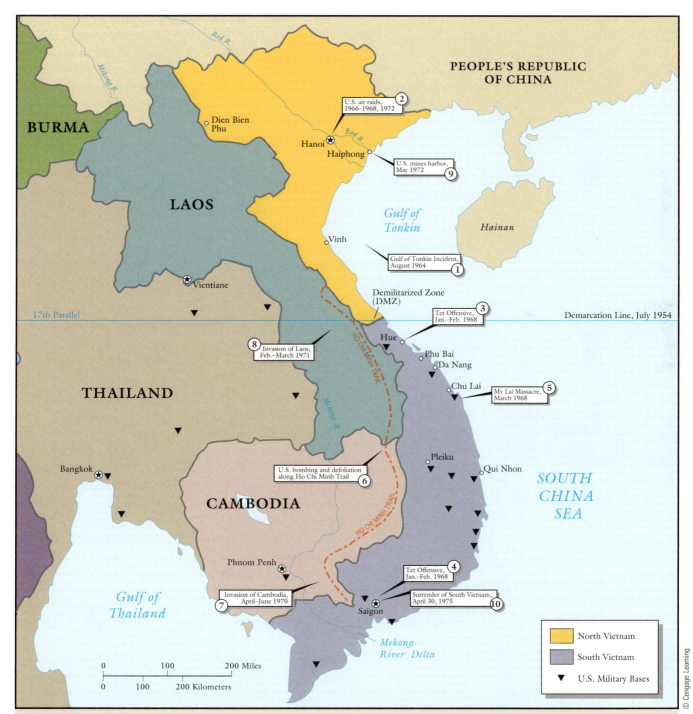

Map 29.1 Vietnam War. *The war in Vietnam spread into neighboring countries as the United States sought to prevent North Vietnam from bringing supplies and troops southward along a network called the Ho Chi Minh Trail. Unlike the Korean War (see Map 27.3 on p. 640), the guerrilla-style war in Indochina had few conventional battle "fronts."*

State George Ball warned that "no one has demonstrated that a white ground force of whatever size can win a guerrilla war . . . in jungle terrain in the midst of a population that refuses cooperation to the white forces."

Although Johnson still privately doubted the chances for success, he became obsessed about the political and diplomatic consequences of a U.S. pullout. Domestic criticism of any communist victory could endanger his Great Society programs. Johnson also accepted the "domino theory," the claim that a U.S. withdrawal could lead to further communist aggression and damage U.S. credibility around the world.

Ultimately, Johnson greatly expanded U.S. military involvement. He ordered a sustained campaign of bombing in North Vietnam, code-named "Rolling Thunder." Washington also deployed U.S. ground forces to regain lost territory, expanded covert operations, and boosted economic aid to the beleaguered South Vietnamese government. Only six months after the 1964 election, with his advisers still divided, Johnson committed the United States to a wider war.

The War Continues to Widen

Hoping to break the enemy's spirit, U.S. military commanders sought to inflict massive casualties during 1965. The Johnson administration authorized the use of napalm, a chemical that charred both foliage and people, and allowed the Air Force to bomb new targets. Additional U.S. combat troops arrived. After North Vietnam rejected a Johnson peace plan that Hanoi viewed as a form of surrender, the United States again escalated its effort. North Vietnam's leadership, pursuing a long-term strategy of attrition, became convinced that Johnson would eventually lose public and congressional support for the costly war.

In spring 1965, as another South Vietnamese government was forming in Saigon, General William Westmoreland, who directed the U.S. effort, recommended using "search and destroy" missions against communist forces. "Body count"—the number of enemy forces killed or disabled—became the key measure of success for these missions. In July, Johnson publicly agreed to send 50,000 additional military personnel to Vietnam. Privately, he pledged to send another 50,000 and left open the possibility of sending even more. LBJ also approved saturation bombing in the South Vietnamese countryside and intensified bombardment of the North.

Some advisers urged Johnson to inform the public about the expanded U.S. effort. They recommended seeking an outright declaration of war from Congress or at least legislation granting the president broader powers during wartime. But Johnson worried about expanding a still-small antiwar movement. Instead, he stressed the administration's willingness to negotiate and acted as if the war he was escalating was not really a war, apparently hoping that most Americans would remain largely in the dark about events in Vietnam. Over the next three years, U.S. involvement steadily increased. The number of U.S. troops in Vietnam grew to 535,000. Overall, U.S. planes dropped approximately 1.5 million tons of bombs— more than all the tonnage dropped during the Second World War.

Despite this level of violence, Vietnam remained a "limited" war. The United States avoided doing anything that might provoke China or the Soviet Union. The strategy remained one of containing the NLF and North Vietnam by steadily escalating the cost they would pay, in lost lives and bombed-out infrastructure. Body count remained the primary measure for gauging progress. Estimates that a kill ratio of 10 to 1 would force North Vietnam and the NLF to pull back encouraged the U.S. military command to unleash more firepower and further inflate enemy casualty figures. Whenever the number of enemy forces seemed to increase, the Pentagon required more troops to maintain the desired kill ratio.

QUICK REVIEW

JOHNSON'S DECISION TO ESCALATE THE WAR IN VIETNAM

- Containment policy and domino theory warned against allowing communist expansion

- Advisers gave conflicting advice about major military involvement

- Danger of direct involvement by China or the Soviet Union limited U.S. military options

- Dubious attack in the Gulf of Tonkin prompted a congressional resolution authorizing the escalation of military action against North Vietnam

VISUAL LINK TO THE PAST

Shocking Images

This 1968 photo, which gained Eddie Adams a Pulitzer Prize, shows a South Vietnamese police chief summarily executing a suspected Viet Cong leader on the streets of Saigon. The photo was widely circulated in the U.S. media. The image seemed to reflect badly on South Vietnam's system of justice and shocked many Americans. It was one of many troubling images that led to new questions about whether the struggle in Vietnam advanced the democratic goals claimed by U.S. leaders. Much later, however, Adams apologized for how his photo had helped disgrace this once respected South Vietnamese military leader. "The general killed the Viet Cong; I killed the general with my camera," wrote Adams.

AP Images/Eddie Adams

Q Why was this image so shocking to many Americans, and what might a careful viewer want to know about the overall context of this image?

Johnson used body-count numbers to justify claims of victory being "just around the corner." But North Vietnam, enjoying material assistance from China, could match every U.S. escalation. The North Vietnamese funneled troops and supplies into the South through the shifting network of roads and paths called the Ho Chi Minh Trail. The "pacification" and "strategic hamlet" programs, which gathered Vietnamese farmers into tightly guarded villages, sounded viable in Washington but created greater instability and animosity by uprooting many South Vietnamese from their villages and ancestral lands. By the end of 1967, several of Johnson's key aides, most notably Secretary of Defense Robert McNamara, decided that the United States could not sustain its commitment to South Vietnam. The majority of Johnson's advisers refused to accept McNamara's assessment.

The Media and the War

The destruction wreaked by U.S. forces was giving NLF, North Vietnamese, Chinese, and Soviet leaders a propaganda advantage. Pictures from Southeast Asia allowed critics from around the world to condemn the U.S. bombardments. Antiwar protesters at home constantly hounded the president and members of his administration. They also assailed what they considered the media's uncritical reporting of the war.

With television making Vietnam a "living room war"—one that people could watch in their own homes—Johnson kept three sets playing in his office in order to monitor what viewers were seeing. Most of what he saw, early on, he liked. In time, however, media coverage changed. Images of unrelenting destruction undercut the optimistic words coming from the White House and U.S. officials in Saigon. LBJ started telephoning network executives, castigating them for critical broadcasts. More and more journalists and reporters, finally following the lead of David Halberstam, began challenging the reassuring reports.

As the conflict dragged on, the media began to talk about a "war at home." In time, it came to seem as if the fundamental structures of domestic politics, society, and culture might soon be in danger of unraveling.

THE WAR AT HOME

FOCUS QUESTION

What domestic social-political movements emerged during America's longest war? How did they seek to change U.S. political culture and the direction of public policy? What role did commercial media play in the "movement of movements"?

Even as Lyndon Johnson's policy in Southeast Asia was coming under attack from antiwar activists, a broader culture of dissent emerged.

The Movement of Movements

No single group can lay exclusive claim to "the Sixties," the period from roughly 1963 to 1974 that coincided with America's longest war. Still, those on the political and cultural left, especially when gaining recruits from the huge baby boom generation, initially dominated media accounts and the earliest histories of the era. Iconic images from the 1960s provide a kaleidoscopic panorama of what can be called a "movement of movements" on the political and cultural left. This movement of movements rejected a dominant ideal of the 1950s and early 1960s: the faith that political pluralism would almost always unite the nation (see Chapter 28). Activists increasingly questioned the existing political system. At the same time, disparate movements based on deeply held values—involving issues such as war and peace, race relations, gender politics, the environment, and sexuality—took shape. Four of the earliest and most prominent of the movements involved a New Left, a counterculture, a Black Power movement, and an antiwar insurgency.

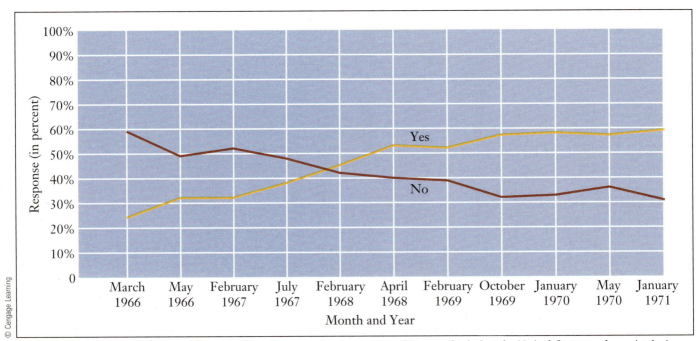

© Cengage Learning

AMERICAN ATTITUDES TOWARD THE VIETNAM WAR. *Responses to the question: "Do you think that the United States made a mistake in sending troops to fight there?"*

A New Left

While relatively few college students actually joined left-leaning movements, the activities of a **New Left** dominated politics on many campuses, attracted significant media attention, and in time generated popular controversy.

In 1962, two years after the new conservatism had given birth to Young Americans for Freedom (see Chapter 28), the left-leaning Students for a Democratic Society (SDS) emerged. Although SDS endorsed familiar causes, especially civil rights, it also attracted attention for the personalized style of its politics. SDS's *Port Huron Statement* (1962) pledged to fight the "loneliness, estrangement, isolation" that supposedly afflicted many people. Charging that the dominant political culture valued bureaucratic expertise over citizen engagement and economic growth over meaningful work, SDS called for "participatory democracy"—grassroots activism and institutions responsive to local needs. Grassroots political efforts, such as Freedom Summer in Mississippi, provided tangible examples of participatory democracy.

New Left activists constantly expanded their view of what counted as "politics." Although voter registration drives remained important in the South, for example, local movements came to place greater emphasis on alternative political forms, such as sit-ins and demonstrations.

On campus, discontent simmered. Dissenting students chafed at courses that seemed irrelevant to the issues of the day and at college bureaucracies that imposed restrictions on their living arrangements and lifestyle choices. Far worse, these dissenters argued, giant universities, accepting funding from the military-industrial complex, seemed oblivious to the social and moral implications of their war-related research. During the "Berkeley Revolt" of 1964 and 1965, students and sympathetic faculty protested how the University of California restricted political activity on campus and then began speaking out against its complicity in the Vietnam War and in racial discrimination. The long-running drama at Berkeley, which disrupted classes and polarized the university, came to symbolize what the media began calling "the war on campus."

The Counterculture

The youth-dominated **counterculture** of the mid-1960s remains a difficult "movement" to identify. Embracing the slogan "Do Your Own Thing," the counterculture elected no officers, held no formal meetings, and maintained no central office. It burst into view in low-income neighborhoods, such as San Francisco's Haight-Ashbury area, and along the streets bordering college campuses, such as Berkeley's Telegraph Avenue. Its self-appointed spokespeople embraced values, lifestyles, and institutions hailed as both utopian and as realistic alternatives to those of the dominant culture.

Countercultural ventures drew on earlier models, especially those of the "Beat movement" of the 1950s. A loosely connected group of writers and poets, the Beats had denied that either the material abundance or conventional spiritual ideals of the 1950s provided fulfillment. Beat writers such as Jack Kerouac, author of *On the Road* (1957), praised rebels and nonconformists for seeking more instinctual and sensual ways of living. The Beat poet Allen Ginsberg, in works such as *Howl* (1956), decried soulless materialism and puritanical moral codes. He celebrated the kind of personal freedom that he found in drugs, Eastern mysticism, and same-sex love affairs.

Countercultural energies during the 1960s left their imprint on a wide range of social and cultural movements, including the cooperative movement, radical feminism, environmentalism, and the fight against legal restrictions on lifestyle choices. The counterculture also affected mainstream consumer culture. The mass media liked to portray countercultural "hippies" as being on the cutting edge of a

New Left *1960s movement that sought to reorient politics by emphasizing more activist forms of participation, especially by young people.*

counterculture *Antiestablishment movement that symbolized the youthful social upheaval of the 1960s. Ridiculing traditional attitudes toward such matters as clothing, hairstyles, and sexuality, the counterculture urged a more open and less regimented approach to daily life.*

massive "youth rebellion" filled with flamboyant clothing, long hair, uninhibited sexuality, communal living arrangements, drug use, and new forms of music, such as the folk rock of the Byrds, the poetic songs of singer-songwriters like Bob Dylan and Joni Mitchell, and the acid rock of the Grateful Dead.

Images and products from the counterculture soon found a ready market among otherwise conventional consumers. The ad agency for Chrysler Motors urged car buyers to break from older patterns and join the "Dodge Rebellion." Recognizing the appeal of bands such as San Francisco's Jefferson Airplane, the music industry, too, saw profits to be made. An early countercultural happening, the "Human Be-In," organized by community activists from San Francisco in early 1967, provided a model for subsequent, commercially dominated music festivals such as Monterey Pop (later in 1967) and Woodstock (in 1969).

Civil Rights and Black Power

The media played an important and controversial role in efforts to achieve liberty and equality for African Americans. Civil rights leaders, of course, had long recognized the value of media coverage. TV images of the violence in Selma, Alabama, in 1965 had helped Dr. King's SCLC galvanize support for federal voting-rights legislation. At one point, ABC television interrupted a special showing of the anti-Nazi film *Judgment at Nuremberg* to show white Alabama state troopers beating peaceful, mostly African American, voting-rights marchers.

The turmoil associated with the civil rights campaigns prompted different views. Conservatives insisted that favorable media coverage of activism actually encouraged conflict and violence. Movement activists who looked to Dr. King replied that racial discrimination, lack of opportunity, and inadequate government remedies produced the frustration that spawned violence. Other more militant voices within the broad movement of movements argued that governments could not effectively address race-related issues and that aggrieved groups needed to mobilize themselves.

This debate intensified in 1965 in the wake of racial conflict in Los Angeles. An altercation between a white highway patrol officer and a black motorist escalated into six days of violence, centered in the largely African American community of Watts. Thirty-four people died; hundreds of businesses and homes were burned; armed National Guard troops patrolled the streets; and television camera crews broadcast the destruction.

A stunned Lyndon Johnson ordered up new social-welfare resources for Watts. The mayor and police chief of Los Angeles, conversely, blamed civil rights "agitators." When Dr. King rushed to the scene, preaching the politics of nonviolence, local activists generally ignored or even ridiculed him. They endorsed more militant action to gain political power and access to more equitable policing practices, higher paying jobs, and better housing. The basic structure of the post-Watts debate changed relatively little as more than 300 cases of serious urban violence occurred between 1965 and 1969, usually during the summer.

How do these "long, hot summers" fit into a history of the 1960s? The earliest narratives of civil rights movements in the 1960s saw escalating violence producing radical **Black Power** movements that splintered the earlier, more united, civil rights cause. The competing story about a "movement of movements," however, suggests that there never was a single civil rights *movement* that could have splintered. Long before Watts, a variety of black activist movements were advocating different ways to gain greater power for black communities.

Many Black Power efforts during the late 1950s and early 1960s looked to **Malcolm X,** who had initially gained attention as a minister in the Nation of Islam, a North America-based group popularly known as the "Black Muslims." Malcolm

Black Power *Mid-1960s movements that called for modifying integrationist goals in favor of gaining political and economic power for separate black-directed institutions and emphasized pride in African American heritage.*

Malcolm X *Charismatic African American leader who urged the creation of separate black economic and cultural institutions and became a hero to members of Black Power movements.*

X criticized Dr. King's gradual, nonviolent approach as largely irrelevant to the everyday problems of most African Americans and questioned the desirability or feasibility of racial integration. Malcolm X never advocated initiating confrontation, but he did endorse self-defense "by any means necessary."

Portrayed as a dangerous subversive by the FBI and most mainstream media, Malcolm X offered more than angry rhetoric. Malcolm urged African Americans to "recapture our heritage and identity" and "launch a cultural revolution to unbrainwash an entire people." Seeking a broad movement, Malcolm X eventually broke from the Black Muslims and established his own Organization of Afro-American Unity. Murdered in 1965 by enemies from the Nation of Islam, Malcolm X remained, especially after the posthumous publication of his *Autobiography* (1965), a powerful symbol for black-centered political and cultural visions of the future.

Events in the South highlighted other variations within the movement. In June 1966, a KKK gunman shot James Meredith, who had integrated the University of Mississippi several years earlier and was conducting a one-person "March against Fear" from Tennessee to Jackson, Mississippi. An enlarged March against Fear, which would complete Meredith's walk, did not seek new civil rights legislation as the 1963 March on Washington had. It sought, instead, to dramatize that movements for liberty and equality could focus on everyday struggles for safety, dignity, pride, and empowerment.

During the march, SNCC leader Stokely Carmichael played to the omnipresent TV cameras. Carmichael's rise to prominence had begun the previous year, when he organized a third-party political movement, bearing the striking logo of a coiled black panther, in Lowndes County, Alabama. In Mississippi, he questioned an unwavering commitment to nonviolence and urged that the civil rights struggle not remain just one for "Freedom," the byword of the SCLC, but for "Black Power." As Carmichael later explained, Black Power was "a call for black people in this country to unite, to recognize their heritage, to build a sense of community." They should "define their own goals" and "lead their own organizations."

Black Power thus provided a sometimes inflammatory label for an often pragmatic set of claims that local civil rights groups had been making for some time. They sought greater on-the-ground power both in and for their own communities. Operating from this perspective, in 1966, several college students from Oakland announced a new Black Power organization that borrowed its name and logo from Carmichael's earlier movement in Lowndes County. This Black Panther Party's platform employed militant rhetoric on behalf of 10 objectives, including greater opportunities for housing, education, and employment; legal protections, especially against police misconduct; and improved health and nutrition initiatives in low-income black neighborhoods. A 1967 rally in Sacramento, California, on behalf of a Second Amendment right to use firearms for self-defense attracted the notice of J. Edgar Hoover. He made destroying the Black Panther Party a key goal of his FBI.

Within this volatile context, Congress passed the **Civil Rights Act of 1968**. One provision of this omnibus measure, popularly known as the "Fair Housing Act," sought to eliminate racial discrimination in the national real estate market. But the act contained exemptions that enfeebled its own enforcement. Another section in the law declared it a crime to cross state lines in order to incite a "riot." Supporters hailed this provision as a law-and-order measure, while critics countered that it targeted political activists, especially those in the Black Power movement.

The Antiwar Movement

Meanwhile, another of these multifaceted movements was coming to overshadow all others: that to end the war in Vietnam. On college campuses, supporters and

Civil Rights Act of 1968
Measure that banned racial discrimination in housing, made interference with a person's civil rights a federal crime, and stipulated that crossing state lines to incite a riot was a federal offense.

opponents of the war debated at "teach-ins." which soon gave way to demonstra-tions and sit-ins. A draft-resistance effort emerged, often symbolized by the burning of draft cards. This movement gained its most celebrated member when the heavy-weight boxing champion Muhammad Ali refused induction into the military. Campus protests passed into a new phase when a pitched, bloody battle broke out between antiwar demonstrators and police at the University of Wisconsin in Madison in 1967.

Dr. Martin Luther King, Jr., now faced pressure from antiwar clergy to proclaim publicly his opposition to the war, connect it to the civil rights cause, and elaborate his moral-spiritual position. Speaking at New York's Riverside Church in April 1967, Dr. King noted that African American troops, mostly from low-income communities, served and died in numbers far greater than their proportion of the U.S. population "for a nation that has been unable to seat them together in the same schools" with the white soldiers now at their side in Vietnam. The immoral "madness" in Vietnam "must cease," Dr. King concluded. Many voices from the political-media mainstream condemned King's address, and, as King continued to broaden his political agenda, criticism from onetime supporters followed.

Meanwhile, a massive 1967 antiwar demonstration in Washington under-scored how the politics of the New Left and the spirit of the counterculture could march together, at least when opposing LBJ's policies in Vietnam. A small group of activists had invented a kind of "nonmovement movement" that bypassed mobili-zation and organization in favor of making the media its primary constituency. Two members of this group, Abbie Hoffman and Jerry Rubin, proclaimed themselves leaders of a (nonexistent) Youth International Party (or YIPPIE!) and waited for media coverage to surround their activities, as they knew it would. In one incident, they mocked the symbolic value of stocks on the New York Stock Exchange by tossing dollar bills onto the trading floor. Invoking the sit-in movement, they joked about staging department store "loot-ins." Their contribution to the 1967 antiwar march in Washington would be a separate trek to the Pentagon, where marchers would try to levitate the building.

Although the Pentagon remained firmly planted, the march against it gener-ated eye-catching media imagery. The event also gained the novelist and antiwar activist Norman Mailer a National Book Award for his account, *Armies of the Night* (1968). Mailer's book, which wove together personal impressions and journalistic observation, helped to reinvent political reporting. Cultural observers identified accounts such as Mailer's as a "New Journalism" and saw this form of reportage paralleling how political activists were creating a "New Politics" that expanded ideas about what counted as political involvement.

1968

FOCUS QUESTION

What helped to make the single year of 1968, even as it was still unfolding, seem such an important time in the history of America's longest war and of the Sixties?

But the relationship between this New Politics and the media seemed uncertain. Might not images of colorful quipsters such as Hoffman and Rubin help fuel cultural polarization rather than political action? Was the media's taste for specta-cular demonstrations trivializing underlying issues? Such questions became even more pressing during the tumultuous 12 months of 1968.

Turmoil in Vietnam

At the end of January 1968, during a supposed truce in observance of Tet, the Vietnamese lunar New Year celebration, NLF and North Vietnamese forces suddenly went on the attack throughout South Vietnam. Militarily, this **Tet Offensive** gained the NLF and the North relatively little territory at a very high cost. The NLF lost three-quarters of its military forces and much of its civilian support structure. But in the United States, the Tet Offensive became a turning point. It undercut the optimistic story that the Johnson administration had been spinning. After CBS-TV anchor Walter Cronkite returned from a post-Tet trip to Vietnam, he told a national audience that the United States would never prevail militarily. Lyndon Johnson reportedly lamented that if he had lost "the most trusted person in America," as Cronkite was then known, he had lost the rest of the country.

Johnson received more bad news after summoning his most trusted advisers and a select group of senior outsiders, including Dean Acheson, for advice on General Westmoreland's call for an additional 206,000 U.S. troops. Most rejected Westmoreland's request and insisted that South Vietnamese troops shoulder more of the military burden. Acheson, an architect of America's global containment policy following the Second World War, now advised that the United States "could no longer do the job we set out to do in the time we have left, and we must begin to take steps to disengage." As public opinion polls showed rapidly declining confidence in U.S. policy, Johnson changed his guiding assumption about Vietnam. The cost of continuing the U.S. intervention vastly outweighed whatever benefit might accrue. He turned toward negotiations but found little success.

Turmoil at Home

The Tet Offensive also destroyed Johnson's political plans. The antiwar wing of the Democratic Party was already trying to deny Johnson renomination. The dissidents backed Senator Eugene McCarthy of Minnesota, the only prominent Democrat willing to challenge LBJ. Johnson's forces won the New Hampshire primary, but McCarthy came close enough to claim a symbolic victory. Polls predicted he would easily beat Johnson, head-to-head, in the upcoming Wisconsin primary.

Even before the Wisconsin contest, Senator Robert Kennedy of New York, brother of the slain president, jumped into the race. Facing two Democratic challengers, President Johnson surprised all but his closest confidants when, during a live TV address in late March about Vietnam, he suddenly announced that he would not seek reelection. He also limited U.S. bombing of North Vietnam and signaled a readiness to begin peace negotiations in Paris.

LBJ's withdrawal created a three-way race for the Democratic nomination. McCarthy now faced Bobby Kennedy and Johnson's ever-loyal vice president, Hubert H. Humphrey, who had entered the fray after LBJ's surprise announcement. The Democratic Party's A-level celebrities generally divided their support between McCarthy and Kennedy, while Humphrey courted the Democratic power brokers who had been allied with LBJ.

Martin Luther King, Jr., welcomed LBJ's withdrawal and hoped that an antiwar candidate, ideally Kennedy, would head the Democratic ticket in November. On April 4, 1968, however, Dr. King was assassinated in Memphis, Tennessee, where he was supporting a strike by African American sanitation workers. Law enforcement officials identified James Earl Ray, a career criminal, as the lone killer. Ray waived a jury trial, pled guilty, and received a 99-year prison sentence. Subsequently, he recanted and claimed to have been a pawn in a conspiracy directed by white supremacists. He died in prison still insisting on his innocence, but few people credit his claims.

As news of Dr. King's murder spread, violence swept through more than 100 cities and towns. Thirty-nine people died; 75,000 regular and National Guard troops were called to duty. When President Johnson proclaimed Sunday, April 7, as a day

Tet Offensive *Surprise NLF attack during the lunar New Year holiday in 1968 that brought high casualties to the NLF but fueled pessimism about the war's outcome in the United States.*

THE FUNERAL PROCESSION OF DR. MARTIN LUTHER KING, APRIL 9, 1968. *A vast crowd of mourners, including ordinary people and dignitaries, accompanied the body of Dr. King through the streets of Atlanta, Georgia. The simple, mule-drawn wagon had become the symbol of one of his final efforts, a Poor People's Campaign, that was to include a march on the nation's capital. After Dr. King's assassination in Memphis, a wagon would bear his body through the streets of the city in which he had grown up, gone to college, and would be buried.*

QUICK REVIEW

1968: A VIOLENT YEAR

- Tet Offensive in Vietnam challenged the claim of U.S. progress toward victory

- Martin Luther King, Jr., was assassinated

- Robert F. Kennedy was assassinated

- Violence between police and demonstrators rocked the Democratic convention in Chicago

- Television coverage spread graphic images of all these events

of national mourning for the slain civil rights leader, parts of the nation's capital city remained ablaze.

Following Dr. King's memorial service, Gene McCarthy and Robert Kennedy returned to campaigning. Kennedy sought to demonstrate that popular opinion endorsed his candidacy. He also hoped to convince party insiders that only a Democrat without ties to Lyndon Johnson, especially another Kennedy, could capture the White House in November.

On June 5, an ebullient Kennedy defeated McCarthy in California's Democratic primary. While preparing to leave the hotel that had hosted his victory celebration, Kennedy was slain by yet another political assassin. Bystanders grabbed Sirhan Sirhan, a Palestinian immigrant, who was later convicted of the killing. Television coverage of Kennedy's body being returned by train to Washington and his state funeral were reminders of Dr. King's recent murder and of the 1963 assassination of RFK's own brother. Bowing to the reality of Humphrey's delegate total, McCarthy effectively closed down his campaign.

The violence of 1968 continued. That summer, thousands of antiwar demonstrators converged on Chicago, site of the Democratic Party's convention, to protest the nomination of Hubert Humphrey, who still supported Johnson's policy in Vietnam. Responding to provocative acts by some demonstrators, including Abbie Hoffman and Jerry Rubin, police officers attacked antiwar protestors and journalists. Opinion polls showed that most people supported the use of force against the demonstrators, and the Democratic Party emerged from Chicago badly divided.

The Election of 1968

Both Humphrey and the Republican candidate, former vice president Richard Nixon, worried about Alabama's George Wallace, a southern Democrat who was running for president as a third-party candidate on the American Independent ticket. Wallace concentrated his fire on the counterculture and the antiwar movement. If any "hippie" protestor ever blocked his motorcade, he once announced, it would "be the last car he'll ever lay down in front of." Wallace also courted voters who saw themselves as captives to "tax-and-spend" bureaucracies in Washington. He never expected to gain the presidency. But if a candidate from the two major parties failed to win a majority of the electoral votes, the Constitution required that the president be selected by the House of Representatives, where Wallace hoped to play the power-broker role.

Nixon, who promised to restore order at home and hinted at a secret plan for ending U.S. involvement in Vietnam, narrowly prevailed in November. Although he won 56 percent of the electoral vote, Nixon outpolled Humphrey in the popular vote by less than 1 percent. Wallace's plan collapsed when he picked up only 46 electoral votes, all from the Deep South, and just 13.5 percent of the popular vote nationwide. Nixon won five crucial southern states and attracted, all across the country, votes from people whom he called "the forgotten Americans, the non-shouters, the non-demonstrators."

		Electoral Vote		Popular Vote	
		Number	%	Number	%
◼ (green)	Humphrey (Democrat)	191	35.5	31,275,166	42.9
◼ (blue)	Nixon (Republican)	301	56.0	31,785,480	43.6
◼ (tan)	Wallace (American Independent)	46	8.5	9,906,473	13.5

© Cengage Learning

***Map 29.2* Presidential Election, 1968.** *George Wallace sought to throw the 1968 presidential election into the House of Representatives with his third-party candidacy. What does this map suggest about the political changes already sweeping through the once solidly Democratic South?*

CONTINUED POLARIZATION, 1969–1974

Raised as a Quaker, Richard Nixon had campaigned as someone able to restore the kind of tranquility he had known when growing up in Yorba Linda, California. His presidency, however, failed to calm the troubled waters.

Lawbreaking, Violence, and a New President

A handful of people on the leftist fringe embraced violence. There were nearly 200 actual and attempted bombings on college campuses during the 1969–1970 academic year. Attacks also rocked several large banks and the U.S. Capitol building. In 1970, three members of a small faction that had broken with SDS, "the Weather Underground," blew themselves apart when their bomb factory in New York City exploded.

At the same time, government officials stepped up their use of violent force. Fred Hampton of the Black Panthers and prison activist George Jackson died under circumstances their supporters called political assassination and public officials considered normal law enforcement. J. Edgar Hoover's FBI harassed activists, planted damaging rumors, and even operated as *agent provocateurs* who incited protesters to undertake actions that officials could later prosecute as crimes.

FOCUS QUESTION

Why did the polarization that had developed over the 1960s continue into the 1970s? What foreign and domestic events contributed to the continued polarization?

State and local officials redoubled their efforts to bring order. During the fall of 1971, New York's Governor Nelson Rockefeller broke off negotiations with inmates at Attica State Prison, who had seized several cell blocks and taken guards hostage in a protest over living conditions. He then ordered heavily armed state troopers and National Guard forces into the complex. When this "Attica Uprising" finally ended, 29 prisoners and 11 guards lay dead.

Social Policy

Richard Nixon insisted that his vast public experience made him the ideal leader for such turbulent times. Although Nixon considered foreign policy his specialty, he initially crafted an ambitious domestic agenda. At the urging of Democrat Daniel Patrick Moynihan, a special presidential adviser on domestic issues, Nixon decided he could push through bolder programs than any Democratic president. In 1969, he proposed his Family Assistance Plan (FAP), which called for replacing most existing welfare measures, including the controversial Aid to Families with Dependent Children (AFDC). AFDC provided government payments to cover the basic costs of care for low-income children who had lost the support of a breadwinning parent.

Under FAP, *every* low-income family would be guaranteed an annual income of $1,600. Moynihan and Nixon touted FAP as advancing equality since it replaced existing arrangements that assisted only those with special circumstances, but it debuted to tepid reviews. Conservatives claimed that income supplements for families with regularly employed, albeit low-paid, wage earners would be too costly. Proponents of more generous governmental assistance programs argued that FAP's income guarantee was too miserly. The House of Representatives approved a modified version of FAP in 1970, but it failed to pass the Senate.

Congress did pass Nixon's revenue-sharing plan, part of his "new federalism." It returned a portion of federal tax dollars to state and local governments, which could spend these "block grants" as they saw fit. A Democratic-controlled Congress and a Republican White House also cooperated to continue and even increase funding for many Great Society initiatives: Medicare, Medicaid, rent subsidies for low-income people, and Supplementary Security Insurance (SSI) payments to those who were elderly, blind, or disabled.

Nixon had adopted a complicated approach to civil rights during his campaign. He commonly criticized existing policies, such as the busing of children to advance school integration, but carefully distinguished his stance from that of George Wallace. The administration allowed, and sometimes urged, federal bureaucracies to extend the reach of civil rights measures passed during the Great Society. In line with candidate Nixon's call for supporting "black capitalism" through small business loans, the new president helped extend the plan to other minority entrepreneurs, particularly Hispanics. His administration also helped implement the bilingual education programs that had been authorized in 1968 legislation. Indeed, the reach of many federal social welfare programs expanded during Nixon's first term, and the percentage of people living below the poverty line declined.

Environmentalism

Nixon also worked with the new environmental movement that became a significant political force during his presidency. Landmark legislation of the 1960s had already protected large areas of the country from commercial development. In the 1970s, a broader environmental movement focused on people's health and on ecological balances. Accounts such as *The Silent Spring* (1962) by Rachel Carson had raised concerns that the pesticides used in agriculture, especially DDT, threatened bird populations. Air pollution in cities such as Los Angeles had become so toxic that simply breathing became equivalent to smoking several packs of cigarettes per day. Industrial processes, atomic weapons testing, and nuclear power plants prompted fear of cancer-causing materials. Earth Day, a countercultural-style festival first held in 1970, aimed to raise awareness about the many newly publicized hazards of environmental degradation.

The Nixon administration, although remaining aloof from Earth Day, took environmental issues seriously. The president supported creation of the Environmental Protection Agency (EPA) and signed major pieces of congressional legislation, including the Clean Air Act of 1970 and the Endangered Species Act of 1973. National parks and wilderness areas were expanded, and a new law required that "environmental impact statements" be prepared in advance of any major government project.

Controversies over Rights

Activism on social and environmental concerns accompanied fierce debate over the federal government's responsibility to protect the rights and liberties of citizens. Nixon had campaigned for president as an opponent of the Warren Court and promised to appoint federal judges who would "apply" rather than "make" the law. After Warren announced his retirement, Lyndon Johnson's plan to anoint his close confidant, Associate Justice Abe Fortas, stalled. Consequently, the victorious Nixon could appoint a Republican loyalist, Warren Burger, as chief justice. Subsequent vacancies allowed Nixon to appoint three other Republicans to the High Court.

This new "Burger Court" immediately faced controversial rights-related cases. Lawyers sympathetic to the Great Society vision of social welfare advanced the argument that access to adequate economic assistance from the federal government was a constitutionally protected right. The Burger Court rejected this claim, holding that states could limit the amount they paid to welfare recipients.

Rights-related claims involving health and safety legislation generally fared better. A vigorous consumer movement, which had drawn inspiration from Ralph Nader's exposé about auto safety (*Unsafe at Any Speed*, 1965), joined with environmentalists to bolster rights claims to workplace safety, consumer protection, and nontoxic environments. Their efforts found expression in such legislation as the Occupational Safety Act of 1973 and stronger consumer and environmental protection laws. The Burger Court supported the constitutionality of these measures.

At the same time, the newly energized women's rights movement pressed another set of issues. The **Equal Rights Amendment (ERA)**, initially proposed during the 1920s, promised to guarantee women the same legal rights as men. Easily passed by Congress in 1972 and quickly ratified by more than half the states, the ERA suddenly stalled. Conservative women's groups, such as Phyllis Schlafly's "Stop ERA," charged that this constitutional change would undermine traditional "family values" and expose women to new dangers such as military service. The ERA failed to attain approval from the three-quarters of states needed for ratification. Ultimately, women's groups abandoned the ERA effort in favor of using the courts to adjudicate equal rights claims on a case-by-case, issue-by-issue basis.

One of these issues, whether a woman possessed a constitutional right to terminate a pregnancy, became far more controversial than the ERA. In *Roe v. Wade* (1973), the Burger Supreme Court ruled, in a 7-2 decision, that a state law making abortion a criminal offense violated a woman's "right to privacy." Two of the three justices appointed by Nixon voted with the majority. The *Roe* decision outraged antiabortion groups, who rallied under the "Right-to-Life" banner on behalf of the unborn fetus, providing new support for the expanding conservative wing of the

Equal Rights Amendment *Proposed amendment to the Constitution providing that equal rights could not be abridged on account of sex. It won congressional approval in 1972 but failed to gain ratification by the states.*

Roe v. Wade *Supreme Court decision in 1973 that ruled that a blanket prohibition against abortion violated a woman's right to privacy and prompted decades of political controversy.*

WOMEN'S RIGHTS DEMONSTRATORS, AUGUST 16, 1970. *Activists, who have gathered in Washington, D.C., to demonstrate on behalf of women's rights, take time to rest. Symbolically, they effectively "occupy" a statue erected in honor of a 19th-century military hero, Admiral David G. Farragut.*

Republican Party. On the other side, feminist groups made the issue of individual choice in reproductive decisions a central rallying point.

Meanwhile, with little controversy, President Nixon signed an extension of the Voting Rights Act of 1965, and in 1972 approved another civil rights measure popularly known as "Title IX." It banned sexual discrimination in higher education and became the legal basis for requiring colleges and universities to adopt "gender equity" in all areas, including intercollegiate athletics. The Nixon administration also refined the "affirmative action" concept, which had surfaced during Lyndon Johnson's presidency, and required that all hiring and contracting that depended on federal funding take "affirmative" steps to enroll greater numbers of African Americans as union apprentices.

The Economy

Nixon eventually confronted economic problems that had been unthinkable only a decade earlier. The expensive war in Vietnam, along with increased domestic spending and a volatile international economy, began to curtail growth. Johnson had been determined to contain communism in Indochina without cutting Great Society programs or raising taxes, and he had thus concealed the true costs of the war. Nixon inherited a deteriorating (although still favorable) balance of trade and rising rate of inflation.

By 1971, the unemployment rate topped 6 percent. According to conventional wisdom, when unemployment rises, prices should remain constant or even decline. Yet *both* unemployment and inflation numbers rose simultaneously. Economists coined the term "stagflation" to describe this puzzling convergence of economic stagnation and price inflation. Along with stagflation, U.S. exports were becoming less competitive in international markets, and in 1971, for the first time in the 20th century, the United States ran a trade deficit, importing more products than it exported.

Long critical of economic regulations, but fearful of the political consequences of stagflation and trade imbalances, Nixon now needed a quick cure for the nation's economic ills. "I am now a Keynesian in economics," he suddenly announced in January 1971. In August, he unveiled a "New Economic Policy" that included a 90-day freeze on any increases in wages and prices, to be followed by government monitoring to detect "excessive" increases in either. He simultaneously took an even more daring step and abandoned the fixed gold-to-dollar ratio, the gold standard. Henceforth, the U.S. dollar would "float" in value against the prevailing market price for gold and against all other currencies in the world. This change would devalue the dollar and hopefully make American exports more competitive in the global marketplace.

In October 1973, oil-producing nations in the Middle East further changed international economic arrangements. Citing the declining U.S dollar and falling oil revenues as justifications, petroleum producers began curtailing exports s a means of raising prices. About a week later, in response to U.S. military aid for Israel, then engaged in the Yom Kippur War with Egypt and Syria, the Organization of Petroleum Exporting Countries (OPEC) temporarily embargoed oil shipments to the United States. Nixon and Congress responded with a series of measures that included rationing, deceased speed limits, and the naming of a new "energy czar." For the United States, the days of cheap oil were coming to an end.

FOREIGN POLICY IN A TIME OF TURMOIL, 1969–1974

Even as it wrestled with divisive domestic concerns, the Nixon administration was far more interested in international affairs. Henry Kissinger, Nixon's national security adviser and then secretary of state, laid out a grand strategy: **détente** with the Soviet Union, normalization of relations with China, and disengagement from direct military involvement in South Vietnam.

Détente

Although Nixon had built his early political career on hard-line anticommunism, he and Kissinger worked to ease tensions with the Soviet Union and China. They expected that improved relations might lead these nations to reduce their support for North Vietnam, increasing chances for a successful pullback of U.S. combat troops.

Arms control talks took top priority in U.S.-Soviet relations. In 1969, the two superpowers opened the Strategic Arms Limitation Talks (SALT); after several years of high-level diplomacy, they signed an agreement (SALT I) that limited further development of antiballistic missiles and offensive intercontinental ballistic missiles. SALT I's impact on the arms race was limited because it said nothing about the number of nuclear warheads that a single missile might carry. Still, the ability to conclude any arms-control pact signaled improving relations.

FOCUS QUESTION

What were the major aims of U.S. foreign policy during the presidency of Richard Nixon? How successful was the Nixon administration in carrying out these policies?

détente *An easing of tensions, particularly between the Soviet Union and the United States.*

Nixon's overtures toward the People's Republic of China brought an even more dramatic break with the Cold War past. Secret negotiations, often conducted personally by Kissinger, led to a slight easing of U.S. trade restrictions and, then, to an invitation from China for Americans to compete in a table-tennis match. This much-celebrated "ping-pong diplomacy" presaged more significant diplomatic exchanges. Most spectacularly, Nixon visited China in 1972, posing for photos with Mao Zedong and strolling along the Great Wall. A few months later, the UN admitted the People's Republic as the sole representative of China, and in 1973 the United States and China exchanged informal diplomatic missions.

Vietnamization and the Nixon Doctrine

Nixon Doctrine *Pledged that the United States would extend military assistance to anticommunist governments in Asia but would require them to supply their own combat forces.*

My Lai Incident *The murder by U.S. troops of more than 200 civilians, most of them women and children, in the small South Vietnamese village of My Lai in 1968.*

In Vietnam, the Nixon administration decided to speed withdrawal of U.S. ground forces by embracing a policy, called "Vietnamization," which had already informally begun under Lyndon Johnson's administration. Put simply, it meant that South Vietnamese, rather than U.S. troops, should bear the burden of ground combat operations. In July 1969, the **Nixon Doctrine** announced a broader version of this approach. It pledged that the United States would extend military assistance to anticommunist governments in Asia but would require them to supply their own combat forces. From the outset, the Nixon Doctrine for Vietnam envisioned the eventual removal of U.S. ground troops without accepting compromise or defeat. While officially adhering to Johnson's 1968 bombing halt over the North, Nixon and Kissinger accelerated both the ground and air wars by launching new offensives and by approving a military "incursion" into Cambodia, an ostensibly neutral country.

The 1970 invasion of Cambodia set off a new wave of protest. U.S. campuses exploded in angry demonstrations, and a number of institutions began the summer vacation early. White police officers fatally shot two students at the all-black Jackson State College in Mississippi, and National Guard troops at Kent State University in Ohio fired on unarmed protesters, killing four students.

A continuing controversy over the **My Lai Incident** further polarized sentiment over the war. Shortly after the 1968 Tet Offensive, U.S. troops had entered the small South Vietnamese hamlet of My Lai and murdered more than 200 civilians, most of them women and children. This massacre became public in 1969. Military courts convicted only one officer, Lieutenant William Calley, of any offense. Critics charged that the military was using Calley as a scapegoat for a failed strategy that emphasized body counts and lax rules of engagement. Ultimately, Calley was ordered released based on procedural irregularities.

The Nixon administration widened military operations to include Laos as well as Cambodia. Although it denied waging any such campaign, large areas of those agricultural countries were ravaged. As the number of Cambodian refugees swelled and food supplies dwindled, the communist guerrilla force there—the Khmer Rouge—came to power and, in a murderous attempt to eliminate dissent, turned Cambodia into a "killing field." It slaughtered more than one million Cambodians.

© Bettmann/CORBIS

JACKSON STATE. *The era of America's longest war was a time of violence overseas and at home. In May 1970, police gunfire killed two students and wounded 15 others at Jackson State University in Mississippi. This picture was taken through a bullet-riddled window in a women's dorm.*

Even greater violence was yet to come. During spring 1972, North Vietnam's "Easter Offensive" approached within 30 miles of Saigon before falling back. Nixon responded with an escalation far greater than that by Lyndon Johnson in 1965. Nixon ordered the systematic bombing of North Vietnam, the mining of its harbors, and the institution of a naval blockade. Just weeks before the November 1972 elections in the United States, Henry Kissinger declared that "peace is at hand" and announced a cease-fire. After Nixon's reelection, however, the impending peace deal fell apart in Paris, and the United States unleashed even greater firepower. During the "Christmas bombing" of December 1972, the heaviest bombardment in history, B-52 planes pounded military and civilian targets in North Vietnam around the clock. North Vietnam, which was also feeling diplomatic pressure from the Soviet Union and China, decided to conclude peace negotiations with Washington and Saigon.

The United States Leaves Vietnam

Much of the U.S. media, Congress, and public were also calling for an end to the war. U.S. soldiers questioned the purpose of their sacrifices; some refused to engage the enemy; and a few openly defied their superiors. At home, Vietnam Veterans Against the War (VVAW), a new organization, joined the antiwar coalition. Running out of nonbombing options, Nixon proceeded with full-scale Vietnamization.

In January 1973, the warring parties signed peace accords in Paris that provided for the withdrawal of U.S. troops. As U.S. ground forces departed, the South Vietnamese government, headed by Nguyen Van Thieu, continued to fight, increasingly demoralized and ineffectual. In spring 1975, nearly two years after the Paris accords, South Vietnam's army and Thieu's government collapsed as North Vietnamese armies entered the capital of Saigon. America's longest war ended with its objective, maintaining a noncommunist Vietnam, unfulfilled.

Between 1960 and 1973, approximately 3.5 million American men and women served in Vietnam; 58,000 died, 150,000 were wounded, and 2,000 were classified as missing. Americans struggled to understand why their country failed to defeat a small, barely industrialized nation. Those still supporting the war blamed an irresponsible media, a disloyal antiwar movement, and a Congress afflicted by a "failure of will." By contrast, the war's opponents stressed the overextension of U.S. power, the misguided belief in national omnipotence, and the miscalculations of decision makers.

Regardless of their position on the war, most Americans seemed to agree on a single proposition: There should be "no more Vietnams." The United States should not undertake another military operation unless it involved clear and compelling political objectives, sustained public support, and realistic means to accomplish its goals. Eventually, people who wanted to reassert U.S. power in the world dismissed this caution as "the Vietnam syndrome."

Expanding the Nixon Doctrine

Although the Nixon Doctrine initially applied to the Vietnamization of the war in Indochina, Nixon and Kissinger extended its premise to the entire world. The White House made clear that the United States would not dispatch its troops but would generously aid anticommunist regimes or factions willing to fight their own battles. In one of its most controversial foreign policies, the administration employed covert action against the elected socialist government of Salvador Allende Gossens in Chile in 1970. On September 11, 1973, the Chilean military overthrew Allende, immediately suspended democratic rule, and announced that Allende had committed suicide.

A CRISIS OF GOVERNANCE, 1972–1974

FOCUS QUESTION

How did the political controversies of the early 1970s lead the nation into a crisis of governance? How did this crisis ultimately undermine Richard Nixon's presidency and force his resignation?

A political loner who ruminated about taking revenge against his enemies, Nixon often seemed his own greatest foe. During the summer of 1971, Daniel Ellsberg, an antiwar activist who had once worked in the national security bureaucracy, leaked to the press a top-secret, highly critical history of U.S. involvement in the Vietnam War, subsequently known as the "Pentagon Papers." Nixon responded by seeking, unsuccessfully, a court injunction to stop publication and, more ominously, by unleashing his own secret intelligence unit, "the Plumbers," to stop leaks to the media. Searching for something that might discredit Ellsberg, the Plumbers burglarized his psychiatrist's office. Thus began a series of secretive political "dirty tricks" and clear-cut crimes, sometimes financed by funds solicited for Nixon's 1972 reelection campaign.

The Election of 1972

Nixon's political strategists worried that domestic troubles and the war in Vietnam might deny the president another term. Creating a campaign organization separate from that of the Republican Party, with the ironic acronym of CREEP (Committee to Re-elect the President), they secretly raised millions of dollars, much of it from illegal contributions.

As the 1972 campaign took shape, Nixon's chances for reelection dramatically improved. An assassin's bullet crippled George Wallace. Senator Edmund Muskie of Maine, initially Nixon's leading Democratic challenger, made a series of blunders (some of them, perhaps, precipitated by Republican "dirty tricksters"). Eventually, Senator George McGovern of South Dakota, an outspoken opponent of the Vietnam War but a lackluster campaigner, won the Democratic nomination.

McGovern never seriously challenged Nixon. He called for higher taxes on the wealthy, a guaranteed minimum income for all Americans, amnesty for Vietnam War draft resisters, and the decriminalization of marijuana. In foreign policy, he urged deep cuts in defense spending and peace in Vietnam—proposals which Nixon successfully portrayed as signs of weakness. Nixon won an easy victory in November, receiving the Electoral College votes of all but one state and the District of Columbia.

While helping achieve this victory, the president's supporters left a trail of crime and corruption that eventually led to a crisis of governance. In June 1972, a surveillance team with links to both CREEP and the White House had been arrested while fine-tuning eavesdropping equipment in the Democratic Party's headquarters in Washington's Watergate office complex. In public, Nixon's spokespeople dismissed the Watergate break-in as a "third-rate burglary;" privately, the president and his inner circle launched a cover-up. They paid hush money to the Watergate burglars and ordered CIA officials to misinform the FBI that any investigation into the burglary would jeopardize national security. Nixon contained the political damage through the 1972 election, but events associated with **Watergate** soon overtook him.

Watergate *Business and residential complex in Washington, D.C., that came to stand for the illegal political espionage and cover-ups directed by the Nixon administration. The complicated web of crimes brought about Nixon's resignation in 1974.*

The Watergate Investigations

While reporters from the *Washington Post* pursued the taint of scandal coming from the election, Congress, the federal courts, and government prosecutors also sought evidence of lawbreaking. Federal District Judge John Sirica, a Republican appointee presiding over the trial of the Watergate burglars, suspected a cover-up. In May 1973, U.S. Senate leaders convened a special, bipartisan Watergate Committee, headed by North Carolina's conservative Democratic senator Sam Ervin, to investigate. The Ervin hearings, carried live on TV, eventually attracted the most public attention. Testimony from John Dean, once the president's chief legal counsel, linked Nixon himself to attempts to cover up Watergate and to other illegal activities. The president denied Dean's charges.

Along the way, though, Senate investigators discovered that a voice-activated taping system had recorded conversations involving Nixon and his aides. These tapes made it possible to determine whether the president or Dean, Nixon's primary accuser, was lying. While contending he was not "a crook," Nixon also claimed an "executive privilege" to keep the tapes from being released, but Judge Sirica, Archibald Cox (a special, independent prosecutor in the Watergate case), and Congress all demanded access to them.

If Nixon's Watergate-related problems were not enough, his vice president, Spiro Agnew, suddenly resigned in October 1973 after pleading no contest to income-tax evasion. He agreed to a plea-bargain arrangement to avoid prosecution for having accepted illegal kickbacks while in Maryland politics. Acting under the Twenty-fifth Amendment (ratified in 1967), Nixon appointed—and both houses of Congress confirmed—Representative Gerald R. Ford of Michigan as the new vice president.

Nixon's Resignation

Nixon's clumsy efforts to protect himself backfired. During the fall of 1973, Nixon had abruptly fired Archibald Cox, hoping to prevent him from gaining access to the tapes. Nixon's own release of edited transcripts of some Watergate-related conversations, a key one containing an 18-minute gap in one tape, merely strengthened demand for the original recordings. Finally, by proclaiming that he would obey only a "definitive" Supreme Court decision, Nixon all but invited the justices to deliver a unanimous ruling against his withholding of the tapes. On July 24, 1974, the Court did just that in the case of *United States v. Nixon.* After televised deliberations, a bipartisan majority of the House Judiciary Committee voted three formal articles of impeachment against the president for obstruction of justice, violation of constitutional liberties, and refusal to produce evidence.

Nixon promised to rebut these accusations before the Senate, but his aides were already orchestrating his departure. One of his own attorneys had discovered that a tape Nixon had been withholding contained the long-sought "smoking gun," clear evidence of a criminal offense. It confirmed that during a 1972 conversation, Nixon had helped hatch the plan by which the CIA would advance the fraudulent claim of national security in order to stop the FBI from investigating the Watergate break-in. Nixon went on television on August 8, 1974, to announce his resignation. On August 9, Gerald Ford became the nation's 38th chief executive. He assumed the post having been elected neither president nor even vice president.

In 1974, most people told pollsters that the string of abuses collectively known as "Watergate" was one of the gravest crises in the history of the republic and that the Nixon administration had posed a serious threat to constitutional governance. But opinion polls conducted on the 20th anniversary of Nixon's resignation suggested that Americans by then only dimly recalled the Watergate episode.

What might account for this change? First, the president avoided prosecution; Gerald Ford granted him an unconditional pardon. The nation was denied an authoritative accounting, in a court of law, of Nixon's misdeeds. Another reason for fading memories may be the media's habit of attaching the suffix *gate* to nearly every political scandal—grave and trivial—of the post-Nixon era. Finally, images of Watergate have tended to blend into the broader picture of turmoil that accompanied U.S. involvement in the nation's longest war.

Conclusion

The power of the national government expanded between 1963 and 1974. Lyndon Johnson's Great Society provided a blueprint for policy-making at home even as his administration dramatically escalated the war in Vietnam. This growth of governmental power prompted divisive debates that polarized the country. During Johnson's presidency, both the war effort and the economy faltered. The use of presidential power by Johnson's Republican successor, Richard Nixon, prompted a crisis of governance that ultimately forced Nixon from office. The hopes of the early 1960s ended in frustration.

The era of America's longest war was a time of political passion, cultural and racial conflict, and differing definitions of patriotism. It saw an antiwar movement, youthful dissent, Black Power, women's activism, and contests over what constituted Americans' basic rights. Different groups have invoked divergent explanations for the fates of both the Great Society and the war effort, and the divisions from this era shaped politics and culture for years to come. Many Americans became skeptical, even cynical, about expanding the power of the federal government in the name of expanding liberty and equality.

CHAPTER REVIEW

Review Questions

1. How did the Johnson administration define its domestic goals, and how did it approach problem solving? Why did Johnson's "Great Society" produce so much controversy?

2. Through what incremental steps did the Johnson administration involve the United States ever more deeply in Vietnam? What was its major goal in Vietnam?

3. What domestic social-political movements emerged during America's longest war? How did they seek to change U.S. political culture and the direction of public policy? What role did commercial media play in the "movement of movements"?

4. What helped to make the single year of 1968, even as it was still unfolding, seem such an important time in the history of America's longest war and of the Sixties?

5. Why did the polarization that had developed over the 1960s continue into the 1970s? What foreign and domestic events contributed to the continued polarization?

6. What were the major aims of U.S. foreign policy during the presidency of Richard Nixon? How successful was the Nixon administration in carrying out these policies?

7. How did the political controversies of the early 1970s lead the nation into a crisis of governance? How did this crisis ultimately undermine Richard Nixon's presidency and force his resignation?

Critical Thinking Questions

1. What long-term repercussions did America's longest war exact on America's economy, social fabric, culture, and foreign policy?

2. Great Society proposals reinvigorated long-term debates over the extension of government power and over definitions of civil and personal liberties. What roles did issues of race, gender, and the distribution of wealth and income play in these debates?

3. Why was the era of America's longest war marked by so much protest and unrest? How would the polarization of views during that era continue to affect how people saw the history and future of the United States?

Identifications

Review your understanding of the following key terms, people, and events for this chapter.

Civil Rights Act of 1964, p. 687

Freedom Summer, p. 688

Great Society, p. 689

Voting Rights Act of 1965, p. 689

Immigration and Nationality Act of 1965, p. 689

Gulf of Tonkin Resolution, p. 690

New Left, p. 695

counterculture, p. 695

Black Power, p. 696

Malcolm X, p. 696

Civil Rights Act of 1968, p. 697

Tet Offensive, p. 699

Equal Rights Amendment (ERA), p. 703

Roe v. Wade, p. 703

détente, p. 705

Nixon Doctrine, p. 706

My Lai Incident, p. 706

Watergate, p. 708

DISCOVERY

How did American involvement in the Vietnam War affect American government and society?

In thinking about this question, begin by breaking it down into the components shown below. A discussion of the significance of each component should appear in your answer.

Culture and Society

Think about the reading in this chapter and examine the graph on American attitudes toward the Vietnam War on page 694. What happened between March of 1966 and January of 1971 to change people's feelings so dramatically?

Look at the Visual Link to the Past box, "Shocking Images," on page 693 and the photo of Jackson State on page 706. How are these pictures similar? What feelings do they convey? Was the increase in violence in American society in the late 1960s and early 1970s connected to the violence that Americans were seeing unfold in Vietnam? Did the war influence the civil rights movement and the student movement? If so, how? More broadly, how do you think the visual media—most notably television and photographs—influenced American politics?

JACKSON STATE

30

UNCERTAIN TIMES, 1974–1992

SEARCHING FOR DIRECTION, 1974–1980
- A Faltering Economy
- Welfare and Energy Initiatives
- Negotiation and Confrontation in Foreign Policy
- The New Right

THE REAGAN REVOLUTION, 1981–1992
- The Election of 1980
- Supply-Side Economics
- Curtailing Unions, Regulations, and Welfare
- Reagan to Bush

RENEWING AND ENDING THE COLD WAR
- The Defense Buildup
- Deploying Military Power

- The Iran-*Contra* Controversy
- The Cold War Eases
- Post–Cold War Policy and the Persian Gulf War
- The Election of 1992

THE POLITICS OF SOCIAL MOVEMENTS
- Women's Issues
- Sexual Politics
- Activism among African Americans
- Activism among American Indians
- Activism in Spanish-Speaking Communities
- Activism among Asian Americans
- Anti-Government Activism

Events of the 1960s and early 1970s, particularly Vietnam and Watergate, shook Americans' faith in government. During the 1970s and 1980s, the nation debated how to respond to an aging industrial economy, a ballooning federal deficit, and a beleaguered social welfare system. Did the country need new governmental programs, or might conditions improve if Washington reduced its role?

Disagreement extended to foreign policy. Should the United States set aside anticommunism to pursue other goals, as Democratic president Jimmy Carter (1977–1981) initially urged, or should it wage the Cold War even more vigorously, as his successor, Republican Ronald Reagan

(1981–1989), advocated? After 1989, when the Cold War ended unexpectedly, the United States needed to find a foreign policy for a post–Cold War world.

Meanwhile, the "movement of movements," a legacy of the 1960s, refused to fade away. Social movements associated with women's rights, gay rights, and racial and ethnic identities affected how Americans saw themselves and their nation's future. Some of the goals of these movements, however, met strident opposition from the New Right that had helped build Reagan's popularity. Political polarization deepened and broadened, sparking new controversies over issues such as abortion, taxation, affirmative action, and environmental regulations.

TIMELINE

1972	1976	1980	1984	1988	1992

■ **1974**
Nixon resigns and Ford becomes president; Ford soon pardons Nixon

■ **1975**
South Vietnam falls to North Vietnam

■ **1976**
Jimmy Carter elected president • OPEC sharply raises oil prices

■ **1978**
Carter helps negotiate Camp David Peace Accords on Middle East

■ **1979**
Soviet Union invades Afghanistan • *Sandinistas* come to power in Nicaragua
• U.S. hostages seized in Iran

■ **1980**
Reagan elected president • U.S. hostages in Iran released

■ **1981**
Reagan tax cut passed

■ **1983**
Reagan announces SDI ("Star Wars") program

■ **1984**
Reagan defeats Walter Mondale • U.S. troops removed from Lebanon

■ **1986**
Reagan administration rocked by revelation of Iran-*Contra* affair

1988 ■
George H. W. Bush defeats Michael Dukakis in presidential election
• Congress enacts Indian Gaming Regulation Act

■ **1989**
Communist regimes in Eastern Europe collapse;
Berlin Wall falls • Cold War, in effect, ends

■ **1990**
Bush angers conservative Republicans by
agreeing to a tax increase

1991 ■
Bush orchestrates Persian Gulf War against Iraq

■ **1992**
Bill Clinton defeats Bush

SEARCHING FOR DIRECTION, 1974–1980

When Richard Nixon resigned in August 1974, **Gerald R. Ford**, his vice president, moved from one office to which voters had never elected him to another, the presidency. Ford promised to "heal the land," but he achieved limited success. His attempt to present his administration as an updated version of the modern Republicanism of the 1950s quickly foundered. His appointment of Nelson Rockefeller as vice president infuriated GOP conservatives, and his pardoning of former president Nixon, in September 1974, angered almost everyone. In the election of 1976, Ford nearly lost the GOP's presidential nomination to Ronald Reagan, who campaigned as a "true conservative," owing nothing to Washington insiders.

FOCUS QUESTION

How did the legacies of the Vietnam War and Watergate help shape U.S. politics in the decade that followed?

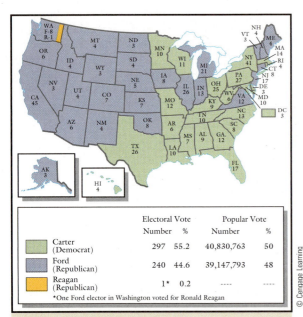

© Cengage Learning

	Electoral Vote		Popular Vote	
	Number	%	Number	%
Carter (Democrat)	297	55.2	40,830,763	50
Ford (Republican)	240	44.6	39,147,793	48
Reagan (Republican)	1*	0.2	----	----

*One Ford elector in Washington voted for Ronald Reagan

Map 30.1 **Presidential Election, 1976.** *This map shows the low voter turnout and the very close election that made Jimmy Carter president. Notice how Carter, from Georgia, drew votes from southern states.*

Gerald R. Ford *A GOP member of the House of Representatives, Ford became the first person to be appointed vice president of the United States. When Richard Nixon resigned, Ford became president.*

Jimmy Carter *Democratic president (1977–1981) whose single term in office was marked by inflation, fuel shortages, and a hostage crisis.*

The Democrats did turn to an outsider, **James Earl (Jimmy) Carter**. A retired naval officer, engineer, peanut farmer, and former governor of Georgia, Carter campaigned by stressing personal character. He highlighted his small-town roots and his Southern Baptist faith. Carter defeated Ford, but the election was close, and voter turnout hit its lowest mark (54 percent) since the end of the Second World War.

Once in office, Carter's lack of a popular mandate and his outsider status proved serious handicaps. Moreover, he was caught between advisers who claimed that the national government exercised too much power and those who argued that Washington did too little. His policies often seemed hesitant and inconsistent.

The 865-day presidency of Ford and the one-term administration of Carter reflected the uncertainties of post-Vietnam and post-Watergate America. The sense of national crisis seemed unrelenting, as politicians and citizens alike attempted to cope with a faltering economy, disruptive energy shortages, and sensationalized foreign challenges.

A Faltering Economy

Economic problems dominated the domestic side of Ford's caretaker presidency. Ford first touted a program called "Whip Inflation Now" (WIN), which included a one-year surcharge on income taxes and cuts in federal spending. WIN proved to be a loser. During 1975, unemployment reached 8.5 percent, and the inflation rate topped 9 percent. Ford also clashed with the Democratic-controlled Congress over how to deal with the ever-rising price of oil and with stagflation. Democrats charged that Ford could not implement coherent programs of his own, and many Republicans complained that he could not stand up to congressional Democrats.

Once Carter took office, economic problems only worsened. Carter pushed for tax cuts, increased public-works spending, and pro-growth Federal Reserve Board policies, but these measures did not bring the sustained recovery that had also eluded Carter's Republican predecessors. By 1980, the economy had virtually stopped expanding; unemployment (after temporarily dipping) continued to rise; and inflation topped 13 percent. Voters told pollsters that their economic fortunes had deteriorated while Carter was in office.

Economic distress spread beyond individuals. New York City faced bankruptcy. According to one estimate, Chicago lost 200,000 manufacturing jobs during the 1970s. Soaring unemployment, rising crime rates, deteriorating downtowns, and shrinking tax revenues afflicted most urban areas, even as inflation further eroded the buying power of city budgets.

Conservative economists and business interests argued that domestic programs favored by most congressional Democrats contributed to economic distress. Increasing the minimum wage and enforcing excessive safety and antipollution regulations, they asserted, drove up the cost of doing business and forced companies to raise prices to consumers. During his last two years in office, Carter seemed to agree with some of this analysis. Defying many Democrats in Congress, he cut spending for social programs, sought to reduce capital-gains taxes to encourage investment, and inaugurated the process of "deregulating" various industries, beginning with the financial and transportation sectors.

Welfare and Energy Initiatives

Carter puzzled over welfare policy. His staff differed over whether to propose increasing monetary assistance to low-income families or to advocate federal spending to create several million public service jobs. A proposed compromise failed in Congress.

The president pushed harder on energy issues. The United States obtained 90 percent of its energy from fossil fuels, much of it from imported petroleum. In 1978, as in 1973, the Organization of Petroleum Exporting Countries (OPEC), a cartel dominated by oil-rich nations in the Middle East, dramatically raised the price of crude oil and precipitated acute worldwide shortages. As gasoline became expensive and scarce, drivers denounced high prices and long lines at the pumps. Carter promised to make the United States less dependent on imported fossil fuel. Without consulting Congress or even members of his own administration, he offered a complex plan that featured more than 100 interrelated provisions and included increased taxation, deregulation, and the promotion of coal and nuclear power.

Congress quickly rejected it. Gas and oil interests opposed higher taxes. Consumer activists blocked deregulation. Environmentalists charged that greater use of coal would increase air pollution. Although, in theory, nuclear reactors could provide inexpensive, almost limitless amounts of energy, the cost of building and maintaining them far exceeded original estimates and posed safety risks. In 1979, a serious reactor malfunction at **Three Mile Island**, Pennsylvania, heightened fears of a nuclear-reactor meltdown. Power companies canceled orders for new reactors, and the nuclear power industry's expansion halted. Meanwhile, OPEC oil prices continued to rise, from about $3.60 a barrel in 1971 to nearly $36 a decade later, at the end of Carter's presidency.

Negotiation and Confrontation in Foreign Policy

Foreign policy lurched along a similar uncertain course during the mid- and late 1970s. Ford's initiatives, which included extending Nixon's policy of détente with the Soviet Union and pursuing peace negotiations in the Middle East, achieved little. Ford pledged a renewal of U.S. military support to the government in South Vietnam, if North Vietnam ever directly threatened its survival, but the antiwar mood in the United States and battlefield conditions in Vietnam made fulfilling this commitment impossible. North Vietnam's armies stormed across the South in March 1975, and Congress refused any new American involvement. The following month, Khmer Rouge forces in Cambodia drove a U.S.-backed government from the capital of Phnom Penh, and North Vietnamese troops overran the South Vietnamese capital of Saigon, renaming it Ho Chi Minh City.

Carter had little background in foreign policy, but his faith in negotiation and in his own skills as a facilitator yielded some successes. On the issue of the Panama Canal, the object of diplomatic negotiations for 13 years, Carter secured treaties that granted Panama increasing authority over the waterway and full control in 2000. Carter convinced skeptical senators, whose votes he needed to ratify any treaty, that the canal was no longer an economic or strategic necessity. Carter's personal skills also shaped the **Camp David Peace Talks of 1978**. Relations between Egypt and Israel had been strained since the Yom Kippur War of 1973, when Israel repelled an Egyptian attack and seized the Sinai Peninsula and territory along the West Bank (of the Jordan River). Reviving earlier Republican efforts to broker a peace settlement, Carter brought Menachem Begin and Anwar Sadat, leaders of Israel and Egypt, respectively, to the presidential retreat at Camp David. After 13 days of difficult bargaining, the three leaders announced a framework for further

Three Mile Island *Site of a nuclear power plant in Pennsylvania that experienced a major reactor malfunction in 1979; the industry stopped development following this event.*

Camp David Peace Talks of 1978 *Talks in which President Carter negotiated a peace treaty with Menachem Begin and Anwar Sadat, leaders of Israel and Egypt.*

negotiations and a peace treaty. Middle East tensions hardly vanished, but these Camp David Accords kept alive high-level discussions, lowered the level of acrimony between Egypt and Israel, and bound both nations to the United States through Carter's promises of economic aid.

In Asia, the Carter administration built on Nixon's initiative, expanding economic and cultural relations with China. The United States finally established formal diplomatic ties with the People's Republic on New Year's Day 1979.

Carter's foreign policy became best known for its emphasis on human rights. Carter argued that Cold War alliances with repressive dictatorships, even in the name of anticommunism, undermined U.S. influence in the world. The human rights policy, however, proved difficult to orchestrate. Carter's administration continued to support some harsh dictators, such as Ferdinand Marcos in the Philippines. Moreover, rhetoric about human rights helped justify uprisings against longstanding dictator-allies in Nicaragua and Iran. Revolutions in these countries, fueled by resentment against the United States, brought anti-American regimes to power and presented Carter with difficult choices.

In Nicaragua, the *Sandinista* movement toppled the dictatorship of Anastasio Somoza, which the United States had long supported. The *Sandinistas*, initially a coalition of moderate democrats and leftists, soon tilted toward a militant Marxism. Republican critics charged that Carter's policies had given a green light to communism throughout Central America, and some pledged to oust the *Sandinistas*.

If events in Nicaragua brought dilemmas to Carter, those in Iran and Afghanistan all but shattered his presidency. The United States had steadfastly supported the dictatorial Shah Reza Pahlavi, who had reigned in oil-rich Iran since an American-supported coup in 1953. The shah's overthrow in the **Iranian Revolution of January 1979**, by a revolutionary movement dominated by Islamic fundamentalists, signaled a massive repudiation of U.S. influence. When the White House allowed the deposed shah to enter the United States for medical treatment in November, Iranians seized the U.S. embassy in Tehran and 66 American hostages. Iran demanded the return of the shah in exchange for the hostages' release.

Iranian Revolution of January 1979 *Rebellion in which Islamic fundamentalists overthrew Iranian dictator Shah Reza Pahlavi; led to 66 Americans being taken hostage when Carter allowed the shah into the United States for medical assistance.*

AMERICAN HOSTAGES IN IRAN. *The Iranian government presents American hostages to the press under a banner protesting Carter's decision to admit the shah into the United States to obtain medical treatment.*

© Bettmann/CORBIS

In response, Carter turned to tough talk, levied economic sanctions against Iran, and sent a combat team to rescue the hostages. This military effort ended in an embarrassing failure. Carter's critics cited this "hostage crisis" as conclusive proof of his incompetence. After Carter's defeat in the 1980 election, diplomatic efforts finally freed the hostages, but the United States and Iran remained at odds.

Criticism of Carter also focused on the Soviet Union's 1979 invasion of Afghanistan, a move primarily sparked by Soviet fear of the growing influence of Islamic fundamentalists along its borders. Carter halted grain exports to the Soviet Union (angering his farm constituency), organized a boycott of the 1980 Summer Olympic Games in Moscow, withdrew a new Strategic Arms Limitation Treaty (SALT) from the Senate, and revived registration for the military draft. Still, Republicans (along with some Democrats) charged Carter with allowing U.S. power and prestige to decline as the Soviet Union embarked on a new campaign to expand communism.

For a time, after Senator Edward Kennedy of Massachusetts entered the 1980 presidential primaries, it seemed as if Carter's own Democratic Party might deny him a second term. Although Kennedy's challenge fizzled, it popularized anti-Carter themes that Republicans would gleefully embrace. "It's time to say no more hostages, no more high interest rates, no more high inflation, and no more Jimmy Carter," was Kennedy's standard stump speech.

The New Right

By 1976, the idea of preventing another Carter or another Kennedy presidency animated a diverse coalition of conservatives: a **New Right**. This broadly based movement succeeded in holding together several different constituencies. One was the already disparate group that had initially gathered around William F. Buckley's *National Review* during the 1950s. Buckley reached out to new converts through television; his long-running interview show, *Firing Line*, debuted on PBS in 1971. The economist Milton Friedman—a frequent Buckley guest, a 1976 Nobel laureate, and creator of a PBS series touting free-market economic principles—provided another important link between the conservatism of the 1950s and 1970s. In addition, many of the then-youthful conservatives who had energized Barry Goldwater's 1964 presidential campaign, such as Patrick Buchanan, came to the New Right after having worked in Richard Nixon's administration.

In contrast, the **"neoconservative"** (or "neocon") wing of the New Right of the 1970s had generally identified with Democrats during the 1950s and much of the 1960s. Anticommunist writers and academics such as Jeane Kirkpatrick and Irving Kristol viewed most domestic movements of the 1960s as threatening the social stability and intellectual values they admired. This initial generation of neoconservatives, often the offspring of European-Jewish immigrants, also complained that U.S. foreign policy, even under Nixon, failed to support Israel strongly enough.

Conservative business leaders provided another important New Right constituency. In their view, new regulatory legislation accepted by the Nixon administration, especially measures dealing with workplace safety and environmental concerns, threatened "economic freedom" and "entrepreneurial liberty." Convinced that anti-corporate professors and students dominated most colleges and universities, conservative business leaders and their philanthropic foundations generously funded new research institutions, such as the Heritage Foundation (established in 1973) and the CATO Institute (founded in 1977).

New Right *A diverse coalition of conservatives that focused on social issues and national sovereignty; they supported the Republican party under the leadership of Ronald Reagan.*

neoconservatives *Group of intellectuals, many of whom had been anticommunist Democrats during the 1950s and 1960s, who came to emphasize hard-line foreign policies and conservative social stances after 1968.*

The New Right of the 1970s also attracted support from Protestants in fundamentalist and evangelical churches. People from these religious groups had generally stayed clear of overtly partisan politics since the 1920s but continued to express concern about public issues that involved spiritual and social matters. Already angered by Supreme Court decisions that seemed to eliminate sectarian prayers from public schools, many expressed greater outrage over *Roe v. Wade* (1973), the landmark abortion ruling. Reaching out to antiabortion Catholics, people whom most members of southern Protestant congregations would have shunned a generation earlier, a "Religious Right" slowly took shape. The Reverend Jerry Falwell of the Thomas Road Baptist Church and The Old Time Gospel Hour television ministry declared *Roe* showed the necessity of political action. Antireligious elites in Washington "have been imposing morality on us for the last fifty years," Falwell proclaimed.

Leaders of the Religious Right insisted that sacred values should actively shape political policy making. They viewed clear separation between church and state as a violation of the First Amendment right to the "free exercise of religion." Particularly in the South, conservatives embarked on a lengthy legal crusade to prevent the Internal Revenue Service from denying tax exempt status to private Christian colleges and academies that opposed racial integration. Most spokespeople for the Religious Right championed foreign policies that maximized use of U.S. military power, especially on behalf of Israel.

In 1976, most evangelicals and fundamentalists from the South, including Falwell, supported Jimmy Carter. His religious background made him seem less committed to the *Roe* decision than Gerald Ford, whose spouse, Betty Ford, often identified herself with women's issues. Very soon, however, Falwell and others on the Religious Right began realigning their politics with those of the GOP's conservative bloc, placing their growing movement behind a refashioned Republican party under the leadership of Ronald Reagan.

THE REAGAN REVOLUTION, 1981–1992

FOCUS QUESTION

To what extent did Ronald Reagan's administration represent a victory for the New Right agenda in both domestic and foreign policy?

Ronald Reagan courted the New Right on national security, economic, and social issues. He used the hostage crisis with Iran as a symbol of Carter's failures, while his revitalized anticommunist rhetoric called for a stronger military posture and greater defense spending. A "taxpayer revolt" that had swept through California politics during the late 1970s provided a model for Reagan's attack on "tax-and-spend" domestic policymaking at the federal level. (The situation was ironic, since California's tax revolt had emerged in response to tax increases adopted while Reagan was governor.) Reagan also opposed abortion rights, advocated prayer in school, and extolled conservative family values.

The Election of 1980

Easily capturing the Republican nomination, and anointing one of his defeated rivals, George H.W. Bush, as a running mate, Ronald Reagan advanced an optimistic vision of a rejuvenated America. Punctuating his speeches with quips inspired by Hollywood movies, he stressed his opposition to domestic social spending and high taxes while promising support for a stronger

Ronald Reagan *Republican president (1981–1989) who steered domestic politics in a conservative direction and sponsored a huge military buildup.*

national defense. To underscore the nation's economic problems under Carter, Reagan asked repeatedly, "Are you better off now than you were four years ago?"

The Reagan-Bush team swept to victory, capturing the Electoral College tally by a 489 to 49 margin. Republicans also took away 12 Democratic Senate seats, gaining control of the Senate, though not the House of Representatives.

The new president focused on three major priorities: cutting federal taxes, reducing the governmental regulatory structure, and boosting national security capabilities.

Supply-Side Economics

To justify cutting taxes, Reagan touted **supply-side economics**. This economic theory held that tax reductions targeted toward investors and businesses would stimulate production, create jobs, and ameliorate the economic stagnation of the 1970s. Reagan pushed a tax-reduction plan, endorsed by many Democrats, through Congress in 1981. At the same time, the Federal Reserve Board kept interest rates high to drive down inflation.

A severe economic downturn in 1981 and 1982 sent the president's approval ratings diving to 35 percent, and the Republican Party experienced losses in the off-year election of 1982. Slowly, however, inflation moderated, and the economy rebounded to enter a period of noninflationary growth. According to one study, the economy added nearly 17 million new jobs, and inflation dropped from double digits to around 2 percent. Although unemployment figures did not fall as sharply, Reagan's supporters hailed a "Reagan revolution."

This revival and its causes were controversial. Reagan had not matched tax cuts with budget reductions, and budget deficits soared. Reagan constantly inveighed against deficits and "big spenders," but his eight years in Washington saw annual deficits triple to nearly $300 billion. To finance such deficit spending, the United States borrowed abroad and piled up the largest foreign debt in the world.

Although partisans of the Reagan revolution argued that its effects would ultimately "trickle down" and benefit everyone, its detractors countered that the country was developing a "Swiss-cheese" economy, one in which many groups were falling through the holes. Mortgage foreclosures, reminiscent of the 1930s, hit the farm states. Cities saw a dramatic reduction in federal spending, even as they tried to cope with growing unemployment, disinvestment, population loss, and collapsing local tax revenue. The minimum wage, when adjusted for inflation, also declined in value during Reagan's presidency.

The mixed economic picture especially applied to African Americans. The number of African American families earning a solid middle-class income, for example, more than doubled between 1970 and 1990. African American college graduates could expect incomes comparable to those of their white classmates. Partly as a result of affirmative action hiring plans put in place by the Nixon and Carter administrations, many could afford to leave problem-plagued inner-city neighborhoods. But the situation looked different for those who remained persistently unemployed, perhaps trapped in declining urban centers. At the end of the 1980s one-third of all African American families lived in poverty, and the number

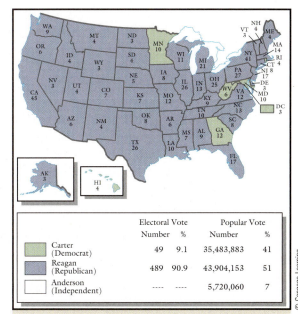

Map 30.2 Presidential Election, 1980. *Compare this map with the one showing the election of Jimmy Carter four years earlier. What factors might explain such a sudden downturn in Democratic fortunes?*

supply-side economics
Economic theory that tax reductions targeted toward investors and businesses would stimulate production and eventually create jobs.

earning less than $15,000 per year had doubled since 1970. In inner cities, fewer than half of African American children were completing high school, and more than 60 percent were unemployed. The gap between the well off and the disadvantaged widened during the 1980s.

Curtailing Unions, Regulations, and Welfare

Meanwhile, Reagan pursued his second major goal: cutting back the role of the federal government in supporting labor unions and regulatory structures.

In 1981, Reagan fired the nation's air traffic controllers after their union refused to halt a nationwide strike. The action portended more aggressive anti-union strategies that his administration and business interests would introduce during the 1980s. The percentage of unionized workers fell to just 16 percent by the end of Reagan's presidency.

Reagan had entered office promising to tame OPEC by encouraging the development of new sources of supply. Rejecting environmentalists' calls to decrease U.S. dependence on fossil fuels by promotion of renewable sources, Reagan and his successor, George H. W. Bush, pursued a "cheap oil" policy. The tapping of new oil fields at home and abroad, together with rivalries among OPEC's members, weakened the cartel's hold on the world market and reduced energy costs.

To oversee environmental issues, Reagan appointed James Watt, an outspoken critic of governmental regulation, as secretary of the Department of the Interior. Watt supported the so-called "sagebrush rebellion," in which western states demanded fewer restrictions on the use of public lands within their borders. In both the Interior and Energy departments, the White House relaxed enforcement of federal safety and environmental regulations.

Reagan's agenda for **deregulation** focused especially on the financial system. His economic advisers embraced the idea that financial markets were self-regulating and self-correcting. Minimal governmental interference in the marketplace, they argued, would bring greater economic efficiencies and therefore greater prosperity overall. The Carter administration had previously pursued programs of deregulation, and many Democrats in Congress now joined Republicans in crafting a looser environment for financial institutions. Several pieces of legislation in the 1980s wiped away lending regulations. More credit became available to more people, as a new "subprime loan" industry boomed.

But there were hazards. Savings and loan (S & L) companies had ventured into risky loans, particularly in real estate, and bankruptcies began to cascade through the S & L industry, eventually closing 747 institutions. Many people lost their savings. Finally, in 1989, Congress created a bailout plan designed to save some S & Ls and to transfer assets from already failed institutions to solvent ones. The plan proved astronomically expensive, and taxpayers footed the bill that eventually reached around $125 billion.

The Reagan administration also sought a somewhat more limited role for government in social welfare spending. It rejected suggestions for eliminating the basic set of New Deal–Great Society programs—particularly Social Security and Medicare—but it did decrease funding for various kinds of public-benefit programs, particularly Aid to Families with Dependent Children (AFDC). Reductions in food stamps and other programs increased poverty rates and fell disproportionately on female-headed households and on children. By the end of the 1980s, one of every five children was growing up in a household where the income fell below the official poverty line.

deregulation *Reduction or removal of governmental rules or policies; Reagan's deregulation agenda focused on the financial system.*

The Reagan administration seized the opportunity to place its conservative stamp on the federal legal system. Almost immediately, Reagan nominated a Supreme Court justice, Sandra Day O'Connor (the first woman to sit on the Court), who appeared to be a conservative. The resignation of Warren Burger allowed Reagan to elevate **William Rehnquist** to the position of chief justice and to appoint Antonin Scalia, a staunch conservative, to replace Rehnquist as an associate justice. Reagan also named prominent conservative jurists to lower federal courts and staffed the Justice Department with young conservative attorneys, such as John Roberts and Samuel Alito.

By 1990, because of retirements, about half of all federal judges had reached the bench during Ronald Reagan's presidency. The New Right welcomed the influx of conservative judges, while civil libertarians complained that the federal courts were becoming less hospitable to legal arguments made by criminal defendants, labor unions, and political dissenters.

No matter what problems beset his administration, criticism rarely stuck to Reagan, whom one frustrated Democrat dubbed the "Teflon president." His genial optimism seemed unshakable. He even appeared to rebound quickly—although close observers noted a clear decline in his energies—after being shot by a would-be assassin in March 1981.

Reagan to Bush

Democrats continually underestimated Reagan's appeal—a miscalculation that doomed their 1984 presidential effort. Walter Mondale, Jimmy Carter's vice president, ran on a platform calling for an expansion of social welfare programs. Mondale proposed higher taxes to fund this agenda and chose as his running mate Representative Geraldine Ferraro of New York, the first woman to stand for president or vice president on a major party ticket.

Republican campaign ads—often framed by the slogan "It's Morning Again in America"—portrayed a glowing landscape of bustling small towns and lush farmlands. They attacked Mondale's support from labor unions and civil rights groups as a vestige of the "old politics" of "special interests" and his tax proposal as a return to the policies popularly associated with the stagflation of the 1970s. The 1984 presidential election ended with Mondale carrying only his home state of Minnesota and the District of Columbia.

The election signified that the Reagan revolution had significantly challenged the nation's political vocabulary. Democrats had once invoked "liberalism" to stand for governmental initiatives to stimulate the economy, promote greater equality, and advance liberty for all. Republicans recast the term "liberal" as a code word for wasteful social programs devised by a bloated federal government that gouged hardworking people and squandered their dollars. The term "conservative," as used by New Right Republicans, came to stand for economic growth through the curtailment of governmental power and support for traditional sociocultural values. The once-dominant Democratic Party of the New Deal, Fair Deal, and Great Society confronted an uncertain future.

©Galen Rowell/CORBIS

RIDING THE PRESIDENTIAL RANGE. *Ronald Reagan, a master of both imagery and rhetoric, could casually and effectively adopt poses indebted to the Hollywood westerns in which he had once appeared. Here, the septuagenarian president, decked out in denim, stars in a western-themed parade.*

William Rehnquist *Elevated to chief justice of the United States Supreme Court by President Reagan in 1986.*

HISTORY THROUGH FILM

The First Movie-Star President

Ronald Reagan began his presidency in Hollywood. The political career of the "Great Communicator" built on, rather than broke away from, his days in the entertainment industry. His media advisers could count on directing a seasoned professional. Reagan always knew where to stand; how to deliver lines effectively; how to convey emotions through both body language and dialogue; and when to melt into the background so that other players in the cast of his presidency might carry a crucial scene.

Several of Reagan's movies provided rehearsals for roles he would play in the White House. Initially, Reagan's opponents thought that his old film parts, particularly in *Bedtime for Bonzo* (1947), in which he costarred with a chimpanzee, would be political liabilities. Instead of disavowing his days in Hollywood, Reagan accentuated his fluency with film-related imagery. His efforts to cheer on the nation during the 1980s consciously invoked his favorite film role, that of the 1920s Notre Dame football star, George Gipp, who Reagan played in *Knute Rockne, All American* (1940). Similarly, when tilting with a Democratic-controlled Congress over tax policy, Reagan invoked Clint Eastwood's famous screen character "Dirty Harry," promising to shoot down any tax increase. "Go ahead, make my day," he taunted. On another occasion, he cited *Rambo* (1982), an action thriller set in post-1975 Vietnam as a possible blueprint for dealing with countries that had seized U.S. hostages. As he freely drew from Hollywood motion pictures, Reagan occasionally seemed unable to separate "reel" from "real" life. During one session with reporters, he erroneously referred to his own dog as "Lassie," the canine performer who had been Reagan's Hollywood contemporary during the 1940s and 1950s.

Life in Hollywood also provided a prologue to President Reagan's conservative policies. Early in his film career, Reagan appeared in four films as the same character, a government agent named "Brass Bancroft." In these B-grade thrillers, Reagan developed an image that he later deployed in politics: the action-oriented character who could distinguish (good) friends from (evil) foes. *Murder in the Air* (1940), one of the Brass Bancroft movies, even featured a science fiction–style "death ray" that resembled the SDI ("Star Wars") armaments that President Reagan would champion more than 40 years later.

Subsequent film roles refined his Hollywood image. Poor eyesight kept Reagan out of combat during the Second World War, but he served long hours as an Army Air Corps officer, producing movies in support of the war effort. He appeared in several films, such as *For God and Country* (1943), and more often provided upbeat voice-overs, once even sharing a soundtrack with President Franklin Roosevelt. He also starred, on loan from the Air Corps, in *This Is the Army* (1943), one of the most successful of wartime Hollywood's military-oriented musicals. After the war, Reagan increasingly directed his energies toward Cold War politics in the film capital. His tenure as the anticommunist president of the Screen Actors Guild—and as a secret FBI informant—likely speeded his conversion from New Deal Democrat to right-leaning Republican. In his final onscreen roles Reagan usually portrayed the kind of independent, rugged individualist—often in westerns such as *Law and Order* (1953)—that he would later lionize in his political speeches.

Nancy Reagan, who costarred with her husband in *Hellcats of the Navy* (1957) and later as the nation's First Lady, offered her close-up view of the relationship between Reagan the actor and Reagan the politician: "There are not two Ronald Reagans." During the 1980s Hollywood and Washington, D.C., became embodied in the same character, Ronald Wilson Reagan.

Ronald Reagan as the "Gipper" in Knute Rockne, All American.

In the election of 1988, the Reagan legacy fell to the president's heir apparent, Vice President **George H. W. Bush.** Born into a wealthy Republican family and educated at Yale, Bush had prospered in the oil business, served in the House of Representatives, and headed the CIA. To court the New Right, he pledged "no new taxes" and chose Senator J. Danforth (Dan) Quayle, a youthful conservative from Indiana, as a running mate. Quayle would soon delight political comedians, who highlighted his verbal blunders.

Governor Michael Dukakis of Massachusetts emerged as the Democratic presidential candidate. Dukakis avoided talk of new domestic programs and higher taxes. Instead, he spoke about bringing competence and honesty to the White House.

Although Bush emerged the winner, Democrats retained control of both houses of Congress. The turnout was the lowest for any national election since 1924, and polls suggested that many voters remained unimpressed with either Bush or Dukakis.

Once in the White House, Bush began to lose crucial support. He angered New Right Republicans by agreeing to an increase in the minimum wage and by failing to veto a law that allowed for some affirmative action in the hiring of women and people of color into occupations in which they were underrepresented. Most important, in 1990 Bush broke his "no new taxes" pledge in an attempt to curb the still-rising federal deficit. Worse for the president's political future, the economic growth of the Reagan years began slowing, while the budget deficit continued to grow.

George H. W. Bush *Republican president (1989–1993) who directed an international coalition against Iraq in the Persian Gulf War.*

Renewing and ending the Cold War

In foreign policy, Reagan promised to reverse what he derided as Carter's passivity. He declared that the Vietnam War had been a "noble cause" that politicians had refused to win. Renewing the rhetoric of strident anticommunism, Reagan denounced the USSR as an "evil empire" and promised a military buildup to confront communism. This renewal of the Cold War, however, proved short-lived, and Reagan and Bush presided over its end.

FOCUS QUESTION

What forces and events contributed first to heightened tensions in the Cold War and then to its end?

The Defense Buildup

In response to his campaign promises, Reagan's administration led off with dramatic increases in military spending, even as tax cuts reduced federal revenues. At the height of Reagan's military buildup, which produced gaping budget deficits, the Pentagon was purchasing about 20 percent of the nation's manufacturing output.

In 1983, Reagan proposed the most expensive defense system in history: a space-based shield against incoming missiles. This **Strategic Defense Initiative (SDI)** soon had its own Pentagon agency, which sought $26 billion, over five years, in research costs alone. Skeptics dubbed SDI "Star Wars." Although most scientists dismissed the plan as too speculative, Congress voted appropriations for SDI. Reagan insisted that a defensive shield could work and also suggested that the USSR might collapse under the economic strain of competing in an accelerating arms race.

The CIA, headed by William Casey, stepped up its covert activities during Reagan's time in office. Some became so obvious they hardly qualified as covert. It was no secret, for instance, that the United States sent aid to anticommunist forces in Afghanistan, many of them radical Islamic fundamentalist groups. The CIA also

Strategic Defense Initiative (SDI) *Popularly termed "Star Wars," a proposal to develop technology for the creation of a space-based defensive missile shield around the United States.*

helped train and support the *contras* in Nicaragua, a military force fighting to topple the *Sandinista* government. To contain the power of Iran, assistance went to its bitter enemy, Saddam Hussein in Iraq.

Deploying Military Power

In renewing the global Cold War, Reagan promised military support to "democratic" revolutions anywhere. The United States thus funded opposition forces in countries aligned with the Soviet Union: Ethiopia, Angola, South Yemen, Cambodia, Guatemala, Grenada, Afghanistan, and Nicaragua. Reagan called the participants in such anticommunist insurgencies "freedom fighters," although few displayed any visible commitment to democratic values or institutions.

The Reagan administration also deployed U.S. military power, initially in southern Lebanon in 1982. Here, Israeli troops faced off against Islamic groups supported by Syria and Iran. The Reagan administration convinced Israel to withdraw and sent 1,600 U.S. Marines as part of an international "peacekeeping force" to restore stability. Islamic militias then turned against the U.S. forces. After a massive truck bomb attack against a military compound killed 241 U.S. troops, mostly Marines, in April 1983, Reagan decided to end this ill-defined undertaking. In February 1984, he ordered the withdrawal of U.S. troops.

Another military intervention seemed more successful. In October 1983, Reagan sent 2,000 U.S. troops to the tiny Caribbean island of Grenada, whose socialist leader was forging ties with Castro's Cuba. U.S. troops swept aside Grenada's government and installed one friendlier to U.S. policies.

Buoyed by Grenada, the Reagan administration fixed its sights on Nicaragua, where the Marxist-leaning *Sandinista* government was trying to break Nicaragua's dependence on the United States. The administration responded with economic pressure, a propaganda campaign, and greater assistance to the *contras*—initiatives that stirred considerable controversy because of mounting evidence of the *contras'* corruption and brutality. Finally, Democrats in Congress barred additional military aid to the *contras*.

Meanwhile, violence continued to escalate throughout the Middle East. Militant Islamic groups increased attacks against Israel and Western powers. Bombings and kidnappings of Westerners became more frequent. Apparently, Libya's Muammar al-Qaddafi and Iranian leaders encouraged such activities. In the spring of 1986, the United States launched an air strike into Qaddafi's personal compound. It killed his young daughter, but Qaddafi and his government survived. Despite what looked like a long-range assassination attempt against a foreign leader, an action outlawed by Congress, Americans generally approved of using strong measures against sponsors of terrorism and hostage taking.

The Iran-*Contra* Controversy

In November 1986, a magazine in Lebanon reported that the Reagan administration was selling arms to Iran in order to secure the release of Americans being held hostage by Islamic militants. These alleged deals violated the Reagan administration's own pledges against selling arms to Iran or rewarding hostage taking by negotiating for the release of captives. During the 1980 campaign, Reagan had made hostages in Iran a symbol of U.S. weakness under Carter. When Iranian-backed groups continued to kidnap Americans during Reagan's own presidency, it seemed that Reagan had sought clandestine ways to recover hostages and avoid such charges being leveled at him.

As Congress began to investigate, the story became more bizarre. It appeared that the Reagan administration had not only sold arms to Iran but had funneled profits from these back-channel deals to the *contra* forces in Nicaragua, thereby circumventing the congressional ban on U.S. military aid. Oliver North, an aide in the office of the national security adviser, had directed the effort, working with international arms dealers and private go-betweens. North's covert machinations seemingly violated both the stated policy of the White House and an act of Congress.

This **Iran-*Contra* Affair** never reached the proportions of the Watergate scandal. Reagan stepped forward and testified, through a deposition, that he could not recall any details about either the release of hostages or the funding of the *contras*. Vice President George H. W. Bush also claimed ignorance. Several officials in the Reagan administration were convicted of felonies, including falsifying documents and lying to Congress, but appellate courts later overturned these verdicts. Finally, in 1992, just a few days before the end of his presidency, George H. W. Bush pardoned six former Reagan-era officials connected to the Iran-*Contra* Controversy.

The Cold War Eases

After six years of renewed Cold War confrontations, Reagan's last two years saw a sudden thaw in U.S.-Soviet relations. The economic cost of superpower rivalry was burdening both nations, and political change sweeping the Soviet Union eliminated reasons for confrontation. **Mikhail Gorbachev**, who became general secretary of the Communist Party in 1985, understood that his isolated country faced economic stagnation and environmental problems brought on by decades of poorly planned industrial development. To redirect the Soviet Union's course, he withdrew troops from Afghanistan, reduced commitments to Cuba and Nicaragua, proclaimed a policy of *glasnost* ("openness"), and began to implement *perestroika* ("economic liberalization") at home.

Gorbachev's policies gained him acclaim throughout the West, and summit meetings with the United States yielded breakthroughs in arms control. At Reykjavik, Iceland, in October 1986, Reagan shocked both Gorbachev and his own advisers by proposing a wholesale ban on nuclear weapons. In December 1987, Reagan and Gorbachev signed a major arms treaty that reduced each nation's supply of intermediate-range missiles and allowed for on-site verification, which the Soviets had never before permitted. The next year, Gorbachev scrapped the policy that forbade nations under Soviet influence from renouncing communism. In effect, he declared an end to the Cold War.

Within the next few years, communist states began to topple like dominoes. In 1989, the first year of Bush's presidency, Poland's anticommunist labor movement, Solidarity, ousted the pro-Soviet regime. The pro-Moscow government in East Germany fell in November 1989. West and East Germans hacked down the Berlin Wall and began the difficult process of reunification. Yugoslavia quickly disintegrated, and warfare ensued as rival ethnic groups re-created separate states in Slovenia, Serbia, Bosnia, and Croatia. Latvia, Lithuania, and Estonia, which had been under Soviet control since the Second World War, declared their independence. In December 1991, Boris Yeltsin, the president of the new state of Russia, brokered a plan to abolish the Soviet Union and replace it with 11 separate republics, loosely joined in a commonwealth arrangement.

Iran-*Contra* Affair *Reagan administration scandal in which the United States secretly sold arms to Iran, a country implicated in holding American hostages, and diverted the money to finance the attempt by the* contras *to overthrow the Sandinista government of Nicaragua.*

Mikhail Gorbachev *Became general secretary of the Communist Party in 1985; he agreed to Reagan's proposal to ban nuclear weapons and eliminated the policy that prohibited nations under Soviet influence from rejecting communism, which brought an end to the Cold War.*

©Owen Franken/CORBIS

BERLIN WALL, 1989 *Berliners celebrated the end of the Cold War by chiseling away at the Berlin Wall, which the communist East German state had erected in 1962 to prevent the flow of refugees to West Berlin. Pieces of the Berlin Wall became coveted symbols of the fall of communism.*

Post–Cold War Policy and the Persian Gulf War

The Bush administration set about redefining U.S. national security in a post–Cold War era. The collapse of the Soviet Union weakened support for the leftist insurgencies in Central America that had so preoccupied the Reagan administration. Nicaraguans voted out the *Sandinistas*. Consequently, the Pentagon pondered new military missions, imagining rapid, sharply targeted strikes rather than lengthy, conventional campaigns. The armed forces assessed, for example, how they might serve in the "war against drugs," an effort that Bush had suggested during his 1988 presidential campaign.

General Manuel Noriega, the president of Panama, was deeply involved in the drug trade, and the Reagan administration had secured an indictment against him for international narcotics trafficking. Confronting Noriega posed a potentially embarrassing problem for Bush: The anticommunist general had been recruited as a CIA "asset" during the mid-1970s, when Bush had headed the agency. Nevertheless, the United States needed a friendly and stable government in Panama in order to complete the transfer of the Panama Canal to Panamanian sovereignty in 2000, and Bush decided to topple Noriega. During "Operation Just Cause," U.S. Marines landed in Panama in December 1989 and laid siege to the president's headquarters. Noriega soon surrendered, was extradited to Florida, and went to prison after a 1992 conviction for trafficking in cocaine.

Deposing the leader of a foreign government by unilateral military action raised questions of international law, but the Panamanian operation, which involved 25,000 U.S. troops and few casualties, provided a new model for the post–Cold War era. The Pentagon firmed up plans for creating highly mobile, rapid deployment forces. A test of its new strategy came during the Persian Gulf War of 1991.

On August 2, 1990, Iraq's Saddam Hussein ordered his troops to occupy the neighboring oil-rich emirate of Kuwait. U.S. intelligence analysts had been caught off guard, and they now warned that Iraq's next target might be Saudi Arabia, the largest oil exporter in the Middle East and a longtime U.S. ally.

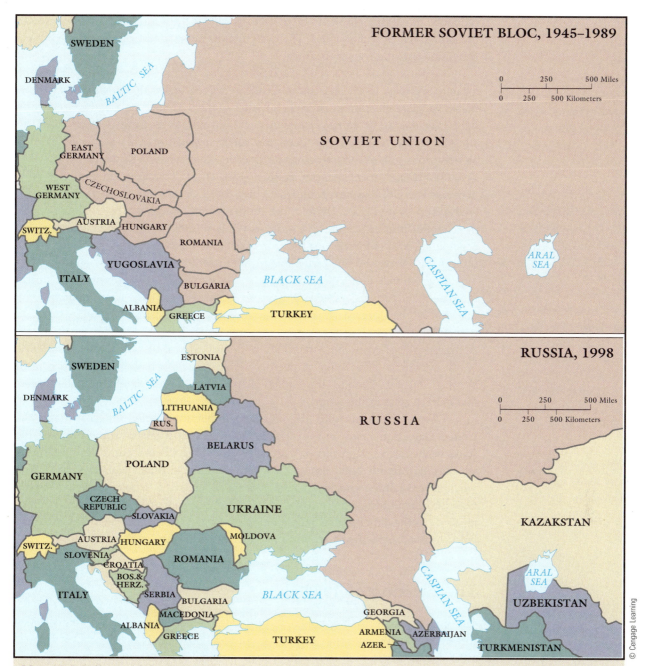

Map 30.3 Collapse of the Soviet Bloc. *These contrasting maps show the Soviet Union and the countries it dominated before and after the fall of communist governments. What countries in Eastern Europe escaped Russian control after 1989? What new countries emerged out of the old Soviet Union?*

Moving swiftly, Bush orchestrated a multilateral, international response. Four days after Iraq's invasion of Kuwait, he launched Operation Desert Shield by sending several hundred thousand U.S. troops to Saudi Arabia. After consulting with European leaders, Bush approached the UN, which denounced Iraqi aggression, ordered economic sanctions against Iraq, and authorized the United States to lead an international force to Kuwait if Hussein's troops did not withdraw.

Bush assembled a massive coalition force, ultimately nearly 500,000 troops from the United States and some 200,000 from other countries. He claimed a moral obligation to rescue Kuwait, and his policy-makers also spoke frankly about the economic threat that Hussein's aggression posed for the oil-dependent economies of the United States and its allies. These arguments persuaded Congress to approve a resolution backing the use of force.

In mid-January 1991, the United States launched an air war on Iraq. It began a ground offensive in late February. Coalition forces, enjoying air supremacy, decimated Saddam Hussein's armies in a matter of days. U.S. casualties were relatively light (148 deaths in battle). Estimates of Iraqi casualties ranged from 25,000 to 100,000 deaths. Although this **Persian Gulf War** lasted scarcely six weeks, it took an enormous toll on infrastructure facilities in both Iraq and Kuwait.

In a controversial decision, Bush stopped short of ousting Saddam Hussein, a goal that the UN had never approved and that U.S military planners had considered too costly and risky. Instead, the United States, backed by the UN, maintained its economic pressure, ordered the dismantling of Iraq's nuclear and bacteriological capabilities, and enforced "no-fly" zones over northern and southern Iraq to help protect the Kurds and Shi'a Muslims from Hussein's continued persecution.

The Persian Gulf War temporarily boosted Bush's popularity, but voters ultimately judged the president's record on foreign affairs as something of a muddle. He had organized an international coalition against Iraq and assisted a peaceful post–Cold War transition in Russia and Eastern Europe. He had also embraced global economic integration and supported (but been unable to pass) a North American Free Trade Agreement (NAFTA), which would eliminate tariff barriers and join Canada, the United States, and Mexico together in the largest free-market zone in the world.

Despite this leadership, the president publicly projected indecisiveness. The United States remained on the sidelines as full-scale warfare erupted among the states of the former Yugoslavia, with Serbs launching a brutal campaign of territorial aggrandizement and "ethnic cleansing" against Bosnian Muslims. In Africa, when severe famine wracked Somalia, Bush ordered U.S. troops to secure supply lines for humanitarian aid, but the American public remained wary of this military mission. As the old objective of containing the Soviet Union became irrelevant, Bush failed to excite Americans around any new foreign policy goal.

The Election of 1992

The inability to project a coherent vision for either domestic or foreign policy threatened Bush's reelection and forced concessions to the New Right. Dan Quayle, although clearly a liability with voters outside his conservative constituency, returned as Bush's running mate. The president allowed New Right activists, who talked about "a religious war" for "the soul of America," to dominate the 1992 Republican National Convention. Conservative Democrats and independents, who had supported Reagan and Bush in the previous three presidential elections, found this rhetoric unsettling.

Bush's Democratic challenger, Governor William Jefferson Clinton of Arkansas, stressed economic issues. Campaigning as a "New Democrat," Bill Clinton promised job creation, deficit reduction, and an overhaul of the nation's health-care system. Sounding almost like a moderate Republican, Clinton pledged to shrink the size of government and to "end this [welfare] system as we know it." This platform made it difficult for Bush to label Clinton as a "big-government liberal."

Clinton's focus on the economy helped deflect attention from the sociocultural issues on which he was vulnerable. As a college student, he had avoided service in Vietnam and, while in England as a Rhodes Scholar, had demonstrated against the war. When Bush, a decorated veteran of the Second World War, challenged the

Persian Gulf War *After Saddam Hussein invaded Kuwait, the United States formed a military coalition to restore Kuwait's sovereignty. The conflict between Iraq and the U.S.-led coalition lasted six weeks in 1991.*

patriotism of his Democratic challenger, Clinton emphasized, rather than repudiated, his roots in the 1960s. He appeared on MTV and touted his devotion to (relatively soft) rock music. In addition, he chose Senator Albert Gore of Tennessee, a Vietnam veteran, as his running mate.

The 1992 election brought Clinton a surprisingly easy victory. The quixotic campaign of Ross Perot, a Texas billionaire who spent more than $60 million of his own money on a third-party run, took more votes from Bush than from Clinton. With Perot in the race, Clinton garnered only 43 percent of the popular vote but won 370 electoral votes by carrying 32 states and the District of Columbia. Bush won a majority only among white Protestants in the South. Clinton carried the Jewish, African American, and Latino votes by large margins and even gained a plurality among people who had served in the Vietnam War. He also ran well among independents who had supported Reagan and Bush during the 1980s. Perhaps most surprising, about 55 percent of eligible voters went to the polls, a turnout that reversed 32 years of steady decline in voter participation.

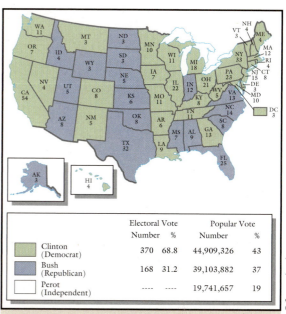

		Electoral Vote		Popular Vote	
		Number	%	Number	%
▢	Clinton (Democrat)	370	68.8	44,909,326	43
▢	Bush (Republican)	168	31.2	39,103,882	37
▢	Perot (Independent)	----	----	19,741,657	19

© Cengage Learning

Map 30.4 Presidential Election, 1992. *Notice the substantial number of votes cast for an independent candidate, Ross Perot. How did Perot's vote totals affect Bill Clinton's mandate as president?*

THE POLITICS OF SOCIAL MOVEMENTS

The activism associated with the 1960s became firmly embedded in most areas of American life in the decades that followed. Mass demonstrations reminiscent of those against the Vietnam War remained one tool of advocacy and protest. Both anti-abortion and pro-choice forces, for example, regularly demonstrated in Washington, D.C. In nearly every major city and many smaller towns, women's groups staged annual Take Back the Night rallies to call attention to the danger of sexual assault.

The media increasingly ignored most mass demonstrations, however, unless they sparked violent conflict. In 1991, for example, 30,000 Korean Americans staged a march for racial peace in Los Angeles. Although it was the largest demonstration ever conducted by any Asian American group, even the local media failed to cover it.

Women's Issues

In this environment, women's groups adopted a range of methods to rally new supporters and reenergize their core constituencies. Struggles over gender-related issues had emerged within the labor movement and the civil rights and antiwar movements of the 1960s. Initially, many of the men involved in these causes complained that issues of gender equality interfered with broader fights to redirect labor, racial, or foreign policies, but women insisted on calling attention to their second-class status in movements that claimed to be egalitarian. The continued spread of the birth control pill gave women greater control over reproductive choices but also complicated the meaning of "sexual freedom." Throughout the 1970s women promoted "consciousness-raising" sessions to discuss how *political* empowerment was inseparable from *personal* power relationships involving housework, child rearing, sexuality, and economic independence. "The personal is political" became a watchword for the new women's movement.

FOCUS QUESTION

How did social movements of the post-1960s era affect social life, culture, and the ways people saw their own personal identities?

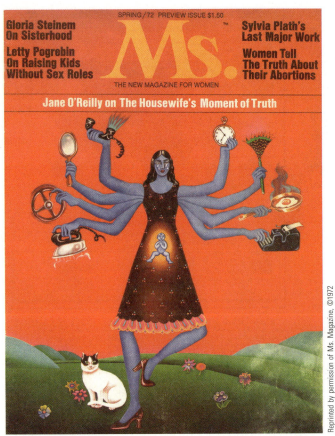

Ms. DEBUTS. *Eventually styling itself as "More than a Magazine— a Movement," Ms. has always featured eye-catching covers that help to chart the changing priorities of many feminist activists. Initially an experimental offshoot of New York magazine, Ms. debuted on its own in January 1972, under the editorship of Gloria Steinem, with this surrealistic, vividly symbolic cover.*

The number of groups addressing issues of concern to women continually expanded. The National Organization for Women (NOW) became generally identified with the rights-based agenda of the mainstream of the Democratic Party. African American women often formed separate organizations that emphasized issues of cultural and ethnic identity. Chicana groups coalesced within the United Farm Workers' (UFW) movement and alongside many Mexican American organizations. Lesbians organized their own groups, often allying with an emerging gay rights movement. Many U.S. feminist organizations joined with groups in other nations on behalf of international women's rights. Although never embracing the word "feminism," conservative women played leadership roles in causes associated with the New Right.

With agendas often varying along lines of class, race, ethnicity, and religion, the women's movement remained highly diverse, but women from different backgrounds often cooperated to build new institutions and networks. Their efforts included battered-women's shelters; rape crisis centers; union-organizing efforts; organizations of women in specific businesses or professions; women and gender studies programs in colleges and universities; and academic journals and popular magazines devoted to women's issues. Pressure for gender equity also affected existing institutions. Many Protestant denominations came to accept women into the ministry, and Reform Judaism placed women in its pulpits. Educational institutions adopted "gender-fair" hiring practices and instructional materials.

Economic self-sufficiency became an especially pressing issue. Reagan-era budget cuts for social programs took their toll. Homeless shelters, which once catered almost exclusively to single men, began taking in women and children. As this feminization of poverty gained attention, proposals on the state and federal level called for reshaping patterns of public support by limiting direct governmental payments and emphasizing strategies to move women, even those with young children, into the workforce.

The job market, however, remained laced with inequalities. The average female worker earned around 75 cents for every dollar taken home by men. "Glass ceilings" limited women's chances for promotion, and child-care expenses often fell disproportionately on women who worked outside the home.

Sexual harassment in the workplace became a highly charged issue. In 1986, the U.S. Supreme Court ruled that sexual harassment constituted a form of discrimination under the Civil Rights Act of 1964. In 1991, the issue gained national attention when Anita Hill, an African American law professor, accused Clarence Thomas, an African American nominee for the U.S. Supreme Court, of having sexually harassed her when both worked for the federal government. Feminists denounced the all-male Senate Judiciary Committee, which was responsible for considering Thomas's nomination, for failing even to understand, let alone investigate seriously, the issue of sexual harassment. Although the Senate narrowly approved Thomas for the High Court, women's groups mobilized female voters and elected four women as U.S. senators in 1992.

LINK TO THE PAST

Cultural Disagreements: Equality for Women?

The changing role of women in America dramatically altered family and civic life during this era. Many of the cultural and political disputes of these years revolved around issues related to gender. Advocates of "full equality" for women, such as the National Organization for Women (NOW), clashed with New Right activists, who opposed gender equality as an affront to the "natural" order.

National Organization for Woman (Now)

Statement of Purpose, 1966 ("Statement of Purpose," mimeographed, Washington, D.C., p. 1)

The purpose of NOW is to take action to bring women into full participation in the mainstream of American society now, exercising all the privileges and responsibilities thereof in truly equal partnership with men. . . . We reject the current assumptions that a man must carry the sole burden of supporting himself, his wife, and family, and that a woman is automatically entitled to lifelong support by a man upon her marriage, or that marriage, home and family are primarily woman's world and responsibility. . . . We believe that a true partnership between the sexes demands a different concept of marriage, an equitable sharing of the responsibilities of home and children and of the economic burdens of their support. . . .

We will strive to ensure that no party, candidate, president, senator, governor, congressman, or any public official who betrays or ignores the principle of full equality between the sexes is elected or appointed to office.

Jerry Falwell

calling for a "Moral Majority" in his 1980 book, *Listen America!* (New York, Doubleday. 1980, pp. 150–151)

I believe that at the foundation of the women's liberation movement there is a minority core of women who were once bored with life, whose real problems are spiritual problems. Many women have never accepted their God-given roles. . . . God Almighty created men and women biologically different and with differing needs and roles.

He made men and women to complement each other and to love each other. Not all the women involved in the feminist movement are radicals. Some are misinformed, and some are lonely. . . . I believe that women deserve more than equal rights. . . . Men and women have differing strengths. . . . Because a woman is weaker does not mean that she is less important.

Q Different assumptions about gender roles led to public policy disputes, especially in areas related to military service, families and reproduction, and labor rights. What specific social and political issues seemed to have been grounded in the contest over women's rights?

Sexual Politics

Issues involving gays and lesbians also became more public and political. In 1969, New York City police raided the Stonewall Inn, a bar in Greenwich Village with a largely homosexual clientele. Patrons resisted arrest, and the resultant confrontations pitted the neighborhood's gay and lesbian activists, who claimed to be the victims of police harassment, against law enforcement officials.

Recent studies emphasize that Lesbian-Gay-Bisexual-Transgendered (LGBT) activism did not suddenly emerge in 1969 but, instead, grew out of earlier movements, such as the Mattachine Society, and cultural communities such as the Beats (see Chapter 29). Still, the events at the Stonewall Inn, because of the prominence they received in mainstream and alternative media, marked an important benchmark in sexual politics. Gay and lesbian activism became an important part of the larger "movement of movements" that continued into the 1970s and 1980s. Thousands of advocacy and support groups, such as New York City's Gay Activist Alliance (GAA), sprang up. As many individuals "came out of the closet," newspapers, theaters, nightspots, and religious groups proudly identified themselves as activists. LGBT communities asserted constitutional claims to equal access to housing, jobs, and benefits for domestic partners.

One issue, with international implications, was especially urgent. A human immunodeficiency virus produced an immune deficiency syndrome, HIV-AIDS, a contagious disease for which medical science offered virtually nothing in the way of cure. The disease could be transmitted through the careless use of intravenous drugs, tainted blood supplies, and unprotected sexual intercourse. At first, the incidence of HIV-AIDS in the United States was primarily limited to gay men, and activists charged that, as a consequence, cultural and religious conservatives placed a low priority on medical efforts to understand its causes, check its spread, or devise a cure. The resultant controversy over medical funding galvanized empowerment efforts among LGBT organizations, such as Aids Coalition to Unleash Power, or ACT UP. With the development of prevention programs and drugs that could combat HIV-AIDS, however, most public figures came to support new efforts both at home and overseas, particularly in Africa, to address HIV-AIDS. It has remained a modern health threat in many parts of the world, but its specific identification with LGBT rights has faded.

AIDS ACT-UP Campaign. *Health-care issues increasingly galvanized grassroots activists. In 1989, members of ACT-UP, a group that embraced direct action, protested what they saw as the federal government's inattention to the issue of AIDS during the 1980s.*

Activism among African Americans

The emphasis on group identity as the fulcrum for social activism became especially strong among racial and ethnic communities. Having accomplished many of the legislative goals of the older civil rights movement, African American activists, one observed, were "heading into a completely new era, and we don't know what to make of it." Mobilization to promote political and cultural change proceeded along many fronts.

African American leaders became increasingly prominent in national and local politics. One media spotlight fell on the Reverend Jesse Jackson, a former associate of Dr. Martin Luther King, Jr. In 1971, he created a Chicago-based organization, Operation PUSH, which pressured public officials and corporations to create jobs and promote community development projects. Abundant media coverage made Reverend Jackson better known for addressing a wide range of national and international issues, including the status of the Palestinians and apartheid in South Africa. During the 1980s, he formed the Rainbow Coalition to provide a national umbrella for his movement and to facilitate campaigns for the Democratic Party's presidential nomination in 1984 and 1988. Jackson's efforts garnered several primary victories and helped shape Democratic Party politics.

Other types of political activism also left a significant imprint on electoral politics during the 1970s and 1980s. In 1970, 13 African American members of Congress established the Congressional Black Caucus (CBC) to form a common front on a wide range of foreign and domestic issues. By the end of the 1980s, more than 7,000 African Americans (including nearly 1,500 women) held political office. The year the Voting Rights Act had passed, 1965, there had been fewer than 200. Urban centers with significant African American populations, such as Gary and Detroit, elected black mayors, and so did cities such as Denver, where African American candidates successfully formed cross-ethnic alliances. This form of black political activism confronted clear limits. Few mayors, whatever their ethnic identity, could mobilize the economic resources that large cities required to deal with rising crime rates, decaying infrastructures, and galloping inflation.

In addition to political activism, a diverse set of cultural movements emerged. The hyperviolent cycle of 1970s "Blaxploitation movies," such as *Shaft* (1971) and *Coffy* (1973) prompted heated debate over whether representing urban black life "like it [supposedly] was," rather than "like it [supposedly] should be," advanced African American interests. The 1980s movies of Spike Lee also created controversy. *Do the Right Thing* (1989) provided a complex meditation about African American heroes, multiculturalism, law enforcement patterns, and personal activism amidst the uncertainties of urban life. Prominent academics such as **Henry Louis Gates, Jr.**, worked to expand the study of the African American experience and to challenge a movement that advocated creating an "Afro-centric" school curriculum. Gates insisted that cultural works of African Americans could simultaneously be seen as unique and different, *and also* be viewed in relationship to broader cultural traditions.

Activism among American Indians

American Indians had, of course, longstanding identities based on their tribal affiliation, and many issues, particularly those involving land and treaty disputes, turned on specific, tribal-based claims. Other questions, which seemed to require strategies that extended beyond a single tribe or band, became identified as "pan-Indian" in nature.

Henry Louis Gates, Jr.
Innovative voice in African American and American studies.

In 1969, people from several tribes began a two-year sit-in designed to dramatize a history of broken treaty promises, at the former federal prison on Alcatraz Island in San Francisco harbor. Expanding on this tactic, the American Indian Movement (AIM), created in 1968 by young activists from several Northern Plains tribes, adopted even more confrontational approaches. Clashes with both federal officials and older American Indian leaders erupted in 1973 on the Pine Ridge Reservation in South Dakota. In response, federal officials targeted members of AIM with illegal surveillance and a series of controversial criminal prosecutions.

Meanwhile, important social and legal changes were taking place. In the Civil Rights Act of 1968, which contained several sections that became known as the "Indian Bill of Rights," Congress extended most of the provisions of the constitutional Bill of Rights to Native Americans living on reservations, while reconfirming the legitimacy of tribal laws. Federal legislation and several Supreme Court decisions in the 1970s subsequently reinforced the principle of "tribal self-determination." By the early 21st century, the federal government officially recognized nearly 600 separate tribes and bands. After 1978, Congress also provided funds for educational institutions that would build job skills and preserve tribal cultures.

American Indians also sued to protect tribal water rights and traditional religious ceremonies, some of which included the ritualistic use of drugs such as peyote. In 1990, Congress passed the Native American Graves Protection and Repatriation Act, which required universities and museums to return human remains and sacred objects to tribes that requested them.

Claiming exemption from state gaming laws, Native Americans began to open bingo halls and then full-blown casinos. In 1988, the U.S. Supreme Court ruled that states could not prohibit gambling operations on tribal land, and Congress immediately responded with the Indian Gaming Regulatory Act. Gambling emerged as one of the most lucrative sectors of the nation's entertainment business, and many Indian-owned casinos thrived. Ironically, the glitzy, tribal-owned casinos often financed tribal powwows and other efforts to nurture traditional cultural practices.

To forestall the disappearance of native languages and cultures, American Indian activists urged bilingualism and renewed attention to tribal rituals. Indian groups also denounced the use of stereotypical nicknames, such as "Chiefs" and "Redskins," and Indian-related logos in sports. The federal government assisted this cultural-pride movement by funding two National Museums of the American Indian. The National Park Service changed the name of "Custer Battlefield" in Montana to "Little Bighorn Battlefield," redesigning its exhibits to honor American Indian culture.

Activism in Spanish-Speaking Communities

Spanish-speaking Americans, who constituted the fastest-growing ethnic group in the United States, highlighted the diversity and complexity of identity. Many Spanish-speaking people, especially in the Southwest, preferred the umbrella term "Latino," whereas others, particularly in Florida, used the term "Hispanic."

Mexican Americans, members of the oldest and most numerous Spanish-speaking group, could tap a long tradition of social activism. The late 1960s saw an emerging spirit of *Chicanismo*, a populist-style pride in a heritage that could be traced back to the ancient civilizations of Middle America. Young activists made "Chicano/a," terms of derision that older Mexican Americans had generally

Chicanismo Populistic pride in the Mexican American heritage that emerged in the late 1960s.

©Andre Jenny/The Image Works

GAMING AT POTAWATOMI CASINO. *During the 1980s, casino-style gaming began to emerge as one of the nation's leading entertainment enterprises. Native Americans embraced casinos, such as this one located in Milwaukee, Wisconsin, as important ways to generate jobs and capital on Indian reservations. The Potawatomi complex, which opened in 1991, juxtaposes traditional-style sculptures, an Indian heritage center and gift shop, an imaginatively designed building, more than 1,000 slot machines, and a cabaret-style dinner theater patterned after ones in Las Vegas.*

avoided in the past, into a rallying cry. New Spanish-language newspapers and journals reinforced a growing sense of pride, and Mexican Americans successfully pushed for programs in Chicano and Chicana Studies at colleges and universities.

Mexican Americans also organized politically. In San Antonio in the 1970s, Ernesto Cortes, Jr., took the lead in founding Communities Organized for Public Service (COPS), a group that brought the energy and talents of Mexican Americans, particularly women, into the city's public arena for the first time. On the national level, the Mexican American Legal Defense and Education Fund (MALDEF), established in 1968, emerged as a highly visible advocacy group ready to lobby or litigate. Professional groups, such as the National Network of Hispanic Women, also proliferated.

Efforts to organize agricultural workers, who were largely of Mexican and Filipino descent, dramatized both the successes and the difficulties of expanding the union movement to largely immigrant workers. **Dolores Huerta and Cesar Chavez**, charismatic leaders who emulated the nonviolent tactics of Martin Luther King, Jr., vaulted the United Farm Workers (UFW) into public attention during the 1970s. Chavez undertook personal hunger strikes and Huerta helped organize well-publicized consumer boycotts of lettuce and grapes to pressure growers into collective bargaining agreements with the UFW. Despite some successes, strong anti-union stands by growers and the continued influx of new immigrants eager for work increasingly undercut the UFW's efforts.

Dolores Huerta and Cesar Chavez *Political activists who vaulted the United Farm Workers into public attention during the 1970s.*

Social activism among Puerto Ricans in the United States emerged more slowly. Some stateside Puerto Ricans focused their political energy on the persistent "status" question—that is, whether Puerto Rico should seek independence, strive for statehood, or retain a commonwealth connection to the mainland. Over time, activism increasingly shifted its emphasis away from the island. The Puerto Rican Legal Defense and Education Fund and allied groups helped Puerto Ricans surmount political-legal obstacles and achieve social and economic gains.

Cuban Americans, who had begun immigrating in large numbers to southern Florida after Fidel Castro came to power, generally enjoyed greater access to education and higher incomes. They also tended to be politically conservative, generally voting Republican and lobbying for a hard line toward Castro's communist government. Cuban Americans developed a dense network of institutions that leveraged them into positions of power in Florida politics and civic affairs.

Beneath a common Spanish language, then, lay great diversity. In more recent years, immigrants from the Dominican Republic and Central America, who were among the most economically deprived and least organized, have also added their voices and concerns.

Activism among Asian Americans

Americans of Chinese, Japanese, Korean, Filipino, and other backgrounds began to create an Asian American movement in the 1970s. Organizations such as the Asian Pacific Planning Council (APPCON), founded in 1976, lobbied to obtain government funding for projects that benefited Asian American communities. During the 1970s, Asian American studies programs also took shape at colleges and universities, particularly on the West Coast. By the early 1980s, Asian American political activists enjoyed growing influence, especially within the Democratic Party, and began gaining public office.

Emphasizing this broad, Asian American identity raised questions of inclusion, exclusion, and rivalry. Filipino American activists, members of the second largest Asian American group in the United States in 2010, often resisted the Asian American label because they believed that Chinese Americans or Japanese Americans dominated groups such as APPCON. Many people of Filipino descent focused on specific goals, particularly an effort to obtain citizenship and veterans' benefits for former soldiers of the Second World War who had fought against Japan. Japanese American groups also lobbied on behalf of specific issues, and in 1988 Congress formally apologized and voted to approve a reparations payment of $20,000 to every living Japanese American who had been confined in internment camps during the Second World War (see Chapter 26).

As a result of combined pressure from different ethnic groups, the federal government finally designated "Asian or Pacific Islanders" (API) as a single pan-ethnic category in the censuses from 1990 on. It also provided nine specifically enumerated subcategories (such as Native Hawaiian or Filipino) and allowed other API groups (such as Hmong or Samoan) to write in their respective ethnic identifications. Thus, the term Asian American—which by the second decade of the 21st century applied to more than 16 million people and dozens of different ethnicities—both reflected, and was challenged by, the new emphasis on ethnic identity.

Anti-Government Activism

Ronald Reagan's first Inaugural Address, in 1981, declared that "government is not the solution to our problem; government is the problem." As president, Reagan exempted national security institutions from this principle and rarely applied it literally to basic safety-net programs such as Social Security and Medicare. His claim that government action was almost always harmful, however, did appeal to the New Right wing of the larger Reagan coalition. During the 1980s, denunciations of federal power spread throughout the culture, propelled especially by controversies over affirmative action and various regulatory rules.

Affirmative action programs had grown from bipartisan roots in the administrations of Lyndon Johnson and Richard Nixon. Public officials, proponents argued, should act "affirmatively" to make sure that people who belonged to groups with a shared history of discrimination—especially African Americans, Latinos, and women—could actually obtain an equitable share of the nation's jobs, public spending, and educational programs. Affirmative action would help compensate for past discrimination and for continued, sometimes hidden, prejudice.

Critics of affirmative action began to identify it as one of the most dangerous examples of increased governmental power. They often quoted Dr. King's words about judging people by the "content of their character" rather than the "color of their skin" and argued that government should remain "blind" to color and gender. Even some beneficiaries of these programs, such as Supreme Court Justice Clarence Thomas, charged that the derogatory label of "affirmative action applicant" threw into question the talents and capabilities of individuals. More broadly, critics of affirmative action programs denounced "set-aside" job programs and special educational admission procedures for previously disadvantaged groups as examples of illegal quotas, violations of constitutional guarantees, and even harbingers of totalitarianism. Did not affirmative action *on behalf of* people in some groups always constitute "reverse discrimination" *against* those in others?

In the midst of this controversy, federal courts struck down affirmative action plans that contained inflexible quotas but upheld less rigid ones that made group identity only one of several criteria for making hiring or educational decisions. In the celebrated Supreme Court decision popularly known as the *Bakke* case (1978), a majority of justices ruled that affirmative action programs in educational settings could pass constitutional muster because they aimed at redressing past discrimination *and* because they contributed to diversity, an intangible social and psychological quality important in any social, educational, or business environment.

Opposition to affirmative action mobilized anti-government activists, who found a close ally in "New Right radio." In 1984, Rush Hudson Limbaugh, III, took over a limited-market New Right talk show in California. A decade later, Rush Limbaugh's ability to galvanize anti-government listeners had propelled him to the top ranks of a rapidly expanding, informal network for anti-government activism.

The New Right radio programs almost always endorsed a central tenet of the new anti-government activism: "Free markets," not government, provided the best structure for enhancing individual freedom and ensuring social-economic progress. A widening circle of academic and legal proponents of these anti-government ideas also pressed this case. New economic textbooks challenged the Keynesian-oriented ones that

ANTIABORTION PROTEST, 1989. *Legalized abortions became a major political issue after the 1973 Supreme Court decision in* Roe v. Wade. *Here, on the 16th anniversary of* Roe, *protesters assemble in front of the Supreme Court building.*

had once dominated college and university classrooms. A new legal field, called "law and economics," attracted lawyers and judges who crafted doctrines that accorded with free-market assumptions rather than the pro-regulatory ones that had guided New Deal–Great Society jurisprudence. Taking advantage of loosened regulations, the business and financial world began to test the theories of self-regulating markets on Wall Street by devising new modes of investment and unusual new financial instruments.

Anti-government activists, like other activists, hardly moved in lockstep. Some cared deeply about opposing new rules for affirmative action; others placed greater priority on economic or environmental deregulation. But anti-government activism (always linked to anti-tax sentiment) successfully challenged the once-dominant political agendas of the Democratic Party. It propelled the mainstream of the Republican Party decidedly rightward, established a strong foothold in public-policy and media discussions, and succeeded in remapping the nation's cultural and informational landscape.

Conclusion

The "Reagan revolution" of the 1980s rested on a conservative movement that had been taking shape for several decades. New Right Republicans distrusted extending federal government power, advocated sharp tax cuts with deregulation, and stressed a sociocultural agenda emphasizing "traditional" values. The dozen years of Republican dominance of the White House, from 1980 to 1992, helped shift the terms of political debate in the United States. The "liberal" label became one that most Democrats sought to avoid. In the international realm, the Reagan and Bush presidencies facilitated the end of the Cold War, a struggle that had defined U.S. foreign policy since the end of the Second World War.

Meanwhile, American society seemed to fragment into specialized identifications. Social activism increasingly organized around sexual, racial, ethnic, and ideological identities. The New Right's stress on limiting the power of government and promoting conservative values reconfigured discussions about how government power could best promote liberty and equality.

CHAPTER REVIEW

Review Questions

1. How did the legacies of the Vietnam War and Watergate help shape U.S. politics in the decade that followed?

2. To what extent did Ronald Reagan's administration represent a victory for the New Right agenda in both domestic and foreign policy?

3. What forces and events contributed first to heightened tensions in the Cold War and then to its end?

4. How did social movements of the post-1960s era affect social life, culture, and the ways people saw their own personal identities?

Critical Thinking Questions

1. In domestic policy, the Reagan presidency represented a swing away from the liberal Democratic dominance that had dated from the New Deal. Discuss this proposition.

2. Discuss the many ways in which social activism continued to play an important role in politics and culture during the 1970s and 1980s.

Identifications

Review your understanding of the following key terms, people, and events for this chapter.

Gerald R. Ford, p. 713
Jimmy Carter, p. 714
Three Mile Island, p. 715
Camp David Peace Talks of 1978, p. 715
Iranian Revolution of January 1979, p. 716

New Right, p. 717
neoconservatives, p. 717
Ronald Reagan, p. 718
supply-side economics, p. 719
deregulation, p. 720
William Rehnquist, p. 721

George H. W. Bush, p. 723
Strategic Defense Initiative (SDI), p. 723
Iran-*Contra* Affair, p. 725
Mikhail Gorbachev, p. 725
Persian Gulf War, p. 728

Henry Louis Gates, Jr., p. 733
Chicanismo, p. 734
Dolores Huerta and Cesar Chavez, p. 735

DISCOVERY

What were some of the key issues that helped shape American elections in the 18 years between 1974 and 1992?

In thinking about this question, begin by breaking it down into the components shown below. A discussion of the significance of each component should appear in your answer.

Foreign Policy

Study Map 30.3 (below) and Map 23.2 on page 542. Examine the effects of the Soviet Union's 1989 collapse on the geography of Europe and Asia. How many independent nations in Europe and Asia emerged after 1989 from lands that had either been part of the Soviet Union or under Soviet control? What happened after 1989 to Czechoslovakia, Yugoslavia, Lithuania, Latvia, and Estonia, countries that the Treaty of Versailles had first brought into being in 1919? From your examination of Map 30.3,

what conclusions might you draw about the likely effects of the Soviet Union's collapse on politics in Europe, the Middle East, and Asia? Do you think the power of the Soviet Union is likely to be broadly dispersed among the many nations that once made it up, or do you think it will flow to and be reconsolidated by Russia? From your reading of this map, what would you identify as the likely geopolitical implications of the Soviet Union's collapse for the United States?

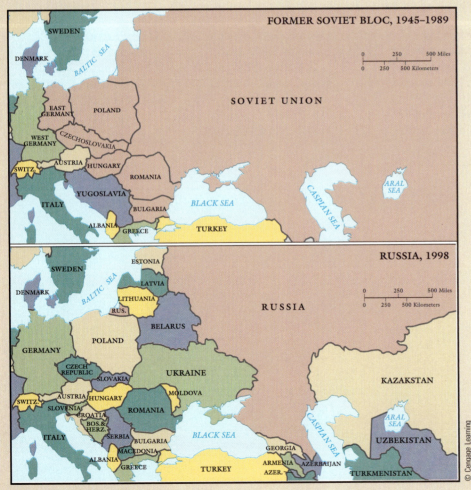

Map 30.3 Collapse of the Soviet Bloc

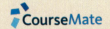
Visit the CourseMate website at www.cengagebrain.com for additional study tools and review materials for this chapter.

31

ECONOMIC, SOCIAL, AND CULTURAL CHANGE IN THE LATE 20TH CENTURY

A CHANGING PEOPLE
  An Aging, Shifting Population
  The New Immigration
  The Metropolitan Nation

ECONOMIC TRANSFORMATIONS
  New Technologies
  Changes in the Structure and Operations of Business
  The Financial Sector
  The Sports-Entertainment Industry

CULTURE AND MEDIA
  The Video Revolution
  Hollywood
  The Changing Media Environment for Pop Music
  The New Mass Culture Debate
  The Religious Landscape

The final decades of the 20th century brought sweeping change to American life. A dramatic increase in immigration, along with movements of people throughout metropolitan areas and into states in the West and South, altered the demographic landscape. The continuing decline of employment in the manufacturing sector changed the workplace. A digital revolution transfigured how people communicated. A vast entertainment-information complex, with an emphasis on professional sports, also emerged. At the same time, religious life became more diverse and more closely intertwined with the nation's politics.

1972	1976	1980	1984	1988	1992	1996

■ **1971**
Starbucks Coffee opens first store

■ **1972**
Congress passes Title IX (Patsy Mink Equal Opportunity in Education Act)

■ **1977**
Congress passes Community Reinvestment Act

■ **1978**
Supreme Court decision frees banks to relocate credit-card operations

■ **1979**
ESPN joins the cable-TV lineup

■ **1981**
MTV and CNN debut on cable TV

■ **1982**
Congress relaxes regulations on S & Ls

■ **1986**
Congress passes Immigration Reform and Control Act

1987 ■
Prices crash on New York Stock Exchange and then rebound

■ **1988**
FOX television network begins

■ **1989**
Congress enacts bailout plan for S & L industry

■ **1990**
Congress passes another Immigration Act

■ **1991**
First McDonalds opens in Moscow

1995 ■
Amazon.com begins selling books online

1996 ■
FOX News Channel debuts

2
Human Genome Project issues preliminary dr

A CHANGING PEOPLE

FOCUS QUESTION

What major demographic trends characterized the post-1970 United States? How did they help to change daily life?

America's population changed significantly during the final three decades of the 20th century, becoming older, more metropolitan, and more ethnically and racially diverse. Moreover, the nation's centers of power continued shifting away from the Northeast and toward the South and West.

An Aging, Shifting Population

During the 1950s, the height of the baby boom, the population had grown by 1.8 percent per year; after 1970, even with new waves of immigration and longer life expectancies, the growth rate slowed to about 1 percent per year. Younger people were delaying marriage until well into their 20s; most raised smaller families than had their parents; and many adults remained unmarried for much of their lives. The number of households with at least one child under 18 continually shrank. In

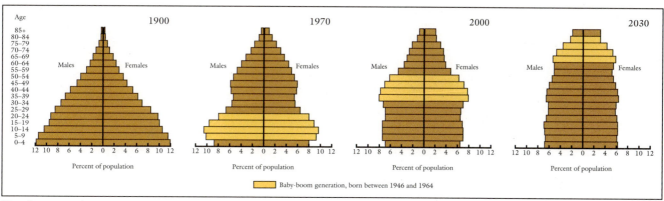

THE AGING OF AMERICA

Source: U.S. Census Bureau. Adapted from C. L. Himes, "Elderly Americans," Population Bulletin 2002, 56(4): p. 4.

1960, nearly half fell into this category; by 1999, only about a third of U.S. house-holds contained even one person under the age of 18. Consequently, by the mid-1980s, people in the 25 to 44 age category constituted a larger slice of the U.S. population than any other, and the number in their teens to early twenties was relatively small.

The steady rise of the median age of the population brought public policy, as well as personal, dilemmas. As aging baby boomers pondered retirement, policy-makers began exploring various ways of covering projected Social Security and Medicare payouts. Trend watchers of the 1960s had talked of a "youth revolt." By the end of the 20th century, their counterparts pondered the "graying of America."

The changing geographical distribution of America's population restructured political and economic power. After 1970, most of the population growth occurred in the South and the West. Between 1990 and 2001, California gained eight seats in the House of Representatives, Florida added six, New York lost five, and several northeastern states shed two or three. Presidential politics increasingly focused on Florida, Texas, and California. Many reasons helped account for this demographic shift: affordable air-conditioning; the expansion of tourism and new retirement communities; and businesses attracted by lower labor costs and the absence of strong unions.

The development of high-tech industries connected to military-related spending and the computer revolution also played an important role. California's Santa Clara County, propelled by spectacular growth in its semiconductor industry and its network of computer-related enterprises, became known as "Silicon Valley" during the early 1970s. It spawned companies such as Google and Yahoo!

The government-financed space program, directed from the National Aeronautics and Space Administration (NASA) installations in Texas and Florida, signified the shift of research and technology to the Sun Belt. In 1961, President Kennedy had announced plans for the manned Apollo program, and in July 1969, astronaut Neil Armstrong had walked on the lunar surface. Apollo flights continued until 1972, when NASA began to develop a space station. In the 1980s, NASA started operating space shuttles. In early 1986, the program suffered a tragic setback when the *Challenger* shuttle exploded shortly after liftoff. After a hiatus of more than two years, the program resumed its operations, with new safety procedures in place.

Individual entrepreneurs and giant corporations also migrated to the Sun Belt and crafted multiple versions of a single product: *entertainment*. The Sun Belt

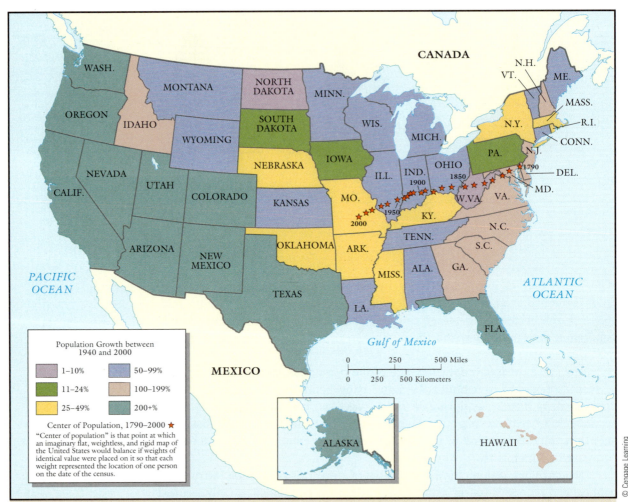

Map 31.1 Population Shifts toward the Sun Belt. *In the era after the Second World War, Americans gravitated toward the South and West. Which states grew the fastest? What might be some of the causes and consequences of such population shifts?*

featured a host of "magical" places such as Disneyland and Las Vegas. These tourist destinations predated the 1970s, but they boomed during the final decades of the 20th century.

The New Immigration

A dramatic increase in immigration from countries mostly to the south and west of the United States accounted for much of the U.S. population growth in the late 20th century. The vast bulk of post-1970 immigration came from Asia, Oceania, Latin America, and Africa. In 2000, roughly 12 percent of the U.S. population had been born outside the United States, compared to the all-time high of 15 percent in 1890.

The number of Spanish-speaking people in the United States at the end of the 20th century exceeded that of all but four countries of Latin America. The largest number of non-European immigrants came from Mexico. Responding to labor shortages in the United States and poor economic prospects at home, immigration from Mexico rose substantially in every decade. Ninety percent of all Mexican Americans lived in the Southwest, primarily Texas and California.

Most people moving from Puerto Rico to the mainland settled around New York City, but sizable Puerto Rican communities developed in Chicago and in cities

21ST-CENTURY LOS ANGELES. *Billboards such as these, one in English and the other in Chinese, showed how the advertising industry, like other American institutions, adjusted to growing linguistic diversity.*

in New England and Ohio as well. By 2000, the Puerto Rican population on the U.S. mainland totaled about three million, compared to a population of nearly four million in Puerto Rico.

Cubans had begun immigrating in large numbers in response to Fidel Castro's revolution. In 1962, Congress had designated people fleeing from Castro's Cuba as refugees eligible for admittance, and during the next 20 years, more than 800,000 Cubans from every strata of society came to the United States. The greatest impact came in south Florida; by 2000, about half of all Miamians were of Cuban descent.

These changes in immigration patterns began with the landmark Immigration and Nationality Act of 1965, which abolished quotas based on national origins (see Chapter 24). Instead, it placed a ceiling of 20,000 immigrants for every country, gave preference to people with close family ties in the United States, and accorded priority to those with special skills and those classified as "refugees." Although largely unforeseen at the time, this legislation laid the basis not only for a resumption of high-volume immigration but also for a substantial shift in region of origin.

International events also affected U.S. immigration policy. Following the American withdrawal from Vietnam, for example, U.S. officials facilitated the admittance of many Vietnamese, Cambodians, Laotians, and Hmong (an ethnically distinct people who inhabited lands extending across the borders of these three Asian countries). The goal was to resettle some of the people who had allied with the United States during the Vietnam War and whose families were consequently in peril.

In response to the growing number of people seeking admission to the United States, Congress passed the Refugee Act of 1980. It favored political refugees, "those fleeing overt persecution," over people seeking simply to improve their economic circumstances. In practice, U.S. officials interpreted the terms "political" and "economic" so that people leaving communist regimes were generally admitted but those fleeing right-wing dictatorships were often turned away or deported. For example, Cubans and Soviet Jews were admitted, but many Guatemalans and Salvadorans, hoping to escape repressive military governments backed by the United States during the 1980s, usually were not.

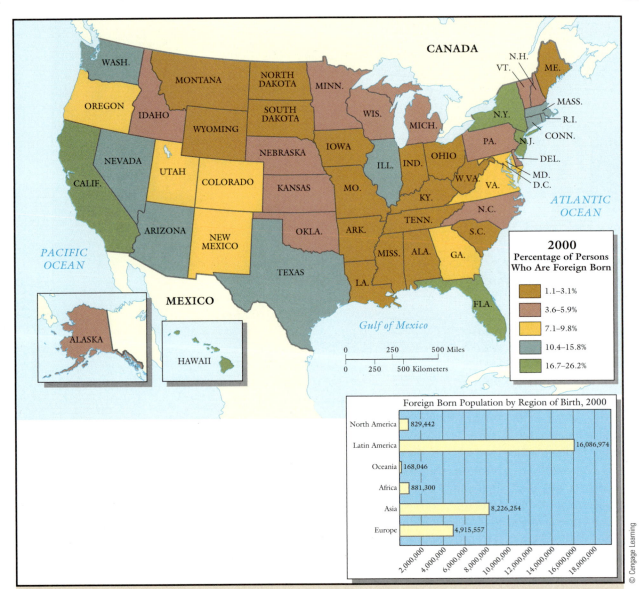

Map 31.2 New Americans: Percentage of Persons Who Are Foreign Born and Foreign-Born Population by Region of Birth, 2000. *This map and chart illustrate the wave of new immigration into the United States. Which regions of the world contributed the most immigrants? Which states received the most, and the least, immigration?*

Source: Data from U.S. Census Bureau, Census 2000.

Immigration Reform and Control Act of 1986 (Simpson-Mazzoli Act) *Created stricter requirements for businesses hiring undocumented workers and granted amnesty for undocumented immigrants who had lived continuously in the United States since 1982.*

Immigration became an ongoing political issue. The **Immigration Reform and Control Act of 1986** (or the **Simpson-Mazzoli Act**) imposed stricter requirements on businesses employing undocumented workers and granted amnesty to those who could prove that they had been living in the United States continuously since 1982. Immigration continued to soar as the economic upturn of the 1990s acted as a magnet for newcomers. Another Immigration Act in 1990 raised the number of immigrants who could be admitted on the basis of special job skills or the investment capital they could bring into the United States. Those favoring continued high levels of immigration saw the entire nation benefiting, but proponents of more rigorous restrictions insisted that the United States could not bear the economic, social, or cultural burden that newcomers supposedly posed. Conflicting perspectives stalemated any further change in immigration policy.

The Metropolitan Nation

Urban-suburban demographics, too, were in a state of flux. At the end of the 20th century, more than 80 percent of Americans lived in vast metropolitan areas. With the overall population growing, the relationship between central cities and adjacent suburbs changed. The suburbs melded into "urban corridors," metropolitan strips running between older cities such as Seattle and Tacoma or Washington and Baltimore. Outlying areas sprouted "edge cities," such as Irvine in California or Boca Raton in Florida, which competed with older urban centers for businesses, job opportunities, and residents. Residents of edge cities, according to surveys, rarely found the need to visit the nearby center cities such as Los Angeles or Miami.

Demographic patterns within suburban areas also changed. Especially in the last decade of the century, more people from non-European backgrounds began moving to suburbs, just as more Americans of European descent were relocating in cities. As a result, the percentage of African Americans residing in urban centers steadily declined, and the percentage living in suburbia increased. With immigrants settling outside central cites, some suburbs—even in metropolitan areas such as Chicago and Minneapolis—came to contain more foreign-born residents than the central cities they surrounded.

Moreover, new suburbs sprouted up farther and farther away from either core or edge cities. A frenzy of new construction, financed by innovative lending arrangements, transformed farmland and small towns into a series of sprawling housing developments, which demographers called **"exurbs."** Built on relatively inexpensive land, exurbs offered homebuyers more space for less money. When commuting to work, however, these exurbanites could easily spend several hours every day trapped inside a car.

Meanwhile, central cities were transformed. During the 1970s and 1980s, as manufacturing jobs left urban areas and as retail shopping shifted to suburban malls, cities became primarily financial, administrative, and entertainment centers. Many large cities faced rising rates of homelessness and crime and deterioration in schools and infrastructure, especially sewage and water systems. Big-city mayors complained that the government in Washington did little to address urban problems. Federal funding decreased from $64 per urban resident in 1980 to less than $30 by the early 1990s.

At the same time, certain areas within many central cities underwent stunning revivals. A building boom brought new office towers, residential buildings, and sports and arts complexes to many downtowns across the country. People with cash or credit to spend on housing, restaurants, and entertainment began returning to selected areas, which came to be labeled as "gentrified."

This urban renaissance, which gained momentum during the 1990s, sprang from many sources. A vibrant national economy and improved air and water quality helped. Innovative urban design skillfully integrated diverse architectural styles with new green spaces. Community development corporations (CDCs), grassroots efforts indebted to movement cultures of the 1960s, supported initiatives for affordable housing, child-care facilities, and employment opportunities. The **Community Reinvestment Act of 1977**, which encouraged banks to finance more home buying in low-income neighborhoods, stimulated economic activity. Community policing, a trend toward harsher sentencing, and an aging population lowered urban crime rates during the 1990s. Commuters discovered that they could save both time and money by moving from distant suburbs to the revitalizing downtowns. New immigrants repopulated once-declining neighborhoods, refurbishing property and reviving commercial zones. Many U.S. cities featured vibrant, transnational spaces.

exurbs *Housing developments that expanded farther away from larger cities into farmlands and small towns.*

Community Reinvestment Act of 1977 *Encouraged banks to finance development and home buying in low-income neighborhoods to stimulate economic activity.*

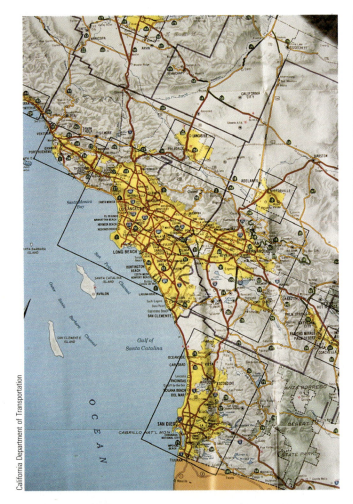

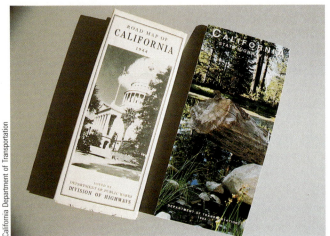

URBAN CORRIDORS. *These official California road maps, from the 1940s and the 1990s, show development of urban corridors in the Los Angeles area.*

The ability to live and play in the new metropolitan spaces, of course, largely depended on household income. During the two decades after 1980, households in the top 10 percent of the income pyramid saw a substantial increase in their incomes. Those at the *very* top, the super wealthy, fared even better. The vast majority of individuals and families, by contrast, saw far more modest gains. An important part of this story involved the transformations that were occurring throughout the U.S. and international economies.

Economic transformations

A latter-day Rip van Winkle, awakening from a 30-year sleep in 1999, would have marveled at the consumer products in daily use. People could awaken to sounds from a digital device; glance at the morning news on a personal computer; use the same PC or Mac to work from home; and later watch a daytime TV program they had recorded earlier. They could also enter a fantasy world through a video game or catch up with the world and friends via the Internet or a mobile phone. If one could look past large pockets of persistent poverty, it could seem as if Americans lived in a consumption paradise provided by new technologies and innovative businesses.

FOCUS QUESTION

What were the most important post-1970 technological and economic changes? How did technological change create both new problems and new possibilities?

New Technologies

The computer revolution, which had begun during the 1940s, entered a new phase after 1970. Microchips increased hardware capacity and reduced the size and cost of computers. Microsoft and Apple, two companies founded during the 1970s, challenged mighty IBM for supremacy in the personal computer market and introduced competing operating systems and Web browsers. Their celebrity CEOs, Bill Gates and Steve Jobs, became two of the wealthiest and most influential people in the world. Although Microsoft quickly beat out Apple for domination in the war over lucrative operating systems, the companies continued to battle over virtually everything else, including that all-important intangible: the loyalty of customers who saw their computers, especially if they owned a Mac, as part of their personal identity.

Changes in the speed and accessibility of informational systems rearranged how people interacted with the larger economy and lived their daily lives. Enhanced by new communications technologies, such as fiber-optic networks and then satellite transmission, successive generations of computers fueled an **"information revolution."** Libraries replaced card catalogs with networked computer databases; screens replaced paper. Voice mail, faxes, e-mail, and text messaging came to supplement or substitute for posted mail and telephone conversations. The use of cellular phones spread rapidly during the 1990s and, along with improved computer access, made telecommuting from home to work an attractive option.

Technological innovations in other fields such as biotechnology promised to produce the same kind of dramatic effects. Beginning in 1990, for example, the **Human Genome Project** sought to map the human genetic code. This international effort, which unveiled a preliminary draft of the human genome in 2000, sought to provide new techniques for gene transfer, embryo manipulation, tissue regeneration, and even cloning. Other biotechnological research portended new approaches to the treatment of cancer and other diseases. Still further research revolutionized farming. Large food producers heralded the use of genetically modified crops as an extension of the earlier "green revolution," which had boosted agricultural yields.

These new technologies raised legal and ethical questions. How would the computer revolution, for example, affect traditional ideas and laws about privacy? Biotechnological research generated even more controversial questions. Almost immediately after the Supreme Court decided the abortion case of *Roe v. Wade* (1973), Congress banned federal funding for research involving fetal tissue. Fears that experimentation with embryonic stem cells would increase abortions blocked federal support for research, except when an executive order from President Bill Clinton was briefly in effect. Proponents of stem cell research, sustained by other

information revolution
Acceleration of the speed and availability of information due to computer and satellite systems.

Human Genome Project
Program launched in 1990 to map all genetic material in the 24 human chromosomes. It sparked ongoing debate over potential consequences of genetic research and manipulation.

sources of funding, argued for its benefits in regenerating human tissue. Controversy, more gradually, came to swirl around genetically modified (GM, for short) foods. By the end of the 20th century, critics wondered if GM crops could harm biodiversity.

Changes in the Structure and Operations of Business

Computerization encouraged businesses to change their modes of operation. Computer networks helped lower costs and boost productivity (the output of goods per labor hour). Companies increasingly abandoned paperwork in favor of more efficient computerized tracking systems.

The computer revolution also speeded the continued expansion of chain and franchise businesses. McDonald's and Holiday Inn had pioneered nationwide standardization in the fast-food and travel industries during the late 1950s. Other businesses adapted their models. Starbucks Coffee Company began as a local operation in 1971, rapidly expanded beyond Seattle during the 1980s, and opened a new store somewhere in the world every day during the 1990s. Starbucks elevated coffee into a pricey designer commodity.

Sam Walton's Wal-Mart chain prospered by moving in the opposite direction: The company promised customers it was constantly rolling back prices. Wal-Mart initially avoided upscale metropolitan areas where Starbucks was thriving, focusing instead on small towns and exurban areas. Here, the company could find employees, called "associates," willing to work part time at relatively low pay. Wal-Mart became the largest private employer in the United States; by the end of the century, 1 of about every 120 workers, and nearly 1 of every 20 in the retail sector, worked for the retailing giant. Wal-Mart did offer consumers a greater array of merchandise and lower prices, but it also crushed local, independent retailers in thousands of midsized and small towns.

U.S. chain and franchise businesses also expanded overseas, especially after the end of the Cold War. In 1991, McDonald's opened to great fanfare in Moscow.

LATTES IN SHANGHAI. *American chain businesses spread throughout the world, part of the process known as globalization.*

Pepsi and Coke carried their ongoing "cola wars" into new territory. During the 1970s, Pepsi had struck a special deal with the Kremlin that had made its cola the first American product sold in the USSR. During the 1990s, Coca-Cola debuted and quickly challenged its rival for cola supremacy in Russia's newly competitive soft-drink market.

Launched in 1995, Amazon.com led a different kind of retailing revolution—e-commerce, or the practice of selling over the Internet. Toward the very end of the 1990s, a wave of new "dot-com" businesses flooded the Internet and set off a short-term bubble in dot-com stocks that Amazon managed to survive. Buying and selling over the Internet quickly became a settled feature of consumer culture. Amazon and eBay, the online auction site, became models for doing business in cyberspace.

As suppliers and markets increasingly gave businesses worldwide scope, commercial publications began to refer to the process as **"globalization."** U.S. automakers, for example, increasingly looked outside the United States to procure parts and even to assemble their automobiles and trucks. Conversely, foreign buyers purchased U.S. companies and real estate holdings, including RCA, Double-day, Mack Truck, and Goodyear. By the end of the 20th century, it became difficult to define what constituted a U.S. company or a foreign one.

New technologies and globalization interacted to change the basic structure of American businesses and their workforces. Citing pressure from declining profits and international competitors, which usually paid workers a fraction of the U.S. wage rate, many industrial companies cut back their labor forces and trimmed their management staffs. This process became known as **"downsizing."** The U.S. auto industry began to lay off thousands of workers, and many older steel plants closed entirely.

As employment in traditional manufacturing and extractive sectors (such as mining) declined, jobs in service, high-tech, and information and entertainment sectors increased. Positions in financial services, computing, and other high-tech industries offered high salaries—astronomical ones for top management—but most jobs in the rapidly expanding service sector, such as clerks and cleaners, remained low-paying, part time, and nonunionized. Wal-Mart's enormous nonunion workforce, for example, earned an average of $7 to $8 per hour and had limited, or no, health benefits. U.S. manufacturers wanting to lower costs moved plants to countries with cheap labor environments, further contributing to the decline of relatively better-paid manufacturing jobs in the United States.

Some economists worried that this shift toward a "postindustrial" service economy would effectively change the domestic wage structure, "de-skill" the American labor force, and eventually erode the nation's standard of living. Others argued that globalization and corporate downsizing would temporarily mean lost jobs, but gains in productivity would soon translate into lower consumer prices and rising living standards for everyone. Real wages did rise a little in the late 1990s, especially for women.

The structure of the labor market changed in other ways. Skilled workers during the middle of the 20th century had tended to stick to one profession and even the same place of employment throughout their working life. By the end of the century, however, both

globalization *Development of an increasingly integrated global economy, as trade and investment expanded worldwide.*

downsizing *Process of cutting back labor forces and management staffs by businesses.*

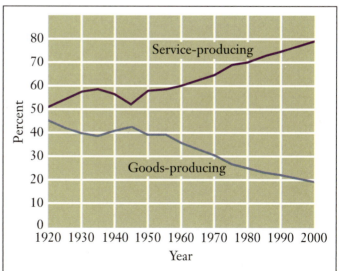

GROWTH OF SERVICE SECTOR JOBS, 1920–2000

Source: Data from the U.S. Census Bureau.

blue-collar and white-collar workers were likely to switch employers several times before retiring.

Economic restructuring also contributed to a dramatic drop in labor union membership. During the 1950s, more than 30 percent of American workers belonged to a union. By the end of the 20th century, the figure stood at only 13 percent. Although the labor movement mounted organizing drives among clerical, restaurant, and hotel workers, it struggled to make inroads into these sectors of the economy.

Most businesses adamantly fought unionization, and the health and retirement benefits that American companies had once proudly offered began to disappear. During the 1940s and 1950s, a generous benefit package helped employers attract workers without having to pay dramatically higher wages and salaries. In addition, the amount of money a company paid toward its share of a health plan did not count, under federal law, as part of an employee's taxable compensation. Labor and management both stood to gain, it had seemed, from generous benefit programs.

Things began to change during the 1970s as U.S. companies faced increasing foreign competition and rising costs for health care. In 1960, only about 7 percent of the entire U.S. GDP went for health care; some 40 years later, the comparable figure neared 15 percent, a greater percentage than people paid for food. (In Canada, by contrast, health care totaled less than 10 percent of GDP.) The annual cost of providing health care for a family, according to most estimates, came to about what a full-time, minimum-wage worker would earn over a year and twice the pay of the average Wal-Mart employee. U.S. companies facing foreign competition, such as the large auto manufacturers, complained about maintaining extensive benefit packages that included health care for their aging workforces.

Individuals and families increasingly maintained their lifestyles by incurring debt. Economists began to analyze the **"household deficit"**—the difference between what U.S. households earned and what they actually spent. As late as 1980, the rate of indebtedness for households, though higher than that during the 1950s, still remained lower than it had been during the 1920s. The 1980s, however, inaugurated a trend that would accelerate into the next century. As more people shouldered greater debt, the number of personal bankruptcies increased, and the rate of personal savings in the United States fell to the lowest in the industrialized world.

The Financial Sector

The household deficit became intertwined with one of the most dramatic post-1970 economic changes: the expansion of a vast, highly innovative financial industry. A wide range of financial institutions—from international "superbanks" such as Citigroup, to payday loan institutions like Moneytree, to pawn shop chains such as Pawn America, right on down to illegal loan-sharking operations—profited from people unable to balance their personal books. By the end of the century, loans to homebuyers who lacked the resources to afford them were helping to sustain the financial industry. It also thrived, however, on wealthy investors who appeared awash in assets to invest. By the end of the 20th century, according to one estimate, more than 40 percent of U.S. corporate profits came from the financial services sector, while only about 10 percent derived from manufacturing.

The computer revolution helped the financial industry expand and changed its everyday relationship to customers. Bank-issued credit cards, monitored through new informational systems, vastly expanded their reach after 1970. Banks deluged

household deficit *Difference between what U.S. households earned and what they spent.*

potential cardholders, particularly college students, with competing enticements. "Free" credit cards, once interest and service charges began piling up, proved anything but free to those who used them. Other innovations of the 1980s and1990s—automated teller machines (ATMs), automatic deposits, debit cards, and electronic bill payment—moved Americans ever closer to a cashless economy.

The financial system increasingly shed the regulatory restrictions crafted earlier in the century, particularly during the New Deal (see Chapter 25). Free-market economists argued that deregulating the financial industry was an obvious way to free up the flow of investment capital and to cure the economic malaise of the 1970s. This deregulation had led to the collapse and subsequent bailout of the savings and loan (S & L) industry during the 1980s (see Chapter 30). The problems elsewhere in the financial sector, however, seemed limited to individual firms and to specific times, such as the meltdown on the New York Stock Exchange in October 1987. A rapid rebound seemingly confirmed claims that all markets were self-correcting, even self-regulating. The S & L debacle, from this perspective, signaled no structural problem in the larger financial industry.

During the last two decades of the 20th century, then, most observers applauded the financial sector's growth and dynamism. Wall Street investment firms, such as Lehman Brothers, and large banks, such as Chase Manhattan, did well. Newer types of financial ventures, such as the "hedge fund" operations, which managed complicated investment portfolios for a limited number of affluent clients, performed *very* well. These funds came to make up a "shadow banking system"—one whose financial dealings were not covered by the regulatory system that oversaw more traditional banking institutions. Financial investments still risked losing money, but a new generation of managers claimed the ability to forecast and thus *manage* risk.

The financial sector could also create, and then trade, new forms of investment that carried the generic name of "derivatives," because they had been "derived" from other financial transactions. During the late 1980s, for example, entrepreneurs in the financial sector began purchasing individual home-loan contracts. Combining those of dubious value with sounder ones, they would market the resultant package of loan contracts as a new form of investment called a "collateralized debt obligation" (CDO). Financial analysts argued that the chance of so many different loan contracts defaulting at the same time were so slim that the CDO carried virtually no risk to investors.

CDOs based on home loans were only one of many different types of new securities derived from various other kinds of financial transactions. This part of the larger financial system produced huge profits. It provided similarly outsized payouts, in bonuses and stock options, to the people who worked in this largely unregulated, little-understood enterprise. Economists and public officials, including those who worked at the Treasury Department and the Federal Reserve System, cheered the creation of new types of securities. Governmental regulation of them, according to Alan Greenspan, chairman of the Federal Reserve Board from 1987 to 2006, would discourage innovation and prevent the financial system from delivering an ever-increasing array of secure investments to clients all over the world. Deregulation and globalization in the financial industry, then, echoed other economic transformations of the last three decades of the 20th century. The hazards would become apparent in 2008.

The Sports-Entertainment Industry

The sports-entertainment industry also grew exponentially during this era. Metropolitan areas competed to obtain—or retain—professional teams. TV contracts and tax write-offs tempted tycoons such as George Steinbrenner of the New York Yankees to run a sporting empire.

Baseball led off this expansionist era. Seeking a better fit with emerging economic, demographic, and social forces, the leadership of Major League Baseball (MLB) realigned the "national pastime." During the 1970s, MLB shuffled teams in and out of Milwaukee, Seattle, and Washington, D.C. By relocating franchises from struggling to thriving metropolitan areas, MLB acquired new ticket buyers, TV deals, and stadiums financed by public money. If moving existing franchises made sense, creating new ones seemed an even shrewder option. During the mid-1950s, there had been only 16 Big League teams, none located west of Chicago; at the end of the 20th century, 30 MLB franchises stretched across the United States and into Canada.

Other sports followed baseball's lead. The National Football League (NFL) also expanded into new metropolitan areas. Just in time for the 1970 season, the NFL merged with the American Football League (AFL), with which it had been playing a "Super Bowl" since 1967. In contrast to the economic philosophy of MLB, that of the revamped NFL helped small-market teams such as the Green Bay Packers remain competitive with larger-market franchises. During the 1970s, ABC began televising an NFL game during prime-time hours, and the success of *Monday Night Football* signaled the growing importance of football to TV and to the nation's popular culture.

Basketball's small court made National Basketball Association (NBA) games extremely TV-friendly, and entrepreneurs easily gained television contracts to underwrite new professional franchises. The NBA came to feature high-profile African American stars such as Julius ("Dr. J") Irving and Michael Jordan, who became the preeminent symbol for marketing the NBA. The NBA also elevated African Americans into coaching and management positions far more quickly than did the NFL and MLB.

Several efforts to make soccer a major attraction in the United States faltered, but most other sports-entertainment operations flourished. By the end of the 20th century, the National Hockey League (NHL) supported 28 franchises. Professional play in tennis, aided by TV coverage, featured rapidly expanding tours for both men and women. Professional golf continually grew in popularity, especially after it found its own marketable star, Eldrick (Tiger) Woods, during the mid-1990s. Auto racing thrived as well. The Indianapolis 500 initially vied with the Super Bowl for recognition as the most spectacular one-day event in sports, but events sponsored by the National Association for Stock Car Racing (NASCAR), once associated only with the South, eventually overtook those of Indy-style racing.

College sports grew in similar fashion. Television coverage mushroomed, especially after TV entrepreneurs created **ESPN** (1979–), a cable network devoted entirely to sports. ESPN initially helped so-called "minor" collegiate sports, such as gymnastics and lacrosse, gain TV time, but college football and basketball, with their highly rated postseason contests, ultimately benefited far more. University administrators often claimed that success on their playing fields and arenas, which became ever more luxurious, translated into greater visibility, prestige, and donations for the educational mission of their institutions.

The glamour and excitement generated by the sports-entertainment industry increasingly merged with political culture. Candidates competed to sign up prominent athletes for their campaign squads, and some retired players, including football's Jack Kemp and Hall of Fame hurler Jim Bunning, made the transition from the sports to the political field. In addition to tapping his family connections, George W. Bush used his partial ownership of the Texas Rangers baseball team as an entrée into electoral politics.

With the business of sports booming, its legal foundations inevitably shifted. MLB's star players, armed with union advisers and their own attorneys, successfully

ESPN *First cable network devoted entirely to sports.*

spearheaded new legal challenges to old doctrines that contractually bound players to a single franchise year after year. Court rulings eventually brought differing versions of "free agency" to the major team sports. Although some fans and sportswriters grumbled when highly paid players seemed to underperform, owners discovered that steadily rising TV revenues, tax breaks, and favorable stadium deals allowed them to adjust to the new salary structures and strong union movements.

Sports and legal disputes also became intertwined with social issues. Women's rights advocates condemned big-time sports for promoting sexism—pointing, for example, to NFL cheerleading squads that resembled Las Vegas chorus lines—and urged equality for women athletes. One result of this pressure was **"Title IX"** of a 1972 congressional measure, which was later retitled the **Patsy Mink Equal Opportunity in Education Act**. By mandating gender equity in intercollegiate sports activities, Title IX forced colleges and universities to upgrade the financing and promotion of women's sports.

The sports-entertainment industry continued to provide a cultural mirror on racial issues. The effort to measure how much opportunity sports really offered to African American athletes, especially at the collegiate level, remained a persistent concern. By the end of the 20th century, the number of African Americans playing professional baseball was in decline, while the number of Latino ballplayers was soaring. And as NBA scouts began identifying talented international players, especially from Eastern Europe, some observers predicted that the strong African American presence in the NBA might suffer as well.

While the sports-entertainment complex was growing in visibility and profitability, traditionalists detected signs of decline. The familiar complaint about intercollegiate athletics corrupting educational standards gained new force. Critics also found sporting enterprises awash in hypercommercialism, financial double-dealing, and on-field cheating. MLB, for example, seemingly owed much of its success to home-run hitters led by Mark McGwire of the St. Louis Cardinals. It soon became arguable, however, that performance-enhancing drugs—and, perhaps, souped-up baseballs—were aiding sluggers like McGwire. Sports historians now argue that the late 1980s ushered in baseball's "Steroid Era."

Title IX (Patsy Mink Equal Opportunity in Education Act) *(1972) Required colleges and universities to improve the financing and promotion of women's sports.*

CULTURE AND MEDIA

New technologies significantly altered how people received and used books, movies, TV, music, and other sources of information and entertainment. By the end of the 20th century, virtually every home or apartment had at least one television and an accompanying recording device. About 80 percent had a personal computer. People looked to the Internet for access to newspapers, books, music, and movies. E-mail became, even before the popularity of text messaging, the first choice for contacting friends. The omnipresent video screen, more portable than ever before, seemed the preeminent symbol of American culture.

The Video Revolution

At the beginning of the 1970s, the three broadcast TV networks could promise advertisers that a rough cross section of the American public would be watching their nighttime sales pitches. During the 1970s, however, viewing trends increasingly

FOCUS QUESTION

How did new forms of media change the ways in which people received entertainment, information, and even religious instruction? How did the debate over popular culture in the 1980s and 1990s differ from the earlier debate of the 1950s?

forced the networks to embrace the strategy called **"narrowcasting,"** in which programmers fragmented the TV audience into carefully targeted segments. CBS replaced several highly watched programs, such as *The Beverly Hillbillies*, with "edgier" shows aimed at viewers under the age of 40, who were coveted by advertisers because they were most likely to purchase products and services. *All in the Family*, a sitcom about intergenerational conflict within a blue-collar family, made its proudly bigoted protagonist, Archie Bunker, a lightning rod for issues involving race and gender. Although *The Mary Tyler Moore Show* rarely took overtly feminist positions, it did address the personal politics of working women.

With CBS leading the way, the new programming strategy helped the entire TV industry prosper between the mid-1970s and mid-1980s, but a decade later network programmers were struggling. Prime-time programs garnered disappointing ratings, and the networks responded by slashing budgets and staff, especially in their news divisions. Local stations, which had been limping along without a network affiliation, began picking up viewers who were deserting network offerings. These independents programmed older Hollywood films, sporting events, and reruns of canceled prime-time shows now being syndicated to individual stations. Several hundred independent television stations debuted during the 1980s.

Capitalizing on the rise of these independents, the media mogul Rupert Murdoch introduced his FOX TV network in 1988. Using a pattern later imitated by far less-successful challengers, FOX offered a limited schedule to previously nonaffiliated stations. FOX's first big hit, *The Simpsons* (1989–), an animated send-up of the standard family sitcom, became a pop culture phenomenon and mass-marketing bonanza. In 1993, FOX outbid CBS for the TV rights to carry NFL games. FOX and the other fledgling networks introduced programs—such as *In Living Color* and *Buffy the Vampire Slayer*—for audiences that contained more minority, young, and urban viewers than those of the three older networks.

New technologies, which promised viewers greater choice, challenged all four networks. The remote control and videocassette recorders (VCRs) allowed viewers control over their television offerings. The primary challenge came from cable television, which had wired nearly three-quarters of the nation's homes by 2000. The expansion of cable during the 1980s accelerated audience fragmentation and narrowcasting. Atlanta's Ted Turner led the way by introducing the Cable News Network (CNN), several movie channels, and an all-cartoon network before his communication empire merged with that of Time Warner in 1996. Challenging the networks and cable, companies selling direct satellite transmission began gaining an important share of the viewing audience. By the end of the 20th century, the percentage of viewers watching prime-time network programs had fallen to less than 60 percent.

Hollywood

Hollywood also adopted new business arrangements and technologies. With movie attendance in 1970 about the same as it had been in 1960, Hollywood studios began raising ticket prices, betting on a few blockbuster films such as the highly profitable *Star Wars* series (1977–2005), and hoping for a surprise hit such as *The Blair Witch Project* (1999). Although Hollywood endured super expensive flops such as *Heaven's Gate* (1980) or *Eyes Wide Shut* (1999), motion pictures survived and even thrived through adaptation.

Volatility in the movie market encouraged most filmmakers to play it safe. Many recycled titles and special effects that had made money in the past. They transferred popular stories, such as *How the Grinch Stole Christmas* (2000), and TV

narrowcasting *Tactic used by TV programmers to target specific audiences with corresponding shows.*

FAMILY GUY. *As the U.S. TV audience began to fragment, animated shows increasingly found exceedingly loyal niche markets. FOX network introduced* Family Guy *in 1999 but canceled the series in 2000. Noting the popularity of* Family Guy *in reruns and the strong DVD sales, FOX soon began producing new episodes. Although the inept antihero of the series, Peter Griffin, recalls Fred Flintstone and Homer Simpson, aficionados of this series consider his antics and* Family Guy's *references to popular culture several cuts above those found on* The Flintstones *and* The Simpsons.

shows, such as *The Brady Bunch* (1995), to the big screen and produced sequels for any movie, such as *Speed* (1992), that had even approached blockbuster status. In addition, Hollywood expanded the older practice of targeting younger viewers with movies such as *Ferris Bueller's Day Off* (1986). Meanwhile, celebratory stories that tapped themes in popular history, such as *Titanic* (1997), impressed both ticket buyers and industry insiders.

At the same time, however, a cultural complex that nurtured "independent" movies emerged. Woody Allen became one of the first U.S. filmmakers to specialize in movies, such as *Annie Hall* (1977), which borrowed techniques and themes from European cinema. In 1981, Robert Redford launched the Sundance Film Institute in hopes of encouraging innovative screenwriting and direction. Its annual Sundance Festival, held in Park City, Utah, began attracting Hollywood moguls. They sought the next small movie, such as *The Brothers McMullan* (1995), that might find a large audience. Sundance supported the work of African American, Latino, and Asian American directors by showcasing movies such as *Hoop Dreams* (1994), *El Mariachi* (1993), and *Picture Bride* (1995). It also celebrated women directors such as Lizzie Borden (*Working Girls*, 1986) and Barbara Kopple (*American Dream*, 1990).

Hollywood became increasingly intertwined with the television establishment, once its feared rival, and with the emerging home-viewing industries. Hollywood gained badly needed revenue by licensing its offerings to TV and for VCR and DVD distribution. For a brief time, during the early 1990s, the United States could claim more video rental outlets than movie theaters. But filmmakers also had to confront new "pirating" technologies that meant their movies might appear in bootlegged editions at virtually the same time they debuted in theaters.

The Changing Media Environment for Pop Music

New business ventures and technologies also transformed the relationship between the media and the lucrative pop music industry. A Music Television channel (MTV) debuted in 1981 and subsequently adjusted to changes in the cable TV and music industries. Initially offering a 24-hour supply of rock videos, MTV came under fire for portraying women as sex objects and excluding artists of color. The network eventually defused complaints, especially after featuring Michael Jackson's 29-minute video based on his hit single "Thriller" (1983). By the end of the 20th century, MTV and other cable channels regularly programmed videos that represented the increasingly multiethnic nature of the music industry. MTV seemed on the cutting edge of changes in programming as well. During the 1990s, it introduced a wide range of youth-oriented shows such as *The Real World* (1992–), which inaugurated the "reality genre" that spread to other cable channels and the broadcast networks.

Entertainment conglomerates began marketing music in ever-newer formats. The 45-rpm record and the long-play album (LP), associated with the musical revolutions of the 1950s and 1960s, all but disappeared. Analog cassette tapes, which could be played through a variety of portable devices including Sony's Walkman, arrived during the 1970s. The compact discs (CDs) of the early 1980s changed not only the technology for delivering pop music but also the nature of the product and the listening experience. The now-classic rock LPs of the 1960s and early 1970s, such as the Beatles' *Magical Mystery Tour* (1967), had featured 10 to 12 songs, split between the two sides and often organized around a core concept. By the late 1990s, CD offerings were coming to mirror those that MP3 technology was just beginning to provide by offering unusual musical mixes that generally lacked any unifying theme.

New formats enabled listeners to obtain, preserve, and exchange music in entirely new ways. After several years in which Internet users experimented with the sharing of musical files, in 1999 a college student introduced Napster. This short-lived venture provided a technology by which users could share music gleaned from commercially produced CDs. Artists as well as corporate executives confronted a serious threat to CD sales—and the future of their industry. They charged Internet technologies with facilitating the "pirating" of copyrighted material. Their legal actions promoted a prolonged battle—which extended into the new century—over how music was made, stored, and distributed.

The New Mass Culture Debate

New trends in mass commercial culture generated other controversies. In 1975, the Federal Communications Commission (FCC) ordered the television networks to dedicate the first 60 minutes of prime time each evening to "family" programming free of violence and "mature" themes. Federal courts struck down this family-hour requirement as a violation of the First Amendment. Demands that Congress regulate rock lyrics and album covers also ran afoul of complaints that this kind of legislation would be unconstitutional. TV programmers, record producers, and new Internet gaming ventures, following the example of the Hollywood film industry, began to adopt "warning labels" that supposedly informed parents about products with violent and sexually explicit imagery.

Commercial pop culture also produced new aesthetic disputes. Unlike the cultural critics of the 1950s, who had dismissed mass fare as trivial and degenerate (see Chapter 28), analysts from the new academic field of "cultural studies" often seemed unabashed fans of the commercial products they studied. They jettisoned any bright-line distinction between lowbrow and highbrow as untenable. The music of the Beatles could be studied along with that of Beethoven, the lyrics of Bob Dylan alongside classic poetry. Rejecting the elitist-themed criticism of the 1950s, which had seen consumers as cultural dupes who passively soaked up junk, cultural studies stressed people's creative interaction with commercial culture. Scholarly accounts of *Star Trek,* for example, examined how, through self-produced magazines (called "fanzines"), conventions, and the Internet, Trekkies created a grassroots subculture that used the original TV series and its spinoffs to launch serious discussions about social and political issues. The cultural studies approach also tended to embrace multiculturalism, highlighting works produced by women, political outsiders, and non-Western writers and artists. It encouraged students to see traditional texts within their political and historical contexts rather than as timeless works. Traditionalists condemned this "cultural turn" as a legacy of the counterculture of the 1960s and blamed it for eroding settled ideas about the quality and value of artistic expression.

Some of the fiercest debates over popular culture involved the impact of an "infotainment" complex. An imprecise cultural category, infotainment signaled that the always-delicate balance between actually informing and merely amusing audiences had tilted decisively toward the latter.

Cable TV's news operations emphasized infotainment in ways that the major networks had long avoided. While maintaining a 24/7 schedule, CNN initially followed the networks in pursuing a "hard-news" agenda from camera crews and correspondents stationed around the globe. Yet it also introduced programs such as *Crossfire,* which featured the in-studio pyrotechnics of verbally dueling pundits. CNN's eventual rival, the FOX News Channel (FNC), which debuted in 1996, retrofitted the *Crossfire* approach to much of its programming. FNC featured verbally nimble personalities who covered the news from studio sets and emphasized, despite labels such as "fair and balanced," political opinions that leaned toward those of the New Right.

Public affairs broadcasting on cable TV increasingly adopted a narrowcasting strategy. FNC made clear that its idea of "balance" aimed at attracting viewers who saw the major networks and CNN as "biased." CNN and MSNBC, in response, began positioning their coverage toward people uncomfortable with FNC. This new approach, critics charged, featured news programming that reinforced rather than broadened the perspectives of core constituencies. A "fake" news program, *The Daily Show,* satirized the narrowness of its cable TV counterparts. It also arguably produced—or simply attracted—viewers more broadly informed about issues than were the aficionados of "real" newscasts.

The Religious Landscape

A pervasive religiosity differentiated the United States from most European nations during the last decades of the 20th century. Attention commonly focused on Americans drawn to the Religious Right, but a propensity to see daily life and world events through religious teachings spanned the political and cultural spectrum. Polls taken at the end of the 20th century suggested that more than three-quarters of Americans believed in a divine being that performed miracles on earth.

QUICK REVIEW

VIDEO-SCREEN REVOLUTION

- New products placed video screens at the center of personal and social communication

- "Narrowcasting" intensified audience segmentation

- New aesthetic forms, especially ones using computers, emerged

- A new debate erupted over the effects of mass commercial culture on social and political life

MUSICAL LINK TO THE PAST

Hip-Hop Leaps In

Songwriters: E. Fletcher, M. Glover, C. Chase, S. Robinson
Title: "The Message" (1982)
Performers: Grandmaster Flash and the Furious Five

Black radio formats in the early 1980s were generally staid and conservative, favoring such easy listening, corporate-associated artists as Lionel Richie. According to critic Nelson George, New York–based black music professionals "were so office-bound, taking meetings with managers and listening to tapes from song publishers [in midtown Manhattan], that they failed to venture up the road to Harlem and the South Bronx, where, in the middle of the nation's most depressing urban rot, something wonderful was happening." That "wonderful" innovation was hip-hop music, which began in the mid-1970s with DJs using other artists' records (Chic's "Good Times" was a perennial favorite) as instrumental backing tracks for live rappers. Hip-hop assembled elaborate rhyming stories, messages, and boasts—often improvised on the spot.

Although early hits such as the Sugar Hill Gang's 1979 "Rapper's Delight" promoted a genial party mood, "The Message" presented a sobering litany of inner-city ghetto life: police brutality, junkies, pimps, homeless people "pissing on the stairs," and random violence, punctuated with the mantra of "sometimes it makes me wonder, how I keep from going under." It presaged the even harder-edged, more politically minded, and economically successful rap artists, such as Public Enemy, NWA, and KRS-One. Despite commercial success ("The Message" achieved top-five R&B hit

status), major-label executives veered away from the angry black, mostly male, performers of rap music until the mid-1980s. Like earlier controversial American music innovations such as bebop and rock 'n' roll, rap was initially confined to independent label distribution.

Hip-hop also introduced revolutionary musical approaches. DJ Grandmaster Flash, who was unable to afford studio-recording time in the mid-1970s, created his own backing tracks by manipulating turntables and vinyl records in new ways. He, along with DJ Kool Herc, pioneered the effects of "scratching" (turning records manually to make the needle repeat brief lengths of groove) and "phasing" (altering turntable speeds to change the sound of recordings). These and other new technologies enabled "The Message" to offer a complex soundscape that represented the urban atmosphere of the early 1980s.

Q How did hip-hop artists convert a turntable into a musical instrument?

Q What might this use of a century-old technology say about the role of technology in musical change and the specific cultural climate that gave birth to hip-hop?

Source: "The Message" by Melvin Glover, Nathanial Glover, Charles Morris, Joseph R. Saddler, Robert K. Wiggins, and Guy T. Williams. Copyright © 1982 E/A Music, Inc. and Grandmaster Flash Publishing Inc. Used by permission.

The nation's religious landscape showed greater diversity than ever before. During the 1950s, Will Herberg could see his book entitled *Protestant-Catholic-Jew* (1955) as characterizing the religious dimensions of the "American way of life." A half-century later, these three faiths represented only some of the religious denominations in the United States.

After about 1970, cultural and social change helped produce this religious diversity. Movements such as the Jesus People were loosely associated with the counterculture. A few other countercultural groups withdrew to communal retreats organized around religious teachings. Many people drawn to alternative cultures also embraced spiritual and religious impulses outside of the Protestant-Catholic-Jewish triad. Asian-inspired traditions, such as Transcendental Meditation and Buddhism, proved particularly appealing.

Meanwhile, immigration swelled the numbers in faiths, especially Islam, that had held only a minimal presence in the United States prior to 1970. The Black Power impulse had attracted new converts to the homegrown Nation of Islam during the 1960s, and post-1960s immigration from countries with large Islamic populations brought several million people who practiced more orthodox versions of Islam to the United States. According to some estimates (the official U.S. Census does not track religious affiliations), the number of residents practicing Islam by the year 2000 surpassed those practicing Judaism, and even those identifying with several mainline Protestant denominations, including Presbyterianism and Episcopalianism. Adapting to American cultural practices, mosques began making Sunday, rather than the traditional Friday, the week's major Islamic holy day. The faith's leading institutions, such as the Islamic Center of Southern California, provided a variety of religious and nonreligious services. They also sought to inform non-Muslims about Islam, which could claim more followers worldwide than any other religion.

Other religions experienced similar growth spurts. The number of Protestant evangelicals grew faster than the U.S. population. Between 1970 and the late 1990s, the Southern Baptist Convention expanded beyond its traditional regional base and added six million new members. The Church of Jesus Christ of Latter-day Saints (the Mormon faith) gained more than half that many. Along with augmenting their membership rolls at home, many of these groups greatly expanded their international missionary activities.

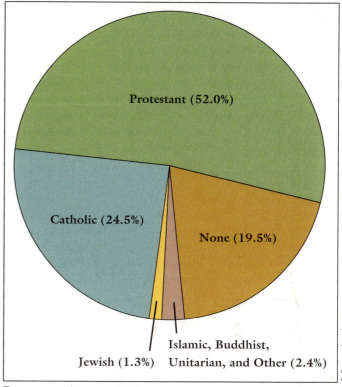

RELIGION IN AMERICA, 2001
This chart shows the self-described religious affiliations of the American people compiled through sampling techniques.

Source: Data adapted from *The American Religious Identification Survey*, Graduate Center, City University of New York.

Religious faith did not always determine political belief. Most fundamentalists and evangelicals favored the politics of the New Right, but there were evangelical groups, such as the Sojourners, that pursued many of the "social justice" issues identified with the political left. Moreover, some evangelicals joined mainline religious movements in espousing environmental causes that were, generally, anathema to the New Right.

Most organized religious groups struggled with the relationship between their spiritual faith and other social and cultural causes. Religious communities offered very different responses, for example, to the emergence of Lesbian-Gay-Bisexual-Transgendered (LGBT) movements. Most leaders of the Religious Right, such as Jerry Falwell and Pat Robertson, mobilized against what they saw as the "moral decay" posed by LGBT activism. Orthodox Judaism, Islam, and Catholicism, without mobilizing on the scale of the Religious Right, still labeled same-sex relationships as sinful. In stark contrast, a minority of churches, synagogues, and temples—especially in larger cities—welcomed LGBT members. A few denominations accepted gays and lesbians as ministers and rabbis, and recognizable bodies of "gay theology," grounded in specific biblical passages and on more general principles of tolerance, began to emerge. Churches also faced, along with the nation at large, growing pressure to confront the legality of gay marriages (see Chapter 32).

Religious divisions emerged over foreign policy questions. The movement to contain the spread of nuclear weaponry attracted a number of religious groups.

©REBECCA COOK/Reuters/CORBIS

THE ISLAMIC CENTER OF AMERICA, DEARBORN, MICHIGAN. *This 70,000-square-foot facility dramatizes the growing presence of Islam in the United States. It features building materials imported from throughout the world, a gold dome, twin minarets, and a prayer hall that can accommodate 1,000 worshippers.*

After prolonged internal debate, the Conference of Catholic Bishops issued a pastoral letter entitled "The Challenge of Peace" (1983). It joined statements by several Protestant groups and, in effect, declared U.S. nuclear policy in conflict with religious teachings. At about the same time, some Catholic priests joined dissident Protestant congregations in offering sanctuary to undocumented refugees from Latin America, particularly El Salvador and Guatemala, who were fleeing U.S.-supported military regimes and, once they reached the United States, American immigration authorities. On the other hand, many spiritual leaders and laypeople, particularly those associated with evangelical churches, gravitated toward the fervent anticommunist initiatives supported by the New Right and the Reagan administration.

Three prominent religious figures who entered the partisan arena exemplified the diversity of religion's relationship to political action. Father Robert F. Drinan, a member of the U.S. House of Representatives from 1971 to 1981, often embraced positions on issues, such as abortion, contrary to the pronouncements of his own Roman Catholic Church. Eventually, the Church hierarchy decreed that no priest should hold a political office, and Father Drinan resigned. The presidential bids, in 1984 and 1988, of the Reverend Jesse Jackson, a Baptist, recalled a movement-style politics that looked back to the religious fervor of the civil rights crusade but also moved in step with the largely secular multiculturalism of the 1980s. Pat Robertson, in contrast, hoped he could use his firm identification with the Religious Right to successfully challenge Vice President George H. W. Bush for the 1988 GOP presidential nomination.

Although his presidential bid failed, Robertson did shore up his religious empire at a time when several other media-enabled religious movements were being swamped by controversy. Jim and Tammy Faye Bakker of the "Praise the Lord" (PTL) movement and Jimmy Lee Swaggart saw their multimillion-dollar, multimedia operations collapse when they violated the financial and moral values their ministries preached. After being convicted on multiple counts of fraud, Jim Bakker landed in jail. Swaggart's dalliances with prostitutes left his ministry, which had once claimed a worldwide media audience of more than 500 million people, relegated to cable TV's public access channels.

Other religious ministries prospered in the manner of Pat Robertson's. The Billy Graham Evangelistic Association crusade (created in 1950) avoided even the hint of financial or moral malfeasance, and Reverend Graham himself remained one of the nation's most admired—and officially nonpartisan—citizens. Another charismatic Baptist minister, Rick Warren, painstakingly established one of the important evangelical "mega-churches" in Southern California in 1980. Within 20 years, Warren's Saddleback Church ranked among the 10 largest congregations in the country.

Successful movements on the Religious Right, such as Falwell's and Warren's, became cultural conglomerates. They established publishing enterprises, bookstores, radio and TV outlets, Christian academies and other "charter" schools, religiously affiliated colleges and seminaries, and even schools of law and of public policy. Apocalyptic novels—such as the *Left Behind* series by Tim LaHaye and Jerry B. Jenkins—and Christian-themed movies—including *A Thief in the Night* (1972)—found a large audience. The Christian music industry easily surpassed the classical and jazz genres in sales by the end of the 20th century.

Conclusion

Sweeping changes occurred in demographics, economics, culture, and society during the last quarter of the 20th century. The nation aged, and more of its people gravitated to the Sun Belt. Sprawling urban corridors challenged older central cities as sites for development. Rapid technological change fueled the growth of globalized industries and the restructuring of the labor force to fit a postindustrial economy.

The most prominent development in American popular culture was the proliferation of the video screen. Television, motion pictures, the Internet, and even services for phones increasingly targeted specific audiences, and the fragmented nature of cultural reception was exemplified by the rise of new, particularistic media ventures.

CHAPTER REVIEW

Review Questions

1. What major demographic trends characterized the post-1970 United States? How did they contribute to changing daily life?

2. What were the most important post-1970 technological and economic changes? How did technological change create both new problems and new possibilities?

3. How did new forms of media change the ways in which people received entertainment, information, and even religious instruction? How did the debate over popular culture in the 1980s and 1990s differ from the earlier debate of the 1950s?

Critical Thinking Questions

1. In what ways might the major demographic changes of the late 20th century have accelerated economic restructuring?

2. How did the spread of video screens help to change so many areas of cultural life?

Identifications

Review your understanding of the following key terms, people, and events for this chapter.

Immigration Reform and Control Act of 1986 (Simpson-Mazzoli Act), p. 746
exurbs, p. 747

Community Reinvestment Act of 1977, p. 747
information revolution, p. 749
Human Genome Project, p. 749

globalization, p. 751
downsizing, p. 751
household deficit, p. 752
ESPN, p. 754

Title IX (Patsy Mink Equal Opportunity in Education Act), p. 755
narrowcasting, p. 756

DISCOVERY

How have the various social movements and demographic changes of the post-1960 period affected U.S. culture?

In thinking about this question, begin by breaking it down into the components shown below. A discussion of the significance of each component should appear in your answer.

Geography

Examine Map 31.1 on page 744 and Map 31.2 on page 746. What areas of the country (and states) have seen the largest population growth since 1940? What might account for this growth? What benefits accrue to states with rapidly growing populations? What potential problems might these increased populations create? Which states had the densest populations of foreign-born inhabitants in 2000? To what extent are these states the same as those that have experienced the largest population growth since 1940? How close does the correlation appear to be between immigrant density and general population growth? How do you think the growth of immigrant populations is affecting local societies and governments?

Economy and Technology

Look at the two photos below. How has the growing diversity of America's population shaped the marketing strategies of American businesses? Both the presence of immigrants in the United States and the presence of American corporations such as Starbucks in foreign countries underscore globalizing trends in commerce, trade, and migration. How do you assess the effect of globalization on the American economy, society, and culture?

21ST-CENTURY LOS ANGELES

LATTES IN SHANGHAI

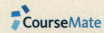

Visit the CourseMate website at www.cengagebrain.com for additional study tools and review materials for this chapter.

32

A TIME OF HOPE AND FEAR, 1993–2012

THE POLITICS OF POLARIZATION, 1993–2008

A New Democrat
A Decade of Legal Investigations and Trials
The Investigation and Trial of a President
The Long Election and Trials of 2000
A Conservative Washington, 2001–2008
Politics and Social-Cultural Issues

FOREIGN POLICIES OF HOPE AND TERROR: 1993–2008

Clinton's Internationalist Agenda
Globalization
Protecting the Planet
September 11, 2001, and the Bush Doctrine

Unilateralism and the Iraq War
National Security and Presidential Power
Divisions over Foreign Policy Direction

AN ECONOMY OF BUBBLE AND BUST, 1993–2008

Deregulation of the Financial Sector during the 1990s
Economics for a New Century, 2000–2006
The Bubble Bursts, 2006–2008
The Election of 2008

CHANGING TIMES, 2009–

Political Polarization
The Culture of Social Networking and Liberty,
    Equality, Power

The decades that directly preceded and followed the turn of the 21st century featured a tension between hope and fear. With the collapse of the Soviet Union, it seemed that America's military, economic, and cultural structure had not only survived the challenge of communism but had become the envy of the world.

Hopes for a bright future, however, found their match in new fears. Could the nation's economic and cultural institutions withstand domestic changes such as the restructuring of the economy and increased immigration? Was its political system flexible enough to meet the challenges of 21st-century governance? Could the world's preeminent economic and military power overcome new threats from terrorist networks? Might new measures for fighting terrorism endanger liberty and equality at home?

Presidents Bill Clinton and George W. Bush tried, in different ways, to redesign the political landscape, yet the nation's politics remained polarized. The sudden economic meltdown in 2008 helped bring a new Democratic face to the White House, Barack Obama. The first African American president and the second youngest in U.S. history, Obama offered what he called "the audacity of hope" in a time of war and economic uncertainty.

TIMELINE

| 1993 | 1995 | 1997 | 1999 | 2001 | 2003 | 2005 | 2007 | 2009 | 2011 |

1993
Congress approves North American Free Trade Agreement (NAFTA)

1994
Republicans gain control of Congress • O. J. Simpson saga begins

1996
Congress overhauls national welfare system • Clinton reelected president • FOX News Channel debuts

1997
Congress and White House agree on deficit reduction plan

1998
House of Representatives impeaches Clinton

1999
Senate trial ends with Clinton's acquittal

2000
Bush v. Gore decision clears way for George W. Bush to become president

2001
Congress passes Bush tax cut • Terrorists from al-Qaeda destroy World Trade Center and attack Pentagon • Congress passes Patriot Act • U.S. forces invade Afghanistana

2002
National Security Strategy of 2002 reasserts the Bush Doctrine

2003
Bush secures another tax cut

2004
Bush defeats Kerry in the presidential race • Facebook debuts at Harvard

2005
Hurricane Katrina hits Gulf Coast • YouTube goes online • Insurgency in Iraq continues as permanent Iraqi government debuts

2006
Democrats gain control of Congress • Housing "bubble" reaches its peak

2007
New U.S. strategy adopted in Iraq • Housing "bubble" bursts

2008
Bush administration and Federal Reserve Board respond to financial meltdown • Great Recession, worst since 1930s, begins • Barack Obama wins presidential race

2009
Obama administration passes economic stimulus plan • U.S. devotes more resources to war in Afghanistan

2010
Republicans surge at national, state, and local levels in elections of 2010

2011
A White House-ordered, CIA-directed raid into Pakistan by Navy SEALs kills Osama bin Laden in early May

2012
Facebook, the social networking site that had been a privately held corporation, begins offering stock shares to the public and initially raises $16 billion dollars • Barack Obama reelected president

THE POLITICS OF POLARIZATION, 1993–2008

FOCUS QUESTION

What political and cultural forces helped to polarize national politics during the years between 1993 and 2008? What impact did this polarization have on public policymaking in Washington?

William Jefferson (Bill) Clinton Democratic president (1993–2001) whose two terms witnessed economic growth and featured sustained attacks, including an impeachment effort, by Republican opponents.

Earned Income Tax Credit (EITC) Tax measure that assisted low- and moderate-income households with children.

"New Democrat" Refers to Democrats such as Clinton whose policy preferences clashed with some classic Democratic positions, including those on criminal justice issues and social welfare measures.

"Contract with America" Sponsored by Newt Gingrich, called for an overhaul of the welfare system, additional anticrime legislation, reform of federal legal procedures, a three-fifths majority for any increase in taxation, and a revised relationship with the UN.

William Jefferson (Bill) Clinton, the first Democratic president since Jimmy Carter, brought images of youth, vitality, and cultural diversity to Washington. His initial cabinet included three African Americans and two Latinos; three cabinet posts went to women. Ruth Bader Ginsburg, his first nominee to the Supreme Court, became only the second woman to sit on the High Court. As ambassador to the United Nations, Clinton named Madeleine Albright, who, during his second term, would become the country's first female secretary of state.

A New Democrat

The Clinton administration moved quickly on the domestic front. It steered a family leave plan for working parents through Congress; helped establish AmeriCorps, a program that allowed students to repay college loans through community service; and secured passage of the Brady Bill, which instituted restrictions on handgun purchases that the Supreme Court subsequently declared unconstitutional. A presidential order ended the Reagan era's ban on federal funding for abortion counseling.

Vice President Al Gore's tiebreaking vote in the Senate allowed passage of Clinton's 1993 economic package. It featured a modest tax increase and a spending-cut package aimed at reducing the federal deficit and lowering interest rates to stimulate economic growth. The plan also expanded an existing governmental program, the **Earned Income Tax Credit (EITC),** which assisted low- and moderate-income households with children.

Identifying himself as a **"New Democrat"** (see also Chapter 30), Clinton broke with his party's recent orthodoxy on criminal justice issues. He backed a 1994 law that provided funding for more police officers and more prisons. His controversial "three strikes" provision required a life sentence for a third felony conviction in federal courts. Clinton later supported limiting appeals by prisoners on death row and an antiterrorist bill opposed by civil libertarian groups.

The administration's ambitious effort to revamp the nation's health-care system, though, ended in failure. A task force chaired by Hillary Rodham Clinton produced a plan containing exceedingly complex mechanisms for financing and delivering health care. Republicans effectively used the proposal, which died in Congress in 1994, to paint the president as a proponent of "big government."

The November 1994 elections brought dramatic victories for the GOP. An aggressive campaign spearheaded by Representative Newt Gingrich of Georgia produced Republican majorities in both houses of Congress for the first time in 40 years. Republicans also won state and local offices, particularly across the South. Gingrich claimed a mandate for what he called a **"Contract with America,"** which called for overhauling the welfare system, enacting additional anticrime legislation, streamlining federal legal procedures, requiring a three-fifths majority for any increase in federal taxation, and revising the nation's relationship to the UN.

Gingrich overplayed his new role as Speaker of the House. A deadlock between a Democratic president and a GOP Congress over spending issues produced two brief shutdowns of federal agencies in late 1995 and early 1996, but most people blamed the Republicans rather than the White House. Indeed, a continually improving economy sustained Clinton's approval ratings. The annual rise in GDP averaged nearly 4 percent. Alan Greenspan, head of the Federal Reserve Board since 1987, kept down inflation by managing interest rates. Economic growth spurred millions of new jobs, decreased the federal deficit, boosted corporate profits, and enabled the astronomical boom in the financial sector. Although the fruits of economic expansion were distributed unequally—the income gulf between the wealthiest 1 percent of households and the other 99 percent deepened—most people did see their economic fortunes improve, however slightly. Unemployment fell, averaging less than 2 percent a year during the 1990s, and real income headed upward for the first time in nearly 15 years.

Surveying the political and economic landscapes, Clinton declared in his 1996 State of the Union address that the era of "big government" was at an end. He suggested a willingness to work with congressional Republicans in reducing social welfare costs. The Personal Responsibility and Work Opportunity Reconciliation Act of 1996 incorporated a series of accommodations between Congress and Clinton, who had vetoed two earlier welfare measures. The new law supplanted the controversial AFDC program with **Temporary Assistance to Needy Families (TANF)**, which allowed the states to design, under general federal guidelines, their own welfare-to-work programs.

TANF worried many traditional Democrats. Provisions limiting governmental assistance over a person's lifetime to five years and authorizing states to suspend benefits if recipients failed to find employment within two years seemed blind to the difficulties faced by people without job skills. TANF's opponents also feared its impact on children. TANF's New Democratic supporters, on the other hand, predicted it would encourage states to devise programs that both reduced welfare costs and created jobs. TANF immediately benefited the Clinton-Gore team, however, by eliminating the welfare issue from partisan debate and re-emphasizing the president's claim that he was reducing the size and cost of government.

In the 1996 election, Clinton and Gore defeated Republicans Robert Dole and Jack Kemp, making Clinton the first Democratic president since Franklin D. Roosevelt to win back-to-back terms. Clinton and Congress, still controlled by Republicans, then agreed on a timetable for decreasing the federal deficit, which the president accurately predicted would begin to disappear. But the nation's political culture was about to start revolving around a legal-constitutional debate over the future of Clinton's presidency rather than policy initiatives.

A Decade of Legal Investigations and Trials

Intensive inquiries into Clinton's public and private life capped a decade of popular fascination with investigations and trials. Americans, of course, had long been drawn to legal spectacles, such as the Scopes Trial of the 1920s (see Chapter 24). During the 1990s, however, investigative and courtroom dramas, both fictional and real, inundated popular culture, as evidenced by the success of novels by John Grisham, films like *A Few Good Men* (1992), and television programs such as *Law & Order* (1990–2010).

Coverage of real trials began a new phase when Court TV (reorganized as truTV in 2008) arrived in 1991. This cable channel helped drive the media feeding frenzy that surrounded the trials of O. J. Simpson, which began in mid-1994 and ran for nearly three years. TV cameras closely followed an investigation into the double homicide of Simpson's former wife and one of her friends that led to the indictment of Simpson, a football star turned actor. Simpson's high-profile attorneys argued to a jury with an African American majority that racist police officers had conspired to frame an innocent black person.

Temporary Assistance to Needy Families (TANF)
Program that allowed each state to design its own welfare-to-work programs under general federal guidelines.

As cable TV news stations fixated on Simpson's case, pundits christened the result "All O. J., All the Time." Television coverage featured legal commentators able to subject the smallest bits of evidence to the maximum amount of analysis. The trial itself finally ended in October 1995 with jurors quickly returning a "not guilty" verdict. Debates over whether their decision represented a reasonable view of the evidence or an emotional rebuke to the police system sustained innumerable media retrospectives. A sequel to this criminal trial featured relatives of the victims winning a civil suit against Simpson for monetary damages.

The Investigation and Trial of a President

Long before the Simpson saga ended, groups on the New Right were bankrolling private inquiries into Bill Clinton's past. One concerned a scandal-plagued real-estate venture in Arkansas called "Whitewater," to which Hillary and Bill Clinton had been financially connected. Confident of rebutting the Whitewater allegations, the Clinton administration asked for the appointment of a special independent prosecutor to investigate them. The president also faced a seemingly frivolous civil suit for monetary damages by Paula Corbin Jones, who alleged that Clinton, while governor of Arkansas, had sexually harassed her. The Jones case became entangled with the Whitewater inquiry when Kenneth Starr replaced the initial head prosecutor. A conservative attorney with Supreme Court ambitions, Starr extended the Whitewater investigation into allegations that Clinton was concealing sexual encounters with other women.

Clinton's denial of sexual liaisons crumbled in early 1998 after conservative activists helped Starr obtain irrefutable evidence of White House trysts between Clinton and a young intern, Monica Lewinsky. Republican leaders in the House of Representatives claimed that Clinton's conduct justified his removal from office. Democrats condemned Clinton's behavior but argued that his private failings did not qualify as the "high crimes or misdemeanors" necessary for impeachment, let alone conviction.

At Newt Gingrich's insistence, Republicans made Clinton's character their major issue during the off-year elections of 1998, but Clinton won this informal political trial. Republicans surprisingly lost five seats in the House. Even worse for Gingrich, public revelation of a long-term extramarital affair forced his resignation. Using evidence gathered by Starr's investigators, the Republican majority in the lame-duck House of Representatives still mobilized enough votes, in mid-December 1998, for two articles of impeachment (one for perjury and another for obstruction of justice) against Clinton. The dramatic Senate trial concluded on February 12, 1999, with both articles of impeachment gaining nowhere near the 67 votes that the Constitution required for conviction.

Although Clinton could justifiably complain about a well-funded public-private campaign to unseat him, the president was hardly an innocent. He would ultimately be ordered to pay $850,000 to settle the Paula Jones lawsuit, be cited for contempt of court for "misleading" testimony, and be forced to surrender his license to practice law.

In addition, the transition from "All O. J., All the Time" to "All Clinton, All the Time" meant that an adversarial, legalistic model would shape media coverage of the president's problems. FOX News Channel's 1996 launch added a spicy new ingredient to the cable TV mix. FOX's rightward political slant was less important initially than its role in refining the adversarial O. J. format for TV news. The channel perfected a cost-cutting technique by which its camera crews gathered eye-catching imagery and brief interviews for re-editing and

HISTORY THROUGH FILM

The Big Lebowski (1998)

Director: Joel Coen

Starring: Jeff Bridges ("The Dude"), John Goodman (Walter),
Steve Buscemi (Donny), and Sam Elliott ("The Stranger")

There are many possible ways of recalling the 1990s and almost as many reasons to begin with *The Big Lebowski*. This loosely structured, irony-soaked comedy is set at the decade's beginning, "just about the time of your conflict with Saddam and the Iraqis," according to its narrator, "The Stranger" (Sam Elliot).

The Big Lebowski meanders through historical events such as military interventions in Korea and Vietnam, the New Left and counterculture of the Sixties, the sexual revolution, and the new immigration. The film also wanders through the history of the Hollywood film industry, drawing snippets from the western, the musical, and the *film noir* of the 1940s, particularly *The Big Sleep* (1945, 1946). It also reworks the Hollywood "bio-pic," a traditional genre that offers highly sanitized biographies of invariably male heroes.

The heroic figure for the Nineties is "Jeffrey Lebowski" (Jeff Bridges). Portrayed as a burnout from the Sixties, he claims that he wrote the initial draft of the *Port Huron Statement* (the 1962 manifesto of the Students for a Democratic Society). Known as "the Dude," he embraces the "slacker life" and concentrates on, in no particular order, White Russian cocktails, pot, and bowling. One of his bowling buddies, Walter Sobchak (John Goodman), is a satirical portrayal of a gun-toting wacko, mocking Hollywood's re-presentation of veterans of the Vietnam War.

The storyline, such as it is, begins with a gang of thugs mistaking "the Dude" for "the Big Lebowski," a paraplegic veteran of the Korean conflict and celebrated philanthropist, whose young wife, "Bunny," owes a gambling debt. The "Big Lebowski" improbably hires "the Dude" to broker a ransom deal for "Bunny," who has allegedly been kidnapped.

Falling into the role of private investigator, "the Dude" must survive a series of trial-like encounters in order to save, as did noble knights of old, a "damsel in distress."

In this film, however, the surreal misadventures of a private investigator of the 1990s provide another opportunity for the reworking of various Hollywood movie clichés. It all ends with "the Dude" drinking beer at his favorite bowling alley, talking to "the Stranger," and telling him (and all of us) that all the "strikes and gutters, ups and downs" of life will never bother or change him.

Initially a box-office disappointment, the movie subsequently spawned the inevitable 10th Anniversary DVD, a series of Facebook sites, and the annual "Lebowski Fests" where the movie's devoted fans bowl, dress in costume, sip White Russians, and shout out its signature line: "I'm a Lebowski. You're a Lebowski."

In *The Big Lebowski*, the 1990s randomly unfolds as a time that lacks a coherent theme. Coming after the end of the Cold War, and with 9/11 still unimaginable, the movie portrays an era that, much like "the Dude," simply "abides."

Polygram/Working Title/ The Kobal Collection

"THE DUDE" ABIDES.

recycling. On-air commentators used fleeting video and brief sound bites as the basis for trading opinions and speculation without leaving the studio or doing any actual reporting.

A medium newer and more adversarial than cable TV—political sites on the Internet—came online at a critical point in the Clinton investigation. The first news of the Clinton-Lewinsky relationship surfaced on *The Drudge Report*, a conservative opinion-gossip Internet site that other media had previously disdained. *The Drudge Report* became a model for subsequent sites that featured an adversarial approach to political coverage. Over the course of the 1990s, in short, discussions of public affairs increasingly took on the accusatory-investigative format that came to envelop—indeed, almost paralyze—the Clinton administration.

The Long Election and Trials of 2000

The lengthy presidential election of 2000 also ended in a legal drama. Vice President Al Gore ran as the Democratic presidential nominee and selected Senator Joseph Lieberman of Connecticut as his running mate. The Republican ballot once more bore the name of Bush. **George W. Bush,** the son of the former president, chose **Richard (Dick) Cheney**—a conservative Republican stalwart who had served in Bush senior's administration—to be his vice-presidential running mate.

George W. Bush *Republican president (2001–2009) elected in the highly disputed 2000 election contest decided by the Supreme Court.*

Richard (Dick) Cheney *Conservative Republican who served as vice president to George W. Bush.*

The campaign of 2000 energized the Republican Party's base but stirred less passion elsewhere. Bush claimed his record as governor of Texas showed he could work with Democrats, appeal to African Americans and Hispanics, and pursue a "compassionate conservatism." Gore's disorganized campaign struggled to articulate coherent themes. By distancing himself from Clinton, the vice president likely squandered his primary asset—eight years of economic prosperity. Barely 50 percent of eligible voters went to the polls. Following a pattern evident since the Reagan presidency of the 1980s, the vote highlighted the gender, racial, and ethnic differences between the two parties. According to exit polls, Bush attracted 54 percent of the ballots cast by men but only 43 percent of those from women. He received 38 percent of the votes from Latinos, 37 percent from Asian Americans, and 9 percent from African Americans.

The election of 2000 ended in a near dead heat. Republicans narrowly maintained control of the House of Representatives, and the Senate ended up evenly split between the two parties. Gore carried the popular vote by about 500,000 ballots, but the only tally that mattered, the one in the Electoral College, turned on the 25 votes from Florida. Only about 1,000 popular votes initially separated the two candidates.

When it became evident that no clear winner had emerged in Florida, cable TV news shifted to an "All Election, All the Time" focus on Florida, where Bush's brother Jeb was governor and the GOP dominated the state legislature. Republican officials declared Bush the victor in Florida by a margin of 930 votes. Democrats charged that numerous irregularities—including antiquated voting machines, deliberately confusing ballots, and apparent efforts to discourage voting by African Americans—had distorted the count. A torrent of lawsuits, by Democrats and Republicans alike, quickly ensued. Florida's highest court finally ordered hand recounts in several counties where Gore's

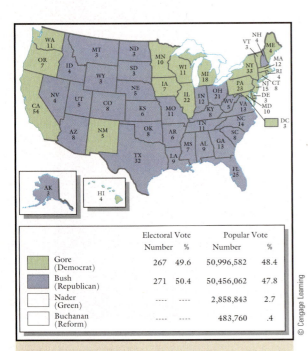

	Electoral Vote		Popular Vote	
	Number	%	Number	%
Gore (Democrat)	267	49.6	50,996,582	48.4
Bush (Republican)	271	50.4	50,456,062	47.8
Nader (Green)	----	----	2,858,843	2.7
Buchanan (Reform)	----	----	483,760	.4

© Cengage Learning

***Map 32.1* Presidential Election, 2000.** *Although Gore won the popular vote, Bush won the electoral vote after a bitter fight over disputed ballots in Florida.*

THE 2000 PRESIDENTIAL CAMPAIGN, PHASE 2. *The inconclusive popular vote in Florida extended the 2000 presidential election process. Partisan activists, especially on the Republican side, rushed to Florida and on TV. GOP demonstrators insisted that George W. Bush had carried the Sunshine State and that the hand counting of ballots was meant to steal his victory.*

totals seemed suspiciously low. When early results seemed to be reducing Bush's already slim margin, Republicans accused Democrats of stealing his victory and appealed to the U.S. Supreme Court.

On the evening of December 12, 2000, the Court handed down its final decision in *Bush v. Gore* (2000). Five conservative Republicans (over the dissents of two other Republicans and two Democrats) ruled that no more ballots could be recounted. Gore conceded political defeat, and George W. Bush became the 43rd president of the United States.

A Conservative Washington, 2001–2008

Bush chose a cabinet and White House staff as diverse as Clinton's. It included General Colin Powell in the key post of secretary of state, three women, two Asian Americans, and even a Democrat who had briefly served in Clinton's administration.

In contrast to Clinton, who preferred intellectual give-and-take sessions with his advisers, Bush favored brief, tightly controlled meetings that moved toward clearly delineated decisions. According to dissident members of his administration, Bush rarely seemed interested in exploring, or sometimes even hearing or reading, ideas in conflict with his instincts. He initially allowed Vice President Cheney and Donald Rumsfeld, the secretary of defense, wide latitude to set policy directions. Bush also proclaimed that religious faith *directly* shaped his political outlook.

Several divisive issues immediately dominated Bush's presidency. An economic downturn accompanied by an early 2001 plunge in U.S stock markets—a consequence of the bursting bubble in high-tech stocks and fraudulent activities by several large corporations—signaled the end of the boom of the 1990s. Federal

Bush v. Gore Court case over the 2000 presidential election; the Court ceased the recounting of ballots in Florida, which made George W. Bush the 43rd president of the United States.

revenue surpluses began dwindling and then turning to deficits. Consumer confidence slumped. The Bush administration responded by urging a tax cut to provide an economic stimulus.

The White House pressed two other proposals. First, Cheney put together an ambitious energy plan, focused on easing restrictions on oil drilling and regulations on pricing. Critics complained that it primarily benefited large oil and gas firms and did little to develop alternative sources of energy. Second, the president personally championed an educational program called "No Child Left Behind" that would require nationwide testing to determine which schools were teaching students effectively.

Bush's initiatives were bolder than either his campaign rhetoric or his loss of the popular vote might have suggested. A revised tax plan, which phased in the substantial cuts that tilted toward the wealthiest 1 percent of Americans, became law in June 2001. "No Child Left Behind," supported by Democratic icon Ted Kennedy, also passed. Opponents of the pro-oil and pro-gas energy bill blocked its passage but only until 2005. In 2003, the administration narrowly secured congressional passage of the Medicare Prescription Drug Improvement Act, a costly addition (the first in 35 years) to the Medicare system.

The president's approval ratings, which had hovered under 50 percent, soared after the attacks on the World Trade Center and the Pentagon on September 11, 2001. (For the foreign policy implications of 9/11, especially in the Middle East, see pp. 778–781.) Bush's popularity carried into the midterm elections of 2002, which left the GOP with secure control of the U.S. Senate and a solid majority in the House of Representatives.

Downplaying the rapidly growing federal deficit, largely the result of Bush's earlier tax reductions, the White House secured yet another tax cut in 2003. Democrats condemned these cuts for tilting toward the already wealthy in an economy that had shed nearly three million jobs and had shown a widening gap between rich and poor.

The White House's political strategy for the 2004 elections, fine-tuned by consultant Karl Rove, stressed Bush's role in combating terrorism. The Democratic nominee, Senator John Kerry of Massachusetts, had served in Vietnam during the 1960s before becoming an antiwar activist. Kerry endorsed the Bush administration's national security initiatives but criticized its strategy and tactics for combating the terrorist threat.

A fiercely partisan campaign ensued. Some Bush supporters disparaged Kerry's Vietnam War record, and his campaign portrayed a Kerry presidency as a danger to national security. Democrats charged Bush with bumbling leadership, saddling future generations with a horrendous burden of debt, and enabling a small percentage of the wealthy to enjoy tax cuts. The GOP's mobilization effort produced an unusually large turnout and charges of voter fraud, especially in Ohio. Bush defeated Kerry by only about 3 percent of the popular vote and 15 electoral ballots.

Bush still claimed an electoral mandate and announced an ambitious second-term agenda that featured substantial overhauls of the Social Security system and the tax code. He barnstormed the country on behalf of these initiatives, but most people appeared wary in light of the shaky economy and a yawning federal deficit. Moreover, a Republican-controlled Congress became a depreciating asset to the White House after revelations of illegal contributions from lobbyists and personal misconduct forced the resignation of several GOP legislators, including the powerful Tom DeLay. Congress's approval rating skidded below that of President Bush.

Politics and Social-Cultural Issues

With the major political parties locked in partisan stalemate, a variety of movement groups tried to seize the initiative on specific issues. Immigration policy emerged as one of the most contentious problems. Entering the United States in near-record numbers, immigrants were now seeking jobs throughout the country, particularly in the South. Organizations that opposed immigration demanded new restrictions, tighter border security, and stronger penalties for employers of undocumented immigrants. Pro-immigrant groups, tapping the power of Spanish-language radio and TV, staged temporary work stoppages and street demonstrations. They cited economic studies that challenged claims that immigrants "took away" jobs and depressed wage levels. The Bush administration angered congressional Republicans by endorsing a "guest worker" arrangement, an option favored by most business interests. Uncertain about how immigration legislation might affect electoral results in 2008, Republicans backed off taking action at the national level.

Differences over the role of government in dealing with environmental concerns also sharpened. Business interests joined prominent Republicans in supporting continued deregulation and opposing new governmental restrictions. In response to this position, environmentalist groups argued that hazardous wastes, though a potential threat to everyone, most directly affected people with low incomes who lacked the political power to keep toxic by-products out of their neighborhoods and off their lands. They further charged that the relatively few corporations that dominated the global production and sale of food brutalized animals, overused antibiotics, depleted soil quality and vital rain forests, and polluted the environment. Governmental regulations, they argued, were needed to protect the quality of soil and water as well as to ensure the health and safety of consumers.

The issue of gay marriage also emerged as a major political-cultural flashpoint, as LGBT movements sought legal recognition of long-term partnerships that they viewed to be as legitimate as heterosexual marriages. When the U.S. Supreme Court struck down state anti-sodomy laws (in *Lawrence v. Texas, 2003*), it signaled that the same constitutional logic might apply to bans on same-sex marriage. Opinion polls suggested sharply divided views about gay marriage but fairly broad support for civil unions or other legal arrangements that would recognize LGBT partnerships. In several states, though, courts held that the bedrock principle of legal constitutional equality guaranteed gays and lesbians a right to marry.

Conservative organizations claimed that gay couples were unsuited for raising children and joined the Bush administration in seeking an amendment to the U.S. Constitution that specifically declared marriage as a "union between a man and a woman." Opponents of this initiative narrowly turned back a congressional effort to send such an amendment to the states for ratification in 2006.

Mobilization on the political right also highlighted conflict between religious belief and scientific-medical research. Moving beyond opposition to abortion, "right-to-life" activists condemned other practices, such as assisted suicide and removal of feeding tubes; anti-pregnancy drugs; and medical research that used stem cells from human embryos. In July 2006, after Congress passed a measure in support of stem cell research, President Bush issued, on live television, the first veto of his presidency, on "culture-of-life" grounds.

Many of these political-cultural issues involved court decisions. The conservative legal movement continued its successful campaign to staff the lower federal courts with rightward-tilting jurists and blocked a Bush nominee for the Supreme Court, Harriet Myers, in part because of an apparently moderate background on issues such as abortion and gay rights. The White House easily obtained Senate

QUICK REVIEW

THE POLITICS OF POLARIZATION

- Clinton worked to reduce the size of government, eliminate the federal deficit, and overhaul the welfare system

- Republicans took over Congress in 1994 with the "Contract for America," but Clinton's policies and a thriving economy undercut their message

- An adversarial media culture accelerated with the trial of O. J. Simpson and the impeachment of Clinton

- Bush implemented a bold conservative agenda despite coming into office without having won the popular vote

- Polarization increased around sociocultural issues such as immigration, the environment, LGBT rights, and scientific-medical research

Roberts Court *The most politically conservative Supreme Court since the 1930s was headed by Chief Justice John Roberts, who could generally count on support from four associate justices who had also been Republican appointees.*

confirmations for two staunchly conservative Supreme Court nominees: John Roberts to replace William Rehnquist as chief justice, and Samuel Alito (rather than Myers) to succeed the retiring Sandra Day O'Connor. The divided decisions of the "**Roberts Court**" limited women's access to abortion, struck down an ordinance regulating gun ownership in the nation's capital, and adopted a restrictive view of the ability of local school districts to use racial identification when assigning students to particular schools in pursuit of desegregation strategies.

FOREIGN POLICIES OF HOPE AND TERROR: 1993–2008

FOCUS QUESTION

How did Bill Clinton's administration attempt to redesign foreign policy for a post–Cold War world? How did the administration of George W. Bush, especially after September 11, 2001, seek to reorient Clinton's approach?

A committed internationalist, Bill Clinton came to the White House with an ambitious foreign policy agenda. Later, George W. Bush sought to reorient Clinton's approach following the attacks of September 11, 2001.

Clinton's Internationalist Agenda

Clinton failed to formulate consistent guidelines about when to employ U.S. military power in localized conflicts that no longer could automatically be connected to the now-defunct Soviet Union. In Somalia, U.S. troops, under the umbrella of a UN mission since May 1992, had been assisting a humanitarian effort to provide food and relief supplies. After a battle in Mogadishu (subsequently portrayed in the book and movie *Black Hawk Down*) took the lives of 18 U.S. service personnel in the fall of 1993, however, domestic criticism mounted. Clinton ordered a pullout the following spring. Recalling the criticism of involvement in Somalia, Clinton withheld support from a UN peacekeeping effort in Rwanda, where 500,000 Tutsis died during a genocidal civil war. In Haiti, though, Clinton dispatched U.S. troops, in cooperation with the UN, to reinstall the elected president, Jean-Bertrand Aristide, who had been ousted in a coup. The White House, in cooperation with NATO, also sent 20,000 U.S. troops to Yugoslavia to prevent Bosnian Serbs from massacring Bosnian Muslims. U.S. forces remained in Bosnia to oversee a cease-fire and peace-building process that resulted from the U.S.-brokered Dayton (Ohio) Peace Accords of 1995.

In March 1999, Clinton supported a NATO bombing campaign to protect Albanian Muslims from an "ethnic cleansing" program in the Serbian province of Kosovo carried out by Serbia's president, Slobodan Milosevic. The Albanian Muslims constituted nearly 90 percent of the population in Kosovo. After 78 days of bombardment, Milosevic withdrew his forces from Kosovo. Serbs soon elected a new president supportive of multiethnic democracy and the West, and Milosevic faced trial before an international human rights court. As in Bosnia, U.S. and allied troops remained in Kosovo as peacekeepers.

Clinton's military moves in Haiti, Bosnia, and Kosovo provoked controversy. Republican critics accused the president of lacking clear guidelines about when, where, and how to employ U.S. force. Suspicious of cooperating with the UN, they denounced peacekeeping and "nation-building" programs, and demanded clear-cut exit strategies to prevent the United States from getting bogged down in lengthy occupations. Defenders of intervention insisted that Clinton's flexibility and willingness to work with NATO and the UN were strengths, not weaknesses, in a post–Cold War world.

Globalization

The Clinton administration placed great emphasis on lowering barriers to trade and expanding global markets to advance the international economic process called "globalization" (see Chapter 31). His stance angered many labor leaders, who claimed that globalization was contributing to the loss of industrial jobs in the United States. It also sparked a highly visible anti-globalization movement that emerged in most nations to challenge transnational economic elites.

In pursuit of globalization, Clinton first promoted the stalled North American Free Trade Agreement (NAFTA) among the United States, Canada, and Mexico. In late 1993, he pushed NAFTA through Congress in a close vote that depended on Republican support and faced fierce opposition from labor unions. Then, in early 1995, Mexico's severe debt crisis and a drastic devaluation of its currency prompted Clinton to extend a $20 billion loan. The loan stabilized the Mexican economy and, within a few years, had been repaid with $1 billion in interest.

Clinton's administration signed more than 300 trade agreements, including the so-called Uruguay Round of the General Agreement on Tariffs and Trade (GATT) in late 1993. In early 1995 GATT was replaced by a more powerful **World Trade Organization (WTO).** Anxious to move China toward a market economy, Clinton reversed his earlier position and backed China's entry into the WTO, in exchange for its promise to relax trade restrictions. Similarly, in February 1994, the United States ended its 19-year-old trade embargo against Vietnam.

Protecting the Planet

International environmental issues were a third area of major concern for the Clinton administration. Clinton's secretary of the interior set aside 16 new national monuments and blocked road construction and logging in nearly 60 million acres of wild areas in national forests. Building on the work of its Republican predecessors, Clinton's administration placed almost 6 million new surface and underwater acres under federal protection.

The U.S. government, however, often seemed to be one of the country's most flagrant polluters. Throughout the Cold War, governmental nuclear facilities had spewed toxic wastes, and workers had been inadequately warned about the dangers of radiation. In 1993, Clinton's energy secretary released long-secret medical records relating to radiation and promised programs to inform and compensate victims.

Most importantly, Clinton supported the environmental movement's increasing focus on international ecological dangers. Environmentalists warned of holes in the ozone layer caused by chlorofluorocarbons (CFCs), potentially catastrophic climate change associated with deforestation and desertification, pollution of the world's oceans, and the decline of biodiversity in plant and animal species. Solutions to global environmental problems seemingly required worldwide cooperation toward "sustainable development." An "Earth Summit" was held in Brazil in 1992. International conventions signed in Kyoto in 1997 and at The Hague in 2000 pointed toward establishing international standards on emissions of CFCs and gases that contributed to global climate changes. Yet, in the United States, the climate-change issue became increasingly polarized as some Republicans began insisting that the issue was a scientific hoax that would cripple the American economy.

Clinton's post–Cold War agenda included several other priorities. Clinton supported nonproliferation of nuclear weapons. He dismantled some of the U.S.

World Trade Organization (WTO) *Established in 1995 to oversee and promote international trade between nations.*

nuclear arsenal and increased economic aid to Ukraine in exchange for a pledge to disarm its 1,600 Soviet-era warheads. After promises of U.S. help, North Korea also agreed to begin halting its fledgling nuclear program and permitting international inspections—agreements it later repudiated. The White House successfully pressed for a new Nuclear Nonproliferation Treaty in the spring of 1995, and three years later neared the brink of war with Iraq to maintain international inspections of Saddam Hussein's weapons programs. After enduring punishing air strikes, Iraq still expelled the investigators and left analysts wondering if Hussein had resumed building weapons of mass destruction (WMDs).

September 11, 2001, and the Bush Doctrine

During the 1990s, intelligence experts highlighted a growing concern about attacks by a foreign terrorist network called al-Qaeda. Its operatives bombed the World Trade Center in New York City in 1993; U.S. embassies in Kenya and Tanzania in 1998; and a U.S. battleship, the *Cole*, docked in Yemen in 2000. As the Clinton administration left office, national security officers worried about what al-Qaeda's leader Osama bin Laden, an Islamic fundamentalist from Saudi Arabia, might be plotting next.

On September 11, 2001, 19 suicide terrorists, organized in separate squads, seized four jetliners, already airborne and loaded with highly flammable jet fuel, for use as high-octane, human-guided missiles. Two planes destroyed the Twin Towers of New York's World Trade Center; another ripped into the Pentagon in Washington; and only the courageous action of passengers on a fourth plane, which crashed in Pennsylvania, prevented a second attack against the nation's capital. Nearly 3,000 people, including several hundred plane passengers and an even larger number of police officers and firefighters in New York City, perished.

George W. Bush, donning the mantle of a wartime president, declared a war on terrorism. Tracing the attacks to Osama bin Laden and al-Qaeda operating out of Afghanistan, the Bush administration organized a multinational invasion force. In December 2001, U.S.-led troops toppled the Taliban regime that had been dominating Afghanistan with bin Laden's help and installed a pro-U.S. government in Afghanistan's capital city of Kabul. This effort failed to secure that nation's countryside or to capture bin Laden and his top aides.

Meanwhile, the president proclaimed what became known as the **Bush Doctrine**. As fully expressed in The National Security Strategy of 2002, it denounced not only terrorist networks but any nation sponsoring terrorism or accumulating WMDs that terrorists might use. The United States henceforth claimed the unilateral authority to wage preemptive war against any force, including any foreign nation, that endangered American security.

Congressional legislation bolstered the Bush doctrine. Many Democrats joined Republicans in passing the USA Patriot Act, which gave the executive branch broad latitude to watch over and detain people it considered threats to national security. A newly created agency, the Department of Homeland Security, launched an array of new measures including screenings for all passengers at airports. Fear of more terrorist attacks strengthened the case for extending the power of the executive branch.

Unilateralism and the Iraq War

As Osama bin Laden dropped from sight, the White House invoked the Bush Doctrine against Iraq and Saddam Hussein, the old nemesis of the president's father, who controlled some of the richest oil reserves in the world. Contending that intelligence reports showed that Saddam possessed WMDs and had ties to

Bush Doctrine *Denounced terrorist networks and claimed authority to wage war against any force that endangered American security.*

GROUND ZERO, SEPTEMBER 11, 2001. *The South Tower of the World Trade Center collapses as the North Tower burns, after terrorists commandeered two airliners and used them as deadly missiles.*

al-Qaeda, the Bush administration asked the UN and other nations to support a military strike to remove Hussein on the claim that Iraq had frustrated the weapons inspections mandated by the Gulf War settlement of 1991. The UN instead favored giving weapons inspectors another try.

Unlike his father, an internationalist who had carefully courted UN backing for the Persian Gulf War, Bush proved determined to overthrow Hussein regardless of the UN's position. Acting without UN authorization, in early 2003 the Bush administration assembled its own "coalition of the willing"—troops from the United States and Great Britain, plus smaller contingents from Poland, Italy, Spain, and several other countries. On March 20, the coalition launched an air and ground

BAGHDAD, IRAQ, 2006. *Bombings aimed at both Iraqis and U.S. personnel followed the fall of Saddam Hussein. In May 2006, a bomb attack hit a news crew from CBS, underscoring the danger that journalists, as well as troops, confronted whenever they left the relative safety of the U.S.-controlled "Green Zone" in central Baghdad.*

AP Images/Khalid Mohammed

assault against Iraq. Overriding military planners who desired at least 300,000 U.S. troops, "Operation Iraqi Freedom" deployed only one-third that many forces. Saddam Hussein's regime did fall in less than two months, and on May 1 President Bush proclaimed, from the deck of the aircraft carrier *Abraham Lincoln*, that "significant combat" had ended in Iraq.

This carefully crafted media event quickly rebounded against the president, as resistance flared against the American-dominated occupation, which aimed at creating a pro-U.S. government and a new economic order closely tied to U.S. companies. An evolving insurgency brought rising American and Iraqi casualties. In part, violence stemmed from Iraq's ethnic, religious, and regional divisions. Under Hussein, Sunni Arabs who lived in areas around Baghdad had dominated political power. The Shi'a Arabs, a majority of the nation's population, who were concentrated in the South, and the northern Kurds, mostly Sunni but non-Arabs, had been persecuted outsiders. They now wanted a share of governmental power. Divisions also emerged between Iraqis who insisted that any new government remain secular (as it had been under Hussein) and those who desired one based on Islamic law. Moreover, terrorist groups from outside Iraq, particularly ones claiming connections to al-Qaeda, joined the insurgency.

Factional struggles, complicated by the presence of Western troops with little knowledge of Iraq's socio-religious dynamics, embroiled the country in civil war.

As U.S. casualties in Iraq mounted, so did the costs. The administration repeatedly asked Congress for additional billions of dollars to fund ongoing operations. Meanwhile, the war in Afghanistan stalled, the Taliban regrouped, and the al-Qaeda leaders who had attacked on September 11, 2001, retreated into mountainous safe havens and into Pakistan.

As the Iraqi operation faltered, the Bush administration's public rationale for having undertaken it fell apart. The White House never documented any connection between al-Qaeda and Saddam Hussein, and an exhaustive official report concluded that Iraq had possessed no WMDs at the time of the invasion. Later evidence suggested that intelligence had been distorted to bolster the justification for war.

As the initial case for war came under fire, so did its conduct. Photographs showing abuse of detained Iraqis, especially at Baghdad's Abu Ghraib prison, and stories of a few U.S. troops deliberately killing civilians called into question the wisdom of having U.S. forces occupy the country. Controversy developed over whether methods of what the Bush administration called "enhanced interrogation" had been a euphemism for what others called "torture."

In 2005, Iraqis elected a national assembly, chose an interim prime minister, and produced a constitution that gained popular approval. But the civil war only intensified, and widespread hatred for U.S. intervention in Muslim lands inflamed many people across the Middle East. Contrary to the Bush Doctrine, it seemed that regime change in Iraq was producing neither a stable nor a pro-American region.

National Security and Presidential Power

Hurricane Katrina, slamming into the U.S. Gulf Coast region in late August 2005, prompted an intense, if temporary, debate over national security on the home front. Local and state officials bumbled through the first post–9/11 emergency. The Department of Homeland Security, presumably created to deal more efficiently with threats that included hurricanes, seemed unprepared. Although the White House would claim no one had "anticipated the breach of levees" intended to protect New Orleans from floodwaters, videotapes later showed the president receiving precisely such a warning. Katrina exacted an especially heavy toll on the Gulf Coast's oldest, poorest, and African American residents. After failing to provide effective aid to hundreds of thousands, neither state nor national authorities could supply a precise figure, presumably in the several thousands, of those who perished as a result of Katrina.

The Bush administration's limited response to Katrina departed from its usual preference for expanding the reach of the executive branch. It convinced Congress to renew the Patriot Act, which otherwise would have automatically expired in 2006. When a bipartisan coalition blocked Bush's nomination of John Bolton to become ambassador to the UN, the administration placed him in this position through an unprecedented interim appointment, which did not require Senate confirmation.

Several issues raised special controversy over presidential power. Initially, when dealing with alleged terrorists captured overseas, especially in Afghanistan, the Bush administration chose to operate outside both domestic and international agreements and detain captives at a new facility in the U.S. enclave at Guantanamo Bay, Cuba. Later, it devised special legal proceedings for trying detainees, which the U.S. Supreme Court, on three separate occasions, declared unconstitutional. The Bush administration also bypassed the Foreign Intelligence Surveillance Act of 1978 (FISA), which mandated special procedures before undertaking domestic wiretaps. Congress and the White House agreed on revisions to FISA, in 2007 and 2008, that granted surveillance agencies, in the name of national security, broader power to monitor communication networks.

HURRICANE KATRINA HITS NEW ORLEANS, 2005. *These photos provide bird's-eye and ground-level views of New Orleans after Hurricane Katrina made landfall. They suggest the devastation that befell the Crescent City and the challenges faced by those charged with devising an effective response. Katrina temporarily highlighted the domestic dimensions of "homeland security."*

Changes in Washington drained some urgency and partisan discord from the issues of the war and presidential powers during the final years of the Bush presidency. An apparent antiwar backlash helped the Democratic Party capture control of Congress in the midterm elections of November 2006. The following month, Bush named Robert Gates, a skillful bureaucratic manager, to replace the mercurial Donald Rumsfeld as head of the Department of Defense. Gates helped the Bush administration adopt a new strategy for Iraq that temporarily increased U.S. troop levels and placed in command General David Petraeus, an expert on counterinsurgency warfare. Deploying U.S. troops more selectively, General Petraeus stepped up training for Iraqi forces and ramped up payments to Sunni factions in exchange for their political participation. The strategy soon reduced the level of civil violence and decreased political tension within Iraq as Bush prepared to leave office.

Divisions over Foreign Policy Direction

By the end of Bush's presidency, the wars in Afghanistan and Iraq had claimed the lives of nearly 5,000 U.S. troops. Iraqi civilian casualties numbered, by the most conservative estimates, in the tens of thousands. The ongoing occupation of Iraq was costing the United States $6 billion per month. Popular support for Bush dropped below 30 percent.

Democratic critics, looking toward the election of 2008, advocated a timetable for removing U.S. combat troops from Iraq, a renewed military and diplomatic effort to stabilize Afghanistan, and a clearer focus on al-Qaeda. In their view, Bush had neglected threats to national security that required international cooperation. One involved securing loose stockpiles of nuclear material before they fell into the hands of terrorists.

Another threat involved climate change. The Bush administration claimed that the science behind climate change remained uncertain. It also objected to the fact that targets would not be applied equally to developed nations and to certain developing nations, especially China. The Republican-dominated Senate failed to approve the Kyoto Protocol, but some prominent Democrats such as the former vice president, Al Gore, continued to publicize the dangers of climate change and advocate rejoining the international forums working on the issue. They also pressed for development of "green energy" sources that would both lessen U.S. reliance on supplies of oil from the Middle East and help reduce carbon output.

AN ECONOMY OF BUBBLE AND BUST, 1993–2008

In 2003, the Nobel Prize–winning economist Robert Lucas credited his generation with effectively mastering the "central problem of depression-prevention." He spoke for those who believed that the U.S. and world economies were enjoying "The Great Moderation," a term that signified a faith that the economy, increasingly free from governmental regulations, would no longer face the extremes of boom and bust. This conviction dominated economic thought and policy-making during the 1990s and the first years of the 21st century. Then, beginning in 2006, the American economy reached the high point of what, in retrospect, was an economic-financial bubble that helped conceal other dismal economic trends. During the 96 months of the Bush presidency, for example, the economy gained only about three million new jobs, a fraction of the total added during the 1990s.

Deregulation of the Financial Sector during the 1990s

The financial sector had become the most dynamic and exciting part of the economy during the 1990s (see Chapter 31). Its leaders could take credit for generating roughly 30 percent of all domestic profits by the middle of the decade.

Clinton's economic brain trust, led by Robert Rubin, formerly of the financial giant Goldman Sachs, argued that the late 20th century economy had outgrown the New Deal regulatory structure, but it still saw an important economic role for government. If the economy were to continue growing, these New Democrats argued, Washington occasionally needed to mount activist rescue efforts. If the economy appeared to be running smoothly, though, government should stay out of the way, except to remove outmoded regulations.

The Clinton administration also resisted regulating new financial products because it feared hampering financial innovation. Its embrace of "Rubinomics" thus sided with forces outside the administration that wanted to translate the dominant faith in minimal regulation into congressional legislation. The administration endorsed the Commodities Futures Modernization Act of 2000, which prohibited Washington from regulating the new financial inventions called "derivatives."

Economics for a New Century, 2000–2006

The administration of Republican George W. Bush surpassed that of New Democrat Bill Clinton in its enthusiasm for supporting deregulation and promoting financial innovation. Henry (Hank) Paulson, who became secretary of the treasury in 2006, was another alumnus of Goldman Sachs. Just before joining the Bush administration, Paulson had successfully pressed federal regulators to exempt the five largest investment houses, including Goldman Sachs, from a rule that required investment firms to reserve a specific amount of capital to cover their debt obligations. This move dramatically increased these five firms' capacity to borrow funds and, consequently, their ability to speculate in risky investments.

Critics of deregulation noted early signs of trouble. During 2002, several fraud-plagued firms fell into bankruptcy. The most spectacular case involved Enron, a Texas-based energy company with close ties to members of the Bush administration. The absence of effective regulation had allowed Enron to engage in legally suspect speculation in the trading of energy-related contracts and in illegal bookkeeping that lifted its profits to fictional heights.

The political and financial impact of the scandals of the early 2000s soon paled in comparison to the systemic problems within the real estate and financial industries. The Bush administration had quickly abandoned its predecessor's commitment to balanced budgets and a small federal deficit, but it retained its goal of promoting homeownership. Like Clinton, Bush urged financial institutions to help low-income buyers find the house of their dreams. By 2006, nearly 70 percent of households lived in their own homes, an all-time high.

Why had the nation become caught up in an unsustainable **housing bubble** rather than a genuine boom? First, as more buyers entered the housing market, prices for new and existing homes skyrocketed. Many people who desired—and were being urged—to become homeowners lacked household incomes that could handle a conventional mortgage.

Second, the home-lending industry responded by devising an array of "non-conventional" mortgages for people whose incomes or credit histories disqualified them from obtaining a fixed rate loan. By 2006, far too many new loans involved **"subprime" mortgages**, meaning that they, unlike those of higher quality, carried a high risk of default. In 2001, less than 10 percent of home mortgages qualified as less than "prime" quality. In contrast, 40 percent of the new loans processed between 2001 and 2006 fell into this category.

Worse, problems extended beyond subprime mortgages. People with houses whose market value had dramatically increased could refinance their existing mortgage at a lower interest rate. As if by magic, refinancing on the basis of the higher valuation gave them more money to spend. Mortgage refinancing helped stimulate overall economic activity but at the risk of creating mortgage holders who would, if the economy seriously faltered, be unable to meet their payments.

Third, people at the commanding heights of the financial system worked overtime to boost the residential housing market. The Federal Reserve Board, under Alan Greenspan (who began a fifth term in 2002) and his successor Ben Bernanke (who took over in 2006), kept interest rates at historic lows. This kept relatively "cheap money" flowing through the financial sector—and kept the residential housing market bubbling.

Finally, the giant firms at the top of the financial structure continued issuing optimistic risk assessments. Compliant investing services such as Moody's gave "low risk" ratings to the mortgage-backed collateralized debt obligations (CDOs) that investment firms such as Goldman Sachs and Lehman Brothers were marketing as top-grade securities (see also Chapter 31).

By 2006, some people detected a bubble about to burst. The famed investor Warren Buffett of Berkshire Hathaway called mortgage-backed CDOs "financial weapons of mass destruction" and forecast trouble for the home loan industry: "Dumb lending always has its consequences."

The Bubble Bursts, 2006–2008

Buffett, hailed as "the Oracle of Omaha," proved prophetic. Beginning in late 2006, the rise in housing prices first slowed and then headed rapidly downward. The financial industry soon fell victim to the housing bubble it had helped inflate. Self-correcting mechanisms, contrary to what free-market economists promised, had never appeared. As loans went into default, the ripple effect cascaded into financial institutions overloaded with mortgage-derived securities. Credit stopped flowing, economies throughout the world began to contract, and unemployment rose.

The Bush administration and the Fed's Bernanke sought to respond. First, the Fed extended massive financial assistance to the financial industry. Then, during spring 2008, Bernanke's Fed and the Treasury Department's Hank Paulson helped J. P. Morgan Chase acquire Bear Stearns, a rival Wall Street firm headed for bankruptcy, but later allowed Lehman Brothers, another Wall Street stalwart, to collapse. The Bush administration and the Fed appeared to be signaling that a short-lived era of governmental rescue was over.

housing bubble *Refers to a housing market, such as that of the early 2000s, in which millions of people who lacked the incomes to handle a conventional mortgage obtained loans and in which home prices shot up dramatically.*

"subprime" mortgages *Mortgages that carry a high risk of default.*

Almost instantaneously, a complete global financial meltdown loomed. In a massive sell-off, the Dow Jones stock average plummeted nearly 20 percent during a single week in early October. People began draining their savings and money market accounts. The world's financial system seized up, as it had done at the start of the Great Depression of the 1930s. The economy began to slip into what some would later call the "Great Recession."

Bush's Treasury Department, the Fed, and governments around the world recognized the need for a coordinated, dramatic response. Paulson hastily designed a rescue plan, and Congress passed a revised version as the Emergency Economic Stabilization Act of 2008, enacted with greater support from Democrats than from Republicans. It included the **Troubled Asset Relief Program (TARP)**. Implicitly based on the principle that giant financial institutions were "too big to fail," TARP empowered the Treasury Department to spread $700 billion throughout the financial system.

The Election of 2008

Differences over how to respond to this Great Recession dominated the 2008 political season. The presidential contest featured septuagenarian Republican Senator John McCain of Arizona and his much-younger senatorial colleague, Democrat **Barack Obama**. The first major-party presidential candidate of African descent, Obama capitalized on a media-savvy campaign staff, an innovative fundraising operation, his skills at oratory, and the unpopularity of the outgoing Bush administration. The Obama campaign also energized many of the movements, such as those opposing immigration restriction and favoring gay rights, which had become so active during the early years of the 21st century. Many voters blamed Bush for the economic morass and viewed McCain, who admitted to knowing little about the economy, as lagging behind Obama in economic sagacity. Obama's campaign featured two words: "hope" and "change."

McCain's zigzag effort undercut his chances for victory. He admirably rejected the tactic of conducting a smear campaign falsely claiming Obama had not been born in the United States or secretly practiced Islam. McCain's biggest gamble, selecting Alaska's half-term governor Sarah Palin as a running mate, pleased conservatives but ultimately produced scant returns at the polls. By inching away from the political center, McCain mollified some of the most conservative Republicans but also lost independents and crossover Democrats.

Although veteran pundits expected a very close finish, younger, Internet-based forecasters correctly predicted a substantial Obama victory. Young voters, especially women and African Americans, turned out in record numbers in November. The turnout among Latinos and Asian Americans also reached all-time highs. In contrast, the percentage of Americans of European descent casting ballots fell slightly from that of 2004. Forty-three percent of this vote, a slight increase from what Kerry had gained four years prior, went to Obama. In addition to the presidency, the Democratic Party picked up seats in both branches of Congress.

Troubled Asset Relief Program (TARP) *Section of the Emergency Economic Stabilization Act of 2008 that authorized the Treasury Department to use $700 billion to rescue the financial system.*

Barack Obama *The 44th president of the United States and the first of African descent; voted into office in 2008 with a campaign offering "hope" and "change."*

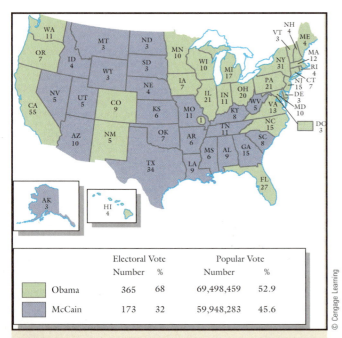

		Electoral Vote		Popular Vote	
		Number	%	Number	%
	Obama	365	68	69,498,459	52.9
	McCain	173	32	59,948,283	45.6

© Cengage Learning

Map 32.2 Presidential Election, 2008. *The victory of Barack Obama over John McCain is illustrated in this state-by-state tally of votes in the Electoral College. How did the 2008 presidential election break from the regional pattern that had boosted George W. Bush to the White House (see map 32.1)? What states did Obama carry that Al Gore failed to win in 2000?*

BARACK, MICHELLE, MALIA, AND SASHA OBAMA. *When the Obama family moved into the White House in 2009, Sasha became the first resident to have been born in the 21st century.*

QUICK REVIEW

THE BUBBLE BURSTS

- Clinton and Bush promoted deregulation of the financial industry

- The financial industry responded with unrealistic assessments of risk, unsound lending practices, and fraudulent activities

- As loans went into default, the financial system began to collapse

- Congress passed TARP in an attempt to rescue the financial industry

- With the faltering economy and the Iraq War as central campaign points, Barack Obama won the presidential election of 2008

CHANGING TIMES, 2009–

Barack Obama's administrative team brought even greater diversity—and more star power—than the teams of Clinton and Bush. The key position of secretary of state went to Hillary Clinton. Steven Chu, a Nobel Prize winner, became secretary of energy. Perhaps most crucially, Robert Gates, a Republican who had been a calming presence toward the end of Bush's presidency, agreed to remain as secretary of defense. The president's inaugural address urged the nation to tackle the current crises with "hope and virtue."

Political Polarization

The appointment of Gates signaled Obama's inclination for continuing some Bush-era policies and thus disappointed supporters hoping for fundamental changes. The new administration set aside Obama's earlier pledge to close the prison facility at Guantanamo and to try terrorist suspects in U.S. courts. On the crucial economic

FOCUS QUESTION

What hopes did the Obama administration bring to Washington and what fears did its arrival produce among Republicans? What hopes and fears did the emerging culture of social networking generate?

front, Timothy Geithner, a Federal Reserve official who had helped devise the Bush administration's financial bailout of 2008, became Obama's treasury secretary, and the new president reappointed Ben Bernanke to lead the Fed.

In the Middle East the Obama administration brought modest changes of emphasis. In Afghanistan and along that nation's border with Pakistan, Obama upped troop levels, placed increased reliance on air attacks by unmanned drones, and budgeted additional financial resources. The United States tried to increase pressure on Afghanistan's leadership to rein in corruption and pressed Pakistan's government to move more determinedly against Taliban forces. These moves won as much support from Republican as Democratic ranks.

Most domestic initiatives, however, produced steadily escalating Republican opposition. The Obama administration could claim some victories, including Senate confirmation of two Supreme Court nominees (Sonia Sotomayor and Elena Kagan) and a law creating a "bill of rights" for credit card holders. It encountered fierce GOP opposition on almost everything else. Only three Republican senators (and no representatives in the House) supported its plan to stimulate the economy through greater government spending. The American Recovery and Reinvestment Act of 2009, popularly known as "the Stimulus," provided $212 billion in tax cuts and $575 billion in federal spending. A congressional measure to reregulate parts of the financial industry passed in the face of Republican criticism.

Months of negotiation among the White House, House Speaker Nancy Pelosi, and Senate Majority Leader Harry Reid also yielded the **Affordable Health Care for America Act (ACA)** of 2010. Republicans revived the strategy used to derail the Clinton health-care plan 16 years earlier and unanimously opposed the measure. ACA's proponents rounded up just enough conservative Democratic votes to pass the law, which would extend, over time, coverage to some 30 million people. The ACA also expanded the Medicaid system, created mechanisms (called "exchanges") for increasing competition among insurance companies, and prohibited insurance companies from denying coverage to people with preexisting health conditions. Its most controversial provision mandated that every American carry health insurance. Critics charged that this complex legislation might cost much more than official estimates, endanger the Medicare program, and create uncertainty throughout the health-care system. The administration countered that it would both save money and bring health-care coverage to nearly all Americans.

Republican resistance to health-care legislation, which they called "Obamacare" and claimed to be unconstitutional, signaled even broader opposition to the Obama presidency. The GOP's most conservative factions rebranded themselves as part of a "Tea Party" movement and threatened primary challenges to any Republican incumbent tempted to support White House initiatives. Pressed by their Tea Party wing, Republicans insisted that cutting governmental programs and lowering the federal deficit should take precedence over increased spending for job creation and aid to unemployed workers. Familiar questions thus resurfaced: Was governmental action the core cause of economic problems or could it be part of their solutions?

The GOP ran squarely against Obama and his domestic policies in the midterm elections of 2010. Primary contests eliminated a number of Republican stalwarts in favor of Tea Party activists and accelerated the party's decades-long move toward the political right. Democratic candidates found themselves burdened by a jobless economic recovery and their own embattled president. In contrast to 2008, many younger voters stayed home in 2010 while older ones, who tended to favor Republican candidates, turned out in higher numbers.

The 2010 midterm elections followed a long-familiar pattern: The party controlling the White House and Congress lost legislative seats. The result of the GOP's

Affordable Health Care for America Act (ACA) *Legislation designed to extend health care to some 30 million people, expand the Medicaid system, create mechanisms for increasing competition among insurance companies, prohibit the use of preexisting health conditions to deny coverage, and provide nearly every American with health insurance.*

VISUAL LINK TO THE PAST

The Future of Print Media?

This final edition of Denver's *Rocky Mountain News*—which appeared on February 27, 2009—offered a poignant and perceptive look at the past and present of newspaper publishing. This tabloid source of news and opinion, which had garnered four coveted Pulitzer Prizes during its final decade of publishing, accompanied many other newspapers around the country into oblivion.

As the arrival of the Internet transformed how people communicated with one another, the familiar medium of the newspaper lost its economic viability. People who wanted to obtain the day's news, sample political opinion, or survey evening entertainment options began firing up their computers rather than glancing at the printed page. Sports fans, especially, found that the morning sports page, long a major incentive for opening up a newspaper, seemed a pale imitation of what they could find on ESPN and its constantly expanding Web site.

Sources of revenue for newspapers steadily shrank. As print papers began developing their own sites in cyberspace, they found that they were "giving away" material that they were still asking print readers to purchase. Moreover, with fewer readers, newspaper publishers saw advertising revenues, the lifeblood of their business, dry up. The economics of publishing meant that most cities, even ones as large as Denver, could no longer support more than one newspaper.

Q Look carefully at this page from the final day in the life of the *Rocky Mountain News*. How do

the paper's publishers seek to tell, in prose, the story of a nearly 150-year relationship with Denver?

Q How does the visual composition of this same page, which harkens back to a time when Denver was not yet a city and Colorado not a state, show that the *Rocky Mountain News* and the citizens of Denver were now living in a different era? What, for example, do you see running down the left-hand side of this re-creation of a mid–19th century newspaper that you might see sprinkled through an early 21st century Web site?

AFP PHOTO/ROCKY MOUNTAIN NEWS / Newscom

well-funded electoral effort, however, exceeded the historical averages and the early projections of most analysts. Republicans took control of the House, cut into the Democrats' majority in the Senate, and gained more than 600 legislative seats and 20 gubernatorial offices in states throughout the country. A national political culture marked by extreme partisanship seemed likely to continue into a new decade.

The Culture of Social Networking and Liberty, Equality, Power

The Obama administration and its critics increasingly drew on the culture of **social networking sites**. The Obama electoral movement had successfully employed the Internet to gain the Democratic nomination and the presidency. It ultimately raised far more money over the Internet than McCain's campaign gathered from all of its outreach to individual contributors.

Use of the Internet to create communities with similar interests that transcended boundaries of time and space became an important new cultural-social force during the early 21st century. LinkedIn and MySpace went online in 2003. Facebook, created in 2004 by undergraduates at Harvard University to facilitate links with other students, quickly attracted wealthy investors from Silicon Valley and tapped enough advertising revenues to make its operations profitable in 2009.

YouTube, developed by Silicon Valley entrepreneurs in 2005, offered a different kind of social networking model. It allowed people to post footage derived from motion picture and TV sources; music from just about anywhere; and, most importantly, original material created by individual users. Its rate of growth surpassed even that of Facebook. Google soon purchased YouTube for $1.65 billion.

The changes brought by the Internet and social networking worried some people. They feared that Internet news and commentary greatly intensified the adversarial framework that had come to dominate cable TV news. They also saw Internet journalism preying on the investigative legwork of writers for print publications. At the same time, online journalism helped to lure readers from print publications and to diminish their value to potential advertisers. Losing readers and revenue, magazines and newspapers began to cease publication. Frequent Internet postings, moreover, seemed to be making the 24/7 news cycle move even faster. Critics also feared that the process of "linking up" threatened traditional notions of privacy as well as the safety of the young and the innocent.

The most enthusiastic champions of social networking, however, praised it— and the larger Internet environment—for creating patterns that could not only transcend old barriers of time and space but also help people reimagine liberty, power, and equality. Freely shared and communally developed software might liberate communication from corporate control. Interactive Internet sites might empower ordinary people and challenge hierarchical arrangements. Political figures used the Web to issue policy pronouncements that bypassed the traditional media gatekeepers. Bloggers took on, and sometimes took down, media commentators and special interests. Wikipedia supplanted hard-copy encyclopedias with a collaboratively written, ever-changing, and controversial source on virtually everything. And even history textbooks began to devise more participatory formats.

social networking sites
Internet-based sites that unite communities of people based on similar interests, including partisan political identity.

The Election of 2012

Intense partisanship shaped the 2012 election season. The Republican leader in the U.S. Senate had made clear his legislative priority: making Obama a one-term president by blocking any legislation that could help Obama's re-election. When conservative

Chief Justice John Roberts, a Republican, voted to uphold the constitutionality of the Obama-sponsored Affordable Care Act of 2010, many GOP leaders denounced his apparent non-partisanship as tantamount to political treason.

As the Republican Party continued to move rightward, W. Mitt Romney struggled to gain its presidential nomination. The GOP's right wing had long distrusted Romney's commitment to its views on issues such as abortion, taxes, immigration, and health care. Romney—a wealthy venture capitalist from a devout Mormon family with a long

© Joe Raedle/Getty Images

THE PRESIDENTIAL CONTEST, 2012. *The televised debates between Democratic incumbent Barack H. Obama and Republican challenger W. Mitt Romney invariably came to focus on their differing claims about economic issues.*

record of governmental service—embraced their views by pledging to scale back government regulations, slash taxes, and expand the military—all while addressing the federal budget deficit. Seeking to mobilize the Republican base, Romney advocated repeal of "Obamacare," termination of federal funding for Planned Parenthood, and cutting or abolishing the disaster relief programs of the Federal Emergency Management Agency (FEMA). He also selected U.S. Representative Paul Ryan of Wisconsin, a conservative favorite, as his running mate. The broader Republican campaign denounced Obama's presidency as "socialistic," and some fiercely anti-Obama spokespeople fuelled suspicion of the president's racial heritage and misinformation about his religious faith.

As the election neared, the Romney campaign tried to hit the reset button. The candidate moved toward the center, cautiously endorsing most of Obama's foreign policy moves, praising popular provisions of the Affordable Care Act, and promising to work with congressional Democrats on taxes and spending. The Romney camp enjoyed lavish funding as a consequence of the Supreme Court's decision to strike down previous limits on political contributions in its *Citizens United* decision (2010).

The Obama campaign, which also garnered massive donations, remained focused on a few central themes. It touted Obama's first term for achieving health care legislation, for improving economic conditions and saving the auto industry, for killing Osama bin Laden, and for winding down two unpopular wars. More often, though, Democrats were on the attack. They assailed Romney as beholden to ultra-conservatives on social issues, such as abortion and contraception, and to the very wealthy on tax policy. They also charged the Romney-Ryan ticket with failing to document how its vague economic proposals could actually generate a promised "12 million new jobs." Moreover, Democrats firmly backed immigration reform. The Romney camp expected a victory and ridiculed independent, statistically based polls that showed Obama maintaining a solid lead.

Predictions of an Obama victory proved accurate. The president dominated the electoral vote and gained the popular one as well. The Romney campaign did best among white voters, especially men, over the age of 50, while Obama won overwhelming majorities among African Americans, Hispanics, and Asian Americans. About 55 percent of women voters broke for Obama, and people between the ages of 18 and 29, who voted in record numbers, strongly supported the president.

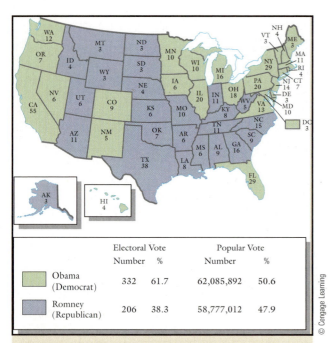

	Electoral Vote		Popular Vote	
	Number	%	Number	%
Obama (Democrat)	332	61.7	62,085,892	50.6
Romney (Republican)	206	38.3	58,777,012	47.9

© Cengage Learning

Map 32.3 Presidential Election, 2012. *President Barack Obama won a second term by dominating the Electoral College vote. He also captured the popular vote.*

The post-electoral cycle of partisan spin, informal "tweets," and scholarly analysis quickly began. While dueling Republican strategists were debating fears that their party now rested on an inevitably shrinking demographic base, those from the Democratic side were hoping the nation's changing demography offered the opportunity to forge a new, Democratic-dominated political era. A system of national governance divided along partisan lines, however, remained the immediate reality. Democrats solidified their hold over the Senate in 2012, but Republicans maintained their majority in the House. Instant analyses suggested the two parties would be further apart on key issues in the newly elected Congress than they had been in the outgoing one, a prediction that portended future showdowns over crucial legislation, especially those involving fiscal and spending priorities.

Conclusion

Two presidents, one Democrat and one Republican, dominated political life at the end of the 20th and the beginning of the 21st centuries. Bill Clinton's administration pressed a modest domestic agenda that moved the Democratic Party away from its "big government" image. It cut back the welfare system and eliminated the federal deficit. As political polarization escalated during the 1990s, however, Clinton's personal behavior ensnared him in legal investigations that stalled his presidency. The Bush administration's conservative agenda featured tax cuts, deregulation, and reform of education. It also converted the budget surplus left by Clinton into a rising federal deficit. The political parties of these years launched partisan attacks that exaggerated the buoyant hopes and the deepest fears of the age.

Both Clinton and Bush tried to chart foreign policies for a post–Cold War world. Clinton's internationalist policy deployed military power selectively and concentrated on measures fostering the globalization of economic relationships. After the terrorist attacks of 9/11, the Bush administration focused its unilateralist foreign policy on fighting a global "war on terror." The United States first invaded Afghanistan and then attacked Iraq, where it began the kind of expensive "nation-building" project that Republicans had once opposed.

The U.S. economy enjoyed its longest period of sustained growth during the 1990s, but the early years of the 21st century produced a mixed picture. The financial industry continued to reap phenomenal profits, aided by a spectacular bubble in the residential housing market. In 2007, declining home prices and a wave of mortgage foreclosures rocked the financial sector, and the impact rippled quickly through the entire global economy. Although the Bush administration and the Federal Reserve Board, with more Democratic than Republican support, rescued the financial industry, the larger economy slid into the Great Recession, the worst since the 1930s.

President Bush's unpopularity and the country's economic distress helped the Democratic Party regain control of Congress in 2006 and lifted its standard-bearer, Barack Obama, to the presidency in 2008 and again in 2012. Backing a flurry of new initiatives, Obama sought to shift the military focus from Iraq to Afghanistan, revamp the health-care system, and return some greater regulation to the financial system. Discussions of social policy, international relations, and economic recovery continued against the backdrops of hope and fear that circulated within rapidly changing forms of media.

CHAPTER REVIEW

Review Questions

1. What political and cultural forces helped to polarize national politics during the years between 1993 and 2008? What impact did this polarization have on the policy-making process in Washington?

2. How did the Clinton administration attempt to redesign foreign policy for a post–Cold War world? How did the administration of George W. Bush, especially after September 11, 2001, seek to reorient Clinton's approach?

3. What forces fueled the various economic bubbles from the late 1990s to 2008? How did governmental officials respond to the financial meltdown of 2008 and the subsequent recession?

4. What hopes did the Obama administration bring to Washington and what fears did its arrival produce among its critics? What hopes and fears did the emerging culture of social networking generate?

Critical Thinking Questions

1. Before the 1980s, Republicans had generally opposed expensive domestic programs and large deficits, which they identified with Democratic administrations. What factors help explain how, between 1980 and 2000, Republican administrations created large government deficits, while New Democrats offered their party as the guarantor of fiscal prudence? How did the financial meltdown of 2008 and the subsequent recession alter the situation?

2. How did Bill Clinton and George W. Bush, who espoused differing visions of government power and social policy, generate different popular followings? How could Bush, who generally lacked the strong approval ratings of Clinton, become such a "strong" chief executive, especially during the early years of his two-term presidency?

Identifications

Review your understanding of the following key terms, people, and events for this chapter.

William Jefferson (Bill) Clinton, p. 768
Earned Income Tax Credit (EITC), p. 768
"New Democrat," p. 768
"Contract with America," p. 768

Temporary Assistance to Needy Families (TANF), p. 769
George W. Bush, p. 772
Richard (Dick) Cheney, p. 772
Bush v. Gore, p. 773

Roberts Court, p. 776
World Trade Organization (WTO), p. 777
Bush Doctrine, p. 778
housing bubble, p. 785
"subprime" mortgages, p. 785

Troubled Asset Relief Program (TARP), p. 786
Barack Obama, p. 786
Affordable Health Care for America Act (ACA), p. 788
social networking sites, p. 790

DISCOVERY

How well did the Electoral College system, part of an 18th-century Constitution that was drafted and ratified before the emergence of organized political parties, fit with the political and demographic conditions that shaped the presidential election of 2000?

In thinking about this question, begin by breaking it down into the components shown below. A discussion of the significance of each component should appear in your answer.

Political Conditions

Map 32.1 on page 772 shows the election of 2000, dramatically underscoring the role that the Electoral College system still plays in presidential selection. It is the winner in the race for 270 out of a total of 538 Electoral College votes, not the victor in popular votes, who becomes the president of the United States. Refer to the text of the U.S. Constitution, available in the Appendix to this book, and review the system for choosing a president that the Founding Fathers devised.

How closely, during the presidential election of 2000, did the number of votes that the Electoral College system assigned to the individual states actually represent the political alignment that had emerged during the final decades of the 20th century? In what states, in 2000, would the presidential candidate of the Republican Party have had virtually no chance of winning *any* electoral votes? In what states would this same political reality have confronted the Democratic presidential candidate? What states, then, would become the focus of presidential politicking in 2000? How might the Electoral College arrangement have affected popular voter turnout in 2000? Might a system in which the winner of a state does not automatically receive *all* of that state's electoral votes have changed the political dynamics in 2000?

Demographic Conditions

Looking at the same map, how might it be argued that the Electoral College system continued to work well in 2000 because the Constitution requires that states with larger populations cast more electoral votes than less populated states? How, alternatively, might it also be claimed that the Electoral College system still, unfairly, failed to accurately represent *actual* population differentials in 2000? (How many electoral votes must every state, no matter how small its actual population, be permitted to cast?)

Revisit Map 31.1 on page 744 and review recent shifts in population. How might these shifts have affected the dynamics of Electoral College politics in 2000? Similarly, review Map. 31.2 on page 746, which represents the "new immigration" that took place during the last decades of the 20th century. How might these trends affect Electoral College politics in the presidential elections that would follow that of 2000? Which states, looking forward, seem likely to gain electoral votes as new immigrants and their children become citizens? Which states, given the recalculation of electoral votes, will likely become more politically important in presidential politics?

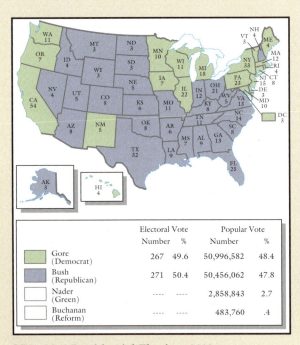

		Electoral Vote		Popular Vote	
		Number	%	Number	%
	Gore (Democrat)	267	49.6	50,996,582	48.4
	Bush (Republican)	271	50.4	50,456,062	47.8
	Nader (Green)	----	----	2,858,843	2.7
	Buchanan (Reform)	----	----	483,760	.4

Map 32.1 Presidential Election, 2000

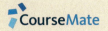
CourseMate

Visit the CourseMate website at www.cengagebrain.com for additional study tools and review materials for this chapter.

THE DECLARATION OF INDEPENDENCE

The Unanimous Declaration of the Thirteen United States of America

When in the Course of human events it becomes necessary for one people to dissolve the political bands which have connected them with another, and to assume among the Powers of the earth, the separate and equal station to which the Laws of Nature and of Nature's God entitle them, a decent respect to the opinions of mankind requires that they should declare the causes which impel them to the separation.

We hold these truths to be self-evident, that all men are created equal, that they are endowed by their Creator with certain unalienable Rights, that among these are Life, Liberty and the pursuit of Happiness. That to secure these rights, Governments are instituted among Men, deriving their just Powers from the consent of the governed. That whenever any Form of Government becomes destructive of these ends, it is the Right of the People to alter or to abolish it, and to institute new Government, laying its foundation on such principles and organizing its Powers in such form, as to them shall seem most likely to effect their Safety and Happiness. Prudence, indeed, will dictate that Governments long established should not be changed for light and transient causes; and accordingly all experience hath shewn, that mankind are more disposed to suffer, while evils are sufferable, than to right themselves by abolishing the forms to which they are accustomed. But when a long train of abuses and usurpations, pursuing invariably the same Object evinces a design to reduce them under absolute Despotism, it is their right, it is their duty, to throw off such Government, and to provide new Guards for their future security. Such has been the patient sufferance of these Colonies; and such is now the necessity which constrains them to alter their former Systems of Government. The history of the present King of Great Britain is a history of repeated injuries and usurpations, all having in direct object the establishment of an absolute Tyranny over these States. To prove this, let Facts be submitted to a candid world.

He has refused his Assent to Laws, the most wholesome and necessary for the public good.

He has forbidden his Governors to pass Laws of immediate and pressing importance, unless suspended in their operation till his Assent should be obtained; and when so suspended, he has utterly neglected to attend to them.

He has refused to pass other Laws for the accommodation of large districts of people, unless those people would relinquish the right of Representation in the Legislature, a right inestimable to them and formidable to tyrants only.

He has called together legislative bodies at places unusual, uncomfortable, and distant from the depository of their Public Records, for the sole Purpose of fatiguing them into compliance with his measures.

He has dissolved Representative Houses repeatedly, for opposing with manly firmness his invasions on the rights of the People.

He has refused for a long time, after such dissolutions, to cause others to be elected; whereby the Legislative Powers, incapable of Annihilation, have returned to the People at large for their exercise; the State remaining in the mean time exposed to all the dangers of invasion from without, and convulsions within.

He has endeavoured to prevent the Population of these States; for that purpose obstructing the Laws for Naturalization of Foreigners; refusing to pass others to encourage their migrations hither, and raising the conditions of new Appropriations of Lands.

He has obstructed the Administration of Justice, by refusing his Assent to Laws for establishing Judiciary Powers.

He has made Judges dependent on his Will alone, for the tenure of their offices, and the amount and payment of their salaries.

He has erected a multitude of New Offices, and sent hither swarms of Officers to harass our People, and eat out their substance.

He has kept among us, in times of peace, Standing Armies without the Consent of our legislatures.

He has affected to render the Military independent of and superior to the Civil Power.

He has combined with others to subject us to a jurisdiction foreign to our constitution, and unacknowledged by our laws; giving his Assent to their Acts of pretended Legislation: For Quartering large bodies of armed troops among us: For protecting them, by a mock Trial, from Punishment for any Murders which they should commit on the Inhabitants of these States: For cutting off our Trade with all parts of the world: For imposing Taxes on us without our Consent: For depriving us in many cases, of the benefits of Trial by Jury: For transporting us beyond Seas to be tried for pretended offences: For abolishing the free System of English Laws in a neighbouring Province, establishing therein an Arbitrary government, and enlarging its Boundaries so as to render it at once an example and fit instrument for introducing the same absolute rule into these Colonies: For taking away our Charters, abolishing our most valuable Laws, and altering fundamentally the Forms of our Governments: For suspending our own Legislatures, and declaring themselves invested with Power to legislate for us in all cases whatsoever.

He has abdicated Government here, by declaring us out of his Protection, and waging War against us.

He has plundered our seas, ravaged our Coasts, burnt our towns, and destroyed the lives of our people.

He is at this time transporting large Armies of foreign Mercenaries to compleat the works of death, desolation and tyranny, already begun with circumstances of Cruelty and perfidy scarcely paralleled in the most barbarous ages, and totally unworthy the Head of a civilized nation.

He has constrained our fellow Citizens taken Captive on the high Seas to bear Arms against their Country, to become the executioners of their friends and Brethren, or to fall themselves by their Hands.

He has excited domestic insurrections amongst us, and has endeavoured to bring on the inhabitants of our frontiers, the merciless Indian Savages, whose known rule of warfare, is an undistinguished destruction of all ages, sexes and conditions.

In every stage of these Oppressions We have Petitioned for Redress in the most humble terms: Our repeated Petitions have been answered only by repeated injury. A Prince, whose character is thus marked by every act which may define a Tyrant, is unfit to be the ruler of a free People.

Nor have We been wanting in attentions to our British brethren. We have warned them from time to time of attempts by their legislature to extend an unwarrantable jurisdiction over us. We have reminded them of the circumstances of our emigration and settlement here. We have appealed to their native justice and magnanimity, and we have conjured them by the ties of our common kindred to disavow these usurpations, which, would inevitably interrupt our connections and correspondence. They too have been deaf to the voice of justice and of consanguinity. We must, therefore, acquiesce in the necessity, which denounces our Separation, and hold them, as we hold the rest of mankind, Enemies in War, in Peace Friends.

We, therefore, the Representatives of the United States of America, in General Congress, Assembled, appealing to the Supreme Judge of the world for the rectitude of our intentions, do, in the Name, and by Authority of the good People of these Colonies, solemnly publish and declare, That these United Colonies are, and of Right ought to be Free and Independent States; that they are Absolved from all Allegiance to the British Crown, and that all political connection between them and the State of Great Britain, is and ought to be totally dissolved; and that, as Free and Independent States, they have full Power to levy War, conclude Peace, contract Alliances, establish Commerce, and to do all other Acts and Things which Independent States may of right do. And for the support of this Declaration, with a firm reliance on the protection of divine Providence, we mutually pledge to each other our Lives, our Fortunes and our sacred Honor.

THE CONSTITUTION OF THE UNITED STATES OF AMERICA

We the People of the United States, in Order to form a more perfect Union, establish Justice, insure domestic Tranquility, provide for the common defence, promote the general Welfare, and secure the Blessings of Liberty to ourselves and our Posterity, do ordain and establish this Constitution for the United States of America.

Article I.

SECTION 1. All legislative Powers herein granted shall be vested in a Congress of the United States, which shall consist of a Senate and House of Representatives.

SECTION 2. The House of Representatives shall be composed of Members chosen every second Year by the People of the several States, and the Electors in each State shall have the Qualifications requisite for Electors of the most numerous Branch of the State Legislature.

No Person shall be a Representative who shall not have attained to the Age of twenty five Years, and been seven Years a Citizen of the United States, and who shall not, when elected, be an Inhabitant of that State in which he shall be chosen.

Representatives and direct Taxes[1] shall be apportioned among the several States which may be included within this Union, according to their respective Numbers, which shall be determined by adding to the whole Number of free Persons, including those bound to Service for a Term of Years, and excluding Indians not taxed, three fifths of all other Persons.[2]

The actual Enumeration shall be made within three Years after the first Meeting of the Congress of the United States, and within every subsequent Term of ten Years, in such Manner as they shall by Law direct. The Number of Representatives shall not exceed one for every thirty Thousand, but each State shall have at Least one Representative; and until such enumeration shall be made, the State of New Hampshire shall be entitled to chuse three; Massachusetts eight; Rhode Island and Providence Plantations one; Connecticut five; New York six; New Jersey four; Pennsylvania eight; Delaware one; Maryland six; Virginia ten; North Carolina five; South Carolina five; and Georgia three.

When vacancies happen in the Representation from any State, the Executive Authority thereof shall issue Writs of Election to fill such Vacancies.

The House of Representatives shall chuse their Speaker and other Officers; and shall have the sole Power of Impeachment.

SECTION 3. The Senate of the United States shall be composed of two Senators from each State, chosen by the Legislature thereof, for six Years; and each Senator shall have one Vote.[3]

Immediately after they shall be assembled in Consequence of the first Election, they shall be divided as equally as may be into three Classes. The Seats of the Senators of the first Class shall be vacated at the Expiration of the second Year, of the second Class at the Expiration of the fourth Year, and of the third Class at the Expiration of the sixth Year, so that one third may be chosen every second Year; and if Vacancies happen by Resignation, or otherwise, during the Recess of the Legislature of any State, the Executive thereof may make temporary Appointments until the next Meeting of the Legislature, which shall then fill such Vacancies.[4]

No Person shall be a Senator who shall not have attained to the Age of thirty Years, and been nine Years a Citizen of the United States, and who shall not, when elected, be an Inhabitant of that State for which he shall be chosen.

The Vice President of the United States shall be President of the Senate, but shall have no Vote, unless they be equally divided.

The Senate shall chuse their other Officers, and also a President pro tempore, in the Absence of the Vice President, or when he shall exercise the Office of President of the United States.

The Senate shall have the sole Power to try all Impeachments. When sitting for that Purpose, they shall be on Oath or Affirmation. When the President of the United States is tried, the Chief Justice shall preside: And no Person shall be convicted without the Concurrence of two thirds of the Members present.

Judgment in Cases of Impeachment shall not extend further than to removal from Office, and disqualification to hold and enjoy any Office of honor, Trust or Profit under the United States: but the Party convicted shall nevertheless be liable and subject to Indictment, Trial, Judgment and Punishment, according to Law.

SECTION 4. The Times, Places and Manner of holding Elections for Senators and Representatives, shall be prescribed in each State by the Legislature thereof, but the Congress may at any time by Law make or alter such Regulation, except as to the Places of chusing Senators.

The Congress shall assemble at least once in every Year, and such Meeting shall be on the first Monday in December, unless they shall by Law appoint a different Day.[5]

SECTION 5. Each House shall be the Judge of the Elections, Returns and Qualifications of its own Members, and a Majority of each shall constitute a Quorum to do Business; but a smaller Number may adjourn from day to day, and may be

---

Text is from the engrossed copy in the National Archives. Original spelling, capitalization, and punctuation have been retained.

[1]Modified by the Sixteenth Amendment.

[2]Replaced by the Fourteenth Amendment.

[3]Superseded by the Seventeenth Amendment.

[4]Modified by the Seventeenth Amendment.

[5]Superseded by the Twentieth Amendment.

authorized to compel the Attendance of absent Members, in such Manner, and under such Penalties as each House may provide.

Each House may determine the Rules of its Proceedings, punish its Members for disorderly Behaviour, and, with the Concurrence of two thirds, expel a Member.

Each House shall keep a Journal of its Proceedings, and from time to time publish the same, excepting such Parts as may in their Judgment require Secrecy; and the Yeas and Nays of the Members of either House on any question shall, at the Desire of one fifth of those Present, be entered on the Journal.

Neither House, during the Session of Congress, shall, without the Consent of the other, adjourn for more than three days, nor to any other Place than that in which the two Houses shall be sitting.

SECTION 6. The Senators and Representatives shall receive a Compensation for their Services, to be ascertained by Law, and paid out of the Treasury of the United States. They shall in all Cases, except Treason, Felony and Breach of the Peace, be privileged from Arrest during their Attendance at the Session of their respective Houses, and in going to and returning from the same; and for any Speech or Debate in either House, they shall not be questioned in any other Place.

No Senator or Representative shall, during the Time for which he was elected, be appointed to any civil Office under the Authority of the United States, which shall have been created, or the Emoluments whereof shall have been encreased during such time; and no Person holding any Office under the United States, shall be a Member of either House during his Continuance in Office.

SECTION 7. All Bills for raising Revenue shall originate in the House of Representatives; but the Senate may propose or concur with Amendments as on other Bills.

Every Bill which shall have passed the House of Representatives and the Senate shall, before it become a Law, be presented to the President of the United States; If he approve he shall sign it, but if not he shall return it, with his Objections to that House in which it shall have originated, who shall enter the Objections at large on their Journal, and proceed to reconsider it. If after such Reconsideration two thirds of that House shall agree to pass the Bill, it shall be sent, together with the Objections, to the other House, by which it shall likewise be reconsidered, and if approved by two thirds of that House, it shall become a Law. But in all such Cases the Votes of both Houses shall be determined by yeas and Nays, and the Names of the Persons voting for and against the Bill shall be entered on the Journal of each House respectively. If any Bill shall not be returned by the President within ten Days (Sundays excepted) after it shall have been presented to him, the Same shall be a Law, in like Manner as if he had signed it, unless the Congress by their Adjournment prevent its Return, in which Case it shall not be a Law.

Every Order, Resolution, or Vote to which the Concurrence of the Senate and House of Representatives may be necessary (except on a question of Adjournment) shall be presented to the President of the United States; and before the Same shall take Effect, shall be approved by him, or being disapproved by him shall be repassed by two thirds of the Senate and House of Representatives, according to the Rules and Limitations prescribed in the Case of a Bill.

SECTION 8. The Congress shall have power To lay and collect Taxes, Duties, Imposts and Excises, to pay the Debts and provide for the common Defence and general Welfare of the United States; but all Duties, Imposts and Excises shall be uniform throughout the United States; To borrow Money on the credit of the United States; To regulate Commerce with foreign Nations, and among the several States, and with the Indian Tribes; To establish an uniform Rule of Naturalization, and uniform Laws on the subject of Bankruptcies throughout the United States; To coin Money, regulate the Value thereof, and of foreign Coin, and fix the Standard of Weights and Measures; To provide for the Punishment of counterfeiting the Securities and current Coin of the United States; To establish Post Offices and post Roads; To promote the Progress of Science and useful Arts, by securing for limited Times to Authors and Inventors the exclusive Right to their respective Writings and Discoveries; To constitute Tribunals inferior to the supreme Court; To define and punish Piracies and Felonies committed on the high Seas, and Offences against the Law of Nations;

To declare War, grant Letters of Marque and Reprisal, and make Rules concerning Captures on Land and Water; To raise and support Armies, but no Appropriation of Money to that Use shall be for a longer Term than two Years; To provide and maintain a Navy; To make Rules for the Government and Regulation of the land and naval Forces; To provide for calling forth the Militia to execute the Laws of the Union, suppress Insurrections and repel Invasions; To provide for organizing, arming, and disciplining, the Militia, and for governing such Part of them as may be employed in the Service of the United States, reserving to the States respectively, the Appointment of the Officers, and the Authority of training the Militia according to the discipline prescribed by Congress; To exercise exclusive Legislation in all Cases whatsoever, over such District (not exceeding ten Miles square) as may, by Cession of particular States, and the Acceptance of Congress, become the Seat of the Government of the United States, and to exercise like Authority over all Places purchased by the Consent of the Legislature of the State in which the Same shall be, for the Erection of Forts, Magazines, Arsenals, dock-Yards, and other needful Buildings;—And To make all Laws which shall be necessary and proper for carrying into Execution the foregoing Powers, and all other Powers vested by this Constitution in the Government of the United States, or in any Department or Officer thereof.

SECTION 9. The Migration or Importation of such Persons as any of the States now existing shall think proper to admit, shall not be prohibited by the Congress prior to the Year one thousand eight hundred and eight, but a Tax or duty may be imposed on such Importation, not exceeding ten dollars for each Person.

The Privilege of the Writ of Habeas Corpus shall not be suspended, unless when in Cases of Rebellion or Invasion the public Safety may require it.

No Bill of Attainder or ex post facto Law shall be passed.

No Capitation, or other direct, Tax shall be laid, unless in Proportion to the Census or Enumeration herein before directed to be taken.

No Tax or Duty shall be laid on Articles exported from any State.

No Preference shall be given by any Regulation of Commerce or Revenue to the Ports of one State over those of another: nor shall Vessels bound to, or from, one State, be obliged to enter, clear, or pay Duties in another.

No Money shall be drawn from the Treasury, but in Consequence of Appropriations made by Law, and a regular Statement and Account of the Receipts and Expenditures of all public Money shall be published from time to time.

No Title of Nobility shall be granted by the United States: And no Person holding any Office of Profit or Trust under them, shall, without the Consent of the Congress, accept of any present, Emolument, Office, or Title, of any kind whatever, from any King, Prince, or foreign State.

SECTION 10. No State shall enter into any Treaty, Alliance, or Confederation; grant Letters of Marque and Reprisal; coin Money; emit Bills of Credit; make any Thing but gold and silver Coin a Tender in Payment of Debts; pass any Bill of Attainder, ex post facto Law, or Law impairing the Obligation of Contracts, or grant any Title of Nobility.

No State shall, without the Consent of the Congress, lay any Imposts or Duties on Imports or Exports, except what may be absolutely necessary for executing its inspection Laws: and the net Produce of all Duties and Imposts, laid by any State on Imports or Exports, shall be for the Use of the Treasury of the United States; and all such Laws shall be subject to the Revision and Controul of the Congress.

No State shall, without the Consent of Congress, lay any Duty of Tonnage, keep Troops, or Ships of War in time of Peace, enter into any Agreement or Compact with another State, or with a foreign Power, or engage in War, unless actually invaded, or in such imminent Danger as will not admit of delay.

Article II.

SECTION 1. The executive Power shall be vested in a President of the United States of America. He shall hold his Office during the Term of four Years, and, together with the Vice President, chosen for the same Term, be elected, as follows: Each State shall appoint, in such Manner as the Legislature thereof may direct, a Number of Electors, equal to the whole Number of Senators and Representatives to which the State may be entitled in the Congress: but no Senator or Representative, or Person holding an Office of Trust or Profit under the United States, shall be appointed an Elector.

The Electors shall meet in their respective States, and vote by Ballot for two Persons, of whom one at least shall not be an Inhabitant of the same State with themselves. And they shall make a List of all the Persons voted for, and of the Number of Votes for each; which List they shall sign and certify, and transmit sealed to the Seat of the Government of the United States, directed to the President of the Senate. The President of the Senate shall, in the Presence of the Senate and House of Representatives, open all the Certificates, and the Votes shall then be counted. The Person having the greatest Number of Votes shall be the President, if such Number be a Majority of the whole Number of Electors appointed;

and if there be more than one who have such Majority, and have an equal Number of Votes, then the House of Representatives shall immediately chuse by Ballot one of them for President; and if no Person have a Majority, then from the five highest on the List the said House shall in like Manner chuse the President. But in chusing the President, the Votes shall be taken by States, the Representation from each State having one Vote; A quorum for this Purpose shall consist of a Member or Members from two thirds of the States, and a Majority of all the States shall be necessary to a Choice. In every Case, after the Choice of the President, the Person having the greatest Number of Votes of the Electors shall be the Vice President. But if there should remain two or more who have equal Votes, the Senate shall chuse from them by Ballot the Vice President.[6]

The Congress may determine the Time of chusing the Electors, and the Day on which they shall give their Votes; which Day shall be the same throughout the United States.

No Person except a natural born Citizen, or a Citizen of the United States, at the time of the Adoption of this Constitution, shall be eligible to the Office of President, neither shall any Person be eligible to that Office who shall not have attained to the Age of thirty five Years, and been fourteen Years a Resident within the United States.

In Case of the Removal of the President from Office, or of his Death, Resignation, or Inability to discharge the Powers and Duties of the said Office, the Same shall devolve on the Vice President, and the Congress may by Law provide for the Case of Removal, Death, Resignation or Inability, both of the President and Vice President, declaring what Officer shall then act as President, and such Officer shall act accordingly, until the Disability be removed, or a President shall be elected.[7]

The President shall, at stated Times, receive for his Services, a Compensation, which shall neither be increased nor diminished during the Period for which he shall have been elected, and he shall not receive within that Period any other Emolument from the United States, or any of them.

Before he enter on the Execution of his Office, he shall take the following Oath or Affirmation:—"I do solemnly swear (or affirm) that I will faithfully execute the Office of President of the United States, and will to the best of my Ability, preserve, protect and defend the Constitution of the United States."

SECTION 2. The President shall be Commander in Chief of the Army and Navy of the United States, and of the Militia of the several States, when called into the actual Service of the United States; he may require the Opinion, in writing, of the principal Officer in each of the executive Departments, upon any Subject relating to the Duties of their respective Offices, and he shall have Power to grant Reprieves and Pardons for Offences against the United States, except in Cases of Impeachment.

He shall have Power, by and with the Advice and Consent of the Senate, to make Treaties, provided two thirds of the Senators present concur; and he shall nominate, and by and with the Advice and Consent of the Senate, shall appoint Ambassadors, other public Ministers and Consuls, Judges of

[6]Superseded by the Twelfth Amendment.
[7]Modified by the Twenty-fifth Amendment.

the supreme Court, and all other Officers of the United States, whose Appointments are not herein otherwise provided for, and which shall be established by Law; but the Congress may by Law vest the Appointment of such inferior Officers, as they think proper, in the President alone, in the Courts of Law, or in the Heads of Departments.

The President shall have Power to fill up all Vacancies that may happen during the Recess of the Senate, by granting Commissions which shall expire at the End of their next Session.

SECTION 3. He shall from time to time give the Congress Information of the State of the Union, and recommend to their Consideration such Measures as he shall judge necessary and expedient; he may, on extraordinary Occasions, convene both Houses, or either of them, and in Case of Disagreement between them, with Respect to the Time of Adjournment, he may adjourn them to such Time as he shall think proper; he shall receive Ambassadors and other public Ministers; he shall take Care that the Laws be faithfully executed, and shall Commission all the Officers of the United States.

SECTION 4. The President, Vice President and all civil Officers of the United States, shall be removed from Office on Impeachment for, and Conviction of, Treason, Bribery, or other high Crimes and Misdemeanors.

Article III.

SECTION 1. The judicial Power of the United States, shall be vested in one supreme Court, and in such inferior Courts as the Congress may from time to time ordain and establish.

The Judges, both of the supreme and inferior Courts, shall hold their Offices during good Behaviour, and shall, at stated Times, receive for their Services, a Compensation, which shall not be diminished during their Continuance in Office.

SECTION 2. The judicial Power shall extend to all Cases, in Law and Equity, arising under this Constitution, the Laws of the United States, and Treaties made, or which shall be made, under their Authority;—to all Cases affecting Ambassadors, other public Ministers and Consuls;—to all Cases of admiralty and maritime Jurisdiction;—to Controversies to which the United States shall be a Party;—to Controversies between two or more States;—between a State and Citizens of another State;[8]—between Citizens of different States,—between Citizens of the same State claiming Lands under Grants of different States, and between a State, or the Citizens thereof, and foreign States, Citizens or Subjects.

In all Cases affecting Ambassadors, other public Ministers and Consuls, and those in which a State shall be Party, the supreme Court shall have original Jurisdiction. In all the other Cases before mentioned, the supreme Court shall have appellate Jurisdiction, both as to Law and Fact, with such Exceptions, and under such Regulations as the Congress shall make.

The Trial of all Crimes, except in Cases of Impeachment, shall be by Jury; and such Trial shall be held in the State where the said Crimes shall have been committed; but when not committed within any State, the Trial shall be at such Place or Places as the Congress may by Law have directed.

SECTION 3. Treason against the United States, shall consist only in levying War against them, or in adhering to their Enemies, giving them Aid and Comfort. No Person shall be convicted of Treason unless on the Testimony of two Witnesses to the same overt Act, or on Confession in open Court.

The Congress shall have Power to declare the Punishment of Treason, but no Attainder of Treason shall work Corruption of Blood, or Forfeiture except during the Life of the Person attainted.

Article IV.

SECTION 1. Full Faith and Credit shall be given in each State to the public Acts, Records, and judicial Proceedings of every other State. And the Congress may by general Laws prescribe the Manner in which such Acts, Records and Proceedings shall be proved, and the Effect thereof.

SECTION 2. The Citizens of each State shall be entitled to all Privileges and Immunities of Citizens in the several States.

A Person charged in any State with Treason, Felony, or other Crime, who shall flee from Justice, and be found in another State, shall on Demand of the executive Authority of the State from which he fled, be delivered up, to be removed to the State having Jurisdiction of the Crime.

No Person held to Service or Labour in one State, under the Laws thereof, escaping into another, shall, in Consequence of any Law or Regulation therein, be discharged from such Service or Labour, but shall be delivered up on Claim of the Party to whom such Service or Labour may be due.

SECTION 3. New States may be admitted by the Congress into this Union; but no new State shall be formed or erected within the Jurisdiction of any other State, nor any State be formed by the Junction of two or more States, or Parts of States, without the Consent of the Legislatures of the States concerned as well as of the Congress.

The Congress shall have Power to dispose of and make all needful Rules and Regulations respecting the Territory or other Property belonging to the United States; and nothing in this Constitution shall be so construed as to Prejudice any Claims of the United States, or of any particular State.

SECTION 4. The United States shall guarantee to every State in this Union a Republican Form of Government, and shall protect each of them against Invasion; and on Application of the Legislature, or of the Executive (when the Legislature cannot be convened) against domestic Violence.

Article V.

The Congress, whenever two thirds of both Houses shall deem it necessary, shall propose Amendments to this Constitution, or, on the Application of the Legislatures of two thirds of the several States, shall call a Convention for proposing Amendments, which, in either Case, shall be valid to all Intents and Purposes, as Part of this Constitution, when

[8]Modified by the Eleventh Amendment.

ratified by the Legislatures of three fourths of the several States, or by Conventions in three fourths thereof, as the one or the other Mode of Ratification may be proposed by the Congress; Provided that no Amendment which may be made prior to the Year One thousand eight hundred and eight shall in any Manner affect the first and fourth Clauses in the Ninth Section of the first Article; and that no State, without its Consent, shall be deprived of its equal Suffrage in the Senate.

Article VI.

All Debts contracted and Engagements entered into, before the Adoption of this Constitution, shall be as valid against the United States under this Constitution, as under the Confederation.

This Constitution, and the Laws of the United States which shall be made in Pursuance thereof; and all Treaties made, or which shall be made, under the Authority of the United States, shall be the supreme Law of the Land; and the Judges in every State shall be bound thereby, any Thing in the Constitution or Laws of any State to the Contrary notwithstanding.

The Senators and Representatives before mentioned, and the Members of the several State Legislatures, and all executive and judicial Officers, both of the United States and of the several States, shall be bound by Oath or Affirmation, to support this Constitution; but no religious Test shall ever be required as a Qualification to any Office or public Trust under the United States.

Article VII.

The Ratification of the Conventions of nine States, shall be sufficient for the Establishment of this Constitution between the States so ratifying the Same.

Done in Convention by the Unanimous Consent of the States present the Seventeenth Day of September in the Year of our Lord one thousand seven hundred and Eighty seven and of the Independence of the United States of America the Twelfth. In witness whereof We have hereunto subscribed our Names,

Articles in Addition to, and Amendment of, the Constitution of the United States of America, Proposed by Congress, and Ratified by the Legislatures of the Several States, Pursuant to the Fifth Article of the Original Constitution.

Amendment I[9]

Congress shall make no law respecting an establishment of religion, or prohibiting the free exercise thereof; or abridging the freedom of speech, or of the press; or the right of the people peaceably to assemble, and to petition the Government for a redress of grievances.

Amendment II

A well regulated Militia, being necessary to the security of a free State, the right of the people to keep and bear Arms shall not be infringed.

Amendment III

No Soldier shall, in time of peace, be quartered in any house, without the consent of the Owner, nor in time of war, but in a manner to be prescribed by law.

Amendment IV

The right of the people to be secure in their persons, houses, papers, and effects, against unreasonable searches and seizures, shall not be violated, and no Warrants shall issue, but upon probable cause, supported by Oath or affirmation, and particularly describing the place to be searched, and the persons or things to be seized.

Amendment V

No person shall be held to answer for a capital or otherwise infamous crime, unless on a presentment or indictment of a Grand Jury, except in cases arising in the land or naval forces, or in the Militia, when in actual service in time of War or public danger; nor shall any person be subject for the same offence to be twice put in jeopardy of life or limb; nor shall be compelled in any criminal case to be a witness against himself, nor be deprived of life, liberty, or property, without due process of law; nor shall private property be taken for public use, without just compensation.

Amendment VI

In all criminal prosecutions, the accused shall enjoy the right to a speedy and public trial, by an impartial jury of the State and district wherein the crime shall have been committed, which district shall have been previously ascertained by law, and to be informed of the nature and cause of the accusation; to be confronted with the witnesses against him; to have compulsory process for obtaining witnesses in his favor, and to have the Assistance of Counsel for his defence.

Amendment VII

In suits at common law, where the value in controversy shall exceed twenty dollars, the right of trial by jury shall be preserved, and no fact tried by a jury, shall be otherwise reexamined in any Court of the United States, than according to the rules of the common law.

Amendment VIII

Excessive bail shall not be required, nor excessive fines imposed, nor cruel and unusual punishments inflicted.

Amendment IX

The enumeration in the Constitution, of certain rights, shall not be construed to deny or disparage others retained by the people.

[9]The first ten amendments were passed by Congress September 25, 1789. They were ratified by three-fourths of the states December 15, 1791.

Amendment X

The powers not delegated to the United States by the Constitution; nor prohibited by it to the States, are reserved to the States respectively, or to the people.

Amendment XI[10]

The Judicial power of the United States shall not be construed to extend to any suit in law or equity, commenced or prosecuted against one of the United States by Citizens of another State, or by Citizens or Subjects of any Foreign State.

Amendment XII[11]

The Electors shall meet in their respective States and vote by ballot for President and Vice-President, one of whom, at least, shall not be an inhabitant of the same State with themselves; they shall name in their ballots the person voted for as President, and in distinct ballots the person voted for as Vice-President, and they shall make distinct lists of all persons voted for as President, and of all persons voted for as Vice-President, and of the number of votes for each, which lists they shall sign and certify, and transmit sealed to the seat of the government of the United States, directed to the President of the Senate;—The President of the Senate shall, in the presence of the Senate and House of Representatives, open all the certificates and the votes shall then be counted;—The person having the greatest number of votes for President, shall be the President, if such number be a majority of the whole number of Electors appointed; and if no person have such majority, then from the persons having the highest numbers not exceeding three on the list of those voted for as President, the House of Representatives shall choose immediately, by ballot, the President.

But in choosing the President, the votes shall be taken by states, the representation from each state having one vote; a quorum for this purpose shall consist of a member or members from two-thirds of the states, and a majority of all the states shall be necessary to a choice. And if the House of Representatives shall not choose a President whenever the right of choice shall devolve upon them, before the fourth day of March next following, then the Vice-President shall act as President, as in the case of the death or other constitutional disability of the President.—The person having the greatest number of votes as Vice-President, shall be the Vice-President, if such number be a majority of the whole number of Electors appointed, and if no person have a majority, then from the two highest numbers on the list, the Senate shall choose the Vice-President; a quorum for the purpose shall consist of two-thirds of the whole number of Senators, and a majority of the whole number shall be necessary to a choice. But no person constitutionally ineligible to the office of President shall be eligible to that of Vice-President of the United States.

Amendment XIII[12]

SECTION 1. Neither slavery nor involuntary servitude, except as a punishment for crime whereof the party shall have been duly convicted, shall exist within the United States, or any place subject to their jurisdiction.

SECTION 2. Congress shall have power to enforce this article by appropriate legislation.

Amendment XIV[13]

SECTION 1. All persons born or naturalized in the United States, and subject to the jurisdiction thereof, are citizens of the United States and of the State wherein they reside. No State shall make or enforce any law which shall abridge the privileges or immunities of citizens of the United States; nor shall any State deprive any person of life, liberty, or property, without due process of law; nor deny to any person within its jurisdiction the equal protection of the laws.

SECTION 2. Representatives shall be apportioned among the several States according to their respective numbers, counting the whole number of persons in each State, excluding Indians not taxed. But when the right to vote at any election for the choice of electors for President and Vice-President of the United States, Representatives in Congress, the Executive and Judicial officers of a State, or the members of the Legislature thereof, is denied to any of the male inhabitants of such State, being twenty-one years of age, and citizens of the United States, or in any way abridged, except for participation in rebellion, or other crime, the basis of representation therein shall be reduced in the proportion which the number of such male citizens shall bear to the whole number of male citizens twenty-one years of age in such State.

SECTION 3. No person shall be a Senator or Representative in Congress, or elector of President and Vice-President, or hold any office, civil or military, under the United States, or under any State, who, having previously taken an oath, as a member of Congress, or as an officer of the United States, or as a member of any State legislature, or as an executive or judicial officer of any State, to support the Constitution of the United States, shall have engaged in insurrection or rebellion against the same, or given aid or comfort to the enemies thereof. But Congress may by a vote of two-thirds of each House, remove such disability.

SECTION 4. The validity of the public debt of the United States, authorized by law, including debts incurred for payment of pensions and bounties for services in suppressing insurrection or rebellion, shall not be questioned. But neither the United States nor any State shall assume or pay any debt or obligation incurred in aid of insurrection or rebellion against the United States, or any claim for the loss or

---

[10]Passed March 4, 1794. Ratified January 23, 1795.
[11]Passed December 9, 1803. Ratified June 15, 1804.
[12]Passed January 31, 1865. Ratified December 6, 1865.
[13]Passed June 13, 1866. Ratified July 9, 1868.

emancipation of any slave; but all such debts, obligations, and claims shall be held illegal and void.

SECTION 5. The Congress shall have the power to enforce, by appropriate legislation, the provisions of this article.

Amendment XV[14]

SECTION 1. The right of citizens of the United States to vote shall not be denied or abridged by the United States or by any State on account of race, color, or previous conditions of servitude—

SECTION 2. The Congress shall have power to enforce this article by appropriate legislation.

Amendment XVI[15]

The Congress shall have power to lay and collect taxes on incomes, from whatever source derived, without apportionment among the several States, and without regard to any census or enumeration.

Amendment XVII[16]

The Senate of the United States shall be composed of two Senators from each State, elected by the people thereof, for six years; and each Senator shall have one vote. The electors in each State shall have the qualifications requisite for electors of the most numerous branch of the State legislatures.

When vacancies happen in the representation of any State in the Senate, the executive authority of such State shall issue writs of election to fill such vacancies: Provided, That the legislature of any State may empower the executive thereof to make temporary appointments until the people fill the vacancies by election as the legislature may direct.

This amendment shall not be so construed as to affect the election or term of any Senator chosen before it becomes valid as part of the Constitution.

Amendment XVIII[17]

SECTION 1. After one year from the ratification of this article the manufacture, sale, or transportation of intoxicating liquors within, the importation thereof into, or the exportation thereof from the United States and all territory subject to the jurisdiction thereof for beverage purposes is hereby prohibited.

SECTION 2. The Congress and the several States shall have concurrent power to enforce this article by appropriate legislation.

SECTION 3. This article shall be inoperative unless it shall have been ratified as an amendment to the Constitution by the legislatures of the several States, as provided in the Constitution, within seven years from the date of the submission hereof to the States by the Congress.

Amendment XIX[18]

The right of citizens of the United States to vote shall not be denied or abridged by the United States or by any State on account of sex.

Congress shall have power to enforce this article by appropriate legislation.

Amendment XX[19]

SECTION 1. The terms of the President and Vice-President shall end at noon on the 20th day of January, and the terms of Senators and Representatives at noon on the 3d day of January, of the years in which such terms would have ended if this article had not been ratified; and the terms of their successors shall then begin.

SECTION 2. The Congress shall assemble at least once in every year, and such meeting shall begin at noon on the 3d day of January, unless they shall by law appoint a different day.

SECTION 3. If, at the time fixed for the beginning of the term of the President, the President elect shall have died, the Vice-President elect shall become President. If a President shall not have been chosen before the time fixed for the beginning of his term, or if the President elect shall have failed to qualify, then the Vice-President elect shall act as President until a President shall have qualified; and the Congress may by law provide for the case wherein neither a President elect nor a Vice-President elect shall have qualified, declaring who shall then act as President, or the manner in which one who is to act shall be selected, and such person shall act accordingly until a President or Vice-President shall have qualified.

SECTION 4. The Congress may by law provide for the case of the death of any of the persons from whom the House of Representatives may choose a President whenever the right of choice shall have devolved upon them, and for the case of the death of any of the persons from whom the Senate may choose a Vice-President whenever the right of choice shall have devolved upon them.

SECTION 5. Sections 1 and 2 shall take effect on the 15th day of October following the ratification of this article.

SECTION 6. This article shall be inoperative unless it shall have been ratified as an amendment to the Constitution by the legislatures of three-fourths of the several States within seven years from the date of its submission.

---

[14]Passed February 26, 1869. Ratified February 2, 1870.
[15]Passed July 12, 1909. Ratified February 3, 1913.
[16]Passed May 13, 1912. Ratified April 8, 1913.
[17]Passed December 18, 1917. Ratified January 16, 1919.
[18]Passed June 4, 1919. Ratified August 18, 1920.
[19]Passed March 2, 1932. Ratified January 23, 1933.

Amendment XXI[20]

SECTION 1. The eighteenth article of amendment to the Constitution of the United States is hereby repealed.

SECTION 2. The transportation or importation into any State, Territory, or possession of the United States for delivery or use therein of intoxicating liquors, in violation of the laws thereof, is hereby prohibited.

SECTION 3. This article shall be inoperative unless it shall have been ratified as an amendment to the Constitution by conventions in the several States, as provided in the Constitution, within seven years from the date of the submission hereof to the States by the Congress.

Amendment XXII[21]

No person shall be elected to the office of the President more than twice, and no person who has held the office of President, or acted as President, for more than two years of a term to which some other person was elected President shall be elected to the office of the President more than once.

But this Article shall not apply to any person holding the office of President when this Article was proposed by the Congress, and shall not prevent any person who may be holding the office of President, or acting as President, during the term within which this Article becomes operative from holding the office of President or acting as President during the remainder of such term.

Amendment XXIII[22]

SECTION 1. The District constituting the seat of Government of the United States shall appoint in such manner as the Congress may direct: A number of electors of President and Vice President equal to the whole number of Senators and Representatives in Congress to which the District would be entitled if it were a State, but in no event more than the least populous State; they shall be in addition to those appointed by the States, but they shall be considered, for the purposes of the election of President and Vice President, to be electors appointed by the State; and they shall meet in the District and perform such duties as provided by the twelfth article of amendment.

SECTION 2. The Congress shall have power to enforce this article by appropriate legislation.

Amendment XXIV[23]

SECTION 1. The right of citizens of the United States to vote in any primary or other election for President or Vice President, or for Senator or Representative in Congress, shall not be denied or abridged by the United States or any State by reason of failure to pay any poll tax or other tax.

SECTION 2. The Congress shall have power to enforce this article by appropriate legislation.

Amendment XXV[24]

SECTION 1. In case of the removal of the President from office or of his death or resignation, the Vice President shall become President.

SECTION 2. Whenever there is a vacancy in the office of the Vice President, the President shall nominate a Vice President who shall take office upon confirmation by a majority vote of both Houses of Congress.

SECTION 3. Whenever the President transmits to the President pro tempore of the Senate and the Speaker of the House of Representatives his written declaration that he is unable to discharge the powers and duties of his office, and until he transmits them a written declaration to the contrary, such powers and duties shall be discharged by the Vice President as Acting President.

SECTION 4. Whenever the Vice President and a majority of either the principal officers of the executive department or of such other body as Congress may by law provide, transmit to the President pro tempore of the Senate and the Speaker of the House of Representatives their written declaration that the President is unable to discharge the powers and duties of his office, the Vice President shall immediately assume the powers and duties of the office of Acting President.

Thereafter, when the President transmits to the President pro tempore of the Senate and the Speaker of the House of Representatives his written declaration that no inability exists, he shall resume the powers and duties of his office unless the Vice President and a majority of either the principal officers of the executive department or of such other body as Congress may by law provide, transmit within four days to the President pro tempore of the Senate and the Speaker of the House of Representatives their written declaration that the President is unable to discharge the powers and duties of his office. Thereupon Congress shall decide the issue, assembling within forty-eight hours for that purpose if not in session. If the Congress, within twenty-one days after receipt of the latter written declaration, or, if Congress is not in session, within twenty-one days after Congress is required to assemble, determines by two-thirds vote of both Houses that the President is unable to discharge the powers and duties of his office, the Vice President shall continue to discharge the same as Acting President; otherwise, the President shall resume the powers and duties of his office.

---

[20]Passed February 20, 1933. Ratified December 5, 1933.
[21]Passed March 12, 1947. Ratified March 1, 1951.
[22]Passed June 16, 1960. Ratified April 3, 1961.
[23]Passed August 27, 1962. Ratified January 23, 1964.
[24]Passed July 6, 1965. Ratified February 11, 1967.

Amendment XXVI[25]

SECTION 1 The right of citizens of the United States, who are eighteen years of age or older, to vote shall not be denied or abridged by the United States or by any State on account of age.

SECTION 2. The Congress shall have power to enforce this article by appropriate legislation.

Amendment XXVII[26]

No law, varying the compensation for the service of the Senators and Representatives, shall take effect, until an election of Representatives shall have intervened.

[25]Passed March 23, 1971. Ratified July 5, 1971.
[26]Passed September 25, 1789. Ratified May 7, 1992.

A

AAA. *See* Agricultural Adjustment Administration

Abell, Mary, 416

Abilene, Kansas, 412

Abolition and abolitionism: education for freedpeople and, 390–391; women's rights and, 394

Abortion and abortion rights, 673, 703–704, 718, 729, 775

Abraham Lincoln Brigade, 606

Abu Ghraib prison, 781

Accommodationism, 427, 493

Acheson, Dean, 638, 646, 699

Acquired immune deficiency syndrome. *See* AIDS

Activism: of African Americans, 733; of American Indians, 733–734; anti-government, 736–738; Asian-American, 736; of counterculture, 695–696; gay and lesbian, 645, 731–732; governmental, 478, 668–669; of New Left, 695; of post-1960s movements, 703; Puerto Rican, 736; in Sixties, 694; Spanish-American, 734–736; against Vietnam War, 697–698; by women, 442, 481–482, 673–674, 729–731. *See also* specific issues and movements

ACT UP, 732

Adams, Ansel, 625

Adams, Eddie, 693

Adamson Act, 501

Addams, Jane, 481, 482, 532

Advertising, 664, 665; in 1920s, 553–554; of cigarettes, 437; growth of, 439

AEF. *See* American Expeditionary Force

AFDC. *See* Aid to Families with Dependent Children

Affirmative action, 704, 723, 737

Affluence: in 1950s, 661–665; age of, 657; discontents of, 665–667. *See also* Prosperity; Wealth

Affluent Society, The (Galbraith), 662

Affordable Health Care for America Act (ACA, 2010), 788

Afghanistan, 716, 717, 723, 778, 781, 788

AFL. *See* American Federation of Labor

Africa, 658; immigrants from, after 1970, 744. *See also* African Americans

African Americans: in 1920s, 568–569; in 1980s, 719–720; accommodationism and, 427, 493; activism of, 733; Alliance movement and, 450; in baseball, 650–651; in Black Cabinet, 596; Black Codes and, 389; citizenship and, 392; Columbian Exhibition and, 460; as cowboys, 414; culture in 1920s, 569–571; disfranchisement of, 426, 488; Ellington's music and, 597; as Exodusters, 424; as FBI targets, 645; First World War and, 536; after First World War, 547; in Great Depression, 596; higher education for, 391; homesteading and, 409; Jim Crow laws and, 426, 468; Ku Klux Klan and, 398; labor and community of, 467–469; labor unions and, 447; lynchings of, 425, 426, 493; middle class of, 425–426, 469; migration by, 407, 424, 425, 535, 625–626, 652; as movie directors, 757; NBA and, 754; as officeholders, 397; population shifts (1940–1960), 675 (*map*); as president, 786; in Republican Party, 397; Roosevelt, Theodore, and, 495; in Second World War, 620–621, 623–624; sharecropping and, 390, 467; in South, 395, 423; suffragists and, 490; in urban areas and suburbs, 747; as U.S. soldiers, 511; in Vietnam War, 698; voting and, 387, 392, 393, 401, 426, 592, 677, 688, 689; Washington, Booker T., and, 427; women and, 425–426, 442–443, 483, 673, 730. *See also* Africa; Civil rights movement; Freedpeople; Race and racism; Race riots; Slavery

Afro-Latinos, in sports, 651

Agent provocateurs, 701

Aging, of population, 742–743, 743 (*table*)

Agnew, Spiro, 709

"Agrarians" (southern writers), 573

Agricultural Adjustment Administration (AAA), 584

Agriculture: commercialization of, 461; crop lien system in, 424; immigrant labor in, 462, 464, 466, 678; labor decline in, 440; reforms in, 584–585; in South, 424. *See also* Farms and farming

Agriculture Department, 496

Aguinaldo, Emilio, 513

AIDS, 732

AIDS Coalition to Unleash Power. *See* ACT UP

Aid to Families with Dependent Children (AFDC), 702, 720

Aircraft Production Board, 534

Air Force, 635, 692

Airplanes, 556, 622, 659

Air pollution, 703

Air traffic controllers, firing of, 720

Alabama (commerce raider), 396

"Alabama Claims," 396

Alaska, 453

Albany & Susquehanna Railroad, 435

Albright, Madeleine, 768

Alcatraz Island, Indian sit-in on, 734

Alcohol and alcoholism, 539, 563; cultural conservatism and, 482–483. *See also* Prohibition

Alcott, Louisa May, 442

Ali, Muhammad, 698

Alien and Sedition Acts (1798), 540

Alien Land Law (California, 1913), 466

Alito, Samuel, 721, 776

All-American Canal, 587 (*map*)

Allen, Woody, 757

Allende Gossens, Salvador, 707

Alliance for Progress, 670

Alliances: First World War and, 527, 528–529, 529 (*map*). *See also* National security; specific alliances

Allies (First World War), 527, 528, 531, 533–534, 541. *See also* First World War; specific countries

Allies (Second World War), 607, 610, 612 (*map*); UN and, 627–628. *See also* Second World War; specific countries

Allotment, in Dawes Act, 420, 598

All Quiet on the Western Front (movie), 606
al-Qaeda, 778, 780, 781
Alternating current (AC), 434
Altgeld, John P., 448, 482
Amalgamated Association of Iron, Steel, and Tin Workers, 447
Amalgamated Clothing Workers, 594
Amazon.com, 751
Amendments. *See* specific amendments
American Bar Association, 444
American Civil Liberties Union, Scopes Trial and, 566–567
American Communist Party (CP), 589, 635, 637, 643, 645, 646, 659; McCarthy and, 646–647
American Economic Association, 444
American Equal Rights Association (AERA), 394
American Expeditionary Force (AEF), 533
American Federation of Labor (AFL), 447, 536, 546, 594; CIO and, 594–595, 663; women and, 447, 621
American-Filipino War, 513–514
American Football League (AFL), 754
American Historical Association, 444
American Hospital Association (AHA), 649
American Impressionism, 441
American Indian Movement (AIM), 734
American Indians: activism of, 733–734; assimilation and, 420; boarding schools for, 420–422; buffalo extermination and, 415, 419; Dawes Severalty Act and, 420; Five Civilized Tribes and, 417; Ghost Dance and, 422; Homestead Act and, 409; land and, 417, 678; in New Deal, 598; peace policy for, 420; Plains Indians and, 417–423; reservations for, 417, 418, 418 *(map)*, 419; Sand Creek massacre and, 419; in Second World War, 615, 624; as slaveowners, 418; Termination and Relocation programs for, 677–678; westward expansion of whites and, 417–418;

Wounded Knee massacre against, 422
Americanization: campaigns for, 474; classes at Ford, 492; of immigrants, 466
American Legion, 546
American Medical Association (AMA), 444, 649
American Museum of Natural History, 458, 459
American Protective League, 540, 546
American Railway Union (ARU), 448
American Recovery and Reinvestment Act (2009), 788
American Tobacco Company, 436, 506
American Union Against Militarism, 532
American Woman Suffrage Association, 394
AmeriCorps program, 768
Ames, Adelbert, 401
Amnesty, 386; for ex-Confederates, 388; for undocumented workers, 746
Amsterdam News, 625
Amusement parks, 456, 469
Anarchists and anarchism: Haymarket bombing and, 446; Sacco and Vanzetti case and, 546–547
Anderson, Marian, 596
Angel Island, immigrants in, 463
Anglo-Americans, Mexican American lands and, 414–415
Anglos (whites), 411, 598
Anglo-Saxons, 440, 564
Annuity payments, for Indians, 418
Anshutz, Thomas, 441
Antebellum period, 432
Anthony, Susan B., 394
Antiabortion protest, 737
Anticommunism: CIA and, 636, 642; entertainment industry and, 643; labor movement and, 642; of McCarthy, 646–647, 659; of Reagan, 643, 723; of Truman, 634, 637
Antidiscrimination measures, 677. *See also* Discrimination
Anti-government activism, 736–738
Anti-imperialism, 504, 512
Anti-Imperialist League, 513
Anti-lynching campaign, 425, 426
Antimonopoly parties, 449

Anti-Saloon League, 483
Anti-Semitism, 461, 588, 596, 609. *See also* Jews and Judaism
Antitrust issues, 436, 501; in Second World War, 620
Antiwar movies, 606
Antiwar sentiment: in Chicago (1968), 700–701; in Iraq war, 783; in Vietnam War, 692, 697–698, 706, 707
ANZUS mutual defense pact (1952), 641
Apartheid, in South Africa, 641
API groups, 736
Apollo program, 743
Appalachia, funding for, 672
APPCON, 736
Appeal to Reason (socialist publication), 483
Appeasement, of Hitler, 607
Apple Computer, 749
Appliances, in 1920s, 553
Arab world. *See* Islam; Israel; Middle East
Arbuckle, Roscoe "Fatty," 471, 472
Architecture, of skyscrapers, 457
Area Redevelopment Bill (1961), 672
Are Women People? A Book of Rhymes for Suffrage Times (Miller), 491
Argonne Forest, in First World War, 534
Aristide, Jean-Bertrand, 776
Arizona, 411, 490, 663
Arkansas, 386, 398
Armaments: in Second World War, 607. *See also* Weapons
Armed forces. *See* Military; specific battles and wars
Armies of the Night (Mailer), 698
Armistice, in Spanish-American War, 511
Armories, 446
Arms race, 634, 674, 705
Armstrong, Neil, 743
Army Corps of Engineers, water projects and, 663
Arnold, Henry Harley ("Hap"), 615
Arsenal of democracy, U.S. as, 609
Art and artists: in 1920s, 572–573; FBI dossiers on, 645; in Great Depression, 594, 595; middle-class and, 441; PWA and, 591; realism in, 441, 480. *See also* specific types and individuals
Arthur, Chester A., 428

Article X, of League of Nations Covenant, 543

Artisans: resistance by, 445. *See also* Craft workers

"Aryan race," 606

Asia, 658; Carter and, 716; immigration from, 409, 410–412, 417, 460–461, 462–463, 744; Japanese aggression in, 607. *See also* specific locations

Asian Americans: activism of, 736; as movie directors, 757

Asiatic Barred Zone, 539

Assassinations: attempt on Reagan, 721; of Franz Ferdinand (Sarajevo), 528; of Garfield, 428; of Kennedy, John F., 681, 682; of Kennedy, Robert F., 700; of King, Martin Luther, Jr., 699–700; of McKinley, 494, 518

Assemblies, of Knights of Labor, 445–446

Assembly line, at Ford, 492

Assimilation: immigrants and, 466; of Indians, 420–422, 598, 677–678

Associationalism, 560–561

Aswan Dam, 660

Athletics. *See* Sports

Atlanta Exposition, Washington, Booker T., at, 427

Atlantic Charter (1941), 627

Atlantic Monthly, The, 480

ATMs (automated teller machines), 753

Atomic bomb: in Second World War, 617, 618, 634; Soviets and, 638, 645. *See also* Nuclear power

Attica Uprising, 702

Attrition, in Vietnam War, 692

Australia, ANZUS pact and, 641

Australian ballot (secret ballot), 487

Austria, 659; German annexation of, 607; immigrants from, 538

Austria-Hungary, 542 *(map)*; immigrants from, 416. *See also* First World War

Authority. *See* Power (authority)

Autobiography (Malcolm X), 697

Automobiles and automobile industry: in 1920s, 552, 553, 554; assembly line in, 492; auto racing and, 754; downsizing and, 751; mass-production techniques in, 437

Aviation. *See* Airplanes

Axis Powers, 610

B

Baby and Child Care (Spock), 672

Baby boom and baby boomers, 652, 652 *(table)*, 666, 694; aging of, 743

Bacteriological weapons: in Iraq, 728; in Second World War, 614

Baer, George F., 495

Baghdad, U.S. soldiers in, 780

Baker, Ella, 676

Bakke case, 737

Bakker, Jim and Tammy Faye, 762

Balanced budget, 668

Balance of trade, 705

Balkan region, 528

Ball, George, 692

Ballinger, Richard A., 497

Ballparks, 469

Baltic region, Second World War and, 607

Baltimore and Ohio Railroad, 445

Banks and banking: credit cards and, 752–753; Federal Reserve Act and, 500–501; Morgan, J. P., and, 435; Panic of 1907 and, 497

Bara, Theda, 472

Barton, Bruce, 556

Baruch, Bernard, 534, 634

Baruch Plan, 634

Baseball, 556; color line in, 650–651; sports-entertainment industry and, 753, 754

Bataan, 614

Batista, Fulgencio, 660

Baton Rouge, 676

Battle of Britain, 608

Battles. *See* specific battles and wars

Bay of Pigs (Cuba) invasion, 670–671

Bayonet rule, in South, 400, 401, 404

Beat movement, 696; LGBT activism and, 731

Begin, Menachem, 715–716

Belgium: First World War and, 528, 541; Second World War and, 611

Bell, Alexander Graham, 434

Bellamy, Edward, 441

Benefits: in 1950s, 663; packages of, 752; unemployment, 667

Berkeley Revolt (1964, 1965), 695

Berkman, Alexander, 447

Berlin: airlift in, 636; blockade of, 636; Kennedy, John F., and, 671; zones in, 628, 638 *(map)*

Berlin, Edward A., 468

Berlin, Irving, 468, 595

Berlin Wall, 671, 725, 726

Bernanke, Ben, 785, 788

Berry, Chuck, 666

"Bertha the Sewing Machine Girl:...," 470

Bethune, Mary McLeod, 596

Beveridge, Albert J., 496

Bible, fundamentalism and, 551, 565–566

Bicycles, 441, 444

Big business: mass production, mass distribution and, 437; mining and, 411; railroads as, 434–435; Roosevelt, Franklin D., and, 620. *See also* Business; Corporations

Big Four, at Paris Peace Conference, 541

Big government, Clinton and, 768, 769

Big Lebowski, The (movie), 771

"Big navy" policy, 507, 507 *(table)*

Big Three, at Paris Peace Conference (1919), 541

Bilingual education, 702

Bilingualism, American Indian, 734

Bill of Rights (U.S.), 404. *See also* Second Bill of Rights

Bin Laden, Osama, 778

Biodiversity, decline of, 777

Biotechnology, 749

Bipolar world, after Second World War, 658

Birmingham, racial conflict in, 680

Birth control, 444, 673

Birth of a Nation, The (movie), 399, 564

Birthrate. *See* Baby boom and baby boomers

Bison. *See* Buffalo

Black(s): Cuban revolutionaries and, 510. *See also* African Americans; Slavery

Black Cabinet, 596

Black Codes, 389

Black Hills, Sioux and gold in, 419

"Blacking up," 570

Black Kettle (Chief), 419

Blacklist, in entertainment industry, 643

Black Muslims, 696, 697

Black nationalism (Garvey), 547

Black Panthers, 697, 701

Black Power movement, 696–697; Nation of Islam and, 761

Black Star Line, 547

"Black Tuesday" (October 29, 1929), 576

Blackwell, Elizabeth, 444

Blaine, James G., 428

Blair, Frank, 395

Blair Witch Project, The (movie), 756

Blitzkrieg (lightning war), 607

Block, Herbert (Herblock), 644

Blockade(s): in Berlin, 636; in First World War, 531; in Spanish-American War, 510 *(map)*; in Vietnam War, 707

Block grants, 702

Bloggers, 790

Blood, segregation of, in Second World War, 623

Blue-collar workforce, 752

Blues, 569

Board of Indian Commissioners, 420

Boats. *See* Ships and shipping

"Body count," in Vietnam War, 692, 693, 706

Bohemia, 461

Bolling v. Sharpe, 674

Bolsheviks (Russia), 533

Bolton, John, 781

Bombs and bombings: hydrogen bomb and, 638; by leftist fringe, 701; in Second World War, 615–616, 617, 618; terrorist, 778; in Vietnam War, 691, 692, 707. *See also* Atomic bomb; Nuclear power

Bonsack, James Albert, and Bonsack cigarette machines, 437

Bonus Army, 580

Boom-and-bust cycles, 432

"Boomers," in Indian Territory 420

Borderlands, railroads and, 411

Borrowing, in Great Depression, 590

Bosnia, 528, 725

Bosnian Serbs and Muslims, 776

Bosses (political), 467

Boston, police strike in, 545, 560

Boulder Dam (Hoover Dam), 587

Bourne, Randolph, 475

Boxers and Boxer Rebellion, 518

Boycotts: against Cuba, 660; labor, 642; of lettuce and grapes, 735; Montgomery bus boycott, 676;

of Pullman cars, 448; of Summer Olympic Games (1980), 717

Bracero program, 620, 678

Bradley, Mamie Till, 676

Brandeis, Louis, 501

Brazil, Earth Summit in, 777

Briand, Aristide, 561

Brooklyn Dodgers, 650, 651

Brotherhood of Sleeping Car Porters, 569

Brown v. Board of Education of Topeka (1954), 674, 676; *Brown II* (1955), 674

Bryan, William Jennings, 480, 501, 513; 1896 election and, 451–452, 452 *(map)*; 1900 election and, 453; 1908 election and, 497; "Cross of Gold" speech of, 451; Scopes trial and, 566–567

Bubbles (financial): economy and (1993–2008), 783–786; in housing, 785–786

Buchanan, Patrick, 717, 772

Buckley, William F., Jr., 668, 717

Buddhism, 760

Budget: increases in, 690; military-related spending in, 642; under Reagan, 719. *See also* Deficit

Buffalo, destruction of, 415, 419

Buffett, Warren, 785

Bulgaria, 461, 628

Bulge, Battle of the, 611

Bull Moosers, in 1912, 498, 501

Bunau-Varilla, Philippe, 520

Bundy, McGeorge, 691

Burchard, Samuel, 428

Bureaucracy, 395, 635

Bureau of Immigration and Naturalization, 488

Bureau of Indian Affairs (BIA), 598, 678

Bureau of Reclamation, 587, 588, 663

Bureau of Refugees, Freedmen, and Abandoned Lands. *See* Freedmen's Bureau

Burger, Warren, 703, 721

Burroughs, Edgar Rice, 517

Bus boycott, in Montgomery, 676

Bush, George H. W.: 1980 election and, 718–719; 1988 election and, 723, 762; 1992 election and, 728–729, 729 *(map)*; foreign policy of, 726–728; Iran-*Contra* and, 725

Bush, George W.: 2000 election and, 772–773, 772 *(map)*; 2004 election and, 774; baseball ownership by, 754; cabinet of, 773; economy and, 773–774, 784–786; guest workers and, 775; national security and, 781–783; September 11, 2001, attacks and, 774, 778

Bush Doctrine, 778

Bush v. Gore, 773

Business: in 1920s, 556; black-owned, 469; international relations and, 561–562; military connection with, 661, 662; in New Deal, 592–593; New Right on, 717; organization and practices in, 435–437; overseas expansion by, 506; politics of, 559–562; in Second World War, 619–620; in South, 663; structural and operational changes in, 750–752; Wilson and, 501

Butte, Montana, mining in, 411

Byrds (musical group), 696

C

Cable television, 754, 758; news coverage on, 759, 770

California, 490, 663, 677; Chinese immigrants in, 409–410, 522; federal water projects in New Deal, 587 *(map)*; gold in, 411; immigrants in, 464; Japanese Americans in, 466, 522; Latinos in, 626–627; Mexicans in, 414, 464, 597, 678; migration to, 595; population growth in, 743

Californios, 571–572

Calley, William, 706

Cambodia, 661, 706, 715; immigrants from, 745

"Campaign of Truth" (Truman), 642

Camp David, peace talks at (1978), 715

Canada: immigrants from, 461; NAFTA and, 728, 777; NATO and, 637

Canals, in Panama, 520–521, 521 *(map)*

Canal Zone, 520, 521, 521 *(map)*

Capital (financial): labor and, 545; in South, 423

Capitalism: AFL and, 447; black, 702; Hoover and, 561; in New

Deal, 592–593; "people's," 553; welfare 556
Capitol building, bombing of, 701
Capone, Al, 563
Capra, Frank, 622
Caribbean region: dollar diplomacy in, 522; U.S. empire in, 519 (map), 523; U.S. military in, 562. See also specific locations
Carlisle Institute, 422
Carmichael, Stokely, 697
Carnegie, Andrew, 435, 436; anti-imperialism of, 513; gospel of wealth of, 453; ironworkers strike and, 545
Carnegie foundations, 453
Carnegie Hall (New York), 453
Carnegie-Mellon University, 453
Carnegie Steel Company, 434, 435, 447
Carolina(s). See also North Carolina; South Carolina
Caroline Islands, 629
Carpetbaggers, 393, 397, 401
Carranza, Venustiano, 524
Cars. See Automobiles and automobile industry
Carson, Rachel, 702
Carter, James Earl (Jimmy): 1976 election and, 714, 714 (map); canal zone and, 521; economy and, 714–715; foreign policy of, 715–717; religion of, 718
Carter family, Maybelle, A.P., and Sara, 555
Casablanca meeting, 611
Casey, William, 723
Cash-and-carry provision, 607
Casinos, on Indian lands, 734, 735
Castro, Fidel, 660, 670, 671, 736, 745
Casualties. See specific battles and wars
Catholicism: of Kennedy, John F., 669; McCarthy endorsed by, 646–647; of Mexican Americans, 415; of new immigrants, 461; Protestants and, 563, 564; Roosevelt, Franklin D., and, 593, 596; of Smith, Alfred E., 669; undocumented immigrants and, 762. See also Missions and missionaries; Religion
CATO Institute, 717
Catt, Carrie Chapman, 490, 532
Cattle drives, 412

Cavalry, in Spanish-American War, 510–511
CDO (collateralized debt obligation), 753
CDs (compact discs), 758
Celebrities: in 1920s, 554–556; religious leaders as, 665
Cell phones, 749
Censorship, of comic books, 666
Census, "Asian or Pacific Islander" category on, 736
Central America: canal across, 507, 520–521, 521 (map); Carter and, 716; immigrants from, 736; intervention in, 523, 562. See also specific locations
Central High School (Little Rock), 677
Central Intelligence Agency (CIA), 635–636; covert actions of, 636, 642, 659–660, 661; Cuba and, 660, 670–671; Reagan and, 723–724
Central Pacific Railroad, 409, 410
Central Park (New York), 458–459
Central Powers, in First World War, 531, 533
Century (magazine), 441
Century of Dishonor, A (Jackson, Helen Hunt), 420
Chain businesses, 750–751
"Challenge of Peace, The" (Conference of Catholic Bishops, 1983), 762
Challenger shuttle, 743
Chambers, Whittaker, 643
Chaney, James, 688
Chaplin, Charlie, 556
Chase, William Merritt, 441
Chavez, Cesar, 735
Cheney, Richard (Dick), 772, 773, 774
Cherokee Indians, 418
Cheyenne Indians, 419
Chiang Kai-shek. See Jiang Jieshi
Chicago: 1919 race riot in, 547; 1968 Democratic convention in, 700–701; beef processing in, 412, 483; Haymarket bombing in, 446–447; Hull House in, 481–482; population of, 457; saloons in, 483
Chicago Daily Tribune, 1948 election and, 636
Chicago Defender, 535
Chicago World's Fair. See Columbian Exposition

Chicanismo, 734
Chicano/a studies, 735
Chicanos/as, 592, 598, 674, 734–735. See also Mexican Americans
Chickasaw Indians, 418
Chief Joseph, 419
Child health care, 559
Child labor, 423, 464, 482, 501
Child rearing, 672, 673
Children: Head Start for, 689; immigrant, 460, 461 (table), 463, 466; Indian, 420–422; prenatal and child health care and, 559; in suburbs, 652, 672. See also Education
Children's Bureau, 593
Chile, 707
China: Boxer Rebellion in, 518; Bush, George W., and, 783; Clinton and, 777; communism in, 637–638; diplomatic relations with, 716; dollar diplomacy in, 522; immigration from, 409, 410–412, 417, 460, 462–463, 522, 565; Japan and, 521, 607, 614; Korean War and, 641; missionaries in, 505; Nixon and, 706; Open Door policy in, 516–518; in Second World War, 609, 614; Vietnam and, 661, 693
China lobby, 637
Chinatown, 410
Chinese Americans, 409–411, 736
Chinese Exclusion Act (1882), 410–411, 462, 522
Chinese Revolution (1911), 522
Chisholm Trail, 412
Chivington, John, 419
Chlorofluorocarbons (CFCs), 777
Choctaw Indians, 418
Christianity: fundamentalist and liberal Protestants on, 565–566. See also Evangelicalism; Missions and missionaries; Religion; Religious Right; specific groups
Chu, Steven, 787
Church(es): immigrant, 465. See also Religion; Separation of church and state
Church of Jesus Christ of Latter-Day Saints. See Mormons
CIA. See Central Intelligence Agency
Cigarette-making machines, 437

Cigarettes, 436. *See also* Tobacco and tobacco industry

Cinema. *See* Movies and movie industry

CIO. *See* Committee for Industrial Organization; Congress of Industrial Organizations

Cities: African Americans in, 469, 568, 652, 675; bankruptcies of, 714; core areas in, 458; culture in, 458–459; electricity in, 434, 458; functions of, 747; growth of, 456, 457–460; immigrants in, 461 *(table)*, 465–467; Indian relocation to, 678; movement to, in Second World War, 624; organized crime in, 467; political machines in, 466–467; Puerto Rican communities in, 744–745; reform in, 485–486; sanitation in, 458; suburbs and, 440, 652; transportation and, 458; urbanization and, 562, 563 *(map)*; urban renewal in, 679, 689; walking, 458; water and sewage systems in, 458. *See also* Metropolitan areas; Municipalities; Towns; Urban areas

Citizenship: exclusion of Asians, 462; Fourteenth Amendment and, 392; for Hawaiian citizens, 512; for Indians, 420, 677–678; progressives on, 488; for Puerto Ricans, 515, 516, 678. *See also* Suffrage; Voting and voting rights

City commission plan, 485, 486

City manager plan, 485, 486

Civil disobedience, 676

Civilian Conservation Corps (CCC), 584, 619

Civilization. *See* Culture

Civilized Tribes. *See* Five Civilized Tribes

Civil libertarians, 635, 642, 646

Civil liberties: Haymarket bombing aftermath and, 446. *See also* Civil rights

Civil rights: in 1950s, 665; accommodationism and, 493; Eisenhower and, 674, 677; Fourteenth Amendment and, 392; of freedpeople, 391; of Indians, 677–678; Johnson, Lyndon B., and, 677; Kennedy, John F., and, 669, 680, 681;

Montgomery bus boycott and, 676; NAACP and, 493–494; Nixon and, 702; politics of, 677; Roosevelt, Franklin D., and, 596; in Second World War, 625–627; Spanish-speaking communities and, 678–679; Truman and, 649–650. *See also* Civil rights movement; Rights

Civil Rights Acts: of 1875, 402; of 1957, 677; of 1960, 677; of 1964, 402, 687, 730; of 1968, 697, 734

Civil Rights bills, during congressional Reconstruction, 392

Civil Rights Cases (1883), 402

Civil rights movements, 649–650, 733; from 1953–1963, 674–681; in 1960s, 688; Black Power movement and, 696–697; *Brown* cases and, 674; NAACP and, 493; tactics in, 675, 676, 679–680. *See also* Civil rights

Civil service: reform of, 396, 428, 491; women in, 674

Civil war(s): in China, 614; in Iraq, 780; in Spain, 606

Civil War (U.S.): slavery and, 385. *See also* Lincoln, Abraham

Civil Works Administration (CWA), 584

Clan Na Gael, 465

Clark, Champ, 499

Clarke, Edward H., 444

Classes: distinctions in Gilded Age, 440–441. *See also* Elites; specific classes

Clayton Antitrust Act, 501

Clean Air Act (1970), 703

Clemenceau, Georges, 543

Clergy, women as, 730

Cleveland, Grover, 451; 1884, 1888, 1892 elections and, 427, 428, 429; anti-imperialism of, 513; Cuba and, 508; Hawaii and, 507; Panic of 1893 and, 449; Pullman Strike and, 448; tariffs and, 428–429

Cleveland Indians, 651

Climate: ecological dangers and, 777; of Great Plains, 416

Clinton, Hillary Rodham, 770, 787

Clinton, William Jefferson (Bill), 768; 1992 election and, 728–729, 729 *(map)*; 1996 election and, 769; cabinet of, 768; economy and, 768–769,

784; environmental policy of, 777–778; foreign policy of, 776–777; globalization and, 777; impeachment of, 770; stem cell research and, 749

Closed shops, 642

Clothing and clothing industry: Jews and Italians in, 464. *See also* Textiles and textile industry

Clubwomen, 483

CNN (Cable News Network), 756, 759

Coal and coal industry: in 1920s, 557; railroads and, 434; strikes in, 495, 545

Coalitions: New Deal, 654; Populist-Democratic and Populist-Republican, 451

Cody, Buffalo Bill, 422–423

Coeur d'Alene, Idaho, mining strike at, 412

"Cola wars," 751

Cold War, 632, 657; China and, 637–638; civil rights and, 650, 677; Cuban Missile Crisis during, 671; defense buildup in, 723–724; détente in, 705–706; economy and, 648; end of, 725; fears of subversion during, 635, 643–644, 644–645; foreign policy after, 726–728; Korean War and, 639–641; onset of, 633–634; Third World and, 660–661. *See also* Communism; Containment; Soviet Union

Cole (battleship), terrorist attack on, 778

Colfax Massacre, 398

Collateralized debt obligations (CDOs), 785

Collective bargaining, 446

College(s). *See* Universities and colleges

Collier, John, 598

Colombia, 520, 521

Colonial economy, in South, 423

Colonies and colonization: after First World War, 541; of U.S., 512, 512 *(map)*

Colorado, 419, 488

Colored Farmers' Alliance, 450

Color line, in baseball, 650–651

Columbian Exposition (Chicago, 1893), 459–460

Columbus, New Mexico, Villa in, 524

Comic books, 666

Commerce. *See* Trade

Commerce and Navigation, Treaty of, with Japan, 609

Commerce raiders, 396

Commercial culture, 456, 469–472

Commission on Civil Rights. *See* U.S. Commission on Civil Rights

Commission on Human Rights (UN), 628

Committee for a Sane Nuclear Policy (SANE), 674

Committee for Industrial Organization (CIO), 594, 594 (table). *See also* Congress of Industrial Organizations

Committee on Public Information (CPI), 537

Commodities Futures Modernization Act (2000), 784

Commodity Credit Corporation (1930s), 450

Commons, John R., 491

Commonwealth, in former Soviet Union, 725

Communication(s). *See* Mass media; specific media

Communism: in China, 614, 637–638; Eisenhower and, 659, 661; in French Indochina, 641, 661; Great Fear and, 645–646; Kennedy, John F., and, 670; McCarthy and, 646–647; Red Scare after First World War and, 546; SACB and, 646; Truman and, 635; in Vietnam, 661. *See also* Anticommunism; Containment; Soviet Union

Communist Control Act (1954), 659

Communist Party, 589, 595, 635, 637, 643, 645, 646. *See also* American Communist Party

Communities: African American, 469; ethnic, 465–467

Communities Organized for Public Service (COPS), 735

Community Action Program (CAP), 687, 689

Community development corporations (CDCs), 747

Community Reinvestment Act (1977), 747

Company towns, 423, 448

Competition: corporate restraints on, 435–437; railroad pools and, 449

Compromise of 1877, 403–404

Computer revolution, 749

Computers: business operations and, 750; financial industry and, 752–753; Silicon Valley and, 743. *See also* High-tech industries; Internet

Comstock Law (1872), 444

Concentration camps: Cubans in, 508; Filipinos in, 513

Concentration policy, Indians and, 417

Coney Island, 469, 470

Coney Island (movie), 471

Confederacy (Civil War): Indians and, 418. *See also* Civil War (U.S.)

Confederate States of America. *See* Confederacy

Conference of Catholic Bishops, 762

Conformity, in 1950s, 665–666

Congress (U.S.): ex-Confederates in, 388, 391; Johnson, Andrew, and, 392, 393; war power of, 637

Congressional Black Caucus, 733

Congressional Reconstruction, 391–393

Congress of Industrial Organizations (CIO), 594, 621, 642, 663

Congress on Racial Equality (CORE), 626, 679

Conscience of a Conservative, The (Goldwater), 668

Consciousness-raising, by women, 729

Conscription. *See* Draft (military)

Conservation, 496

Conservatism: 2001–2008, 773–774; cultural, 482–483; FOX News and, 759; immigrants and, 473–474; IRS and, 718; new conservatism and, 667–668, 673, 688–689, 690; New Right on, 721. *See also* New Right

Consolidation, corporate, 435–437

Conspicuous consumption, 440

Constitution(s): during Reconstruction, 388, 393, 394; Southern, disfranchising blacks, 426

Constitution (U.S.), national security and, 647

Consumer goods, 439; economic growth and, 662; in Second World War, 622

Consumers and consumerism: consumer culture and, 439–440; counterculture and, 695–696

Consumer society, in 1920s, 552–553

Consumption: conspicuous, 440; culture of, 439–440, 444

Containment, 653, 681; Eisenhower and, 657, 658–660; Korea and, 641–642; Truman Doctrine and, 634–635; use of term, 635

Contraception. *See* Birth control

Contracts: government, 395; labor, 390; "yellow dog," 557

Contract with America, 768

Contras (Nicaragua), 724, 725

Conventions, state, during Reconstruction, 388, 394

Cooke, Jay, 400, 435

Coolidge, Calvin, 545, 556, 560, 562, 579

Cooperation, Hoover and, 561

Cooperatives: of farmers, 449, 450; of workers, 446

Cooper v. Aaron, 677

Copper, 411

Coral Sea, Battle of the, 614

CORE. *See* Congress on Racial Equality

Corporations: campaign contributions by, 487; consolidation of, 435–437; culture and, 439–441; government support for, 435; in Great Depression, 593; growth of, 434–435; management revolution and, 437–438; multinational, 506; power of, 429; progressivism and, 496; in Second World War, 620; trusts and, 436; white-collar workers for, 440. *See also* Business

Corregidor, 614

Corruption: Homestead Act and, 409; organized crime and, 467; political machines and, 466–467; Republicans and, 400

Cortes, Ernesto, Jr., 735

Cosmopolitanism, of Bourne, 475

Costa Rica, United Fruit in, 523

Cotton and cotton industry, 448; labor for, 423; production of, 424; in South, 424. *See also* Textiles and textile industry

Coughlin, Charles (Father), 588

Council of Economic Advisers, 648
Counterculture, 695–696, 698
Counterinsurgency tactics, in Vietnam, 671
Countervailing power, 664–665
Country music, in 1920s, 555
Court(s): on affirmative action quotas, 737; political-cultural issues and, 775–776; television coverage of, 769–770
Court-packing plan, of Roosevelt, Franklin D., 600
Covenant, of League of Nations, 541
Covert actions, 636, 639, 659–660, 661, 692, 707, 723–724
Cowboys: blacks as, 414; on cattle drives, 412; Mexican Americans as, 414
Cox, Archibald, 709
Cox, James M., 559
Coxey, Jacob, 448
"Coxey's army," 448
Craft unions, 445, 447
Craft workers, in AFL, 447
Crazy Horse, 419
Credit: availability of, 720; contraction in, 785; crop lien system and, 424; farmers', 424, 501; farmers, price deflation, and, 449; Hispanic farmers and, 411
Credit cards, 752–753, 788
Credit Mobilier affair, 395
Creek Indians, 418
Creel, George, 537
CREEP (Committee to Re-elect the President), 708
"Creole Rhapsody" (Ellington), 597
Crime and criminals: organized, 467, 671; during Prohibition, 563
Crimes against humanity: by Nazis, 613. See also Human rights
Cripple Creek, Colorado, mining strike at, 412
Crisis, The, 493
Croatia and Croatian people, 461, 528, 725
Croix de Guerre, for 369th Regiment, 536, 537
Croly, Jane ("Jenny June"), 442
Cronkite, Walter, 699
Crop lien system, 424
"Cross of Gold" speech (Bryan), 451

Cuba, 520; Batista in, 660; Guantanamo facility in, 781; Kennedy, John F., and, 670–671; Roosevelt, Franklin D., and, 599; Soviets and, 725; Spain and, 508; Spanish-American War and, 509–511, 510 (map); subordination to U.S., 514–515
Cuban Americans, 736, 745
Cuban Missile Crisis, 671, 683
Cuen, Rafael, 414, 415
Cultural pluralism, 474–475; Indians and, 598
Cultural pride movement, American Indian, 734
Culture: in 1950s, 665–667; aesthetic disputes over, 759; African American, 569–571; class distinctions in, 441; commercial, 456, 469–472; consumer, 439–440; Great Depression crisis in, 580–581; Indians and, 420–422; labor in, 594–595; mass, 667; media and, 755–763; melting pot and, 474; Mexican American, 415, 572; New Woman in, 443, 444; popular, 444, 759; of poverty, 669; religion and, 759–763; after Second World War, 650–653; social issues, politics, and, 775–776; of Swedish immigrants, 416–417; television, 667; youth, 666. See also Art and artists; Society; specific issues

cummings, e. e., 572
Currency. See Money
Curriculum, Afro-centric, 733
Custer, George A., 419
Czechoslovakia, 607

D

Daily Show, The (TV program), 759
Dakota country, Sioux reservation in, 419
Dams: TVA and, 586, 586 (map); in West, 587–588, 587 (map), 663
Dance halls, 456, 469
Danish West Indies. See Virgin Islands
Darrow, Clarence, 566–567
Darwin, Charles, 440; evolution and, 566
Daughters of Bilitis, 645

Daughters of the American Revolution, 596
Davis, Henry Winter, 387
Davis, John W., 560
Dawes Plan (1924), 561
Dawes Severalty Act (1887), 420, 598
Dayton, city manager plan in, 486
Dayton Peace Accords (1995), 776
D-Day, 611
DDT, 702–703
Dean, John, 709
Death camps, of Nazi Germany, 609
Death rates: for New York City residents (1925), 569 (table)
Debates, Kennedy-Nixon, 669
Debs, Eugene Victor, 448, 484, 485, 540; 1912 election and, 483, 499, 499 (map), 500; 1920 election and, 546
Debt: of farmers, 416, 424; in Mexico, 777. See also National debt
Deep South, 670, 680, 701. See also Slavery; South
Defense Department, 635, 642, 661
Defense industries, 668
Defense spending, 642, 648, 659, 661, 668, 670
Deficit: under Bush, George W., 774; Great Society and, 689; household, 752; Reagan and, 719
Deficit spending, 670
Deflation, 449, 453
Deforestation, 777
DeLay, Tom, 774
De Lôme, Enrique, 508
DeMille, Agnes, 413
Democracy, in 1920s, 573
Democratic Party: 1876 election and, 403–404; 1924 convention of, 568; 1964 convention of, 688; 1968 convention of, 700–701; in 1980s, 721; in 1990s, 768; African Americans in, 675; ethnic voters in, 596; Great Depression coalition in, 592–593; Jackson, Jesse, and, 733; Johnson, Andrew, and, 389, 395; Mississippi Plan and, 401–402; political stalemate and, 427–428; Populists and, 451; Roosevelt, Franklin D., and, 582; in South, 398, 400; urban-ethnic delegates in 1924,

568; white-only primaries of, 426. *See also* Elections; Politics

Demography: shift in, 742–743; urban-suburban, 747–748. *See also* Population; Race and racism; Religion

Demonstrations. *See* Protest(s)

Dempsey, Jack, 556

Dennis v. United States, 646

Denominations (religious). *See* Religion; specific groups

Department stores, 439

Deportation, of immigrants, 463–464, 679

Depressions (financial): of 1873–1878, 400, 433, 445; of 1893–1897, 436, 447, 453; agricultural in 1920s, 562. *See also* Great Depression; Panics (financial)

Deregulation: Carter and, 714, 715; of financial industry, 753, 784; investment risk and, 784–785; Reagan and, 720

Derivatives, 753, 784

Desegregation: of armed forces, 511, 650; of baseball, 650–651; of schools, 674, 679. *See also* Integration

Desertification, 777

Desert Shield, Operation, 727

Destination Tokyo (movie), 622

Destroyers-for-bases deal, 608

Détente policy, 705–706

Detroit, race riot in (1943), 624

Dewey, George, in Philippines, 509

Dewey, John, 573

Dewey, Thomas E., 617, 636

Diaz, Porfirio, 524

Dickens, Charles, 442

Dictators and dictatorships: Carter and, 716; in Latin America, 519, 660; in Third World, 660

Diem, Ngo Dinh, 661, 671, 672, 681, 691

Dien Bien Phu, battle at, 661

Dime novels, 422, 441, 470

Diphtheria, 465

Diplomacy: atomic, 634; with China, 516–518, 716; Nixon and, 706; Roosevelt, Theodore, and, 521–522; of Taft, 522–523. *See also* Foreign policy

Direct election of senators, 450, 487

Direct primary, 487

Disarmament, First World War and, 532

Discrimination: affirmative action and, 737; against African Americans, 468–469, 650, 689; ban on, in hiring, 620; Chinese immigrants and, 410–411; in employment, 677; gender, 674; against Indians, 678; against Mexican Americans, 414, 678; NAACP fight against, 569; in New Deal, 596–598; in public transportation and accommodations, 402; against Puerto Ricans, 678. *See also* Race and racism

Diseases: in cities, 465; flu epidemic after First World War and, 534; in Spanish-American War, 509, 511. *See also* Epidemics; Health and health care; Medicine

Disfranchisement: of blacks, 426, 488; of noncitizen immigrants, 488; progressives and, 487, 488

Disneyland, 744

Dissent and dissenters: student, 695. *See also* Protest(s)

Distribution of wealth. *See* Wealth and wealthy

District of Columbia, 674. *See also* Washington, D.C.

Diversity, in cities, 456

Dixiecrats, 636, 637, 647, 650, 654

DJs, 760

Doak, William N., 597

Doby, Larry, 651

Doctors. *See* Medicine

Dodge City, 412

Dollar, floating, 705

Dollar diplomacy, of Taft, 522–523

Domestic policy. *See* specific presidents

Domestic service, 424

Domestic surveillance, 659

Dominican Republic: immigrants from, 736; intervention in, 519, 523, 562

Domino theory, 661, 692

Dos Passos, John, 572

Dot-com businesses, 751

Do the Right Thing (movie), 733

Double V campaign, 625

Doughboys, 533

Douglass, Frederick, on Supreme Court and civil rights, 402

Dow Jones, plummet in, 786

Downsizing, 751

Draft (military), 717; First World War and, 534; resistance in Vietnam War, 698; Second World War and, 607

Drama. *See* Theater

Dresden, bombings of, 618

Drinan, Robert F., 762

Drudge Report, The, 772

Drugs: American Indians and, 734; for sports figures, 755

Drunkenness, 473. *See also* Alcohol and alcoholism; Temperance

Du Bois, W. E. B., 427, 493, 547, 645

Duck Soup (movie), 581

Dukakis, Michael, 723

Duke, James Buchanan, 436, 437

Dulles, Allen, 660

Dulles, John Foster, 659

Dumbarton Oaks Conference (1944), 627

DuPont Corporation, 434

Durable goods, for consumers, 552

Dust Bowl, 413, 584

Dylan, Bob, 696

E

Eakins, Thomas, 441

Earhart, Amelia, 558

Earned Income Tax Credit (EITC), 768

Earth Day (1970), 703

Earth Summit, 777

East Asia: Roosevelt, Theodore, and, 521–522. *See also* Asia

East Asian Co-Prosperity Sphere, 607, 610

Eastern Europe: Cold War and, 634, 725, 727 (*map*); immigrants from, 461, 565; after Second World War, 628; Soviet Union and, 634

Easter Offensive (Vietnam War), 707

East Germany, 636, 671; fall of communism in, 725

Eastman, Crystal, 473

Eastman, Max, 473

Eastman Kodak, 506

Ebony magazine, 673

Ecology. *See* Environment

E-commerce, 751

Economic and Social Council, 627

Economic inequality, 669

Economic Opportunity Act (1964), 687

Economics, policy toward Third World, 660

Economy: in 1950s, 662–663; in 1990s, 728, 768–769; 1993–2008, 783–786; auto manufacturing and, 437; boom-and-bust cycles in, 432; business operations and, 750–752; finances and, 752–753; First World War and, 534, 535–537; after First World War, 548; globalization of, 751; government and, 495, 536–537, 619, 648; in Great Depression, 582, 584; growth of, 433–434; New Right on, 737–738; scandals in, 784–785; in South, 389, 423; technology and, 749–750; Vietnam War and, 689. *See also* Great Depression; Panics (financial); Trade

Edge cities, 747

Edison, Thomas A., 434

Education: Afro-centric, 733; bilingual, 702; for freedpeople, 390–391; of Indians, 420–422; of managers, 438; national security and, 668; No Child Left Behind program and, 774; segregation in, 450, 674; for women, 444, 482 *(table)*. *See also* Higher education; Public schools; Schools; Teachers

EEOC. *See* Equal Employment Opportunity Commission

Egypt, 424, 705; Camp David Accords and, 715–716; Nasser in, 660

Eighteenth Amendment, 483, 539, 563

Eight-hour day, 445, 446, 501

Einstein, Albert, 617

Eisenhower, Dwight D.: 1952 election and, 654, 654 *(map)*; civil rights and, 674, 677; farewell address of, 661–662; Korea and, 658; modern Republicanism of, 667, 668; and national security, 658–659, 668; new conservatism and, 667–668; in Second World War, 611; Third World and, 660–661; Vietnam and, 661

Eisenhower Doctrine, 660–661

Elections: of 1866, 392; of 1867, 393; of 1868, 395; of 1872, 398–400; of 1874, 400; of 1875, 401–402;

of 1876, 403, 427; from 1876 through 1892, 427–428; of 1880, 428; of 1884, 427, 428; of 1888, 427, 429; of 1890, 429; of 1892, 427, 429, 450–451; of 1894, 451; of 1896, 451–452, 452 *(map)*; of 1900, 453; of 1904, 495; of 1908, 497; of 1910, 498; of 1912, 483, 498, 499–500, 499 *(map)*; of 1916, 532; of 1920, 559; of 1924, 560, 568; of 1928, 579; of 1932, 580, 581 *(map)*; of 1934, 589; of 1936, 592–593, 593 *(map)*; of 1940, 609; of 1942, 619; of 1944, 617; of 1946, 636; of 1948, 636–637, 637 *(map)*; of 1952, 653–654, 654 *(map)*; of 1956, 669; of 1958, 669; of 1960, 669–670, 670 *(map)*; of 1964, 688–689, 690; of 1966, 689; of 1968, 699, 700, 701, 701 *(map)*; of 1972, 708; of 1976, 713; of 1980, 718–719, 719 *(map)*; of 1982, 719; of 1984, 721; of 1988, 723; of 1992, 728–729, 729 *(map)*; of 1994, 768; of 1996, 769; of 2000, 772–773, 772 *(map)*; of 2002, 774; of 2004, 774; of 2008, 688, 786, 786 *(map)*, 787; of 2010, 788–790; of 2012, 790–792; fraud in, 467; of senators, 450, 487; voter participation in, 452, 488. *See also* Voting and voting rights

Electoral College, in 2000, 772–773

Electoral commission, in 1876 election, 403

Electorate, progressives and, 487, 488

Electric Auto-Lite plant, 589

Electricity: in Great Depression, 591; for urban transportation, 458

Electric light, 434

Electronic banking, 753

Elevator, 434, 457

Eliot, T. S., 572

Elites: industrial, 453; urban, 456, 458, 459; urban masses and, 476. *See also* Classes

Ellington, Duke, 468, 571; African-American rhapsody by, 597

Ellis Island, 463

Ellsberg, Daniel, 708

El Salvador, immigrants from, 745

Embargo: on Middle East oil, 705; before Second World War, 606, 609

Embassies, bombings of, 778

Emergency Economic Stabilization Act (2008), 786

Emergency Fleet Corporation, 534

Emergency Relief Appropriation Act (1935), 591

Emergency Unemployment Relief office, 578

Emigrants. *See* Immigrants and immigration; Migration

Emissions, pollution from, 777

Empire, of United States, 512–516, 512 *(map)*

Employment: in 1920s, 556; of African Americans, 623; discrimination in, 677; in Second World War, 620, 623; of women, 673, 730. *See also* Unemployment

Employment Act (1946), 648

Endangered Species Act (1973), 703

Energy: Bush, George W., and, 774; Carter and, 715; green, 783

Engineers, 440

Engines, 434

England (Britain): "Alabama Claims" and, 396; China and, 516; immigrants from, 461; Nazi raids on, 608; Suez crisis and, 660. *See also* First World War; Second World War

Enron, 784

Entertainment: in Great Depression, 581; sports-entertainment industry and, 753–755; Sun Belt production of, 743–744; Wild West Show as, 422–423; working class and commercial, 456, 469–472, 482

Entrepreneurs: blacks as, 469; immigrants as, 465–466

Environment: Bush, George W., and, 775; Clinton and, 777–778; conservationists and, 496; dangers to, 777; mining and, 411; Nixon and, 702–703; Reagan and, 720; regulation of, 495–496

Environmentalism, 695, 702–703

Environmental Protection Agency (EPA), 703

Epidemics. *See also* Diseases

Equal Employment Opportunity Commission (EEOC), 687

Equality: gender, 729–730; for men, 593; racial, 568–569; for women, 593, 731. *See also*

African Americans; Equal rights; Race and racism; Women

Equal Pay Act (1963), 674

Equal rights: Fourteenth Amendment and, 392. *See also* Equality

Equal Rights Amendment (ERA): in 1920s, 559; in 1970s, 703

Ervin, Sam, 709

Espionage. *See* Spies and spying

Espionage, Sabotage, and Sedition Acts (1917 and 1918), 540

ESPN, 754

Estonia: independence of, 725; after Second World War, 628

Ethical issues, genetic codes and, 749–750

Ethiopia, Italian invasion of, 606

Ethnic cleansing, 776

Ethnic groups, in former Yugoslavia, 725

Ethnicity: of Asian Americans, 736; communities based on, 465–467; enclaves of, 416; European American, 567–568; in First World War, 539; Mexican Americans and, 571–572; middle class groups and, 465–466; in New Deal, 596–598; of new immigrants, 461, 462 *(table)*; socialism and, 485. *See also* African Americans

Europe: after First World War, 541, 542 *(map)*; immigration and, 416–417, 460, 461–462; imperialism of, 507; League of Nations and, 544–545; NATO and, 637; Second World War and, 607–609, 608 *(map)*, 611–613. *See also* Colonies and colonization; First World War; Second World War

European American ethnics, 567–568

European Recovery Program. *See* Marshall Plan

Evangelicalism: in 1970s, 718; Sojourners and, 761. *See also* Religion

"Evil empire," Soviet Union as 723

Evolution, Darwin on, 440, 566

Evolutionary socialists, 485

Executive: emergency powers of, 647; increase in power of, 632, 634; national security and, 647, 659. *See also* President

Executive clemency, for Santee Sioux, 419

Executive Orders: 9835 (loyalty program), 635; 9981 (desegregation of military), 650; banning racial discrimination in federal housing, 680

Expansion: by Japan, 609–610; overseas, 504, 505–507; Soviet, 633, 634

Exports: in 1875 and 1915, 506 *(table)*; Nixon and, 705

Extermination campaign, in Second World War, 611

Exurbs, 747

F

Factories (industrial), 434, 445

Factory law, in Illinois, 482

Fair Deal, of Truman, 648–649

Fair Employment Practices Commission (FEPC), 620

Fair Housing Act, 697. *See also* Civil Rights Act, of 1968

Fall, Albert, 560

Falwell, Jerry, 718, 761

Families: gender politics and, 672; as homesteaders, 416–417; immigration and, 461; low-income, 702; sharecropping and, 390; working-class, 464–465; working women and, 673. *See also* Marriage

Family Assistance Plan (FAP), 702

Family Guy (TV series), 757

Fanzines, 759

Farewell address, of Eisenhower, 661–662

Farewell to Arms, A (Hemingway), 572

Farmers' Alliance, 450. *See also* Populists

Farms and farming: in 1920s, 562–567; Alliance movement and, 450; cooperatives for, 449, 450; crop lien system and, 424; free silver movement and, 449, 453; grangers and, 412, 449, 450; in Great Depression, 592; Greenback Party and, 449; green revolution and, 749; Hispanic, 411; Hoover and, 561; immigrant labor for, 678; Japanese, 466; resistance to railroads and, 449; sharecropping and, 390, 424,

467; tenant farmers and, 467; in West, 412, 416. *See also* Agriculture

Farm Security Administration (FSA), 593, 619

Farm workers, Mexican, 571, 674, 678

Farragut, David G., 704

Farrell, James T., 580–581

Fascism: popular front against, 589; in Spain, 606. *See also* Hitler, Adolf; Italy; Mussolini, Benito; Nazi Germany

Fast-food industry, 750

Faubus, Orval, 677

Faulkner, William, 572–573

Federal Bureau of Investigation (FBI), 643, 645, 676, 679, 697, 701

Federal Communications Commission (FCC), 758

Federal Emergency Relief Administration (FERA), 584

Federal government. *See* Government (U.S.)

Federal Housing Administration (FHA), 651, 679

Federal marshals, 398

Federal Republic of Germany. *See* West Germany

Federal Reserve Act (1913), 500

Federal Reserve Board, 500, 714, 719; Great Depression and, 578; Greenspan and, 753

Federal Reserve System, 500–501

Federal Trade Commission (FTC), 501

Federal Trade Commission Act (1914), 501

Feminine Mystique, The (Friedan), 666, 674

Femininity, in Second World War, 623

Feminism, 730; in Great Depression, 593–594; radical, 695; use of term, 473. *See also* Abortion and abortion rights; Women; Women's rights

Feminization, of poverty, 730

Femme fatale, 653

FEPC. *See* Fair Employment Practices Commission

Ferraro, Geraldine, 721

Fiction. *See* Literature; Novels

Field, James G., 451

Fifteenth Amendment, 394, 396, 398, 402, 404, 488, 493

Filibuster, 1876 election and, 404

Filipino Americans, 592, 736

Filipino people, 461, 464, 513

Fillmore, Millard, 428

Film noir, 653

Films. *See* Movies and movie industry

Finances, 752–753; Clinton and, 769; deregulation of, 784; railroads and, 409, 435; regulation of, 753; in Second World War, 619–620. *See also* Economy; Panics (financial)

Financial institutions, 720. *See also* Banks and banking; Savings and loan institutions

Firebombing, of Japan, 615–616, 617

Fireside chats, of Roosevelt, Franklin D., 582, 583

First Amendment, 643; political expression and, 646; Religious Right on, 718; television and, 758

First New Deal (1933–1935), 582–588. *See also* Great Depression; New Deal

First World War, 527, 528–540; Allies in, 527, 528, 531, 533–534, 541; colonies after, 541; end of, 534; labor and, 539, 545; mobilization for, 529, 529 *(map)*, 534–540; neutrality in, 530–533; peace efforts and, 540–545; Russian exit from, 533; society after, 545–547; submarine warfare in, 531; United States and, 533–534; women in, 535–536, 538. *See also* Alliances; Wilson, Woodrow

Fiscal policy: in Great Depression, 590. *See also* Economy; Finances

Fish, Hamilton, 396

Fitzgerald, F. Scott, 551, 572

Five Civilized Tribes, 417

Five-Power Treaty, 561

Flappers, 554, 558

Flexible response, 670, 671–672, 681

Floating exchange rates, 705

Florida, 400; 2000 election and, 772–773; causeway to Key West, 585; Cubans in, 745; population growth in, 743

Flu epidemic, after First World War, 534

Flynn, Elizabeth Gurley, 473

Food(s): healthy, 441; rations in South, 390; regulation of, 495

Food Administration, 534

Food stamp program, 689, 720

Football, 441, 754

Foraker Act (1900), 515

Forbes, Charles R., 560

Ford, Betty, 718

Ford, Gerald R., 709, 713–714, 714 *(map)*; economy and, 714; foreign policy and, 715; Religious Right and, 718

Ford, Henry, 437, 492

Ford Motor Company, 437, 492, 552

Foreign Affairs (journal), 635

Foreign aid: Eisenhower and, 660; to Greece and Turkey, 634; Marshall Plan and, 636, 648

Foreign-born Americans. *See* Immigrants and immigration

Foreign Intelligence Surveillance Act (FISA, 1978), 781

Foreign investment, 506

Foreign Miners Tax (California, 1850), 410, 414

Foreign policy: containment and, 634–635; détente and, 705–706; Good Neighbor Policy and, 599; jingoist, 507; Open Door policy and, 517–519; Second World War and, 607–618; war on terrorism and, 774. *See also* Imperialism; specific presidents

Foreign trade. *See* Trade

Forests, 496; deforestation and, 777

Formosa. *See* Taiwan

Fortas, Abe, 703

Fort Orange. *See* Albany

"40 acres and a mule," 390

Fossil fuels: dependence on, 715; Reagan and, 720. *See also* Energy

442nd Regimental Combat Team, 627

"Four-Minute Men," 537

Fourteen Points, 533, 540, 541, 544 *(table)*

Fourteenth Amendment, 392, 393, 394, 398, 402, 404, 650

Fox News Channel (FNC), 759, 770

FOX TV network, 756

France: China and, 516; Indochina and, 641, 661; New York's 369th Regiment and, 536, 537;

Panama Canal and, 520; in Second World War, 607; Suez crisis and, 660. *See also* First World War; Second World War

Franchise (vote). *See* Disfranchisement; Voting and voting rights

Franchise businesses, 750–751

Franco, Francisco, 606, 607

Frankfurter, Felix, 573

Franz Ferdinand (Austria-Hungary), 528

Fraternal organizations, 425, 465

Free agency, in sports, 755

Freedmen's Bureau, 389–390, 391, 392

Freedom(s): of speech, 540. *See also* Rights

Freedom Democratic Party, 674

Freedom riders, 680

Freedom Singers, 674

Freedom Summer, in Mississippi, 688

Freedpeople, 386, 387, 389, 390–391

Free French, in Second World War, 611

Free labor, 432

Free markets, New Right radio on, 737

Free silver movement, 449, 453

Free Speech (newspaper), 425, 426

French Canadians, as immigrants, 461

French Indochina. *See* Indochina; Vietnam

Frick, Henry Clay, 447

Friedan, Betty, 666, 674

Friedman, Milton, 717

Frontier, Turner's thesis on, 429, 506

"Front-porch campaign," of McKinley 452

FTC. *See* Federal Trade Commission

Fugitive from a Chain Gang (movie), 581

Full employment, 648

Full Employment Bill (1946), 648

Fundamentalism and fundamentalists: in 1920s, 551, 565–566; Islamic, 717; New Right politics of, 761; Protestant, 565–566, 718; rural white Americans and, 562

Fusionism approach, 668

G

Gaither Report (1957), 668

Galbraith, John Kenneth, 662, 664

Galveston, city commission plan in, 486

Gambling, Indian operations of, 734, 735

Gangsters and gangsterism, 467

Garfield, James A., 428

Garment industry, 464, 465, 466

Garrison, Jim, 682

Garvey, Marcus, 547, 548

Gas and water socialists, 485

Gasoline. *See* Oil and oil industry

Gasoline engine. *See* Engines

Gates, Bill, 749

Gates, Henry Louis, Jr., 733

Gates, Robert, 783, 787

GATT. *See* General Agreement on Tariffs and Trade

Gay Activist Alliance (GAA), 732

Gays and lesbians: activism of, 645, 731–732; Lavender Scare and, 645; marriage by, 775. *See also* Homosexuality; Marriage; Same-sex relationships

Gay theology, 761

Geithner, Timothy, 788

Gender: equality of, 394, 473, 704; financial lending and, 652; New Women as threat to roles, 444; politics of, 672–674; in Second World War, 622–623; Western settlement and, 417; women's issues and, 729–730; workforce segregation by, 620. *See also* Men; Women

General Agreement on Tariffs and Trade (GATT), 628, 777

General Assembly (UN), 627

General Motors (GM), 595

General strikes, after Second World War, 642

Genetically modified (GM) foods, 750

Genetic code, 749

Genetics, ethical issues and, 749–750

Geneva, summit conference in (1955), 659

Geneva Medical College (New York), 444

Geneva Peace Accords (1954), 661

Genocide. *See* Holocaust; Rwanda

Gentility, 441

"Gentlemen's agreement" (1907), with Japan, 463, 522

Gentrification, of cities, 747

Geography: of cities, 456; population distribution by, 743

Geopolitics: of Cold War, 638 *(map)*; of Roosevelt, Theodore, 518–522

German Americans: in First World War, 538, 539; in Second World War, 624; *Turnevereins* of, 465

German Democratic Republic. *See* East Germany

German language, in First World War, 539 *(table)*

Germany: China and, 516; after First World War, 541, 542 *(map)*, 561; immigrants from, 416, 461; postwar zones in, 636; Second World War expansion by, 608 *(map)*; after Second World War, 628, 636; zones of occupation in, 628. *See also* East Germany; First World War; Nazi Germany; Second World War; West Germany

Gershwin, George, 468

Ghettos, Harlem as, 568

Ghost Dance, 422

Gibbs, Jonathan, 397

GI Bill (1944), 648–649

GI Bill of Rights (1952), 649

Gilded Age: literature of, 441; Twain and, 440

Gilded Age, The (Twain and Warner), 396

Gilman, Charlotte Perkins, 442

Gingrich, Newt, 689, 768

Ginsberg, Allen, 695

Ginsburg, Ruth Bader, 768

Gitmo. *See* Guantanamo Bay

Glasnost, 725

Globalization, 751; Clinton and, 777; of financial industry, 753

GNP. *See* Gross national product

"God Bless America" (Berlin), 595

Gold, 419, 453; in California, 411; free silver and, 449, 451; greenbacks and, 449

Gold bugs, 449

Gold Rush, in California, 409, 411

Gold standard, 449, 452, 705

Goldwater, Barry, 668, 677, 688–689, 717

Golf, 754

Gompers, Samuel F., 447, 513, 536, 546

Goodman, Andrew, 688

Good Neighbor Policy, 599

Google, 790

Gorbachev, Mikhail, 725

Gore, Albert, 768; 1992 election and, 729; 1996 election and, 769; 2000 election and, 772–773, 772 *(map)*; environment and, 783

Gorras Blancas, Las (the White Caps), 411

Gospel of wealth, of Carnegie, 453

Government(s): attitudes toward, 712; city commission plan and, 485; city manager plan of, 485, 486; Hoover and, 561; progressives on, 478

Government (U.S.): activism of, 668–669; Contract with America and, 768; economic role of, 495, 536–537, 619, 648; in Great Depression, 578; power in Second World War, 621–622; powers of, 710; Reagan on, 736–737; regulation by, 496; relationship with business, 435; trusts and, 436–437, 495

Governors: of Philippines, 513, 514; during Reconstruction, 388

Graft (payments), 466

Graham, Billy, 665, 763

Grain, 448. *See also* Wheat

Grand Coulee Dam, 587

Grandfather clauses, 426, 493

Grange and grangers, 412, 449, 450

Grant, Ulysses S., 401, 654; 1868 election and, 395; 1872 election and, 398–400; administration of, 395–396, 398, 401; civil service reform and, 396; corruption and, 395–396; foreign policy and, 396; Hamburg Massacre and, 403; peace policy toward Indians, 420

Grapes of Wrath, The (Steinbeck), 595

Grateful Dead, 696

Grazing lands, 411, 412, 496

Great Britain. *See* England (Britain)

Great Depression, 576; causes of, 577–579; First New Deal in (1933–1935), 582–588; legislation in "Hundred Days" (1933), 583 *(table)*. *See also* Depressions (financial); Wealth

Great Fear, communism and, 645–646

Great Gatsby, The (Fitzgerald), 572

Great Migration, of African Americans, 535
"Great Moderation, The," 783–784
Great Plains, 416, 584
Great Railroad Strike, 432, 433, 434, 445
Great Recession, 786
Great Society, 689–690, 702
Great War. See First World War
Great White Fleet, 522
Greece, 461, 628, 634
Greeley, Horace, 398–400
Greenback Party, 449
Greenbacks (currency), 449
Green Berets, 671
Green energy, 783
Green revolution, 749
Greenspan, Alan, 753, 769, 785
Greenwich Village, feminists in, 473
Gregory, Thomas, 540
Grey (Lord), 531
Griffith, D. W., 399, 564
Gross domestic product (GDP), health care and, 752
Gross national product (GNP), 648, 686; 1869–1873, 433; 1897–1901, 433; 1940–1945, 619; 1940–1970, 663 (table); in 1950s, 662
Guadalcanal, battle at, 614
Guam: in Second World War, 614; U.S. acquisition of, 511, 512
Guantanamo Bay, U.S. detention facility at, 781, 787
Guatemala, 660, 745
Guerrilla warfare, in Vietnam War, 691 (map)
Guest workers, 775
Guiteau, Charles, 428
Gulf of Tonkin Resolution, 690
Guthrie, Woody, 595
Gypsies, Nazi death camps and, 609, 611

H
Habeas corpus, writ of, 398
Hague convention, 777
Haight-Ashbury district, 695
Haiti, 386; Clinton and, 776; intervention in, 523, 562, 599
Halberstam, David, 694
Half-Breeds, 428
Hamburg Massacre, 403
Hamer, Fannie Lou, 674, 688
Hamilton, Alice, 481
Hampton, Fred, 701

Hampton Institute, 421
Hanna, Mark, 452
Harding, Warren G., 551, 559–560
Harlem, 568
Harlem Renaissance, 569–571
Harper's (magazine), 441, 480
Harrington, Michael, 669
Harrison, Benjamin, 429
Hassam, Childe, 441
Hastie, William, 596
Havana, 508
Hawaii: annexation and, 507, 512; Japanese Americans in, 624; Japanese immigrants to, 462; Pearl Harbor attack in, 609–610
Hawley, Ellis, 560
Hawley-Smoot Tariff (1930), 578
Hay, John, 509, 518
Hay-Bunau-Varilla Treaty (1903), 520
Hayes, Rutherford B., 403–404, 432, 445
Haymarket bombing, 446–447
Hay-Pauncefote Treaty (1901), 520
Haywood, William ("Big Bill"), 473
H-bomb. See Hydrogen bomb
Head Start Program, 689
Head tax, on Mexican immigrants, 565
Health, Education, and Welfare Department, 667
Health and health care: for children, 559; costs of, 752; Medicare, Medicaid, and, 689; Obama and, 788; public, 465. See also Diseases; Medicine
Hearst, William Randolph, 508
Hefner, Hugh, 673
Hellman, Lillian, 643
Hemingway, Ernest, 572, 645
Hepburn Act (1906), 495
Herberg, Will, 665, 760
Herblock, on HUAC, 644
Heritage Foundation, 717
Herran, Tomas, 520
Heterodoxy, 473
Hidden Persuaders, The (Packard), 665
Hierarchy. See Classes
"High" culture, 441
Higher education: for African Americans, 391; funding for, 668; for women, 444, 482 (table). See also Universities and colleges
High-tech industries, 743, 751
Highway Act (1956), 663

Highways. See Roads and highways
Hill, Anita, 730
Hillman, Sidney, 594–595
Hip-hop music, 760
Hippies, 695–696
Hiring, discrimination in, 677
Hiroshima, bombing of, 617, 618, 629
Hispanics, 734–735; in borderland communities, 411; homesteading and, 409; use of term, 734. See also Latinos; Spanish-speaking populations
Hiss, Alger, 643–644
Hitler, Adolf: appeasement of, 607; death camps of, 609; fascist regime of, 606; League of Nations and, 544; on national pride, 600; suicide of, 614. See also Holocaust; Jews and Judaism; Nazi Germany; Second World War
HIV-AIDS, 732
Hmong people, 736, 745
Ho Chi Minh, 641, 661, 671
Ho Chi Minh City, 715
Ho Chi Minh Trail, 691 (map), 693
Hoffman, Abbie, 698, 700
Holding Company Act (1935), 591
Holiday Inn, 750
Holly, Buddy, 666
Hollywood. See Movies and movie industry
Hollywood Ten, 643, 644
Holocaust, 611–614. See also Hitler, Adolf; Jews and Judaism; Nazi Germany
Home front: in Second World War, 619–627; during Vietnam War, 694–698
Homeland Security, Department of, 778, 781
Home loans, 753, 784–785
Homeowners' Loan Corporation (1933), 584
Homestead Act, 408–409, 417
Homesteading, in West, 409, 416–417
Homestead Strike, 447, 545
Homophile movement, 645
Homosexuality: activism and, 731–732; FBI dossiers on, 645; Nazi death camps and, 609, 611. See also Gays and lesbians
Honduras, 523

Hoover, Herbert, 579–580; 1928 election and, 568, 568 (map), 579; 1932 election and, 580, 581 (map); in Food Administration, 534; in Harding cabinet, 560

Hoover, J. Edgar, 644, 645, 701; Black Panthers and, 697; King and, 676

Hoover Dam. See Boulder Dam

Hoover-Stimson Doctrine (1931), 606

Hoovervilles, 576

Hostage crisis (Iran, 1979), 716–717, 724

House, Edward M., 531

House-Grey memorandum (1916), 531

Households: after 1970s, 742; financial deficit in, 752

House of Representatives. See Congress (U.S.)

House Un-American Activities Committee (HUAC), 643, 644

Housing: bubble in, 785–786; discrimination in, 650, 652, 677, 697; housing projects and, 679; individual ownership of, 784; mortgage financing for, 465, 651–652; redlining in, 679; soddies, 416; suburban, 651–652; in urban and suburban areas, 747; of working class, 465

Housing Act (1949), 649

Howells, William Dean, 441

Howl (Ginsberg), 695

How the Other Half Lives (Riis), 481

HUAC. See House Un-American Activities Committee

Huerta, Dolores, 735

Huerta, Victoriano, 524

Hughes, Charles Evans, 561

Hughes, Langston, 569

Huk rebels (Philippines), 641

Hull, Charles J., 481

Hull House, 481, 482

"Human Be-In," 696

Human Genome Project, 749

Human immunodeficiency virus (HIV). See HIV-AIDS

Human rights: Carter and, 716; Milosevic and, 776

Humphrey, Hubert H., 669, 699, 700, 701, 701 (map)

Hundred Days, legislation in (1933), 582, 583 (table)

Hungary, 461, 659

Hunter, Robert, 465

Hunting, 415, 419

Hurricane Katrina (2005), 781, 782

Hurston, Zora Neale, 571

Husbands. See Families; Men

Hussein (Jordan), 661

Hussein, Saddam, 724, 726–728, 778, 779, 780, 781

Hydraulic mining, 411

Hydrogen bomb, 638

Hypercommercialism, 755

I

ICBMs. See Intercontinental ballistic missiles

Idaho, woman suffrage in, 488–490

"I Have a Dream" speech (King), 681

Illegal immigrants, 597–598; Asians as, 463; from Mexico, 679

Illiteracy: black, 391, 397. See also Literacy

IMF. See International Monetary Fund

Immigrants and immigration, 454, 456, 460–465, 775; in 1930s, 596; from Asia, 410–411, 466; Catholicism of, 461; Chinese, 565; communities of, 465–467; conservatives' views of, 473–474; Cuban, 736; disfranchisement of, 488; from Eastern Europe, 565; as homesteaders, 409, 416–417; institutions of, 465; international events and, 745; Japanese, 565; labor of, 441, 464–465; living conditions of, 465; McCarran-Walter Act and, 644; melting pot, cultural pluralism, and cosmopolitanism and, 474–475; from Mexico, 597–598, 678–679; "national origins" system for, 689; new, 461, 744–746; old, 461; political machines and, 467; population of, 460, 461, 461 (table); prohibition movement and, 483; quotas on, 564–565, 565 (table), 609; rate of return to countries of origin, 461–462; reading test for, 539; reasons for, 461–462, 462–463; religion and, 761; restrictions on, 410–411, 462, 463, 564–565; rural white Americans and,

562; socialism and, 485; sources of, 462 (table); Spanish-speaking, 736; voting rights and, 488; in West, 462–463. See also Migration

Immigration Act (1990), 746

Immigration and Nationality Act (1965), 689, 745

Immigration Reform and Control Act (Simpson-Mazzoli Act, 1986), 746

Immigration Restriction Act: of 1917, 539, 540; of 1924 (Johnson-Reed Act), 564, 565 (table)

Impeachment: of Clinton, 770; of Johnson, Andrew, 393; of Nixon, 709

Imperialism, 504, 517; overseas economic expansion and, 506–507; U.S. acquisitions and, 512. See also Empire(s)

Income: distribution of, 579 (table), 769; federal supplements to, 702; per capita rural (1920s), 562; wealth gap and, 748. See also Wages; Wealth and wealthy

Income tax, 450

Independence, for Cuba, 508, 514

Independent films, 757

India, 424

Indiana, 427–428

Indianapolis 500, 754

Indian Bill of Rights, 734

Indian Gaming Regulatory Act (1988), 734

Indian policy: concentration policy, 417; peace policy, 420; reservation, 418, 418 (map), 419; Termination and Relocation programs, 677–678. See also American Indians

Indian Reorganization Act (IRA, 1934), 598

Indians. See American Indians specific groups

Indian Territory, 412; five civilized tribes in, 418; land opened to white settlement in, 420

Indochina, 610, 641, 661. See also Cambodia; Laos; Vietnam; Vietnam War

Indonesia, 610

Industrial accidents, 411, 445, 464

Industrial democracy, labor movement and, 536

Industrialists, philanthropy by, 453 (*table*)

Industrialization. *See* Industry and industrialization

Industrial Relations Commission (U.S.), 491–492

Industrial Workers of the World (IWW), 473, 485; First World War and, 540

Industry and industrialization: in 1900–1920, 438 (*map*); in 1920s, 553; African American migration to, 467; electric-powered, 434; First World War and, 534; immigrants and, 464; railroads and, 409; of ranching, 414; in Second World War, 619; in South, 423–427, 467–468; in West, 408–417; workers in, 444–448, 557

Inflation: in 1975, 714; Nixon and, 705; Reagan and, 719. *See also* Economy

Influence of Sea Power upon History, The (Mahan), 506–507

Information revolution, 749

Infotainment, 759

Infrastructure, in Great Depression, 585

"In God We Trust," as national motto 665

Initiative, 487

Injunctions, strikes and, 447, 448

Inner cities, African Americans in, 720

Installment purchasing, 553

Institutions: black, 425–426, 469; ethnic, 465

Insurance companies: national health care and, 649; in Second World War, 621–622

Integration: in South, 680. *See also* African Americans; Desegregation; Segregation

Intellectual thought: on American nationality, 473–475; FBI dossiers and, 645; "Lost Generation" and, 572–573; new conservatism and, 668; realism and, 480; Social Darwinism and, 440. *See also* Art and artists; Literature

Intercontinental ballistic missiles (ICBMs), 705

Interest-group pluralism, 664

Interior Department, 496

International Harvester factory, 434, 506

International Monetary Fund (IMF), 628

International organizations: after Second World War, 627–628; World Bank and, 628; World Trade Organization as, 777. *See also* League of Nations

International relations: in 1920s, 561–562; trade and, 599–600. *See also* Treaties

International trade. *See* Trade

Internet, 759; political sites on, 772; social networking sites and, 790

Internment, of Japanese Americans, 624–625, 736

Interstate Commerce Act (1887), 449

Interstate Commerce Commission (ICC), 449, 495

Interstate highways, 662

Inventions and inventors, economic growth and, 434

Investment: borrowing for, 784; derivatives as, 753; foreign, 506; in Germany, 561; U.S. global and Latin American (1914), 523 (*table*)

Investment firms, 753, 784

Iran: Carter and, 716; CIA and coup in, 660; hostage crisis in, 716–717, 724; U.S. arms sales to, 724; violence by, 724

Iran-*Contra* Affair, 724–725

Iranian Revolution (1979), 716

Iraq: Bush, George W., and, 779–780; Hussein in, 724; Persian Gulf War and, 726–728; weapons in, 778

Iraqi Freedom, Operation, 780

Iraq war, unilateralism and, 778–781

Ireland: immigrants from, 462. *See also* Irish Americans

Irish Americans, 409; Clan Na Gael and, 465. *See also* Ireland

Iron and iron industry, in South, 423

Irreconcilables, 542

Irrigation, in West, 587, 587 (*map*), 663

Irving, Julius ("Dr. J."), 754

Islam, 761; fundamentalist, 717, 723. *See also* Muslims

Islamic Centers: of America (Dearborn, Michigan), 762; of Southern California, 761

Isolationism, Second World War and, 604, 609

Israel, 705; Camp David Accords and, 715–716; Middle East conflict and, 660, 705

Issei, 624

Isthmus of Panama. *See* Panama

Italian Americans, in Second World War, 624

Italians, Sacco, Vanzetti, and, 567

Italy: as Axis power, 610; after First World War, 541, 542 (*map*); immigrants from, 461, 462; Second World War and, 606, 611. *See also* First World War

Itinerant laborers, 415–416

Iwo Jima, battle at, 615

IWW. *See* Industrial Workers of the World

J

Jackson, George, 701

Jackson, Helen Hunt, 420

Jackson, Jesse, 733, 762

Jackson, Michael, 758

Jackson State College, killings at, 706

Japan: aggression by, 606, 607, 609–610; atomic bombings of, 617, 618; as Axis power, 610; brutality by, 614; China and, 516, 607; after First World War, 541; gentlemen's agreement with, 522; immigrants from, 461, 462–463, 466, 565; Korea and, 639; occupation of, 629; Pearl Harbor attack by, 609–610; in Second World War, 614, 615–616; treaty with, 641; war with Russia, 521

Japanese Americans, 522, 736; in agriculture, 466; internment of, 624–625, 736; in military, 627

Jazz (music), 569–571

"Jazz Age," 551

Jazz Singer, The (movie), 570

Jefferson Airplane, 696

Jesus People, 760

Jewish Chaplain's Organization, 665

Jews and Judaism: Holocaust and, 611–614; immigration and, 461, 609; Nazi Germany and, 606; Nazi thefts from, 613; as neoconservatives, 717; Protestants and, 563, 564; Roosevelt, Franklin D., and,

593, 596; Soviet Jewish immigrants and, 745; on Supreme Court, 501; tailoring and, 466; Zionism after Second World War, 629. *See also* Anti-Semitism; Religion

JFK (movie), 682

Jiang Jieshi, 614, 637, 638

Jim Crow laws, 426, 468

Jingoism, 507, 508

Job Corps, 687

Job creation, in Second World War, 619

Jobs: civil service, 428. *See also* Employment

Jobs, Steve, 749

Johnson, Andrew, 387–388, 395, 428; Congress and, 392; Fourteenth Amendment and, 392; impeachment of, 393; Reconstruction policy of, 388

Johnson, Hiram W., 498

Johnson, Lyndon B.: 1960 election and, 669, 670; 1964 election and, 688–689, 690; 1968 election and, 699; civil rights and, 677, 688, 696–697; economy and, 686; Great Society and, 689–690; New Frontier and, 686–688; as president, 681, 685, 687; Vietnam War and, 690–694, 699

Johnson, Tom, 485

Johnson County War, 412

Johnson-O'Malley Act (1934), 598

Johnson-Reed Act (1924), 564, 565 *(table)*

Joint Chiefs of Staff, in Second World War, 610, 615

Jolson, Al, 570

Jones, Paula Corbin, 770

Joplin, Scott, 468

Jordan, 661

Jordan, Michael, 754

Joseph (Chief), 410

Journalism: muckrakers in, 480; New Journalism and, 698; online, 790; women in, 442, 453, 558; yellow journalism and, 508

Judeo-Christian tradition, 665

Jungle, The (Sinclair), 483

Just Cause, Operation, 726

Justice Department, 650

K

Kagan, Elena, 788

Kaiser Corporation, 620

Kallen, Horace, 474–475

Kansas, 412, 424, 490

Kansas Pacific Railroad, 412

Kansas Territory, policy for Indians in, 417

Katrina (Hurricane), 781, 782

Kazan, Elia, 643

Keating-Owen Act, 501

Keaton, Buster, 471, 472

Kelley, Florence, 481, 482

Kellogg, Frank, 561

Kellogg-Briand Pact (1928), 561–562, 606

Kennan, George, 635

Kennedy, Edward (Ted), 717, 774

Kennedy, Jacqueline Bouvier, 669, 670

Kennedy, John F., 657; 1960 election and, 669–670, 670 *(map)*; assassination of, 681; Berlin and, 671; civil rights and, 669, 680, 681; domestic policy of, 672; foreign policy of, 670–672; space exploration and, 743; Vietnam and, 671–672, 681; women's issues and, 674

Kennedy, Robert F., 699, 700

Kent State University, killings at, 706

Kenya, embassy bombing in, 778

Kern-McGillicuddy Act, 501

Kerouac, Jack, 695

Kerry, John, 774

Kettle Hill, battle at, 511

Key, David, 404

Keynes, John Maynard, 648; and Keynesianism, 590

Khmer Rouge, 706, 715

Khrushchev, Nikita, 659, 671

Kim Il-sung, 639, 640

King, Martin Luther, Jr., 676, 696, 697; assassination of, 699–700; FBI and, 676; "I Have a Dream" speech of, 681; Kennedy, John F., and, 669; Vietnam War and, 698

Kinsey, Alfred, 645

Kinsey Report, 645

Kirkpatrick, Jeane, 717

Kissinger, Henry, 705, 706, 707

Knights of Labor, 445–446, 446–447, 450

Knights of the White Camelia, 398

Knox, Philander C., 522, 523

Kodak camera, 434. *See also* Eastman Kodak

Korea, 521; containment and, 641–642; division of, 629; Japan and, 521, 639; zones of occupation in, 639. *See also* Korean War

Korean War, 639–641, 640 *(map)*, 649, 654, 658, 661

Korematsu v. United States 624–625, 626

Kosovo, 776

Kristol, Irving, 717

Ku Klux Klan, 399, 676; in 1920s, 547, 564; rural white Americans and, 562; terrorism by, 394, 395, 398, 697

Ku Klux Klan Act (1871), 398

Kurds, 728, 780

Kuwait, Persian Gulf War and, 726, 727

Kyoto convention, 777

Kyoto Protocol, Bush, George W., and, 783

L

Labor: in 1920s, 557; of African Americans, 467–468; agricultural, 440; capital conflicts with, 432, 445, 456, 545; after Civil War, 389; in First World War, 535, 539; during Great Depression, 588–589, 594–595; immigrant, 441, 464–465; itinerant, 415–416; management accord with, 438, 663; Mexican, 565, 571–572; in New Deal, 588–589, 594–595; for railroads, 409, 410; rights of, 491; scientific management and, 438; seasonal, 416; in Second World War, 621; for southern industries, 423; structural changes in, 751–752; of women, 559. *See also* Labor unions; Management; Strikes; Workers

Labor Department, 593

Labor force. *See* Workforce

Labor-Management Relations Act. *See* Taft-Hartley Act

Labor movement: anticommunism and, 642; in Great Depression, 594–595. *See also* Labor unions

Labor Reform Party, 445

Labor's Non-Partisan League (LNPL), 595

Labor strikes. *See* Strikes

Labor unions: in 1920s, 557; in 1950s, 663; African Americans and, 447; anticommunism and,

642; Brotherhood of Sleeping Car Porters, 569; economic changes and, 751, 752; ethnic groups in, 596; in First World War, 531; in Great Depression, 589; growth of, 445–446, 447; immigrants and, 464; membership in (1933–1945), 595 (table); in mining, 412; NLRB and, 590–591; Reagan and, 720; in Second World War, 621; women in, 447; workers and, 445. See also Trade unions

Ladies' Home Journal, 439, 480

La Follette, Philip, 589

La Follette, Robert, 490–492, 496, 589

Laissez-faire, Coolidge's politics and, 560

Land: black ownership of, 424; conservation and, 496; for cotton vs. land for food crops, 424; federal protection of, 777; for freedpeople, 387, 390; Homestead Act and, 408–409; Indians and, 417, 420, 598, 678; Mexican Americans' loss of, 414–415; sagebrush rebellion and, 720; in South, 389, 424

Landon, Alf, 592, 593 (map)

Language(s): American Indian, 734; German in First World War, 539 (table); in Los Angeles, 745

Laos, 661, 706; immigrants from, 745

Las Vegas, 744

Lathrop, Julia, 481, 482

Latin America, 658, 671; direct military aid to, 641; Eisenhower and, 660; Good Neighbor Policy and, 599; immigrants from, after 1970, 744; Kennedy, John F., and, 670; Roosevelt, Theodore, and, 519–520, 520–521; United States in (1895–1934), 519 (map); Wilson and, 523–524. See also Central America; specific locations

Latinos: in California, 626–627; as movie directors, 757; in sports, 651; use of term, 734. See also Spanish-speaking populations

Latvia: independence of, 725; after Second World War, 628

Lavender Scare, 645, 646

Law: antitrust, 436; consumer and environmental protection, 703; Granger, 449. See also specific acts

Lawyers, women as, 442

League of Nations, 541, 543; Japanese aggression and, 606; Second World War and, 627; trusteeships of, 541; Wilson and, 532, 543. See also Versailles Treaty

League of United Latin American Citizens (LULAC), 627, 679

League of Women Voters, 559

Lease, Mary, 451

Lebanon, 661

Lee, Spike, 733

Left Behind series, 763

Left wing (political), 701. See also Communism; New Left; Socialists and socialism

Legal Redress Committee (NAACP), 493

Legal system. See Law; Supreme Court

Legislation: in Great Depression, 583 (table), 590–591; regulating women's labor, 559. See also Law; specific acts

Leisure, for workers, 456

LeMay, Curtis, 616

Lend-Lease Act, 609

Lend-lease assistance, to Soviets, 634

Lenin, Vladimir, 533

Lesbian-Gay-Bisexual-Transgendered (LGBT) movement, 731–732, 761

Lesbians. See Gays and lesbians; Homosexuality

Levitt, William, 652

Levittown, New York, 651, 652

Lewinsky, Monica, 770

Lewis, John L. (UMW), 594–595

LGBT movement. See Lesbian-Gay-Bisexual-Transgendered movement

Libbey, Laura Jane, 470

Liberal Protestants, 566

Liberal Republicans, 398

Liberals and liberalism: in New Deal, 582; Republicans on, 721

Liberty(ies). See also Rights; specific rights and liberties

Liberty Bonds, for First World War, 536–537

Libraries, Carnegie-funded, 453

Libya, 724

Life expectancy, of Indians, 678

Lifestyle: of counterculture, 695–696; of homesteaders, 416–417; in late 20th century, 741; of workers, 465, 466

Lighting, electric, 434

Liliuokalani (Hawaii), 507

Limbaugh, Rush, 737

Limited war: Korean War as, 641; Vietnam War as, 692

Lincoln, Abraham: and executive clemency for Santee Sioux, 419; Gettysburg Address of, 385; Wartime Reconstruction and, 386–387

Lindbergh, Charles A., 556

LinkedIn, 790

Lippmann, Walter, 573

Liquor. See Alcohol and alcoholism

"Liquor trust," 480

Literacy, voting and, 426, 488, 493

Literature: in 1920s, 572–573; in 1950s, 665–666; of Beats, 695; parenting, 672, 673; on plantation South, 425; popular, 470; realism in, 441; sentimental, 441; on working women, 442, 470. See also Novels; specific works and writers

Lithography, 439

Lithuania, 461; independence of, 725; after Second World War, 628

Little Bighorn, Battle of, 419

Little Caesar (movie), 581

Little Crow (chief), 418

"Little Richard," 666

Little Rock, school desegregation in, 677

Livestock, 411

Lloyd George, David, 543

Loans: defaults on, 753, 785; in First World War, 531; home, 753, 784–785; reconstruction, after World War II, 634; small business, 702

Loan sharks, 752

Lobbyists: financial contributions from, 774; restrictions on, 487

Lochner v. New York, 447

Locke, Alain, 474, 569

Lockouts, 447

Lodge, Henry Cabot, 543

Lonely Crowd, The (Riesman), 665–666

Long, Huey, 588
Longhorn cattle, 412
Longshoremen, strikes by, 589
Looking Backward (Bellamy), 441
Los Alamos, 617
Los Angeles: linguistic diversity in, 745; Mexican American culture in, 572; race riots in, 624, 696
Losing Ground (Murray), 689
Lost Cause, of South, 425
Lost Generation, 572–573
Louisiana, 398, 400; reorganization of, 386, 387
Lower classes, 440. *See also* Classes; Working class
Loyalty Program (Truman), 635, 644
LPs, 758
Lucas, Robert, 783
Luftwaffe, England and, 608
LULAC. *See* League of United Latin American Citizens
Lusitania (ship), sinking of, 531
Luxury goods, in Second World War, 622
Lymon, Frankie, 666
Lynchings: of blacks, 425, 426, 493; of German immigrant, 539; legislation against, 650
Lynd, Robert and Helen, 553, 573

M
MacArthur, Arthur, 514
MacArthur, Douglas, 514, 614–615, 641
Macedonian immigrants, 461
Machines (political). *See* Political machines
Macy's, R. H., 439
Maddox (ship), 691
Madero, Francisco, 524
Mafia, 467
Magazines, 439, 480
Mahan, Alfred Thayer, 506–507
Mail, 444
Mailer, Norman, 698
Mail-order catalogs, 439–440
Maine (ship), 508
Major League Baseball (MLB), 650–651, 754
Malaria, 509, 521
Malcolm X, 696–697
MALDEF. *See* Mexican American Legal Defense and Educational Fund
Management, 437–438, 445, 492, 663
Manchukuo, 606

Manchuria, 521, 606
Manhattan Project, 617, 634
Manhattan Transfer (Dos Passos), 572
Manila, 509, 512, 513
Mann Act (1910), 473
Man That Nobody Knows, The (Barton), 556
Manufacturing: employment in, 751; in First World War, 534; in Great Depression, 585; growth in, 433, 434; immigrant, 464, 466; small manufacturers, 466
Mao Zedong, 614, 637, 706
"Maple Leaf Rag" (Joplin), 468
March, Peyton, 536
March against Fear, 697
March on Washington (1941), 625
March on Washington for Jobs and Freedom (1963), 680–681
Marcos, Ferdinand, 716
Mariana Islands, 629
Marines (U.S.): in Cuba, 520; in Korean War, 641; in Latin America, 523, 562, 599; in Lebanon, 661; in Mexico, 524; in Panama, 726
Market(s), foreign, 504, 506, 516
Marketing: mass, in 1920s, 553–554; of music, 758
Marne River, Battle of, 533
Marriage: in 1920s, 554; same-sex, 775; sex before, 472
Married women, 594, 620
"Marse Chan" (Page), 425
Marshall, George C., 617, 636, 646
Marshall, Thurgood, 674
Marshall Field & Co., 439
Marshall Islands, 615, 629
Marshall Plan, 636, 648
Marx Brothers, movies of, 581
Mary Tyler Moore Show (TV program), 756
Masculinity, in Second World War, 623
Mass culture: in 1950s, 667; debate over, 758–759
Mass distribution, 437
Masses, The (artistic journal), 473
Mass execution, of Santee Sioux, 419
Massive retaliation policy, 659
Mass marketing, in 1920s, 553–554
Mass media: antiwar movement and, 698; civil rights movement and, 696; culture and, 755–759; future of print media and,

789; Vietnam War and, 693–694. *See also* specific media
Mass production, 437, 492
Mattachine Society, 645, 731
Matthews, Joseph Warren, 416
Mayors: reform, 485; socialist, 484 (*map*)
McCain, John, 786, 790
McCarran Internal Security Act (1950), 644
McCarthy, Eugene, 699, 700
McCarthy, Joseph, and McCarthyism, 646–647, 659
McClure's Magazine, 480
McCormick farm machinery plant strike, 446
McDonald's, 750
McGovern, George, 708
McKinley, William, 452–453, 507; 1896 election and, 451–452, 452 (*map*); 1900 election and, 453; assassination of, 494, 518; Cuba and, 508, 514; imperialism and, 512, 513
McKinley Tariff (1890), 429
McNamara, Robert, 670, 693
Meat Inspection Act (1906), 495
Meatpacking industry, 483
Media. *See* Mass media
Medicaid, 689, 702, 788
Medicare, 689, 702, 720, 737, 788
Medicare Prescription Drug Improvement Act (2003), 774
Medicine: biotechnology and, 749; fee-for-service system, 649; regulation of, 495; women and, 442, 444. *See also* Health and health care
Melting pot, 474
Melting Pot, The (Zangwill), 474
Memphis, 392, 699; racial violence in, 425
Men: gay, 645; Homestead Act and, 409; as immigrants, 461, 462; in New Deal programs, 593; separate sphere of, 672; virility and "strenuous life" for, 441; in West, 417; in workforce, 620. *See also* Gender
Mencken, H. L., and Scopes trial, 566–567
Merchants: in crop lien system, 424. *See also* Business; Commerce
Meredith, James, 697
Merger movement, 436

Metropolitan areas, 458. *See also* Cities; Suburbs; Urban areas

Metropolitan Museum of Art (New York), 458, 459

Mexican American Legal Defense and Educational Fund (MALDEF), 735

Mexican Americans, 571–572, 734–735; as agricultural labor, 464; *bracero* program and, 678; civil rights of, 679; culture of, 415; as immigrants, 415, 461; loss of lands, 414–415; in military, 627; in New Deal, 597–598; school desegregation and, 650, 679; as vaqueros (cowboys), 414; Zoot Suit Riots and, 624. *See also* Mexico

Mexican Revolution (1910), 524

Mexican War, 516

Mexico: after 1970, 744; debt crisis in, 777; immigrants from, 415, 461, 678–679; labor from, 565; NAFTA and, 728, 777; Wilson and, 504, 523–524; Zimmerman telegram and, 532. *See also* Mexican Americans

Miami, Cubans in, 745

Microchips, 749

Microsoft, 749

Middle class, 433; in 1920s, 554; black, 425–426, 469; corporate, 440; ethnic, 465–466; Jewish, 466; management in, 438; progressives in, 479; "realism" and, 480; women and, 442–444, 674

Middle East, 658; Bush, George W., and, 774; Carter and, 715; Eisenhower Doctrine toward, 660–661; Obama and, 788; oil exports from, 705; Reagan and, 724; after Second World War, 629. *See also* Near East; specific countries

Midvale Steel Company, 492

Midway, Battle of, 614

Midway Plaisance (Columbian Exposition), 459–460

Midwest, immigrants in, 416

Migrant workers, Mexican, 571

Migration: of African Americans, 424, 425, 467, 535, 568, 652, 675 (*map*); to cities, 557, 624, 625–626. *See also* Immigrants and immigration

Militarism, in Japan, 609–610

Military: blacks in, 511, 536; desegregation of, 650; Eisenhower and, 659; GI Bill for, 648–649; Great Railroad Strike and, 432, 445; McCarthy and, 659; Navy Department and, 635; NSC-68 and, 639, 641–642; Pullman Strike and, 448; Reagan and, 724; in Reconstruction South, 389; segregation of, 511, 536; in Vietnam, 671, 692, 707; women in Second World War, 623. *See also* specific battles and wars

Military bases: in Middle East, 641; in Okinawa, 641. *See also* Naval bases

Military districts, in South, 393

Military draft. *See* Draft (military)

Military-industrial complex, 661, 662

Military occupation. *See* Occupation (military), Zones of occupation

Military rule, of South, 389, 393, 400

Militia: black, in South, 403; Republican, in South, 398, 400; strikes and, 445, 447, 448; used in riots, 493

Miller, Alice Duer, 491

Miller & Lux (industrial ranching company), 414, 416

Millionaires, in 1890s, 440

Milosevic, Slobodan, 776

Mines and mining: labor for, 410, 464; Mexican Americans and, 414; strikes in, 412, 495, 642; in West, 411–412. *See also* Coal and coal industry; Gold

Minimum wage, 390, 667, 672, 714, 719

Mining camps, 417

Minnesota, 416

Minnesota Farmer-Labor Party, 589

Minorities: in New Deal, 596–597, 596–598; political influence of, 486; professional organizations and, 444; voting rights of, 487; women in workforce and, 620. *See also* Ethnicity; Race and racism; specific groups

Minoso, Orestes (Minnie), 651

Minstrelsy, 469

Missile gap, 670

Missiles, 671, 705

Missions and missionaries, Protestant, 417, 505

Mississippi: 1875 election and, 401; Freedom Summer in, 688; Till, Emmett, murder in, 676

Mississippi Freedom Democratic Party (MFDP), 688

Mississippi Plan, 401–402

Missouri Pacific Railroad, 446

Mitchell, John (UMW), 495

Mitchell, Joni, 696

Model Cities Program, 689

Model T Ford, 437, 492

Modern Republicanism, of Eisenhower, 667, 668

Mogadishu, 776

Mondale, Walter, 721

Monday Night Football, 754

Money Power, 450

Mongoose, Operation, 671

Monopolies, 436

Monroe Doctrine, 516; Roosevelt Corollary to, 519–520

Montenegrin immigrants, 461

Monterey Pop festival, 696

Montgomery bus boycott, 676

Montgomery Ward (store), 439–440

Morgan, J. P. (John Pierpont), 435, 436, 497

Morgan, J. P., Jr., 561

Mormons, 761

Mortgage-backed CDOs, 785

Mortgages, 465, 651–652, 679, 785

Moscow Conference (1943), 627

Moslems. *See* Muslims

Motion pictures. *See* Movies

Movies and movie industry, 756–758; in 1920s, 556, 564; antiwar, 606; blacklist in, 643; Blaxpoitation, 733; development of, 470–472, 473; *film noir* in, 653; in First World War, 538; in Great Depression, 595; religious, 763; after Second World War, 652–653

Moynihan, Daniel Patrick, 702

Mr. Deeds Goes to Town (movie), 595

Mr. Smith Goes to Washington (movie), 595

MS. magazine, 730

MTV (Music Television channel), 758

Muckrakers, 480, 483

Mugwumps, 428

Multiculturalism, 475; of 1980s, 762

Multinational corporations, 506

Muncie, Indiana, study of, 553

Munich Conference, 607

Municipalities, socialist officials in, 483, 484 (map)
Munn v. Illinois, 449
Murdoch, Rupert, 756
Murray, Charles, 689
Museums, 458, 459
Music: black, 569; Christian, 763; counterculture, 696; country, 555; by Ellington, 597; file sharing for, 758; hip-hop, 760; patriotic, 515; pop, 758; ragtime, 468, 569; rap, 760; rock 'n' roll, 666
Music halls, 469
Muskie, Edmund, 708
Muslims, 728, 761, 776. See also Islam; Middle East
Mussolini, Benito, 600, 606
Mutual defense pacts, 637
Myers, Harriet, 775
My Lai incident (Vietnam War), 706
MySpace, 790

N
NAACP. See National Association for the Advancement of Colored People
Nader, Ralph, 703, 772
NAFTA. See North American Free Trade Agreement
Nagasaki, 617
Nanjing, Japanese brutality in, 607
Napalm, 692
Napster, 758
Narrowcasting, 756, 759
NASA. See National Aeronautics and Space Administration
NASCAR (National Association for Stock Car Racing), 754
Nasser, Gamal Abdel, 660
Nast, Thomas, cartoons of, 400
National Aeronautics and Space Administration (NASA), 668, 743
National American Woman Suffrage Association (NAWSA), 488, 490, 532, 559
National Association for the Advancement of Colored People (NAACP), 493–494, 569; Brown cases and, 674
National Association of Colored Women, 425–426
National Association of Manufacturers (NAM), 647

National bank. See Banks and banking
National Basketball Association (NBA), 754
National debt, 619
National Defense Education Act (1958), 668
National Farmers' Alliance and Industrial Union, 450
National Football League (NFL), 754
National forests, 777
National Forest Service, 496, 497
National government. See Government (U.S.)
National Guard, 412, 677, 680, 696, 706
National health insurance program, 649
National Hockey League (NHL), 754
National Industrial Recovery Act (NIRA, 1933), 585, 589
Nationalism, 507
Nationalist Chinese, 614, 637
Nationalist Party (South Africa), 641
Nationality, American, views on, 473–475
National Labor Relations Act (NLRA, 1935), 590–591, 595, 600
National Labor Relations Board (NLRB), 590–591, 595, 663
National Labor Union, 445
National Liberation Front (NLF), 671, 691
National monuments, 495, 777
National Network of Hispanic Women, 735
National Organization for Women (NOW), 730, 731
"National origins" system, for immigration, 689
National parks, 495, 703
National Park Service, 495
National Recovery Administration (NRA), 585
National Review, 668, 717
National security, 632, 654; 1948 election and, 636, 637; ANZUS pact and, 641; Bush, George W., and, 781–783; after Cold War, 726; domestic policy and, 642–647; economic growth and, 639; education policies and, 668; Eisenhower and,

658–659, 668; executive power and, 647; homosexuals and, 645; Kennedy, John F., and, 670; risks to, 635; spending and, 648; Truman and, 634–635, 641–642. See also Communism
National Security Act (1947), 635–636
National Security Council (NSC), 635, 660; NSC-68 of, 639, 641
National Security Strategy Act (2002), 778
National Socialist (Nazi) Party. See Nazi Germany
National Union of Social Justice (NUSJ), 588
National Union Party, 392
National Urban League, 494
National War Labor Board (NWLB), 536
National Woman Suffrage Association, 394
National Women's Party (NWP), 490, 559
National Youth Administration (NYA), 619
Nation-building programs, 776
Nation of Islam, 696, 697; Black Power movement and, 761
Native American Graves Protection and Repatriation Act (1990), 734
Native Americans. See American Indians
Native peoples. See American Indians
Native Son (Wright), 645
Nativism, 565
NATO. See North Atlantic Treaty Organization
Natural resources, scientific management of, 496
Navajo Signal Corps, 615
Naval bases, in Second World War, 608
Navies. See Navy (U.S.), Royal Navy
Navy (U.S.): expenditures and battleship size (1890–1914), 507 (table); Great White Fleet and, 522; Mahan on, 506–507; in Spanish-American War, 509, 511. See also Royal Navy
Navy (U.S.). See also First World War; Second World War

Nazi Germany: as Axis power, 610; collapse of, 613 (map); death camps of, 609; expansion of, 608 (map); fascist regime in, 606. See also Germany; Hitler, Adolf; Second World War

Nazi gold, 613

Nazi-Soviet nonaggression pact, 607

Near East: after First World War, 541, 542 (map). See also Middle East

Nebraska, 417

Negro National Baseball League, 650

Negro rule, 397, 427

Negro World, The, 547

Neighborhoods, black, 469

Neoconservatives (neocons), 717

Neutrality: in First World War, 530–533; in Third World, 660, 661

Neutrality Acts (1935, 1936, 1937), 606, 609

New conservatism, 667–668, 673, 688–689, 690

New Deal, 647; coalition against, 619; First (1933–1935), 582–588; labor in, 588–589, 594–595; minorities in, 596–598; overseas relations during, 599–600; politics in (1934–1935), 588–589; Second (1935–1937), 590–595; West and, 586–588, 587 (map). See also Great Depression

New Democrats, 768–769, 784

"New Economic Policy" (Nixon), 705

New federalism, of Nixon, 702

New Freedom, 499

New Frontier, 669–670, 686–687

New Guinea, 615

New immigrants, 461, 744–746. See also Immigrants and immigration

New Jersey, government of, 486

"New Journalism," 698

New Left, 695, 698

New Look, of Eisenhower, 659

New Mexico, 411; Mexican Americans and Anglo-Americans in, 415

New Nationalism: of Roosevelt, Theodore, 498, 499; Wilson and, 501

"New Negro," 569–571

New Orleans: Hurricane Katrina in (2005), 781, 782; race riot in, 392

"New Politics," in 1960s 698

New Right, 717–718; Bush, George H. W., and, 723; on gender equality, 731; Protestant fundamentalists, evangelicals, and, 718, 761; radio of, 737; Reagan and, 737

News, television coverage of, 759

New South, 423–427. See also South

Newspapers, 470; foreign-language, 465; investigative reporting in, 480; socialist, 483; spread of, 439

New Woman, 443, 444

New world order, Wilson on, 532

New York (city): garment workers strike in, 545; population of, 457; Puerto Ricans in, 678; Tammany Hall in, 395; WPA projects in (1938), 592 (table)

New York (state): political parties in, 427–428; population loss in, 743; prisons in, 702

New York Journal, 508

New York Press Club, 442

New York's 369th Regiment, 536, 537

New York Stock Exchange, 435, 577, 698; 1987 meltdown of, 753. See also Stock market

New York Tribune, 398

New York World, 508

New Zealand, ANZUS pact and, 641

Nez Percé Indians, 419

Niagara movement, 493

Nicaragua: canal across, 520; Carter and, 716; contras in, 724, 725; intervention in, 562, 599; Sandinistas in, 716, 724, 726; Soviets and, 725

Nicholas II (Russia), 532

Nickelodeons, 456, 469, 470

Nicodemus, 424

Nimitz, Chester W., 614, 615

Nineteenth Amendment, 490, 558

9th and 10th Negro Cavalries, 511

NIRA. See National Industrial Recovery Act

Nisei, 624

Nitze, Paul, 639

Nixon, Richard M.: 1952 election and, 653, 654; 1960 election and, 669, 670, 670 (map); 1968 election and, 701, 701 (map); 1972 election and, 708; China and, 706; civil rights and, 702, 703–704; economy under, 704–705; environmentalism and, 702–703; foreign policy of, 705–707; Hiss and, 643–644; impeachment of, 709; pardon of, 709; resignation of, 709, 714; social policy under, 702; Vietnamization policy of, 706–707; Watergate and, 708–709

Nixon Doctrine, 706, 707

NLF. See National Liberation Front

NLRB. See National Labor Relations Board

Nobel Prize, to Roosevelt, Theodore, 521

No Child Left Behind program, 774

Nonaggression pact, Nazi-Soviet, 607

Nonrecognition policy, toward Manchukuo, 606

Nonviolent protest, 679, 697. See also Protest(s)

Noriega, Manuel (Panama), 726

"Normalcy," Harding on 551

Normandy landings, 611

North (region): African Americans in, 467, 469, 535, 568, 675; investment in southern industry by, 423; political parties in, 427–428; racism in, 547

North Africa, in Second World War, 610–611

North American Free Trade Agreement (NAFTA), 728, 777

North Atlantic Treaty Organization (NATO), 637, 638 (map), 641, 776

North Carolina A&T College, sit-in movement and, 679

Northeast, unions in, 663

Northern Ireland. See Ireland

Northern Pacific Railroad, 400, 435

Northern Securities Company, 494–495

North Korea, 639, 778. See also Korea; Korean War

North Vietnam, 661, 690, 715; bombings of, 707; Tet Offensive and, 698–699. See also Vietnam War

Novels: apocalyptic, 763; dime, 422, 441, 470; women and, 470. See also Literature

NOW. *See* National Organization for Women

NRA. *See* National Recovery Administration

NSC-68, 639, 641

Nuclear Nonproliferation Treaty (1995), 777

Nuclear power: atomic bomb and, 634; ban on weapons, 725; Clinton and, 777–778; Cuban Missile Crisis and, 671; Eisenhower and, 659; as energy source, 715; religious groups on containment, 761–762; Soviet Union and, 634, 638; Three Mile Island accident and, 715; weapons testing and, 659

Nuremberg trials, 613

Nursing, women in, 442

Nye, Gerald P., 606

O

Oath of allegiance, for ex-Confederates, 386, 387

Obama, Barack, 786; 2008 election and, 786, 786 *(map)*, 787; 2012 election and, 790–792; cabinet of, 787; economy and, 787–788; foreign policy of, 788

"Obamacare," 788

Ocala, Florida, Farmers' Alliance convention at, 450

Occupation (military): of Berlin, 628; of Germany, 628; of Japan, 629; of South, 389, 393. *See also* Zones of occupation

Occupational Safety Act (1973), 703

Occupations (jobs): women and, 538. *See also* Jobs; Professions

Oceania, immigrants from, after 1970, 744

O'Connor, Sandra Day, 673, 721, 776

Odets, Clifford, 595

OEO. *See* Office of Economic Opportunity

Officeholders: blacks as, 397; ex-Confederates as, 387, 388, 391, 392; socialists as, 483, 484 *(map)*

Office of Economic Opportunity (OEO), 687

Office of Price Administration, 619

Office of Scientific Research and Development, 619

Office of War Information (OWI), 622

Office work, women in, 442

Ohio, political parties in, 427–428

Oil and oil industry: Bush, George W., and, 774; Carter and, 714, 715; environment and, 783; Reagan's "cheap oil" policy, 720; Rockefeller in, 436. *See also* Energy; Organization of Petroleum Exporting Countries

Okies, 413, 595

Okinawa, 615, 641

Oklahoma! (musical), 413

Oklahoma, in Great Depression, 585

Older people, Social Security for, 649

Old Guard (Republican Party). *See* Republican Party

Old immigrants, 461

Olmsted, Frederick Law, 459

Olympic Games, boycott of (1980), 717

Omaha Beach landing, 611

100th Battalion, of Nisei, 627

O'Neill, Eugene, 572

Online activities. *See* Computers Internet Social networking sites

On the Road (Kerouac), 695

OPEC. *See* Organization of Petroleum Exporting Countries

Open Door notes, 518

Open Door policy, 516–518

Open housing, 677

Open-range grazing, 411, 412

Operas, 458, 459

Operation Desert Shield, 727

Operation Iraqi Freedom, 780

Operation Just Cause, 726

Operation Mongoose, 671

Operation OVERLORD, 611–614

Operation PUSH, 733

Operation TORCH, 611

Operation Wetback, 679

Oregon, 487, 490

Organization (business), 435–437

Organization Man, The (Whyte), 665

Organization of Afro-American Unity, 697

Organization of Petroleum Exporting Countries (OPEC), 705, 715, 720

Organized crime, 467, 563, 671

Organized labor. *See* Labor unions

Orthodoxy, of new immigrants, 461

Oswald, Lee Harvey, 681, 682

Ottoman Empire, 527; after First World War, 541, 542 *(map)*. *See also* First World War

Overland trails. *See* Trails

OVERLORD, Operation, 611–614

Ozone layer, 777

P

Pacification policy, in Vietnam, 693

Pacific Ocean region, 507; Second World War in, 614–616, 616 *(map)*; U.S. empire in, 512 *(map)*

Pacific Railroad Act (1862), 409

Pacifists: in First World War, 532; in Second World War, 609

Packard, Vance, 665

Page, Thomas Nelson, 425

Pago Pago, U.S. rights to, 507

Pahlavi, Reza (Shah), 716

Painting: American Impressionism and, 441; realism in, 441. *See also* Art and artists

Paiute Indians, 422

Pakistan, 788

Palestine: after First World War, 541, 542 *(map)*; Jewish state and, 629

Palin, Sarah, 786

Palmer, A. Mitchell, and Palmer raids, 546

Panama: intervention in, 520–521, 726; Noriega and, 726; Roosevelt, Franklin D., and, 599

Panama Canal, 520–521, 521 *(map)*, 599, 726; Carter and, 715; return to Panama in 2000, 521

Panay incident, 607

Panics (financial): of 1873, 400, 427, 435; of 1893, 427, 447, 448, 449, 451; of 1907, 496–497

Pan-Indian issues, 733–734

Paramilitary organizations, 400

Pardons: for ex-Confederates, 386, 388, 389; for Nixon, 709, 713; for Reagan-era Iran-*Contra* officials, 725

Paris: Peace Conference in (1919), 541; Second World War Allies in, 611; Vietnam peace accords in, 707

Paris, Treaty of, of 1898, 511, 513

Parker, Alton B., 495

Parks, Rosa, 676

Parks, urban, 458–459

Patriot Act, 778

Patriotism: in First World War, 537, 538, 540; music for, 515

Patronage, 396

Patrons of Husbandry. *See* Grange

Patsy Mink Equal Opportunity in Education Act (Title IX, 1972), 755

Paul, Alice, 490, 559

Paulson, Henry (Hank), 784, 785, 786

Pawn shops, 752

Payday loan institutions, 752

Payne-Aldrich Tariff, 497

Peace: First World War and, 540–545; after Second World War, 627–629

Peace accords (1973), for Vietnam War, 707

Peace Corps, 670

Peacekeeping missions, 640, 776

Peace movements: in First World War, 532. See also Antiwar sentiment

Peace policy, Indians and, 420

"Peace without victory," Wilson on 527

Pearl Harbor: Japanese attack on, 609–610; U.S. control of, 507, 512

Peasants, 461

Pelosi, Nancy, 788

Pendleton Act (1883), 396, 428

Penicillin, 619

Penniman, "Little Richard," 666

Pennsylvania, terrorist attacks and, 778

Pensions: for Union veterans, 429. See also Benefits; Social Security

Pentagon, 610; terrorist attack on, 778

Pentagon Papers, 708

Peonage, of Mexican Americans, 415

People, the, progressives and, 487, 494

People of color: voting rights of, 490. See also specific groups

"People's capitalism," in 1920s 553

People's Party. See Populists

People's Republic of China. See China

Perestroika, 725

Perishable goods, 552

Perkins, Frances, 593

Perot, Ross, 729, 729 (map)

Pershing, John J. ("Black Jack"), 524, 533, 536

Persian Gulf War (1991), 726–728

Personal registration laws, in states, 487–488

Personal Responsibility and Work Opportunity Reconciliation Act (1996), 769

Personnel department, 492

Pesticides, 702–703

Petraeus, David, 783

Petroleum industry. See Oil and oil industry

Phelps, Elizabeth Stuart, 442

Philadelphia, population of, 457

Philanthropy, by industrialists, 453, 453 (table)

Philippines: American-Filipino War and, 513–514; CIA activity in, 660; military aid to, 641; in Second World War, 610, 614, 615; in Spanish-American War, 509, 511; U.S. acquisition of, 511, 512, 513. See also Filipino Americans

Photography, 481, 693

Physical fitness, 441

Physicians. See Medicine

Picketing, 447, 490

Pill, the, 673

Pinchot, Gifford, 496, 497–498

Pine Ridge Reservation, 422, 734

"Ping-pong diplomacy," 706

Pingree, Hazen S., 485

Pinkerton guards, Homestead strike and, 447

"Pinups," in Second World War 623

Plain people. See Popular culture

Plains Indians, 417–423

Platt Amendment, 514, 599

Playboy magazine, 673

Pledge of Allegiance, "under God" added to, 665

Plessy v. Ferguson, 426, 650

Plumbers unit, Nixon and, 708

Pluralism: cultural, 474–475, 598; political, 663–665, 694; religion and, 665

Pneumonia, 465

Poets and poetry: Beat, 695; on woman suffrage, 491

Poison gas, in First World War, 530

Poland: after First World War, 541; immigrants from, 461; Second World War and, 607; after Second World War, 628–629; Solidarity movement in, 725

Polarization, political, 712, 768–776, 787–790

Police: community, 747; Haymarket bombing and, 446; strike in Boston, 545, 560

Political campaigns, of 1964 688

Political culture: sports-entertainment industry and, 754. See also Culture

Political machines, 396, 466–467, 482

Political parties: labor, 445; progressives and, 485; in states, 486. See also Elections; specific parties

Political power. See Power (authority)

Politics: of associationalism, 560–561; "attack," 647; blacks and 469; bureaucracy and, 396; of business, 559–562; of civil rights, 677; of gender and sex, 672–674; labor in, 594–595; in New Deal (1934–1935), 588–589; of New Left, 696; pluralism in, 663–665; of polarization, 712, 768–776, 787–790; of race, 423; reform and, 486; Religious Right and, 718, 762; sexual, 731–732; social-cultural issues and, 775–776; of social movements, 729–738; of stalemate in late 1800s, 427–429; women and, 442. See also Political parties

Poll taxes, 488, 493

Pollution, 703; Clinton and, 777. See also Environment

Polynesian people, 507

Pools (business), 449

Poor people: political influence of, 486; voting rights for, 487, 488. See also Poverty

Poor People's Campaign, 700

Pop music, 758

Popular culture, 444, 759

Popular front, 589

Population: African American, 675 (map); aging of, 742–743, 743 (table); changes after 1970, 742–744; of Chinese immigrants, 411; in cities, 457; of immigrants, 460, 461, 461 (table); in Sun Belt, 744, 745 (map); of West, 407

Populists: 1896 election and, 451; platform of, 450–451

Pornography, 473

Port Arthur, China, 521

Port Huron Statement (1962), 695

Postindustrial service economy, 751

Potawatomi casino, 735

Potsdam Conference (1945), 634

Potter, David, 662

Poverty: in 1950s, 669; feminization of, 730; reduction in, 690, 702; in South, 424; urban, 458; war on, 687. *See also* Poor people; Wealth gap

Poverty (Hunter), 465

Powderly, Terence V., 445, 446

Powell, Colin, 773

Power (authority): countervailing, 664–665; of government, 495–496, 632; presidential, 647, 781–783; of United States worldwide, 504, 505–507. *See also* Imperialism

Power (energy). *See* Energy, Nuclear power

"Praise the Lord" (PTL) movement, 762

Predatory pricing, 436

Prejudice. *See* Race and racism

Prenatal care, 559

Presidency. *See* President

President: national security authority of, 647; power of, 647, 781–783; terms of office for, 647. *See also* specific individuals

Presidential Commission on the Status of Women, 674

Presidential elections. *See* Elections

Presley, Elvis, 666, 667

Press. *See* Mass media, Newspapers

Primary elections, direct, 487

Principles of Scientific Management, The (Taylor), 492

Printing, technological innovations in, 439

Print media: future of, 789. *See also* Newspapers

Private property. *See* Property

Proclamation of Amnesty and Reconstruction (1863), 386

Production: in late 19th century, 433; military, 642; in Second World War, 619. *See also* Mass production

Professions and professionals: in corporations, 440; "female" professions and, 558; organizations for, 444; women in, 442, 444, 673

Progressive Party: of 1912, 478, 498, 499–500, 499 (*map*); of 1948, 636, 637, 637 (*map*); in Wisconsin, 589

Progressives and progressivism, 478; accomplishments of, 500–501; civil rights campaign and, 493–494; cultural conservatism of, 482–483; municipal reform and, 485–486; Protestant spirit and, 479–480; Roosevelt, Theodore, and, 494–496; socialism and, 485; state political reforms and, 487–488; Taft and, 497–498; white Americans and, 562; Wilson and, 500–501; in Wisconsin, 490–492; women's activism and, 481–482, 483, 488–490

Prohibition, 562; Eighteenth Amendment and, 483, 539; repeal of, 582; rural white Americans and, 562; Volstead Act and, 540

Promontory Summit, Utah, transcontinental railroad at, 400, 410

Propaganda: anticommunist, 642; Cold War, 642, 659; in First World War, 537–540; in Second World War, 622; in Vietnam War, 693–694

Property: Indian, 420; voting rights and, 426, 488

Prosperity: in 1920s, 552–559; of black middle class, 426; economic growth and, 433. *See also* Affluence; Wealth

Prostitution, 417, 473, 480

Protectorates: Hawaii as, 507; Samoa as, 507

Protest(s): antiabortion, 737; labor, 588–589; in Sixties, 695, 697–698; suffragist, 490; by women, 674. *See also* Resistance

Protestant-Catholic-Jew (Herberg), 665, 760

Protestants and Protestantism: fundamentalist vs. liberal, 565–566; immigrants and, 564–565; overseas missionaries and, 505; progressivism and, 479–480; Prohibition and, 563. *See also* Religion

Provisional governors, during Reconstruction, 388

Psychological warfare, 659

Public Enemy, The (movie), 581

Public health. *See* Health; Health and health care

Public housing, 648, 649, 652, 679. *See also* Housing

Public lands: Ballinger-Pinchot controversy over, 497–498; Homestead Act and, 408–409; Roosevelt, Theodore, and, 496

Public Lands Commission, 496

Public schools: in South, 394. *See also* Education; Schools

Public works, 448; interstate highway program, 662; kickbacks for, 458

Public Works Administration (PWA), 585

Pueblo Relief Act (1933), 598

Puerto Rican-Hispanic Leadership Forum, 678

Puerto Rican Legal Defense and Education Fund, 736

Puerto Ricans, 744–745; activism of, 678, 736

Puerto Rico: Spanish-American War and, 509; U.S. acquisition of, 511, 512, 515–516

Pulitzer, Joseph, 508

Pullman, George M., 448

Pullman Strike, 448

Pure Food and Drug Act (1906), 495

PUSH, Operation, 733

PWA. *See* Public Works Administration

Q

al-Qaddafi, Muammar (Libya), 724

Quarantine: of Cuba, 671; before Second World War, 606–607

Quayle, J. Danforth (Dan), 723

Queens College. *See* Rutgers University

Quotas: affirmative action, 737; on immigration, 564–565, 565 (*table*), 609

R

Race and racism: Asians and, 462; Chinese immigrants and, 410–411; after First World War, 547; immigration restriction and, 564–565; industrialization and, 423; Japan and, 614; in New South, 425; in North, 425, 468–469; Second World War and, 614, 623–624, 625–627; in South, 676, 679–680; in South Africa, 641; in Spanish-American War, 510. *See also* Civil rights movement; Equality; Slavery

Race riots: in Chicago (1919), 547; in Detroit (1943), 624; after King's assassination, 699–700; in Los Angeles, 624, 696; during Reconstruction, 392; in Springfield, Illinois, 493; in Watts (1965), 696; in Wilmington, North Carolina, 426

Racial discrimination. See Discrimination

Racial fitness, 441

Racial segregation. See Segregation

Racial superiority, 441

Radar, 610, 619

Radical Republicans, 387, 388

Radicals and radicalism: after First World War, 545–547; in Great Depression, 589

Radio, 659; hip-hop music on, 760; New Right and, 737

Radio Asia, 659

Radio Free Europe, 659

Radio Liberty, 659

Radio priest, Coughlin as, 588

Ragtime music, 468, 569

Railheads, 412

Railroads: as big business, 434–435; borderland communities and, 411; economic growth and, 433; expansion of (1870–1890), 410 (map); farmers' resistance to, 449; financing of, 409, 435; after First World War, 545; Granger laws and, 449; labor for, 409, 410, 462, 464; mining and, 411; pools in, 449; ranching and, 412, 414; refrigerated rail cars and, 412; regulation of, 449, 495; in South, 423, 467–468; standard time zones and, 439; strikes against, 432, 433, 434, 445, 446, 448, 642; subsidies for, 409, 435; technological advances for, 434; in West, 409. See also Transcontinental railroad

Rainbow Coalition, 733

Ranching, 411, 412–414; industrial, 414; longhorn cattle and, 412; seasonal labor in, 416

Randolph, A. Philip, 569, 625, 650

Range wars, 412, 413

Rap music, 760

Ratification, of Versailles Treaty, 542–545

Rationing, 619

Rauschenbusch, Walter, 480

Ray, James Earl, 699

Reading. See Literacy

Reading Railroad, 495

Reagan, Ronald, 718–721; 1976 election and, 713; 1980 election and, 718–719, 719 (map); anticommunism and, 643; arms treaty and, 725; domestic policy of, 719–721; foreign policy of, 723–725; Inaugural Address by (1981), 736; as movie star, 722; new conservatism of, 688

Reagan revolution, 719

Reagon, Bernice Johnson, 673–674

Realism, 441, 480, 481

Reality shows, on television, 758

Real wages. See Wages

"Reason Why the Colored American Is Not in the World's Columbian Exposition, The" (Wells), 460

Rebates, on rail shipments, 436, 449

Recall, 487

Recession(s): of 1937–1938, 600; in 1950s, 662; Great Recession and, 786. See also Depressions (financial); Economy; Panics (financial)

Reciprocal Trade Agreement (1934), 599

Reconstruction, 385, 396–398; 1868 election and, 395; Black Codes during, 389; black officeholders in, 397; congressional, 391–393; end of, 394, 404; Fifteenth Amendment and, 394; Fourteenth Amendment and, 392; freedpeople during, 386, 387, 389–391; Ku Klux Klan during, 394, 395, 398; movie about, 399; presidential, 388–389; Radical Republicans and, 387; Supreme Court and, 402; Wartime, 386–387

Reconstruction acts (1867), 393, 395

Reconstruction Finance Corporation (RFC), 580

Recordings, music, 758

Red China. See China

Redford, Robert, 757

Redistribution of income, in Second World War, 619

Redlining, 679

Red Scare: in Cold War, 635, 642–647; after First World War, 545–547; McCarthy and, 646–647. See also National security; Subversion

Red Shirts, 400, 403

Referendum, 487

Refinancing, of property, 785

Reform(s): agricultural, 584–585; civil service reform, 396, 428; in Great Depression, 585, 593–594; for Indians, 420; muckrakers and, 480; municipal, 485–486; in New Deal, 593–594; political machines and, 467; by Roosevelt, Franklin D., 582; in states, 486–492; suffrage and, 488–490; Wilson and, 500–501; women and, 442–443, 481–482, 483. See also New Deal; Progressives and progressivism

Refrigeration: of perishables, 552; in railroad cars, 412

Refugee Act (1980), 745

Refugees: Jewish, 609, 611; political, 745; Second World War scientific innovation and, 619

Regions. See specific regions

Regulation: Bush, George W., and, 775; environmental, 495–496; of financial system, 753; government role in, 496; New Right on, 717; of railroads, 449, 495, 496; Reagan and, 720; of trusts, 436–437, 494–495

Rehnquist, William, 689, 721, 776

Reid, Harry, 788

Relief programs, in Great Depression, 580, 584, 591, 598

Religion: in 1950s, 665; in 2001, 761 (table); Ghost Dance and, 422; in late 20th century, 759–763; of new immigrants, 461; nuclear policy and, 761–762; same-sex relationships and, 761. See also Fundamentalism; Missions and missionaries; specific groups

Religious Right, 718, 761, 762

Relocation program, for Indians, 677–678

"Remember the Maine" slogan, 508, 509

Rent subsidies, 689, 702

Reparations: German, after First World War, 541, 561; for interned Japanese Americans, 736

Repression, in First World War, 537–540

Reproduction: choice and, 729; literature on, 444

Republican Party: 1876 election and, 403–404; in 1968, 701; in 1990s, 768; factions in, 428; Ku Klux Klan and, 394, 395, 398; Mississippi Plan and, 401–402; Old Guard in, 496, 497, 498; political stalemate and, 427–428; Populists and, 451; in South, 397–398, 400, 675; "Tea Party" wing of, 788; Versailles Treaty and, 542, 543, 544; Wartime Reconstruction and, 386–387. *See also* Elections; Reagan, Ronald

Republicans (Spain), 606

Research departments, 438

Reservations (Indian), 678; in 1875 and 1900, 418 (*map*); expansion of, 418, 419

Reservoirs, in West, 663

Resistance: to desegregation, 676; by farmers, 448–450; by Hispanics, 411; Indian, 418–419; by workers, 444–448. *See also* Protest(s)

Resources, conservation of, 496

Restraint of trade, 436, 448

Restrictive covenants, 650, 652

Retailing, 750, 751

Reuben James (ship), sinking of, 609

Revenue Act, of 1926, 560

Revenue-sharing plan, 702

Revisionist historians, 633

Revolts and rebellions. *See* Resistance; specific rebellions

Revolution(s): in Cuba, 508; in Iran (1979), 716; in Nicaragua, 716; in Russia (1917), 533

Revolutionary socialists, 485

Rhee, Syngman, 639, 640

Rhineland, 606

Riesman, David, 665–666

Rifle Clubs, 400, 401

Rights: Nixon and, 703–704. *See also* Civil rights; Freedom(s); Women's rights

Right-to-life activists, 703–704, 775

Right wing (political): Bush, George W., and, 775; New Right and, 717–718; Religious Right and, 718. *See also* Conservatism; New Right; Religious Right

Riis, Jacob, 481

Rio Arriba County, New Mexico, 411

Rio Grande region, 414

Riots: anti-Asian, 522. *See also* Race riots

Risk, financial, 784–785

Roads and highways: in 1920s, 552; in 1950s, 663; interstate highways and, 662, 663

Robber barons, 453. *See also* Industrialists

Roberts, John, 721, 776

Roberts, Owen J., 600

Roberts Court, 776

Robertson, Pat, 761, 762

Robeson, Paul, 645

Robinson, Jackie, 650–651

Rockefeller, John D., 436, 453, 480

Rockefeller, Nelson, 702, 713

Rockefeller Foundation, 453

Rockefeller University, 453

Rock 'n' roll music, 666

Rodgers and Hammerstein, 413

Roe v. Wade, 703–704, 718, 737, 749

Rolling Thunder, 692

Roman Catholicism. *See* Catholicism

Romances (novels), 470

Romania, after Second World War, 628

Romney, Mitt, 2012 election and, 790–792

Roosevelt, Eleanor, 581, 593; Anderson, Marian, and, 596; social activism of, 626; UN and, 628; women's issues and, 674

Roosevelt, Franklin Delano, 637; 1932 election and, 581 (*map*); 1936 election and, 592–593, 593 (*map*); 1940 election and, 609; 1944 election and, 617; about, 576, 581–582; big business and, 620; Black Cabinet of, 596; cabinet of, 593; death of, 617; recession of 1937–1938 and, 600; Second Bill of Rights of, 647; Supreme Court and, 600; at Yalta, 644. *See also* Great Depression; New Deal; Second World War

Roosevelt, Theodore: 1904 election and, 495; 1908 election and, 497; 1912 election and, 498, 499–500, 499 (*map*); conservation and, 496; East

Asia and, 521–522; environment and, 495–496; First World War and, 539; geopolitics of, 518–522; imperialism of, 504; lifestyle and, 441; muckrakers and, 480; Navy and, 507; Panama Canal and, 520–521; Progressive Party and, 478; Russo-Japanese War and, 521; in Spanish-American War, 510–511; Square Deal of, 495; as trust-buster, 494–495; on Zangwill play, 474

Roosevelt Corollary, to Monroe Doctrine, 519–520

Roosevelt liberalism, 582

Root-Takahira Agreement (1908), 521

Rosenbergs, Julius and Ethel, 645

Rough Riders, 510–511

Rove, Karl, 774

Royal Air Force (RAF), 608

Royal Navy (England), in First World War, 531

Rubin, Jerry, 698, 700

Rubin, Robert, 784

Ruby, Jack, 681

Ruhr valley, 561

Rumsfeld, Donald, 773, 783

Rural areas: Indians in (1940–1980), 678 (*table*); Mexican Americans in, 678; migration from, 557; in South, 424. *See also* Farms and farming

Rural Electrification Administration (REA), 619

Russia: China and, 516; after Cold War, 727 (*map*), 728, 740, 740 (*map*); democratic government in, 532–533; immigrants from, 461. *See also* First World War; Soviet Union

Russo-Japanese War, 521

Rustin, Bayard, 645, 676

Rustlers, 412

Rutgers University, 442

Ruth, George Herman ("Babe"), 556

Rwanda, 776

S

Saar River region, 541

Sacco, Nicola, 546–547

Sacco and Vanzetti case, 546

Sadat, Anwar, 715–716

Saddleback Church, 763

Safety, rights-related claims and, 703

"Sagebrush rebellion," 720

Saigon, 707, 715. *See also* South Vietnam; Vietnam War

Saipan, 615

Sakhalin Island, Japan and, 521

Saloons, 483

SALT talks. *See* Strategic Arms Limitation Talks

SALT Treaty. *See* Strategic Arms Limitation Treaty (SALT)

Same-sex relationships, 761; marriage as, 775. *See also* Homosexuality; Lesbian-Gay-Bisexual-Transgendered (LGBT) movement

Samoa, 507

Samoan people, 736

Sand Creek massacre, 419

Sandinistas (Nicaragua), 716, 724, 726

San Francisco region, 695; Asian immigrants in, 410, 463, 522; longshoremen's strike in (1934), 589; prostitution in, 417

Sanitation, in cities, 458, 465

San Juan Hill, battle at, 511

Santee Sioux, conflict with, 418–419

Santiago, Cuba, 510, 510 (*map*), 511

Santo Domingo (Dominican Republic), 396

Sarajevo, Franz Ferdinand assassination in, 528

Sargent, John Singer, 443, 530

Satellites (space), Sputnik as, 668

Saturation bombing, 692

Saudi Arabia, Persian Gulf War and, 726, 727

Saving Private Ryan (movie), 612

Savings and loan institutions (S&Ls), 720, 753

Scabs, 446

Scalawags, 393, 397–398

Scandinavia, immigrants from, 416, 461

Schlafly, Phyllis, 673, 703

Schofield, John M., 393

Schools: black, 398; desegregation of, 674, 677; for freedpeople, 390–391; for Indian children, 420–422; public, 394; segregation of, 394, 522, 650; in South, 394. *See also* Education; Higher education; Universities and colleges

Schwerner, Michael, 688

Sciences: vs. scripture, 562. *See also* Social Darwinism; Technology

Scientific management, 438, 492, 496

SCLC. *See* Southern Christian Leadership Conference

Scopes, John T., and Scopes Trial, 566–567

Screen Actors Guild, Reagan and, 643

Scribner's (magazine), 440

SDI. *See* Strategic Defense Initiative

SDS. *See* Students for a Democratic Society

Seattle, strike in, 545

Second Bill of Rights, 621, 622, 647

Second Front, in Second World War, 611

Second New Deal (1935–1937), 590–595. *See also* Great Depression; New Deal

Second World War, 604–629; African Americans in, 620–621; aggressor states and, 606; Allies in, 613 (*map*); American Indians in, 624; atomic bomb in, 617, 618; Axis Powers and, 610; Europe and, 607–609, 608 (*map*), 611–613; events leading to, 605–606; gender issues in, 622–623; home front in, 619–627; Japanese Americans during, 624–625; Latinos during, 626–627; in Pacific Ocean region, 614–616, 616 (*map*); peace after, 627–629; race and racism during, 614, 623–624, 625–626; society in, 622–627; spheres of interest after, 628–629; U.S. entry into, 610; U.S. neutrality before, 606; wartime conferences and, 634; women in, 620. *See also* Allies

Secret ballot, 487

Sectionalism, 449

Securities, 753, 785

Security. *See* National security

Security Council (UN), 627

Sedalia, Missouri, 412

Seduction of the Innocent, The (Wertham), 666

Segregation: in baseball, 650–651; of blood in Second World War, 623; in cities, 568; Jim Crow laws and, 426, 468; of military, 511, 536; of public facilities, 426; Roosevelt, Franklin D.,

and, 596; of schools, 394, 522, 650, 674; in southern industries, 423; suburban, 652; Supreme Court on, 674. *See also* Desegregation

Selective Training and Service Act (1940), 607

Self-defense, Malcolm X on, 697

Self-determination, 540, 541

Self-government, for Indians, 598

Self-regulation, of stock market, 738

Seminole Indians, 418

Semiskilled laborers, 446

Senate (U.S.), election to, 450, 487

Seneca Falls Convention, 488

Seoul, battle at, 641

Separate but equal principle, 426, 650

Separate spheres, in new suburbs, 672–673

Separation of church and state, 718

Separatism, black, 547

September 11, 2001, terrorist attacks on, 774, 778, 779

Serbia, 528, 529, 725

Serbs (Serbians), 461; Bosnian, 776

Serviceman's Readjustment Act (1944). *See* GI Bill

Service sector of economy, 751; jobs in, 751 (*table*)

"Set-aside" job programs, 737

Settlement houses, 481–482

Seventeenth Amendment, 487

Seventh Cavalry, 419, 422

Sewage systems, 458

Sex and sexuality: in 1920s, 554; counterculture and, 695, 696; cultural conservatism and, 482; Hollywood warning labels about, 758; Kinsey on, 645; in movies, 472; new sexuality and, 472–473; of "new woman," 444. *See also* Gender; Homosexuality

Sexism, in sports, 755

Sexual discrimination, in higher education, 704

Sexual harassment: Clinton and, 770; Hill-Thomas case and workplace, 730

Sexual politics, 731–732

Sexual slavery, 417

Seymour, Horatio, 395

Shah of Iran. *See* Pahlavi, Reza

Shakespeare, William, 441

Sharecroppers and sharecropping, 390, 424; African American, 390, 467; Great Depression and, 585, 592

Share the Wealth clubs, 588

Share wages, 390

Shasta Dam, 587 (map)

Sheep, 411, 412

Sheppard-Towner Act (1921), 559

Sheridan, Philip, 419

Sherman, William T., 390

Sherman Antitrust Act (1890), 436, 447, 448

Sherman Silver Purchase Act (1890), 449, 451

Sherry, Michael, 742

Shi'a Muslims, 728, 780

Ships and shipping: in First World War, 531; Five-Power Treaty and, 561. See also Railroads; Roads and highways; Transportation

Silent Spring, The (Carson), 702–703

Silicon Valley, 743

Silver, "free silver" movement, 449, 451, 453

Simmons, William, 564

Simpson, O. J., 769–770

Simpson-Mazzoli Act (1986), 746

Simpsons, The (TV program), 756, 757

Sinai Peninsula, 715

Sinclair, Upton, 483

Singapore, 610, 614

Singer Sewing Machine, 506

Singleton, Benjamin, 424

Sioux Indians, 418–419; Battle of Little Big Horn and, 419; Ghost Dance and, 422

Sirhan, Sirhan, 700

Sirica, John, 708, 709

Sit-down strikes, 595

Sit-in movement: in civil rights movement, 679; during Vietnam War, 698

Sitting Bull, 419, 422

Sixteenth Street Baptist Church (Birmingham), bombing of, 680

"Sixties," 694

Skilled labor, 437, 445, 464

Skyscrapers, 457

Slavery: Indians and, 418; Lincoln and, 386; as war issue, 385. See also Abolition and abolitionism; African Americans

Slavs, as immigrants, 461

Slovak immigrants, 461

Slovene immigrants, 461

Slovenia, 725

Slums. See Tenements

Smith, Alfred E., 568, 568 (map) 582, 669

Smith-Connally Act (1943), 621

SNCC. See Student Nonviolent Coordinating Committee

Soccer, 754

Social activism. See Activism

Social classes. See Classes

Social Darwinism, 440, 441

Social Gospel, 480

Socialist Party, 483; 1912 election and, 483, 484, 499, 499 (map) 500; First World War and, 540

Socialists and socialism, 446, 483–485; black, 569; after First World War, 545–546; immigrants and, 485; of mayors, 484 (map). See also Bolsheviks

Social mobility, 466

Social movements, politics of, 729–738

Social networking sites, 790

Social orders. See Classes

Social programs, of Nixon, 702

Social reform. See Reform(s)

Social sciences: in 1920s, 553; growth of, 440

Social Security, 667, 720; Bush, George W., and, 774; coverage by, 594; Reagan and, 737; Truman and, 648, 649

Social Security Act: of 1935, 590, 592, 600; of 1950, 649

Social welfare. See Welfare

Social workers, at Ford, 492

Society: in 1950s, 661–665, 665–667; after First World War, 545–547; militarization of, 642; politics and, 775–776; in Second World War, 622–627; Social Darwinism and, 440; sports and legal issues and, 755. See also Families; Gender; Men; Women

Sociology department, at Ford Motor Company, 492

Soddies (sod house), 416

Soil Conservation and Domestic Allotment Act (1936), 585

Sojourners, 761

Soldiers: African American, 511; in First World War, 533. See also Military; specific battles and wars

Solidarity movement (Poland), 725

Solid South, 403

Solomon Islands, 614

Somalia, 776

Songs and songwriters. See Music

Sororal organizations, 425

Sorosis, 442

Sotomayor, Sonia, 788

Souls of Black Folk, The (Du Bois), 427

Sousa, John Philip, 515

South: in 1950s, 675; 1968 election and, 701; African American migration and, 467, 535, 675; agriculture in, 424; black clubwomen in, 483; Black Codes in, 389; black officeholders in, 397; carpetbaggers in, 393, 397; after Civil War, 388–389; Democratic Party in, 395, 398, 400, 401–402; disfranchisement in, 426, 488; freedom rides in, 679–680; Ku Klux Klan in, 394, 398, 676; labor in, 663; military districts in, 393; opposition to desegregation in, 676; political parties in, 427–428; population growth in, 743; race in, 425, 426; railroads in, 423; Reconstruction Acts and, 393; Reconstruction in, 388–389, 394, 396–398; Republican Party in, 395, 397, 398; scalawags in, 393, 397–398; sharecropping in, 390, 424; textiles in, 423; voter participation in, 489 (table). See also Confederacy; Deep South; New South; Reconstruction; Slavery

South Africa, 453; U.S. alliance with, 641

South Carolina, 398, 400

Southeast Asia, Kennedy, John F., and, 671–672

Southern Baptists, 761

Southern Christian Leadership Conference (SCLC), 676

Southern Europe, immigrants from, 461

Southern Farmers' Alliance, 450

Southern Manifesto (1956), 676

"Southern Question," 396

South Korea, 639. See also Korea; Korean War

South Manchurian Railroad, 521, 522

South Vietnam, 661, 671–672, 681, 691, 707, 715. *See also* Vietnam War

Southwest: Mexican Americans in, 744; Mexicans in, 597; Spanish-speaking peoples in, 415, 678. *See also* Deep South

Sovereignty, of nations, 518

Soviet Union: Berlin blockade by, 636; Carter and, 717; Cuba and, 660, 671; détente with, 705; end of Cold War and, 725, 727 *(map)*; Kennedy, John F., and, 671; Korean War and, 639; NATO and, 637; nuclear weapons of, 634, 638; in Second World War, 611; after Second World War, 628–629; U.S. relations with, 659; Vietnam and, 661. *See also* Cold War; Russia; Stalin, Joseph

Soyer, Moses, 591

Space exploration, 668, 743

Space station, 743

Spain: Cuba and, 508. *See also* Spanish-American War

Spanish-American activism, 734–736

Spanish-American War, 504, 508–511, 510 *(map)*

Spanish-speaking populations: civil rights and, 678–679. *See also* Hispanics

Speculation: Great Depression and, 577–578; Panic of 1873 and, 400; in railroads, 435; in risky investments, 784

Speech, freedom of, 540

Spencer, Herbert, 440

Spending. *See* Borrowing Defense spending

Spheres of influence, 506, 634; after Second World War, 628–629

Spies and spying: Cold War fears of, 635, 644, 646; spy planes and, 659

Spillane, Mickey, 623

Spirit of St. Louis, The (airplane), 556

Spock, Benjamin, 672

Spoils system, 396

Sports, 441; gender equity in, 704

Sports-entertainment industry, 753–755

Springfield, Illinois, race riots in, 493

Sputnik, 668

Square Deal, 495

SSI. *See* Supplementary Security Insurance

Stagflation, 705, 714

Stalin, Joseph: Cold War and, 633–634; nonaggression pact with Hitler, 607

Stalingrad, Battle of, 611

Stalwarts, 428

Standard of living. *See* Lifestyle

Standard Oil Company, 436, 453, 480, 506

Standard time zones, 439

Stanton, Edwin M., 393

Stanton, Elizabeth Cady, 394

Starbucks, 750

Stark, John, publisher of "Maple Leaf Rag," 468

Starr, Ellen Gates, 481

Starr, Kenneth, 770

"Stars and Stripes Forever" (Sousa), 515

Star Wars (missile system). *See* Strategic Defense Initiative

Star Wars (movies), 756

State(s): political reform in, 486–492; readmission of, 386, 387, 394; woman suffrage in, 488–490, 490 *(map)*

States' Rights (Dixiecrat) Party. *See* Dixiecrats

Stearns, Harold, 572

Steel industry, 457; consolidation in, 436; labor for, 464; railroads and, 434; strikes against, 447, 545; Truman and, 647

Steeplechase Park (Coney Island), 469

Steffens, Lincoln, 480

Stein, Gertrude, 572

Steinbeck, John, 595, 645

Steinbrenner, George, 753

Steinem, Gloria, 730

Stem cell research, 749–750, 775

Stephens, Alexander H., 388

Stereotypes, of African Americans, 397

Steroids, sports figures and, 755

Stevens, Thaddeus, 399

Stevenson, Adlai, 653, 654 *(map)*

Stimson, Henry, 611, 617

"Stimulus," 788

Stock Growers' Association, 412

Stock market, 497; in 2001, 773–774; collapse of (1873), 435; in Great Depression, 577–578; self-regulation of, 738. *See also* New York Stock Exchange

Stocks, of railroads, 409

Stokes, Edith Minturn, portrait of, 443

Stone, Oliver, 682

Stonewall riot, 731–732

Story of Avis, The (Phelps), 442

Strategic Air Command, Cuban Missile Crisis and, 671

Strategic Arms Limitation Talks (SALT), 705; SALT I and, 705

Strategic Arms Limitation Treaty (SALT), 717

Strategic Defense Initiative (SDI), 723

Strategic hamlet program, in Vietnam, 693

Strikes: in coal mines, 495, 545; during depressions, 433; in First World War, 536; after First World War, 545; in Great Depression, 589; Great Railroad Strike, 432, 433, 434, 445; Haymarket bombing and, 446; Homestead, 447; injunctions and, 447; Knights of Labor and, 446; at McCormick farm machinery plant, 446; in mining, 412; Pullman, 448; against railroads, 446, 448; in Second World War, 621; after Second World War, 642; sit-down, 595; by steelworkers, 447, 545

Student Nonviolent Coordinating Committee (SNCC), 679, 688, 697

Students for a Democratic Society (SDS), 695

Studs Lonigan trilogy, 580–581

Subcultures, gay and lesbian, 645

Submarines: in First World War, 531; in Second World War, 610

Subprime loans, 720; mortgages as, 785

Subsidies: for railroads, 409, 435; rent, 689, 702, 689

Subtreasuries (federal warehouses), 450

Suburbs: demographics of, 747; development of, 440; gender politics and, 672–673; housing in, 651–652, 679

Subversion: Cold War and, 635, 643–644; homosexuality and, 645

Subversive Activities Control Act (1950), 646, 659

Subversive Activities Control Board (SACB), 646
Subways, 458
Sudetenland, 607
Suez crisis (1956), 660
Suffrage: universal male, 394; for women, 394, 442, 488–490, 490 (map). *See also* Voting and voting rights
Suffragists, 488, 489, 490
Sugar and sugar industry, 513; in Cuba, 514; in Hawaii, 512; in Second World War, 620
Summit meetings: Eisenhower and, 659; with Gorbachev, 725
Sumter, South Carolina, city manager plan in, 486
Sun Belt, 668, 688, 743, 744 (map)
Sundance Festival, 757
Sunday, Billy, 480
Sunni Muslims, 780
Sun Records, 666
Superbanks, 752
Super Bowl, 754
Superman (comic-strip hero), 594
Superpowers. *See* Cold War, Soviet Union
Supplementary Security Insurance (SSI), 702
Supply-side economics, 719–720
Supreme Court (U.S.): on anti-integregation efforts, 677; big business and, 436–437; *Brown* cases and, 674; under Burger, 703–704; on Communist Party leaders, 646; on disfranchisement clauses, 426; Douglass, Frederick, speech on, 402; on executive power, 647; on grandfather clauses, 426, 493; Hill-Thomas issue and, 730; movie industry and, 653; Nixon and, 703, 709; Reagan and, 721; Reconstruction and, 402; on regulation, 449; Roosevelt, Franklin D., and, 600; on segregation, 650; on separate but equal facilities, 426, 650; trusts and, 495; under Warren, 674, 703; women on, 673, 721; on workday hours, 447
Survey Graphic (magazine), 569
Survival of the fittest, 440
Sussex (ship), sinking of, 531
Swaggert, Jimmy Lee, 762
Sweatshops, 466

Sweden, immigrants from, 416–417
Swedish Lutheran church, 417
Symphonies, 458, 459
Synagogues, immigrant, 465
Syria, 705

T
Taft, Robert, 637
Taft, William Howard: 1908 election and, 497; 1912 election and, 498, 499–500, 499 (map); dollar diplomacy of, 522–523; First World War and, 536; as governor of Philippines, 514; tariffs and, 497
Taft-Hartley Act (1947), 642, 647, 648
Taft-Katsura Agreement (1905), 521
Tailoring, 466
Taiwan, 637, 638
Take Back the Night rallies, 729
Taliban, 778, 781, 788
Tammany Hall, 395
TANF. *See* Temporary Assistance to Needy Families
Tanzania, embassy bombing in, 778
Tarbell, Ida, 453, 480
Tariff(s): Cleveland and, 428–429; Hawley-Smoot, 578; McKinley, 429; Payne-Aldrich, 497; Roosevelt, Franklin D., and, 599; Underwood-Simmons, 500
Tariff Act (1930). *See* Hawley-Smoot Tariff
TARP. *See* Troubled Asset Relief Program
Tarzan, the Ape Man (movie), 517
Taxation: Bush, George H. W., and, 723; Bush, George W., and, 774; capital-gains, 714; income, 450; Kennedy, John F., and, 672, 681, 686; Reagan and, 718, 719; in Second World War, 619. *See also* Income tax; Tariff(s)
Taxpayer revolt, in 1970s, 718
Taylor, Frederick Winslow, 492
Teachers: blacks as, 390; women as, 390, 442
Teach-ins, 698
"Tea Party" movement, 788
Teapot Dome scandal, 560
Technology, 749–750; consumer, 672; innovations in, 434; in mining, 411; in Sun Belt, 743. *See also* Weapons

Teens. *See* Young people
Tehran Conference (1943), 628
Tejanos (Mexican Texans), 414–415
Telephone, 434
Television: in 1952 election, 654; blacklist in, 643; critique of, 667; family-hour requirement on, 758; fathers portrayed on, 673; football on, 754; Kennedy-Nixon debates on, 669; McCarthy and, 659; movie industry and, 653, 757–758; racial violence on, 680, 696; sports coverage by, 754; video revolution and, 755–756; Vietnam War and, 693–694; Watergate hearings on, 709
Television evangelists, 718
Teller Amendment, 508
Temperance: women and, 443. *See also* Prohibition
Temporary Assistance to Needy Families (TANF), 769
Tenant farming: African Americans and, 467; Great Depression and, 585
Tenements, workers in, 465
Tennessee, 386, 398; reconstruction of, 392; Scopes Trial in, 566–567
Tennessee Valley Authority (TVA, 1933), 585–586, 586 (map)
Tennis, 754
Tenure of Office Act (1867), 393
Termination and Relocation, for Indians, 677–678
Terrell, Mary Church, 426
Territories, Puerto Rico as, 515
Terrorism: bombings and, 778; Iraq war and, 780; of Ku Klux Klan, 394, 395, 398; on September 11, 2001, 774, 778, 779
Tesla, Nikola, 434
Test-ban agreements, 659
Tet Offensive (Vietnam), 698–699
Texas, 450, 663; cattle in, 412; in Great Depression, 585; tejanos and Anglos in, 414–415
Texas Rangers, as vigilante force, 415
Textiles and textile industry: in 1920s, 557; in South, 423; strikes in, 589. *See also* Clothing and clothing industry; Cotton and cotton industry
Theater, Zangwill in, 474
Theology: gay, 761. *See also* Religion

Thief in the Night, A (movie), 763

Thieu, Nguyen Van, 707

Third parties: in 1968, 701; in Great Depression, 589. *See also* specific groups

Third Reich (Germany), 606, 609, 611–614

Third World, 658; American civil rights record and, 677; Kennedy, John F., on, 670; U.S. policy toward, 660

Thirteenth Amendment, 388, 404

"This Land Is Your Land" (Guthrie), 595

Thomas, Clarence, 730; and affirmative action, 737

369th Regiment, 536, 537

Three Mile Island, nuclear reactor at, 715

Thurmond, Strom, 636, 637, 637 *(map)*

Tilden, Samuel J., 403–404

Till, Emmett, 676

Time, standardization of, 439

Time-and-motion studies, 492

Time Warner, 756

Title VII, of Civil Rights Act (1964), 687

Title IX (1972) (Patsy Mink Equal Opportunity in Education Act), 704, 755

Tobacco and tobacco industry: Duke and, 436; mass distribution in, 437; in South, 423

Tokyo, air raids on, 616

Toledo, Ohio, strike in, 589

Too big to fail institutions, 786

Tootle, the Engine, 666

TORCH, Operation, 611

Torture, in Iraq war, 781

"To Secure These Rights," 650

Totalitarian movement, communism as, 634

Total war, First World War as, 534

Towns: company, 423. *See also* Cities

Townsend, Francis E., 588

Toynbee Hall (London), 481

Trade: in borderland communities, 411; with China, 516, 706; with Cuba, 515; with Germany, 531; globalization of, 777; international, 599–600; NAFTA and, 728, 777; in prostitution, 417; before Second World War, 606

Trade unions, 447; in 1920s, 557; Filipino workers and, 513; Socialist, 545–546; Wilson and, 501. *See also* Labor unions

Trading with the Enemy Act, 538

Trails, Chisholm, 412

Transatlantic flight: by Earhart, 556; by Lindbergh, 556

Transcendental Meditation, 760

Transcontinental railroad, 400, 409, 410

Transit systems, electric-powered, 458

"Trans-National America" (Bourne), 475

Transportation: in cities, 458; desegregation of, 676; racial discrimination in, 426. *See also* Automobiles and automobile industry; Canals; Railroads; Ships and shipping

Traverse des Sioux, Treaty of (1851), 418

Treasury notes, 449

Treaties: between Confederacy and five civilized tribes, 418; Indians and, 418; with Japan (1951), 641. *See also* specific treaties

Trekkies, 759

Trials: of Clinton, Bill, 770–772; of Simpson, O. J., 769–770. *See also* Impeachment

Triangle Shirtwaist Company fire, 464

Tribes: termination of, 678. *See also* American Indians; specific tribes

Triborough Bridge, 585

Tripartite Pact (1940), 607

Triple Alliance, 527, 528. *See also* Central Powers

Triple Entente, 527, 528. *See also* Allies (First World War)

Troops. *See* Military; Soldiers

Trotter, Monroe, 493

Troubled Asset Relief Program (TARP), 786

Truce, ending Korean War, 658

Truman, Harry S, 617; 1948 election and, 636–637, 637 *(map)*; 1952 election and, 653; anticommunism of, 634, 637, 644; atomic bombs and, 634; civil rights and, 649–650; Cold War and, 633–634; containment and, 634–635;

economy and, 648; Fair Deal of, 648–649; Korean War and, 640; labor and, 642; loyalty program of, 635; MacArthur and, 641; national security and, 634–635; presidential power and, 647

Truman Doctrine (1947), 634–635

Trusteeships, of League of Nations, 541

Trusts, 436–437, 480, 494–495, 499, 501

Trust Territories of the Pacific, 629

Tugwell, Rexford, 573

Turkey: Cuban Missile Crisis and, 671; foreign aid to, 634. *See also* Ottoman Empire

Turner, Frederick Jackson, 429; "frontier thesis" of, 429, 506

Turner, George Kibbe, 480

Turner, Ted, 756

Turnevereins, 465

Tuskegee Institute, 427

Tutsi people, 776

TVA. *See* Tennessee Valley Authority

Twain, Mark, 396, 440

Tweed, William Marcy ("Boss"), 395

Twenties, 551–573

24th and 25th Negro Infantry Regiments, 511

Twenty-fifth Amendment, 709

Twenty-second Amendment, 647

Tyler, John, 428

Typhoid fever, 465

U

UAW. *See* United Auto Workers

U-boats. *See* Submarines

Ukraine, 461

UMW. *See* United Mine Workers

UN. *See* United Nations

Unconditional surrender policy, in Second World War, 616

Underconsumptionism, 590

Understanding clauses, 426

Undocumented immigrants: regulation of, 746; religious groups and, 762. *See also* Illegal immigrants

Unemployment: in 1975, 714; Clinton and, 769; in Great Depression, 576, 578; in male and female occupations (1930), 594, 594 *(table)*; Nixon and, 705; in nonfarm labor force

(1929–1945), 599 (table); Panic of 1873 and, 400; Panic of 1893 and, 447; in recession of 1937–1938, 600. See also Employment

Unemployment benefits, 667

Unilateralism, Iraq war and, 778–781

Unionists, 392

Union Leagues, in Reconstruction South, 393, 397

Union Pacific Railroad, 395, 409, 446

Union Party, 387

United Auto Workers (UAW), 595

United Daughters of the Confederacy (UDC), 425

United Farm Workers (UFW), 735

United Fruit Company, 523

United Mine Workers (UMW), 495, 594, 621

United Nations (UN), 706; Clinton and, 776; Iraq war and, 779; Korean War and, 640; peacekeeping by, 640, 776; Persian Gulf War and, 727; Second World War and, 627

U.S. Bureau of Immigration, 463

U.S. Commission on Civil Rights, 677

U.S. Immigration Service, 597

U.S. Information Agency (USIA), 659

U.S. Steel Corporation, 436, 464, 595

U.S. v. Cruikshank, 402

U.S. v. E. C. Knight Company, 436–437

U.S. v. Nixon, 709

U.S. v. Reese, 402

Unity League, 679

Universal Declaration of Human Rights (UN, 1948), 628

Universal male suffrage, 394

Universal Negro Improvement Association (UNIA), 547

Universal suffrage. See Voting and voting rights

Universities and colleges: antiwar movement in, 697–698; athletics at, 441; black, 391, 425; bombings at, 701; desegregation of, 697; GI Bill and, 648–649; New Left in, 695; Title IX in, 704; women in, 444, 673; work-study programs in, 687. See also Higher education

University of California (Berkeley), student protests at, 695

University of Chicago, 453

University of Mississippi, desegregation of, 697

University of Wisconsin, 698

Unsafe at Any Speed (Nader), 703

Unskilled laborers, 446

Urban areas: African Americans activism in, 733; armories in, 446; black culture in, 569; demographics of, 747–748; economic problems in, 714; growth of, 457, 747–748; Indians in (1940–1980), 678 (table); Mexican Americans in, 678; poverty in, 458; problems in, 747; transportation in, 458. See also Cities

Urban corridors, 747, 748

Urbanization, in 1920s, 562, 563 (map)

Urban League. See National Urban League

Urban renewal, 679, 689

Uruguay Round, of GATT, 777

USA Patriot Act. See Patriot Act

USSR. See Soviet Union

Utah, 490

Utilities: in Great Depression, 592; municipal reform and, 485

U-2 spy planes, 659, 671

V

Valentino, Rudolph, 556

Valenzuela, Richard (Richie Valens), 666

Value added, by economic sector (1869–1899), 434 (table)

"Vamps," in movies 472

Vandenberg, Arthur, 634

Vanzetti, Bartolomeo, 546–547

Vaqueros, 414

Vassar, 444

Vaudeville shows, 469

Veblen, Thorstein, 440

Venezuela, 519

VENONA files, 635

Veracruz, 524

Versailles Treaty (1919), 541, 542 (map); ratification fight and, 542–545

Vertical integration, 435

Veterans: GI Bill for, 648–649; of Korean War, 649; of Second World War, 648–649; Union, 429

Veterans' Readjustment Assistance Act (1952). See GI Bill of Rights

Veto: Johnson, Andrew, and, 392, 393; Truman and, 642

Vice commissions, 473

Vice president, 428. See also specific individuals

Vichy France, 607

Victory (magazine), 622

Video revolution, 755–756, 757–758

Viet Cong, 693

Vietnam: Eisenhower and, 661; Ford and, 715; France and, 641; immigrants from, 745; Kennedy, John F., and, 671–672, 681; trade with, 777. See also Indochina

Vietnamization policy, 706–707

Vietnam syndrome, 707

Vietnam Veterans Against the War, 707

Vietnam War, 691 (map); American attitudes toward, 694 (table); antiwar movement during, 697–698, 706, 707; draft resistance in, 698; escalation of, 690–694; Nixon and, 706–707; Pentagon Papers and, 708; Tet Offensive in, 698–699

Vigilantes, white, 389, 415

Villa, Francisco ("Pancho"), 524

Virgin Islands, U.S. purchase of, 523

Virtuous electorate, 487

V-J Day, 618, 619

Voice of America, 659

Volstead Act, 540

Volunteers, Spanish-American War, 509

Volunteers in Service to America (VISTA), 687

Voting and voting rights: in 2008, 786; African Americans and, 387, 392, 393, 426, 592, 677, 688, 689; bulldozing and, 403; disfranchisement and, 426, 488; by ethnic groups, 596; Fifteenth Amendment and, 394; grandfather clauses and, 426, 493; interference as federal offense, 398; Mississippi Plan and, 401–402; participation in, 452, 488, 489 (table); reforms in, 487–488; in South, 393, 426, 489 (table), 688; universal male suffrage and, 394; women and, 394, 488–490, 490 (map), 537. See also Elections; Suffrage

Voting Rights Act (1965), 689, 704, 733

W

Wade, Benjamin, 387
Wade-Davis reconstruction bill, 387
Wage labor, 411, 416
Wages, 751; in 1920s, 557–558; in 1950s and 1960s, 663; at Ford, 492; gender and, 673, 674; in manufacturing, 464; minimum, 390, 667, 672; real, 663; in Second World War, 621; in South, 390, 423; of working class, 445
Wagner, Robert, 582, 590
Wagner Act (1935). *See* National Labor Relations Act
Wagner-Rogers bill (1939), 609
Waiting for Lefty (Odets), 595
Wake Island, in Second World War, 614
Walker, Madame C. J., 469
Walking cities, 458
Wallace, George, 688, 689, 708
Wallace, Henry A., 634, 636, 637, 637 *(map)*
Wall Street, market self-regulation on, 738
Walton, Sam, and Wal-Mart, 750
War against drugs, 726
War bonds, 619
Ward, A. Montgomery, 439–440
War Democrats, 387
War Department, 393, 610, 635. *See also* Defense Department
War Industries Board (WIB), 534
War Labor Board, 619, 620, 621
Warner, Charles Dudley, 396
War on poverty, 687
War on terrorism, 778
Warren, Earl, 674, 681, 703
Warren, Rick, 763
Warren Commission, 681, 682
Wars and warfare. *See* specific battles and wars
Warsaw Pact, 638 *(map)*
Wartime Reconstruction, 386–387
Washington (state), 490
Washington, Booker T., 427, 469, 493; at White House, 495
Washington, D.C.: antiwar demonstration in (1967), 698; Coxey's army in, 448; September 11, 2001, terrorist attack on, 778

Washington, Treaty of (1871), 396
Washington Conference on the Limitation of Armaments, 561, 606
Washington Post, Watergate scandal and, 708
Waste Land, The (Eliot), 572
Water: in cities, 458; in West, 663
"Water cure" in Philippines, 514
Watergate scandal, 708–709
Water projects, in West, 587–588, 587 *(map)*
Watt, Jame, 720
Watts riot (1965), 696
"Waving the bloody shirt" rhetoric, 427
Wealth and wealthy: distribution of wealth and, 619, 748, 769; gospel of wealth and, 453; maldistribution of wealth and, 578–579; Social Darwinism and, 440
Wealth gap: income distribution and, 748, 769; under Reagan, 720; in Second World War, 619
Wealth Tax Act (1935), 592
Weapons: Clinton and, 777–778; in Cuban Missile Crisis, 671, 683; in First World War, 530; in Iraq, 778; of mass destruction, 778, 779, 781; napalm as, 692; U.S. sales to Iran, 724. *See also* Armaments; Bombs and bombings; Nuclear power
Weather Underground, 701
Weaver, James B., 451
Weaver, Robert, 596
Web. *See* Internet
Weeks, Philip, 417
Welfare: Carter and, 715; Clinton and, 768, 769; federal spending on, 669; Great Society and, 689–690; of Indians, 598; Kennedy, John F., and, 672; Nixon and, 702; Reagan and, 720; Sheppard-Towner Act and, 559; Social Security Act and, 590; in South, 394; Supreme Court on, 703
Welfare capitalism, 556
Welfare state, 648
Wells, Ida B., 425, 426, 460, 493
Wertham, Frederick, 666
West: Asian immigrants in, 462–463; Chinese immigrants in, 409–411; conservation in, 496; farmers in, 412, 416; free silver

and, 449; gender and settlement of, 417; Hispanics vs. Anglos in, 411; homesteading in, 409, 416–417; Indians in, 417–423; industrialization in, 408–417; itinerant labor in, 415–416; Mexican Americans in, 414–415; migration to, 407; mining in, 411–412; myths of, 422–423; New Deal and, 586–588, 587 *(map)*; population in, 407, 743; railroads in, 409, 410; ranching in, 411, 412–414; water projects in, 663; woman suffrage in, 488–490, 490 *(map)*
West Bank (of Jordan River), 715
West Berlin, 636, 671
Western Europe, Marshall Plan in, 636
Western Federation of Miners, 412
Western Hemisphere: Monroe Doctrine and, 516; Roosevelt, Theodore, and, 519–520
Westerns (novels), 441
West Germany, 636, 641
Westinghouse, George, 434
Westminster School District v. Mendez, 650, 679
Westmoreland, William, 692, 699
Wetback, Operation, 679
Weyler, Valeriano ("Butcher"), 508
Wheat, 448
Whip Inflation Now (WIN) program, 714
White City (Columbian Exposition), 459, 460
White-collar workers, 440, 557, 752
White Leagues, 400
Whites: as Anglos, 597; Klan and, 564; movement to suburbs, 652; in NAACP, 494; in South, 400, 676; in West, 409; in workforce, 620
"White slave trade," 473
White supremacy, 425, 426, 451, 564, 647, 680; of Johnson, Andrew, 388
Whitewater scandal, 770
Whyte, William H., Jr., 665
Wikipedia, 790
Wildcat strikes, in Second World War, 621
Wildlife reserves, 495
Wild West Show, 422–423
Wilhelm II (Germany), 529
Willard, Frances, 442, 444

Williams v. Mississippi, 426
Willkie, Wendell, 609
Wilson, Edmund, 580
Wilson, Henry Lane, 524
Wilson, Woodrow: 1912 election and, 499–500, 499 (map); 1916 election and, 532; failure of peace and, 540–545; First World War and, 527, 530; foreign policy of, 523–524; Fourteen Points and, 533, 540; illness of, 543–544; on immigrants, 474; labor and, 536; League of Nations and, 532; Mexico and, 504, 523–524; New Freedom of, 499; New Nationalism and, 501; at Paris Peace Conference, 541, 543; presidency of, 500–501; repression and, 537–540
Wiretaps, 781
Wisconsin idea, 490–493
Wisconsin Industrial Commission, 491
Wisconsin Progressive Party, 589
"Witch hunts," after Second World War 642
Wives. *See* Families Women
WMD. *See* Weapons, of mass destruction
Woman's Christian Temperance Union (WCTU), 443, 483
Woman suffrage, 394, 488–490; before 1920, 490 (map); humor and, 491
Women: in 1920s, 551, 555; activism by, 442, 481–482; African American, 425–426, 442–443; Chinese, 417; in Clinton cabinet, 768; in cotton mills, 423; equality for, 731; "feminine mystique" and, 666; in *film noir*, 653; in First World War, 535–536, 538; gender politics and, 672–673; in Grange, 450; in higher education (1870–1930), 482 (table); Homestead Act and, 409; as homesteaders, 416, 417; Indian, 421; in labor unions, 447; lesbian, 645; in middle class, 442–444; as movie directors, 757; in New Deal programs, 593; New Woman and, 443, 444; in organized labor, 621; physical activities by, 441; as Populists, 451;

prostitution and, 417; protective labor legislation for, 559; in Second World War, 620; sexual and gender equality and, 472–473; in suburbs, 672–673; on Supreme Court, 673; voting rights of, 487, 488–490, 490 (map); 537; wages for, 751; in workforce, 442, 464, 470, 535–536, 557, 673. *See also* Gender; Woman suffrage
Women of the Ku Klux Klan, 564
Women's Airforce Service Pilots (WASPs), 622
Women's Bureau, 593
Women's club movement, 425–426, 442–443, 483
Women's movement, 673–674, 687, 729–730; in 1920s, 558–559; Kennedy administration and, 674. *See also* Feminism; Women; Women's rights; Women's rights movement
Women's Peace Party, 532
Women's rights: ERA and, 703; sports and, 755. *See also* Feminism; Women's movement
Women's rights movement, 488, 703, 704; Fifteenth Amendment and, 394
Women's Strike for Peace, 674
Wood, Leonard, 510, 514
Woods, Eldrick (Tiger), 754
Woodstock festival, 696
Work (Alcott), 442
Workday, 545; eight-hour, 445, 446, 501; industrial, 464
Workers, 751–752; African American, 423; on assembly lines, 492; cultural institutions and, 459; in First World War, 535–536; industrial, 557; management and, 438; on railroads, 409, 410; resistance by, 444–448; after Second World War, 642, 643; in South, 423; in sweatshops, 466; women as, 442, 673. *See also* Labor; Working class
Workforce: distribution of (1870–1920), 436 (table); globalization and, 751; immigrants in, 464; in Second World War, 620; women in, 557, 730. *See also* Women

Working class, 433; commercial culture and, 469–472, 482; families in, 464–465; popular culture of, 456
Workmen's compensation, 445, 501
Workplace: accidents in, 411, 441, 445, 464; conditions in, 445; mines as, 411–412; sexual harassment in, 730. *See also* Safety
Works Progress Administration (WPA), 591, 592 (table), 619
World Bank, 628
World power, United States as, 512–518, 524–525
World Trade Center: bombing of (1993), 778; terrorist destruction of (2001), 774, 778
World Trade Organization (WTO), 777
World War I. *See* First World War
World War II. *See* Second World War
World Wide Web. *See* Internet
Worship. *See* Freedom(s), Religion
Wounded Knee, massacre at, 422
Wovoka (Paiute shaman), 422
WPA. *See* Works Progress Administration
Wright, Richard, 645
Writing. *See* Literature specific titles and authors
WTO. *See* World Trade Organization
Wyoming, woman suffrage in, 488

Y
Yalta Conference (1945), 628, 644
"Yellow dog" contracts, 557
Yellow fever, Panama Canal and, 521
Yellow journalism, 508
Yellow Wallpaper, The (Gilman), 442
Yeltsin, Boris, 725
Yemen, *Cole* attack in, 778
YIPPIES, 698
Yom Kippur War (1973), 705, 715
Young Americans for Freedom (YAF), 668, 695
Young people: counterculture and, 695–696; in Peace Corps, 670; sexuality and, 472; sexual revolution of, 456; youth culture of, 666
Youngstown Sheet & Tube Company v. Sawyer, 647
Youth. *See* Young people

Youth International Party (Yippies). *See* Yippies

YouTube, 790

Yugoslavia, 541, 542 *(map)*; Bosnian Serbs and Muslims in, 776; former, 725

Z

Zangwill, Israel, 474

Zelaya, José Santos, 523

Zimmermann, Arthur, 532

Zimmermann telegram, 532

Zionism, 629

Zitkala-Sa, 420, 422

Zones of occupation: in Germany, 628, 636; in Japan, 629; in Korea, 629, 639

Zoot Suit Riots (Los Angeles), 624